CONTEMPORARY CRITICAL THEORY

DAN LATIMER

Auburn Unive

HBJ

Harcourt Brace Jovanovich, Publishers

San Diego   New York   Chicago   Austin   Washington, D.C.
London   Sydney   Tokyo   Toronto

CONTEMPORARY CRITICAL THEORY

ISBN: 0-15-513494-9

Library of Congress Catalog Card Number: 88-80626

Printed in the United States of America

PREFACE

Contemporary Critical Theory grew out of the plaintive requests of undergraduate and graduate students for an accessible introduction to the major theoretical developments of the last twenty years. The history of these students' bewilderment, as I reconstruct it, begins with what usually draws them to the liberal arts in the first place: the pleasure they feel in losing themselves in stories, or in the cadences of poetry. It would be puritanical to deny students these seductions, to despise these pleasures of imaginative sympathy, which are as genuine as they are mysterious. In their benign form, they are the source of what we have at times sentimentalized as "humanism," or the "humane." To lose the capacity for them completely does no one any good. It may seem inappropriate to say then that at some point we recognize the need for protection from these powerful impulses and texts. Perhaps we simply want to understand, like Freud in "Creative Writers and Day-Dreaming" (1908), why this kind of fantasy and role-playing is so important and serious, why it persists beyond childhood, or why, as Schiller claims, we must pass through aesthetics before we can arrive at ethics.[1] Perhaps we simply find ourselves in contexts, such as classrooms, where such imaginative experiences are shared with others, where we need a vocabulary. Or, we find that a conversation has been underway for some time and we've arrived late on the scene. We hear words used in strange ways. The effect must be rather alarming, even apocalyptic at first. We hear of gaps, horizons, destruction, aporias, castration, mirrors, and fetishes—of open and closed economies, panoptic gazes, tropes, secondary revision, potlatch, phalli, Essentialism, and Otherness. What we eventually come to understand is that literary studies are no longer exhausted by belles lettres—those stories and poems we thought we had license, as liberal arts majors, simply to enjoy. But no, we must plunge into other fields as well, not because they study the "reality" of which art is the "reflection," but because, since Structuralism, everything, even earnest, hoarse lieutenant colonels with bemedaled uniforms, beautiful secretaries, and daughters in leotards, becomes a text to be read. This is in general a salutary development; it frees the sensibilities of literature students

---

[1] Friedrich Schiller, *On the Aesthetic Education of Man,* tr. Reginald Snell. (New York: Ungar, 1983) 110.

v

to engage themselves in contexts from which they had always thought themselves exiled, whether they wanted to be or not. (And sometimes they wanted to be, believing that it was their privilege.)

But "textuality" does not need to mean "consciousness" or "solipsism" alone. I quote Gayatri Spivak: " . . . human textuality can be seen not only *as* world and self, *as* the representation of a world . . . , but also *in* the world and self, implicated in an 'intertextuality.' " This textbook should provide an occasion to consider to what extent words are material and to what extent material things, such as food, buildings, clothes, are, in their way, words; how these words can be both our world and our consciousness—or, in medievalist Umberto Eco's amusing example of the too-tight jeans of the young, our world and our *lack* of consciousness: A monk's loose robes leave the body unaware of itself, he says. "Thought abhors tights."[2]

There is a limit to what one book can do. It would be ideal, perhaps, to have read Hegel before Blanchot, or Marx before Voloshinov. But we know students often read *Ulysses* before they read the *Odyssey*, or Pound's *Cantos* before they pick up the *Metamorphoses*. The fact that Hegel or Marx, Homer or Ovid have been made contemporary is the main reason we read them in the first place. We do not read them without first knowing, from our contemporary standpoint, that they are still significant. There is always a point in a conversation where one must reconstruct what was being said before one arrived on the scene; we learn in reverse—a fact for which it is absurd to feel shame, since it is the fate of us all.

I want to express my indebtedness to all those who shared with me their ideas and experiences, especially those colleagues, students and professors, who participated in the Auburn Theory Group founded by Ashton Nichols and Alan Richardson in 1985. It was they who created an atmosphere in which a book like this begins to make sense. I am grateful to the National Endowment for the Humanities, whose repeated generosity made it possible for me to study with Edward Said at Columbia (1978), Paul de Man at Yale (1981), and Ernst Behler at the University of Washington (1985). I want to thank the School of Criticism and Theory for admitting me to its 1982 session at Northwestern University, and the Auburn Humanities Fund, then administered by Caine Campbell, for allowing me to attend. Thanks go to the University of Illinois for its stimulating Marxism Institute of 1983, which introduced me to Perry Anderson, Fredric Jameson, Gayatri Spivak, and many others whose work continues to be an inspiration. Thanks go to Vanderbilt University and the Mellon Foundation for their Regional Mellon Fellowships which provided me with an opportunity to hear Mark Taylor and David Krell in 1986. On these and other occasions, I have benefited from conversations with Susan David Bernstein, Robin Blackburn, Mark Conroy, Allen Dunn,

---

[2] Umberto Eco, "Lumbar Thought," in *Travels in Hyperreality, Essays*, tr. William Weaver (New York: Harcourt Brace Jovanovich, 1986) 191–5.

Celia Easton, Ralph Flores, John McGowan, Christopher Norris, Ken Watson, and sixteen years of patient Auburn students. I thank them all for their good advice and apologize for not always being able to follow it. I hope the book will be useful to them. Space considerations forced the omission of many important theorists. I can only name those my colleagues explicitly hoped could be included: Terry Eagleton, Gérard Genette, Gerald Graff, A.J. Greimas, Neil Hertz, Ngugi wa Thiong'o, Michael Riffaterre, and Tzvetan Todorov.

I would also like to thank Stuart McDougal, at the University of Michigan, Bruce Robbins, at Rutgers University, and James Sosnoski, at Miami University, for their careful review of the manuscript.

The material in this textbook is arranged in six theoretically and chronologically overlapping classifications. As an aid to memory alone, it seemed useful to have them, even if the writers whom we have placed under one classification could in some cases also appear under quite a different one. The headnotes have been written primarily to suggest the contents of the individual anthologized selection. They may also be read consecutively as a general introduction to the critical strategy under which they are assembled.

Lastly, thanks to Deb Burling whose secretarial help truly made this book a joint project, and to my parents in Colorado City, Texas, where in the summer my daughter is happy.

CONTENTS

▲
THREE
▼

MARXISM

▲
FOUR
▼

HERMENEUTICS AND RECEPTION THEORY

▲
FIVE
▼

PSYCHOANALYSIS AND MYTH CRITICISM

◆ SIX ◆

FEMINISM

PART ONE

STRUCTURALISM

FERDINAND DE SAUSSURE

Between 1907 and 1911, Ferdinand de Saussure gave a series of lectures on linguistics at the University of Geneva. After his death in 1913, his students collated his lecture notes and published them in 1916 as the *Course in General Linguistics* (English, 1959). The crucial point the book makes is that in the system of signs which constitutes language, the relationship between a given sound and the mental image it evokes is completely arbitrary, based on convention only. The consequences of this fact, says Saussure, are "numberless." One consequence is that languages seem to constitute worlds of convention independent of each other and of the physical world. "Reality" comes to mean the self-referential sign/language system which has adopted us; hence, the world we see is organized by the language we speak. "There is no outside-the-text," as Derrida says in *Of Grammatology.** Saussure imagines the science of "semiology" as a *systematic study of how meaning is conventionally generated by collective behavior.* At the same time, he warns that language's radical arbitrariness makes it a unique medium. For instance, fashion in dress, customs, economic relations—all objects of later semiological analysis by Structuralists—are not as arbitrary as language. Clothes must conform to the human body. The value of a farmer's field is dependent on the food it produces. Once a daughter becomes a wife, she can no longer be "spent" by her father to gain power or property, while a word can be used again and again, inalienably.†

---

*Jacques Derrida, *Of Grammatology,* trans. Gayatri Spivak (Baltimore: Johns Hopkins University Press, 1976) 158.
†Perry Anderson, *In the Tracks of Historical Materialism* (London: Verso, 1983) 42–43.

Nature of the Linguistic Sign

Translated by Wade Baskin

1. Sign, Signified, Signifier

Some people regard language, when reduced to its elements, as a naming-process only—a list of words, each corresponding to the thing that it names. For example:

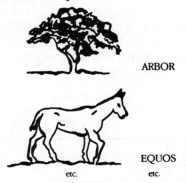

ARBOR

EQUOS

etc.   etc.

This conception is open to criticism at several points. It assumes that ready-made ideas exist before words; it does not tell us whether a name is vocal or psychological in nature (*arbor*, for instance, can be considered from either viewpoint); finally, it lets us assume that the linking of a name and a thing is a very simple operation—an assumption that is anything but true. But this rather naïve approach can bring us near the truth by showing us that the linguistic unit is a double entity, one formed by the associating of two terms.

NATURE OF THE LINGUISTIC SIGN   from *Course in General Linguistics* by Ferdinand de Saussure (first published in 1916); translated from the French by Wade Baskin. Copyright © 1959 by Philosophical Library. Reprinted by permission of Philosophical Library, New York.

We have seen in considering the speaking-circuit that both terms involved in the linguistic sign are psychological and are united in the brain by an associative bond. This point must be emphasized.

The linguistic sign unites, not a thing and a name, but a concept and a sound-image. The latter is not the material sound, a purely physical thing, but the psychological imprint of the sound, the impression that it makes on our senses. The sound-image is sensory, and if I happen to call it 'material', it is only in that sense, and by way of opposing it to the other term of the association, the concept, which is generally more abstract.

The psychological character of our sound-images becomes apparent when we observe our own speech. Without moving our lips or tongue, we can talk to ourselves or recite mentally a selection of verse. Because we regard the words of our language as sound-images, we must avoid speaking of the 'phonemes' that make up the words. This term, which suggests vocal activity, is applicable to the spoken word only, to the realization of the inner image in discourse. We can avoid that misunderstanding by speaking of the *sounds* and *syllables* of a word provided we remember that the names refer to the sound-image.

The linguistic sign is then a two-sided psychological entity that can be represented by the drawing:

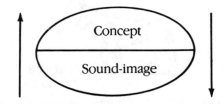

The two elements are intimately united, and each recalls the other. Whether we try to find the meaning of the Latin word *arbor* or the word that Latin uses to designate the concept 'tree', it is clear that only the associations sanctioned by that language appear to us to conform to reality, and we disregard whatever others might be imagined.

Our definition of the linguistic sign poses an important question of terminology. I call the combination of a concept and a sound-image a *sign,* but in current usage the term generally designates only a sound-image, a word, for example (*arbor,* etc.). One tends to forget that *arbor* is called a sign only because it carries the concept 'tree', with the result that the idea of the sensory part implies the idea of the whole.

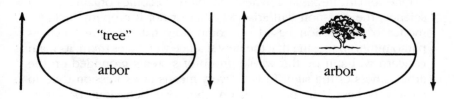

Ambiguity would disappear if the three notions involved here were designated by three names, each suggesting and opposing the others. I propose to retain the word *sign (signe)* to designate the whole and to replace *concept* and *sound-image* respectively by *signified (signifié)* and *signifier (significant);* the last two terms have the advantage of indicating the opposition that separates them from each other and from the whole of which they are parts. As regards *sign,* if I am satisfied with it, this is simply because I do not know of any word to replace it, the ordinary language suggesting no other.

The linguistic sign, as defined, has two primordial characteristics. In enunciating them I am also positing the basic principles of any study of this type.

2. Principle I: The Arbitrary Nature of the Sign

The bond between the signifier and the signified is arbitrary. Since I mean by sign the whole that results from the associating of the signifier with the signified, I can simply say: *the linguistic sign is arbitrary.*

The idea of 'sister' is not linked by any inner relationship to the succession of sounds *s-ö-r* which serves as its signifier in French; that it could be represented equally by just any other sequence is proved by differences among languages and by the very existence of different languages: the signified 'ox' has as its signifier *b-ö-f* on one side of the border and *o-k-s (Ochs)* on the other.

No one disputes the principle of the arbitrary nature of the sign, but it is often easier to discover a truth than to assign to it its proper place. Principle I dominates all the linguistics of language; its consequences are numberless. It is true that not all of them are equally obvious at first glance; only after many detours does one discover them, and with them the primordial importance of the principle.

One remark in passing: when semiology becomes organized as a science, the question will arise whether or not it properly includes modes of expression based on completely natural signs, such as pantomime. Supposing that the new science welcomes them, its main concern will still be the whole group of systems grounded on the arbitrariness of the sign. In fact, every means of expression used in society is based, in principle, on collective behaviour or—what amounts to the same thing—on convention. Polite formulas, for instance, though often imbued with a certain natural expressiveness (as in the case of a Chinese who greets his emperor by bowing down to the ground nine times), are none the less fixed by rule; it is this rule and not the intrinsic value of the gestures that obliges one to use them. Signs that are wholly arbitrary realize better than the others the ideal of the semiological process; that is why language, the most complex and universal of all systems of expression, is also the most characteristic; in this sense linguistics can become the master-pattern for all branches of semiology although language is only one particular semiological system.

The word *symbol* has been used to designate the linguistic sign, or, more specifically, what is here called the signifier. Principle I in particular weighs against the use of this term. One characteristic of the symbol is that it is never wholly arbitrary; it is not empty, for there is the rudiment of a natural bond between the signifier and the signified. The symbol of justice, a pair of scales, could not be replaced by just any other symbol, such as a chariot.

The word *arbitrary* also calls for comment. The term should not imply that the choice of the signifier is left entirely to the speaker; I mean that it is unmotivated, i.e. arbitrary in that it actually has no natural connection with the signified. . . .

3. Principle II: The Linear Nature of the Signifier

The signifier, being auditory, is unfolded solely in time from which it gets the following characteristics: (a) it represents a span, and (b) the span is measurable in a single dimension; it is a line.

While Principle II is obvious, apparently linguists have always neglected to state it, doubtless because they found it too simple; nevertheless, it is fundamental, and its consequences are incalculable. Its importance equals that of Principle I; the whole mechanism of language depends upon it. In contrast to visual signifiers (nautical signals, etc.) which can offer simultaneous groupings in several dimensions, auditory signifiers have at their command only the dimension of time. Their elements are presented in succession; they form a chain. This feature becomes readily apparent when they are represented in writing and the spatial line of graphic marks is substituted for succession in time.

Sometimes the linear nature of the signifier is not obvious. When I accent a syllable, for instance, it seems that I am concentrating more than one significant element on the same point. But this is an illusion; the syllable and its accent constitute only one phonational act. There is no duality within the act but only different oppositions to what precedes and what follows.

IMMUTABILITY AND MUTABILITY OF THE SIGN

1. Immutability

The signifier, though to all appearances freely chosen with respect to the idea that it represents, is fixed, not free, with respect to the linguistic community that uses it. The masses have no voice in the matter, and the signifier chosen by language could be replaced by no other. This fact, which seems to embody a contradiction, might be called colloquially 'the stacked deck'. We say to language: 'Choose!' but we add: 'It must be this sign and no other.' No individual, even if he willed it, could modify in any way at all the choice that has been made; and what is more, the community itself cannot control so much as a single word; it is bound to the existing language.

No longer can language be identified with a contract pure and simple, and it is precisely from this viewpoint that the linguistic sign is a particularly interesting object of study; for language furnishes the best proof that a law accepted by a community is a thing that is tolerated and not a rule to which all freely consent.

Let us first see why we cannot control the linguistic sign and then draw together the important consequences that issue from the phenomenon.

No matter what period we choose or how far back we go, language always appears as a heritage of the preceding period. We might conceive of an act by which, at a given moment, names were assigned to things and a contract was formed between concepts and sound-images; but such an act has never been recorded. The notion that things might have happened like that was prompted by our acute awareness of the arbitrary nature of the sign.

No society, in fact, knows or has ever known language other than as a product inherited from preceding generations, and one to be accepted as such. That is why the question of the origin of speech is not so important as it is generally assumed to be. The question is not even worth asking; the only real object of linguistics is the normal, regular life of an existing idiom. A particular language-state is always the product of historical forces, and these forces explain why the sign is unchangeable, i.e., why it resists any arbitrary substitution.

Nothing is explained by saying that language is something inherited and leaving it at that. Cannot existing and inherited laws be modified from one moment to the next?

To meet that objection, we must put language into its social setting and frame the question just as we would for any other social institution. How are other social institutions transmitted? This more general question includes the question of immutability. We must first determine the greater or lesser amounts of freedom that the other institutions enjoy; in each instance it will be seen that a different proportion exists between fixed tradition and the free action of society. The next step is to discover why, in a given category, the forces of the first type carry more weight or less weight than those of the second. Finally, coming back to language, we must ask why the historical factor of transmission dominates it entirely and prohibits any sudden widespread change.

There are many possible answers to the question. For example, one might point to the fact that succeeding generations are not superimposed on one another like the drawers of a piece of furniture, but fuse and interpenetrate, each generation embracing individuals of all ages—with the result that modifications of language are not tied to the succession of generations. One might also recall the sum of the efforts required for learning the mother language and conclude that a general change would be impossible. Again, it might be added that reflection does not enter into the active use of an idiom—speakers are largely unconscious of the laws of language; and if they are unaware of them, how can they modify them? Even if they were aware of these laws, we may be sure that their awareness would seldom lead to criticism, for people are generally satisfied with the language they have received.

The foregoing considerations are important but not topical. The following are more basic and direct, and all the others depend on them.

(i) *The arbitrary nature of the sign* Above, we had to accept the theoretical possibility of change; further reflection suggests that the arbitrary nature of the sign is really what protects language from any attempt to modify it. Even if people were more conscious of language than they are, they would still not know how to discuss it. The reason is simply that any subject in order to be discussed must have a reasonable basis. It is possible, for instance, to discuss whether the monogamous form of marriage is more reasonable than the polygamous form and to advance arguments to support either side. One could also argue about a system of symbols, for the symbol has a rational relationship with the thing signified; but language is a system of arbitrary signs and lacks the necessary basis, the solid ground for discussion. There is no reason for preferring *sœur* to *sister, Ochs* to *bœuf,* etc.

(ii) *The multiplicity of signs necessary to form any language* Another important deterrent to linguistic change is the great number of signs that must go into the making of any language. A system of writing comprising twenty to forty letters can in case of need be replaced by another system. The same would be true of language if it contained a limited number of elements; but linguistic signs are numberless.

(iii) *The over-complexity of the system* A language constitutes a system. In this one respect language is not completely arbitrary but is ruled to some extent by logic; it is here also, however, that the inability of the masses to transform it becomes apparent. The system is a complex mechanism that can be grasped only through reflection; the very ones who use it daily are ignorant of it. We can conceive of a change only through the intervention of specialists, grammarians, logicians, etc.; but experience shows us that all such meddlings have failed.

(iv) *Collective inertia towards innovation* Language—and this consideration surpasses all the others—is at every moment everybody's concern; spread throughout society and manipulated by it, language is something used daily by all. Here we are unable to set up any comparison between it and other institutions. The prescriptions of codes, religious rites, nautical signals, etc., involve only a certain number of individuals simultaneously and then only during a limited period of time; in language, on the contrary, everyone participates at all times, and that is why it is constantly being influenced by all. This capital fact suffices to show the impossibility of revolution. Of all social institutions, language is least amenable to initiative. It blends with the life of society, and the latter, inert by nature, is a prime conservative force.

But to say that language is a product of social forces does not suffice to show clearly that it is unfree; remembering that it is always the heritage of the preceding period, we must add that these social forces are linked with time. Language is checked not only by the weight of the collectivity but also by time. These two are inseparable. At every moment solidarity with the past checks freedom of choice. We say *man* and *dog*. This does not prevent the existence in the total phenomenon of a bond between the two antithetical forces —arbitrary convention, by virtue of which choice is free, and time, which causes choice to be fixed. Because the sign is arbitrary, it follows no law other than that of tradition, and because it is based on tradition, it is arbitrary.

2. Mutability

Time, which insures the continuity of language, wields another influence apparently contradictory to the first: the more or less rapid change of linguistic signs. In a certain sense, therefore, we can speak of both the immutability and the mutability of the sign.

In the last analysis, the two facts are interdependent: the sign is exposed to alteration because it perpetuates itself. What predominates in all change is the persistence of the old substance; disregard for the past is only relative. That is why the principle of change is based on the principle of continuity.

Change in time takes many forms, on any one of which an important chapter in linguistics might be written. Without entering into detail, let us see what things need to be delineated.

First, let there be no mistake about the meaning that we attach to the word 'change'. One might think that it deals especially with phonetic changes undergone by the signifier, or perhaps changes in meaning which affect the signified concept. That view would be inadequate. Regardless of what the forces of change are, whether in isolation or in combination, they always result in *a shift in the relationship between the signified and the signifier.*

Here are some examples. Latin *necāre* 'kill' became *noyer* 'drown' in French. Both the sound-image and the concept changed; but it is useless to separate the two parts of the phenomenon; it is sufficient to state with respect to the whole that the bond between the idea and the sign was loosened, and that there was a shift in their relationship. If, instead of comparing Classical Latin *necāre* with French *noyer,* we contrast the former term with *necare* of Vulgar Latin of the fourth or fifth century meaning 'drown', the case is a little different; but here again, although there is no appreciable change in the signifier, there is a shift in the relationship between the idea and the sign.

Old German *dritteil* 'one-third' became *Drittel* in Modern German. Here, although the concept remained the same, the relationship was changed in two ways: the signifier was changed not only in its material aspect but also in its grammatical form; the idea of *Teil* 'part' is no longer implied; *Drittel* is a simple word. In one way or another there is always a shift in the relationship.

In Anglo-Saxon the pre-literary form *fot* 'foot' remained while its plural *★fōti* became *fēt* (Modern English *feet*). Regardless of the other changes that are implied, one thing is certain: there was a shift in their relationship; other correspondences between the phonetic substance and the idea emerged.

Language is radically powerless to defend itself against the forces which from one moment to the next are shifting the relationship between the signified and the signifier. This is one of the consequences of the arbitrary nature of the sign.

Unlike language, other human institutions—customs, laws, etc. —are all based in varying degrees on the natural relations of things; all have of necessity adapted the means employed to the ends pursued. Even fashion in dress is not entirely arbitrary; we can deviate only slightly from the conditions dictated by the human body. Language is limited by nothing in the choice of means, for apparently nothing would prevent the associating of any idea whatsoever with just any sequence of sounds.

To emphasize the fact that language is a genuine institution, Whitney quite justly insisted upon the arbitrary nature of signs; and, by so doing, he placed linguistics on its true axis. But he did not follow through and see that the arbitrariness of language radically separates it from all other institutions. This is apparent from the way in which language evolves. Nothing could be more complex. As it is a product of both the social force and time, no one can change anything in it, and, on the other hand, the arbitrariness of its signs theoretically entails the freedom of establishing just any relationship between phonetic substance and ideas. The result is that each of the two elements united in the sign maintains its own life to a degree unknown elsewhere, and that language changes, or rather evolves, under the influence of all the forces which can affect either sounds or meanings. The evolution is inevitable; there is no example of a single language that resists it. After a certain period of time, some obvious shifts can always be recorded.

Mutability is so inescapable that it even holds true for artificial languages: Whoever creates a language controls it only so long as it is not in circulation; from the moment when it fulfils its mission and becomes the property of everyone, control is lost. Take Esperanto as an example; if it succeeds, will it escape the inexorable law? Once launched, it is quite likely that Esperanto will enter upon a fully semiological life; it will be transmitted according to laws which have nothing in common with those of its logical creation, and there will be no turning back. A man proposing a fixed language that posterity would have to accept for what it was would be like a hen hatching a duck's egg: the language created by him would be borne along, willy-nilly, by the current that engulfs all languages.

Signs are governed by a principle of general semiology: continuity in time is coupled to change in time; this is confirmed by orthographic systems, the speech of deaf-mutes, etc.

But what supports the necessity for change? I might be reproached for not having been as explicit on this point as on the principle of immutability. This is because I failed to distinguish between the different forces of change. We must consider their great variety in order to understand the extent to which they are necessary.

The causes of continuity are a priori within the scope of the observer, but the causes of change in time are not. It is better not to attempt giving an exact account at this point, but to restrict discussion to the shifting of relationships in general. Time changes all things; there is no reason why language should escape this universal law.

Let us review the main points of our discussion and relate them to the principles set up in the Introduction.[1]
1. Avoiding sterile word definitions, within the total phenomenon represented by speech we first singled out two parts: 'langue' and 'parole'. Langue is speech less speaking. It is the whole set of linguistic habits which allow an individual to understand and to be understood.

---

1. See Introduction, pp. 1–37, to *Course in General Linguistics,* not reprinted here.

2. But this definition still leaves language outside its social context; it makes language something artificial, since it includes only the individual part of reality; for the realization of language, a community of speakers *(masse parlante)* is necessary. Contrary to all appearances, language never exists apart from the social fact, for it is a semiological phenomenon. Its social nature is one of its inner characteristics. Its complete definition confronts us with two inseparable entities. [See below.]

But under the conditions described language is not living—it has only potential life; we have considered only the social, not the historical, fact.

3. The linguistic sign is arbitrary; language, as defined, would therefore seem to be a system which, because it depends solely on a rational principle, is free and can be organized at will. Its social nature, considered independently, does not definitely rule out this viewpoint. Doubtless it is not on a purely logical basis that group psychology operates; one must consider everything that deflects reason in actual contacts between individuals. But the thing which keeps language from being a simple convention that can be modified at the whim of interested parties is not its social nature; it is rather the action of time combined with the social force. If time is left out, the linguistic facts are incomplete and no conclusion is possible.

If we considered language in time, without the community of speakers—imagine an isolated individual living for several centuries—we should probably notice no change; time would not influence language. Conversely, if we considered the community of the social forces that influence language. To represent

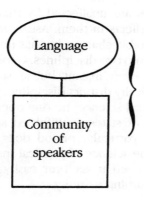

the actual facts, we must then add to our first drawing a sign to indicate the passage of time:

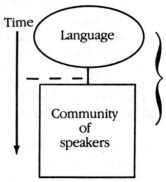

Language is no longer free, for time will allow the social forces at work on it to carry out their effects. This brings us back to the principle of continuity, which cancels freedom. But continuity necessarily implies change, varying degrees of shifts in the relationship between the signified and the signifier.

STATIC AND EVOLUTIONARY LINGUISTICS

Inner Duality of All Sciences Concerned with Values

Very few linguists suspect that the intervention of the factor of time creates difficulties peculiar to linguistics and opens to their science two completely divergent paths.

Most other sciences are unaffected by this radical duality; time produces no special effects in them. Astronomy has found that the stars undergo considerable changes but has not been obliged on this account to split itself into two disciplines. Geology is concerned with successions at almost every instant, but its study of strata does not thereby become a radically distinct discipline. Law has its descriptive science and its historical science; no one opposes one to the other. The political history of states is unfolded solely in time, but an historian depicting a particular period does not work apart from history. Conversely, the science of political institutions is essentially descriptive, but if the need arises it can easily deal with an historical question without disturbing its unity.

On the other hand, that duality is already forcing itself upon the economic sciences. Here, in contrast to the other sciences, political economy and economic history constitute two clearly separated disciplines within a single science; the works that have recently appeared on these subjects point up the distinction. Proceeding as they have, economists are—without being well aware of it—obeying an inner necessity. A similar necessity obliges us to divide linguistics into two parts, each with its own principle. Here as in political economy we are confronted with the notion of *value;* both sciences are concerned with *a system for equating things of different orders* —labour and wages in one and a signified and a signifier in the other.

Certainly all sciences would profit by indicating more precisely the co-ordinates along which their subject-matter is aligned. Everywhere distinctions should be made, according to the following illustration, between (I) *the axis of simultaneities (AB),* which stands for the relations of coexisting things and from which the intervention of time is excluded; and (2) *the axis of successions (CD),* on which only one thing can be considered at a time but upon which are located all things on the first axis together with their changes. [See below.]

For a science concerned with values the distinction is a practical necessity and sometimes an absolute one. In these fields scholars cannot organize their research rigorously without considering both co-ordinates and making a distinction between the system of values *per se* and the same values as they relate to time.

This distinction has to be heeded by the linguist above all others, for language is a system of pure values which are determined by nothing except the momentary arrangement of its terms. A value—so

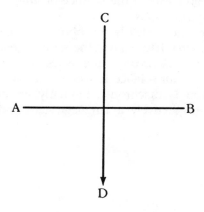

long as it is somehow rooted in things and in their natural relations, as happens with economics (the value of a plot of ground, for instance, is related to its productivity)—can to some extent be traced in time if we remember that it depends at each moment upon a system of coexisting values. Its link with things gives it, perforce, a natural basis, and the judgments that we base on such values are therefore never completely arbitrary; their variability is limited. But we have just seen that natural data have no place in linguistics.

Again, the more complex and rigorously organized a system of values is, the more it is necessary, because of its very complexity, to study it according to both co-ordinates. No other system embodies this feature to the same extent as language. Nowhere else do we find such precise values at stake and such a great number and diversity of terms, all so rigidly interdependent. The multiplicity of signs, which we have already used to explain the continuity of language, makes it absolutely impossible to study simultaneously relations in time and relations within the system.

The reasons for distinguishing two sciences of language are clear. How should the sciences be designated? Available terms do not all bring out the distinction with equal sharpness. 'Linguistic history' and 'Historical linguistics' are too vague. Since political history includes the description of different periods as well as the narration of events, the student might think that he is studying a language according to the axis of time when he describes its successive states, but this would require a separate study of the phenomena that make language pass from one state to another. *Evolution* and *evolutionary linguistics* are more precise, and I shall use these expressions often; in contrast, we can speak of the science of *language-states (états de langue)* or *static linguistics.*

But to indicate more clearly the opposition and crossing of two orders of phenomena that relate to the same object, I prefer to speak of *synchronic* and *diachronic* linguistics. Everything that relates to the static side of our science is synchronic; everything that has to do with evolution is diachronic. Similarly, *synchrony* and *diachrony* designate respectively a language-state and an evolutionary phase. . . .

ROMAN JAKOBSON

Roman Jakobson's career as an influential linguist began before the October Revolution (1917). He was a central figure in The Moscow Linguistic Circle, founded in 1915, in The Society for the Study of Poetic Language (Opojaz) of St. Petersburg, and later in The Prague Linguistic Circle, founded in 1926, to which René Wellek also belonged. These societies produced a theory of literary language that is now called Russian Formalism. Formalists were impatient with theories too slavishly interested in the lives of poets—for example, in whether Pushkin was addicted to smoking, as Osip Brik derisively said.* They rejected mimetic theories of art: for Shklovsky, the opaqueness of literary language was designed to defamiliarize perception, to "make strange" (76). "Art was always free of life . . ." said Shklovsky (77). They dismissed the occult theories of Symbolists like Bely, for whom poetic language evoked supernatural realities (35–36). Formalists were of a scientific bent. Theory was to be based on "the scientific study of facts," said Boris Eichenbaum (72). And for Roman Jakobson, literary history would become a science as soon as it recognized that "the artistic device" was its "only concern" (76–77).

Jakobson's central "scientific" contribution to Formalism, and later to Structuralism, is based on his belief that beneath the apparent diversity of cultures, there are simple abstract patterns or formal principles valid for "all verbal behavior and for human behavior in general," as he says in his study of speech disorders (the second of two selections reprinted here). This pattern is binary in nature. When normal language use breaks down, one of two principles is involved—substitution or combination, that is, the capacity to employ metaphor or the capacity to employ metonymy, respectively. In the former case, for example, naming is lost; and in the latter, syntax is lost. These axes of language are related to Saussure's synchronic and diachronic principles, to Freud's first two operations of the dream-work, condensation and displacement, and to Lévi-Strauss' practice of reading myths like an orchestra score, harmonically or melodically.

*Victor Erlich, *Russian Formalism, History-Doctrine,* 3rd edition (New Haven and London: Yale University Press, 1981) 54. All page citations refer to Erlich.

The Twofold Character of Language
1956

Speech implies a selection of certain linguistic entities and their combination into linguistic units of a higher degree of complexity. At the lexical level this is readily apparent: the speaker selects words and combines them into sentences according to the syntactic system of the language he is using; sentences are in their turn combined into utterances. But the speaker is by no means a completely free agent in his choice of words: his selection (except for the rare case of actual neology) must be made from the lexical storehouse which he and his addressee possess in common. The communication engineer most properly approaches the essence of the speech event when he assumes that in the optimal exchange of information the speaker and the listener have at their disposal more or less the same "filing cabinet of *prefabricated* representations": the addresser of a verbal message selects one of these "preconceived possibilities" and the addressee is supposed to make an identical choice from the same assembly of "possibilities already foreseen and provided for".[1] Thus the efficiency of a speech event demands the use of a common code by its participants.

" 'Did you say *pig* or *fig?*' said the Cat. 'I said *pig,*' replied Alice."[2] In this peculiar utterance the feline addressee attempts to recapture a linguistic choice made by the addresser. In the common code of the Cat and Alice, i.e. in spoken English, the difference between a stop and a continuant, other things being equal, may change the meaning

THE TWOFOLD CHARACTER OF LANGUAGE from *Fundamentals of Language* by Roman Jakobson and Morris Halle (Janua Linguarum, Series Minor, I, The Hague: Mouton, 1956). Reprinted by kind permission of the Jakobson Trust and Dr. Stephen Rudy.

1. D. M. MacKay, "In search of basic symbols," *Cybernetics,* Transactions of the Eighth Conference (New York, 1952), p. 183.
2. Lewis Carroll, *Alice's Adventures in Wonderland,* Chapter VI.

of the message. Alice had used the distinctive feature "stop *vs.* continuant", rejecting the latter and choosing the former of the two opposites; and in the same act of speech she combined this solution with certain other simultaneous features, using the gravity and the tenseness of /p/ in contradistinction to the acuteness of /t/ and to the laxness of /b/. Thus all these attributes have been combined into a bundle of distinctive features, the so-called phoneme. The phoneme /p/ was then followed by the phonemes /i/ and /g/, themselves bundles of simultaneously produced distinctive features. Hence the concurrence of simultaneous entities and the concatenation of successive entities are the two ways in which we speakers combine linguistic constituents.

Neither such bundles as /p/ or /f/ nor such sequences of bundles as /pig/ or /fig/ are invented by the speaker who uses them. Neither can the distinctive feature "stop *versus* continuant" nor the phoneme /p/ occur out of a context. The stop feature appears in combination with certain other concurrent features, and the repertory of combinations of these features into phonemes such as /p/, /b/, /t/, /d/, /k/, /g/, etc. is limited by the code of the given language. The code sets limitations on the possible combinations of the phoneme /p/ with other following and/or preceding phonemes; and only a part of the permissible phoneme-sequences are actually utilized in the lexical stock of a given language. Even when other combinations of phonemes are theoretically possible, the speaker, as a rule, is only a word-user, not a word-coiner. When facing with individual words, we expect them to be coded units. In order to grasp the word *nylon* one must know the meaning assigned to this vocable in the lexical code of modern English.

In any language, there exist also coded word-groups called phrase-words. The meaning of the idiom *how do you do* cannot be derived by adding together the meanings of its lexical constituents; the whole is not equal to the sum of its parts. Those word-groups which in this respect behave like single words are a common but nonetheless only marginal case. In order to comprehend the overwhelming majority of word-groups, we must be familiar only with the constituent words and with the syntactical rules of their combination. Within these limitations we are free to set words in new contexts. Of course, this freedom is relative, and the pressure of current clichés upon our choice of combinations is considerable. But the freedom to compose quite new contexts is undeniable, despite the relatively low statistical probability of their occurrence.

Thus in the combination of linguistic units there is an ascending scale of freedom. In the combination of distinctive features into phonemes, the freedom of the individual speaker is zero; the code has already established all the possibilities which may be utilized in the given language. Freedom to combine phonemes into words is circumscribed, it is limited to the marginal situation of word-coinage. In the forming of sentences out of words the speaker is less constrained. And finally, in the combination of sentences into utterances, the action of compulsory syntactical rules ceases and the freedom of any individual speaker to create novel contexts increases substantially, although again the numerous stereotyped utterances are not to be overlooked.

Any linguistic sign involves two modes of arrangement.

1. *Combination*   Any sign is made up of constituent signs and/or occurs only in combination with other signs. This means that any linguistic unit at one and the same time serves as a context for simpler units and/or finds its own context in a more complex linguistic unit. Hence any actual grouping of linguistic units binds them into a superior unit: combination and contexture are two faces of the same operation.

2. *Selection*   A selection between alternatives implies the possibility of substituting one for the other, equivalent to the former in one respect and different from it in another. Actually, selection and substitution are two faces of the same operation.

The fundamental role which these two operations play in language was clearly realized by Ferdinand de Saussure. Yet from the two varieties of combination—concurrence and concatenation—it was only the latter, the temporal sequence, which was recognized by the Geneva linguist. Despite his own insight into the phoneme as a set of concurrent distinctive features *(éléments différentiels des phonèmes),* the scholar succumbed to the traditional belief in the linear character of language *"qui exclut la possibilité de prononcer deux éléments à la fois".*[3]

In order to delimit the two modes of arrangement which we have described as combination and selection, F. de Saussure states that the former "is *in presentia:* it is based on two or several terms jointly present in an actual series," whereas the latter "connects terms *in absentia* as members of a virtual mnemonic series". That is to say, selection (and, correspondingly, substitution) deals with entities

3. F. de Saussure, *Cours de linguistique générale,* 2nd ed. (Paris, 1922), pp. 68f. and 170f.

conjoined in the code but not in the given message, whereas, in the case of combination, the entities are conjoined in both or only in the actual message. The addressee perceives that the given utterance (message) is a combination of constituent parts (sentences, words, phonemes, etc.) selected from the repository of all possible constituent parts (code). The constituents of a context are in a status of contiguity, while in a substitution set signs are linked by various degrees of similarity which fluctuate between the equivalence of synonyms and the common core of antonyms.

These two operations provide each linguistic sign with two sets of interpretants, to utilize the effective concept introduced by Charles Sanders Peirce:[4] there are two references which serve to interpret the sign—one to the code, and the other to the context, whether coded or free; and in each of these ways the sign is related to another set of linguistic signs, through an alternation in the former case and through an alignment in the latter. A given significative unit may be replaced by other, more explicit signs of the same code, whereby its general meaning is revealed, while its contextual meaning is determined by its connection with other signs within the same sequence.

The constituents of any message are necessarily linked with the code by an internal relation and with the message by an external relation. Language in its various aspects deals with both modes of relation. Whether messages are exchanged or communication proceeds unilaterally from the addresser to the addressee, there must be some kind of contiguity between the participants of any speech event to assure the transmission of the message. The separation in space, and often in time, between two individuals, the addresser and the addressee, is bridged by an internal relation: there must be a certain equivalence between the symbols used by the addresser and those known and interpreted by the addressee. Without such an equivalence the message is fruitless—even when it reaches the receiver it does not affect him. . . .

4. C. S. Peirce, *Collected Papers,* II and IV (Cambridge, Mass., 1932, 1934)—see Index of subjects.

The Metaphoric and Metonymic Poles

The varieties of aphasia are numerous and diverse, but all of them oscillate between the two polar types just described. Every form of aphasic disturbance consists in some impairment, more or less severe, either of the faculty for selection and substitution or for combination and contexture. The former affliction involves a deterioration of metalinguistic operations, while the latter damages the capacity for maintaining the hierarchy of linguistic units. The relation of similarity is suppressed in the former, the relation of contiguity in the latter type of aphasia. Metaphor is alien to the similarity disorder, and metonymy to the contiguity disorder.

The development of a discourse may take place along two different semantic lines: one topic may lead to another either through their similarity or through their contiguity. The metaphoric way would be the most appropriate term for the first case and the metonymic way for the second, since they find their most condensed expression in metaphor and metonymy respectively. In aphasia one or the other of these two processes is restricted or totally blocked—an effect which makes the study of aphasia particularly illuminating for the linguist. In normal verbal behavior both processes are continually operative, but careful observation will reveal that under the influence of a cultural pattern, personality, and verbal style, preference is given to one of the two processes over the other.

In a well-known psychological test, children are confronted with some noun and told to utter the first verbal response that comes into their heads. In this experiment two opposite linguistic predilections are invariably exhibited: the response is intended either as a substitute for, or as a complement to the stimulus. In the latter case the stimulus and the response together form a proper syntactic construction, most usually a sentence. These two types of reaction have been labeled substitutive and predicative.

THE METAPHORIC AND METONYMIC POLES   from *Fundamentals of Language* by Roman Jakobson and Morris Halle (Janua Linguarum, Series Minor, I, The Hague: Mouton, 1956). Reprinted by kind permission of the Jakobson Trust and Dr. Stephen Rudy.

To the stimulus *hut* one response was *burnt out;* another, *is a poor little house.* Both reactions are predicative; but the first creates a purely narrative context, while in the second there is a double connection with the subject *hut:* on the one hand, a positional (namely, syntactic) contiguity, and on the other a semantic similarity.

The same stimulus produced the following substitutive reactions: the tautology *hut;* the synonyms *cabin* and *hovel;* the antonym *palace,* and the metaphors *den* and *burrow.* The capacity of two words to replace one another is an instance of positional similarity, and, in addition, all these responses are linked to the stimulus by semantic similarity (or contrast). Metonymical responses to the same stimulus, such as *thatch, litter,* or *poverty,* combine and contrast the positional similarity with semantic contiguity.

In manipulating these two kinds of connection (similarity and contiguity) in both their aspects (positional and semantic) —selecting, combining, and ranking them—an individual exhibits his personal style, his verbal predilections and preferences.

In verbal art the interaction of these two elements is especially pronounced. Rich material for the study of this relationship is to be found in verse patterns which require a compulsory parallelism between adjacent lines, for example in Biblical poetry or in the West Finnic and, to some extent, the Russian oral traditions. This provides an objective criterion of what in the given speech community acts as a correspondence. Since on any verbal level—morphemic, lexical, syntactic, and phraseological—either of these two relations (similarity and contiguity) can appear—and each in either of two aspects—, an impressive range of possible configurations is created. Either of the two gravitational poles may prevail. In Russian lyrical songs, for example, metaphoric constructions predominate, while in the heroic epics the metonymic way is preponderant.

In poetry there are various motives which determine the choice between these alternants. The primacy of the metaphoric process in the literary schools of romanticism and symbolism has been repeatedly acknowledged, but it is still insufficiently realized that it is the predominance of metonymy which underlies and actually predetermines the so-called "realistic" trend, which belongs to an intermediary stage between the decline of romanticism and the rise of symbolism and is opposed to both. Following the path of contiguous relationships, the realistic author metonymically digresses from the plot to the atmosphere and from the characters to the setting in space and time. He is fond of synecdochic details. In the scene of Anna Karenina's suicide Tolstoi's artistic attention is focused on the heroine's handbag; and in *War and Peace* the synecdoches "hair on the upper lip" or "bare shoulders" are used by the same writer to stand for the female characters to whom these features belong. The alternative predominance of one or the other of these two processes is by no means confined to verbal art. The same oscillation occurs in sign systems other than language.[1] A salient example from the history of painting is the manifestly metonymical orientation of cubism, where the object is transformed into a set of synecdoches; the surrealist painters responded with a patently metaphorical attitude. Ever since the productions of D. W. Griffith, the art of the cinema, with its highly developed capacity for changing the angle, perspective and focus of "shots", has broken with the tradition of the theater and ranged an unprecedented variety of synecdochic "close-ups" and metonymic "set-ups" in general. In such pictures as those of Charlie Chaplin, these devices in turn were superseded by a novel, metaphoric "montage" with its "lap dissolves"—the filmic similes.[2]

The bipolar structure of language (or other semiotic systems), and, in aphasia, the fixation on one of these poles to the exclusion of the other require systematic comparative study. The retention of either of these alternatives in the two types of aphasia must be confronted with the predominance of the same pole in certain styles, personal habits, current fashions, etc. A careful analysis and comparison of these phenomena with the whole syndrome of the corresponding type of aphasia is an imperative task for joint research by experts in psychopathology, psychology, linguistics, poetics, and semiotic, the general science of signs. The dichotomy here discussed appears to be of primal significance and consequence for all verbal behavior and for human behavior in general.[3]

1. I ventured a few sketchy remarks on the metonymical turn in verbal art ('Pro realizm u mystectvi,' *Vaplite*, Kharkov, 1927, No. 2; 'Randbemerkungen zur Prosa des Dichters Pasternak,' *Slavische Rundschau*, VII, 1935), in painting ('Futurizm,' *Iskusstvo*, Moscow, Aug. 2, 1919) and in motion pictures ('*Úpadek filmu,' Listy pro umění a kritiku*, I, Prague, 1933), but the crucial problem of the two polar processes awaits a detailed investigation.
2. Cf. B. Balazs, *Theory of the Film* (London, 1952).
3. For the psychological and sociological aspects of this dichotomy see Bateson's views on "progressional" and "selective integration" and Parsons' on the "conjunction-disjunction dichotomy" in children's development: J. Ruesch and G. Bateson, *Communication, the Social Matrix of Psychiatry* (New York, 1951), pp. 183ff.; T. Parsons and R. F. Bales, *Family, Socialization and Interaction Process (Glencoe, 1955), pp. 119f.*

To indicate the possibilities of the projected comparative research, we choose an example from a Russian folktale which employs parallelism as a comic device: "Thomas is a bachelor; Jeremiah is unmarried" *(Fomá xólost; Erjóma neženát)*. Here the predicates in the two parallel clauses are associated by similarity: they are in fact synonymous. The subjects of both clauses are masculine proper names and hence morphologically similar, while on the other hand they denote two contiguous heroes of the same tale, created to perform identical actions and thus to justify the use of synonymous pairs of predicates. A somewhat modified version of the same construction occurs in a familiar wedding song in which each of the wedding guests is addressed in turn by his first name and patronymic: "Gleb is a bachelor; Ivanovič is unmarried." While both predicates here are again synonyms, the relationship between the two subjects is changed: both are proper names denoting the same man and are normally used contiguously as a mode of polite address.

In the quotation from the folk tale the two parallel clauses refer to two separate facts, the marital status of Thomas and the similar status of Jeremiah. In the verse from the wedding song, however, the two clauses are synonymous: they redundantly reiterate the celibacy of the same hero, splitting him into two verbal hypostases.

The Russian novelist Gleb Ivanovič Uspenskij (1840–1902) in the last years of his life suffered from a mental illness involving a speech disorder. His first name and patronymic, *Gleb Ivanovič,* traditionally combined in polite intercourse, for him split into two distinct names designating two separate beings: Gleb was endowed with all his virtues, while Ivanovič, the name relating the son to the father, became the incarnation of all Uspenskij's vices. The linguistic aspect of this split personality is the patient's inability to use two symbols for the same thing, and it is thus a similarity disorder. Since the similarity disorder is bound up with the metonymical bent, an examination of the literary manner Uspenskij had employed as a young writer takes on particular interest. And the study of Anatolij Kamegulov, who analyzed Uspenskij's style, bears out our theoretical expectations. He shows that Uspenskij had a particular penchant for metonymy, and especially for synecdoche, and that he carried it so far that "the reader is crushed by the multiplicity of detail unloaded on him in a limited verbal space, and is physically unable to grasp the whole, so that the portrait is often lost."[4]

4. A Kamegulov, *Stil' Gleba Uspenskogo* (Leningrad, 1930), pp. 65, 145. One of such

To be sure, the metonymical style in Uspenskij is obviously prompted by the prevailing literary canon of his time, late nineteenth-century "realism"; but the personal stamp of Gleb Ivanovič made his pen particularly suitable for this artistic trend in its extreme manifestations and finally left its mark upon the verbal aspect of his mental illness.

A competition between both devices, metonymic and metaphoric, is manifest in any symbolic process, either intrapersonal or social. Thus in an inquiry into the structure of dreams, the decisive question is whether the symbols and the temporal sequences used are based on contiguity (Freud's metonymic "displacement" and synecdochic "condensation") or on similarity (Freud's "identification and symbolism").[5] The principles underlying magic rites have been resolved by Frazer into two types: charms based on the law of similarity and those founded on association by contiguity. The first of these two great branches of sympathetic magic has been called "homoeopathic" or "imitative", and the second, "contagious magic".[6] This bipartition is indeed illuminating. Nonetheless, for the most part, the question of the two poles is still neglected, despite its wide scope and importance for the study of any symbolic behavior, especially verbal, and of its impairments. What is the main reason for this neglect?

Similarity in meaning connects the symbols of a metalanguage with the symbols of the language referred to. Similarity connects a metaphorical term with the term for which it is substituted. Consequently, when constructing a metalanguage to interpret tropes, the researcher possesses more homogeneous means to handle metaphor, whereas metonymy, based on a different principle, easily defies interpretation. Therefore nothing comparable to the rich literature on

---

disintegrated portraits cited by the monograph: "From underneath an ancient straw cap with a black spot on its shield, there peeked two braids resembling the tusks of a wild boar; a chin grown fat and pendulous definitively spread over the greasy collars of the calico dicky and in thick layer lay on the coarse collar of the canvas coat, firmly buttoned on the neck. From below this coat to the eyes of the observer there protruded massive hands with a ring, which had eaten into the fat finger, a cane with a copper top, a significant bulge of the stomach and the presence of very broad pants, almost of muslin quality, in the broad ends of which hid the toes of the boots."

5. S. Freud, *Die Traumdeutung,* 9th ed. (Vienna, 1950).

6. J. G. Frazer, *The Golden Bough: A Study in Magic and Religion,* Part I, 3rd ed. (Vienna, 1950), chapter III.

metaphor[7] can be cited for the theory of metonymy. For the same reason, it is generally realized that romanticism is closely linked with metaphor, whereas the equally intimate ties of realism with metonymy usually remain unnoticed. Not only the tool of the observer but also the object of observation is responsible for the preponderance of metaphor over metonymy in scholarship. Since poetry is focused upon sign, and pragmatical prose primarily upon referent, tropes and figures were studied mainly as poetical devices. The principle of similarity underlies poetry; the metrical parallelism of lines or the phonic equivalence of rhyming words prompts the question of semantic similarity and contrast; there exist, for instance, grammatical and anti-grammatical but never agrammatical rhymes. Prose, on the contrary, is forwarded essentially by contiguity. Thus, for poetry, metaphor, and for prose, metonymy is the line of least resistance and, consequently, the study of poetical tropes is directed chiefly toward metaphor. The actual bipolarity has been artificially replaced in these studies by an amputated, unipolar scheme which, strikingly enough, coincides with one of the two aphasic patterns, namely with the contiguity disorder.[8]

7. C. F. P. Stutterheim, *Het begrip metaphoor* (Amsterdam, 1941).
8. Thanks are due to Hugh McLean for his valuable assistance and to Justinia Besharov for her original observations on tropes and figures.

CLAUDE LÉVI-STRAUSS

Claude Lévi-Strauss was born in Brussels and educated in Paris in law and philosophy. From 1934–39 he lectured at the University of São Paolo in Brazil, where he became interested in social anthropology in general and the Nambikwara Indians in particular. When he returned to France in 1939, he tried to write a novel about his experiences in Brazil.* This work became the prototype of *Tristes Tropiques,* published by Lévi-Strauss in 1955 after he had spent almost ten years in the United States as a refugee from World War II. It was in New York at the New School for Social Research that he met Roman Jakobson, who introduced him to Saussure and structural linguistics. He was interested in particular in two aspects of Saussure's theories: (1) the notion of the "unmotivated" sign and (2) the fundamental binary axes of human language—the selective (or synchronic) axis and the combinative (or diachronic) axis (160–61). Lévi-Strauss then applied the linguistic method of analysis to the study of culture in general, especially to myths, one result of which can be seen in "The Structural Study of Myth" (1955). In this essay, the deep structure of the Oedipus legend is used to explore whether mankind is generated from the earth (the plant model) or from the bisexual reproduction of men and women.† The Oedipus legend is an example of savage cognition and is not, by any means, illogical for being primitive, as Lévi-Strauss explains in "The Science of the Concrete," the first chapter of *The Savage Mind* (1962).

Tristes Tropiques is Lévi-Strauss' most accessible work. It is so "beautifully written" that it would have won the Prix Goncourt had it not been retooled by Lévi-Strauss as non-fiction for a public "hungry for science" (Pace:20). The selection reprinted here from *Tristes Tropiques* is a meditation on the corruption of writing, which he connects with the creation of cities and colonial empires, the facilitation of slavery, and the birth of architecture. Lévi-Strauss' nostalgia for the neolithic is reminiscent not only of Rousseau but also of Heidegger's hostility for technology and his recommendation in *Der Satz vom Grund* (1957) to be more like the rose of Angelus Silesius, the German mystic, who says that the rose does not ask the human "why," but simply blooms because it blooms. Similarly, Lévi-Strauss' ultimate goal in *The Savage Mind* (247) is to ". . . dissolve man, to reintegrate culture in nature and finally life within the whole of its physico-chemical conditions."

---

*David Pace, *Claude Lévi-Strauss, The Bearer of Ashes* (Boston: Routledge and Kegan Paul, 1983) 20.
†Thomas Sebeok, ed., *Myth, A Symposium* (Bloomington and London: Indiana University Press, 1971) 88–93.

A Writing Lesson
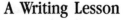
1955

Translated by John Russell

I wanted somehow to arrive at a figure, however approximate, for the total of the Nambikwara population. In 1915 Rondon had put it at twenty thousand, which was probably too high. But at that time the nomadic bands were of several hundred people apiece, and all the indications I had collected along the line pointed to a rapid decline. Thirty years ago, for instance, the known fraction of the Sabané group comprised more than a thousand individuals; when that same group visited the telegraph station of Campos Novos in 1928 it consisted of one hundred and twenty-seven men, plus their women and children. In November 1929, moreover, an influenza epidemic broke out when the group was camping at the point known as Espirro. The disease turned into a form of pulmonary oedema, and three hundred Indians died of it within forty-eight hours. The whole group disintegrated, leaving the sick and dying to fend for themselves. Of the thousand Sabané who had once been known of, only nineteen men and their families were still alive in 1938. This decline is due not only to the epidemic, but also to the fact that some years ago the Sabané were in a state of war with some of their easterly neighbours. But a large group installed not far from Tres Buritis was wiped out by influenza in 1927: of the six or seven survivors, only three were still alive in 1938. The Tarundé group, once one of the largest, numbered twelve men, with their families, in 1936: three years later these twelve were reduced to four.

What was the position at the time of my arrival? Probably a bare two thousand Indians were scattered about the territory. I could not hope to make a systematic count, because certain groups were always hostile, and because, during the nomadic season, all the bands were continually on the move. But I tried to persuade my friends at Utiarity to take me to their village at a time when a rendezvous had been arranged with other allied or related bands. Thus I hoped to estimate the present size of a gathering of this sort and to compare it with the reunions that had been scrutinized in earlier years. I promised to bring them presents, and effect some exchanges, but the leader of the band remained hesitant: he was not sure of his guests, and if my companions and I were to disappear in the region where no white men had penetrated since the incident of the seven telegraph-workers in 1925, then the precarious peace which existed there would be compromised for a long time to come.

In the end he agreed, on condition that we cut down the size of our party, and took only four oxen to carry our presents. Even so, he said, we should have to forswear the usual tracks, because our beasts would never get through the dense vegetation which abounded in the lower reaches of each valley. We should have to go by the plateau, improvising our route as we went along.

This was a very dangerous expedition, but it now seems to me largely grotesque. We had hardly left Juruena when my Brazilian colleague remarked to me on the absence of the Nambikwara women and children: only the men were with us, each armed with bow and arrows. All the literature of travel indicated this as a sign that an attack was imminent. Our feelings were mixed, therefore, as we went forward, verifying from time to time the position of our Smith and Wesson revolvers ('Cemite Vechetone' was our men's name for them) and our rifles. These fears proved misplaced: towards the half-way point of the day's march we caught up with the remainder of the band, whom their provident chief had sent on ahead of us, the day before, knowing that our mules would make much better time than the women, laden as these were with their baskets and encumbered with little children.

Soon after this, however, the Indians got lost. The new itinerary was not as straightforward as they had supposed. Towards evening we had to come to a halt in the bush. We had been promised that there would be game thereabouts and the Indians, counting on our rifles, had brought no food with them. We, for our part, had brought only emergency rations which could not be shared out all round. A troop of deer which had been nibbling away at the edge of a spring fled at our approach. The next morning everybody was in a thoroughly bad humour: ostensibly, this took for its object the leader of the band, whom they considered to be responsible for the venture which he and I had devised between us. Instead of going off to hunt or collect wild food on their own account, they decided to spend the day lying in the shade, leaving it to their leader to find the solution to their problem. He went off, accompanied by one of his wives: towards evening we saw them coming back with their baskets heavy-laden with grasshoppers that they had spent the entire day in collecting. Grasshopper pie is not one of their favourite dishes, but the entire party fell on it, none the less, with relish. Good humour broke out on all sides, and on the next morning we got under way again.

And, at last, we got to the rendezvous. This was a sandy terrace above a watercourse, bordered with trees between which the Indians had laid out some little gardens. Incoming groups arrived at intervals during the day and by the evening there were seventy-five people in all: seventeen families, grouped under thirteen crude shelters hardly more solid than those which served in camp. I was told that when the rains began the whole company would take refuge in five round huts built for several months' wear. Many of the natives seemed never to have seen a white man, and their more than dubious welcome combined with their leader's extreme nervousness seemed to suggest that he had forced their hand, somewhat, in the whole matter. Neither we nor the Indians felt at all at our ease and, as there were no trees, we had to lie, like the Nambikwaras, on the bare ground. No one slept: we kept, all night long, a polite watch upon one another.

It would have been rash to prolong the adventure, and I suggested to the leader that we should get down to our exchanges without further delay. It was then that there occurred an extraordinary incident which forces me to go back a little in time. That the Nambikwara could not write goes without saying. But they were also unable to draw, except for a few dots and zigzags on their calabashes. I distributed pencils and paper among them, none the less, as I had done with the Caduveo. At first they made no use of them. Then, one day, I saw that they were all busy drawing wavy horizontal lines on the paper. What were they trying to do? I could only conclude that they were writing—or, more exactly, that they were trying to do as I did with my pencils. As I had never tried to amuse them with drawings, they could not conceive of any other use for this implement. With most of them, that was as far as they got: but their leader saw further into the problem. Doubtless he was the only one among them to have understood what writing was for. So he asked me for one of my notepads; and when we were working together he did not give me his answers in words, but traced a wavy line or two on the paper and gave it to me, as if I could read what he had to say. He himself was all but deceived by his own play-acting. Each time he drew a line he would examine it with great care, as if its meaning must suddenly leap to the eye; and every time a look of disappointment came over his face. But he would never give up trying, and there was an unspoken agreement between us that his scribblings had a meaning that I did my best to decipher; his own verbal commentary was so prompt in coming that I had no need to ask him to explain what he had written.

And now, no sooner was everyone assembled than he drew forth from a basket a piece of paper covered with scribbled lines and pretended to read from it. With a show of hesitation he looked up and down his 'list' for the objects to be given in exchange for his people's presents. So-and-so was to receive a machete in return for his bow and arrows, and another a string of beads in return for his necklaces —and so on for two solid hours. What was he hoping for? To deceive himself, perhaps: but, even more, to amaze his companions and persuade them that *his* intermediacy was responsible for the exchanges. He had allied himself with the white man, as equal with equal, and could now share in his secrets. We were in a hurry to get away, since there would obviously be a moment of real danger at which all the marvels I had brought would have been handed over. . . . So I did not go further into the matter and we set off on the return journey, still guided by the Indians.

There had been something intensely irritating about our abortive meeting, and about the mystifications of which I had just been the unknowing instrument. Added to that, my mule was suffering from aphtha, and its mouth was causing it pain, so that by turns it hurried impatiently forward and stopped dead in its tracks. We got into a quarrel with one another and, quite suddenly, without realizing how it happened, I found myself alone, and lost, in the middle of the bush.

What was I to do? What people do in books: fire a shot in the air to let my companions know what had happened. I dismounted and did so. No reply. I fired again, and as there seemed to be an answer I fired a third shot. This scared my mule, who went off at a trot and pulled up some distance away.

I put weapons and photographic equipment neatly at the foot of a tree, memorized its position, and ran off to recapture my mule, who seemed quite peaceably disposed. He let me get right up to him and then, just as I reached for the reins, he made off at full speed. This happened more than once until in despair I jumped at him and threw both my arms round his tail. This unusual proceeding took him by surprise, and he decided to give in. Back in the saddle, I made as if to collect my belongings, only to find that we had twisted and turned so often that I had no idea where they were.

Demoralized by this episode, I decided to rejoin our troop. Neither my mule nor I knew where they had gone. Sometimes I would head him in a direction that he refused to take; sometimes I would let him lead, only to find that he was simply turning in a circle. The sun was going down, I was no longer armed, and I expected at every moment to be the target of a volley of arrows. I was not, admittedly, the first white man to penetrate that hostile zone. But none of my predecessors had come back alive and, quite apart from myself, my mule was a tempting prey for people who rarely have anything very much to get their teeth into. These dark thoughts passed, one by one, through my mind as I waited for the sun to go down, thinking that since I at least had some matches with me I could start a bush-fire. Just as I was about to strike the first match I heard voices: two of the Nambikwara had turned back, the moment my absence was noticed, and had been following me all afternoon. For them to recover my equipment was child's play and, at nightfall, they led me to the camp where our whole troop was waiting for me.

Still tormented by this absurd incident, I slept badly. To while away the hours I went back, in my mind, to the scene of the previous morning. So the Nambikwara had learnt what it meant to write! But not at all, as one might have supposed, as the result of a laborious apprenticeship. The symbol had been borrowed, but the reality remained quite foreign to them. Even the borrowing had had a sociological, rather than an intellectual object: for it was not a question of knowing specific things, or understanding them, or keeping them in mind, but merely of enhancing the prestige and authority of one individual—or one function—at the expense of the rest of the party. A native, still in the period of the stone age, had realized that even if he could not himself understand the great instrument of understanding he could at least make it serve other ends. For thousands of years, after all, and still today in a great part of the world, writing has existed as an institution in societies in which the vast majority of people are quite unable to write. The villages where I stayed in the Chittagong hills in Pakistan are populated by illiterates; yet each village has a scribe who fulfils his function for the benefit both of individual citizens and of the village as a whole. They all know what writing is and, if need be, *can* write: but they do it from outside as if it were a mediator, foreign to themselves, with whom they communicate by an oral process. But the scribe is rarely a functionary or an employee of the group as a whole; his knowledge is a source of power—so much so, in fact, that the functions of scribe and usurer are often united in the same human being. This is not merely because the usurer needs to be able to read and write to carry on his trade, but because he has thus a twofold empire over his fellows.

Writing is a strange thing. It would seem as if its appearance could not have failed to wreak profound changes in the living conditions of our race, and that these transformations must have been above all intellectual in character. Once men know how to write, they are enormously more able to keep in being a large body of knowledge. Writing might, that is to say, be regarded as a form of artificial memory, whose development should be accompanied by a deeper knowledge of the past and, therefore, by a greater ability to organize the present and the future. Of all the criteria by which people habitually distinguish civilization from barbarism, this should be the one most worth retaining: that certain peoples write and others do not. The first group can accumulate a body of knowledge that helps it to move ever faster towards the goal that it has assigned to itself; the second is confined within limits that the memory of individuals can never hope to extend, and it must remain the prisoner of a history worked out from day to day, with neither a clear knowledge of its own origins nor a consecutive idea of what its future should be.

Yet nothing of what we know of writing, or of its role in evolution, can be said to justify this conception. One of the most creative phases in human history took place with the onset of the neolithic era: agriculture and the domestication of animals are only two of the developments which may be traced to this period. It must have had behind it thousands of years during which small societies of human beings were noting, experimenting, and passing on to one another the fruits of their knowledge. The very success of this immense enterprise bears witness to the rigour and the continuity of its preparation, at a time when writing was quite unknown. If writing first made its appearance between the fourth and third millennium before our era, we must see it not, in any degree, as a conditioning factor in the neolithic revolution, but rather as an already-distant and doubtless indirect result of that revolution. With what great innovation can it be linked? Where technique is concerned, architecture alone can be called into question. Yet the architecture of the Egyptians or the Sumerians was no better than the work of certain American Indians who, at the time America was discovered, were ignorant of writing. Conversely, between the invention of writing and the birth of modern science, the western world has lived through some five thousand years, during which time the sum of its knowledge has rather gone up and down than known a steady increase. It has often been remarked that there was no great difference between the life of a Greek or Roman citizen and that of a member of the well-to-do European classes in the eighteenth century. In the neolithic age, humanity made immense strides forward without any help from writing; and writing did not save the civilizations of the western world from long periods of stagnation. Doubtless the scientific expansion of the nineteenth and twentieth centuries could hardly have occurred, had writing not existed. But this condition, however necessary, cannot in itself explain that expansion.

If we want to correlate the appearance of writing with certain other characteristics of civilization, we must look elsewhere. The one phenomenon which has invariably accompanied it is the formation of cities and empires: the integration into a political system, that is to say, of a considerable number of individuals, and the distribution of those individuals into a hierarchy of castes and classes. Such is, at any rate, the type of development which we find, from Egypt right across to China, at the moment when writing makes its débuts; it seems to favour rather the exploitation than the enlightenment of mankind. This exploitation made it possible to assemble workpeople by the thousand and set them tasks that taxed them to the limits of their strength: to this, surely, we must attribute the beginnings of architecture as we know it. If my hypothesis is correct, the primary function of writing, as a means of communication, is to facilitate the enslavement of other human beings. The use of writing for disinterested ends, and with a view to satisfactions of the mind in the fields either of science or the arts, is a secondary result of its invention—and may even be no more than a way of reinforcing, justifying, or dissimulating its primary function.

There are, however, exceptions to this rule. Ancient Africa included empires in which several hundred thousand subjects acknowledged a single rule; in pre-Colombian America, the Inca empire numbered several million subjects. But, alike in Africa and in America, these ventures were notably unstable: we know, for instance, that the Inca empire was established in the twelfth century or thereabouts. Pizarro's soldiers would never have conquered it so easily if it had not already, three centuries later, been largely decomposed. And, from the little we know of the ancient history of Africa, we can divine an analogous situation: massive political groups seem to have appeared and disappeared within the space of not many decades. It may be, therefore, that these instances confirm, instead of refuting, our hypothesis. Writing may not have sufficed to consolidate human knowledge, but it may well have been indispensable to the establishment of an enduring dominion. To bring the matter nearer to our own time: the European-wide movement towards compulsory education in the nineteenth century went hand in hand with the extension of military service and the systematization of the proletariat. The struggle against illiteracy is indistinguishable, at times, from the increased powers exerted over the individual citizen by the central authority. For it is only when everyone can read that Authority can decree that 'ignorance of the law is no defence'.

All this moved rapidly from the national to the international level, thanks to the mutual complicity which sprang up between new-born states—confronted as these were with the problems that had been our own, a century or two ago—and an international society of peoples long privileged. These latter recognize that their stability may well be endangered by nations whose knowledge of the written word has not, as yet, empowered them to think in formulae which can be modified at will. Such nations are not yet ready to be 'edified'; and when they are first given the freedom of the library shelves they are perilously vulnerable to the ever more deliberately misleading effects of the printed word. Doubtless the die is already cast, in that respect. But in my Nambikwara village people were not so easily taken in. Shortly after my visit the leader lost the confidence of most of his people. Those who moved away from him, after he had tried to play the civilized man, must have had a confused understanding of the fact that writing, on this its first appearance in their midst, had allied itself with falsehood; and so they had taken refuge, deeper in the bush, to win themselves a respite. And yet I could not but admire the genius of their leader, for he had divined in a flash that writing could redouble his hold upon the others and, in so doing, he had got, as it were, to the bottom of an institution which he did not as yet know how to work. The episode also drew my attention to a further aspect of Nambikwara life: the political relations between individuals and groups. This I was shortly to be able to scrutinize more directly.

We were still at Utiarity when an epidemic of purulent ophthalmia broke out among the natives. This infection, gonococchic in origin, soon spread to every one of them. Apart from being terribly painful, it led to what threatened to be permanent blindness. For several days the entire band was paralysed. They treated their eyes with water, in which a certain kind of bark had been soaked: this they introduced into the eye with the help of leaves rolled into the shape of a funnel. The disease spread to my own group. My wife was the first to catch it. She had taken part in all our previous expeditions and had taken her full share in the study of material culture: but now she was so seriously ill that I had to send her back home. Most of our bearers went sick, and so did my Brazilian associate. Before long it was out of the question to go any farther. I ordered the main body of our party to rest, left our doctor behind to do what he could for them, and myself pushed on with two men and a few animals to the station of Campos Novos, near which a number of Indian bands had been reported. There I spent a fortnight in semi-idleness, picking the barely ripe fruit of an orchard which had 'gone back to Nature': guavas whose bitter taste and stony texture belied the promise of their scent; *caju,* vivid in colour as any parakeet, with a flesh that concealed within its spongy cells an astringent, delicately flavoured juice. And when the larder was empty we had only to get up at dawn and make our way to a thicket, a few hundred yards from the camp, where wood-pigeons would turn up, sharp on time every day, and offer themselves as our prey. At Campos Novos, too, I met two bands which had arrived from the north, drawn by the rumour of the presents I had brought with me.

These two bands were as ill disposed towards one another as they were towards me. From the outset, my gifts were not so much solicited as exacted. During the first few days only one of the bands was in evidence, together with a native from the Utiarity group who had gone on ahead of me. Did he show too much interest in a young woman who belonged to our hosts' group? I believe he did. Relations were bad, almost from the start, between the strangers and their visitor, and he dropped into the habit of coming over to my camp in search of a more cordial welcome. He also shared my meals. This fact was taken note of: and one day when he was out hunting I was visited by a delegation of four Indians. There was a distinct menace in the tone of voice in which they urged me to put poison into his food. They would bring me all that I needed: four little tubes bound together with cotton and filled with grey powder. I was very much put out: yet, as an outright refusal would turn the whole band against me,

I felt it best to go carefully, in view of their maleficent intentions. So I decided to know less of their language than I really did. Faced with my look of total incomprehension, the Indians repeated to me over and over again that my guest was *kakoré*, very wicked, and that I should get rid of him as soon as possible. Eventually they made off, with every sign of discontentment. I warned my guest of what had occurred, and he at once took to his heels; not till months later, when I revisited the region, did I see him again.

Luckily the second band arrived on the following day, giving the Indians a new target for their hostility. The meeting took place at my camp, which was both neutral ground and the terminal-point of their respective journeyings. I had, therefore, a front seat in the stalls. The men of each party came up on their own; a lengthy conversation followed between their respective leaders, consisting mainly of monologues, in alternation, on a plaintive, nasal note that I did not remember having encountered before. 'We are very angry!' one group kept on whining. 'You are our enemies!' To which the others replied: 'We are not at all angry! We are your brothers! Friends! We can understand each other!' and so on. Once this exchange of protests and provocations was over, a common camp was set up, close to my own. After some dancing and singing, during which each group played down its own contribution and glorified that of its adversaries —'The Tamaindé sang so well! And we sing so badly!'—quarrelling began again, and before long tempers began to run high. The night had hardly begun when the noise of argument-cum-singing set up a tremendous row, the significance of which was lost upon me. Threatening gestures could be seen, and once or twice men actually came to blows and had to be separated. The menaces consisted, in every case, of gestures relating in some way to the sexual organs. A Nambikwara shows hostility by taking his penis in both hands and pointing it towards his adversary. This is the prelude to an attack on the adversary in question, with a view to wrenching off the tuft of *buriti* straw that hangs down from the front of his belt, just above his private parts. These parts are 'hidden by the straw' and the point of fighting is to get the other man's straw away from him. This is an entirely symbolic action, for the masculine *cachesexe* is so fragile, and in any case so insubstantial, that it serves neither to protect nor, in any true sense, to dissimulate the parts in question. Another mark of victory is to wrest your opponent's bow and arrows from him and put them down some distance away. At all such times the Indians take on attitudes of extreme intensity, as if in a state of violent contained rage.

Eventually these individual quarrels end up in a general pitched battle. But on this occasion they died down at dawn. Still in the same state of evident exasperation, and with the roughest of gestures, the adversaries began to scrutinize one another closely, fingering an ear-ring here and a cotton bracelet or feathered ornament there, and muttering rapidly throughout: 'Give . . . give . . . give . . . look at that . . . how pretty!' to which the owner would reply: 'No, no . . . it's ugly, old, worn-out. . . .'

This reconciliatory inspection marks the end of the conflict. It introduces, as between the two groups, another kind of relationship: that of the commercial exchange. The material culture of the Nambikwara may be of the rudest, but each band's manufactures are, none the less, highly prized in the outer world. Those in the east are short of pottery and seed-beads. Those in the north consider that their southerly neighbours make particularly beautiful necklaces. The meeting of two groups, once established upon a pacific level, will therefore engender a whole series of reciprocal gifts: the battlefield turns into a market-place.

But the exchanges go forward almost imperceptibly: the morning after the quarrelling everyone went about his normal occupations, and objects or products changed hands without either donor or recipient making any outward allusion to what was going forward. Balls of thread and raw cotton; lumps of wax or resin; urucu paste; shells, earrings, bracelets, and necklaces; tobacco and seed-beads; feathers and strips of bamboo that could be made into arrowheads; bunches of palm-fibres and porcupine-quills; complete pots and potsherds; calabashes. This mysterious traffic went on until the day was half over, when the two groups separated and went off, each on his own way.

The Nambikwara leave everything, on such occasions, to the generosity of their 'opposite number'. Totally foreign to them is the notion that anyone could set a price on any object, discuss that price, haggle over it, insist on getting it, or 'chalk it up' as a debt. I once offered an Indian a forest-knife in return for his having carried a message to a nearby group. When he came back I did not immediately give him the knife, because I assumed that he would come and ask for it. But nothing of the kind: and the next day I couldn't find him anywhere. His friends told me that he had gone away in a rage, and I never saw him again. I had to entrust the present to another Indian. This being so, it is not surprising that when the exchanges are over one side or the other is often discontented with the result; and that, as weeks and then months go by, and he counts up, over and over again, the presents he received, and compares them with those he has given, he becomes more and more bitter. Often this bitterness turns to aggression. Many a war has broken out for no other reason. There are other causes, of course: a murder, or a rape to be either brought off or avenged. It does not seem as if a band feels itself bound to take collective reprisals for an injury done to any one of its members. But such is the animosity which reigns between groups that often every advantage is taken of pretexts of this kind, especially if the group in question feels itself in a strong position. The case is then presented by a warrior, who sets out his grievances in the same tone and in much the style of the encounter-ritual: 'Hallo there! Come here! Now look here—I'm very angry! Really very angry indeed! Arrows! Big arrows!'

Specially dressed for the occasion—tufts of *buriti* straw striped with red, jaguar-skin helmets—the men assemble behind their leader and dance. A divinatory rite must be observed: the chief, or the sorcerer, if one exists, hides an arrow in a corner of the bush. The next day the men search for the arrow and, if it is stained with blood, war is declared: if not, they call it all off. Many expeditions that begin in this way come to an end after a few miles' march. The war-party loses all its enthusiasm and excitement and turns back towards home. But sometimes the venture is pressed to its conclusion, and blood is shed. The Nambikwara attack at dawn, after having first scattered to create the conditions of an ambush. The signal to attack passes from man to man by means of the whistle that each carries round his neck. This whistle, made up of two tubes of bamboo tied together with cotton, makes a noise like that of the cricket and, doubtless for that reason, bears the same name. The war-arrows are those used in peace-time for hunting the bigger game, but their points are cut to a saw-edge. Arrows poisoned with curare, though common in hunting, are never used in battle, because anyone wounded by one of them would get it out before the poison had had time to get into his veins.

ROLAND BARTHES

Lévi-Strauss studied non-linguistic cultural phenomena, like kinship systems, marriage, and the preparation of food, as all being part of a great language. Knowledge of this language revealed the unconscious attitudes of the society that "spoke" it. Roland Barthes dates his own semiological interests from "around 1954," when it occurred to him to combine Saussure and Brecht to produce a social criticism useful for the demystification of bourgeois stereotypes.* These stereotypes Barthes called "myths." They erroneously present artificial, historically determined phenomena as natural phenomena. History is mistaken for Nature on many levels. Hence, myth is speech that has been "depoliticized."† Barthes could study photographs, films, newspaper articles, wrestling matches, cuisine, and clothing without ever changing his "linguistic" method of analysis. His collection of these articles, written monthly between 1954 and 1956, is called *Mythologies* (1957). Barthes is cagey about whether, in demystifying, he is himself the victim of a mythology, whether he is able to rise beyond ideology, what Plato called *doxa*, to truth. He finally decides his readings are Olympian, as opposed to Brechtian, and suggests that sarcasm may be the contemporary "condition of truth" (12).

In "The Great Family of Man," the first of three selections reprinted here, Barthes shows how an emotive word like "family" can fill us with sentimental feelings of common purpose and universality, feelings which would not be so objectionable if they did not hide the real advantages that one branch of the "family" has over other branches. For example, family feeling has not discouraged the economic or military leverage we apply—when it is in our interests—to our human "brothers and sisters." The fact that we all laugh and cry and work and play is hardly the point. And when we think of the hyperbolic intelligibility represented in "The World of Wrestling," where the signs for good and evil are clearly marked, it is troubling to realize that many governments in their foreign policy interpret the world with no greater "textual" sophistication than wrestlers do, and yet these signs are taken seriously when they designate their global "salaud."

"The Death of the Author" (1968) is perhaps the most succinct presentation of the Structuralist notion of the text-produced "scriptor," a

---

*"Inaugural Lecture, College de France," trans. Richard Howard, in *A Barthes Reader,* ed. Susan Sontag (New York: Hill and Wang, 1982) 471.
†Roland Barthes, *Mythologies,* trans. Annette Lavers (New York: Hill and Wang, 1972) 143 ff.

theory generated in opposition to the worshipful bourgeois positivist myth of the "author," who is in literary manuals the anterior source of his textual confidences, the sacred interiority for which his writings are the fallen artifact. For Barthes, the author's text is a network of unconscious quotations spoken by language itself with the author's identity but a holographic phantom generated by the movement of his pen. With the death of the author comes the liberation of the reader, who no longer needs to treat the text theologically as having only one secret. Meaning is thus infinitely pluralized, secularized.

The Great Family of Man

1957

Translated by Annette Lavers

A big exhibition of photographs has been held in Paris, the aim of which was to show the universality of human actions in the daily life of all the countries of the world: birth, death, work, knowledge, play, always impose the same types of behaviour; there is a family of Man.

The Family of Man, such at any rate was the original title of the exhibition which came here from the United States. The French have translated it as: *The Great Family of Man.* So what could originally pass for a phrase belonging to zoology, keeping only the similarity in behaviour, the unity of a species, is here amply moralized and sentimentalized. We are at the outset directed to this ambiguous myth of the human 'community', which serves as an alibi to a large part of our humanism.

This myth functions in two stages: first the difference between human morphologies is asserted, exoticism is insistently stressed, the infinite variations of the species, the diversity in skins, skulls and customs are made manifest, the image of Babel is complacently projected over that of the world. Then, from this pluralism, a type of unity is magically produced: man is born, works, laughs and dies everywhere in the same way; and if there still remains in these actions some ethnic peculiarity, at least one hints that there is underlying each one an identical 'nature', that their diversity is only formal and does not belie the existence of a common mould. Of course this means postulating a human essence, and here is God re-introduced into our Exhibition: the diversity of men proclaims his power, his richness; the unity of their gestures demonstrates his will. This is what the introductory leaflet confides to us when it states, by the pen of M. André Chamson, that *'this look over the human condition must somewhat resemble the benevolent gaze of God on our absurd and sublime ant-hill'.* The pietistic intention is underlined by the quotations which accompany each chapter of the Exhibition: these quotations often are 'primitive' proverbs or verses from the Old Testament. They all define an eternal wisdom, a class of assertions which escape History: *'The Earth is a Mother who never dies, Eat bread and salt and speak the truth, etc.'* This is the reign of gnomic truths, the meeting of all the ages of humanity at the most neutral point of their nature, the point where the obviousness of the truism has no longer any value except in the realm of a purely 'poetic' language. Everything here, the content and appeal of the pictures, the discourse which justifies them, aims to suppress the determining weight of History: we are held back at the surface of an identity, prevented precisely by sentimentality from penetrating into this ulterior zone of human behaviour where historical alienation introduces some 'differences' which we shall here quite simply call 'injustices'.

This myth of the human 'condition' rests on a very old mystification, which always consists in placing Nature at the bottom of History. Any classic humanism postulates that in scratching the history of men a little, the relativity of their institutions or the superficial diversity of their skins (but why not ask the parents of Emmet Till, the young Negro assassinated by the Whites what *they* think of *The Great Family of Man?*), one very quickly reaches the solid rock of a universal human nature. Progressive humanism, on the contrary, must always remember to reverse the terms of this very old imposture, constantly to scour nature, its 'laws' and its 'limits' in order to discover History there, and at last to establish Nature itself as historical.

Examples? Here they are: those of our Exhibition. Birth, death? Yes, these are facts of nature, universal facts. But if one removes History from them, there is nothing more to be said about them; any comment about them becomes purely tautological. The failure of photography seems to me to be flagrant in this connection: to reproduce death or birth tells us, literally, nothing. For these natural facts to gain access to a true language, they must be inserted into a category of knowledge which means postulating that one can transform them, and precisely subject their naturalness to our human criticism. For however universal, they are the signs of an historical writing. True, children are *always* born: but in the whole mass of the human problem, what does the 'essence' of this process matter to us, compared to its modes which, as for them, are perfectly historical? Whether or not the child is born with ease or difficulty, whether or not his birth causes suffering to his mother, whether or not he is threatened by a high mortality rate, whether or not such and such a type of future is open to him: this is what your Exhibitions should be telling people, instead of an eternal lyricism of birth. The same goes for death: must we really celebrate its essence once more, and thus risk forgetting that there is still so much we can do to fight it? It is this very young, far too young power that we must exalt, and not the sterile identity of 'natural' death.

And what can be said about work, which the Exhibition places among great universal facts, putting it on the same plane as birth and death, as if it was quite evident that it belongs to the same order of fate? That work is an age-old fact does not in the least prevent it from remaining a perfectly historical fact. Firstly, and evidently, because of its modes, its motivations, its ends and its benefits, which matter to such an extent that it will never be fair to confuse in a purely gestural identity the colonial and the Western worker (let us also ask the North African workers of the Goutte d'Or district in Paris what they think of *The Great Family of Man*). Secondly, because of the very differences in its inevitability: we know very well that work is 'natural' just as long as it is 'profitable', and that in modifying the inevitability of the profit, we shall perhaps one day modify the inevitability of labour. It is this entirely historified work which we should be told about, instead of an eternal aesthetics of laborious gestures.

So that I rather fear that the final justification of all this Adamism is to give to the immobility of the world the alibi of a 'wisdom' and a 'lyricism' which only make the gestures of man look eternal the better to defuse them.

The World of Wrestling

1957

Translated by Annette Lavers

The grandiloquent truth of gestures
on life's great occasions.

Baudelaire

The virtue of all-in wrestling is that it is the spectacle of excess. Here we find a grandiloquence which must have been that of ancient theatres. And in fact wrestling is an open-air spectacle, for what makes the circus or the arena what they are is not the sky (a romantic value suited rather to fashionable occasions), it is the drenching and vertical quality of the flood of light. Even hidden in the most squalid Parisian halls, wrestling partakes of the nature of the great solar spectacles, Greek drama and bullfights: in both, a light without shadow generates an emotion without reserve.

There are people who think that wrestling is an ignoble sport. Wrestling is not a sport, it is a spectacle, and it is no more ignoble to attend a wrestled performance of Suffering than a performance of the sorrows of Arnolphe or Andromaque.[1] Of course, there exists a false wrestling, in which the participants unnecessarily go to great lengths to make a show of a fair fight; this is of no interest. True wrestling, wrongly called amateur wrestling, is performed in second-rate halls, where the public spontaneously attunes itself to the spectacular nature of the contest, like the audience at a suburban cinema. Then these same people wax indignant because wrestling is a stage-managed sport (which ought, by the way, to mitigate its ignominy). The public is completely uninterested in knowing whether the

1. In Molière's *L'École des Femmes* and Racine's *Andromaque*.

contest is rigged or not, and rightly so; it abandons itself to the primary virtue of the spectacle, which is to abolish all motives and all consequences: what matters is not what it thinks but what it sees. This public knows very well the distinction between wrestling and boxing; it knows that boxing is a Jansenist sport, based on a demonstration of excellence. One can bet on the outcome of a boxing-match: with wrestling, it would make no sense. A boxing-match is a story which is constructed before the eyes of the spectator; in wrestling, on the contrary, it is each moment which is intelligible, not the passage of time. The spectator is not interested in the rise and fall of fortunes; he expects the transient image of certain passions. Wrestling therefore demands an immediate reading of the juxtaposed meanings, so that there is no need to connect them. The logical conclusion of the contest does not interest the wrestling-fan, while on the contrary a boxing-match always implies a science of the future. In other words, wrestling is a sum of spectacles, of which no single one is a function: each moment imposes the total knowledge of a passion which rises erect and alone, without ever extending to the crowning moment of a result.

Thus the function of the wrestler is not to win; it is to go exactly through the motions which are expected of him. It is said that judo contains a hidden symbolic aspect; even in the midst of efficiency, its gestures are measured, precise but restricted, drawn accurately but by a stroke without volume. Wrestling, on the contrary, offers excessive gestures, exploited to the limit of their meaning. In judo, a man who is down is hardly down at all, he rolls over, he draws back, he eludes defeat, or, if the latter is obvious, he immediately disappears; in wrestling, a man who is down is exaggeratedly so, and completely fills the eyes of the spectators with the intolerable spectacle of his powerlessness.

This function of grandiloquence is indeed the same as that of ancient theatre, whose principle, language and props (masks and buskins) concurred in the exaggeratedly visible explanation of a Necessity. The gesture of the vanquished wrestler signifying to the world a defeat which, far from disguising, he emphasizes and holds like a pause in music, corresponds to the mask of antiquity meant to signify the tragic mode of the spectacle. In wrestling, as on the stage in antiquity, one is not ashamed of one's suffering, one knows how to cry, one has a liking for tears.

Each sign in wrestling is therefore endowed with an absolute clarity, since one must always understand everything on the spot. As soon as the adversaries are in the ring, the public is overwhelmed with the obviousness of the roles. As in the theatre, each physical type expresses to excess the part which has been assigned to the contestant. Thauvin, a fifty-year-old with an obese and sagging body, whose type of asexual hideousness always inspires feminine nicknames, displays in his flesh the characters of baseness, for his part is to represent what, in the classical concept of the *salaud*, the 'bastard' (the key-concept of any wrestling-match), appears as organically repugnant. The nausea voluntarily provoked by Thauvin shows therefore a very extended use of signs: not only is ugliness used here in order to signify baseness, but in addition ugliness is wholly gathered into a particularly repulsive quality of matter: the pallid collapse of dead flesh (the public calls Thauvin *la barbaque*, 'stinking meat'), so that the passionate condemnation of the crowd no longer stems from its judgment, but instead from the very depth of its humours. It will thereafter let itself be frenetically embroiled in an idea of Thauvin which will conform entirely with this physical origin: his actions will perfectly correspond to the essential viscosity of his personage.

It is therefore in the body of the wrestler that we find the first key to the contest. I know from the start that all of Thauvin's actions, his treacheries, cruelties and acts of cowardice, will not fail to measure up to the first image of ignobility he gave me; I can trust him to carry out intelligently and to the last detail all the gestures of a kind of amorphous baseness, and thus fill to the brim the image of the most repugnant bastard there is: the bastard-octopus. Wrestlers therefore have a physique as peremptory as those of the characters of the *Commedia dell' Arte,* who display in advance, in their costumes and attitudes, the future contents of their parts: just as Pantaloon can never be anything but a ridiculous cuckold, Harlequin an astute servant and the Doctor a stupid pedant, in the same way Thauvin will never be anything but an ignoble traitor, Reinières (a tall blond fellow with a limp body and unkempt hair) the moving image of passivity, Mazaud (short and arrogant like a cock) that of grotesque conceit, and Orsano (an effeminate teddy-boy first seen in a blue-and-pink dressing-gown) that, doubly humorous, of a vindictive *salope,* or bitch (for I do not think that the public of the Elysée-Montmartre, like Littré, believes the word *salope* to be a masculine).

The physique of the wrestlers therefore constitutes a basic sign, which like a seed contains the whole fight. But this seed proliferates, for it is at every turn during the fight, in each new situation, that the body of the wrestler casts to the public the magical entertainment of a temperament which finds its natural expression in a gesture. The different strata of meaning throw light on each other, and form the most intelligible of spectacles. Wrestling is like a diacritic writing: above the fundamental meaning of his body, the wrestler arranges comments which are episodic but always opportune, and constantly help the reading of the fight by means of gestures, attitudes and mimicry which make the intention utterly obvious. Sometimes the wrestler triumphs with a repulsive sneer while kneeling on the good sportsman; sometimes he gives the crowd a conceited smile which forebodes an early revenge; sometimes, pinned to the ground, he hits the floor ostentatiously to make evident to all the intolerable nature of his situation; and sometimes he erects a complicated set of signs meant to make the public understand that he legitimately personifies the ever-entertaining image of the grumbler, endlessly confabulating about his displeasure.

We are therefore dealing with a real Human Comedy, where the most socially-inspired nuances of passion (conceit, rightfulness, refined cruelty, a sense of 'paying one's debts') always felicitously find the clearest sign which can receive them, express them and triumphantly carry them to the confines of the hall. It is obvious that at such a pitch, it no longer matters whether the passion is genuine or not. What the public wants is the image of passion, not passion itself. There is no more a problem of truth in wrestling than in the theatre. In both, what is expected is the intelligible representation of moral situations which are usually private. This emptying out of interiority to the benefit of its exterior signs, this exhaustion of the content by the form, is the very principle of triumphant classical art. Wrestling is an immediate pantomime, infinitely more efficient than the dramatic pantomime, for the wrestler's gesture needs no anecdote, no decor, in short no transference in order to appear true.

Each moment in wrestling is therefore like an algebra which instantaneously unveils the relationship between a cause and its represented effect. Wrestling fans certainly experience a kind of intellectual pleasure in *seeing* the moral mechanism function so perfectly. Some wrestlers, who are great comedians, entertain as much as a Molière character, because they succeed in imposing an immediate reading of their inner nature: Armand Mazaud, a wrestler of an arrogant and ridiculous character (as one says that Harpagon[2] is

2. In Molière's *L'Avare*.

a character), always delights the audience by the mathematical rigour of his transcriptions, carrying the form of his gestures to the furthest reaches of their meaning, and giving to his manner of fighting the kind of vehemence and precision found in a great scholastic disputation, in which what is at stake is at once the triumph of pride and the formal concern with truth.

What is thus displayed for the public is the great spectacle of Suffering, Defeat, and Justice. Wrestling presents man's suffering with all the amplification of tragic masks. The wrestler who suffers in a hold which is reputedly cruel (an arm-lock, a twisted leg) offers an excessive portrayal of Suffering; like a primitive Pietà, he exhibits for all to see his face, exaggeratedly contorted by an intolerable affliction. It is obvious, of course, that in wrestling reserve would be out of place, since it is opposed to the voluntary ostentation of the spectacle, to this Exhibition of Suffering which is the very aim of the fight. This is why all the actions which produce suffering are particularly spectacular, like the gesture of a conjuror who holds out his cards clearly to the public. Suffering which appeared without intelligible cause would not be understood; a concealed action that was actually cruel would transgress the unwritten rules of wrestling and would have no more sociological efficacy than a mad or parasitic gesture. On the contrary suffering appears as inflicted with emphasis and conviction, for everyone must not only see that the man suffers, but also and above all understand why he suffers. What wrestlers call a hold, that is, any figure which allows one to immobilize the adversary indefinitely and to have him at one's mercy, has precisely the function of preparing in a conventional, therefore intelligible, fashion the spectacle of suffering, of methodically establishing the conditions of suffering. The inertia of the vanquished allows the (temporary) victor to settle in his cruelty and to convey to the public this terrifying slowness of the torturer who is certain about the outcome of his actions; to grind the face of one's powerless adversary or to scrape his spine with one's fist with a deep and regular movement, or at least to produce the superficial appearance of such gestures: wrestling is the only sport which gives such an externalized image of torture. But here again, only the image is involved in the game, and the spectator does not wish for the actual suffering of the contestant; he only enjoys the perfection of an iconography. It is not true that wrestling is a sadistic spectacle: it is only an intelligible spectacle.

There is another figure, more spectacular still than a hold; it is the forearm smash, this loud slap of the forearm, this embryonic punch with which one clouts the chest of one's adversary, and which is accompanied by a dull noise and the exaggerated sagging of a vanquished body. In the forearm smash, catastrophe is brought to the point of maximum obviousness, so much so that ultimately the gesture appears as no more than a symbol; this is going too far, this is transgressing the moral rules of wrestling, where all signs must be excessively clear, but must not let the intention of clarity be seen. The public then shouts 'He's laying it on!', not because it regrets the absence of real suffering, but because it condemns artifice: as in the theatre, one fails to put the part across as much by an excess of sincerity as by an excess of formalism.

We have already seen to what extent wrestlers exploit the resources of a given physical style, developed and put to use in order to unfold before the eyes of the public a total image of Defeat. The flaccidity of tall white bodies which collapse with one blow or crash into the ropes with arms flailing, the inertia of massive wrestlers rebounding pitiably off all the elastic surfaces of the ring, nothing can signify more clearly and more passionately the exemplary abasement of the vanquished. Deprived of all resilience, the wrestler's flesh is no longer anything but an unspeakable heap spread out on the floor, where it solicits relentless reviling and jubilation. There is here a paroxysm of meaning in the style of antiquity, which can only recall the heavily underlined intentions in Roman triumphs. At other times, there is another ancient posture which appears in the coupling of the wrestlers, that of the suppliant who, at the mercy of his opponent, on bended knees, his arms raised above his head, is slowly brought down by the vertical pressure of the victor. In wrestling, unlike judo, Defeat is not a conventional sign, abandoned as soon as it is understood; it is not an outcome, but quite the contrary, it is a duration, a display, it takes up the ancient myths of public Suffering and Humiliation: the cross and the pillory. It is as if the wrestler is crucified in broad daylight and in the sight of all. I have heard it said of a wrestler stretched on the ground: 'He is dead, little Jesus, there, on the cross,' and these ironic words revealed the hidden roots of a spectacle which enacts the exact gestures of the most ancient purifications.

But what wrestling is above all meant to portray is a purely moral concept: that of justice. The idea of 'paying' is essential to wrestling, and the crowd's 'Give it to him' means above all else 'Make him pay'. This is therefore, needless to say, an immanent justice. The baser the action of the 'bastard', the more delighted the public is by the blow which he justly receives in return. If the villain—who is of course a coward—takes refuge behind the ropes, claiming unfairly to have a right to do so by a brazen mimicry, he is inexorably pursued there and caught, and the crowd is jubilant at seeing the rules broken for the sake of a deserved punishment. Wrestlers know very well how to play up to the capacity for indignation of the public by presenting the very limit of the concept of Justice, this outermost zone of confrontation where it is enough to infringe the rules a little more to open the gates of a world without restraints. For a wrestling-fan, nothing is finer than the revengeful fury of a betrayed fighter who throws himself vehemently not on a successful opponent but on the smarting image of foul play. Naturally, it is the pattern of Justice which matters here, much more than its content: wrestling is above all a quantitative sequence of compensations (an eye for an eye, a tooth for a tooth). This explains why sudden changes of circumstances have in the eyes of wrestling habitués a sort of moral beauty: they enjoy them as they would enjoy an inspired episode in a novel, and the greater the contrast between the success of a move and the reversal of fortune, the nearer the good luck of a contestant to his downfall, the more satisfying the dramatic mime is felt to be. Justice is therefore the embodiment of a possible transgression; it is from the fact that there is a Law that the spectacle of the passions which infringe it derives its value.

It is therefore easy to understand why out of five wrestling-matches, only about one is fair. One must realize, let it be repeated, that 'fairness' here is a role or a genre, as in the theatre: the rules do not at all constitute a real constraint; they are the conventional appearance of fairness. So that in actual fact a fair fight is nothing but an exaggeratedly polite one: the contestants confront each other with zeal, not rage; they can remain in control of their passions, they do not punish their beaten opponent relentlessly, they stop fighting as soon as they are ordered to do so, and congratulate each other at the end of a particularly arduous episode, during which, however, they have not ceased to be fair. One must of course understand here that all these polite actions are brought to the notice of the public by the most conventional gestures of fairness: shaking hands, raising the arms, ostensibly avoiding a fruitless hold which would detract from the perfection of the contest.

Conversely, foul play exists only in its excessive signs: administering a big kick to one's beaten opponent, taking refuge behind the ropes while ostensibly invoking a purely formal right, refusing to shake hands with one's opponent before or after the fight, taking advantage of the end of the round to rush treacherously at the adversary from behind, fouling him while the referee is not looking (a move which obviously only has any value or function because in fact half the audience can see it and get indignant about it). Since Evil is the natural climate of wrestling, a fair fight has chiefly the value of being an exception. It surprises the aficionado, who greets it when he sees it as an anachronism and a rather sentimental throwback to the sporting tradition ('Aren't they playing fair, those two'); he feels suddenly moved at the sight of the general kindness of the world, but would probably die of boredom and indifference if wrestlers did not quickly return to the orgy of evil which alone makes good wrestling.

Extrapolated, fair wrestling could lead only to boxing or judo, whereas true wrestling derives its originality from all the excesses which make it a spectacle and not a sport. The ending of a boxing-match or a judo-contest is abrupt, like the full-stop which closes a demonstration. The rhythm of wrestling is quite different, for its natural meaning is that of rhetorical amplification: the emotional magniloquence, the repeated paroxysms, the exasperation of the retorts can only find their natural outcome in the most baroque confusion. Some fights, among the most successful kind, are crowned by a final charivari, a sort of unrestrained fantasia where the rules, the laws of the genre, the referee's censuring and the limits of the ring are abolished, swept away by a triumphant disorder which overflows into the hall and carries off pell-mell wrestlers, seconds, referee and spectators.

It has already been noted that in America wrestling represents a sort of mythological fight between Good and Evil (of a quasi-political nature, the 'bad' wrestler always being supposed to be a Red). The process of creating heroes in French wrestling is very different, being based on ethics and not on politics. What the public is looking for here is the gradual construction of a highly moral image: that of the perfect 'bastard'. One comes to wrestling in order to attend the continuing adventures of a single major leading character, permanent and multiform like Punch or Scapino, inventive in unexpected figures and yet always faithful to his role. The 'bastard' is here revealed as a Molière character or a 'portrait' by La Bruyère, that is to say as a classical entity, an essence, whose acts are only significant epiphenomena arranged in time. This stylized character does not belong to any particular nation or party, and whether the wrestler is called Kuzchenko (nicknamed Moustache after Stalin), Yerpazian, Gaspardi, Jo Vignola or Nollières, the aficionado does not attribute to him any country except 'fairness'—observing the rules.

What then is a 'bastard' for this audience composed in part, we are told, of people who are themselves outside the rules of society? Essentially someone unstable, who accepts the rules only when they are useful to him and transgresses the formal continuity of attitudes. He is unpredictable, therefore asocial. He takes refuge behind the law when he considers that it is in his favour, and breaks it when he finds it useful to do so. Sometimes he rejects the formal boundaries of the ring and goes on hitting an adversary legally protected by the ropes, sometimes he reestablishes these boundaries and claims the protection of what he did not respect a few minutes earlier. This inconsistency, far more than treachery or cruelty, sends the audience beside itself with rage: offended not in its morality but in its logic, it considers the contradiction of arguments as the basest of crimes. The forbidden move becomes dirty only when it destroys a quantitative equilibrium and disturbs the rigorous reckoning of compensations; what is condemned by the audience is not at all the transgression of insipid official rules, it is the lack of revenge, the absence of a punishment. So that there is nothing more exciting for a crowd than the grandiloquent kick given to a vanquished 'bastard'; the joy of punishing is at its climax when it is supported by a mathematical justification; contempt is then unrestrained. One is no longer dealing with a *salaud* but with a *salope*—the verbal gesture of the ultimate degradation.

Such a precise finality demands that wrestling should be exactly what the public expects of it. Wrestlers, who are very experienced, know perfectly how to direct the spontaneous episodes of the fight so as to make them conform to the image which the public has of the great legendary themes of its mythology. A wrestler can irritate or disgust, he never disappoints, for he always accomplishes completely, by a progressive solidification of signs, what the public expects of him. In wrestling, nothing exists except in the absolute, there is no symbol, no allusion, everything is presented exhaustively. Leaving nothing in the shade, each action discards all parasitic meanings and ceremonially offers to the public a pure and full signification, rounded like Nature. This grandiloquence is nothing but the popular and age-old image of the perfect intelligibility of reality. What is portrayed by wrestling is therefore an ideal understanding of things; it is the euphoria of men raised for a while above the constitutive ambiguity of everyday situations and placed before the panoramic view of a univocal Nature, in which signs at last correspond to causes, without obstacle, without evasion, without contradiction.

When the hero or the villain of the drama, the man who was seen a few minutes earlier possessed by moral rage, magnified into a sort of metaphysical sign, leaves the wrestling hall, impassive, anonymous, carrying a small suitcase and arm-in-arm with his wife, no one can doubt that wrestling holds that power of transmutation which is common to the Spectacle and to Religious Worship. In the ring, and even in the depths of their voluntary ignominy, wrestlers remain gods because they are, for a few moments, the key which opens Nature, the pure gesture which separates Good from Evil, and unveils the form of a Justice which is at last intelligible.

The Death of the Author

1968

Translated by Richard Howard

I n his tale *Sarrasine,* Balzac, speaking of a castrato disguised as a woman, writes this sentence: "She was Woman, with her sudden fears, her inexplicable whims, her instinctive fears, her meaningless bravado, her defiance, and her delicious delicacy of feeling." Who speaks in this way? Is it the hero of the tale, who would prefer not to recognize the castrato hidden beneath the "woman"? Is it Balzac the man, whose personal experience has provided him with a philosophy of Woman? Is it Balzac the author, professing certain "literary" ideas about femininity? Is it universal wisdom? Romantic psychology? We can never know, for the good reason that writing is the destruction of every voice, every origin. Writing is that neuter, that composite, that

THE DEATH OF THE AUTHOR   from *The Rustle of Language* by Roland Barthes. English translation copyright © 1986 by Farrar, Straus and Giroux, Inc. Reprinted by permission of Hill and Wang, a division of Farrar, Straus and Giroux, Inc.

obliquity into which our subject flees, the black-and-white where all identity is lost, beginning with the very identity of the body that writes.

No doubt it has always been so: once a fact is *recounted*—for intransitive purposes, and no longer to act directly upon reality, i.e., exclusive of any function except that exercise of the symbol itself —this gap appears, the voice loses its origin, the author enters into his own death, writing begins. However, the affect of this phenomenon has been variable; in ethnographic societies, narrative is never assumed by a person but by a mediator, shaman, or reciter, whose "performance" (i.e., his mastery of the narrative code) can be admired, but never his "genius." The *author* is a modern character, no doubt produced by our society as it emerged from the Middle Ages, inflected by English empiricism, French rationalism, and the personal faith of the Reformation, thereby discovering the prestige of the individual, or, as we say more nobly, of the "human person." Hence, it is logical that in literary matters it should be positivism, crown and conclusion of capitalist ideology, which has granted the greatest importance to the author's "person." The *author* still reigns in manuals of literary history, in biographies of writers, magazine interviews, and in the very consciousness of litterateurs eager to unite, by means of private journals, their person and their work; the image of literature to be found in contemporary culture is tyrannically centered on the author, his person, his history, his tastes, his passions; criticism still largely consists in saying that Baudelaire's oeuvre is the failure of the man Baudelaire, Van Gogh's is his madness, Tchaikovsky's his vice: *explanation* of the work is still sought in the person of its producer, as if, through the more or less transparent allegory of fiction, it was always, ultimately, the voice of one and the same person, the *author,* which was transmitting his "confidences."

Though the Author's empire is still very powerful (the new criticism has quite often merely consolidated it), we know that certain writers have already tried to subvert it. In France, Mallarmé, no doubt the first, saw and foresaw in all its scope the necessity to substitute language itself for the subject hitherto supposed to be its owner; for Mallarmé, as for us, it is language which speaks, not the author; to write is to reach, through a preliminary impersonality —which we can at no moment identify with the realistic novelist's castrating "objectivity"—that point where not "I" but only language functions, "performs": Mallarmé's whole poetics consists in suppressing the author in favor of writing (and thereby restoring, as we shall see, the reader's place). Valéry, entangled in a psychology of the ego, greatly edulcorated Mallarmean theory, but led by a preference for classicism to conform to the lessons of Rhetoric, he continued to cast the Author into doubt and derision, emphasized the linguistic and "accidental" nature of his activity, and throughout his prose works championed the essentially verbal condition of literature, as opposed to which any resort to the writer's interiority seemed to him pure superstition. Proust himself, despite the apparently psychological character of what is called his *analyses,* visibly undertook to blur by an extreme subtilization the relation of the writer and his characters: by making the narrator not the one who has seen or felt, or even the one who writes, but the one who *is going to write* (the young man of the novel—but, as a matter of fact, how old is he and *who* is he?—wants to write but cannot, and the novel ends when writing finally becomes possible), Proust has given modern writing its epic: by a radical reversal, instead of putting his life into his novel, as is so often said, he made his life itself a work of which his own book was the model, so that it is quite clear to us that it is not Charlus who imitates Montesquiou, but Montesquiou, in his anecdotal, historical reality, who is only a secondary, derived fragment of Charlus. Finally Surrealism, to keep to this prehistory of modernity, could doubtless not attribute a sovereign place to language, since language is system, and what this movement sought was, romantically, a direct subversion of the codes—an illusory subversion, moreover, for a code cannot be destroyed, only "flouted"; yet, by constantly striving to disappoint expected meanings (this was the famous surrealist "shock"), by urging the hand to write as fast as possible what the head was unaware of (this was automatic writing), by accepting the principle and the experiment of collective writing, Surrealism helped desacralize the image of the Author. Last, outside literature itself (in fact, such distinctions are becoming quite dated), linguistics furnishes the destruction of the Author with a precious analytic instrument, showing that the speech-act in its entirety is an "empty" process, which functions perfectly without its being necessary to "fill" it with the person of the interlocutors: linguistically, the author is nothing but the one who writes, just as *I* is nothing but the one who says *I:* language knows a "subject," not a "person," and this subject, empty outside of the very speech-act which defines it, suffices to "hold" language, i.e., to exhaust it.

The removal of the Author (with Brecht, we might speak here of a veritable *distancing,* the Author diminishing like a figure at the far end of the literary stage) is not only a historical fact or an act of writing: it utterly transforms the modern text (or—which is the same thing—the text is henceforth produced and read so that the author absents himself from it at every level). Time, first of all, is no longer the same. The Author, when we believe in him, is always conceived as the past of his own book: book and author are voluntarily placed on one and the same line, distributed as a *before* and an *after:* the Author is supposed to *feed* the book, i.e., he lives before it, thinks, suffers, lives for it; he has the same relation of antecedence with his work that a father sustains with his child. Quite the contrary, the modern *scriptor* is born *at the same time* as his text; he is not furnished with a being which precedes or exceeds his writing, he is not the subject of which his book would be the predicate; there is no time other than that of the speech-act, and every text is written eternally *here* and *now.* This is because (or it follows that) *writing* can no longer designate an operation of recording, of observation, of representation, of "painting" (as the Classics used to say), but instead what the linguists, following Oxfordian philosophy, call a performative, a rare verbal form (exclusively found in the first person and in the present), in which the speech-act has no other content (no other statement) than the act by which it is uttered: something like the *I declare* of kings or the *I sing* of the earliest poets; the modern *scriptor,* having buried the Author, can therefore no longer believe, according to the pathos of his predecessors, that his hand is slower than his passion and that in consequence, making a law of necessity, he must emphasize this delay and endlessly "elaborate" his form; for him, on the contrary, his hand, detached from any voice, borne by a pure gesture of inscription (and not of expression), traces a field without origin—or at least with no origin but language itself, i.e., the very thing which ceaselessly calls any origin into question.

We know now that a text consists not of a line of words, releasing a single "theological" meaning (the "message" of the Author-God), but of a multi-dimensional space in which are married and contested several writings, none of which is original: the text is a fabric of quotations, resulting from a thousand sources of culture. Like Bouvard and Pécuchet, those eternal copyists, at once sublime and comical, whose profound absurdity *precisely* designates the truth of writing, the writer can only imitate an ever anterior, never original gesture; his sole power is to mingle writings, to counter some by others, so as never to rely on just one; if he seeks to *express himself,* at least he knows that the interior "thing" he claims to "translate" is itself no more than a ready-made lexicon, whose words can be explained only through other words, and this ad infinitum: an adventure which exemplarily befell young Thomas De Quincey, so versed in his Greek that in order to translate certain absolutely modern ideas and images into this dead language, Baudelaire tells us, "he had a dictionary made for himself, one much more complex and extensive than the kind produced by the vulgar patience of purely literary themes" *(Les Paradis artificiels);* succeeding the Author, the *scriptor* no longer contains passions, moods, sentiments, impressions, but that immense dictionary from which he draws a writing which will be incessant: life merely imitates the book, and this book itself is but a tissue of signs, endless imitation, infinitely postponed.

Once the Author is distanced, the claim to "decipher" a text becomes entirely futile. To assign an Author to a text is to impose a brake on it, to furnish it with a final signified, to close writing. This conception is quite suited to criticism, which then undertakes the important task of discovering the Author (or his hypostases: society, history, the psyche, freedom) beneath the work: once the Author is found, the text is "explained," the critic has won; hence, it is hardly surprising that historically the Author's empire has been the Critic's as well, and also that (even new) criticism is today unsettled at the same time as the Author. In multiple writing, in effect, everything is to be *disentangled,* but nothing *deciphered,* structure can be followed, "threaded" (as we say of a run in a stocking) in all its reprises, all its stages, but there is no end to it, no bottom; the space of writing is to be traversed, not pierced; writing constantly posits meaning, but always in order to evaporate it: writing seeks a systematic exemption of meaning. Thereby, literature (it would be better, from now on, to say *writing),* by refusing to assign to the text (and to the world-as-text) a "secret," i.e., an ultimate meaning, liberates an activity we may call countertheological, properly revolutionary, for to refuse to halt meaning is finally to refuse God and his hypostases, reason, science, the law.

To return to Balzac's sentence. No one (i.e., no "person") says it: its source, its voice is not the true site of writing, it is reading. Another very specific example will help us here: recent investigations (J.-P. Vernant) have shed some light on the constitutively ambiguous nature of Greek tragedy, whose text is "woven" of words with double meanings, words which each character understands unilaterally (this perpetual misunderstanding is precisely what we call the "tragic"); there is, however, someone who understands each word in its duplicity, and further understands, one may say, the very deafness of the characters speaking in his presence: this "someone" is precisely the reader (or here the listener). Here we discern the total being of writing: a text consists of multiple writings, proceeding from several cultures and entering into dialogue, into parody, into contestation; but there is a site where this multiplicity is collected, and this site is not the author, as has hitherto been claimed, but the reader: the reader is the very space in which are inscribed, without any of them being lost, all the citations out of which a writing is made; the unity of a text is not in its origin but in its destination, but this destination can no longer be personal: the reader is a man without history, without biography, without psychology; he is only that *someone* who holds collected into one and the same field all of the traces from which writing is constituted. That is why it is absurd to hear the new writing condemned in the name of a humanism which hypocritically claims to champion the reader's rights. Classical criticism has never been concerned with the reader; for that criticism, there is no other man in literature than the one who writes. We are no longer so willing to be the dupes of such antiphrases, by which a society proudly recriminates in favor of precisely what it discards, ignores, muffles, or destroys; we know that in order to restore writing to its future, we must reverse the myth: the birth of the reader must be requited by the death of the Author.

Manteia, 1968

LOUIS ALTHUSSER

Lévi-Strauss says in *The Raw and the Cooked* (1964) that ". . . myths operate in men's minds without their being aware of the fact."* Althusser's *ideology* plays essentially the same role in Althusser's system of thought as does *myth* in the system of Lévi-Strauss or *doxa* in that of Barthes. It is the network of shared, unexamined assumptions that holds a given society together. It is an imaginary representation of the real conditions of existence, a form of self-delusion. Ideology is not a system of lies deliberately and cynically devised by despots to dominate the masses. It is an atmosphere of consent generated spontaneously by the social structures in which the "subject" is entangled simply by being born. His name awaits him as does his place in a given family. His alien identity is generated for him by the subjecting structures. Later he (or she) becomes the "bearer" of these structures himself, unconsciously reproducing for others the mystifications which have held him (or her) in thrall. For Althusser, as for Aristotle in the *Politics* (VIIIi), the schools are the ultimate modern ideological state apparatus. For others, like Michèle Barrett, the family plays the crucial role, producing an ideology of cooperation, sharing, communality, warmth, and love, while actually training children in the most ferocious aspects of capitalist society: selfishness, submission to male authority, exclusion of the atypical, and paranoia vis à vis other groups unconnected genetically to one's own.† It seems to be possible for Althusser and other powerful thinkers, like Marx or Freud, to rise above mystification to the truth, to penetrate *doxa* and to reveal the structural *epistémé*.‡ But for most people, it is not. Moreover, ideology will remain a necessary condition even for socialist societies; for the operation of ideology is, like Freud's unconscious, eternal. It is Althusser's emphasis on the inevitability of subject-formation and the passivity of the subject in his or her social context that differentiates Althusser from Sartrean notions of Voluntarism (people are free agents) and Historicism (we make things happen by intentional acts) and which finally makes Althusser more of a Structuralist than a Marxist.

---

*Claude Lévi-Strauss, *The Raw and the Cooked*, trans. John and Doreen Weightman (London: Cape, 1970) 12.

†Michèle Barrett and Mary McIntosh, *The Anti-Social Family* (London: Verso, 1982) 46–80.

‡Norman Geras, *Literature of Revolution* (London: Verso, 1986) 130. By the time Plato's term becomes Foucault's, truth has become "truth," and *episfeme* has become *épistème*.

Ideology and Ideological State Apparatuses

1970

Translated by Ben Brewster

ON THE REPRODUCTION OF THE CONDITIONS OF PRODUCTION[1]

I must now expose more fully something which was briefly glimpsed in my analysis when I spoke of the necessity to renew the means of production if production is to be possible. That was a passing hint. Now I shall consider it for itself.

As Marx said, every child knows that a social formation which did not reproduce the conditions of production at the same time as it produced would not last a year.[2] The ultimate condition of production is therefore the reproduction of the conditions of production. This may be 'simple' (reproducing exactly the previous conditions of production) or 'on an extended scale' (expanding them). Let us ignore this last distinction for the moment.

What, then, is *the reproduction of the conditions of production?*

Here we are entering a domain which is both very familiar (since *Capital* Volume Two) and uniquely ignored. The tenacious obviousnesses (ideological obviousnesses of an empiricist type) of the point of view of production alone, or even of that of mere productive practice (itself abstract in relation to the process of production) are so integrated into our everyday 'consciousness' that

IDEOLOGY AND IDEOLOGICAL STATE APPARATUSES by Louis Althusser from *Lenin and Philosophy and other Essays*, tr. Ben Brewster. Copyright © 1971 by New Left Books. Reprinted by permission of Monthly Review Foundation.

1. This text is made up of two extracts from an ongoing study. The sub-title 'Notes towards an Investigation' is the author's own [deleted here]. The ideas expounded should not be regarded as more than the introduction to a discussion.
2. Marx to Kugelmann, 11 July 1868, *Selected Correspondence*, Moscow, 1955, p. 209.

it is extremely hard, not to say almost impossible, to raise oneself to the *point of view of reproduction.* Nevertheless, everything outside this point of view remains abstract (worse than one-sided: distorted) —even at the level of production, and, *a fortiori,* at that of mere practice.

Let us try and examine the matter methodically.

To simplify my exposition, and assuming that every social formation arises from a dominant mode of production, I can say that the process of production sets to work the existing productive forces in and under definite relations of production.

It follows that, in order to exist, every social formation must reproduce the conditions of its production at the same time as it produces, and in order to be able to produce. It must therefore reproduce:

1. the productive forces,
2. the existing relations of production.

Reproduction of the Means of Production

Everyone (including the bourgeois economists whose work is national accounting, or the modern 'macro-economic' 'theoreticians') now recognizes, because Marx compellingly proved it in *Capital* Volume Two, that no production is possible which does not allow for the reproduction of the material conditions of production: the reproduction of the means of production.

The average economist, who is no different in this than the average capitalist, knows that each year it is essential to foresee what is needed to replace what has been used up or worn out in production: raw material, fixed installations (buildings), instruments of production (machines), etc. I say the average economist = the average capitalist, for they both express the point of view of the firm, regarding it as sufficient simply to give a commentary on the terms of the firm's financial accounting practice.

But thanks to the genius of Quesnay who first posed this 'glaring' problem, and to the genius of Marx who resolved it, we know that the reproduction of the material conditions of production cannot be thought at the level of the firm, because it does not exist at that level in its real conditions. What happens at the level of the firm is an effect, which only gives an idea of the necessity of reproduction, but absolutely fails to allow its conditions and mechanisms to be thought.

A moment's reflection is enough to be convinced of this: Mr X, a capitalist who produces woollen yarn in his spinning-mill, has to 'reproduce' his raw material, his machines, etc. But *he* does not produce them for his own production—other capitalists do: an Australian sheepfarmer, Mr Y, a heavy engineer producing machine-tools, Mr Z, etc., etc. And Mr Y and Mr Z, in order to produce those products which are the condition of the reproduction of Mr X's conditions of production, also have to reproduce the conditions of their own production, and so on to infinity—the whole in proportions such that, on the national and even the world market, the demand for means of production (for reproduction) can be satisfied by the supply.

In order to think this mechanism, which leads to a kind of 'endless chain', it is necessary to follow Marx's 'global' procedure, and to study in particular the relations of the circulation of capital between Department I (production of means of production) and Department II (production of means of consumption), and the realization of surplus-value, in *Capital,* Volumes Two and Three.

We shall not go into the analysis of this question. It is enough to have mentioned the existence of the necessity of the reproduction of the material conditions of production.

Reproduction of Labour-Power

However, the reader will not have failed to note one thing. We have discussed the reproduction of the means of production—but not the reproduction of the productive forces. We have therefore ignored the reproduction of what distinguishes the productive forces from the means of production, i.e. the reproduction of labour power.

From the observation of what takes place in the firm, in particular from the examination of the financial accounting practice which predicts amortization and investment, we have been able to obtain an approximate idea of the existence of the material process of reproduction, but we are now entering a domain in which the observation of what happens in the firm is, if not totally blind, at least almost entirely so, and for good reason: the reproduction of labour power takes place essentially outside the firm.

How is the reproduction of labour power ensured?

It is ensured by giving labour power the material means with which to reproduce itself: by wages. Wages feature in the accounting of each enterprise, but as 'wage capital',[3] not at all as a condition of the material reproduction of labour power.

However, that is in fact how it 'works', since wages represents only that part of the value produced by the expenditure of labour power which is indispensable for its reproduction: sc. indispensable to the reconstitution of the labour power of the wage-earner (the wherewithal to pay for housing, food and clothing, in short to enable the wage-earner to present himself again at the factory gate the next day—and every further day God grants him); and we should add: indispensable for raising and educating the children in whom the proletarian reproduces himself (in n models where n = 0, 1, 2, etc. . . .) as labour power.

Remember that this quantity of value (wages) necessary for the reproduction of labour power is determined not by the needs of a 'biological' Guaranteed Minimum Wage *(Salaire Minimum Interprofessionnel Garanti)* alone, but by the needs of a historical minimum (Marx noted that English workers need beer while French proletarians need wine)—i.e. a historically variable minimum.

I should also like to point out that this minimum is doubly historical in that it is not defined by the historical needs of the working class 'recognized' by the capitalist class, but by the historical needs imposed by the proletarian class struggle (a double class struggle: against the lengthening of the working day and against the reduction of wages).

However, it is not enough to ensure for labour power the material conditions of its reproduction if it is to be reproduced as labour power. I have said that the available labour power must be 'competent', i.e. suitable to be set to work in the complex system of the process of production. The development of the productive forces and the type of unity historically constitutive of the productive forces at a given moment produce the result that the labour power has to be (diversely) skilled and therefore reproduced as such. Diversely: according to the requirements of the socio-technical division of labour, its different 'jobs' and 'posts'.

How is this reproduction of the (diversified) skills of labour power provided for in a capitalist regime? Here, unlike social formations characterized by slavery or serfdom, this reproduction of the skills of labour power tends (this is a tendential law) decreasingly to be provided for 'on the spot' (apprenticeship within production itself),

---

3. Marx gave it its scientific concept: *variable capital.*

but is achieved more and more outside production: by the capitalist education system, and by other instances and institutions.

What do children learn at school? They go varying distances in their studies, but at any rate they learn to read, to write and to add—i.e. a number of techniques, and a number of other things as well, including elements (which may be rudimentary or on the contrary thoroughgoing) of 'scientific' or 'literary culture', which are directly useful in the different jobs in production (one instruction for manual workers, another for technicians, a third for engineers, a final one for higher management, etc.). Thus they learn 'know-how'.

But besides these techniques and knowledges, and in learning them, children at school also learn the 'rules' of good behaviour, i.e. the attitude that should be observed by every agent in the division of labour, according to the job he is 'destined' for: rules of morality, civic and professional conscience, which actually means rules of respect for the socio-technical division of labour and ultimately the rules of the order established by class domination. They also learn to 'speak proper French', to 'handle' the workers correctly, i.e. actually (for the future capitalists and their servants) to 'order them about' properly, i.e. (ideally) to 'speak to them' in the right way, etc.

To put this more scientifically, I shall say that the reproduction of labour power requires not only a reproduction of its skills, but also, at the same time, a reproduction of its submission to the rules of the established order, i.e. a reproduction of submission to the ruling ideology for the workers, and a reproduction of the ability to manipulate the ruling ideology correctly for the agents of exploitation and repression, so that they, too, will provide for the domination of the ruling class 'in words'.

In other words, the school (but also other State institutions like the Church, or other apparatuses like the Army) teaches 'know-how', but in forms which ensure *subjection to the ruling ideology* or the mastery of its 'practice'. All the agents of production, exploitation and repression, not to speak of the 'professionals of ideology' (Marx), must in one way or another be 'steeped' in this ideology in order to perform their tasks 'conscientiously'—the tasks of the exploited (the proletarians), of the exploiters (the capitalists), of the exploiters' auxiliaries (the managers), or of the high priests of the ruling ideology (its 'functionaries'), etc.

The reproduction of labour power thus reveals as its *sine qua non* not only the reproduction of its 'skills' but also the reproduction of its subjection to the ruling ideology or of the 'practice' of that ideology, with the proviso that it is not enough to say 'not only but also', for it is clear that *it is in the forms and under the forms of ideological subjection that provision is made for the reproduction of the skills of labour power.*

But this is to recognize the effective presence of a new reality: *ideology.*

Here I shall make two comments.

The first is to round off my analysis of reproduction.

I have just given a rapid survey of the forms of the reproduction of the productive forces, i.e. of the means of production on the one hand, and of labour power on the other.

But I have not yet approached the question of the *reproduction of the relations of production.* This is a *crucial question* for the Marxist theory of the mode of production. To let it pass would be a theoretical omission—worse, a serious political error.

I shall therefore discuss it. But in order to obtain the means to discuss it, I shall have to make another long detour.

The second comment is that in order to make this detour, I am obliged to re-raise my old question: what is a society?

INFRASTRUCTURE AND SUPERSTRUCTURE

On a number of occasions[4] I have insisted on the revolutionary character of the Marxist conception of the 'social whole' insofar as it is distinct from the Hegelian 'totality' I said (and this thesis only repeats famous propositions of historical materialism) that Marx conceived the structure of every society as constituted by 'levels' or 'instances' articulated by a specific determination: the *infrastructure,* or economic base (the 'unity' of the productive forces and the relations of production) and the *superstructure,* which itself contains two 'levels' or 'instances': the politico-legal (law and the State) and ideology (the different ideologies, religious, ethical, legal, political, etc.).

Besides its theoretico-didactic interest (it reveals the difference between Marx and Hegel), this representation has the following crucial theoretical advantage: it makes it possible to inscribe in the theoretical apparatus of its essential concepts what I have called their

4. In *For Marx* and *Reading Capital,* 1965 (English editions 1969 and 1970 respectively).

respective indices of effectivity. What does this mean?

It is easy to see that this representation of the structure of every society as an edifice containing a base (infrastructure) on which are erected the two 'floors' of the superstructure, is a metaphor, to be quite precise, a spatial metaphor: the metaphor of a topography *(topique).*[5] Like every metaphor, this metaphor suggests something, makes something visible. What? Precisely this: that the upper floors could not 'stay up' (in the air) alone, if they did not rest precisely on their base.

Thus the object of the metaphor of the edifice is to represent above all the 'determination in the last instance' by the economic base. The effect of this spatial metaphor is to endow the base with an index of effectivity known by the famous terms: the determination in the last instance of what happens in the upper 'floors' (of the superstructure) by what happens in the economic base.

Given this index of effectivity 'in the last instance', the 'floors' of the superstructure are clearly endowed with different indices of effectivity. What kind of indices?

It is possible to say that the floors of the superstructure are not determinant in the last instance, but that they are determined by the effectivity of the base; that if they are determinant in their own (as yet undefined) ways, this is true only insofar as they are determined by the base.

Their index of effectivity (or determination), as determined by the determination in the last instance of the base, is thought by the Marxist tradition in two ways: (1) there is a 'relative autonomy' of the superstructure with respect to the base; (2) there is a 'reciprocal action' of the superstructure on the base.

We can therefore say that the great theoretical advantage of the Marxist topography, i.e. of the spatial metaphor of the edifice (base and superstructure) is simultaneously that it reveals that questions of determination (or of index of effectivity) are crucial; that it reveals that it is the base which in the last instance determines the whole edifice; and that, as a consequence, it obliges us to pose the theoretical problem of the types of 'derivatory' effectivity peculiar to the superstructure, i.e. it obliges us to think what the Marxist tradition calls conjointly the relative autonomy of the superstructure and the

---

5. *Topography* from the Greek *topos:* place. A topography represents in a definite space the respective *sites* occupied by several realities: thus the economic is *at the bottom* (the base), the superstructure *above it.*

reciprocal action of the superstructure on the base.

The greatest disadvantage of this representation of the structure of every society by the spatial metaphor of an edifice, is obviously the fact that it is metaphorical: i.e. it remains *descriptive*.

It now seems to me that it is possible and desirable to represent things differently. NB, I do not mean by this that I want to reject the classical metaphor, for that metaphor itself requires that we go beyond it. And I am not going beyond it in order to reject it as outworn. I simply want to attempt to think what it gives us in the form of a description.

I believe that it is possible and necessary to think what characterizes the essential of the existence and nature of the superstructure *on the basis of reproduction*. Once one takes the point of view of reproduction, many of the questions whose existence was indicated by the spatial metaphor of the edifice, but to which it could not give a conceptual answer, are immediately illuminated.

My basic thesis is that it is not possible to pose these questions (and therefore to answer them) *except from the point of view of reproduction*.

I shall give a short analysis of Law, the State and Ideology *from this point of view*. And I shall reveal what happens both from the point of view of practice and production on the one hand, and from that of reproduction on the other.

THE STATE

The Marxist tradition is strict, here: in the *Communist Manifesto* and the *Eighteenth Brumaire* (and in all the later classical texts, above all in Marx's writings on the Paris Commune and Lenin's on *State and Revolution*), the State is explicitly conceived as a repressive apparatus. The State is a 'machine' of repression, which enables the ruling classes (in the nineteenth century the bourgeois class and the 'class' of big landowners) to ensure their domination over the working class, thus enabling the former to subject the latter to the process of surplus-value extortion (i.e. to capitalist exploitation).

The State is thus first of all what the Marxist classics have called *the State apparatus*. This term means: not only the specialized apparatus (in the narrow sense) whose existence and necessity I have recognized in relation to the requirements of legal practice, i.e. the police, the courts, the prisons; but also the army, which (the proletariat has paid for this experience with its blood) intervenes directly as a supplementary repressive force in the last instance, when the police and its specialized auxiliary corps are 'outrun by events'; and above this ensemble, the head of State, the government and the administration.

Presented in this form, the Marxist-Leninist 'theory' of the State has its finger on the essential point, and not for one moment can there be any question of rejecting the fact that this really is the essential point. The State apparatus, which defines the State as a force of repressive execution and intervention 'in the interests of the ruling classes' in the class struggle conducted by the bourgeoisie and its allies against the proletariat, is quite certainly the State, and quite certainly defines its basic 'function'.

From Descriptive Theory to Theory as Such

Nevertheless, here too, as I pointed out with respect to the metaphor of the edifice (infrastructure and superstructure), this presentation of the nature of the State is still partly descriptive.

As I shall often have occasion to use this adjective (descriptive), a word of explanation is necessary in order to remove any ambiguity.

Whenever, in speaking of the metaphor of the edifice or of the Marxist 'theory' of the State, I have said that these are descriptive conceptions or representations of their objects, I had no ulterior critical motives. On the contrary, I have every grounds to think that great scientific discoveries cannot help but pass through the phase of what I shall call *descriptive 'theory'*. This is the first phase of every theory, at least in the domain which concerns us (that of the science of social formations). As such, one might—and in my opinion one must—envisage this phase as a transitional one, necessary to the development of the theory. That it is transitional is inscribed in my expression: 'descriptive theory', which reveals in its conjunction of terms the equivalent of a kind of 'contradiction'. In fact, the term theory 'clashes' to some extent with the adjective 'descriptive' which I have attached to it. This means quite precisely: (1) that the 'descriptive theory' really is, without a shadow of a doubt, the irreversible beginning of the theory; but (2) that the 'descriptive' form in which the theory is presented requires, precisely as an effect of this 'contradiction', a development of the theory which goes beyond the form of 'description'.

Let me make this idea clearer by returning to our present object: the State.

When I say that the Marxist 'theory' of the State available to us is still partly 'descriptive', that means first and foremost that this descriptive 'theory' is without the shadow of a doubt precisely the beginning of the Marxist theory of the State, and that this beginning gives us the essential point, i.e. the decisive principle of every later development of the theory.

Indeed, I shall call the descriptive theory of the State correct, since it is perfectly possible to make the vast majority of the facts in the domain with which it is concerned correspond to the definition it gives of its object. Thus, the definition of the State as a class State, existing in the repressive State apparatus, casts a brilliant light on all the facts observable in the various orders of repression whatever their domains: from the massacres of June 1848 and of the Paris Commune, of Bloody Sunday, May 1905 in Petrograd, of the Resistance, of Charonne, etc., to the mere (and relatively anodyne) interventions of a 'censorship' which has banned Diderot's *La Réligieuse* or a play by Gatti on Franco; it casts light on all the direct or indirect forms of exploitation and extermination of the masses of the people (imperialist wars); it casts light on that subtle everyday domination beneath which can be glimpsed, in the forms of political democracy, for example, what Lenin, following Marx, called the dictatorship of the bourgeoisie.

And yet the descriptive theory of the State represents a phase in the constitution of the theory which itself demands the 'supersession' of this phase. For it is clear that if the definition in question really does give us the means to identify and recognize the facts of oppression by relating them to the State, conceived as the repressive State apparatus, this 'interrelationship' gives rise to a very special kind of obviousness, about which I shall have something to say in a moment: 'Yes, that's how it is, that's really true!'[6] And the accumulation of facts within the definition of the State may multiply examples, but it does not really advance the definition of the State, i.e. the scientific theory of the State. Every descriptive theory thus runs the risk of 'blocking' the development of the theory, and yet that development is essential.

That is why I think that, in order to develop this descriptive theory into theory as such, i.e. in order to understand further the mechanisms of the State in its functioning, I think that it is indispensable to

6. See p. 84, *On Ideology*.

add something to the classical definition of the State as a State apparatus.

The Essentials of the Marxist Theory of the State

Let me first clarify one important point: the State (and its existence in its apparatus) has no meaning except as a function of *State power.* The whole of the political class struggle revolves around the State. By which I mean around the possession, i.e. the seizure and conservation of State power by a certain class or by an alliance between classes or class fractions. This first clarification obliges me to distinguish between State power (conservation of State power or seizure of State power), the objective of the political class struggle on the one hand, and the State apparatus on the other.

We know that the State apparatus may survive, as is proved by bourgeois 'revolutions' in nineteenth-century France (1830, 1848), by *coups d'état* (2 December, May 1958), by collapses of the State (the fall of the Empire in 1870, of the Third Republic in 1940), or by the political rise of the petty bourgeoisie (1890–95 in France), etc., without the State apparatus being affected or modified: it may survive political events which affect the possession of State power.

Even after a social revolution like that of 1917, a large part of the State apparatus survived after the seizure of State power by the alliance of the proletariat and the small peasantry: Lenin repeated the fact again and again.

It is possible to describe the distinction between State power and State apparatus as part of the 'Marxist theory' of the State, explicitly present since Marx's *Eighteenth Brumaire* and *Class Struggles in France.*

To summarize the 'Marxist theory of the State' on this point, it can be said that the Marxist classics have always claimed that (1) the State is the repressive State apparatus, (2) State power and State apparatus must be distinguished, (3) the objective of the class struggle concerns State power, and in consequence the use of the State apparatus by the classes (or alliance of classes or of fractions of classes) holding State power as a function of their class objectives, and (4) the proletariat must seize State power in order to destroy the existing bourgeois State apparatus and, in a first phase, replace it with a quite different, proletarian, State apparatus, then in later phases set in motion a radical process, that of the destruction of the State (the end of State power, the end of every State apparatus). In this perspective, therefore, what I would propose to add to the 'Marxist theory' of the State is already there in so many words. But it seems to me that even with this supplement, this theory is still in part descriptive, although it does now contain complex and differential elements whose functioning and action cannot be understood without recourse to further supplementary theoretical development.

The State Ideological Apparatuses

Thus, what has to be added to the 'Marxist theory' of the State is something else.

Here we must advance cautiously in a terrain which, in fact, the Marxist classics entered long before us, but without having systematized in theoretical form the decisive advances implied by their experiences and procedures. Their experiences and procedures were indeed restricted in the main to the terrain of political practice.

In fact, i.e. in their political practice, the Marxist classics treated the State as a more complex reality than the definition of it given in the 'Marxist theory of the State', even when it has been supplemented as I have just suggested. They recognized this complexity in their practice, but they did not express it in a corresponding theory.[7]

I should like to attempt a very schematic outline of this corresponding theory. To that end, I propose the following thesis.

In order to advance the theory of the State it is indispensable to take into account not only the distinction between *State power* and *State apparatus*, but also another reality which is clearly on the side of the (repressive) State apparatus, but must not be confused with it. I shall call this reality by its concept: *the ideological State apparatuses*.

What are the ideological State apparatuses (ISAs)?

They must not be confused with the (repressive) State apparatus. Remember that in Marxist theory, the State Apparatus (SA) contains:

---

7. To my knowledge, Gramsci is the only one who went any distance in the road I am taking. He had the 'remarkable' idea that the State could not be reduced to the (Repressive) State Apparatus, but included, as he put it, a certain number of institutions from '*civil society*': the Church, the Schools, the trade unions, etc. Unfortunately, Gramsci did not systematize his institutions, which remained in the state of acute but fragmentary notes (cf. Gramsci, *Selections from the Prison Notebooks,* International Publishers, 1971, pp. 12, 259, 260–3; see also the letter to Tatiana Schucht, 7 September 1931, in *Lettre del Carcere,* Einaudi, 1968, p. 479, *Letters from Prison,* tr. Lynne Lawner (New York: Harper and Row, 1973).

the Government, the Administration, the Army, the Police, the Courts, the Prisons, etc., which constitute what I shall in future call the Repressive State Apparatus. Repressive suggests that the State Apparatus in question 'functions by violence'—at least ultimately (since repression, e.g. administrative repression, may take non-physical forms).

I shall call Ideological State Apparatuses a certain number of realities which present themselves to the immediate observer in the form of distinct and specialized institutions. I propose an empirical list of these which will obviously have to be examined in detail, tested, corrected and reorganized. With all the reservations implied by this requirement, we can for the moment regard the following institutions as Ideological State Apparatuses (the order in which I have listed them has no particular significance):

—the religious ISA (the system of the different Churches),
—the educational ISA (the system of the different public and private 'Schools'),
—the family ISA,[8]
—the legal ISA,[9]
—the political ISA (the political system, including the different Parties),
—the trade-union ISA,
—the communications ISA (press, radio and television, etc.),
—the cultural ISA (Literature, the Arts, sports, etc.).

I have said that the ISAs must not be confused with the (Repressive) State Apparatus. What constitutes the difference?

As a first moment, it is clear that while there is *one* (Repressive) State Apparatus, there is a *plurality* of Ideological State Apparatuses. Even presupposing that it exists, the unity that constitutes this plurality of ISAs as a body is not immediately visible.

As a second moment, it is clear that whereas the—unified —(Repressive) State Apparatus belongs entirely to the *public* domain, much the larger part of the Ideological State Apparatuses (in their apparent dispersion) are part, on the contrary, of the *private* domain. Churches, Parties, Trade Unions, families, some schools, most newspapers, cultural ventures, etc., etc., are private.

---

8. The family obviously has other 'functions' than that of an ISA. It intervenes in the reproduction of labour power. In different modes of production it is the unit of production and/or the unit of consumption.
9. The 'Law' belongs both to the (Repressive) State Apparatus and to the system of the ISAs.

We can ignore the first observation for the moment. But someone is bound to question the second, asking me by what right I regard as Ideological *State* Apparatuses, institutions which for the most part do not possess public status, but are quite simply *private* institutions. As a conscious Marxist, Gramsci already forestalled this objection in one sentence. The distinction between the public and the private is a distinction internal to bourgeois law, and valid in the (subordinate) domains in which bourgeois law exercises its 'authority'. The domain of the State escapes it because the latter is 'above the law': the State, which is the State *of* the ruling class, is neither public nor private; on the contrary, it is the precondition for any distinction between public and private. The same thing can be said from the starting-point of our State Ideological Apparatuses. It is unimportant whether the institutions in which they are realized are 'public' or 'private'. What matters is how they function. Private institutions can perfectly well 'function' as Ideological State Apparatuses. A reasonably thorough analysis of any one of the ISAs proves it.

But now for what is essential. What distinguishes the ISAs from the (Repressive) State Apparatus is the following basic difference: the Repressive State Apparatus functions 'by violence', whereas the Ideological State Apparatuses *function 'by ideology'*.

I can clarify matters by correcting this distinction. I shall say rather that every State Apparatus, whether Repressive or Ideological, 'functions' both by violence and by ideology, but with one very important distinction which makes it imperative not to confuse the Ideological State Apparatuses with the (Repressive) State Apparatus.

This is the fact that the (Repressive) State Apparatus functions massively and predominantly *by repression* (including physical repression), while functioning secondarily by ideology. (There is no such thing as a purely repressive apparatus.) For example, the Army and the Police also function by ideology both to ensure their own cohesion and reproduction, and in the 'values' they propound externally.

In the same way, but inversely, it is essential to say that for their part the Ideological State Apparatuses function massively and predominantly *by ideology,* but they also function secondarily by repression, even if ultimately, but only ultimately, this is very attenuated and concealed, even symbolic. (There is no such thing as a purely ideological apparatus.) Thus Schools and Churches use suitable methods of punishment, expulsion, selection, etc., to 'discipline' not only their shepherds, but also their flocks. The same is true of the Family. . . . The same is true of the cultural IS Apparatus (censorship, among other things), etc.

Is it necessary to add that this determination of the double 'functioning' (predominantly, secondarily) by repression and by ideology, according to whether it is a matter of the (Repressive) State Apparatus or the Ideological State Apparatuses, makes it clear that very subtle explicit or tacit combinations may be woven from the interplay of the (Repressive) State Apparatus and the Ideological State Apparatuses? Everyday life provides us with innumerable examples of this, but they must be studied in detail if we are to go further than this mere observation.

Nevertheless, this remark leads us towards an understanding of what constitutes the unity of the apparently disparate body of the ISAs. If the ISAs 'function' massively and predominantly by ideology, what unifies their diversity is precisely this functioning, insofar as the ideology by which they function is always in fact unified, despite its diversity and its contradictions, *beneath the ruling ideology,* which is the ideology of 'the ruling class'. Given the fact that the 'ruling class' in principle holds State power (openly or more often by means of alliances between classes or class fractions), and therefore has at its disposal the (Repressive) State Apparatus, we can accept the fact that this same ruling class is active in the Ideological State Apparatuses insofar as it is ultimately the ruling ideology which is realized in the Ideological State Apparatuses, precisely in its contradictions. Of course, it is a quite different thing to act by laws and decrees in the (Repressive) State Apparatus and to 'act' through the intermediary of the ruling ideology in the Ideological State Apparatuses. We must go into the details of this difference—but it cannot mask the reality of a profound identity. To my knowledge, *no class can hold State power over a long period without at the same time exercising its hegemony over and in the State Ideological Apparatuses.* I only need one example and proof of this: Lenin's anguished concern to revolutionize the educational Ideological State Apparatus (among others), simply to make it possible for the Soviet proletariat, who had seized State power, to secure the future of the dictatorship of the proletariat and the transition to socialism.[10]

This last comment puts us in a position to understand that the

10. In a text written in 1937, Krupskaya relates the history of Lenin's desperate efforts and what she regards as his failure.

Ideological State Apparatuses may be not only the *stake,* but also the *site* of class struggle, and often of bitter forms of class struggle. The class (or class alliance) in power cannot lay down the law in the ISAs as easily as it can in the (repressive) State apparatus, not only because the former ruling classes are able to retain strong positions there for a long time, but also because the resistance of the exploited classes is able to find means and occasions to express itself there, either by the utilization of their contradictions, or by conquering combat positions in them in struggle.[11]

Let me run through my comments.

If the thesis I have proposed is well-founded, it leads me back to the classical Marxist theory of the State, while making it more precise in one point. I argue that it is necessary to distinguish between State power (and its possession by . . .) on the one hand, and the State Apparatus on the other. But I add that the State Apparatus contains two bodies: the body of institutions which represent the Repressive State Apparatus on the one hand, and the body of institutions which represent the body of Ideological State Apparatuses on the other.

But if this is the case, the following question is bound to be asked, even in the very summary state of my suggestions: what exactly is the extent of the role of the Ideological State Apparatuses? What is their importance based on? In other words: to what does the 'function' of these Ideological State Apparatuses, which do not function by repression but by ideology, correspond?

---

11. What I have said in these few brief words about the class struggle in the ISAs is obviously far from exhausting the question of the class struggle.

To approach this question, two principles must be borne in mind:

The first principle was formulated by Marx in the Preface to *A Contribution to the Critique of Political Economy:* 'In considering such transformations [a social revolution] a distinction should always be made between the material transformation of the economic conditions of production, which can be determined with the precision of natural science, and the legal, political, religious, aesthetic or philosophic—in short, ideological forms in which men become conscious of this conflict and fight it out.' The class struggle is thus expressed and exercised in ideological forms, thus also in the ideological forms of the ISAs. But the class struggle *extends far beyond* these forms, and it is because it extends beyond them that the struggle of the exploited classes may also be exercised in the forms of the ISAs, and thus turn the weapon of ideology against the classes in power.

This by virtue of the *second principle:* the class struggle extends beyond the ISAs because it is rooted elsewhere than in ideology, in the Infrastructure, in the relations of production, which are relations of exploitation and constitute the base for class relations.

ON THE REPRODUCTION OF THE RELATIONS OF PRODUCTION

I can now answer the central question which I have left in suspense for many long pages: *how is the reproduction of the relations of production secured?*

In the topographical language (Infrastructure, Superstructure), I can say: for the most part,[12] it is secured by the legal-political and ideological superstructure.

But as I have argued that it is essential to go beyond this still descriptive language, I shall say: for the most part,[12] it is secured by the exercise of State power in the State Apparatuses, on the one hand the (Repressive) State Apparatus, on the other the Ideological State Apparatuses.

What I have just said must also be taken into account, and it can be assembled in the form of the following three features:

1. All the State Apparatuses function both by repression and by ideology, with the difference that the (Repressive) State Apparatus functions massively and predominantly by repression, whereas the Ideological State Apparatuses function massively and predominantly by ideology.

2. Whereas the (Repressive) State Apparatus constitutes an organized whole whose different parts are centralized beneath a commanding unity, that of the politics of class struggle applied by the political representatives of the ruling classes in possession of State power, the Ideological State Apparatuses are multiple, distinct, 'relatively autonomous' and capable of providing an objective field to contradictions which express, in forms which may be limited or extreme, the effects of the clashes between the capitalist class struggle and the proletarian class struggle, as well as their subordinate forms.

3. Whereas the unity of the (Repressive) State Apparatus is secured by its unified and centralized organization under the leadership of the representatives of the classes in power executing the politics of the class struggle of the classes in power, the unity of the different Ideological State Apparatuses is secured, usually in contradictory forms, by the ruling ideology, the ideology of the ruling class.

12. For the most part. For the relations of production are first reproduced by the materiality of the processes of production and circulation. But it should not be forgotten that ideological relations are immediately present in these same processes.

Taking these features into account, it is possible to represent the reproduction of the relations of production[13] in the following way, according to a kind of 'division of labour'.

The role of the repressive State apparatus, insofar as it is a repressive apparatus, consists essentially in securing by force (physical or otherwise) the political conditions of the reproduction of relations of production which are in the last resort *relations of exploitation.* Not only does the State apparatus contribute generously to its own reproduction (the capitalist State contains political dynasties, military dynasties, etc.), but also and above all, the State apparatus secures by repression (from the most brutal physical force, via mere administrative commands and interdictions, to open and tacit censorship) the political conditions for the action of the Ideological State Apparatuses.

In fact, it is the latter which largely secure the reproduction specifically of the relations of production, behind a 'shield' provided by the repressive State apparatus. It is here that the role of the ruling ideology is heavily concentrated, the ideology of the ruling class, which holds State power. It is the intermediation of the ruling ideology that ensures a (sometimes teeth-gritting) 'harmony' between the repressive State apparatus and the Ideological State Apparatuses, and between the different State Ideological Apparatuses.

We are thus led to envisage the following hypothesis, as a function precisely of the diversity of ideological State Apparatuses in their single, because shared, role of the reproduction of the relations of production.

Indeed we have listed a relatively large number of ideological State apparatuses in contemporary capitalist social formations: the educational apparatus, the religious apparatus, the family apparatus, the political apparatus, the trade-union apparatus, the communications apparatus, the 'cultural' apparatus, etc.

But in the social formations of that mode of production characterized by 'serfdom' (usually called the feudal mode of production), we observe that although there is a single repressive State apparatus which, since the earliest known Ancient States, let alone the Absolute Monarchies, has been formally very similar to the one we know today, the number of Ideological State Apparatuses is smaller and their

13. *For that part* of reproduction to which the Repressive State Apparatus and the Ideological State Apparatus *contribute.*

individual types are different. For example, we observe that during the Middle Ages, the Church (the religious ideological State apparatus) accumulated a number of functions which have today devolved on to several distinct ideological State apparatuses, new ones in relation to the past I am invoking, in particular educational and cultural functions. Alongside the Church there was the family Ideological State Apparatus, which played a considerable part, incommensurable with its role in capitalist social formations. Despite appearances, the Church and the Family were not the only Ideological State Apparatuses. There was also a political Ideological State Apparatus (the Estates General, the *Parlement*, the different political factions and Leagues, the ancestors or the modern political parties, and the whole political system of the free Communes and then of the *Villes*). There was also a powerful 'proto-trade-union' Ideological State Apparatus, if I may venture such an anachronistic term (the powerful merchants' and bankers' guilds and the journeymen's associations, etc.). Publishing and Communications, even, saw an indisputable development, as did the theatre; initially both were integral parts of the Church, then they became more and more independent of it.

In the pre-capitalist historical period which I have examined extremely broadly, it is absolutely clear that *there was one dominant Ideological State Apparatus, the Church,* which concentrated within it not only religious functions, but also educational ones, and a large proportion of the functions of communications and 'culture'. It is no accident that all ideological struggle, from the sixteenth to the eighteenth century, starting with the first shocks of the Reformation, was *concentrated* in an anti-clerical and anti-religious struggle; rather this is a function precisely of the dominant position of the religious ideological State apparatus.

The foremost objective and achievement of the French Revolution was not just to transfer State power from the feudal aristocracy to the merchant-capitalist bourgeoisie, to break part of the former repressive State apparatus and replace it with a new one (e.g., the national popular Army)—but also to attack the number-one Ideological State Apparatus: the Church. Hence the civil constitution of the clergy, the confiscation of ecclesiastical wealth, and the creation of new ideological State apparatuses to replace the religious ideological State apparatus in its dominant role.

Naturally, these things did not happen automatically: witness the Concordat, the Restoration and the long class struggle between the

landed aristocracy and the industrial bourgeoisie throughout the
nineteenth century for the establishment of bourgeois hegemony
over the functions formerly fulfilled by the Church: above all by the
Schools. It can be said that the bourgeoisie relied on the new
political, parliamentary-democratic, ideological State apparatus, installed in the earliest years of the Revolution, then restored after long
and violent struggles, for a few months in 1848 and for decades after
the fall of the Second Empire, in order to conduct its struggle against
the Church and wrest its ideological functions away from it, in other
words, to ensure not only its own political hegemony, but also the
ideological hegemony indispensable to the reproduction of capitalist
relations of production.

That is why I believe that I am justified in advancing the following
Thesis, however precarious it is. I believe that the ideological State
apparatus which has been installed in the *dominant* position in
mature capitalist social formations as a result of a violent political and
ideological class struggle against the old dominant ideological State
apparatus, is the *educational ideological apparatus.*

This thesis may seem paradoxical, given that for everyone, i.e. in
the ideological representation that the bourgeoisie has tried to give
itself and the classes it exploits, it really seems that the dominant
ideological State apparatus in capitalist social formations is not the
Schools, but the political ideological State apparatus, i.e. the regime
of parliamentary democracy combining universal suffrage and party
struggle.

However, history, even recent history, shows that the bourgeoisie
has been and still is able to accommodate itself to political ideological State apparatuses other than parliamentary democracy: the First
and Second Empires, Constitutional Monarchy (Louis XVIII and
Charles X), Parliamentary Monarchy (Louis-Philippe), Presidential
Democracy (de Gaulle), to mention only France. In England this is
even clearer. The Revolution was particularly 'successful' there from
the bourgeois point of view, since unlike France, where the bourgeoisie, partly because of the stupidity of the petty aristocracy, had to
agree to being carried to power by peasant and plebeian *'journées
révolutionnaires',* something for which it had to pay a high price, the
English bourgeoisie was able to 'compromise' with the aristocracy
and "share" State power and the use of the State apparatus with it for
a long time (peace among all men of good will in the ruling classes!).
In Germany it is even more striking, since it was behind a political
ideological State apparatus in which the imperial Junkers (epito-

mized by Bismarck), their army and their police provided it with a shield and leading personnel, that the imperialist bourgeoisie made its shattering entry into history, before 'traversing' the Weimar Republic and entrusting itself to Nazism.

Hence I believe I have good reasons for thinking that behind the scenes of its political Ideological State Apparatus, which occupies the front of the stage, what the bourgeoisie has installed as its number-one, i.e. as its dominant ideological State apparatus, is the educational apparatus, which has in fact replaced in its functions the previously dominant ideological State apparatus, the Church. One might even add: the School-Family couple has replaced the Church-Family couple.

Why is the educational apparatus in fact the dominant ideological State apparatus in capitalist social formations, and how does it function?

For the moment it must suffice to say:

1. All ideological State apparatuses, whatever they are, contribute to the same result: the reproduction of the relations of production, i.e. of capitalist relations of exploitation.

2. Each of them contributes towards this single result in the way proper to it. The political apparatus by subjecting individuals to the political State ideology, the 'indirect' (parliamentary) or 'direct' (plebiscitary or fascist) 'democratic' ideology. The communications apparatus by cramming every 'citizen' with daily doses of nationalism, chauvinism, liberalism, moralism, etc, by means of the press, the radio and television. The same goes for the cultural apparatus (the role of sport in chauvinism is of the first importance), etc. The religious apparatus by recalling in sermons and the other great ceremonies of Birth, Marriage and Death, that man is only ashes, unless he loves his neighbour to the extent of turning the other cheek to whoever strikes first. The family apparatus . . . but there is no need to go on.

3. This concert is dominated by a single score, occasionally disturbed by contradictions (those of the remnants of former ruling classes, those of the proletarians and their organizations): the score of the Ideology of the current ruling class which integrates into its music the great themes of the Humanism of the Great Forefathers, who produced the Greek Miracle even before Christianity, and afterwards the Glory of Rome, the Eternal City, and the themes of Interest, particular and general, etc. nationalism, moralism and economism.

4. Nevertheless, in this concert, one ideological State apparatus certainly has the dominant role, although hardly anyone lends an ear to its music: it is so silent! This is the School.

It takes children from every class at infant-school age, and then for years, the years in which the child is most 'vulnerable', squeezed between the family State apparatus and the educational State apparatus, it drums into them, whether it uses new or old methods, a certain amount of 'know-how' wrapped in the ruling ideology (French, arithmetic, natural history, the sciences, literature) or simply the ruling ideology in its pure state (ethics, civic instruction, philosophy). Somewhere around the age of sixteen, a huge mass of children are ejected 'into production': these are the workers or small peasants. Another portion of scholastically adapted youth carries on: and, for better or worse, it goes somewhat further, until it falls by the wayside and fills the posts of small and middle technicians, white-collar workers, small and middle executives, petty bourgeois of all kinds. A last portion reaches the summit, either to fall into intellectual semi-employment, or to provide, as well as the 'intellectuals of the collective labourer', the agents of exploitation (capitalists, managers), the agents of repression (soldiers, policemen, politicians, administrators, etc.) and the professional ideologists (priests of all sorts, most of whom are convinced 'laymen').

Each mass ejected *en route* is practically provided with the ideology which suits the role it has to fulfil in class society: the role of the exploited (with a 'highly-developed' 'professional', 'ethical', 'civic', 'national' and a-political consciousness); the role of the agent of exploitation (ability to give the workers orders and speak to them: 'human relations'), of the agent of repression (ability to give orders and enforce obedience 'without discussion', or ability to manipulate the demagogy of a political leader's rhetoric), or of the professional ideologist (ability to treat consciousnesses with the respect, i.e. with the contempt, blackmail, and demagogy they deserve, adapted to the accents of Morality, of Virtue, of 'Transcendence', of the Nation, of France's World Role, etc.).

Of course, many of these contrasting Virtues (modesty, resignation, submissiveness on the one hand, cynicism, contempt, arrogance, confidence, self-importance, even smooth talk and cunning on the other) are also taught in the Family, in the Church, in the Army, in Good Books, in films and even in the football stadium. But no other ideological State apparatus has the obligatory (and not least, free) audience of the totality of the children in the capitalist social formation, eight hours a day for five or six days out of seven.

But it is by an apprenticeship in a variety of know-how wrapped up in the massive inculcation of the ideology of the ruling class that the *relations of production* in a capitalist social formation, i.e. the relations of exploited to exploiters and exploiters to exploited, are largely reproduced. The mechanisms which produce this vital result for the capitalist regime are naturally covered up and concealed by a universally reigning ideology of the School, universally reigning because it is one of the essential forms of the ruling bourgeois ideology: an ideology which represents the School as a neutral environment purged of ideology (because it is . . . lay), where teachers respectful of the 'conscience' and 'freedom' of the children who are entrusted to them (in complete confidence) by their 'parents' (who are free, too, i.e. the owners of their children) open up for them the path to the freedom, morality and responsibility of adults by their own example, by knowledge, literature and their 'liberating' virtues.

I ask the pardon of those teachers who, in dreadful conditions, attempt to turn the few weapons they can find in the history and learning they 'teach' against the ideology, the system and the practices in which they are trapped. They are a kind of hero. But they are rare and how many (the majority) do not even begin to suspect the 'work' the system (which is bigger than they are and crushes them) forces them to do, or worse, put all their heart and ingenuity into performing it with the most advanced awareness (the famous new methods!). So little do they suspect it that their own devotion contributes to the maintenance and nourishment of this ideological representation of the School, which makes the School today as 'natural', indispensable-useful and even beneficial for our contemporaries as the Church was 'natural', indispensable and generous for our ancestors a few centuries ago.

In fact, the Church has been replaced today *in its role as the dominant Ideological State Apparatus* by the School. It is coupled with the Family just as the Church was once coupled with the Family. We can now claim that the unprecedentedly deep crisis which is now shaking the education system of so many States across the globe, often in conjunction with a crisis (already proclaimed in the *Communist Manifesto*) shaking the family system, takes on a political meaning, given that the School (and the School-Family couple) constitutes the dominant Ideological State Apparatus, the Apparatus playing a determinant part in the reproduction of the relations of production of a mode of production threatened in its existence by the world class struggle.

ON IDEOLOGY

When I put forward the concept of an Ideological State Apparatus, when I said that the ISAs 'function by ideology', I invoked a reality which needs a little discussion: ideology.

It is well known that the expression 'ideology' was invented by Cabanis, Destutt de Tracy and their friends, who assigned to it as an object the (genetic) theory of ideas. When Marx took up the term fifty years later, he gave it a quite different meaning, even in his Early Works. Here, ideology is the system of the ideas and representations which dominate the mind of a man or a social group. The ideologico-political struggle conducted by Marx as early as his articles in the *Rheinische Zeitung* inevitably and quickly brought him face to face with this reality and forced him to take his earliest intuitions further.

However, here we come upon a rather astonishing paradox. Everything seems to lead Marx to formulate a theory of ideology. In fact, *The German Ideology* does offer us, after the *1844 Manuscripts,* an explicit theory of ideology, but . . . it is not Marxist (we shall see why in a moment). As for *Capital,* although it does contain many hints towards a theory of ideologies (most visibly, the ideology of the vulgar economists), it does not contain that theory itself, which depends for the most part on a theory of ideology in general.

I should like to venture a first and very schematic outline of such a theory. The theses I am about to put forward are certainly not off the cuff, but they cannot be sustained and tested, i.e. confirmed or rejected, except by much thorough study and analysis.

Ideology has no History

One word first of all to expound the reason in principle which seems to me to found, or at least to justify, the project of a theory of ideology *in general,* and not a theory of particular ideolog*ies,* which, whatever their form (religious, ethical, legal, political), always express *class positions.*

It is quite obvious that it is necessary to proceed towards a theory of ideolog*ies* in the two respects I have just suggested. It will then be clear that a theory of ideolog*ies* depends in the last resort on the history of social formations, and thus of the modes of production combined in social formations, and of the class struggles which develop in them. In this sense it is clear that there can be no question of a theory of ideolog*ies in general,* since ideolog*ies* (defined in the double respect suggested above: regional and class) have a history, whose determination in the last instance is clearly situated outside ideologies alone, although it involves them.

On the contrary, if I am able to put forward the project of a theory of ideology *in general,* and if this theory really is one of the elements on which theories of ideolog*ies* depend, that entails an apparently paradoxical proposition which I shall express in the following terms: *ideology has no history.*

As we know, this formulation appears in so many words in a passage from *The German Ideology.* Marx utters it with respect to metaphysics, which, he says, has no more history than ethics (meaning also the other forms of ideology).

In *The German Ideology,* this formulation appears in a plainly positivist context. Ideology is conceived as a pure illusion, a pure dream, i.e. as nothingness. All its reality is external to it. Ideology is thus thought as an imaginary construction whose status is exactly like the theoretical status of the dream among writers before Freud. For these writers, the dream was the purely imaginary, i.e. null, result of 'day's residues', presented in an arbitrary arrangement and order, sometimes even 'inverted,' in other words, in 'disorder.' For them, the dream was the imaginary, it was empty, null and arbitrarily 'stuck together' *(bricolé),* once the eyes had closed, from the residues of the only full and positive reality, the reality of the day. This is exactly the status of philosophy and ideology (since in this book philosophy is ideology *par excellence*) in *The German Ideology.*

Ideology, then, is for Marx an imaginary assemblage *(bricolage),* a pure dream, empty and vain, constituted by the 'day's residues' from the only full and positive reality, that of the concrete history of concrete material individuals materially producing their existence. It is on this basis that ideology has no history in *The German Ideology,* since its history is outside it, where the only existing history is, the history of concrete individuals, etc. In *The German Ideology,* the thesis that ideology has no history is therefore a purely negative thesis, since it means both:

1. ideology is nothing insofar as it is a pure dream (manufactured by who knows what power: if not by the alienation of the division of labour, but that, too, is a *negative* determination);

2. ideology has no history, which emphatically does not mean that

there is no history in it (on the contrary, for it is merely the pale, empty and inverted reflection of real history) but that it has no history *of its own.*

Now, while the thesis I wish to defend formally speaking adopts the terms of *The German Ideology* ('ideology has no history'), it is radically different from the positivist and historicist thesis of *The German Ideology.*

For on the one hand, I think it is possible to hold that ideolog*ies have a history of their own* (although it is determined in the last instance by the class struggle); and on the other, I think it is possible to hold that ideology *in general has no history,* not in a negative sense (its history is external to it), but in an absolutely positive sense.

This sense is a positive one if it is true that the peculiarity of ideology is that it is endowed with a structure and a functioning such as to make it a non-historical reality, i.e. an *omni-historical* reality, in the sense in which that structure and functioning are immutable, present in the same form throughout what we can call history, in the sense in which the *Communist Manifesto* defines history as the history of class struggles, i.e. the history of class societies.

To give a theoretical reference-point here, I might say that, to return to our example of the dream, in its Freudian conception this time, our proposition: ideology has no history, can and must (and in a way which has absolutely nothing arbitrary about it, but, quite the reverse, is theoretically necessary, for there is an organic link between the two propositions) be related directly to Freud's proposition that the *unconscious is eternal,* i.e. that it has no history.

If eternal means, not transcendent to all (temporal) history, but omnipresent, trans-historical and therefore immutable in form throughout the extent of history, I shall adopt Freud's expression word for word, and write *ideology is eternal,* exactly like the unconscious. And I add that I find this comparison theoretically justified by the fact that the eternity of the unconscious is not unrelated to the eternity of ideology in general.

That is why I believe I am justified, hypothetically at least, in proposing a theory of ideology *in general,* in the sense that Freud presented a theory of the unconscious *in general.*

To simplify the phrase, it is convenient, taking into account what has been said about ideologies, to use the plain term ideology to designate ideology in general, which I have just said has no history, or, what comes to the same thing, is eternal, i.e. omnipresent in its immutable form throughout history (= the history of social formations containing social classes). For the moment I shall restrict myself to 'class societies' and their history.

Ideology is a 'Representation' of the Imaginary Relationship of Individuals to their Real Conditions of Existence

In order to approach my central thesis on the structure and functioning of ideology, I shall first present two theses, one negative, the other positive. The first concerns the object which is 'represented' in the imaginary form of ideology, the second concerns the materiality of ideology.

THESIS I: Ideology represents the imaginary relationship of individuals to their real conditions of existence.

We commonly call religious ideology, ethical ideology, legal ideology, political ideology, etc., so many 'world outlooks'. Of course, assuming that we do not live one of these ideologies as the truth (e.g. 'believe' in God, Duty, Justice, etc. . . .), we admit that the ideology we are discussing from a critical point of view, examining it as the ethnologist examines the myths of a 'primitive society', that these 'world outlooks' are largely imaginary, i.e. do not 'correspond to reality'.

However, while admitting that they do not correspond to reality, i.e. that they constitute an illusion, we admit that they do make allusion to reality, and that they need only be 'interpreted' to discover the reality of the world behind their imaginary representation of that world (ideology = *illusion/allusion*).

There are different types of interpretation, the most famous of which are the *mechanistic* type, current in the eighteenth century (God is the imaginary representation of the real King), and the *'hermeneutic'* interpretation, inaugurated by the earliest Church Fathers, and revived by Feuerbach and the theologico-philosophical school which descends from him, e.g. the theologian Barth (to Feuerbach, for example, God is the essence of real Man). The essential point is that on condition that we interpret the imaginary transposition (and inversion) of ideology we arrive at the conclusion that in ideology 'men represent their real conditions of existence to themselves in an imaginary form'.

Unfortunately, this interpretation leaves one small problem unsettled: why do men 'need' this imaginary transposition of their real conditions of existence in order to 'represent to themselves' their real conditions of existence?

The first answer (that of the eighteenth century) proposes a simple solution: Priests or Despots are responsible. They 'forged' the Beautiful Lies so that, in the belief that they were obeying God, men would in fact obey the Priests and Despots, who are usually in alliance in their imposture, the Priests acting in the interests of the Despots or *vice versa,* according to the political positions of the 'theoreticians' concerned. There is therefore a cause for the imaginary transposition of the real conditions of existence: that cause is the existence of a small number of cynical men who base their domination and exploitation of the 'people' on a falsified representation of the world which they have imagined in order to enslave other minds by dominating their imaginations.

The second answer (that of Feuerbach, taken over word for word by Marx in his Early Works) is more 'profound,' i.e. just as false. It, too, seeks and finds a cause for the imaginary transposition and distortion of men's real conditions of existence, in short, for the alienation in the imaginary of the representation of men's conditions of existence. This cause is no longer Priests or Despots, nor their active imagination and the passive imagination of their victims. This cause is the material alienation which reigns in the conditions of existence of men themselves. This is how, in *The Jewish Question* and elsewhere, Marx defends the Feuerbachian idea that men make themselves an alienated (= imaginary) representation of their conditions of existence because these conditions of existence are themselves alienating (in the *1844 Manuscripts:* because these conditions are dominated by the essence of alienated society— *'alienated labour').*

All these interpretations thus take literally the thesis which they presuppose, and on which they depend, i.e. that what is reflected in the imaginary representation of the world found in an ideology is the conditions of existence of men, i.e. their real world.

Now I can return to a thesis which I have already advanced: it is not their real conditions of existence, their real world, that 'men' 'represent to themselves' in ideology, but above all it is their relation to those conditions of existence which is represented to them there. It is this relation which is at the centre of every ideological, i.e. imaginary, representation of the real world. It is this relation that contains the 'cause' which has to explain the imaginary distortion of the ideological representation of the real world. Or rather, to leave aside the language of causality it is necessary to advance the thesis that it is the *imaginary nature of this relation* which underlies all the imaginary distortion that we can observe (if we do not live in its truth) in all ideology.

To speak in a Marxist language, if it is true that the representation of the real conditions of existence of the individuals occupying the posts of agents of production, exploitation, repression, ideologization and scientific practice, does in the last analysis arise from the relations of production, and from relations deriving from the relations of production, we can say the following: all ideology represents in its necessarily imaginary distortion not the existing relations of production (and the other relations that derive from them), but above all the (imaginary) relationship of individuals to the relations of production and the relations that derive from them. What is represented in ideology is therefore not the system of the real relations which govern the existence of individuals, but the imaginary relation of those individuals to the real relations in which they live.

If this is the case, the question of the 'cause' of the imaginary distortion of the real relations in ideology disappears and must be replaced by a different question: why is the representation given to individuals of their (individual) relation to the social relations which govern their conditions of existence and their collective and individual life necessarily an imaginary relation? And what is the nature of this imaginariness? Posed in this way, the question explodes the solution by a 'clique'[14], by a group of individuals (Priests or Despots) who are the authors of the great ideological mystification, just as it explodes the solution by the alienated character of the real world. We shall see why later in my exposition. For the moment I shall go no further.

THESIS II: Ideology has a material existence.

I have already touched on this thesis by saying that the 'ideas' or 'representations', etc., which seem to make up ideology do not have an ideal *(idéale or idéelle)* or spiritual existence, but a material existence. I even suggested that the ideal *(idéale, idéelle)* and spiritual existence of 'ideas' arises exclusively in an ideology of the 'idea' and of ideology, and let me add, in an ideology of what seems to have 'founded' this conception since the emergence of the sciences, i.e. what the practicians of the sciences represent to

14. I use this very modern term deliberately. For even in Communist circles, unfortunately, it is a commonplace to 'explain' some political deviation (left or right opportunism) by the action of a 'clique'.

themselves in their spontaneous ideology as 'ideas', true or false. Of course, presented in affirmative form, this thesis is unproven. I simply ask that the reader be favourably disposed towards it, say, in the name of materialism. A long series of arguments would be necessary to prove it.

This hypothetical thesis of the not spiritual but material existence of 'ideas' or other 'representations' is indeed necessary if we are to advance in our analysis of the nature of ideology. Or rather, it is merely useful to us in order the better to reveal what every at all serious analysis of any ideology will immediately and empirically show to every observer, however critical.

While discussing the ideological State apparatuses and their practices, I said that each of them was the realization of an ideology (the unity of these different regional ideologies—religious, ethical, legal, political, aesthetic, etc.—being assured by their subjection to the ruling ideology). I now return to this thesis: an ideology always exists in an apparatus, and its practice, or practices. This existence is material.

Of course, the material existence of the ideology in an apparatus and its practices does not have the same modality as the material existence of a paving-stone or a rifle. But, at the risk of being taken for a Neo-Aristotelian (NB Marx had a very high regard for Aristotle), I shall say that 'matter is discussed in many senses', or rather that it exists in different modalities, all rooted in the last instance in 'physical' matter.

Having said this, let me move straight on and see what happens to the 'individuals' who live in ideology, i.e. in a determinate (religious, ethical, etc.) representation of the world whose imaginary distortion depends on their imaginary relation to their conditions of existence, in other words, in the last instance, to the relations of production and to class relations (ideology = an imaginary relation to real relations). I shall say that this imaginary relation is itself endowed with a material existence.

Now I observe the following.

An individual believes in God, or Duty, or Justice, etc. This belief derives (for everyone, i.e. for all those who live in an ideological representation of ideology, which reduces ideology to ideas endowed by definition with a spiritual existence) from the ideas of the individual concerned, i.e. from him as a subject with a consciousness which contains the ideas of his belief. In this way, i.e. by means of the absolutely ideological 'conceptual' device *(dispositif)* thus set up (a subject endowed with a consciousness in which he freely forms or freely recognizes ideas in which he believes), the (material) attitude of the subject concerned naturally follows.

The individual in question behaves in such and such a way, adopts such and such a practical attitude, and, what is more, participates in certain regular practices which are those of the ideological apparatus on which 'depend' the ideas which he has in all consciousness freely chosen as a subject. If he believes in God, he goes to Church to attend Mass, kneels, prays, confesses, does penance (once it was material in the ordinary sense of the term) and naturally repents and so on. If he believes in Duty, he will have the corresponding attitudes, inscribed in ritual practices 'according to the correct principles'. If he believes in Justice, he will submit unconditionally to the rules of the Law, and may even protest when they are violated, sign petitions, take part in a demonstration, etc.

Throughout this schema we observe that the ideological representation of ideology is itself forced to recognize that every 'subject' endowed with a 'consciousness' and believing in the 'ideas' that his 'consciousness' inspires in him and freely accepts, must '*act* according to his ideas', must therefore inscribe his own ideas as a free subject in the actions of his material practice. If he does not do so, 'that is wicked'.

Indeed, if he does not do what he ought to do as a function of what he believes, it is because he does something else, which, still as a function of the same idealist scheme, implies that he has other ideas in his head as well as those he proclaims, and that he acts according to these other ideas, as a man who is either 'inconsistent' ('no one is willingly evil') or cynical, or perverse.

In every case, the ideology of ideology thus recognizes, despite its imaginary distortion, that the 'ideas' of a human subject exist in his actions, or ought to exist in his actions, and if that is not the case, it lends him other ideas corresponding to the actions (however perverse) that he does perform. This ideology talks of actions: I shall talk of actions inserted into *practices*. And I shall point out that these practices are governed by the *rituals* in which these practices are inscribed, within the *material existence of an ideological apparatus*, be it only a small part of that apparatus: a small mass in a small church, a funeral, a minor match at a sports' club, a school day, a political party meeting, etc.

Besides, we are indebted to Pascal's defensive 'dialectic' for the wonderful formula which will enable us to invert the order of the notional schema of ideology. Pascal says more or less: 'Kneel down, move your lips in prayer, and you will believe.' He thus scandalously inverts the order of things, bringing, like Christ, not peace but strife, and in addition something hardly Christian (for woe to him who brings scandal into the world!)—scandal itself. A fortunate scandal which makes him stick with Jansenist defiance to a language that directly names the reality.

I will be allowed to leave Pascal to the arguments of his ideological struggle with the religious ideological State apparatus of his day. And I shall be expected to use a more directly Marxist vocabulary, if that is possible, for we are advancing in still poorly explored domains.

I shall therefore say that, where only a single subject (such and such an individual) is concerned, the existence of the ideas of his belief is material in that *his ideas are his material actions inserted into material practices governed by material rituals which are themselves defined by the material ideological apparatus from which derive the ideas of that subject.* Naturally, the four inscriptions of the adjective 'material' in my proposition must be affected by different modalities: the materialities of a displacement for going to mass, of kneeling down, of the gesture of the sign of the cross, or of the *mea culpa,* of a sentence, of a prayer, of an act of contrition, of a penitence, of a gaze, of a hand-shake, of an external verbal discourse or an 'internal' verbal discourse (consciousness), are not one and the same materiality. I shall leave on one side the problem of a theory of the differences between the modalities of materiality.

It remains that in this inverted presentation of things, we are not dealing with an 'inversion' at all, since it is clear that certain notions have purely and simply disappeared from our presentation, whereas others on the contrary survive, and new terms appear.

Disappeared: the term *ideas.*

Survive: the terms *subject, consciousness, belief, actions.*

Appear: the terms *practices, rituals, ideological apparatus.*

It is therefore not an inversion or overturning (except in the sense in which one might say a government or a glass is overturned), but a reshuffle (of a non-ministerial type), a rather strange reshuffle, since we obtain the following result.

Ideas have disappeared as such (insofar as they are endowed with an ideal or spiritual existence), to the precise extent that it has emerged that their existence is inscribed in the actions of practices governed by rituals defined in the last instance by an ideological apparatus. It therefore appears that the subject acts insofar as he is acted by the following system (set out in the order of its real determination): ideology existing in a material ideological apparatus, prescribing material practices governed by a material ritual, which practices exist in the material actions of a subject acting in all consciousness according to his belief.

But this very presentation reveals that we have retained the following notions: subject, consciousness, belief, actions. From this series I shall immediately extract the decisive central term on which everything else depends: the notion of the *subject.*

And I shall immediately set down two conjoint theses:

1. there is no practice except by and in an ideology;
2. there is no ideology except by the subject and for subjects.

I can now come to my central thesis.

Ideology Interpellates Individuals as Subjects

This thesis is simply a matter of making my last proposition explicit: there is no ideology except by the subject and for subjects. Meaning, there is no ideology except for concrete subjects, and this destination for ideology is only made possible by the subject: meaning, *by the category of the subject* and its functioning.

By this I mean that, even if it only appears under this name (the subject) with the rise of bourgeois ideology, above all with the rise of legal ideology,[15] the category of the subject (which may function under other names: e.g., as the soul in Plato, as God, etc.) is the constitutive category of all ideology, whatever its determination (regional or class) and whatever its historical date—since ideology has no history.

I say: the category of the subject is constitutive of all ideology, but at the same time and immediately I add that *the category of the subject is only constitutive of all ideology insofar as all ideology has the function (which defines it) of 'constituting' concrete individuals as subjects.* In the interaction of this double constitution exists the functioning of all ideology, ideology being nothing but its functioning in the material forms of existence of that functioning.

In order to grasp what follows, it is essential to realize that both he who is writing these lines and the reader who reads them are

15. Which borrowed the legal category of 'subject in law' to make an ideological notion: man is by nature a subject.

themselves subjects, and therefore ideological subjects (a tautological proposition), i.e. that the author and the reader of these lines both live 'spontaneously' or 'naturally' in ideology in the sense in which I have said that 'man is an ideological animal by nature'.

That the author, insofar as he writes the lines of a discourse which claims to be scientific, is completely absent as a 'subject' from 'his' scientific discourse (for all scientific discourse is by definition a subject-less discourse, there is no 'Subject of science' except in an ideology of science) is a different question which I shall leave on one side for the moment.

As St. Paul admirably put it, it is in the 'Logos', meaning in ideology, that we 'live, move and have our being.' It follows that, for you and for me, the category of the subject is a primary 'obviousness' (obviousnesses are always primary): it is clear that you and I are subjects (free, ethical, etc. . . .). Like all obviousnesses, including those that make a word 'name a thing' or 'have a meaning' (therefore including the obviousness of the 'transparency' of language), the 'obviousness' that you and I are subjects—and that that does not cause any problems—is an ideological effect, the elementary ideological effect.[16] It is indeed a peculiarity of ideology that it imposes (without appearing to do so, since these are 'obviousnesses') obviousnesses as obviousnesses, which we cannot *fail to recognize* and before which we have the inevitable and natural reaction of crying out (aloud or in the 'still, small voice of conscience'): 'That's obvious! That's right! That's true!'

At work in this reaction is the ideological *recognition* function which is one of the two functions of ideology as such (its inverse being the function of *misrecognition—méconnaissance*).

To take a highly 'concrete' example, we all have friends who, when they knock on our door and we ask, through the door, the question 'Who's there?', answer (since 'it's obvious') 'It's me.' And we recognize that 'it is him,' or 'her.' We open the door, and 'it's true, it really was she who was there.' To take another example, when we recognize somebody of our (previous) acquaintance (*(re)-connaissance)* in the street, we show him that we have recognized him (and have recognized that he has recognized us) by saying to him, 'Hello, my friend,' and shaking his hand (a material ritual practice of ideological

---

16. Linguists and those who appeal to linguistics for various purposes often run up against difficulties which arise because they ignore the action of the ideological effects in all discourses—including even scientific discourses.

recognition in everyday life—in France, at least; elsewhere, there are other rituals).

In this preliminary remark and these concrete illustrations, I only wish to point out that you and I are *always already* subjects, and as such constantly practice the rituals of ideological recognition, which guarantee for us that we are indeed concrete, individual, distinguishable and (naturally) irreplaceable subjects. The writing I am currently executing and the reading you are currently [17] performing are also in this respect rituals of ideological recognition, including the 'obviousness' with which the 'truth' or 'error' of my reflections may impose itself on you.

But to recognize that we are subjects and that we function in the practical rituals of the most elementary everyday life (the hand-shake, the fact of calling you by your name, the fact of knowing, even if I do not know what it is, that you 'have' a name of your own, which means that you are recognized as a unique subject, etc.)—this recognition only gives us the 'consciousness' of our incessant (eternal) practice of ideological recognition—its consciousness, i.e. its *recognition* —but in no sense does it give us the (scientific) *knowledge* of the mechanism of this recognition. Now it is this knowledge that we have to reach, if you will, while speaking in ideology, and from within ideology we have to outline a discourse which tries to break with ideology, in order to dare to be the beginning of a scientific (i.e. subjectless) discourse on ideology.

Thus in order to represent why the category of the 'subject' is constitutive of ideology, which only exists by constituting concrete subjects as subjects, I shall employ a special mode of exposition: 'concrete' enough to be recognized, but abstract enough to be thinkable and thought, giving rise to a knowledge.

As a first formulation I shall say: *all ideology hails or interpellates concrete individuals as concrete subjects,* by the functioning of the category of the subject.

This is a proposition which entails that we distinguish for the moment between concrete individuals on the one hand and concrete subjects on the other, although at this level concrete subjects only exist insofar as they are supported by a concrete individual.

I shall then suggest that ideology 'acts' or 'functions' in such a way

17. NB: this double 'currently' is one more proof of the fact that ideology is 'eternal', since these two 'currently's are separated by an indefinite interval; I am writing these lines on 6 April 1969, you may read them at any subsequent time.

that it 'recruits' subjects among the individuals (it recruits them all), or 'transforms' the individuals into subjects (it transforms them all) by that very precise operation which I have called *interpellation* or hailing, and which can be imagined along the lines of the most commonplace everyday police (or other) hailing: 'Hey, you there!'[18]

Assuming that the theoretical scene I have imagined takes place in the street, the hailed individual will turn round. By this mere one-hundred-and-eighty-degree physical conversion, he becomes a *subject.* Why? Because he has recognized that the hail was 'really' addressed to him, and that 'it was *really him* who was hailed' (and not someone else). Experience shows that the practical telecommunication of hailings is such that they hardly ever miss their man: verbal call or whistle, the one hailed always recognizes that it is really him who is being hailed. And yet it is a strange phenomenon, and one which cannot be explained solely by 'guilt feelings', despite the large numbers who 'have something on their consciences'.

Naturally for the convenience and clarity of my little theoretical theatre I have had to present things in the form of a sequence, with a before and an after, and thus in the form of a temporal succession. There are individuals walking along. Somewhere (usually behind them) the hail rings out: 'Hey, you there!' One individual (nine times out of ten it is the right one) turns round, believing/suspecting/knowing that it is for him, i.e. recognizing that 'it really is he' who is meant by the hailing. But in reality these things happen without any succession. The existence of ideology and the hailing or interpellation of individuals as subjects are one and the same thing.

I might add: what thus seems to take place outside ideology (to be precise, in the street), in reality takes place in ideology. What really takes place in ideology seems therefore to take place outside it. That is why those who are in ideology believe themselves by definition outside ideology: one of the effects of ideology is the practical *denegation* of the ideological character of ideology by ideology: ideology never says, 'I am ideological'. It is necessary to be outside ideology, i.e. in scientific knowledge, to be able to say: I am in ideology (a quite exceptional case) or (the general case): I was in ideology. As is well known, the accusation of being in ideology only applies to others, never to oneself (unless one is really a Spinozist or

---

18. Hailing as an everyday practice subject to a precise ritual takes a quite 'special' form in the policeman's practice of 'hailing' which concerns the hailing of 'suspects'.

a Marxist, which, in this matter, is to be exactly the same thing). Which amounts to saying that ideology *has no outside* (for itself), but at the same time *that it is nothing but outside* (for science and reality).

Spinoza explained this completely two centuries before Marx, who practised it but without explaining it in detail. But let us leave this point, although it is heavy with consequences, consequences which are not just theoretical, but also directly political, since, for example, the whole theory of criticism and self-criticism, the golden rule of the Marxist-Leninist practice of the class struggle, depends on it.

Thus ideology hails or interpellates individuals as subjects. As ideology is eternal, I must now suppress the temporal form in which I have presented the functioning of ideology, and say: ideology has always-already interpellated individuals as subjects, which amounts to making it clear that individuals are always-ready interpellated by ideology as subjects, which necessarily leads us to one last proposition: *individuals are always-already subjects.* Hence individuals are 'abstract' with respect to the subjects which they always-already are. This proposition might seem paradoxical.

That an individual is always-already a subject, even before he is born, is nevertheless the plain reality, accessible to everyone and not a paradox at all. Freud shows that individuals are always 'abstract' with respect to the subjects they always-already are, simply by noting the ideological ritual that surrounds the expectation of a 'birth,' that 'happy event'. Everyone knows how much and in what way an unborn child is expected. Which amounts to saying, very prosaically, if we agree to drop the 'sentiments', i.e. the forms of family ideology (paternal/maternal/conjugal/fraternal) in which the unborn child is expected: it is certain in advance that it will bear its Father's Name, and will therefore have an identity and be irreplaceable. Before its birth, the child is therefore always-already a subject, appointed as a subject in and by the specific familial ideological configuration in which it is 'expected' once it has been conceived. I hardly need add that this familial ideological configuration is, in its uniqueness, highly structured, and that it is in this implacable and more or less 'pathological' (presupposing that any meaning can be assigned to that term) structure that the former subject-to-be will have to 'find' 'its' place, i.e. 'become' the sexual subject (boy or girl) which it already is in advance. It is clear that this ideological constraint and pre-appointment, and all the rituals of rearing and then education in the family, have some relationship with what Freud studied in the forms of the pre-genital and genital 'stages' of sexuality, i.e. in the 'grip' of what Freud registered by its effects as being the unconscious. But let us leave this point, too, on one side.

Let me go one step further. What I shall now turn my attention to is the way the 'actors' in this *mise en scène* of interpellation, and their respective roles, are reflected in the very structure of all ideology.

An Example: The Christian Religious Ideology

As the formal structure of all ideology is always the same, I shall restrict my analysis to a single example, one accessible to everyone, that of religious ideology, with the proviso that the same demonstration can be produced for ethical, legal, political, aesthetic ideology, etc.

Let us therefore consider the Christian religious ideology. I shall use a rhetorical figure and 'make it speak', i.e. collect into a fictional discourse what it 'says' not only in its two Testaments, its Theologians, Sermons, but also in its practices, its rituals, its ceremonies and its sacraments. The Christian religious ideology says something like this:

It says: I address myself to you, a human individual called Peter (every individual is called by his name, in the passive sense, it is never he who provides his own name), in order to tell you that God exists and that you are answerable to Him. It adds: God addresses himself to you through my voice (Scripture having collected the Word of God, Tradition having transmitted it, Papal Infallibility fixing it for ever on 'nice' points). It says: this is who you are: you are Peter! This is your origin, you were created by God for all eternity, although you were born in the 1920th year of Our Lord! This is your place in the world! This is what you must do! By these means, if you observe the 'law of love' you will be saved, you, Peter, and will become part of the Glorious Body of Christ! Etc. . . .

Now this is quite a familiar and banal discourse, but at the same time quite a surprising one.

Surprising because if we consider that religious ideology is indeed addressed to individuals,[19] in order to 'transform them into subjects,' by interpellating the individual, Peter, in order to make him a subject, free to obey or disobey the appeal, i.e. God's commandments; if it

---

19. Although we know that the individual is always already a subject, we go on using this term, convenient because of the contrasting effect it produces.

calls these individuals by their names, thus recognizing that they are always-already interpellated as subjects with a personal identity (to the extent that Pascal's Christ says: 'It is for you that I have shed this drop of my blood!'); if it interpellates them in such a way that the subject responds: *Yes, it really is me!*' if it obtains from them the *recognition* that they really do occupy the place it designates for them as theirs in the world, a fixed residence: 'It really is me, I am here, a worker, a boss or a soldier!' in this vale of tears; if it obtains from them the recognition of a destination (eternal life or damnation) according to the respect or contempt they show to 'God's Commandments,' Law become Love; —if everything does happen in this way (in the practices of the well-known rituals of baptism, confirmation, communion, confession and extreme unction, etc. . . .), we should note that all this 'procedure' to set up Christian religious subjects is dominated by a strange phenomenon: the fact that there can only be such a multitude of possible religious subjects on the absolute condition that there is a Unique, Absolute, *Other Subject,* i.e. God.

It is convenient to designate this new and remarkable Subject by writing Subject with a capital S to distinguish it from ordinary subjects, with a small s.

It then emerges that the interpellation of individuals as subjects presupposes the 'existence' of a Unique and central Other Subject, in whose Name the religious ideology interpellates all individuals as subjects. All this is clearly[20] written in what is rightly called the Scriptures. 'And it came to pass at that time that God the Lord (Yahweh) spoke to Moses in the cloud. And the Lord cried to Moses, "Moses!" And Moses replied "It is (really)I! I am Moses thy servant, speak and I shall listen!" And the Lord spoke to Moses and said to him, *"I am that I am"*'.

God thus defines himself as the Subject *par excellence,* he who is through himself and for himself ('I am that I am'), and he who interpellates his subject, the individual subjected to him by his very interpellation, i.e. the individual named Moses. And Moses, interpellated-called by his Name, having recognized that it 'really' was he who was called by God, recognizes that he is a subject, a subject *of* God, a subject subjected to God, *a subject through the Subject and subjected to the Subject.* The proof: he obeys him, and makes his people obey God's Commandments.

God is thus the Subject, and Moses and the innumerable subjects of God's people, the Subject's interlocutors-interpellates: his *mirrors,*

---

20. I am quoting in a combined way, not to the letter but 'in spirit and truth'.

his *reflections.* Were not men made *in the image* of God? As all theological reflection proves, whereas He 'could' perfectly well have done without men, God needs them, the Subject needs the subjects, just as men need God, the subjects need the Subject. Better: God needs men, the great Subject needs subjects, even in the terrible inversion of his image in them (when the subjects wallow in debauchery, i.e. sin).

Better: God duplicates himself and sends his Son to the Earth, as a mere subject 'forsaken' by him (the long complaint of the Garden of Olives which ends in the Crucifixion), subject but Subject, man but God, to do what prepares the way for the final Redemption, the Resurrection of Christ. God thus needs to 'make himself' a man, the Subject needs to become a subject, as if to show empirically, visibly to the eye, tangibly to the hands (see St. Thomas) of the subjects, that, if they are subjects, subjected to the Subject, that is solely in order that finally, on Judgement Day, they will re-enter the Lord's Bosom, like Christ, i.e. re-enter the Subject.[21]

Let us decipher into theoretical language this wonderful necessity for the duplication of *the Subject into subjects* and of *the Subject itself into a subject-Subject.*

We observe that the structure of all ideology, interpellating individuals as subjects in the name of a Unique and Absolute Subject is *speculary,* i.e. a mirror-structure, and *doubly* speculary: this mirror duplication is constitutive of ideology and ensures its functioning. Which means that all ideology is *centred,* that the Absolute Subject occupies the unique place of the Centre, and interpellates around it the infinity of individuals into subjects in a double mirror-connexion such that it *subjects* the subjects to the Subject, while giving them in the Subject in which each subject can contemplate its own image (present and future) the *guarantee* that this really concerns them and Him, and that since everything takes place in the Family (the Holy Family: the Family is in essence Holy), 'God will *recognize* his own in it', i.e. those who have recognized God, and have recognized themselves in Him, will be saved.

Let me summarize what we have discovered about ideology in general.

The duplicate mirror-structure of ideology ensures simultaneously:

---

21. The dogma of the Trinity is precisely the theory of the duplication of the Subject (the Father) into a subject (the Son) and of their mirror-connexion (the Holy Spirit).

1. the interpellation of 'individuals' as subjects;
2. their subjection to the Subject;
3. the mutual recognition of subjects and Subject, the subjects' recognition of each other, and finally the subject's recognition of himself;[22]
4. the absolute guarantee that everything really is so, and that on condition that the subjects recognize what they are and behave accordingly, everything will be all right: Amen — 'So be it'.

Result: caught in this quadruple system of interpellation as subjects, of subjection to the Subject, of universal recognition and of absolute guarantee, the subjects 'work', they 'work by themselves' in the vast majority of cases, with the exception of the 'bad subjects' who on occasion provoke the intervention of one of the detachments of the (repressive) State apparatus. But the vast majority of (good) subjects work all right 'all by themselves', i.e. by ideology (whose concrete forms are realized in the Ideological State Apparatuses). They are inserted into practices governed by the rituals of the ISAs. They 'recognize' the existing state of affairs *(das Bestehende)*, that 'it really is true that it is so and not otherwise', and that they must be obedient to God, to their conscience, to the priest, to de Gaulle, to the boss, to the engineer, that thou shalt 'love thy neighbor as thyself', etc. Their concrete, material behaviour is simply the inscription in life of the admirable words of the prayer: *'Amen —So be it'.*

Yes, the subjects 'work by themselves'. The whole mystery of this effect lies in the first two moments of the quadruple system I have just discussed, or, if you prefer, in the ambiguity of the term *subject.* In the ordinary use of the term, subject in fact means: (1) a free subjectivity, a centre of initiatives, author of and responsible for its actions; (2) a subjected being, who submits to a higher authority, and is therefore stripped of all freedom except that of freely accepting his submission. This last note gives us the meaning of this ambiguity, which is merely a reflection of the effect which produces it: the individual *is interpellated as a (free) subject in order that he shall submit freely to the commandments of the Subject, i.e. in order that he*

---

22. Hegel is (unknowingly) an admirable 'theoretician' of ideology insofar as he is a 'theoretician' of Universal Recognition who unfortunately ends up in the ideology of Absolute Knowledge. Feuerbach is an astonishing 'theoretician' of the mirror connexion, who unfortunately ends up in the ideology of the Human Essence. To find the material with which to construct a theory of the guarantee, we must turn to Spinoza.

shall (freely) accept his subjection, i.e. in order that he shall make the gestures and actions of his subjection 'all by himself.' *There are no subjects except by and for their subjection.* That is why they 'work all by themselves'.

'*So be it!* . . .' This phrase which registers the effect to be obtained proves that it is not 'naturally' so ('naturally': outside the prayer, i.e. outside the ideological intervention). This phrase proves that it *has* to be so if things are to be what they must be, and let us let the words slip: if the reproduction of the relations of production is to be assured, even in the processes of production and circulation, every day, in the 'consciousness', i.e. in the attitudes of the individual-subjects occupying the posts which the sociotechnical division of labour assigns to them in production, exploitation, repression, ideologization, scientific practice, etc. Indeed, what is really in question in this mechanism of the mirror recognition of the Subject and of the individuals interpellated as subjects, and of the guarantee given by the Subject to the subjects if they freely accept their subjection to the Subject's 'commandments'? The reality in question in this mechanism, the reality which is necessarily *ignored (méconnue)* in the very forms of recognition (ideology =misrecognition/ignorance) is indeed, in the last resort, the reproduction of the relations of production and of the relations deriving from them. . . .

January–April 1969

MICHEL FOUCAULT

In his interview "Truth and Power," Michel Foucault claims that no one could be less of a Structuralist than himself, if one defines Structuralism as making "the most systematic effort to evacuate the concept of the event."* He is, nevertheless, a former pupil of Althusser, who seems to take his mentor's theories of ideology at times beyond even the possibility of science, beyond any hope of transcending *doxa,* or of rising beyond the figures of discourse to truth. Knowledge is perspective, says Foucault in "Nietzsche, Geneology, History."† "Truth" is knowledge from which perspective has been fallaciously erased, a point made so trenchantly by Nietzsche in "On Truth and Lie in an Extra-Moral Sense." This authoritative perspective arises because man is a herd animal. He needs a "regularly valid and obligatory designation of things . . . , and this linguistic legislation . . . furnishes the first laws of truth. . . . ‡ What Nietzsche calls "linguistic legislation" is Foucault's world of "discourse," the *épistème,* the regulative atmosphere according to which one is mad or sane, sick or healthy, perverted or normal. In Foucault's early books, history was a matter of epistemic shifts, each organized around a particular rhetorical figure characteristic of the time.** The notion that reality is linguistic is a central characteristic of the Structuralist view of things. Foucault also has in common with Structuralists the notion that the subject, in voluntaristic times called the "self," is an illusory function of power relations (1980:117). His last books are claustrophobic meditations on the power which is always already there, which is everywhere, which has drenched every human institution to such an extent that we are never outside it (141–2). Perhaps the most terrifying and outrageous paradox of *Discipline and Punish* (1975) is the notion that Damiens, drawn by horses and hacked apart by axes, is freer than we in the Panoptic Age who have internalized the Gaze of Power and have consented to discipline not only each other but ourselves as well.

*Michel Foucault, *Power/Knowledge,* ed. Colin Gordon (New York: Pantheon, 1980) 114.
†Michel Foucault, *Language, Counter-Memory, Practice,* ed. Donald Bouchard (Ithaca, New York: Cornell University Press, 1977) 156.
‡*The Portable Nietzsche,* ed. and trans. Walter Kaufmann (New York: Viking, 1954) 44–47.
**See Hayden White, "Michel Foucault" in *Structuralism and Since,* ed. John Sturrock (Oxford: Oxford University Press, 1979) 81–115. See also the introductory text for Hayden White in this book.

The Structures of Punishment

1975

Translated by Alan Sheridan

On 2 March 1757, Damiens the regicide was condemned 'to make the *amende honorable* before the main door of the Church of Paris', where he was to be 'taken and conveyed in a cart, wearing nothing but a shirt, holding a torch of burning wax weighing two pounds'; then, 'in the said cart, to the Place de Grève, where, on a scaffold that will be erected there, the flesh will be torn from his breasts, arms, thighs and calves with red-hot pincers, his right hand, holding the knife with which he committed the said parricide, burnt with sulphur, and, on those places where the flesh will be torn away, poured molten lead, boiling oil, burning resin, wax and sulphur melted together and then his body drawn and quartered by four horses and his limbs and body consumed by fire, reduced to ashes and his ashes thrown to the winds.'

'Finally, he was quartered,' recounts the *Gazette d'Amsterdam* of 1 April 1757. 'This last operation was very long, because the horses used were not accustomed to drawing; consequently, instead of four, six were needed; and when that did not suffice, they were forced, in order to cut off the wretch's thighs, to sever the sinews and hack at the joints . . .

'It is said that, though he was always a great swearer, no blasphemy escaped his lips; but the excessive pain made him utter horrible cries, and he often repeated: "My God, have pity on me! Jesus, help me!" The spectators were all edified by the solicitude of the parish priest of St Paul's who despite his great age did not spare himself in offering consolation to the patient.'

Bouton, an officer of the watch, left us his account: 'The sulphur was lit, but the flame was so poor that only the top skin of the hand was burnt, and that only slightly. Then the executioner, his sleeves rolled up, took the steel pincers, which had been especially made for the occasion, and which were about a foot and a half long, and pulled first at the calf of the right leg, then at the thigh, and from there at the two fleshy parts of the right arm; then at the breasts. Though a strong, sturdy fellow, this executioner found it so difficult to tear away the pieces of flesh that he set about the same spot two or three times, twisting the pincers as he did so, and what he took away formed at each part a wound about the size of a six-pound crown piece.

'After these tearings with the pincers, Damiens, who cried out profusely, though without swearing, raised his head and looked at himself; the same executioner dipped an iron spoon in the pot containing the boiling potion, which he poured liberally over each wound. Then the ropes that were to be harnessed to the horses were attached with cords to the patient's body; the horses were then harnessed and placed alongside the arms and legs, one at each limb.

'Monsieur Le Breton, the clerk of the court, went up to the patient several times and asked him if he had anything to say. He said he had not; at each torment, he cried out, as the damned in hell are supposed to cry out, "Pardon, my God! Pardon, Lord." Despite all this pain, he raised his head from time to time and looked at himself boldly. The cords had been tied so tightly by the men who pulled the ends that they caused him indescribable pain. Monsieur le Breton went up to him again and asked him if he had anything to say; he said no. Several confessors went up to him and spoke to him at length; he willingly kissed the crucifix that was held out to him; he opened his lips and repeated: "Pardon, Lord."

'The horses tugged hard, each pulling straight on a limb, each horse held by an executioner. After a quarter of an hour, the same ceremony was repeated and finally, after several attempts, the direction of the horses had to be changed, thus: those at the arms were made to pull towards the head, those at the thighs towards the arms, which broke the arms at the joints. This was repeated several times without success. He raised his head and looked at himself. Two more horses had to be added to those harnessed to the thighs, which made six horses in all. Without success.

'Finally, the executioner, Samson, said to Monsieur Le Breton that there was no way or hope of succeeding, and told him to ask their Lordships if they wished him to have the prisoner cut into pieces.

Monsieur Le Breton, who had come down from the town, ordered that renewed efforts be made, and this was done; but the horses gave up and one of those harnessed to the thighs fell to the ground. The confessors returned and spoke to him again. He said to them (I heard him): "Kiss me, gentlemen." The parish priest of St Paul's did not dare to, so Monsieur de Marsilly slipped under the rope holding the left arm and kissed him on the forehead. The executioners gathered round and Damiens told them not to swear, to carry out their task and that he did not think ill of them; he begged them to pray to God for him, and asked the parish priest of St Paul's to pray for him at the first mass.

'After two or three attempts, the executioner Samson and he who had used the pincers each drew out a knife from his pocket and cut the body at the thighs instead of severing the legs at the joints; the four horses gave a tug and carried off the two thighs after them, namely, that of the right side first, the other following; then the same was done to the arms, the shoulders, the arm-pits and the four limbs; the flesh had to be cut almost to the bone, the horses pulling hard carried off the right arm first and the other afterwards.

'When the four limbs had been pulled away, the confessors came to speak to him; but his executioner told them that he was dead, though the truth was that I saw the man move, his lower jaw moving from side to side as if he were talking. One of the executioners even said shortly afterwards that when they had lifted the trunk to throw it on the stake, he was still alive. The four limbs were untied from the ropes and thrown on the stake set up in the enclosure in line with the scaffold, then the trunk and the rest were covered with logs and faggots, and fire was put to the straw mixed with this wood.

'. . . In accordance with the decree, the whole was reduced to ashes. The last piece to be found in the embers was still burning at half-past ten in the evening. The pieces of flesh and the trunk had taken about four hours to burn. The officers of whom I was one, as also was my son, and a detachment of archers remained in the square until nearly eleven o'clock.

'There were those who made something of the fact that a dog had lain the day before on the grass where the fire had been, had been chased away several times, and had always returned. But it is not difficult to understand that an animal found this place warmer than elsewhere.'

. . . The constant division between the normal and the abnormal, to which every individual is subjected, brings us back to our own time, by applying the binary branding and exile of the leper to quite different objects; the existence of a whole set of techniques and institutions for measuring, supervising and correcting the abnormal brings into play the disciplinary mechanisms to which the fear of the plague gave rise. All the mechanisms of power which, even today, are disposed around the abnormal individual, to brand him and to alter him, are composed of those two forms from which they distantly derive.

Bentham's *Panopticon* is the architectural figure of this composition.[1] We know the principle on which it was based: at the periphery, an annular building; at the centre, a tower; this tower is pierced with wide windows that open onto the inner side of the ring; the peripheric building is divided into cells, each of which extends the whole width of the building; they have two windows, one on the inside, corresponding to the windows of the tower; the other, on the outside, allows the light to cross the cell from one end to the other. All that is needed, then, is to place a supervisor in a central tower and to shut up in each cell a madman, a patient, a condemned man, a worker or a schoolboy. By the effect of backlighting, one can observe from the tower, standing out precisely against the light, the small captive shadows in the cells of the periphery. They are like so many cages, so many small theatres, in which each actor is alone, perfectly individualized and constantly visible. The panoptic mechanism arranges spatial unities that make it possible to see constantly and to recognize immediately. In short, it reverses the principle of the dungeon; or rather of its three functions—to enclose, to deprive of light and to hide—it preserves only the first and eliminates the other two. Full lighting and the eye of a supervisor capture better than darkness, which ultimately protected. Visibility is a trap.

To begin with, this made it possible—as a negative effect—to avoid those compact, swarming, howling masses that were to be found in places of confinement, those painted by Goya or described by Howard. Each individual, in his place, is securely confined to a cell from which he is seen from the front by the supervisor; but the side walls prevent him from coming into contact with his companions. He is seen, but he does not see; he is the object of information, never a subject in communication. The arrangement of his room, opposite the central tower, imposes on him an axial visibility; but the divisions of the ring, those separated cells, imply a lateral invisibility. And this invisibility is a guarantee of order. If the inmates are convicts, there is

---

1. In *The Works of Jeremy Bentham*, 11 vols., ed. John Bowring (1838–43, reissued New York: Russell and Russell, 1962).

no danger of a plot, an attempt at collective escape, the planning of new crimes for the future, bad reciprocal influences; if they are patients, there is no danger of contagion; if they are madmen there is no risk of their committing violence upon one another; if they are schoolchildren, there is no copying, no noise, no chatter, no waste of time; if they are workers, there are no disorders, no theft, no coalitions, none of those distractions that slow down the rate of work, make it less perfect or cause accidents. The crowd, a compact mass, a locus of multiple exchanges, individualities merging together, a collective effect, is abolished and replaced by a collection of separated individualities. From the point of view of the guardian, it is replaced by a multiplicity that can be numbered and supervised; from the point of view of the inmates, by a sequestered and observed solitude.

Hence the major effect of the Panopticon: to induce in the inmate a state of conscious and permanent visibility that assures the automatic functioning of power. So to arrange things that the surveillance is permanent in its effects, even if it is discontinuous in its action; that the perfection of power should tend to render its actual exercise unnecessary; that this architectural apparatus should be a machine for creating and sustaining a power relation independent of the person who exercises it; in short, that the inmates should be caught up in a power situation of which they are themselves the bearers. To achieve this, it is at once too much and too little that the prisoner should be constantly observed by an inspector: too little, for what matters is that he knows himself to be observed; too much, because he has no need in fact of being so. In view of this, Bentham laid down the principle that power should be visible and unverifiable. Visible: the inmate will constantly have before his eyes the tall outline of the central tower from which he is spied upon. Unverifiable: the inmate must never know whether he is being looked at at any one moment; but he must be sure that he may always be so. In order to make the presence or absence of the inspector unverifiable, so that the prisoners, in their cells, cannot even see a shadow, Bentham envisaged not only venetian blinds on the windows of the central observation hall, but, on the inside, partitions that intersected the hall at right angles and, in order to pass from one quarter to the other, not doors but zig-zag openings; for the slightest noise, a gleam of light, a brightness in a half-opened door would betray the presence of the guardian. The Panopticon is a machine for dissociating the see/being seen dyad: in the peripheric ring, one is totally seen, without ever seeing; in the central tower, one sees everything without ever being seen.

It is an important mechanism, for it automatizes and disindividualizes power. Power has its principle not so much in a person as in a certain concerted distribution of bodies, surfaces, lights, gazes; in an arrangement whose internal mechanisms produce the relation in which individuals are caught up. The ceremonies, the rituals, the marks by which the sovereign's surplus power was manifested are useless. There is a machinery that assures dissymmetry, disequilibrium, difference. Consequently, it does not matter who exercises power. Any individual, taken almost at random, can operate the machine: in the absence of the director, his family, his friends, his visitors, even his servants. Similarly, it does not matter what motive animates him: the curiosity of the indiscreet, the malice of a child, the thirst for knowledge of a philosopher who wishes to visit this museum of human nature, or the perversity of those who take pleasure in spying and punishing. The more numerous those anonymous and temporary observers are, the greater the risk for the inmate of being surprised and the greater his anxious awareness of being observed. The Panopticon is a marvellous machine which, whatever use one may wish to put it to, produces homogeneous effects of power.

A real subjection is born mechanically from a fictitious relation. So it is not necessary to use force to constrain the convict to good behaviour, the madman to calm, the worker to work, the schoolboy to application, the patient to the observation of the regulations. Bentham was surprised that panoptic institutions could be so light: there were no more bars, no more chains, no more heavy locks; all that was needed was that the separations should be clear and the openings well arranged. The heaviness of the old 'houses of security', with their fortress-like architecture, could be replaced by the simple, economic geometry of a 'house of certainty.' The efficiency of power, its constraining force have, in a sense, passed over to the other side—to the side of its surface of application. He who is subjected to a field of visibility, and who knows it, assumes responsibility for the constraints of power; he makes them play spontaneously upon himself; he inscribes in himself the power relation in which he simultaneously plays both roles; he becomes the principle of his own subjection. By this very fact, the external power may throw off its physical weight; it tends to the non-corporal; and, the more it approaches this limit, the more constant, profound and permanent are its effects: it is a perpetual victory that avoids any physical confrontation and which is always decided in advance.

Bentham does not say whether he was inspired, in his project, by Le Vaux's menagerie at Versailles: the first menagerie in which the different elements are not, as they traditionally were, distributed in a park. At the centre was an octagonal pavilion which, on the first floor, consisted of only a single room, the king's *salon;* on every side large windows looked out onto seven cages (the eighth side was reserved for the entrance), containing different species of animals. By Bentham's time, this menagerie had disappeared. But one finds in the programme of the Panopticon a similar concern with individualizing observation, with characterization and classification, with the analytical arrangement of space. The Panopticon is a royal menagerie; the animal is replaced by man, individual distribution by specific grouping and the king by the machinery of a furtive power. With this exception, the Panopticon also does the work of a naturalist. It makes it possible to draw up differences: among patients, to observe the symptoms of each individual, without the proximity of beds, the circulation of miasmas, the effects of contagion confusing the clinical tables; among schoolchildren, it makes it possible to observe performances (without there being any imitation or copying), to map aptitudes, to assess characters, to draw up rigorous classifications and, in relation to normal development, to distinguish 'laziness and stubbornness' from 'incurable imbecility'; among workers, it makes it possible to note the aptitudes of each worker, compare the time he takes to perform a task, and if they are paid by the day, to calculate their wages.

So much for the question of observation. But the Panopticon was also a laboratory; it could be used as a machine to carry out experiments, to alter behaviour, to train or correct individuals. To experiment with medicines and monitor their effects. To try out different punishments on prisoners, according to their crimes and character, and to seek the most effective ones. To teach different techniques simultaneously to the workers, to decide which is the best. To try out pedagogical experiments—and in particular to take up once again the well-debated problem of secluded education, by using orphans. One would see what would happen when, in their sixteenth or eighteenth year, they were presented with other boys or girls; one could verify whether, as Helvetius thought, anyone could learn anything; one would follow 'the genealogy of every observable idea'; one could bring up different children according to different systems of thought, making certain children believe that two and two do not make four or that the moon is a cheese, then put them together when they are twenty or twenty-five years old; one would then have discussions that would be worth a great deal more than the sermons or lectures on which so much money is spent; one would have at least an opportunity of making discoveries in the domain of metaphysics. The Panopticon is a privileged place for experiments on men, and for analysing with complete certainty the transformations that may be obtained from them. The Panopticon may even provide an apparatus for supervising its own mechanisms. In this central tower, the director may spy on all the employees that he has under his orders: nurses, doctors, foremen, teachers, warders; he will be able to judge them continuously, alter their behaviour, impose upon them the methods he thinks best; and it will even be possible to observe the director himself. An inspector arriving unexpectedly at the centre of the Panopticon will be able to judge at a glance, without anything being concealed from him, how the entire establishment is functioning. And, in any case, enclosed as he is in the middle of this architectural mechanism, is not the director's own fate entirely bound up with it? The incompetent physician who has allowed contagion to spread, the incompetent prison governor or workshop manager will be the first victims of an epidemic or a revolt. ' "By every tie I could devise", said the master of the Panopticon, "my own fate had been bound up by me with theirs." ' The Panopticon functions as a kind of laboratory of power. Thanks to its mechanisms of observation, it gains in efficiency and in the ability to penetrate into men's behaviour; knowledge follows the advances of power, discovering new objects of knowledge over all the surfaces on which power is exercised.

The plague-stricken town, the panoptic establishment—the differences are important. They mark, at a distance of a century and a half, the transformations of the disciplinary programme. In the first case, there is an exceptional situation: against an extraordinary evil, power is mobilized; it makes itself everywhere present and visible; it invents new mechanisms; it separates, it immobilizes, it partitions; it constructs for a time what is both a counter-city and the perfect society; it imposes an ideal functioning, but one that is reduced, in the final analysis, like the evil that it combats, to a simple dualism of life and death: that which moves brings death, and one kills that which moves. The Panopticon, on the other hand, must be understood as a generalizable model of functioning; a way of defining power relations in terms of the everyday life of men. No doubt Bentham presents it as a particular institution, closed in upon itself. Utopias, perfectly closed in upon themselves, are common enough. As opposed to the ruined prisons, littered with mechanisms of torture, to be seen in Piranese's engravings, the Panopticon presents a cruel, ingenious cage. The fact that it should have given rise, even in our own time, to so many variations, projected or realized, is evidence of the imaginary intensity that it has possessed for almost two hundred years. But the Panopticon must not be understood as a dream building: it is the diagram of a mechanism of power reduced to its ideal form; its functioning, abstracted from any obstacle, resistance or friction, must be represented as a pure architectural and optical system: it is in fact a figure of political technology that may and must be detached from any specific use.

It is polyvalent in its applications; it serves to reform prisoners, but also to treat patients, to instruct schoolchildren, to confine the insane, to supervise workers, to put beggars and idlers to work. It is a type of location of bodies in space, of distribution of individuals in relation to one another, of hierarchical organization, of disposition of centres and channels of power, of definition of the instruments and modes of intervention of power, which can be implemented in hospitals, workshops, schools, prisons. Whenever one is dealing with a multiplicity of individuals on whom a task or a particular form of behaviour must be imposed, the panoptic schema may be used. It is—necessary modifications apart—applicable 'to all establishments whatsoever, in which, within a space not too large to be covered or commanded by buildings, a number of persons are meant to be kept under inspection' (although Bentham takes the penitentiary house as his prime example, it is because it has many different functions to fulfil—safe custody, confinement, solitude, forced labour and instruction).

In each of its applications, it makes it possible to perfect the exercise of power. It does this in several ways: because it can reduce the number of those who exercise it, while increasing the number of those on whom it is exercised. Because it is possible to intervene at any moment and because the constant pressure acts even before the offences, mistakes or crimes have been committed. Because, in these conditions, its strength is that it never intervenes, it is exercised spontaneously and without noise, it constitutes a mechanism whose effects follow from one another. Because, without any physical instrument other than architecture and geometry, it acts directly on individuals; it gives 'power of mind over mind'. The panoptic schema makes any apparatus of power more intense: it assures its economy (in material, in personnel, in time); it assures its efficacity by its preventative character, its continuous functioning and its automatic mechanisms. It is a way of obtaining from power 'in hitherto unexampled quantity', 'a great and new instrument of government . . . ; its great excellence consists in the great strength it is capable of giving to *any* institution it may be thought proper to apply it to'.

It's a case of 'it's easy once you've thought of it' in the political sphere. It can in fact be integrated into any function (education, medical treatment, production, punishment); it can increase the effect of this function, by being linked closely with it; it can constitute a mixed mechanism in which relations of power (and of knowledge) may be precisely adjusted, in the smallest detail, to the processes that are to be supervised; it can establish a direct proportion between 'surplus power' and 'surplus production'. In short, it arranges things in such a way that the exercise of power is not added on from the outside, like a rigid, heavy constraint, to the functions it invests, but is so subtly present in them as to increase their efficiency by itself increasing its own points of contact. The panoptic mechanism is not simply a hinge, a point of exchange between a mechanism of power and a function; it is a way of making power relations function in a function, and of making a function function through these power relations. Bentham's Preface to *Panopticon* opens with a list of the benefits to be obtained from his 'inspection-house': '*Morals reformed—health preserved—industry invigorated—instruction diffused—public burthens lightened*—Economy seated, as it were, upon a rock—the gordian knot of the Poor-Laws not cut, but untied—all by a simple idea in architecture!'

Furthermore, the arrangement of this machine is such that its enclosed nature does not preclude a permanent presence from the outside: we have seen that anyone may come and exercise in the central tower the functions of surveillance, and that, this being the case, he can gain a clear idea of the way in which the surveillance is practised. In fact, any panoptic institution, even if it is as rigorously closed as a penitentiary, may without difficulty be subjected to such irregular and constant inspections: and not only by the appointed inspectors, but also by the public; any member of society will have the right to come and see with his own eyes how the schools, hospitals, factories, prisons function. There is no risk, therefore, that the increase of power created by the panoptic machine may degenerate into tyranny; the disciplinary mechanism will be democratically controlled, since it will be constantly accessible 'to the great tribunal committee of the world'. This Panopticon, subtly arranged so that an observer may observe, at a glance, so many different individuals, also enables everyone to come and observe any of the observers. The seeing machine was once a sort of dark room into which individuals spied; it has become a transparent building in which the exercise of power may be supervised by society as a whole.

The panoptic schema, without disappearing as such or losing any of its properties, was destined to spread throughout the social body; its vocation was to become a generalized function. The plague-stricken town provided an exceptional disciplinary model: perfect, but absolutely violent; to the disease that brought death, power opposed its perpetual threat of death; life inside it was reduced to its simplest expression; it was, against the power of death, the meticulous exercise of the right of the sword. The Panopticon, on the other hand, has a role of amplification; although it arranges power, although it is intended to make it more economic and more effective, it does so not for power itself, nor for the immediate salvation of a threatened society: its aim is to strengthen the social forces—to increase production, to develop the economy, spread education, raise the level of public morality; to increase and multiply.

How is power to be strengthened in such a way that, far from impeding progress, far from weighing upon it with its rules and regulations, it actually facilitates such progress? What intensificator of power will be able at the same time to be a multiplicator of production? How will power, by increasing its forces, be able to increase those of society instead of confiscating them or impeding them? The Panopticon's solution to this problem is that the productive increase of power can be assured only if, on the one hand, it can be exercised continuously in the very foundations of society, in the subtlest possible way, and if, on the other hand, it functions outside these sudden, violent, discontinuous forms that are bound up with the exercise of sovereignty. The body of the king, with its strange material and physical presence, with the force that he himself deploys or transmits to some few others, is at the opposite extreme of this new physics of power represented by panopticism; the domain of panopticism is, on the contrary, that whole lower region, that region of irregular bodies, with their details, their multiple movements, their heterogeneous forces, their spatial relations; what are required are mechanisms that analyse distributions, gaps, series, combinations, and which use instruments that render visible, record, differentiate and compare: a physics of a relational and multiple power, which has its maximum intensity not in the person of the king, but in the bodies that can be individualized by these relations. At the theoretical level, Bentham defines another way of analysing the social body and the power relations that traverse it; in terms of practice, he defines a procedure of subordination of bodies and forces that must increase the utility of power while practising the economy of the prince. Panopticism is the general principle of a new 'political anatomy' whose object and end are not the relations of sovereignty but the relations of discipline.

The celebrated, transparent, circular cage, with its high tower, powerful and knowing, may have been for Bentham a project of a perfect disciplinary institution; but he also set out to show how one may 'unlock' the disciplines and get them to function in a diffused, multiple, polyvalent way throughout the whole social body. These disciplines, which the classical age had elaborated in specific, relatively enclosed places—barracks, schools, workshops—and whose total implementation had been imagined only at the limited and temporary scale of a plague-stricken town, Bentham dreamt of transforming into a network of mechanisms that would be every-where and always alert, running through society without interruption in space or in time. The panoptic arrangement provides the formula for this generalization. It programmes, at the level of an elementary and easily transferable mechanism, the basic functioning of a society penetrated through and through with disciplinary mechanisms.

There are two images, then, of discipline. At one extreme, the discipline-blockade, the enclosed institution, established on the edges of society, turned inwards towards negative functions: arresting evil, breaking communications, suspending time. At the other ex-treme, with panopticism, is the discipline-mechanism: a functional mechanism that must improve the exercise of power by making it lighter, more rapid, more effective, a design of subtle coercion for a society to come. The movement from one project to the other, from a schema of exceptional discipline to one of a generalized surveil-lance, rests on a historical transformation: the gradual extension of the mechanisms of discipline throughout the seventeenth and eight-eenth centuries, their spread throughout the whole social body, the formation of what might be called in general the disciplinary society. . . .

'Discipline' may be identified neither with an institution nor with an apparatus; it is a type of power, a modality for its exercise, comprising a whole set of instruments, techniques, procedures, levels of application, targets; it is a 'physics' or an 'anatomy' of power, a technology. And it may be taken over either by 'specialized' institutions (the penitentiaries or 'houses of correction' of the nineteenth century), or by institutions that use it as an essential instrument for a particular end (schools, hospitals), or by pre-existing authorities that find in it a means of reinforcing or reorganizing their internal mechanisms of power (one day we should show how intra-familial relations, essentially in the parents-children cell, have become 'disciplined', absorbing since the classical age external schemata, first educational and military, then medical, psychiatric, psychological, which have made the family the privileged locus of emergence for the disciplinary question of the normal and the abnormal); or by apparatuses that have made discipline their principle of internal functioning (the disciplinarization of the administrative apparatus from the Napoleonic period), or finally by state apparatuses whose major, if not exclusive, function is to assure that discipline reigns over society as a whole (the police).

On the whole, therefore, one can speak of the formation of a disciplinary society in this movement that stretches from the enclosed disciplines, a sort of social 'quarantine', to an indefinitely generalizable mechanism of 'panopticism'. Not because the disciplinary modality of power has replaced all the others; but because it has infiltrated the others, sometimes undermining them, but serving as an intermediary between them, linking them together, extending them and above all making it possible to bring the effects of power to the most minute and distant elements. It assures an infinitesimal distribution of the power relations. . . .

The formation of the disciplinary society is connected with a number of broad historical processes—economic, juridico-political and, lastly, scientific—of which it forms part.

1.   Generally speaking, it might be said that the disciplines are techniques for assuring the ordering of human multiplicities. It is true that there is nothing exceptional or even characteristic in this: every system of power is presented with the same problem. But the peculiarity of the disciplines is that they try to define in relation to the multiplicities a tactics of power that fulfils three criteria: firstly, to obtain the exercise of power at the lowest possible cost (economically, by the low expenditure it involves; politically, by its discretion, its low exteriorization, its relative invisibility, the little resistance it

arouses); secondly, to bring the effects of this social power to their maximum intensity and to extend them as far as possible, without either failure or interval; thirdly, to link this 'economic' growth of power with the output of the apparatuses (educational, military, industrial or medical) within which it is exercised; in short, to increase both the docility and the utility of all the elements of the system. This triple objective of the disciplines corresponds to a well-known historical conjuncture. One aspect of this conjuncture was the large demographic thrust of the eighteenth century; an increase in the floating population (one of the primary objects of discipline is to fix; it is an anti-nomadic technique); a change of quantitative scale in the groups to be supervised or manipulated (from the beginning of the seventeenth century to the eve of the French Revolution, the school population had been increasing rapidly, as had no doubt the hospital population; by the end of the eighteenth century, the peace-time army exceeded 200,000 men). The other aspect of the conjuncture was the growth in the apparatus of production, which was becoming more and more extended and complex; it was also becoming more costly and its profitability had to be increased. The development of the disciplinary methods corresponded to these two processes, or rather, no doubt, to the new need to adjust their correlation. Neither the residual forms of feudal power nor the structures of the administrative monarchy, nor the local mechanisms of supervision, nor the unstable, tangled mass they all formed together could carry out this role: they were hindered from doing so by the irregular and inadequate extension of their network, by their often conflicting functioning, but above all by the 'costly' nature of the power that was exercised in them. It was costly in several senses: because directly it cost a great deal to the Treasury; because the system of corrupt offices and farmed-out taxes weighed indirectly, but very heavily, on the population; because the resistance it encountered forced it into a cycle of perpetual reinforcement; because it proceeded essentially by levying (levying on money or products by royal, seigniorial, ecclesiastical taxation; levying on men or time by *corvées* of press-ganging, by locking up or banishing vagabonds). The development of the disciplines marks the appearance of elementary techniques belonging to a quite different economy: mechanisms of power which, instead of proceeding by deduction, are integrated into the productive efficiency of the apparatuses from within, into the growth of this efficiency and into the use of what it produces. For the old principle of 'levying-violence', which governed the economy of power, the disciplines substitute the principle of 'mildness-production-profit'. These are the techniques that make it possible to adjust the multiplicity of men and the multiplication of the apparatuses of production (and this means not only 'production' in the strict sense, but also the production of knowledge and skills in the school, the production of health in the hospitals, the production of destructive force in the army).

In this task of adjustment, discipline had to solve a number of problems for which the old economy of power was not sufficiently equipped. It could reduce the inefficiency of mass phenomena: reduce what, in a multiplicity, makes it much less manageable than a unity; reduce what is opposed to the use of each of its elements and of their sum; reduce everything that may counter the advantages of number. That is why discipline fixes; it arrests or regulates movements; it clears up confusion; it dissipates compact groupings of individuals wandering about the country in unpredictable ways; it establishes calculated distributions. It must also master all the forces that are formed from the very constitution of an organized multiplicity; it must neutralize the effects of counter-power that spring from them and which form a resistance to the power that wishes to dominate it: agitations, revolts, spontaneous organizations, coalitions —anything that may establish horizontal conjunctions. Hence the fact that the disciplines use procedures of partitioning and verticality, that they introduce, between the different elements at the same level, as solid separations as possible, that they define compact hierarchical networks, in short, that they oppose to the intrinsic, adverse force of multiplicity the technique of the continuous, individualizing pyramid. They must also increase the particular utility of each element of the multiplicity, but by means that are the most rapid and the least costly, that is to say, by using the multiplicity itself as an instrument of this growth. Hence, in order to extract from bodies the maximum time and force, the use of those overall methods known as time-tables, collective training, exercises, total and detailed surveillance. Furthermore, the disciplines must increase the effect of utility proper to the multiplicities, so that each is made more useful than the simple sum of its elements: it is in order to increase the utilizable effects of the multiple that the disciplines define tactics of distribution, reciprocal adjustment of bodies, gestures and rhythms, differentiation of capacities, reciprocal coordination in relation to apparatuses or tasks. Lastly, the disciplines have to bring into play the power relations, not above but inside the very texture of the multiplicity, as discreetly as possible, as well articulated on the other functions of these multiplicities and also in the least expensive way possible:

to this correspond anonymous instruments of power, coextensive with the multiplicity that they regiment, such as hierarchical surveillance, continuous registration, perpetual assessment and classification. In short, to substitute for a power that is manifested through the brilliance of those who exercise it, a power that insidiously objectifies those on whom it is applied; to form a body of knowledge about these individuals, rather than to deploy the ostentatious signs of sovereignty. In a word, the disciplines are the ensemble of minute technical inventions that made it possible to increase the useful size of multiplicities by decreasing the inconveniences of the power which, in order to make them useful, must control them. A multiplicity, whether in a workshop or a nation, an army or a school, reaches the threshold of a discipline when the relation of the one to the other becomes favourable.

If the economic take-off of the West began with the techniques that made possible the accumulation of capital, it might perhaps be said that the methods for administering the accumulation of men made possible a political take-off in relation to the traditional, ritual, costly, violent forms of power, which soon fell into disuse and were superseded by a subtle, calculated technology of subjection. In fact, the two processes—the accumulation of men and the accumulation of capital—cannot be separated; it would not have been possible to solve the problem of the accumulation of men without the growth of an apparatus of production capable of both sustaining them and using them; conversely, the techniques that made the cumulative multiplicity of men useful accelerated the accumulation of capital. At a less general level, the technological mutations of the apparatus of production, the division of labour and the elaboration of the disciplinary techniques sustained an ensemble of very close relations (cf. Marx, *Capital*, vol. 1, chapter XIII and the very interesting analysis in Guerry and Deleule). Each makes the other possible and necessary; each provides a model for the other. The disciplinary pyramid constituted the small cell of power within which the separation, coordination and supervision of tasks was imposed and made efficient; and analytical partitioning of time, gestures and bodily forces constituted an operational schema that could easily be transferred from the groups to be subjected to the mechanisms of production; the massive projection of military methods onto industrial organization was an example of this modelling of the division of labour following the model laid down by the schemata of power. But, on the other hand, the technical analysis of the process of production, its 'mechanical' breaking-down, were projected onto the labour force whose task it was to implement it: the constitution of those disciplinary machines in which the individual forces that they bring together are composed into a whole and therefore increased is the effect of this projection. Let us say that discipline is the unitary technique by which the body is reduced as a 'political' force at the least cost and maximized as a useful force. The growth of a capitalist economy gave rise to the specific modality of disciplinary power, whose general formulas, techniques of submitting forces and bodies, in short, 'political anatomy', could be operated in the most diverse political régimes, apparatuses or institutions.

2. The panoptic modality of power—at the elementary, technical, merely physical level at which it is situated—is not under the immediate dependence or a direct extension of the great juridico-political structures of a society; it is nonetheless not absolutely independent. Historically, the process by which the bourgeoisie became in the course of the eighteenth century the politically dominant class was masked by the establishment of an explicit, coded and formally egalitarian juridical framework, made possible by the organization of a parliamentary, representative régime. But the development and generalization of disciplinary mechanisms constituted the other, dark side of these processes. The general juridical form that guaranteed a system of rights that were egalitarian in principle was supported by these tiny, everyday, physical mechanisms, by all those systems of micro-power that are essentially non-egalitarian and asymmetrical that we call the disciplines. And although, in a formal way, the representative régime makes it possible, directly or indirectly, with or without relays, for the will of all to form the fundamental authority of sovereignty, the disciplines provide, at the base, a guarantee of the submission of forces and bodies. The real, corporal disciplines constituted the foundation of the formal, juridical liberties. The contract may have been regarded as the ideal foundation of law and political power; panopticism constituted the technique, universally widespread, of coercion. It continued to work in depth on the juridical structures of society, in order to make the effective mechanisms of power function in opposition to the formal framework that it had acquired. The 'Enlightenment', which discovered the liberties, also invented the disciplines.

In appearance, the disciplines constitute nothing more than an infra-law. They seem to extend the general forms defined by law to the infinitesimal level of individual lives; or they appear as methods of training that enable individuals to become integrated into these general demands. They seem to constitute the same type of law on a different scale, thereby making it more meticulous and more indulgent. The disciplines should be regarded as a sort of counterlaw. They have the precise role of introducing insuperable asymmetries and excluding reciprocities. First, because discipline creates between individuals a 'private' link, which is a relation of constraints entirely different from contractual obligation; the acceptance of a discipline may be underwritten by contract; the way in which it is imposed, the mechanisms it brings into play, the non-reversible subordination of one group of people by another, the 'surplus' power that is always fixed on the same side, the inequality of position of the different 'partners' in relation to the common regulation, all these distinguish the disciplinary link from the contractual link, and make it possible to distort the contractual link systematically from the moment it has as its content a mechanism of discipline. We know, for example, how many real procedures undermine the legal fiction of the work contract: workshop discipline is not the least important. Moreover, whereas the juridical systems define juridical subjects according to universal norms, the disciplines characterize, classify, specialize; they distribute along a scale, around a norm, hierarchize individuals in relation to one another and, if necessary, disqualify and invalidate. In any case, in the space and during the time in which they exercise their control and bring into play the asymmetries of their power, they effect a suspension of the law that is never total, but is never annulled either. Regular and institutional as it may be, the discipline, in its mechanism, is a 'counter-law'. And, although the universal juridicism of modern society seems to fix limits on the exercise of power, its universally widespread panopticism enables it to operate, on the underside of the law, a machinery that is both immense and minute, which supports, reinforces, multiplies the asymmetry of power and undermines the limits that are traced around the law. The minute disciplines, the panopticisms of every day may well be below the level of emergence of the great apparatuses and the great political struggles. But, in the genealogy of modern society, they have been, with the class domination that traverses it, the political counterpart of the juridical norms according to which power was redistributed. Hence, no doubt, the importance that has been given for so long to the small techniques of discipline, to those apparently insignificant tricks that it has invented, and even to those 'sciences' that give it a respectable face; hence, the fear of abandoning them if one cannot find any substitute; hence, the affirmation that they are at the very foundation of society, and an element in its equilibrium, whereas they are a series of mechanisms for unbalancing power relations definitively and everywhere; hence, the persistence in regarding them as the humble, but concrete form of every morality, whereas they are a set of physico-political techniques.

To return to the problem of legal punishments, the prison with all the corrective technology at its disposal is to be resituated at the point where the codified power to punish turns into a disciplinary power to observe; at the point where the universal punishments of the law are applied selectively to certain individuals and always the same ones; at the point where the redefinition of the juridical subject by the penalty becomes a useful training of the criminal; at the point where the law is inverted and passes outside itself, and where the counter-law becomes the effective and institutionalized content of the juridical forms. What generalizes the power to punish, then, is not the universal consciousness of the law in each juridical subject; it is the regular extension, the infinitely minute web of panoptic techniques. . . .

PART TWO

DECONSTRUCTION PRECURSORS—AND FILIATIONS

MARTIN HEIDEGGER

It may seem odd that the word *deconstruction* once evoked among scholars fantasies of cold-eyed Yale graduates pouring across the country babbling incomprehensibly and converting every sacred cow in sight into shish kebab. Hans-Georg Gadamer, a student of Heidegger, goes to some lengths to assure us that in the 1920s *Destruktion* never meant *destruction* to young professor Heidegger, who so influentially used it. Heidegger could have said *zerstören* had he actually wanted to "destroy."* And yet, Gadamer recalls not only sublime Black Forest bonfires, revolutionary (because rural) fashions in professorial garb, and charismatic speeches like mountain storms emitting audience-stunning lightning flashes, he also recalls Heidegger's sarcastic characterizations of colleagues, iconoclastic hammer blows to beat down "fashionable expectations," and "destabilizing, radical" followers, "arrogant" in-groups, whose questions seemed to older professors to break "all the rules of human decency." In short, Gadamer says frankly, ". . . I would not like to have been a colleague of the Heidegger of that time."†

But when we read the "Destruktion" chapter of *Being and Time* (1927) reprinted here, we have to agree that Heidegger did not mean to destroy. He means to interrogate the "original" sources in his way, make the sources respond to *his* question, and not be deflected from this purpose by the history of what others have said. When one is inquiring into the meaning of human being *(Dasein)*, it takes some aggression not to accept too piously the traditional answers—not to be overwhelmed by received ideas and the prestige of those who have gone before one. What these thinkers have said certainly has had its positive side. But there have been, inevitably, "concealments" as well, which the "destruction" of tradition will expose. "To bury the past in nullity is not the purpose of this destruction; its aim is positive. . . ." As Heidegger works backward toward increasingly "primordial" treatments of the question of human being, he discovers in each case, in Kant, Descartes, medieval scholasticism, and Aristotle, that the essential temporality of human being has never been raised, that Being is historical: that ". . . any *Dasein* is as it already was, and is 'what' it already was. It is its past. . . ." "The truth," as Jürgen Habermas describes Heidegger's hermeneutic insight, "has time at its core."‡

*Ernst Behler, "Deconstruction versus Hermeneutics: Derrida and Gadamer on Text and Interpretation," in *Southern Humanities Review* XXI (Summer 1987) 201–23.
†Hans-Georg Gadamer, *Philosophical Apprenticeships,* trans. Robert Sullivan (Cambridge and London: MIT Press, 1985) 48–50.
‡Jürgen Habermas, *Philosophical-Political Profiles,* trans. Frederick G. Lawrence (Cambridge and London: MIT Press, 1983) 56.

Thinking and *Destruktion*

1927

Translated by John Macquarrie and Edward Robinson

All research—and not least that which operates within the range of the central question of Being—is an ontical possibility of Dasein. Dasein's Being finds its meaning in temporality. But temporality is also the condition which makes historicality possible as a temporal kind of Being which Dasein itself possesses, regardless of whether or how Dasein is an entity 'in time'. Historicality, as a determinate character, is prior to what is called "history" (world-historical historizing).[1]

"Historicality" stands for the state of Being that is constitutive for Dasein's 'historizing' as such; only on the basis of such 'historizing' is anything like 'world-history' possible or can anything belong historically to world-history. In its factical Being, any Dasein is as it already was, and it is 'what' it already was. It *is* its past, whether explicitly or not. And this is so not only in that its past is, as it were, pushing itself along 'behind' it, and that Dasein possesses what is past as a property which is still present-at-hand and which sometimes has after-effects upon it: Dasein 'is' its past in the way of *its* own Being, which, to put it

THINKING AND *DESTRUKTION* from "The Task of Destroying the History of Ontology" (pp. 41–49) in *Being and Time* by Martin Heidegger. Translated by John Macquarrie and Edward Robinson. Copyright © 1962 by SCM Press Ltd. Reprinted by permission of Harper and Row, Publishers, Inc.

1. 'weltgeschichtliches Geschehen'. While the verb 'geschehen' ordinarily means to 'happen', and will often be so translated, Heidegger stresses its etymological kinship to 'Geschichte' or 'history'. To bring out this connection, we have coined the verb 'historize', which might be paraphrased as to 'happen in a historical way'; we shall usually translate 'geschehen' this way in contexts where history is being discussed. We trust that the reader will keep in mind that such 'historizing' is characteristic of all historical entities, and is *not* the sort of thing that is done primarily by historians (as 'philosophizing', for instance, is done by philosophers). (On 'world-historical' see H. 381 ff.)

roughly, 'historizes' out of its future on each occasion.[2] Whatever the way of being it may have at the time, and thus with whatever understanding of Being it may possess, Dasein has grown up both into and in a traditional way of interpreting itself: in terms of this it understands itself proximally and, within a certain range, constantly. By this understanding, the possibilities of its Being are disclosed and regulated. Its own past—and this always means the past of its 'generation'—is not something which *follows along after* Dasein, but something which already goes ahead of it.

This elemental historicality of Dasein may remain hidden from Dasein itself. But there is a way by which it can be discovered and given proper attention. Dasein can discover tradition, preserve it, and study it explicitly. The discovery of tradition and the disclosure of what it 'transmits' and how this is transmitted, can be taken hold of as a task in its own right. In this way Dasein brings itself into the kind of Being which consists in historiological inquiry and research. But historiology—or more precisely historicity[3]—is possible as a kind of Being which the inquiring Dasein may possess, only because historicality is a determining characteristic for Dasein in the very basis of its Being. If this historicality remains hidden from Dasein, and as long as it so remains, Dasein is also denied the possibility of historiological inquiry or the discovery of history. If historiology is wanting, this is not evidence *against* Dasein's historicality; on the contrary, as a deficient mode[4] of this state of Being, it is evidence for it. Only because it is 'historical' can an era be unhistoriological.

On the other hand, if Dasein has seized upon its latent possibility not only of making its own existence transparent to itself but also of inquiring into the meaning of existentiality itself (that is to say, of previously inquiring into the meaning of Being in general), and if by such inquiry its eyes have been opened to its own essential historicality, then one cannot fail to see that the inquiry into Being (the ontico-ontological necessity of which we have already indicated) is itself characterized by historicality. The ownmost meaning of Being which belongs to the inquiry into Being as an historical inquiry, gives

2. 'Das Dasein "ist" seine Vergangenheit in der Weise *seines* Seins, das, roh gesagt, jeweils aus seiner Zukunft her "geschieht".'
3. 'Historizität'. Cf. note 2, p. 31. H. 10 above.
4. 'defizienter Modus'. Heidegger likes to think of certain characteristics as occurring in various ways or 'modes', among which may be included certain ways of 'not occurring' or 'occurring only to an inadequate extent' or, in general, occurring 'deficiently'. It is as if zero and the negative integers were to be thought of as representing 'deficient modes of being a positive integer'.

us the assignment [Anweisung] of inquiring into the history of that inquiry itself, that is, of becoming historiological. In working out the question of Being, we must heed this assignment, so that by positively making the past our own, we may bring ourselves into full possession of the ownmost possibilities of such inquiry. The question of the meaning of Being must be carried through by explicating Dasein beforehand in its temporality and historicality; the question thus brings itself to the point where it understands itself as historiological.

Our preparatory Interpretation of the fundamental structures of Dasein with regard to the average kind of Being which is closest to it (a kind of Being in which it is therefore proximally historical as well), will make manifest, however, not only that Dasein is inclined to fall back upon its world (the world in which it is) and to interpret itself in terms of that world by its reflected light, but also that Dasein simultaneously falls prey to the tradition of which it has more or less explicitly taken hold.[5] This tradition keeps it from providing its own guidance, whether in inquiring or in choosing. This holds true—and by no means least—for that understanding which is rooted in Dasein's ownmost Being, and for the possibility of developing it—namely, for ontological understanding.

When tradition thus becomes master, it does so in such a way that what it 'transmits' is made so inaccessible, proximally and for the most part, that it rather becomes concealed. Tradition takes what has come down to us and delivers it over to self-evidence; it blocks our access to those primordial 'sources' from which the categories and concepts handed down to us have been in part quite genuinely drawn.[6] Indeed it makes us forget that they have had such an origin, and makes us suppose that the necessity of going back to these sources is something which we need not even understand. Dasein has had its historicality so thoroughly uprooted by tradition that it

5. '. . . das Dasein hat nicht nur die Geneigtheit, an seine Welt, in der es ist, zu verfallen und reluzent aus ihr her sich auszulegen, Dasein verfällt in eins damit auch seiner mehr oder minder ausdrücklich ergriffenen Tradition.' The verb 'verfallen' is one which Heidegger will use many times. Though we shall usually translate it simply as 'fall', it has the connotation of *deteriorating, collapsing,* or *falling down.* Neither our 'fall back upon' nor our 'falls prey to' is quite right: but 'fall upon' and 'fall on to', which are more literal, would be misleading for 'an . . . zu verfallen'; and though 'falls to the lot of' and 'devolves upon' would do well for 'verfällt' with the dative in other contexts, they will not do so well here.

6. In this passage Heidegger juxtaposes a number of words beginning with the prefix 'über-': 'übergibt' ('transmits'); 'überantwortet' ('delivers over'); 'das Überkommene' ('what has come down to us'); 'überlieferten' ('handed down to us').

confines its interest to the multiformity of possible types, directions, and standpoints of philosophical activity in the most exotic and alien of cultures; and by this very interest it seeks to veil the fact that it has no ground of its own to stand on. Consequently, despite all its historiological interests and all its zeal for an Interpretation which is philologically 'objective' ["sachliche"], Dasein no longer understands the most elementary conditions which would alone enable it to go back to the past in a positive manner and make it productively its own.

We have shown at the outset (Section 1) not only that the question of the meaning of Being is one that has not been attended to and one that has been inadequately formulated, but that it has become quite forgotten in spite of all our interest in 'metaphysics'. Greek ontology and its history—which, in their numerous filiations and distortions, determine the conceptual character of philosophy even today —prove that when Dasein understands either itself or Being in general, it does so in terms of the 'world', and that the ontology which has thus arisen has deteriorated [verfällt] to a tradition in which it gets reduced to something self-evident—merely material for reworking, as it was for Hegel. In the Middle Ages this uprooted Greek ontology became a fixed body of doctrine. Its systematics, however, is by no means a mere joining together of traditional pieces into a single edifice. Though its basic conceptions of Being have been taken over dogmatically from the Greeks, a great deal of unpretentious work has been carried on further within these limits. With the peculiar character which the Scholastics gave it, Greek ontology has, in its essentials, travelled the path that leads through the *Disputationes metaphysicae* of Suarez to the 'metaphysics' and transcendental philosophy of modern times, determining even the foundations and the aims of Hegel's 'logic'. In the course of this history certain distinctive domains of Being have come into view and have served as the primary guides for subsequent problematics: the *ego cogito* of Descartes, the subject, the "I", reason, spirit, person. But these all remain uninterrogated as to their Being and its structure, in accordance with the thoroughgoing way in which the question of Being has been neglected. It is rather the case that the categorial content of the traditional ontology has been carried over to these entities with corresponding formalizations and purely negative restrictions, or else dialectic has been called in for the purpose of Interpreting the substantiality of the subject ontologically.

If the question of Being is to have its own history made transparent,

then this hardened tradition must be loosened up, and the concealments which it has brought about[7] must be dissolved. We understand
this task as one in which by taking *the question of Being as our clue,*
we are to *destroy* the traditional content of ancient ontology until we
arrive at those primordial experiences in which we achieved our first
ways of determining the nature of Being—the ways which have
guided us ever since.

In thus demonstrating the origin of our basic ontological concepts
by an investigation in which their 'birth certificate' is displayed, we
have nothing to do with a vicious relativizing of ontological standpoints. But this destruction is just as far from having the *negative*
sense of shaking off the ontological tradition. We must, on the
contrary, stake out the positive possibilities of that tradition, and this
always means keeping it within its *limits;* these in turn are given
factically in the way the question is formulated at the time, and in the
way the possible field for investigation is thus bounded off. On its
negative side, this destruction does not relate itself towards the past;
its criticism is aimed at 'today' and at the prevalent way of treating the
history of ontology, whether it is headed towards doxography,
towards intellectual history, or towards a history of problems. But to
bury the past in nullity [Nichtigkeit] is not the purpose of this
destruction; its aim is *positive;* its negative function remains unexpressed and indirect.

The destruction of the history of ontology is essentially bound up
with the way the question of Being is formulated, and it is possible
only within such a formulation. In the framework of our treatise,
which aims at working out that question in principle, we can carry
out this destruction only with regard to stages of that history which
are in principle decisive.

In line with the positive tendencies of this destruction, we must in
the first instance raise the question whether and to what extent the
Interpretation of Being and the phenomenon of time have been
brought together thematically in the course of the history of ontology,
and whether the problematic of Temporality required for this has ever
been worked out in principle or ever could have been. The first and
only person who has gone any stretch of the way towards investigating the dimension of Temporality or has even let himself be drawn
hither by the coercion of the phenomena themselves is Kant. Only

---

7. '. . . der durch sie gezeitigten Verdeckungen.' The verb 'zeitigen' will appear
frequently in later chapters. See H. 304 and our note ad loc.

when we have established the problematic of Temporality, can we succeed in casting light on the obscurity of his doctrine of the schematism. But this will also show us *why* this area is one which had to remain closed off to him in its real dimensions and its central ontological function. Kant himself was aware that he was venturing into an area of obscurity: 'This schematism of our understanding as regards appearances and their mere form is an art hidden in the depths of the human soul, the true devices of which are hardly ever to be divined from Nature and laid uncovered before our eyes.' Here Kant shrinks back, as it were, in the face of something which must be brought to light as a theme and a principle if the expression "Being" is to have any demonstrable meaning. In the end, those very phenomena which will be exhibited under the heading of 'Temporality' in our analysis, are precisely those *most covert* judgments of the 'common reason' for which Kant says it is the 'business of philosophers' to provide an analytic.

In pursuing this task of destruction with the problematic of Temporality as our clue, we shall try to Interpret the chapter on the schematism and the Kantian doctrine of time, taking that chapter as our point of departure. At the same time we shall show why Kant could never achieve an insight into the problematic of Temporality. There were two things that stood in his way: in the first place, he altogether neglected the problem of Being; and, in connection with this, he failed to provide an ontology with Dasein as its theme or (to put this in Kantian language) to give a preliminary ontological analytic of the subjectivity of the subject. Instead of this, Kant took over Descartes' position quite dogmatically, notwithstanding all the essential respects in which he had gone beyond him. Furthermore, in spite of the fact that he was bringing the phenomenon of time back into the subject again, his analysis of it remained oriented towards the traditional way in which time had been ordinarily understood; in the long run this kept him from working out the phenomenon of a 'transcendental determination of time' in its own structure and function. Because of this double effect of tradition the decisive *connection* between *time* and the *'I think'* was shrouded in utter darkness; it did not even become a problem.

In taking over Descartes' ontological position Kant made an essential omission: he failed to provide an ontology of Dasein. This omission was a decisive one in the spirit [im Sinne] of Descartes' ownmost tendencies. With the *'cogito sum'* Descartes had claimed that he was putting philosophy on a new and firm footing. But what he left undetermined when he began in this 'radical' way, was the kind of Being which belongs to the *res cogitans,* or—more precisely —the *meaning of the Being of the 'sum'.*[8] By working out the unexpressed ontological foundations of the *'cogito sum',* we shall complete our sojourn at the second station along the path of our destructive retrospect of the history of ontology. Our Interpretation will not only prove that Descartes had to neglect the question of Being altogether; it will also show why he came to suppose that the absolute 'Being-certain' ["Gewißein"] of the *cogito* exempted him from raising the question of the meaning of the Being which this entity possesses.

Yet Descartes not only continued to neglect this and thus to accept a completely indefinite ontological status for the *res cogitans sive mens sive animus* ['the thing which cognizes, whether it be a mind or spirit']: he regarded this entity as a *fundamentum inconcussum,* and applied the medieval ontology to it in carrying through the fundamental considerations of his *Meditationes.* He defined the *res cogitans* ontologically as an *ens;* and in the medieval ontology the meaning of Being for such an *ens* had been fixed by understanding it as an *ens creatum.* God, as *ens infinitum,* was the *ens increatum.* But createdness [Geschaffenheit] in the widest sense of something's having been produced [Hergestelltheit], was an essential item in the structure of the ancient conception of Being. The seemingly new beginning which Descartes proposed for philosophizing has revealed itself as the implantation of a baleful prejudice, which has kept later generations from making any thematic ontological analytic of the 'mind' ["Gemütes"] such as would take the question of Being as a clue and would at the same time come to grips critically with the traditional ancient ontology.

Everyone who is acquainted with the middle ages sees that Descartes is 'dependent' upon medieval scholasticism and employs its terminology. But with this 'discovery' nothing is achieved philosophically as long as it remains obscure to what a profound extent the medieval ontology has influenced the way in which posterity has determined or failed to determine the ontological character of the *res cogitans.* The full extent of this cannot be estimated until both the meaning and the limitations of the ancient ontology have been exhibited in terms of an orientation directed towards the question of

8. We follow the later editions in reading *'der Seinssinn des "sum"'.* The earlier editions have an anacoluthic 'den' for 'der'.

Being. In other words, in our process of destruction we find ourselves faced with the task of Interpreting the basis of the ancient ontology in the light of the problematic of Temporality. When this is done, it will be manifest that the ancient way of interpreting the Being of entities is oriented towards the 'world' or 'Nature' in the widest sense, and that it is indeed in terms of 'time' that its understanding of Being is obtained. The outward evidence for this (though of course it is *merely* outward evidence) is the treatment of the meaning of Being as παρουσία or οὐσία, which signifies, in ontologico-Temporal terms, 'presence' ["Anwesenheit"].[9] Entities are grasped in their Being as 'presence'; this means that they are understood with regard to a definite mode of time—the *'Present'*.[10]

The problematic of Greek ontology, like that of any other, must take its clues from Dasein itself. In both ordinary and philosophical usage, Dasein, man's Being, is 'defined' as the ζῷον λόγον ἔχον—as that living thing whose Being is essentially determined by the potentiality for discourse.[11] λέγειν is the clue for arriving at those structures of Being which belong to the entities we encounter in

9. The noun οὐσία is derived from one of the stems used in conjugating the irregular verb εἶναι, ('to be'); in the Aristotelian tradition it is usually translated as 'substance', though translators of Plato are more likely to write 'essence', 'existence', or 'being'. Heidegger suggests that οὐσία is to be thought of as synonymous with the derivative noun παρουσία ('being-at', 'presence'). As he points out, παρουσία has a close etymological correspondence with the German 'Anwesenheit', which is similarly derived from the stem of a verb meaning 'to be' (Cf. O.H.G. 'wesan') and a prefix of the place or time at which ('an-'). We shall in general translate 'Anwesenheit' as 'presence', and the participle 'anwesend' as some form of the expression 'have presence'.

10. 'die *"Gegenwart"'*. While this noun may, like παρουσία or 'Anwesenheit', mean the *presence* of someone *at* some place or on some occasion, it more often means the *present*, as distinguished from the past and the future. In its etymological root-structure, however, it means a *waiting-towards*. While Heidegger seems to think of all these meanings as somehow fused, we shall generally translate this noun as 'the Present', reserving 'in the present' for the corresponding adjective 'gegenwärtig'.

11. The phrase ζῷον λόγον ἔχον is traditionally translated as 'rational animal', on the assumption that λόγος refers to the faculty of *reason*. Heidegger, however, points out that λόγος is derived from the same root as the verb λέγειν ('to talk', 'to hold discourse'); he identifies this in turn with νοεῖν ('to cognize', 'to be aware of', 'to know'), and calls attention to the fact that the same stem is found in the adjective διαλεκτικός ('dialectical'). He thus interprets λόγος as 'Rede', which we shall usually translate as 'discourse' or 'talk', depending on the context. See Section 7 B below (H. 32ff.) and Sections 34 and 35, where 'Rede' will be defined and distinguished both from 'Sprache' ('language') and from 'Gerede' ('idle talk') (H. 160 ff.)

addressing ourselves to anything or speaking about it [im Ansprechen und Besprechen]. (Cf. Section 7 B.) This is why the ancient ontology as developed by Plato turns into 'dialectic'. As the ontological clue gets progressively worked out—namely, in the 'hermeneutic' of the λόγος—it becomes increasingly possible to grasp the problem of Being in a more radical fashion. The 'dialectic,' which has been a genuine philosophical embarrassment, becomes superfluous. That is *why* Aristotle 'no longer has any understanding' of it, for he has put it on a more radical footing and raised it to a new level [aufhob]. λέγειν itself—or rather νοεῖν, that simple awareness of something present-at-hand in its sheer presence-at-hand,[12] which Parmenides had already taken to guide him in his own interpretation of Being—has the Temporal structure of a pure 'making-present' of something.[13] Those entities which show themselves in this and for it, and which are understood as entities in the most authentic sense, thus get interpreted with regard to the Present; that is, they are conceived as presence (οὐσία).[14]

Yet the Greeks have managed to interpret Being in this way without any explicit knowledge of the clues which function here, without any

12. '. . . von etwas Vorhandenem in seiner puren Vorhandenheit . . .' The adjective 'vorhanden' means literally 'before the hand', but this signification has long since given way to others. In ordinary German usage it may, for instance, be applied to the stock of goods which a dealer has 'on hand', or to the 'extant' works of an author; and in earlier philosophical writing it could be used, like the word 'Dasein' itself, as a synonym for the Latin *'existentia'*. Heidegger, however, distinguishes quite sharply between 'Dasein' and 'Vorhandenheit', using the latter to designate a kind of Being which belongs to things *other* than Dasein. We shall translate 'vorhanden' as 'present-at-hand', and 'Vorhandenheit' as 'presence-at-hand.' The reader must be careful not to confuse these expressions with our 'presence' ('Anwesenheit') and 'the Present' ('die Gegenwart'), etc., or with a few other verbs and adjectives which we may find it convenient to tranlate by 'present'.

13. '. . . des reinen "Gegenwärtigens" von etwas'. The verb 'gegenwärtigen', which is derived from the adjective 'gegenwärtig', is not a normal German verb, but was used by Husserl and is used extensively by Heidegger. While we shall translate it by various forms of 'make present', it does not necessarily mean 'making physically present', but often means something like 'bringing vividly to mind'.

14. 'Das Seiende, das sich in ihm für es zeigt und das als das eigentliche Seiende verstanden wird, erhält demnach seine Auslegung in Rücksicht auf—Gegen-wart, d.h. es ist als Anwesenheit (οὐσία) begriffen.' The hyphenation of 'Gegen-wart' calls attention to the structure of this word in a way which cannot be reproduced in English. See note 2, p. 47, H. 25 above. The pronouns 'ihm' and 'es' presumably both refer back to λέγειν, though their reference is ambiguous, as our version suggests.

acquaintance with the fundamental ontological function of time or even any understanding of it, and without any insight into the reason why this function is possible. On the contrary, they take time itself as one entity among other entities, and try to grasp it in the structure of its Being, though that way of understanding Being which they have taken as their horizon is one which is itself naïvely and inexplicitly oriented towards time.

Within the framework in which we are about to work out the principles of the question of Being, we cannot present a detailed Temporal Interpretation of the foundations of ancient ontology, particularly not of its loftiest and purest scientific stage, which is reached in Aristotle. Instead we shall give an interpretation of Aristotle's essay on time, which may be chosen as providing a way of *discriminating* the basis and the limitations of the ancient science of Being.

Aristotle's essay on time is the first detailed Interpretation of this phenomenon which has come down to us. Every subsequent account of time, including Bergson's, has been essentially determined by it. When we analyse the Aristotelian conception, it will likewise become clear, as we go back, that the Kantian account of time operates within the structures which Aristotle has set forth; this means that Kant's basic ontological orientation remains that of the Greeks, in spite of all the distinctions which arise in a new inquiry.

The question of Being does not achieve its true concreteness until we have carried through the process of destroying the ontological tradition. In this way we can fully prove that the question of the meaning of Being is one that we cannot avoid, and we can demonstrate what it means to talk about 'restating' this question.

In any investigation in this field, where 'the thing itself is deeply veiled' one must take pains not to overestimate the results. For in such an inquiry one is constantly compelled to face the possibility of disclosing an even more primordial and more universal horizon from which we may draw the answer to the question, "What is *'Being'?''* We can discuss such possibilities seriously and with positive results only if the question of Being has been reawakened and we have arrived at a field where we can come to terms with it in a way that can be controlled.

GEORGES BATAILLE

If the National Endowment for the Humanities could dream, Georges Bataille would be its nightmare. Bataille is a writer so appalling, so funny, so disrespectful of the institutions designed to civilize the young, so revolted by the pabulum of official humanism, that it is difficult at times to imagine the education system assimilating him without putting an end to itself. Human culture and community are based on a system of shared taboos, says Bataille in *Literature and Evil*.* To observe these taboos is to be reasonable and civilized. To be reasonable and civilized is to be good. To be good is to be submissive. The reward for submission is order, calm, and a modest return on our investments. We are permitted a servile occupation in which we dissipate our vitality and slowly crumble to dust. Human communication in these circumstances consists of the banal exchange of standard phrases. The opium of the people is "not so much religion as it is accepted boredom."† There are possible, however, rare moments of passionate intensity, which sweep away lethargy and inertia and release orgiastic explosions of energy. These are moments of festival and carnival; they draw their power from scandal, from the violation of taboos, the negation of interdicts, from criminality, the overturning of idols, from rents, wounds, bloody painful losses and memorable lacerations (1973:171, 173; 1985:251). The great power of the fascists, for example, was that they could touch the emotions of the masses, release collective exaltation, and provide an escape from boredom (1985:167). The power of sacrifice can best be illuminated, perhaps, in the potlatch destruction of whole villages or in the Aztec or Hebraic hecatombs (of Numbers 31, for instance). It is fainter in ritual circumcision or in art. But what power art has derives from the sacred wastage and divine intoxication of unproductive expenditure and sacrifice (120). Art will therefore seem dangerous, even evil, to those who do not understand that it represents the "dream of sacred violence which no settlement with organized society can attenuate" (1973:11). Boredom dreams of scaffolds, as Baudelaire said. Evil is the dream of the good, the expression of the "most ethical" (8, 12). On the bosom of the legal, the criminal is conceived. But the criminal reaffirms the legal. Thus is the outrageous reappropriated for respectability.

"The Big Toe" (1929), the first of two selections by Bataille reprinted

---

*Georges Bataille, *Literature and Evil*, trans. Alastair Hamilton (New York: Urizen Books, 1973) 172.

†Georges Bataille, *Visions of Excess, Selected Writings, 1927-1939*, ed. and introduction by Allan Stoekl, trans. by Allan Stoekl with Carl Lovitt and Donald Leslie, Jr. (Minneapolis: University of Minnesota Press, 1985) 167.

here, examines the human bias in favor of elevation, the privileging of the head over the foot. The latter is repressed as dirt, darkness, and death. Similarly, in Derrida's later analysis of western philosophy, writing is repressed as the fecal extrusion of the pristine phonic. This repression is central to Bataille's conflict with the Surrealists. The prefix *sur* contains precisely the "Icarian" pathology typical of western civilization (1985:32 ff.). The conflict in "The Notion of Expenditure" (1933) is between utility and pleasure, sordid bourgeois rapacity and joyful orgiastic waste. The latter is the toxic source of excitement that powers both revolution and art.

The Big Toe

Translated by Allan Stoekl

The big toe is the most *human* part of the human body, in the sense that no other element of this body is as differentiated from the corresponding element of the anthropoid ape (chimpanzee, gorilla, orangutan, or gibbon). This is due to the fact that the ape is tree dwelling, whereas man moves on the earth without clinging to branches, having himself become a tree, in other words raising himself straight up in the air like a tree, and all the more beautiful for the correctness of his erection. In addition, the function of the human foot consists in giving a firm foundation to the erection of which man is so proud (the big toe, ceasing to grasp branches, is applied to the ground on the same plane as the other toes).

But whatever the role played in the erection by his foot, man, who has a light head, in other words a head raised to the heavens and heavenly things, sees it as spit, on the pretext that he has this foot in the mud.

Although within the body blood flows in equal quantities from high to low and from low to high, there is a bias in favor of that which elevates itself, and human life is erroneously seen as an elevation. The division of the universe into subterranean hell and perfectly pure heaven is an indelible conception, mud and darkness being the *principles* of evil as light and celestial space are the *principles* of good: with their feet in mud but their heads more or less in light, men obstinately imagine a tide that will permanently elevate them, never to return, into pure space. Human life entails, in fact, the rage of seeing oneself as a back and forth movement from refuse to the ideal, and from the ideal to refuse—a rage that is easily directed against an organ as *base* as the foot.

The human foot is commonly subjected to grotesque tortures that deform it and make it rickety. In an imbecilic way it is doomed to corns, calluses, and bunions, and if one takes into account turns of phrase that are only now disappearing, to the most nauseating filthiness: the peasant expression "her hands are as dirty as feet," while no longer true of the entire human collectivity, was so in the seventeenth century.

Man's secret horror of his foot is one of the explanations for the tendency to conceal its length and form as much as possible. Heels of greater or lesser height, depending on the sex, distract from the foot's low and flat character.

Besides, this uneasiness is often confused with a sexual uneasiness; this is especially striking among the Chinese, who, after having atrophied the feet of women, situate them at the most excessive point of deviance. The husband himself must not see the nude feet of his wife, and it is incorrect and immoral in general to look at the feet of women. Catholic confessors, adapting themselves to this aberration, ask their Chinese penitents "if they have not looked at women's feet."

The same aberration is found among the Turks (Volga Turks, Turks of Central Asia), who consider it immoral to show their nude feet and who even go to bed in stockings.

Nothing similar can be cited from classical antiquity (apart from the use of very high soles in tragedies). The most prudish Roman matrons constantly allowed their nude toes to be seen. On the other hand, modesty concerning the feet developed excessively in the modern era and only started to disappear in the nineteenth century. M. Salomon Reinach has studied this development in detail in the article entitled "Pieds pudiques" ["Modest Feet"],[1] insisting on the role of Spain, where women's feet have been the object of the most dreaded anxiety and thus were the cause of crimes. The simple fact of allowing the shod foot to be seen, jutting out from under a skirt, was regarded as indecent. Under no circumstances was it possible to touch the foot of a woman, this liberty being, with one exception, more grave than any other. Of course, the foot of the queen was the object of the most terrifying prohibition. Thus, according to Mme D'Aulnoy, the Count of Villamediana, in love with Queen Elizabeth, had the idea of starting a fire in order to have the pleasure of carrying her in his arms: "Almost the entire house, worth 100,000 écus, was burned, but he was consoled by the fact that, taking advantage of so favorable an occasion, he took the sovereign in his arms and carried her into a small staircase. He took some liberties there, and, *something very much noticed in this country, he even touched her foot.* A little page saw it, reported it to the king, and the latter had his revenge by killing the count with a pistol shot."

It is possible to see in these obsessions, as M. Reinach does, a progressive refinement of modesty that little by little has been able to reach the calf, the ankle, and the foot. This explanation, in part well founded, is however not sufficient if one wants to account for the hilarity commonly produced by simply imagining the *toes.* The play of fantasies and fears, of human necessities and aberrations, is in fact such that fingers have come to signify useful action and firm character, the toes stupor and base idiocy. The vicissitudes of organs, the profusion of stomachs, larynxes, and brains traversing innumerable animal species and individuals, carries the imagination along in an ebb and flow it does not willingly follow, due to a hatred of the still painfully perceptible frenzy of the bloody palpitations of the body. Man willingly imagines himself to be like the god Neptune, stilling his own waves, with majesty; nevertheless, the bellowing waves of the viscera, in more or less incessant inflation and upheaval, brusquely put an end to his dignity. Blind, but tranquil and strangely despising his obscure baseness, a given person, ready to call to mind the grandeurs of human history, as when his glance ascends a monument testifying to the grandeur of his nation, is stopped in mid-flight by an

1. In *L'Anthropologie,* 1903, pp. 733–36; reprinted in *Cultes, mythes et religions,* 1905, vol 1, pp. 105–10.

atrocious pain in his big toe because, though the most noble of animals, he nevertheless has corns on his feet; in other words, he has feet, and these feet independently lead an ignoble life.

Corns on the feet differ from headaches and toothaches by their baseness, and they are only laughable because of an ignominy explicable by the mud in which feet are found. Since by its physical attitude the human race distances itself *as much as it can* from terrestrial mud—whereas a spasmodic laugh carries joy to its summit each time its purest flight lands man's own arrogance spread-eagle in the mud—one can imagine that a toe, always more or less damaged and humiliating, is psychologically analogous to the brutal fall of a man—in other words, to death. The hideously cadaverous and at the same time loud and proud appearance of the big toe corresponds to this derision and gives a very shrill expression to the disorder of the human body, that product of the violent discord of the organs.

The form of the big toe is not, however, specifically monstrous: in this it is different from other parts of the body, the inside of a gaping mouth, for example. Only secondary (but common) deformations have been able to give its ignominy an exceptionally burlesque value. Now it is easy, most often, to account for burlesque values by means of extreme seductiveness. But we are led here to distinguish categorically two radically opposed kinds of seductiveness (whose habitual confusion entails the most absurd misunderstandings of language).

If a seductive element is to be attributed to the big toe, it is evidently not one to satisfy such exalted aspirations as, for example, the perfectly indelible taste that, in most cases, leads one to prefer elegant and correct forms. On the contrary, if one chooses, for example, the case of the Count of Villamediana, one can affirm that the pleasure he derived from touching the queen's foot specifically derived from the ugliness and infection represented by the baseness of the foot, in practice by the most deformed feet. Thus, supposing that the queen's foot was perfectly pretty, it still derived its sacrilegious charm from deformed and muddy feet. Since a queen is *a priori* a more *ideal* and ethereal being than any other, it was human to the point of laceration to touch what in fact was not very different from the stinking foot of a thug. Here one submits to a seduction radically opposed to that caused by light and ideal beauty; the two orders of seduction are often confused because a person constantly moves from one to the other, and, given this back and forth movement, whether it finds its end in one direction or the other, seduction is all the more acute when the movement is more brutal.

As for the big toe, classic foot fetishism leading to the licking of toes categorically indicates that it is a phenomenon of base seduction, which accounts for the burlesque value that is always more or less attached to the pleasures condemned by pure and superficial men.

The meaning of this article lies in its insistence on a direct and explicit questioning of *seductiveness,* without taking into account poetic concoctions that are, ultimately, nothing but a diversion (most human beings are naturally feeble and can only abandon themselves to their instincts when in a poetic haze). A return to reality does not imply any new acceptances, but means that one is seduced in a base manner, without transpositions and to the point of screaming, opening his eyes wide: opening them wide, then, before a big toe.

The Notion of Expenditure
1933

Translated by Allan Stoekl

THE INSUFFICIENCY OF THE PRINCIPLE OF CLASSICAL UTILITY

Every time the meaning of a discussion depends on the fundamental value of the word *useful*—in other words, every time the essential question touching on the life of human societies is raised, no matter who intervenes and what opinions are represented—it is possible to affirm that the debate is necessarily warped and that the fundamental question is eluded. In fact, given the more or less divergent collection of present ideas, there is nothing that permits one to define what is useful to man. This lacuna is made fairly prominent by the fact that

THE NOTION OF EXPENDITURE   by Georges Bataille from *Visions of Excess, Selected Writings 1927–39,* trans. Allan Stoekl, with Carl R. Lovitt and Donald M. Leslie, Jr. Copyright © 1985. Reprinted by permission of University of Minnesota Press.

it is constantly necessary to return, in the most unjustifiable way, to principles that one would like to situate beyond utility and pleasure: *honor* and *duty* are hypocritically employed in schemes of pecuniary interest and, without speaking of God, *Spirit* serves to mask the intellectual disarray of the few people who refuse to accept a closed system.

Current practice, however, is not deterred by these elementary difficulties, and common awareness at first seems able to raise only verbal objections to the principles of classical utility—in other words, to supposedly material utility. The goal of the latter is, theoretically, pleasure—but only in a moderate form, since violent pleasure is seen as *pathological.* On the one hand, this material utility is limited to acquisition (in practice, to production) and to the conservation of goods; on the other, it is limited to reproduction and to the conservation of human life (to which is added, it is true, the struggle against pain, whose importance itself suffices to indicate the negative character of the pleasure principle instituted, in theory, as the basis of utility). In the series of quantitative representations linked to this flat and untenable conception of existence only the question of reproduction seriously lends itself to controversy, because an exaggerated increase in the number of the living threatens to diminish the individual share. But on the whole, any general judgment of social activity implies the principle that all individual effort, in order to be valid, must be reducible to the fundamental necessities of production and conservation. Pleasure, whether art, permissible debauchery, or play, is definitively reduced, in the intellectual representations *in circulation,* to a concession; in other words it is reduced to a diversion whose role is subsidiary. The most appreciable share of life is given as the condition—sometimes even as the regrettable condition—of productive social activity.

It is true that personal experience—if it is a question of a useful man, capable of wasting and destroying without reason—each time gives the lie to this miserable conception. But even when he does not spare himself and destroys himself while making allowance for nothing, the most lucid man will understand nothing, or imagine himself sick; he is incapable of a *utilitarian* justification for his actions, and it does not occur to him that a human society can have, just as he does, an *interest* in considerable losses, in catastrophes that, *while conforming to well-defined needs,* provoke tumultuous depressions, crises of dread, and, in the final analysis, a certain orgiastic state.

In the most crushing way, the contradiction between current social conceptions and the real needs of society recalls the narrowness of judgment that puts the father in opposition to the satisfaction of his son's needs. This narrowness is such that it is impossible for the son to express his will. The father's partially malevolent solicitude is manifested in the things he provides for his son: lodgings, clothes, food, and, when absolutely necessary, a little harmless recreation. But the son does not even have the right to speak about what really gives him a fever; he is obliged to give people the impression that for him no *horror* can enter into consideration. In this respect, it is sad to say that *conscious humanity has remained a minor;* humanity recognizes the right to acquire, to conserve, and to consume rationally, but it excludes in principle *nonproductive expenditure.*

It is true that this exclusion is superficial and that it no more modifies practical activities than prohibitions limit the son, who indulges in his unavowed pleasures as soon as he is no longer in his father's presence. Humanity can allow itself the pleasure of expressing, in the father's interest, conceptions marked with flat paternal sufficiency and blindness. In the practice of life, however, humanity acts in a way that allows for the satisfaction of disarmingly savage needs, and it seems able to subsist only at the limits of horror. Moreover, to the small extent that a man is incapable of yielding to considerations that either are official or are susceptible of becoming so, to the small extent that he is inclined to feel the attraction of a life devoted to the destruction of established authority, it is difficult to believe that a peaceful world, conforming to his interests, could be for him anything other than a convenient illusion.

The difficulties met with in the development of a conception that is not guided by the servile mode of father–son relations are thus not insurmountable. It is possible to admit the historical necessity of vague and disappointing images, used by a majority of people, who do not act without a minimum of error (which they use as if it were a drug)—and who, moreover, in all circumstances refuse to find their way in a labyrinth resulting from human inconsistencies. An extreme simplification represents, for the uncultivated or barely cultivated segments of the population, the only chance to avoid a diminution of aggressive force. But it would be cowardly to accept, as a limit to understanding, the conditions of poverty and necessity in which such simplified images are formed. And if a less arbitrary conception is condemned to remain esoteric, and if as such, in the present circumstances, it comes into conflict with an unhealthy repulsion, then one must stress that this repulsion is precisely the shame of a generation whose rebels are afraid of the noise of their own words. Thus one cannot take it into account.

THE PRINCIPLE OF LOSS

Human activity is not entirely reducible to processes of production and conservation, and consumption must be divided into two distinct parts. The first, reducible part is represented by the use of the minimum necessary for the conservation of life and the continuation of individuals' productive activity in a given society; it is therefore a question simply of the fundamental condition of productive activity. The second part is represented by so-called unproductive expenditures: luxury, mourning, war, cults, the construction of sumptuary monuments, games, spectacles, arts, perverse sexual activity (i.e., deflected from genital finality)—all these represent activities which, at least in primitive circumstances, have no end beyond themselves. Now it is necessary to reserve the use of the word *expenditure* for the designation of these unproductive forms, and not for the designation of all the modes of consumption that serve as a means to the end of production. Even though it is always possible to set the various forms of expenditure in opposition to each other, they constitute a group characterized by the fact that in each case the accent is placed on a *loss* that must be as great as possible in order for that activity to take on its true meaning.

This principle of loss, in other words, of unconditional expenditure, no matter how contrary it might be to the economic principle of balanced accounts (expenditure regularly compensated for by acquisition), only *rational* in the narrow sense of the word, can be illustrated through a small number of examples taken from common experience:

1. Jewels must not only be beautiful and dazzling (which would make the substitution of imitations possible): one sacrifices a fortune, preferring a diamond necklace; such a sacrifice is necessary for the constitution of this necklace's fascinating character. This fact must be seen in relation to the symbolic value of jewels, universal in psychoanalysis. When in a dream a diamond signifies excrement, it is not only a question of association by contrast; in the unconscious, jewels, like excrement, are cursed matter that flows from a wound: they are a part of oneself destined for open sacrifice (they serve, in fact, as sumptuous gifts charged with sexual love). The functional

character of jewels requires their immense material value and alone explains the inconsequence of the most beautiful imitations, which are very nearly useless.

2. Cults require a bloody wasting of men and animals in *sacrifice*. In the etymological sense of the word, sacrifice is nothing other than the production of *sacred* things.

   From the very first, it appears that sacred things are constituted by an operation of loss: in particular, the success of Christianity must be explained by the value of the theme of the Son of God's ignominious crucifixion, which carries human dread to a representation of loss and limitless degradation.

3. In various competitive games, loss in general is produced under complex conditions. Considerable sums of money are spent for the maintenance of quarters, animals, equipment, or men. As much energy as possible is squandered in order to produce a feeling of stupefaction—in any case with an intensity infinitely greater than in productive enterprises. The danger of death is not avoided; on the contrary, it is the object of a strong unconscious attraction. Besides, competitions are sometimes the occasion for the public distribution of prizes. Immense crowds are present; their passions most often burst forth beyond any restraint, and the loss of insane sums of money is set in motion in the form of wagers. It is true that this circulation of money profits a small number of professional bettors, but it is no less true that this circulation can be considered to be a real *charge* of the passions unleashed by competition and that, among a large number of bettors, it leads to losses disproportionate to their means; these even attain such a level of madness that often the only way out for gamblers is prison or death. Beyond this, various modes of unproductive expenditure can be linked, depending on the circumstances, to great competitive spectacles, just as elements moving separately are caught up in a mightier whirlwind. Thus horse races are associated with a sumptuary process of social classification (the existence of Jockey Clubs need only be mentioned) and the ostentatious display of the latest luxurious fashions. It is necessary in any case to observe that the complex of expenditure represented by present-day racing is insignificant when compared to the extravagance of the Byzantines, who tied the totality of their public activity to equestrian competition.

4. From the point of view of expenditure, artistic productions must

be divided into two main categories, the first constituted by architectural construction, music, and dance. This category is comprised of *real* expenditures. Nevertheless, sculpture and painting, not to mention the use of sites for ceremonies and spectacles, introduces even into architecture the principle of the second category, that of *symbolic* expenditure. For their part, music and dance can easily be charged with external significations.

In their major form, literature and theater, which constitute the second category, provoke dread and horror through symbolic representations of tragic loss (degradation or death); in their minor form, they provoke laughter through representations which, though analogously structured, exclude certain seductive elements. The term poetry, applied to the least degraded and least intellectualized forms of the expression of a state of loss, can be considered synonymous with expenditure; it in fact signifies, in the most precise way, creation by means of loss. Its meaning is therefore close to that of *sacrifice*. It is true that the word "poetry" can only be appropriately applied to an extremely rare residue of what it commonly signifies and that, without a preliminary reduction, the worst confusions could result; it is, however, impossible in a first, rapid exposition to speak of the infinitely variable limits separating subsidiary formations from the residual element of poetry. It is easier to indicate that, for the rare human beings who have this element at their disposal, poetic expenditure ceases to be symbolic in its consequences; thus, to a certain extent, the function of representation engages the very life of the one who assumes it. It condemns him to the most disappointing forms of activity, to misery, to despair, to the pursuit of inconsistent shadows that provide nothing but vertigo or rage. The poet frequently can use words only for his own loss; he is often forced to choose between the destiny of a reprobate, who is as profoundly separated from society as dejecta are from apparent life, and a renunciation whose price is a mediocre activity, subordinated to vulgar and superficial needs.

PRODUCTION, EXCHANGE, AND UNPRODUCTIVE ACTIVITY

Once the existence of expenditure as a social function has been established, it is then necessary to consider the relations between this function and those of production and acquisition that are opposed to it. These relations immediately present themselves as those of an *end* with *utility*. And if it is true that production and acquisition in their development and changes of form introduce a variable that must be understood in order to comprehend historical processes, they are, however, still only means subordinated to expenditure. As dreadful as it is, human poverty has never had a strong enough hold on societies to cause the concern for conservation—which gives production the appearance of an end—to dominate the concern for unproductive expenditure. In order to maintain this preeminence, since power is exercised by the classes that expend, poverty was excluded from all social activity. And the poor have no other way of reentering the circle of power than through the revolutionary destruction of the classes occupying that circle—in other words, through a bloody and in no way limited social expenditure.

The secondary character of production and acquisition in relation to expenditure appears most clearly in primitive economic institutions, since exchange is still treated as a sumptuary loss of ceded objects: thus at its *base* exchange presents itself as a process of expenditure, over which a process of acquisition has developed. Classical economics imagined that primitive exchange occurred in the form of barter; it had no reason to assume, in fact, that a means of acquisition such as exchange might have as its origin not the need to acquire that it satisfies today, but the contrary need, the need to destroy and to lose. The traditional conceptions of the origins of economy have only recently been disproved—even so recently that a great number of economists continue arbitrarily to represent barter as the ancestor of commerce.

In opposition to the artificial notion of barter, the archaic form of exchange has been identified by Mauss under the name *potlatch*,[1] borrowed from the Northwestern American Indians who provided such a remarkable example of it. Institutions analogous to the Indian *potlatch*, or their traces, have been very widely found.

The *potlatch* of the Tlingit, the Haida, the Tsimshian, and the Kwakiutl of the northwestern coast has been studied in detail since the end of the nineteenth century (but at that time it was not compared with the archaic forms of exchange of other countries).

1. On *potlatch*, see above all Marcel Mauss, "Essai sur le don, form archaïque de l'échange" in *Année sociologique*, 1925. [Translated as *The Gift: Forms and Functions of Exchange in Archaic Societies*, trans. I. Cunnison (New York: Norton, 1967). Tr.]

The least advanced of these American tribes practice *potlatch* on the occasion of a person's change in situation—initiations, marriages, funerals—and, even in a more evolved form, it can never be separated from a festival; whether it provides the occasion for this festival, or whether it takes place on the festival's occasion. *Potlatch* excludes all bargaining and, in general, it is constituted by a considerable gift of riches, offered openly and with the goal of humiliating, defying, and *obligating* a rival. The exchange value of the gift results from the fact that the donee, in order to efface the humiliation and respond to the challenge, must satisfy the obligation (incurred by him at the time of acceptance) to respond later with a more valuable gift, in other words, to return with interest.

But the gift is not the only form of *potlatch*; it is equally possible to defy rivals through the spectacular destruction of wealth. It is through the intermediary of this last form that *potlatch* is reunited with religious sacrifice, since what is destroyed is theoretically offered to the mythical ancestors of the donees. Relatively recently a Tlingit chief appeared before his rival to slash the throats of some of his own slaves. This destruction was repaid at a given date by the slaughter of a greater number of slaves. The Tchoukchi of far northwestern Siberia, who have institutions analogous to *potlatch*, slaughter dog teams in order to stifle and humiliate another group. In northwestern America, destruction goes as far as the burning of villages and the smashing of flotillas of canoes. Emblazoned copper ingots, a kind of money on which the fictive value of an immense fortune is sometimes placed, are broken or thrown into the sea. The delirium of the festival can be associated equally with hecatombs of property and with gifts accumulated with the intention of stunning and humiliating.

Usury, which regularly intervenes in these operations as obligatory surplus at the time of the returned *potlatch*, gives rise to the observation that the loan with interest must be substituted for barter in the history of the origins of exchange. It must be recognized, in fact, that wealth is multiplied in *potlatch* civilizations in a way that recalls the inflation of credit in banking civilizations; in other words, it would be impossible to realize at once all the wealth possessed by the total number of donors resulting from the obligations contracted by the total number of donees. But this comparison applies only to a secondary characteristic of *potlatch*.

It is the constitution of a positive property of loss—from which spring nobility, honor, and rank in a hierarchy—that gives the institution its significant value. The gift must be considered as a loss and thus as a partial destruction, since the desire to destroy is in part transferred onto the recipient. In unconscious forms, such as those described by psychoanalysis, it symbolizes excretion, which itself is linked to death, in conformity with the fundamental connection between anal eroticism and sadism. The excremental symbolism of emblazoned coppers, which on the Northwest Coast are the gift objects *par excellence,* is based on a very rich mythology. In Melanesia, the donor designates as his excrement magnificent gifts, which he deposits at the feet of the rival chief.

The consequences in the realm of acquisition are only the unwanted result—at least to the extent that the drives that govern the operation have remained primitive—of a process oriented in the opposite direction. "The ideal," indicates Mauss, "would be to give a *potlatch* and not have it returned." This ideal is realized in certain forms of destruction to which custom allows no possible response. On the other hand, since the yields of *potlatch* are in some ways pledged in advance in a new *potlatch,* the archaic principle of wealth is displayed with none of the attenuations that result from the avarice developed at later stages; wealth appears as an acquisition to the extent that power is acquired by a rich man, but it is entirely directed toward loss in the sense that this power is characterized as power to lose. It is only through loss that glory and honor are linked to wealth.

As a game, *potlatch* is the opposite of a principle of conservation: it puts an end to the stability of fortunes as it existed within the totemic economy, where possession was hereditary. An activity of excessive exchange replaced heredity (as source of possession) with a kind of deliriously formed ritual poker. But the players can never retire from the game, their fortunes made; they remain at the mercy of provocation. At no time does a fortune serve to *shelter its owner from need.* On the contrary, it functionally remains—as does its possessor—*at the mercy of a need for limitless loss,* which exists endemically in a social group.

The nonsumptuary production and consumption upon which wealth depends thus appear as relative utility.

THE FUNCTIONAL EXPENDITURE OF THE WEALTHY CLASSES

The notion of *potlatch,* strictly speaking, should be reserved for expenditures of an agonistic type, which are instigated by challenges and which lead to responses. More precisely, it should be reserved for forms which, for archaic societies, are not distinguishable from *exchange.*

It is important to know that exchange, at its origin, was *immediately* subordinated to a human *end;* nevertheless it is evident that its development, linked to progress in the modes of production, only started at the stage at which this subordination ceased to be immediate. The very principle of the function of production requires that products be exempt from loss, at least provisionally.

In the market economy, the processes of exchange have an acquisitive sense. Fortunes are no longer placed on a gambling table; they have become relatively stable. It is only to the extent that stability is assured and can no longer be compromised by even considerable losses that these losses are submitted to the regime of unproductive expenditure. Under these new conditions, the elementary components of *potlatch* are found in forms that are no longer as directly agonistic.[2] Expenditure is still destined to acquire or maintain rank, but in principle it no longer has the goal of causing another to lose his rank.

In spite of these attenuations, ostentatious loss remains universally linked to wealth, as its ultimate function.

More or less narrowly, social rank is linked to the possession of a fortune, but only on the condition that the fortune be partially sacrificed in unproductive social expenditures such as festivals, spectacles, and games. One notes that in primitive societies, where the exploitation of man by man is still fairly weak, the products of human activity not only flow in great quantities to rich men because of the protection or social leadership services these men supposedly provide, but also because of the spectacular collective expenditures for which they must pay. In so-called civilized societies, the fundamental *obligation* of wealth disappeared only in a fairly recent period. The decline of paganism led to a decline of the games and cults for which wealthy Romans were obliged to pay; thus it has been said that Christianity individualized property, giving its possessor total control over his products and abrogating his social function. It abrogated at least the obligation of this expenditure, for Christianity replaced pagan expenditure prescribed by custom with voluntary alms, either in the form of distributions from the rich to the poor, or (and above all) in the form of extremely significant contributions to churches and later to monasteries. And these churches and monasteries precisely

2. In other words: involving rivalry and struggle.

assumed, in the Middle Ages, the major part of the spectacular function.

Today the great and free forms of unproductive social expenditure have disappeared. One must not conclude from this, however, that the very principle of expenditure is no longer the end of economic activity.

A certain evolution of wealth, whose symptoms indicate sickness and exhaustion, leads to shame in oneself accompanied by petty hypocrisy. Everything that was generous, orgiastic, and excessive has disappeared; the themes of rivalry upon which individual activity still depends develop in obscurity, and are as shameful as belching. The representatives of the bourgeoisie have adopted an effaced manner; wealth is now displayed behind closed doors, in accordance with depressing and boring conventions. In addition, people in the middle class—employees and small shopkeepers—having attained mediocre or minute fortunes, have managed to debase and subdivide ostentatious expenditure, of which nothing remains but vain efforts tied to tiresome rancor.

Such trickery has become the principle reason for living, working, and suffering for those who lack the courage to condemn this moldy society to revolutionary destruction. Around modern banks, as around the totem poles of the Kwakiutl, the same desire to dazzle animates individuals and leads them into a system of petty displays that blinds them to each other, as if they were staring into a blinding light. A few steps from the bank, jewels, dresses, and cars wait behind shop windows for the day when they will serve to establish the augmented splendor of a sinister industrialist and his even more sinister old wife. At a lower level, gilded clocks, dining room buffets, and artificial flowers render equally shameful service to a grocer and his wife. Jealousy arises between human beings, as it does among the savages, and with an equivalent brutality; only generosity and nobility have disappeared, and with them the dazzling contrast that the rich provided to the poor.

As the class that possesses the wealth—having received with wealth the obligation of functional expenditure—the modern bourgeoisie is characterized by the refusal in principle of this obligation. It has distinguished itself from the aristocracy through the fact that it has consented only to *spend for itself,* and within itself—in other words, by hiding its expenditures as much as possible from the eyes of the other classes. This particular form was originally due to the development of its wealth in the shadow of a more powerful noble class. The rationalist conceptions developed by the bourgeoisie, starting in the seventeenth century, were a response to these humiliating conceptions of restrained expenditure; this rationalism meant nothing other than the strictly economic representation of the world—economic in the vulgar sense, the bourgeois sense, of the word. The hatred of expenditure is the *raison d'être* of and the justification for the bourgeoisie; it is at the same time the principle of its horrifying hypocrisy. A fundamental grievance of the bourgeois was the prodigality of feudal society and, after coming to power, they believed that, because of their habits of accumulation, they were capable of acceptably dominating the poorer classes. And it is right to recognize that the people are incapable of hating them as much as their former masters, to the extent that they are incapable of loving them, for the bourgeois are incapable of concealing a sordid face, a face so rapacious and lacking in nobility, so frighteningly small, that all human life, upon seeing it, seems degraded.

In opposition, the people's consciousness is reduced to maintaining profoundly the principle of expenditure by representing bourgeois existence as the shame of man and as a sinister cancellation.

CLASS STRUGGLE

In trying to maintain sterility in regard to expenditure, in conformity with a reasoning that balances *accounts*, bourgeois society has only managed to develop a universal meanness. Human life only rediscovers agitation on the scale of irreducible needs through the efforts of those who push the consequences of current rationalist conceptions as far as they will go. What remains of the traditional modes of expenditure has become atrophied, and living sumptuary tumult has been lost in the unprecedented explosion of *class struggle.*

The components of *class struggle* are seen in the process of expenditure, dating back to the archaic period. In *potlatch,* the rich man distributes products furnished him by other, impoverished, men. He tries to rise above a rival who is rich like himself, but the ultimate stage of his foreseen elevation has no more necessary a goal than his further separation from the nature of destitute men. Thus expenditure, even though it might be a social function, immediately leads to an agonistic and apparently antisocial act of separation. The rich man consumes the poor man's losses, creating for him a category of degradation and abjection that leads to slavery. Now it is evident that, from the endlessly transmitted heritage of the sumptuary world, the modern world has received slavery, and has reserved it for the proletariat. Without a doubt bourgeois society, which pretends to govern according to rational principles, and which, through its own actions, moreover, tends to realize a certain human homogeneity, does not accept without protest a division that seems destructive to man himself; it is incapable, however, of pushing this resistance further than theoretical negation. It gives the workers rights equal to those of the masters, and it announces this *equality* by inscribing that word on walls. But the masters, who act as if they were the expression of society itself, are preoccupied—more seriously than with any other concern—with showing that they do not in any way share the abjection of the men they employ. *The end of the workers' activity is to produce in order to live, but the bosses' activity is to produce in order to condemn the working producers to a hideous degradation* —for there is no disjunction possible between, on the one hand, the characterization the bosses seek through their modes of expenditure, which tend to elevate them high above human baseness, and on the other hand this baseness itself, of which this characterization is a function.

In opposition to this conception of agonistic social expenditure, there is the representation of numerous bourgeois efforts to ameliorate the lot of the workers—but this representation is only the expression of the cowardice of the modern upper classes, who no longer have the force to recognize the results of their own destructive acts. The expenditures taken on by the capitalists in order to aid the proletarians and give them a chance to pull themselves up on the social ladder only bear witness to their inability (due to exhaustion) to carry out thoroughly a sumptuary process. Once the loss of the poor man is accomplished, little by little the pleasure of the rich man is emptied and neutralized; it gives way to a kind of apathetic indifference. Under these conditions, in order to maintain a neutral state rendered relatively agreeable by apathy (and which exists in spite of troublesome elements such as sadism and pity), it can be useful to compensate for the expenditure that engenders abjection with a new expenditure, which tends to attenuate it. The bosses' political sense, together with certain partial developments of prosperity, has allowed this process of compensation to be, at times, quite extensive. Thus in the Anglo-Saxon countries, and in particular in the United States of America, the primary process takes place at the expense of only a relatively small portion of the population: to a certain extent, the working class itself has been led to participate in it (above all when this was facilitated by the preliminary existence of a class held to be abject by common accord, as in the case of the blacks). But these subterfuges, whose importance is in any case strictly limited, do not modify in any way the fundamental division between noble and ignoble men. The cruel game of social life does not vary among the different civilized countries, where the insulting splendor of the rich loses and degrades the human nature of the lower class.

It must be added that the attenuation of the masters' brutality —which in any case has less to do with destruction itself than with the psychological tendencies to destroy—corresponds to the general atrophy of the ancient sumptuary processes that characterizes the modern era.

Class struggle, on the contrary, becomes the grandest form of social expenditure when it is taken up again and developed, this time on the part of the workers, and on such a scale that it threatens the very existence of the masters.

CHRISTIANITY AND REVOLUTION

Short of revolt, it has been possible for the provoked poor to refuse all moral participation in a system in which men oppress men; in certain historical circumstances, they succeeded, through the use of symbols even more striking than reality, in lowering all of "human nature" to such a horrifying ignominy that the pleasure found by the rich in measuring the poverty of others suddenly became too acute to be endured without vertigo. Thus, independently of all ritual forms, an exchange of exasperated challenges was established, exacerbated above all by the poor, a *potlatch* in which real refuse and revealed moral filth entered into a rivalry of horrible grandeur with everything in the world that was rich, pure, and brilliant; and an exceptional outlet was found for this form of spasmodic convulsion in religious despair, which was its unreserved exploitation.

In Christianity, the alternations between the exaltation and dread, tortures and orgies constituting religious life were conjoined in a more tragic way and were merged with a sick social structure, which was tearing itself apart with the dirtiest cruelty. The triumphal song of the Christians glorifies God because he has entered into the bloody game of social war, and because he has "hurled the powerful from

the heights of their grandeur and has exalted the miserably poor."
Their myths associate social ignominy and the cadaverous degradation of the torture victim with divine splendor. In this way religion
assumes the total oppositional function manifested by contrary
forces, which up to this point had been divided between the rich and
the poor, with the one group condemning the other to ruin. It is
closely tied to terrestrial despair, since it itself is only an epiphenomenon of the measureless hate that divides men—but an epiphenomenon that tends to substitute itself for the totality of divergent
processes it summarizes. In conformity with the words attributed to
Christ, who said he came to divide and not to reign, religion thus
does not at all try to do away with what others consider the scourge of
man. On the contrary, in its immediate form, it wallows in a revolting
impurity that is indispensable to its ecstatic torment.

The meaning of Christianity is given in the development of the
delirious consequences of the expenditure of classes, in a mental
agonistic orgy practiced at the expense of the real struggle.

However, in spite of the importance that it has had in human
activity, Christian *humiliation* is only an episode in the historic
struggle of the ignoble against the noble, of the impure against the
pure. It is as if society, conscious of its own intolerable splitting, had
become for a time dead drunk in order to enjoy it sadistically. But the
heaviest drunkenness has not done away with the consequences of
human poverty, and, with the exploited classes opposing the superior
classes with greater lucidity, no conceivable limit can be assigned to
hatred. In historical agitation, only the word Revolution dominates
the customary confusion and carries with it the promise that answers
the unlimited demands of the masses. As for the masters and the
exploiters, whose function is to create the contemptuous forms that
exclude human nature—causing this nature to exist at the limits of
the earth, in other words in mud—a simple law of reciprocity
requires that they be condemned to fear, to the *great night* when their
beautiful phrases will be drowned out by death screams in riots. That
is the bloody hope which, each day, is one with the existence of the
people, and which sums up the insubordinate content of the class
struggle.

Class struggle has only one possible end: the loss of those who
have worked to lose "human nature."

But whatever form of development is foreseen, be it revolutionary
or servile, the general convulsions constituted eighteen hundred
years ago by the religious ecstasy of the Christians, and today by the

workers' movement, must equally be represented as a decisive impulse *constraining* society to use the exclusion of one class by another to realize a mode of expenditure as tragic and as free as possible, and at the same time *constraining* it to introduce sacred forms so human that the traditional forms become relatively contemptible. It is the tropic character of such movements that accounts for the total human value of the workers' Revolution, a Revolution capable of exerting a force of attraction as strong as the force that directs simple organisms toward the sun.

THE INSUBORDINATION OF MATERIAL FACTS

Human life, distinct from juridical existence, existing as it does on a globe isolated in celestial space, from night to day and from one country to another—human life cannot in any way be limited to the closed systems assigned to it by reasonable conceptions. The immense travail of recklessness, discharge, and upheaval that constitutes life could be expressed by stating that life starts only with the deficit of these systems; at least what it allows in the way of order and reserve has meaning only from the moment when the ordered and reserved forces liberate and lose themselves for ends that cannot be subordinated to anything one can account for. It is only by such insubordination—even if it is impoverished—that the human race ceases to be isolated in the unconditional splendor of material things.

In fact, in the most universal way, isolated or in groups, men find themselves constantly engaged in processes of expenditure. Variations in form do not in any way alter the fundamental characteristics of these processes, whose principle is loss. A certain excitation, whose sum total is maintained at a noticeably constant level, animates collectivities and individuals. In their intensified form, the *states of excitation,* which are comparable to toxic states, can be defined as the illogical and irresistible impulse to reject material or moral goods that it would have been possible to utilize rationally (in conformity with the balancing of accounts). Connected to the losses that are realized in this way—in the case of the "lost woman" as well as in the case of military expenditure—is the creation of unproductive values; the most absurd of these values, and the one that makes people the most rapacious, is *glory.* Made complete through degradation, glory, appearing in a sometimes sinister and sometimes brilliant form, has never ceased to dominate social existence; it is impossible to attempt to do anything without it when it is dependent on the blind practice of personal or social loss.

In this way the boundless refuse of activity pushes human plans —including those associated with economic operations—into the game of characterizing universal matter; matter, in fact, can only be defined as the *nonlogical difference* that represents in relation to the *economy* of the universe what *crime* represents in relation to the law. The glory that sums up or symbolizes (without exhausting) the object of free expenditure, while it can never exclude crime, cannot be distinguished—at least if one takes into account the only characterization that has a value comparable to matter—from the *insubordinate characterization,* which is not the condition for anything else.

If on the other hand one demonstrates the interest, concurrent with glory (as well as with degradation), which the human community necessarily sees in the qualitative change constantly realized by the movement of history, and if, finally, one demonstrates that this movement is impossible to contain or direct toward a limited end, it becomes possible, having abandoned all reserves, to assign a *relative* value to utility. Men assure their own subsistence or avoid suffering, not because these functions themselves lead to a sufficient result, but in order to accede to the insubordinate function of free expenditure.

MAURICE BLANCHOT

To say what we know about Blanchot the person is to risk talking nonsense. He is someone who is not there. He does not reflect glory on some university administration. He does not give lectures to students or appear in public to receive prizes and be adored. He does not appear on talk shows to pontificate or gossip. He is not photographed at chic parties, nor is he known to take Jackie Kennedy to lunch. In his 20s, according to P. Adams Sitney, he was a right-wing journalist, but during the Days of May general strike in 1968 that routed the Gaullists, he emerged to march in support of the left.* Moreover, to try to say in one's own words what Blanchot says is to fall into a trap, since what he says seems most valid when *he* says it. In his long essay "Literature and the Right to Death" (1949), language is negation, an allusion to destruction, a warning that "death is loose in the world," the annihilation of the thing to which the word refers (42–43). Yet later in the same essay, language in its materiality makes the dead thing live, coerces it to be present outside itself (46–47). Language, then, is absence *and* being, abolition *and* sustenance (48). The life of speech is the death of things. Speech is the life that "maintains itself" in death (46). Surely it is this tendency in Blanchot to reduce his material to mutually interlocking, antinomical relationships that has been so influential to later writers like Paul de Man and Jacques Derrida. The mobility of thought which is never mobile enough (119), the "extremely fatiguing instability," and the cultivation in speech of the "refusal to abide by any definitive statement" define what Derrida in *Of Grammatology* calls the "trembling": the hesitation appropriate to all post-Hegelian projects that has been mistaken—in Nietzsche or Heidegger, for example—for incoherence (24).

In "The Power and the Glory" (1959) reprinted here, Blanchot differentiates two kinds of writers. The "notorious" writer is one who writes for an established public, who says what this public is already thinking. The public understands his books before they are published and thus scarcely needs to read them. He is celebrated, receives prizes, and becomes a public chatterbox. This is a celebration that is, however, the profoundest oblivion, an immediate absorption of one's discourse into the diurnal Styx of public understanding. Below the level of the street is the other, a nocturnal Styx—the writer's proper concern. Orpheus is drawn into the heart of the night when (in another celebrated Blanchot essay, "The Gaze of Orpheus," 1955) he descends into the depths, not finally to drag his sacred shade into the light or to create the *work* and acquire

*P. Adams Sitney, "Afterword," in Maurice Blanchot, *The Gaze of Orpheus,* trans. Lydia Davis (Barrytown, N.Y.: Station Hill Press, 1981) 163–164.

fame but to pursue that experience for its own sake (99–104). When
Orpheus turns to look at Eurydice, he sacrifices the work. All authenticity
depends on gazing on this *other* night without concern for the work, his
song, which henceforth is the trace of his failure to restore Eurydice to the
light. But to give up such failure, Blanchot says, is so much more serious
than to give up success (102). This is precisely the recognition that
caused another poet, Eugenio Montale, to suspect himself of mediocrity,
because he had won the Nobel Prize.†

The Power and the Glory
1959

Translated by Lydia Davis

I would like to make a few brief and simple statements that may
help us to situate literature and the writer.

There was a time when a writer, like an artist, had some relation to
glory. Glorification was his work, glory was the gift he gave and
received. Glory in the ancient sense is the radiance of a presence
(sacred or royal). And Rilke, too, says that to glorify does not mean to
make known; glory is the manifestation of being as it advances in its
magnificence as being, free of what conceals it, secure in the truth of
its exposed presence.

Glory is followed by renown. Renown applies more exactly to the
name. The power of naming, the force of what denominates, the
dangerous assurance of the name (there is danger in being named)
become the privilege of the person who can name and make what he
names be understood. Understanding is subject to notoriety. Speech
eternalized in writing promises immortality. The writer has thrown in

THE POWER AND THE GLORY by Maurice Blanchot from *The Gaze of Orpheus.*
Translation from the French by Lydia Davis. Copyright © 1981. Reprinted by
permission of George Quasha and Station Hill Press.

†Jared Becker, *Eugenio Montale* (Boston: G. K. Hall, 1986) 18.

his lot with what triumphs over death; he knows nothing of what is temporary; he is the friend of the soul, a man of the spirit, guarantor of what is eternal. Even today, many critics seem to believe sincerely that the vocation of art and literature is to eternalize man.

Renown is succeeded by reputation, just as the truth is succeeded by opinion. The fact of publishing—publication—becomes the essential thing. This can be taken in a superficial sense: the writer is known to the public, he has a large reputation, he wants to become prominent, highly valued, because he needs value—which is money. But value is procured by the public, and what excites the public? Publicity. Publicity becomes an art in itself, it is the art of all the arts, it is what is most important, since it determines the power that gives determination to everything else.

Here we are beginning to deal with considerations of a sort that we must not simplify in our polemical enthusiasm. The writer publishes. To publish is to make public; but to make public is not just to bring about a simple displacement, causing something to pass from the private state to the public state, as though from one place—the innermost heart, the closed room—to another place—the outside, the street. Nor is it a matter of revealing a piece of news or a secret to one person in particular. The "public" is not made up of a large or small number of readers, each reading for himself. Writers like to say that they write their books intending them for a single friend. A resolution that is certain to be disappointed. There is no place in the public for a friend. There is no place for a particular person; any more than there is for particular social structures—families, groups, classes, nations. No one is part of the public and yet the whole world belongs to it, and not only the human world but all worlds, all things and no thing: the others. Because of this, no matter what severe censorship is imposed, no matter how faithfully the orders are obeyed, for authority there is always something suspect and displeasing about the act of publishing. This is because it causes the public to exist, and the public, always indeterminate, eludes the firmest political determinations.

To publish is not to cause oneself to be read, and it is not to give anything to be read. What is public is precisely what does not need to be read; it is always known already, in advance, with a kind of knowledge that knows everything and does not want to know anything. The public's interest, which is always excited, insatiable, and yet satisfied, which finds everything interesting but at the same time takes no interest in anything, is a movement that has been very wrongly described in a disparaging way. Here we see the same impersonal power, though in a relaxed and stabilized form, that lies at the origin of the literary effort as both obstacle and resource. The author speaks against an undefined and incessant speech, a speech without beginning or end—against it but also with its help. The reader eventually reads against the public's interest, against that distracted, unstable, versatile and omniscient curiosity, and he emerges with difficulty from that first reading which has already read before it reads: reading against it but even so through it. The reader, participating in a neutral kind of understanding, and the author, participating in a neutral kind of speech, would like to suspend these for a moment to allow room for a clearer form of expression.

Take the institution of literary prizes. It is easily explained by the structure of modern publishing and the social and economic organization of intellectual life. But when we think about the satisfaction that a writer, with rare exceptions, inevitably feels as he receives a prize that often represents nothing, we must explain it not in terms of the fact that his vanity has been flattered, but of his strong need for that communication before communication which is public understanding, in terms of the appeal of the profound and superficial clamor, in which everything appears, disappears, but remains, within a vague presence, a sort of River Styx that flows in broad daylight through our streets and irresistibly draws the living as though they were already shades, eager to become memorable so as to be better forgotten.

Nor is it a question of influence. It is not even a question of the pleasure of being seen by the blind crowd, or of being known by unknown people, a pleasure that implies the transformation of an indeterminate presence into a specific public, already defined, that is, the degeneration of an impalpable movement into a perfectly manipulable and accessible reality. On a slightly lower level, we will find all the political frivolities of the spectacle. But the writer will never win at this game. The most famous writer is not as well known as a daily radio announcer. And if he is eager to have intellectual power, he knows that he is wasting it in this insignificant notoriety. I believe the writer does not want anything for himself or for his work. But the need to be published—that is, to achieve outside existence, to attain that opening onto the outside, that divulgence-dissolution that takes place in our large cities—belongs to the work, like the memory of the impulse it grew out of, an impulse it must keep prolonging even though it wants to overcome it absolutely, an impulse it terminates for an instant, in effect, every time it is a work.

This reign of the "public," by which we mean the "outside" (the attractive force of a presence that is always there—not close, not distant, not familiar, not strange, it has no center, it is a kind of space that assimilates everything and retains nothing) has changed the writer's destination. Just as he has become a stranger to glory, just as he prefers anonymous groping to renown, and has lost all desire for immortality, so is he gradually—although at first glance this may seem less certain—abandoning the kind of pursuit of power that Barrès on the one hand and Monsieur Teste on the other—one by exerting an influence and the other by refusing to exert that influence —incarnated as two very characteristic types. You will say: "But never before have people who write been so involved in politics. Look at the petitions they sign, the interest they show, look how readily they believe they are authorized to judge everything simply because they write." It is true: when two writers meet, they never talk about literature (fortunately); their first remarks are always about politics. I want to suggest that in general writers are quite without any desire to play a role or assert power or hold a magistracy, rather, they are surprisingly modest even in their fame, and very far removed from the cult of personality (actually, this trait is a consistent way to distinguish which of two contemporary writers is a modern writer and which an old-fashioned writer); the fact is that they are the more drawn to politics the more they stand shivering in the outside, at the edge of the public's uneasiness, seeking that communication before communication whose attraction they feel constantly invited to respect.

This can have the worst kind of result. It produces "these omniscient *observers,* these omniscient *chatterboxes,* these omniscient *pedants,* who know everything about everything and settle everything right away, who are quick to make final judgments about things that have just happened, so that soon it will be impossible for us to learn anything: we already know everything," whom Dionys Mascolo describes in his essay "on France's intellectual poverty."[1] Mascolo adds: "People here are informed, intelligent and acquisitive. They understand everything. They understand each thing so quickly that they do not take the time to think about anything. They do not

1. Dionys Mascolo, *Lettre polonaise sur la misère intellectuelle en France (Polish Letter on France's Intellectual Poverty).*

understand anything . . . Just try forcing people who have already understood everything to admit that something *new* has happened!" Exactly these characteristics—though in this description they are slightly exaggerated and pointed, even degenerative—belong to public existence: neutral comprehension, infinite opening, intuitive and presentient understanding in which everyone is always up to date on recent events and has already decided about everything, meanwhile ruining every true value judgment. And so this apparently has the worst sort of result. But it also creates a new kind of situation in which the writer, in some sense losing his own existence and his individual certainty, and experiencing a kind of communication that is still indeterminate and as powerful as it is impotent, as full as it is empty, sees himself, as Mascolo remarks so justly, "reduced to impotence," "but reduced also to simplicity."

We might say that when the writer becomes involved in politics today, with an energy the experts do not like, he is still not involved in politics but rather in the new, scarcely perceived relationship that the literary work and literary language are seeking to arouse through contact with the public presence. This is why, when he talks about politics, he is already talking about something else—ethics; and talking about ethics, he is talking about ontology; talking about ontology, he is talking about poetry; when he talks, finally, about literature, "his only passion," it is only to revert to politics, "his only passion." This mobility is deceptive and can, once again, result in the worst kind of thing: those futile discussions that publicly active men unfailingly call "byzantine" or "intellectual" (qualifiers that are themselves, naturally, a part of that empty loquaciousness, when they do not serve to hide the irritable weakness of powerful men). All we can say about such mobility—whose difficulties and facilities, whose requirements and risks, have been shown us by Surrealism, which Mascolo correctly describes and defines[2]—is that it is never mobile enough, never faithful enough to that anguishing and extremely fatiguing instability that keeps growing and cultivates in all speech the refusal to abide by any definitive statement.

I must add that even though, because of this mobility, the writer is

2. "I must emphasize the extreme importance of Surrealism, the only intellectual movement in France in the first half of the twentieth century. . . . With a rigorousness that can in no way be called outmoded, Surrealism alone, between the two World Wars, was able to issue demands that were at once the demands of pure thought and the direct demands of men. Only Surrealism, with untiring tenacity, was able to recall that *revolution and poetry are the same thing.*"

dissuaded from being any kind of expert, incapable even of being an expert in literature, much less in a particular literary genre, he nevertheless does not strive for the universality which the *honnête homme* of the seventeenth century, then Goethean man, and finally man in the classless society—not to speak of man in the conception of Father Teilhard, who is yet further removed—propose to us as a fantasy and a goal. Just as public understanding has always understood everything already, in advance, but obstructs all true understanding; just as the public clamor is absence and void of all firm and decided speech, always saying something other than what is said (producing a perpetual and formidable mix-up that Ionesco allows us to laugh at); just as the public is indetermination that destroys every group and every class; so the writer, coming under the fascination of what is at stake when he "publishes," and, seeking a reader in the public as Orpheus did Eurydice in Hell, turns to a kind of speech that is the speech of no one and that no one will understand, because it is always addressed to someone else, always awakening another person in the person who hears it, always arousing the expectation of something different. This speech is not universal, not something that would make literature a Promethean or divine power, having rights over everything, but rather the movement of a speech that is dispossessed and rootless, that prefers to say nothing rather than to claim to say everything, and each time it says something, only designates the level beneath which one must still descend if one wants to begin speaking. In our "intellectual poverty," then, there is also the wealth of thought, there is the indigence that gives us the presentiment that to think is always to learn to think less than we think, to think the absence which is also thought, and when we speak, to preserve this absence by bringing it to speech, if only—as is happening today—through an excess of repetitions and prolixity.

Nevertheless, when a writer rushes so eagerly into a concern for the anonymous and neutral existence that is public existence, when he seems to have no other interest, no other horizon, isn't he becoming involved in something that should never occupy him, or at least only indirectly? When Orpheus descends into hell in search of the work, he confronts a completely different Styx: a nocturnal separation that he must enchant with a look, but a look that does not freeze it. This is the essential experience, the only experience in which he must engage himself completely. Once he has returned to daylight, his only role in relation to the exterior powers is to disappear, quickly torn to pieces by their delegates, the Maenads, while the diurnal Styx, the river of public clamor in which his body has been scattered, carries within itself the work, singing, and not only carries it but wants to transform itself into song within it, maintain in the work its own fluid reality, its infinitely murmuring flux, stranger to all shores.

If the writer today, thinking he is descending into Hell, is satisfied with descending as far as the street, this is because the two rivers, the two great movements of primary communication, flow into one another and tend to mingle. This is because the profound primordial clamor—in which something is said but without speech, or something is silent but without silence—is not unlike the speech that does not speak, the understanding that is misunderstood and always listening, that is the public "mind" and "way." The result of this is that very often the work seeks to be published before it exists, it seeks its realization not in the space that is its own but through exterior animation, that life which appears sumptuous but which is dangerously inconsistent as soon as one tries to appropriate it.

Such confusion is not accidental. This extraordinary muddle, which results in the writer publishing before he has written, the public forming and transmitting what it does not understand, the critic judging and defining what he does not read, and lastly the reader being forced to read what has not yet been written—this movement, which confuses all the different moments in the formation of the work by anticipating them each time, also brings them together in a quest for a new unity. Whence the richness and the poverty, the pride and the humility, the extreme disclosure and the extreme solitude of our literary effort, which at least has the merit of desiring neither power nor glory.

JACQUES DERRIDA

Martin Heidegger feels that the entire tradition of western philosophy has managed to forget that time is the essence of Being, and that history must be at the center of any understanding of the human condition. Georges Bataille believes, similarly, *homo erectus* has privileged everything with which elevation braces itself. The glorification of the head and horror of the humble, muddy toe are symptoms of this "Icarian" neurosis. For Derrida, the great conspiracy of 3000 years of western philosophy is the debasement of writing as a fall into exteriority of pure, interior mental experiences. The voice, or spoken word, on the other hand, is indissolubly wedded to the mind, while the written word can only point to the fullness of meaning of which it is the faintest, most inferior representative. Philosophy has despised writing for the same reason Bataille says we despise the toe, for the same reason Plato's divided line privileges intelligible over sensible reality, for the same reason the Christian exalts the soul over the body and God over nature. There is simply a horror— and consequently there is a massive repression—of the material basis upon which all spirituality and all dignified superstructures depend. This repression of the material is the ontological version of all other kinds of oppression in the world, of labor by management, of faculty by administration, of female by male, of the dark races by the white. Susan Handelman, in her book *The Slayers of Moses* (1982), speaks of the Derridian project in part as an outsider's protest against what everyone else takes for granted, in part as a rebellion of the Rabbinical tradition of Midrash (textual commentary) against Greek logocentrism.† Midrash multiplies and proliferates meaning while the Greek impulse is toward unity and simplification. Lévi-Strauss in "The Writing Lesson" made writing the source of hierarchization and tyranny; Derrida wants to show that writing is more often liberation from centralization *(Of Gram.:* 131). Moreover, according to the Talmud, the Torah existed before space and time, even before the creation of the world by God. The Torah consisted of letters of black fire burning against a background of white fire, and when

---

*Jacques Derrida, "Violence and Metaphysics: An Essay on the Thought of Emmanuel Levinas," in *Writing and Difference,* trans. Alan Bass (Chicago: University of Chicago Press, 1978) 83. See also "Racism's Last Word," trans. Peggy Kamuf, *Critical Inquiry* (Autumn 1985) 290–99.

†Susan Handelman, *The Slayers of Moses* (Albany: SUNY Press, 1982) 33. See also the interview with Derrida conducted for *Le Nouvel Observateur* by Catherine David (Spring 1983), trans. David Allison for *Derrida and Difference,* eds. David Wood and Robert Bernasconi (Coventry, England: Parousia Press, 1985) 112–14.

the Holy One created heaven and earth, he looked into the Torah to see
how it was done (Handelman: 37–38). The textual is prior to the natural.
The world is the product of the Torah. There is nothing, in this sense, too,
outside the text *(Of Gram.: 158)*.

The End of the Book and the Beginning of Writing

1967

Translated by Gayatri Spivak

Exergue

1. The one who will shine in the science of writing will shine like
   the sun. A scribe (*EP*, p. 87)
   O Samas (sun-god), by your light you scan the totality of lands as
   if they were cuneiform signs (ibid.).

2. These three ways of writing correspond almost exactly to three
   different stages according to which one can consider men
   gathered into a nation. The depicting of objects is appropriate to
   a savage people; signs of words and of propositions, to a barbaric
   people; and the alphabet to civilized people. J.-J. Rousseau,
   Essai sur l'origine des langues.

3. Alphabetic script is in itself and for itself the most intelligent.
   Hegel, *Enzyklopädie.*

This triple exergue is intended not only to focus attention on the
ethnocentrism which, everywhere and always, had controlled the
concept of writing. Nor merely to focus attention on what I shall call
logocentrism: the metaphysics of phonetic writing (for example, of

THE END OF THE BOOK AND THE BEGINNING OF WRITING   by Jacques Derrida, exerpted
from "Writing Before the Letter" in *Of Grammatology*, trans. Gayatri Spivak. Copyright © 1976. Reprinted by permission of Johns Hopkins University Press. Some
footnotes were omitted.

the alphabet) which was fundamentally—for enigmatic yet essential reasons that are inaccessible to a simple historical relativism —nothing but the most original and powerful ethnocentrism, in the process of imposing itself upon the world, controlling in one and the same *order:*

1. *the concept of writing* in a world where the phoneticization of writing must dissimulate its own history as it is produced;

2. *the history of* (the only) *metaphysics,* which has, in spite of all differences, not only from Plato to Hegel (even including Leibniz) but also, beyond these apparent limits, from the pre-Socratics to Heidegger, always assigned the origin of truth in general to the logos: the history of truth, of the truth of truth, has always been—except for a metaphysical diversion that we shall have to explain—the debasement of writing and its repression outside "full" speech.

3. *the concept of science* or the scientificity of science—what has always been determined as *logic*—a concept that has always been a philosophical concept, even if the practice of science has constantly challenged its imperialism of the logos, by invoking, for example, from the beginning and ever increasingly, nonphonetic writing. No doubt this subversion has always been contained within a system of direct address *[système allocutoire]* which gave birth to the project of science and to the conventions of all nonphonetic characteristics. It could not have been otherwise. Nonetheless, it is a peculiarity of our epoch that, at the moment when the phoneticization of writing—the historical origin and structural possibility of philosophy as of science, the condition of the *epistème*—begins to lay hold on world culture, science, in its advancements, can no longer be satisfied with it. This inadequation had always already begun to make its presence felt. But today something lets it appear as such, allows it a kind of takeover without our being able to translate this novelty into clear cut notions of mutation, explicitation, accumulation, revolution, or tradition. These values belong no doubt to the system whose dislocation is today presented as such, they describe the styles of an historical movement which was meaningful—like the concept of history itself—only within a logocentric epoch.

By alluding to a science of writing reined in by metaphor, metaphysics, and theology, this exergue must not only announce that the science of writing—*grammatology*—shows signs of liberation all over the world, as a result of decisive efforts. These efforts are necessarily discreet, dispersed, almost imperceptible; that is a quality of their meaning and of the milieu within which they produce their operation. I would like to suggest above all that, however fecund and necessary the undertaking might be, and even if, given the most favorable hypothesis, it did overcome all technical and epistemological obstacles as well as all the theological and metaphysical impediments that have limited it hitherto, such a science of writing runs the risk of never being established as such and with that name. Of never being able to define the unity of its project or its object. Of not being able either to write its discourse on method or to describe the limits of its field. For essential reasons: the unity of all that allows itself to be attempted today through the most diverse concepts of science and of writing, is, in principle, more or less covertly yet always, determined by an historico-metaphysical epoch of which we merely glimpse the *closure*. I do not say the *end*. The idea of science and the idea of writing—therefore also of the science of writing—is meaningful for us only in terms of an origin and within a world to which a certain concept of the sign (later I shall call it *the* concept of sign) and a certain concept of the relationships between speech and writing, have *already* been assigned. A most determined relationship, in spite of its privilege, its necessity, and the field of vision that it has controlled for a few millennia, especially in the West, to the point of being now able to produce its own dislocation and itself proclaim its limits.

Perhaps patient meditation and painstaking investigation on and around what is still provisionally called writing, far from falling short of a science of writing or of hastily dismissing it by some obscurantist reaction, letting it rather develop its positivity as far as possible, are the wanderings of a way of thinking that is faithful and attentive to the ineluctable world of the future which proclaims itself at present, beyond the closure of knowledge. The future can only be anticipated in the form of an absolute danger. It is that which breaks absolutely with constituted normality and can only be proclaimed, *presented*, as a sort of monstrosity. For that future world and for that within it which will have put into question the values of sign, word, and writing, for that which guides our future anterior, there is as yet no exergue.

Socrates, he who does not write[1]—Nietzsche

However the topic is considered, the *problem of language* has never been simply one problem among others. But never as much as at present has it invaded, *as such,* the global horizon of the most diverse researches and the most heterogeneous discourses, diverse and heterogeneous in their intention, method, and ideology. The devaluation of the word "language" itself, and how, in the very hold it has upon us, it betrays a loose vocabulary, the temptation of a cheap seduction, the passive yielding to fashion, the consciousness of the avant-garde, in other words—ignorance—are evidences of this effect. This inflation of the sign "language" is the inflation of the sign itself, absolute inflation, inflation itself. Yet, by one of its aspects or shadows, it is itself still a sign: this crisis is also a symptom. It indicates, as if in spite of itself, that a historico-metaphysical epoch *must* finally determine as language the totality of its problematic horizon. It must do so not only because all that desire had wished to wrest from the play of language finds itself recaptured within that play but also because, for the same reason, language itself is menaced in its very life, helpless, adrift in the threat of limitlessness, brought back to its own finitude at the very moment when its limits seem to disappear, when it ceases to be self-assured, contained, and *guaranteed* by the infinite signified which seemed to exceed it.

The Program

By a slow movement whose necessity is hardly perceptible, everything that for at least some twenty centuries tended toward and finally succeeded in being gathered under the name of language is beginning to let itself be transferred to, or at least summarized under, the name of writing. By a hardly perceptible necessity, it seems as though the concept of writing—no longer indicating a particular, derivative, auxiliary form of language in general (whether understood as communication, relation, expression, signification, constitution of meaning or thought, etc.), no longer designating the exterior surface, the insubstantial double of a major signifier, *the signifier of the signifier*

1. "Aus dem Gedankenkreise der Geburt der Tragödie," I. 3. *Nietzsche Werke* (Leipzig, 1903), vol. 9, part 2, i, p.66.

—is beginning to go beyond the extension of language. In all senses of the word, writing thus *comprehends* language. Not that the word "writing" has ceased to designate the signifier of the signifier, but it appears, strange as it may seem, that "signifier of the signifier" no longer defines accidental doubling and fallen secondary. "Signifier of the signifier" describes on the contrary the movement of language: in its origin, to be sure, but one can already suspect that an origin whose structure can be expressed as "signifier of the signifier" conceals and erases itself in its own production. There the signified always already functions as a signifier. The secondarity that it seemed possible to ascribe to writing alone affects all signifieds in general, affects them always already, the moment they *enter the game*. There is not a single signified that escapes, even if recaptured, the play of signifying references that constitute language. The advent of writing is the advent of this play; today such a play is coming into its own, effacing the limit starting from which one had thought to regulate the circulation of signs, drawing along with it all the reassuring signifieds, reducing all the strongholds, all the out-of-bounds shelters that watched over the field of language. This, strictly speaking, amounts to destroying the concept of "sign" and its entire logic. Undoubtedly it is not by chance that this *overwhelming* supervenes at the moment when the extension of the concept of language effaces all its limits. We shall see that this overwhelming and this effacement have the same meaning, are one and the same phenomenon. It is as if the Western concept of language (in terms of what, beyond its plurivocity and beyond the strict and problematic opposition of speech *[parole]* and language *[langue]*, attaches it *in general* to phonematic or glossematic production, to language, to voice, to hearing, to sound and breadth, to speech) were revealed today as the guise or disguise of a primary writing: more fundamental than that which, before this conversion, passed for the simple "supplement to the spoken word" (Rousseau). Either writing was never a simple "supplement," or it is urgently necessary to construct a new logic of the "supplement." It is this urgency which will guide us further in reading Rousseau.

These disguises are not historical contingencies that one might admire or regret. Their movement was absolutely necessary, with a necessity which cannot be judged by any other tribunal. The privilege of the *phonè* does not depend upon a choice that could have been avoided. It responds to a moment of *economy* (let us say of the "life" of "history" or of "being as self-relationship"). The system of "hearing (understanding)-oneself-speak" through the phonic substance—which *presents itself* as the nonexterior, nonmundane, therefore nonempirical or noncontingent signifier—has necessarily dominated the history of the world during an entire epoch, and has even produced the idea of the world, the idea of world-origin, that arises from the difference between the worldly and the non-worldly, the outside and the inside, ideality and nonideality, universal and nonuniversal, transcendental and empirical, etc.

With an irregular and essentially precarious success, this movement would apparently have tended, as toward its *telos,* to confine writing to a secondary and instrumental function: translator of a full speech that was fully *present* (present to itself, to its signified, to the other, the very condition of the theme of presence in general), technics in the service of language, *spokesman,* interpreter of an originary speech itself shielded from interpretation.

Technics in the service of language: I am not invoking a general essence of technics which would be already familiar to us and would help us in *understanding* the narrow and historically determined concept of writing as an example. I believe on the contrary that a certain sort of question about the meaning and origin of writing precedes, or at least merges with, a certain type of question about the meaning and origin of technics. That is why the notion of technique can never simply clarify the notion of writing.

It is therefore as if what we call language could have been in its origin and in its end only a moment, an essential but determined mode, a phenomenon, an aspect, a species of writing. And as if it had succeeded in making us forget this, and *in willfully misleading us,* only in the course of an adventure: as that adventure itself. All in all a short enough adventure. It merges with the history that has associated technics and logocentric metaphysics for nearly three millennia. And it now seems to be approaching what is really its own *exhaustion;* under the circumstances—and this is no more than one example among others—of this death of the civilization of the book, of which so much is said and which manifests itself particularly through a convulsive proliferation of libraries. All appearances to the contrary, this death of the book undoubtedly announces (and in a certain sense always has announced) nothing but a death of speech (of a *so-called* full speech) and a new mutation in the history of writing, in history as writing. Announces it at a distance of a few centuries. It is on that scale that we must reckon it here, being careful not to neglect the quality of a very heterogeneous historical duration: the acceleration is such, and such its qualitative meaning, that one would be equally wrong in making a careful evaluation according to past rhythms. "Death of speech" is of course a metaphor here: before we speak of disappearance, we must think of a new situation for speech, of its subordination within a structure of which it will no longer be the archon.

To affirm in this way that the concept of writing exceeds and comprehends that of language, presupposes of course a certain definition of language and of writing. If we do not attempt to justify it, we shall be giving in to the movement of inflation that we have just mentioned, which has also taken over the word "writing," and that not fortuitously. For some time now, as a matter of fact, here and there, by a gesture and for motives that are profoundly necessary, whose degradation is easier to denounce than it is to disclose their origin, one says "language" for action, movement, thought, reflection, consciousness, unconsciousness, experience, affectivity, etc. Now we tend to say "writing" for all that and more: to designate not only the physical gestures of literal pictographic or ideographic inscription, but also the totality of what makes it possible; and also, beyond the signifying face, the signified face itself. And thus we say "writing" for all that gives rise to an inscription in general, whether it is literal or not and even if what it distributes in space is alien to the order of the voice: cinematography, choreography, of course, but also pictorial, musical, sculptural "writing." One might also speak of athletic writing, and with even greater certainty of military or political writing in view of the techniques that govern those domains today. All this to describe not only the system of notation secondarily connected with these activities but the essence and the content of these activities themselves. It is also in this sense that the contemporary biologist speaks of writing and *pro-gram* in relation to the most elementary processes of information within the living cell. And, finally, whether it has essential limits or not, the entire field covered by the cybernetic *program* will be the field of writing. If the theory of cybernetics is by itself to oust all metaphysical concepts—including the concepts of soul, of life, of value, of choice, of memory—which until recently served to separate the machine from man, it must conserve the notion of writing, trace, grammè [written mark], or grapheme, until its own historico-metaphysical character is also exposed. Even before being determined as human (with all the distinctive characteristics that have always been attributed to man and the entire system of significations that they imply) or nonhuman, the *grammè*—or the *grapheme*—would thus name the element. An element without simplicity. An element, whether it is understood as the medium or as the irreducible atom, of the arche-synthesis in general, of what one must forbid oneself to define within the system of oppositions of metaphysics, of what consequently one should not even call *experience* in general, that is to say the origin of *meaning* in general.

This situation has always already been announced. Why is it today in the process of making itself known *as such* and *after the fact?* This question would call forth an interminable analysis. Let us simply choose some points of departure in order to introduce the limited remarks to which I shall confine myself. I have already alluded to *theoretical* mathematics; its writing—whether understood as a sensible *graphie* [manner of writing] (and that already presupposes an identity, therefore an ideality, of its form, which in principle renders absurd the so easily admitted notion of the "sensible signifier"), or understood as the ideal synthesis of signifieds or a trace operative on another level, or whether it is understood, more profoundly, as the *passage* of the one to the other—has never been absolutely linked with a phonetic production. Within cultures practicing so-called phonetic writing, mathematics is not just an enclave. That is mentioned by all historians of writing; they recall at the same time the imperfections of alphabetic writing, which passed for so long as the most convenient and "the most intelligent" writing. This enclave is also the place where the practice of scientific language challenges intrinsically and with increasing profundity the ideal of phonetic writing and all its implicit metaphysics (metaphysics *itself*), particularly, that is, the philosophical idea of the *epistémè;* also of *istoria,* a concept profoundly related to it in spite of the dissociation or opposition which has distinguished one from the other during one phase of their common progress. History and knowledge, *istoria* and *epistémè* have always been determined (and not only etymologically or philosophically) as detours *for the purpose of* the reappropriation of presence.

But beyond theoretical mathematics, the development of the *practical methods* of information retrieval extends the possibilities of the "message" vastly, to the point where it is no longer the "written" translation of a language, the transporting of a signified which could remain spoken in its integrity. It goes hand in hand with an extension of phonography and of all the means of conserving the spoken language, of making it function without the presence of the speaking subject. This development, coupled with that of anthropology and of the history of writing, teaches us that phonetic writing, the medium of the great metaphysical, scientific, technical, and economic adventure of the West, is limited in space and time and limits itself even as it is in the process of imposing its laws upon the cultural areas that had escaped it. But this nonfortuitous conjunction of cybernetics and the "human sciences" of writing leads to a more profound reversal.

The Signifier and Truth

The "rationality"—but perhaps that word should be abandoned for reasons that will appear at the end of this sentence—which governs a writing thus enlarged and radicalized, no longer issues from a logos. Further, it inaugurates the destruction, not the demolition but the de-sedimentation, the de-construction, of all the significations that have their source in that of the logos. Particularly the signification of *truth*. All the metaphysical determinations of truth, and even the one beyond metaphysical onto-Theology that Heidegger reminds us of, are more or less immediately inseparable from the instance of the logos, or of a reason thought within the lineage of the logos, in whatever sense it is understood: in the pre-Socratic or the philosophical sense, in the sense of God's infinite understanding or in the anthropological sense, in the pre-Hegelian or the post-Hegelian sense. Within this logos, the original and essential link to the *phonè* has never been broken. It would be easy to demonstrate this and I shall attempt such a demonstration later. As has been more or less implicitly determined, the essence of the *phonè* would be immediately proximate to that which within "thought" as logos relates to "meaning," produces it, receives it, speaks it, "composes" it. If, for Aristotle, for example, "spoken words (ta en tē phonē) are the symbols of mental experience (pathēmata tes psychēs) and written words are the symbols of spoken words" *(De interpretatione,* 1, 16a 3) it is because the voice, producer of *the first symbols,* has a relationship of essential and immediate proximity with the mind. Producer of the first signifier, it is not just a simple signifier among others. It signifies "mental experiences" which themselves reflect or mirror things by natural resemblance. Between being and mind, things and feelings, there would be a relationship of translation or natural signification; between mind and logos, a relationship of conventional symbolization. And the *first* convention, which would relate immediately to the order of natural and universal signification, would be produced as spoken language. Written language would establish the conventions, interlinking other conventions with them.

> Just as all men have not the same writing so all men have not the same speech sounds, but mental experiences, of which these are the *primary symbols (semeîa prótos),* are the same for all, as also are those things of which our experiences are the images *(De interpretatione,* 1, 16a. Italics added).

The feelings of the mind, expressing things naturally, constitute a sort of universal language which can then efface itself. It is the stage of transparence. Aristotle can sometimes omit it without risk. In every case, the voice is closest to the signified, whether it is determined strictly as sense (thought or lived) or more loosely as thing. All signifiers, and first and foremost the written signifier, are derivative with regard to what would wed the voice indissolubly to the mind or to the thought of the signified sense, indeed to the thing itself (whether it is done in the Aristotelian manner that we have just indicated or in the manner of medieval theology, determining the *res* as a thing created from its *eidos,* from its sense thought in the logos or in the infinite understanding of God). The written signifier is always technical and representative. It has no constitutive meaning. This derivation is the very origin of the notion of the "signifier." The notion of the sign always implies within itself the distinction between signifier and signified, even if, as Saussure argues, they are distinguished simply as the two faces of one and the same leaf. This notion remains therefore within the heritage of that logocentrism which is also a phonocentrism: absolute proximity of voice and being, of voice and the meaning of being, of voice and the ideality of meaning. Hegel demonstrates very clearly the strange privilege of sound in idealization, the production of the concept and the self-presence of the subject.

> This ideal motion, in which through the sound what is as it were the simple subjectivity *[Subjektivität],* the soul of the material thing expresses itself, the ear receives also in a theoretical *[theoretisch]* way, just as the eye shape and colour, thus allowing the interiority of the object to become interiority itself *[läßt dadurch das Innere der Gegenstände für das Innere selbst werden] (Esthétique,* III. I tr. fr. p. 16).[2] . . . The ear, on the contrary, perceives *[vernimmt]* the result of that interior vibration of material substance without placing itself in a practical relation toward the objects, a result by means of which it is no

2. Georg Wilhelm Friedrich Hegel, *Werke,* Suhrkamp edition (Frankfurt am Main, 1970), vol. 14, p. 256; translated as *The Philosophy of Fine Art* by F. P. Osmaston (London, 1920), vol. 3, pp. 15–16.

longer the material form *[Gestalt]* in its repose, but the first, more ideal activity of the soul itself which is manifested *[zum Vorschein kommt]* (p. 296).[3]

What is said of sound in general is a fortiori valid for the *phonè* by which, by virtue of hearing (understanding) oneself-speak—an indissociable system—the subject affects itself and is related to itself in the element of ideality.

We already have a foreboding that phonocentrism merges with the historical determination of the meaning of being in general as *presence,* with all the subdeterminations which depend on this general form and which organize within it their system and their historical sequence (presence of the thing to the sight as *eidos,* presence as substance/essence/existence *[ousia],* temporal presence as point *[stigmè]* of the now or of the moment *[nun],* the self-presence of the cogito, consciousness, subjectivity, the co-presence of the other and of the self, intersubjectivity as the intentional phenomenon of the ego, and so forth). Logocentrism would thus support the determination of the being of the entity as presence. To the extent that such a logocentrism is not totally absent from Heidegger's thought, perhaps it still holds that thought within the epoch of onto-theology, within the philosophy of presence, that is to say within philosophy *itself.* This would perhaps mean that one does not leave the epoch whose closure one can outline. The movements of belonging or not belonging to the epoch are too subtle, the illusions in that regard are too easy, for us to make a definite judgment.

The epoch of the logos thus debases writing considered as mediation of mediation and as a fall into the exteriority of meaning. To this epoch belongs the difference between signified and signifier, or at least the strange separation of their "parallelism," and the exteriority, however extenuated, of the one to the other. This appurtenance is organized and hierarchized in a history. The difference between signified and signifier belongs in a profound and implicit way to the totality of the great epoch covered by the history of metaphysics, and in a more explicit and more systematically articulated way to the narrower epoch of Christian creationism and infinitism when these appropriate the resources of Greek conceptuality. This appurtenance is essential and irreducible; one cannot retain the convenience or the "scientific truth" of the Stoic

3. Hegel, p. 134; Osmaston, p. 341.

and later medieval opposition between *signans* and *signatum* without also bringing with it all its metaphysico-theological roots. To these roots adheres not only the distinction between the sensible and the intelligible—already a great deal—with all that it controls, namely, metaphysics in its totality. And this distinction is generally accepted as self-evident by the most careful linguists and semiologists, even by those who believe that the scientificity of their work begins where metaphysics ends. Thus, for example:

> As modern structural thought has clearly realized, language is a system of signs and linguistics is part and parcel of the science of signs, or *semiotics* (Saussure's *sémiologie*). The mediaeval definition of sign— *"aliquid stat pro aliquo"*—has been resurrected and put forward as still valid and productive. Thus the constitutive mark of any sign in general and of any linguistic sign in particular is its twofold character: every linguistic unit is bipartite and involves both aspects—one sensible and the other intelligible, or in other words, both the *signans* "signifier" (Saussure's *signifiant)* and the *signatum* "signified" *(signifié)*. These two constituents of a linguistic sign (and of sign in general) necessarily suppose and require each other.[4]

But to these metaphysico-theological roots many other hidden sediments cling. The semiological or, more specifically, linguistic "science" cannot therefore hold on to the difference between signifier and signified—the very idea of the sign—without the difference between sensible and intelligible, certainly, but also not without retaining, more profoundly and more implicitly, and by the same token the reference to a signified able to "take place" in its intelligibility, before its "fall," before any expulsion into the exteriority of the sensible here below. As the face of pure intelligibility, it refers to an absolute logos to which it is immediately united. This absolute logos was an infinite creative subjectivity in medieval theology: the intelligible face of the sign remains turned toward the word and the face of God.

Of course, it is not a question of "rejecting" these notions; they are necessary and, at least at present, nothing is conceivable for us without them. It is a question at first of demonstrating the systematic

---

4. Roman Jakobson, *Essais de linguistique générale,* tr. fr., p. 162 ["The Phonemic and Grammatical Aspects of Language in their Interrelations," *Proceedings of the Sixth International Congress of Linguistics* (Paris, 1949), p. 6]. On this problem, on the tradition of the concept of the sign, and on the originality of Saussure's contribution within this continuity, cf. Ortigues, op. cit., pp. 54 f.

and historical solidarity of the concepts and gestures of thought that one often believes can be innocently separated. The sign and divinity have the same place and time of birth. The age of the sign is essentially theological. Perhaps it will never *end.* Its historical *closure* is, however, outlined.

Since these concepts are indispensable for unsettling the heritage to which they belong, we should be even less prone to renounce them. Within the closure, by an oblique and always perilous movement, constantly risking falling back within what is being deconstructed, it is necessary to surround the critical concepts with a careful and thorough discourse—to mark the conditions, the medium, and the limits of their effectiveness and to designate rigorously their intimate relationship to the machine whose deconstruction they permit; and, in the same process, designate the crevice through which the yet unnameable glimmer beyond the closure can be glimpsed. The concept of the sign is here exemplary. We have just marked its metaphysical appurtenance. We know, however, that the thematics of the sign have been for about a century the agonized labor of a tradition that professed to withdraw meaning, truth, presence, being, etc., from the movement of signification. Treating as suspect, as I just have, the difference between signified and signifier, or the idea of the sign in general, I must state explicitly that it is not a question of doing so in terms of the instance of the present truth, anterior, exterior or superior to the sign, or in terms of the place of the effaced difference. Quite the contrary. We are disturbed by that which, in the concept of the sign—which has never existed or functioned outside the history of (the) philosophy (of presence) —remains systematically and genealogically determined by that history. It is there that the concept and above all the work of deconstruction, its "style," remain by nature exposed to misunderstanding and nonrecognition.

The exteriority of the signifier is the exteriority of writing in general, and I shall try to show later that there is no linguistic sign before writing. Without that exteriority, the very idea of the sign falls into decay. Since our entire world and language would collapse with it, and since its evidence and its value keep, to a certain point of derivation, an indestructible solidity, it would be silly to conclude from its placement within an epoch that it is necessary to "move on to something else," to dispose of the sign, of the term and the notion. For a proper understanding of the gesture that we are sketching here, one must understand the expressions "epoch," "closure of an epoch," "historical genealogy" in a new way; and must first remove them from all relativism.

Thus, within this epoch, reading and writing, the production or interpretation of signs, the text in general as fabric of signs, allow themselves to be confined within secondariness. They are preceded by a truth, or a meaning already constituted by and within the element of the logos. Even when the thing, the "referent," is not immediately related to the logos of a creator God where it began by being the spoken/thought sense, the signified has at any rate an immediate relationship with the logos in general (finite or infinite), and a mediated one with the signifier, that is to say with the exteriority of writing. When it seems to go otherwise, it is because a metaphoric mediation has insinuated itself into the relationship and has simulated immediacy; the writing of truth in the soul, opposed by *Phaedrus* (278a) to bad writing (writing in the "literal" *[propre]* and ordinary sense, "sensible" writing, "in space"), the book of Nature and God's writing, especially in the Middle Ages; all that functions as *metaphor* in these discourses confirms the privilege of the logos and founds the "literal" meaning then given to writing: a sign signifying a signifier itself signifying an eternal verity, eternally thought and spoken in the proximity of a present logos. The paradox to which attention must be paid is this: natural and universal writing, intelligible and nontemporal writing, is thus named by metaphor. A writing that is sensible, finite, and so on, is designated as writing in the literal sense; it is thus thought on the side of culture, technique, and artifice; a human procedure, the ruse of a being accidentally incarnated or of a finite creature. Of course, this metaphor remains enigmatic and refers to a "literal" meaning of writing as the first metaphor. This "literal" meaning is yet unthought by the adherents of this discourse. It is not, therefore, a matter of inverting the literal meaning and the figurative meaning but of determining the "literal" meaning of writing as metaphoricity itself.

In "The Symbolism of the Book," that excellent chapter of *European Literature and the Latin Middle Ages,* E. R. Curtius describes with great wealth of examples the evolution that led from the *Phaedrus* to Calderon, until it seemed to be "precisely the reverse" (tr. fr. p. 372)[5] by the "newly attained position of the book"

---

5. Ernst Robert Curtius, "Das Buch als Symbol," *Europäische Literatur and lateinisches Mittelalter* (Bern, 1948), p. 307. French translation by Jean Bréjoux (Paris, 1956): translated as *European Literature and the Latin Middle Ages,* by Willard R. Trask, Harper Torchbooks edition (New York, 1963), pp. 305, 306.

(p. 374) [p. 306]. But it seems that this modification, however important in fact it might be, conceals a fundamental continuity. As was the case with the Platonic writing of the truth in the soul, in the Middle Ages too it is a writing understood in the metaphoric sense, that is to say a *natural,* eternal, and universal writing, the system of signified truth, which is recognized in its dignity. As in the *Phaedrus,* a certain fallen writing continues to be opposed to it. There remains to be written a history of this metaphor, a metaphor that systematically contrasts divine or natural writing and the human and laborious, finite and artificial inscription. It remains to articulate rigorously the stages of that history, as marked by the quotations below, and to follow the theme of God's book (nature or law, indeed natural law) through all its modifications.

> Rabbi Eliezer said: "If all the seas were of ink, and all ponds planted with reeds, if the sky and the earth were parchments and if all human beings practised the art of writing—they would not exhaust the Torah I have learned, just as the Torah itself would not be diminished any more than is the sea by the water removed by a paint brush dipped in it."[6]

> Galileo: "It [the book of Nature] is written in a mathematical language."[7]

> Descartes: ". . . to read in the great book of Nature . . ."[8]

> Demea, in the name of natural religion, in the *Dialogues,* . . . of Hume: "And this volume of nature contains a great and inexplicable riddle, more than any intelligible discourse or reasoning."[9]

> Bonnet: "It would seem more philosophical to me to presume that our earth is a book that God has given to intelligences far superior to ours to read, and where they study in depth the infinitely multiplied and varied characters of His adorable wisdom."

> G. H. von Schubert: "This language made of images and hiero-glyphs, which supreme Wisdom uses in all its revelations to

6. Cited by Emmanuel Levinas, in *Difficile liberté* [Paris, 1963], p. 44.
7. Quoted in Curtius, op. cit. (German), p. 326, (English), p. 324; Galileo's word is "philosophy" rather than "nature."
8. Ibid. (German) p. 324, (English) p. 322.
9. David Hume, *Dialogues Concerning Natural Religion,* ed. Norman Kemp Smith (Oxford, 1935), p. 193.

humanity—which is found in the inferior *[nieder]* language of poetry—and which, in the most inferior and imperfect way *[auf der allerniedrigsten und unvollkommensten]*, is more like the metaphorical expression of the dream than the prose of wakefulness, . . . we may wonder if this language is not the true and wakeful language of the superior regions. If, when we consider ourselves awakened, we are not plunged in a millennial slumber, or at least in the echo of its dreams, where we only perceive a few isolated and obscure words of God's language, as a sleeper perceives the conversation of the people around him."[10]

Jaspers: "The world is the manuscript of an other, inaccessible to a universal reading, which only existence deciphers."[11]

Above all, the profound differences distinguishing all these treatments of the same metaphor must not be ignored. In the history of this treatment, the most decisive separation appears at the moment when, at the same time as the science of nature, the determination of absolute presence is constituted as self-presence, as subjectivity. It is the moment of the great rationalisms of the seventeenth century. From then on, the condemnation of fallen and finite writing will take another form, within which we still live: it is non-self-presence that will be denounced. Thus the exemplariness of the "Rousseauist" moment, which we shall deal with later, begins to be explained. Rousseau repeats the Platonic gesture by referring to another model of presence: self-presence in the senses, in the sensible cogito, which simultaneously carries in itself the inscription of divine law. On the one hand, *representative,* fallen, secondary, instituted writing, writing in the literal and strict sense, is condemned in *The Essay on the Origin of Languages* (it "enervates" speech; to "judge genius" from books is like "painting a man's portrait from his corpse," etc.). Writing in the common sense is the dead letter, it is the carrier of death. It exhausts life. On the other hand, on the other face of the same proposition, writing in the metaphoric sense, natural, divine, and living writing, is venerated; it is equal in dignity to the origin of value, to the voice of conscience as divine law, to the heart, to sentiment, and so forth.

10. Gotthilf Heinrich von Schubert, *Die Symbolik des Traumes* (Leipzig, 1862), pp. 23–24.
11. Quoted in Paul Ricoeur, *Gabriel Marcel et Karl Jaspers* (Paris, 1947), p. 45.

> The Bible is the most sublime of all books, . . . but it is after all a book. . . . It is not at all in a few sparse pages that one should look for God's law, but in the human heart where His hand deigned to write *(Lettre à Vernes).*[12]

> If the natural law had been written only in the human reason, it would be little capable of directing most of our actions. But it is also engraved in the heart of man in ineffacable characters. . . . There it cries to him *(L'état de guerre.)*[13]

Natural writing is immediately united to the voice and to breath. Its nature is not grammatological but pneumatological. It is hieratic, very close to the interior holy voice of the *Profession of Faith,* to the voice one hears upon retreating into oneself: full and truthful presence of the divine voice to our inner sense: "The more I retreat into myself, the more I consult myself, the more plainly do I read these words written in my soul: be just and you will be happy. . . . I do not derive these rules from the principles of the higher philosophy, I find them in the depths of my heart written by nature in characters which nothing can efface."[14]

There is much to say about the fact that the native unity of the voice and writing is *prescriptive.* Arche-speech is writing because it is a law. A natural law. The beginning word is understood, in the intimacy of self-presence, as the voice of the other and as commandment.

There is therefore a good and a bad writing: the good and natural is the divine inscription in the heart and the soul; the perverse and artful is technique, exiled in the exteriority of the body. A modification well within the Platonic diagram: writing of the soul and of the body, writing of the interior and of the exterior, writing of conscience and of the passions, as there is a voice of the soul and a voice of the body. "Conscience is the voice of the soul, the passions are the voice of the body" [p. 249]. One must constantly go back toward the "voice of nature," the "holy voice of nature," that merges with the divine inscription and prescription; one must encounter oneself within it, enter into a dialogue within its signs, speak and respond to oneself in its pages.

---

12. *Correspondance complète de Jean Jacques Rousseau,* ed. R. A. Leigh (Geneva, 1967), vol. V, pp. 65–66. The original reads "l'évangile" rather than "la Bible."
13. Rousseau, *Oeuvres complètes,* Pléiade edition, vol. III, p. 602.
14. Derrida's reference is *Emile,* Pléiade edition, vol. 4, pp. 589, 594. My reference is *Emile,* tr. Barbara Foxley (London, 1911), pp. 245, 249. Subsequent references to this translation are placed within brackets.

> It was as if nature had spread out all her magnificence in front of our eyes to offer its text for our consideration. . . . I have therefore closed all the books. Only one is open to all eyes. It is the book of Nature. In this great and sublime book I learn to serve and adore its author.

The good writing has therefore always been *comprehended.* Comprehended as that which had to be comprehended: within a nature or a natural law, created or not, but first thought within an eternal presence. Comprehended, therefore, within a totality, and enveloped in a volume or a book. The idea of the book is the idea of a totality, finite or infinite, of the signifier; this totality of the signifier cannot be a totality, unless a totality constituted by the signified preexists it, supervises its inscriptions and its signs, and is independent of it in its ideality. The idea of the book, which always refers to a natural totality, is profoundly alien to the sense of writing. It is the encyclopedic protection of theology and of logocentrism against the disruption of writing, against its aphoristic energy, and, as I shall specify later, against difference in general. If I distinguish the text from the book, I shall say that the destruction of the book, as it is now under way in all domains, denudes the surface of the text. That necessary violence responds to a violence that was no less necessary.

PAUL DE MAN

Georg Lukács in *Soul and Form* (1910) makes a case for the essay as an art form.* There are writers, says Lukács, who deal with ultimate questions in the most occasional of guises, the book review, for example, or the explication of a poem. He speaks of "ultraviolet" experiences, inexpressible by gesture or image, but which nevertheless long for expression—experiences that leave the richness and multiplicity of lived experience for the moon landscapes of ontological reduction. Lukács' ironic essayist treats these occasions as starting points for an entire criticism of life. It is tempting to claim that de Man is a writer of this type. That he would—almost seriously—make the claim for others (Blanchot, certainly, Poulet, or Empson), but not for himself, suggests the Socratic modesty Lukács mentions as typical of the genre. It is possible that even the numerous dangling verbals in de Man's work ("Looking back . . . a recurrent pattern emerges") are functionally self-effacing in this respect, that they derive from an ascetic reluctance to admit the subjective, to grant that some*one* is thinking (or reading, or looking) and not impersonal thought itself.

The ultimate question of de Man's work is the irreparable separation of consciousness from Being, or even more insistently, the separation of expression from the intuition of plenitude. He pursues anyone who claims their identity with a relentlessness that has been identified as "ethical."† Indeed, philosophers, critics, and occasionally poets have made this claim for art, that it calls down gods to walk among us (Yeats), that it is the bridge from the real to the divine (the Russian Symbolists), that it is the "translucence of the eternal . . . in the temporal" (Coleridge). For Heidegger, the poetry of Hölderlin fused Being, the poet, and human *Dasein* into one; it was the *parousia*, the speech of plenitude.‡ Anyone under the spell of Romantic symbol ideology is likely to make such statements. Their motivating nostalgia is regressive, and de Man pressures them until they renounce their theological claims and admit poetry's inevitable enslavement to the merely human and temporal. It is important to understand that the symbolic identification of self with nature involves a self-mystification that conceals death itself beneath the joy of homecoming. The allegory, on the other hand, is a sign that never claims to coincide

* Georg Lukács, *Soul and Form,* trans. Anna Bostock (Cambridge: MIT Press, 1974) 1–18.

† Christopher Norris, "Some Versions of Rhetoric: Empson and de Man," *Genre* (Spring/Summer 1984) 200.

‡ Paul de Man, *Blindness and Insight,* Second Edition, revised. Introduction by Wlad Godzich (Minneapolis: University of Minnesota Press, 1983) 254.

with Being, but rather insists on distance, difference, struggle, and the postponement of the end of anguish, which will come soon enough without our having to clamor for it.

The Rhetoric of Temporality
Part I
1969

ALLEGORY AND SYMBOL

Since the advent, in the course of the nineteenth century, of a subjectivistic critical vocabulary, the traditional forms of rhetoric have fallen into disrepute. It is becoming increasingly clear, however, that this was only a temporary eclipse: recent developments in criticism[1] reveal the possibility of a rhetoric that would no longer be normative or descriptive but that would more or less openly raise the question

THE RHETORIC OF TEMPORALITY   by Paul de Man, exerpted from *Interpretation: Theory and Practice,* ed. Charles Singleton. Copyright ©1969. Reprinted by permission of Johns Hopkins University Press.

1. The trend is apparent in various critical movements that develop independently of one another in several countries. Thus, for example, in the attempt of some French critics to fuse the conceptual terminology of structural linguistics with traditional terms of rhetoric (see, among others, Roland Barthes, "Éléments de sémiologie," in *Communications* 4[1964], trans. Annette Lavers and Colin Smith, *Elements of Semiology* [New York: Hill and Wang, 1967]; Gérard Genette, *Figures* [Paris: Seuil, 1966]; Michel Foucault, *Les Mots et les choses* [Paris: Gallimard, 1966], trans. *The Order of Things* [New York: Random House, Inc., 1970). In Germany a similar trend often takes the form of a rediscovery and reinterpretation of the allegorical and emblematic style of the baroque (see, among others, Walter Benjamin, *Ursprung des deutschen Trauerspiels* [Berlin: 1928; reissued in Frankfurt: Suhrkamp, 1963], trans. John Osborne, *The Origin of German Tragic Drama* [London: NLB, 1977]; Albrecht Schöne, *Emblematik und Drama im Zeitalter des Barock* [Munich: Beck, 1964]). The evolution from the New Criticism to the criticism of Northrop Frye in North America tends in the same direction.

of the intentionality of rhetorical figures. Such concerns are implicitly present in many works in which the terms "mimesis," "metaphor," "allegory," or "irony" play a prominent part. One of the main difficulties that still hamper these investigations stems from the association of rhetorical terms with value judgments that blur distinctions and hide the real structures. In most cases, their use is governed by assumptions that go back at least as far as the romantic period; hence the need for historical clarification as a preliminary to a more systematic treatment of an intentional rhetoric. One has to return, in the history of European literature, to the moment when the rhetorical key-terms undergo significant changes and are at the center of important tensions. A first and obvious example would be the change that takes place in the latter half of the eighteenth century, when the word "symbol" tends to supplant other denominations for figural language, including that of "allegory."

Although the problem is perhaps most in evidence in the history of German literature, we do not intend to retrace the itinerary that led the German writers of the age of Goethe to consider symbol and allegory as antithetical, when they were still synonymous for Winckelmann. The itinerary is too complex for cursory treatment. In *Wahrheit und Methode,* Hans-Georg Gadamer makes the valorization of symbol at the expense of allegory coincide with the growth of an aesthetics that refuses to distinguish between experience and the representation of this experience. The poetic language of genius is capable of transcending this distinction and can thus transform all individual experience directly into general truth. The subjectivity of experience is preserved when it is translated into language; the world is then no longer seen as a configuration of entities that designate a plurality of distinct and isolated meanings, but as a configuration of symbols ultimately leading to a total, single, and universal meaning. This appeal to the infinity of a totality constitutes the main attraction of the symbol as opposed to allegory, a sign that refers to one specific meaning and thus exhausts its suggestive potentialities once it has been deciphered. "Symbol and allegory," writes Gadamer, "are opposed as art is opposed to non-art, in that the former seems endlessly suggestive in the indefiniteness of its meaning, whereas the latter, as soon as its meaning is reached, has run its full course."[2]

---

2. Hans-Georg Gadamer, *Wahrheit und Methode* (Tübingen: J. C. B. Mohr, 1960; 4th ed., 1975), p. 70; trans. G. Barden and J. Cumming, *Truth and Method* (New York: Seabury Press, 1975), p. 67.

Allegory appears as dryly rational and dogmatic in its reference to a meaning that it does not itself constitute, whereas the symbol is founded on an intimate unity between the image that rises up before the senses and the supersensory totality that the image suggests. In this historical perspective, the names of Goethe, Schiller, and Schelling stand out from the background of the classical idea of a unity between incarnate and ideal beauty.

Even within the area of German thought other currents complicate this historical scheme. In the perspective of traditional German classicism, allegory appears as the product of the age of Enlightenment and is vulnerable to the reproach of excessive rationality. Other trends, however, consider allegory as the very place where the contact with a superhuman origin of language has been preserved. Thus the polemical utterances of Hamann against Herder on the problem of the origin of language are closely related to Hamann's considerations on the allegorical nature of all language,[3] as well as with his literary praxis that mingles allegory with irony. It is certainly not in the name of an enlightened rationalism that the idea of a transcendental distance between the incarnate world of man and the divine origin of the word is here being defended. Herder's humanism encounters in Hamann a resistance that reveals the complexity of the intellectual climate in which the debate between symbol and allegory will take place.

These questions have been treated at length in the historiography of the period. We do not have to return to them here, except to indicate how contradictory the origins of the debate appear to be. It is therefore not at all surprising that, even in the case of Goethe, the choice in favor of the symbol is accompanied by all kinds of reservations and qualification. But, as one progresses into the nineteenth century, these qualifications tend to disappear. The supremacy of the symbol, conceived as an expression of unity between the representative and the semantic function of language, becomes a commonplace that underlies literary taste, literary criticism, and literary history. The supremacy of the symbol still functions as the basis of recent French and English studies of the romantic and post-romantic eras, to such an extent that allegory is frequently considered an anachronism and dismissed as non-poetic.

---

3. Johann Georg Hamann, "Die Rezension der Herderschen Preisschrift," in *J. G. Hamann's Hauptschriften erklärt, vol. 4 (Über den Ursprung der Sprache),* Elfriede Büchsel (Gütersloh: Gerd Mohn, 1963).

Yet certain questions remain unsolved. At the very moment when properly symbolic modes, in the full strength of their development, are supplanting allegory, we can witness the growth of metaphorical styles in no way related to the decorative allegorism of the rococo, but that cannot be called "symbolic" in the Goethian sense. Thus it would be difficult to assert that in the poems of Hölderlin, the island Patmos, the river Rhine, or, more generally, the landscapes and places that are often described at the beginning of the poems would be symbolic landscapes or entities that represent, as by analogy, the spiritual truths that appear in the more abstract parts of the text. To state this would be to misjudge the literality of these passages, to ignore that they derive their considerable poetic authority from the fact that they are not synecdoches designating a totality of which they are a part, but are themselves already this totality. They are not the sensorial equivalent of a more general, ideal meaning; they are themselves this idea, just as much as the abstract expression that will appear in philosophical or historical form in the later parts of the poem. A metaphorical style such as Hölderlin's can at any rate not be described in terms of the antimony between allegory and symbol —and the same could be said, albeit in a very different way, of Goethe's late style. Also, when the term "allegory" continues to appear in the writers of the period, such as Friedrich Schlegel, or later in Solger or E. T. A. Hoffmann, one should not assume that its use is merely a matter of habit, devoid of deeper meaning. Between 1800 and 1832, under the influence of Creuzer and Schelling, Friedrich Schlegel substitutes the word "symbolic" for "allegorical" in the oft-quoted passage of the "Gespräch über die Poesie": ". . . alle Schönheit ist Allegorie. Das Höchste kann man eben weil es unaussprechlich ist, nur allegorisch sagen. [. . . all beauty is allegory. The highest beauty one can only express allegorically, precisely because it is inexpressible]."[4] But can we deduce from this, with Schlegel's editor Hans Eichner, that Schlegel "simply uses allegory where we would nowadays say symbol"?[5] It could be shown that, precisely because it suggests a disjunction between the way in which the world appears in reality and the way it appears in language, the

4. Friedrich Schlegel, "Gespräch über die Poesie," in *Kritische Ausgabe*, Band 2, *Charakteristiken und Kritiken I*, (1796–1801), Hans Eichner, ed. (Paderborn: Ferdinand Schöningh, 1967), pp. 324ff.
5. *Ibid.*, p. xci, n. 2.

word "allegory" fits the general problematic of the "Gespräch," whereas the word "symbol" becomes an alien presence in the later version. We must go even further than this. Ever since the study of *topoi* has made us more aware of the importance of tradition in the choice of images, the symbol, in the post-romantic sense of the term, appears more and more as a special case of figural language in general, a special case that can lay no claim to historical or philosophical priority over other figures. After such otherwise divergent studies as those of E. R. Curtius, of Erich Auerbach, of Walter Benjamin,[6] and of H.–G. Gadamer, we can no longer consider the supremacy of the symbol as a "solution" to the problem of metaphorical diction. "The basis of aesthetics during the nineteenth century," writes Gadamer, "was the freedom of the symbolizing power of the mind. But is this still a firm basis? Is the symbolizing activity not actually still bound today by the survival of a mythological and allegorical tradition?"[7]

To make some headway in this difficult question, it may be useful to leave the field of German literature and see how the same problem appears in English and French writers of the same period. Some help may be gained from a broader perspective.

The English contemporary of Goethe who has expressed himself most explicitly in the relationship between allegory and symbol is, of course, Coleridge. We find in Coleridge what appears to be, at first sight, an unqualified assertion of the superiority of the symbol over allegory. The symbol is the product of the organic growth of form; in the world of the symbol, life and form are identical: "such as the life is, such is the form."[8] Its structure is that of the synecdoche, for the symbol is always a part of the totality that it represents. Consequently, in the symbolic imagination, no disjunction of the constitutive faculties takes place, since the material perception and the symbolical imagination are continuous, as the part is continuous with the whole. In contrast, the allegorical form appears purely mechanical, an abstraction whose original meaning is even more devoid of substance than its "phantom proxy," the allegorical representative; it is an

---

6. See note 1 above.
7. Gadamer, p. 76; Eng., p. 72.
8. S. T. Coleridge, *Essays and Lectures on Shakespeare and Some Other Old Poets and Dramatists* (London: Everyman, 1907), p. 46.

immaterial shape that represents a sheer phantom devoid of shape and substance.[9]

But even in the passage from *The Statesman's Manual,* from which this quotation is taken, a certain degree of ambiguity is manifest. After associating the essential thinness of allegory with a lack of substantiality, Coleridge wants to stress, by contrast, the worth of the symbol. One would expect the latter to be valued for its organic or material richness, but instead the notion of "translucence" is suddenly put in evidence: "The symbol is characterized by the translucence of the special in the individual, or of the general in the special, or of the universal in the general; above all by the translucence of the eternal through and in the temporal."[10]

The material substantiality dissolves and becomes a mere reflection of a more original unity that does not exist in the material world. It is all the more surprising to see Coleridge, in the final part of the passage, characterize allegory negatively as being *merely* a reflection. In truth, the spiritualization of the symbol has been carried so far that the moment of material existence by which it was originally defined has now become altogether unimportant; symbol and allegory alike now have a common origin beyond the world of matter. The reference, in both cases, to a transcendental source, is now more important than the kind of relationship that exists between the reflection and its source. It becomes of secondary importance whether this relationship is based, as in the case of the symbol, on the organic coherence of the synecdoche, or whether, as in the case of allegory, it is a pure decision of the mind. Both figures designate, in fact, the transcendental source, albeit in an oblique and ambiguous way. Coleridge stresses the ambiguity in a definition of allegory in which it is said that allegory ". . . convey[s], while in disguise, either moral qualities or conceptions of the mind that are not in themselves objects of the senses . . . ," but then goes on to state that, on the level of language, allegory can "combine the parts to form a consistent whole."[11] Starting out from the assumed superiority of the symbol in terms of organic substantiality, we end up with a description of figural

9. S. T. Coleridge, *The Statesman's Manual,* W. G. T. Shedd, ed. (New York: Harper and Brothers, 1875), pp. 437–38, quoted in Angus Fletcher, *Allegory: The Theory of a Symbolic Mode* (Ithaca, N.Y.: Cornell University Press, 1964), p. 16, n. 29.
10. *Ibid.*
11. S. T. Coleridge, *Miscellaneous Criticism,* T. M. Raysor, ed. (London: Constable and Co., Ltd., 1936), p. 30; also quoted by Fletcher, p. 19.

language as translucence, a description in which the distinction between allegory and symbol has become of secondary importance. It is not, however, in this direction that Coleridge's considerable influence on later English and American criticism has been most manifest. The very prominent place given in this criticism to the study of metaphor and imagery, often considered as more important than problems of metrics or thematic considerations, is well enough known. But the conception of metaphor that is being assumed, often with explicit reference to Coleridge, is that of a dialectic between object and subject, in which the experience of the object takes on the form of a perception or a sensation. The ultimate intent of the image is not, however, as in Coleridge, translucence, but synthesis, and the mode of this synthesis is defined as "symbolic" by the priority conferred on the initial moment of sensory perception.

The main interpretative effort of English and American historians of romanticism has focused on the transition that leads from eighteenth-century to romantic nature poetry. Among American interpreters of romanticism, there is general agreement about the importance of eighteenth-century antecedents for Wordsworth and Coleridge, but when it comes to describing just in what way romantic nature poetry differs from the earlier forms, certain difficulties arise. They center on the tendency shared by all commentators to define the romantic image as a relationship between mind and nature, between subject and object. The fluent transition in romantic diction, from descriptive to inward, meditative passages, bears out the notion that this relationship is indeed of fundamental importance. The same applies to a large extent to eighteenth-century landscape poets who constantly mix descriptions of nature with abstract moralizings; commentators tend to agree, however, that the relationship between mind and nature becomes much more intimate toward the end of the century. Wimsatt was the first to show convincingly, by the juxtaposition of a sonnet of Coleridge and a sonnet of Bowles that, for all external similitudes, a fundamental change in substance and in tone separated the two texts.[12] He points to a greater specificity in Coleridge's details, thus revealing a closer, more faithful observation of the outside object. But this finer attention given to the natural surfaces is accompanied, paradoxically enough, by a greater inwardness, by

12. William Wimsatt, "The Structure of Romantic Nature Imagery," *The Verbal Icon* (Lexington, Ky.: University of Kentucky Press, 1954) pp. 106–10.

experiences of memory and of reverie that stem from deeper regions of subjectivity than in the earlier writer. How this closer attention to surfaces engenders greater depth remains problematic. Wimsatt writes: "The common feat of the romantic nature poets was to read meanings into the landscape. The meaning might be such as we have seen in Coleridge's sonnet, but it might more characteristically be more profound, concerning the spirit or soul of things—'the one life within us and abroad.' And that meaning especially was summoned out of the very surface of nature itself."[13] The synthesis of surface and depth would then be the manifestation, in language, of a fundamental unity that encompasses both mind and object, "the one life within us and abroad." It appears, however, that this unity can be hidden from a subject, who then has to look outside, in nature, for the confirmation of its existence. For Wimsatt, the unifying principle seems to reside primarily within nature, hence the necessity for the poets to start out from natural landscapes, the sources of the unifying, "symbolic" power.

The point receives more development and ampler documentation in recent articles by Meyer Abrams and Earl Wasserman that make use of very similar, at times even identical material.[14] The two interpreters agree on many issues, to the point of overlapping. Both name, for instance, the principle of analogy between mind and nature as the basis for the eighteenth-century habit of treating a moral issue in terms of a descriptive landscape. Abrams refers to Renaissance concepts of theology and philosophy as a main source for the later *paysage moralisé:* ". . . the divine Architect has designed the universe analogically, relating the physical, moral, and spiritual realms by an elaborate system of correspondences. . . . The metaphysics of a symbolic and analogical universe underlay the figurative tactics of the seventeenth-century metaphysical poets."[15] A "tamed and ordered" version of this cosmology, "smoothed to a neo-classic decency" and decorum, then becomes the origin of the eighteenth-century loco-descriptive poem, in which "sensuous phenomena are coupled with moral statements." And Wasserman points to eighteenth-century

---

13. *Ibid.,* p. 110.
14. Meyer Abrams, "Structure and Style in the Greater Romantic Lyric," in *From Sensibility to Romanticism: Essays Presented to F. A. Pottle,* F. W. Hillis and H. Bloom, eds. (New York: Oxford University Press, 1965). Earl Wasserman, "The English Romantics, The Grounds of Knowledge," *Essays in Romanticism,* 4 (Autumn, 1964).
15. Abrams, p. 536.

theoreticians of the imagination, such as Akenside, who "can find [the most intimate relation] between subject and object is that of associative analogy, so that man beholds 'in lifeless things/The Inexpressive semblance of himself,/Of thought and passion.' "[16]

The key concept here is, in Wasserman's correct phrasing, that of an *associative* analogy, as contrasted with a more vital form of analogy in the romantics. Abrams makes it seem, at times, as if the romantic theory of imagination did away with analogy altogether and that Coleridge in particular replaced it by a genuine and working monism. "Nature is made thought and thought nature," he writes, "both by their sustained interaction and by their seamless metaphoric continuity."[17] But he does not really claim that this degree of fusion is achieved and sustained—at most that it corresponds to Coleridge's desire for a unity toward which his thought and poetic strategy strive. Analogy as such is certainly never abandoned as an epistemological pattern for natural images; even within the esoteric vocabulary of as late a version of a monistic universe as Baudelaire's correspondences, the expression *"analogie universelle"* is still being used.[18] Nevertheless, the relationship between mind and nature becomes indeed a lot less formal, less purely associative and external than it is in the eighteenth century. As a result, the critical—and even, at times, the poetic—vocabulary attempts to find terms better suited to express this relationship than is the somewhat formal concept of analogy. Words such as "affinity," or "sympathy," appear instead of the more abstract "analogy." This does not change the fundamental pattern of the structure, which remains that of a formal resemblance between entities that, in other respects, can be antithetical. But the new terminology indicates a gliding away from the formal problem of a congruence between the two poles to that of the ontological priority of the one over the other. For terms such as "affinity" or "sympathy" apply to the relationships between subjects rather than to relationships between a subject and an object. The relationship with nature has been superseded by an intersubjective, interpersonal relationship that, in the last analysis, is a relationship of the subject toward itself. Thus the priority has passed from the outside world entirely within the subject, and we end up with something that resembles a radical

16. Wasserman, p. 19.
17. Abrams, p. 551
18. Charles Baudelaire, "Réflexions sur quelques-uns de mes contemporains, Victor Hugo," in *Curiosités esthétiques: L'Art romantique et autres Oeuvres critiques,* H. Lemaître, ed. (Paris: Garnier, 1962), p. 735.

idealism. Both Abrams and Wasserman offer quotations from Wordsworth and Coleridge, as well as summarizing comments of their own, that seem to suggest that romanticism is, in fact, such an idealism. Both quote Wordsworth: "I was often unable to think of external things as having external existence, and I communed with all that I saw as something not apart from, but inherent in, my own immaterial nature"—and Wasserman comments that "Wordsworth's poetic experience seeks to recapture that condition."[19]

Since the assertion of a radical priority of the subject over objective nature is not easily compatible with the poetic praxis of the romantic poets, who all gave a great deal of importance to the presence of nature, a certain degree of confusion ensues. One can find numerous quotations and examples that plead for the predominance, in romantic poetry, of an analogical imagination that is founded on the priority of natural substances over the consciousness of the self. Coleridge can speak, in nearly Fichtean terms, of the infinite self in opposition to the "necessarily finite" character of natural objects, and insist on the need for the self to give life to the dead forms of nature.[20] But the finite nature of the objective world is seen, at that moment, in spatial terms, and the substitution of vital (i.e., in Coleridge, intersubjective) relationships that are dynamic, for the physical relationships that exist between entities in the natural world is not necessarily convincing. It could very well be argued that Coleridge's own concept of organic unity as a dynamic principle is derived from the movements of nature, not from those of the self. Wordsworth is more clearly conscious of what is involved here when he sees the same dialectic between the self and nature in temporal terms. The movements of nature are for him instances of what Goethe calls *Dauer im Wechsel,* endurance within a pattern of change, the assertion of a metatemporal, stationary state beyond the apparent decay of a mutability that attacks certain outward aspects of nature but leaves the core intact. Hence we have famous passages such as the description of the mountain scenes in *The Prelude* in which a striking temporal paradox is evoked:

> . . . these majestic floods—these shining cliffs
> The untransmuted shapes of many worlds,
> Cerulian ether's pure inhabitants,
> These forests unapproachable by death,
> That shall endure as long as man endures . . . ;

19. Wasserman, p. 26.
20. *Ibid.,* p. 29.

or

> The immeasurable height
> Of woods decaying, never to be decayed
> The stationary blast of waterfalls. . . .

Such paradoxical assertions of eternity in motion can be applied to nature but not to a self caught up entirely within mutability. The temptation exists, then, for the self to borrow, so to speak, the temporal stability that it lacks from nature, and to devise strategies by means of which nature is brought down to a human level while still escaping from "the unimaginable touch of time." This strategy is certainly present in Coleridge. And it is present, though perhaps not consciously, in critics such as Abrams and Wasserman, who see Coleridge as the great synthesizer and who take his dialectic of subject and object to be the authentic pattern of romantic imagery. But this forces them, in fact, into a persistent contradiction. They are obliged, on the one hand, to assert the priority of object over subject that is implicit in an organic conception of language. So Abrams states: "The best Romantic meditations on a landscape, following Coleridge's example, all manifest a transaction between subject and object in which the thought incorporates and makes explicit what was already implicit in the outer scene."[21] This puts the priority unquestionably in the natural world, limiting the task of the mind to interpreting what is given in nature. Yet this statement is taken from the same paragraph in which Abrams quotes the passages from Wordsworth and Coleridge that confer an equally absolute priority to the self over nature. The contradiction reaches a genuine impasse. For what are we to believe? Is romanticism a subjective idealism, open to all the attacks of solipsism that, from Hazlitt to the French structuralists, a succession of de-mystifiers of the self have directed against it? Or is it instead a return to a certain form of naturalism after the forced abstraction of the Enlightenment, but a return which our urban and alienated world can conceive of only as a nostalgic and unreachable past? Wasserman is caught in the same impasse: for him, Wordsworth represents the extreme form of subjectivism whereas Keats, as a quasi-Shakespearean poet of negative capability, exemplifies a sympathetic and objective form of material imagination. Coleridge acts as the synthesis of this antithetical polarity. But Wasserman's claim for Coleridge as the reconciler of what he calls

21. Abrams, p. 551.

"the phenomenal world of understanding with the noumenal world of reason"[22] is based on a quotation in which Coleridge simply substitutes another self for the category of the object and thus removes the problem from nature altogether, reducing it to a purely intersubjective pattern. "To make the object one with us, we must become one with the object—ergo, an object. Ergo, the object must be itself a subject—partially a favorite dog, principally a friend, wholly God, *the* Friend."[23] Wordsworth was never guilty of thus reducing a theocentric to an interpersonal relationship.

Does the confusion originate with the critics, or does it reside in the romantic poets themselves? Were they really unable to move beyond the analogism that they inherited from the eighteenth century and were they trapped in the contradiction of a pseudo dialectic between subject and object? Certain commentators believe this to be the case;[24] before following them, we should make certain that we have indeed been dealing with the main romantic problem when we interpret the romantic image in terms of a subject-object tension. For this dialectic originates, it must be remembered, in the assumed predominance of the symbol as the outstanding characteristic of romantic diction, and this predominance must, in its turn, be put into question.

It might be helpful, at this point, to shift attention from English to French literary history. Because French pre-romanticism occurs, with Rousseau, so early in the eighteenth century, and because the Lockian heritage in France never reached, not even with Condillac, the degree of automaticism against which Coleridge and Wordsworth had to rebel in Hartley, the entire problem of analogy, as connected with the use of nature imagery, is somewhat clearer there than in England. Some of the writers of the period were at least as aware as their later commentators of what was involved in a development of the general taste that felt attracted toward a new kind of landscape. To take one example: in his *De la composition des paysages sur le terrain,* which dates from 1777, the Marquis de Girardin describes a landscape explicitly as "romantic," made up of dark woods, snow-capped mountains, and a crystalline lake with an island on which an idyllic *"ménage rustique"* enjoys a happy combination of sociability

22. Wasserman, p. 30.
23. *Ibid.,* pp. 29–30.
24. As one instance among others, see E. E. Bostetter, *The Romantic Ventriloquists* (Seattle: University of Washington Press, 1963).

and solitude among cascades and rushing brooks. And he comments on the scene as follows: "It is in situations like this that one feels all the strength of this analogy between natural beauty and moral sentiment."[25] One could establish a long list of similar quotations dating from the same general period, all expressing the intimate proximity between nature and its beholder in a language that evokes the material shape of the landscape as well as the mood of its inhabitants.

Later historians and critics have stressed this close unity between mind and nature as a fundamental characteristic of romantic diction. "Often the outer and the inner world are so deeply intermingled," writes Daniel Mornet, "that nothing distinguishes the images perceived by the senses from the chimera of the imagination."[26] The same emphasis, still present in the more recent writings on the period,[27] closely resembles the opinion expressed in Anglo-American criticism. There is the same stress on the analogical unity of nature and consciousness, the same priority given to the symbol as the unit of language in which the subject-object synthesis can take place, the same tendency to transfer into nature attributes of consciousness and to unify it organically with respect to a center that acts, for natural objects, as the identity of the self functions for a consciousness. In French literary history dealing with the period of Rousseau to the present, ambivalences closely akin to those found in the American historians of romanticism could be pointed out, ambivalences derived from an illusionary priority of a subject that had, in fact, to borrow from the outside world a temporal stability which it lacked within itself.

In the case of French romanticism, it is perhaps easier than it is in English literature to designate the historical origin of this tendency. One can point to a certain number of specific texts in which a symbolic language, based on the close interpenetration between observation and passion, begins to acquire a priority that it will never relinquish during the nineteenth and twentieth centuries. Among

25. Quoted by Daniel Mornet, *Le Sentiment de la Nature en France au XVIIIe siècle de Jean-Jacques Rousseau à Bernardin de Saint-Pierre* (Paris, 1932), p. 248.
26. *Ibid.*, p. 187.
27. See, for example, Herbert Dieckmann, "Zur Theorie der Lyrik im 18. Jahrhundert in Frankreich, mit gelegentlicher Berücksichtigung der Englischen Kritik," in *Poetic und Hermeneutik*, vol. 2, W. Iser, ed. (Munich: Wilhelm Fink, 1966), p. 108.

these texts none is more often singled out than Rousseau's novel *La Nouvelle Héloïse*. It forms the basis of Daniel Mornet's study on the sentiment of nature in the eighteenth century.[28] In more recent works, such as Robert Mauzi's *Idée du bonheur dans la littérature française du 18ème siècle*,[29] the same predominant importance is given to Rousseau's novel. "When one knows *Cleveland* and *La Nouvelle Héloïse*, there is little left to discover about the 18th century," Mauzi asserts in his preface.[30] There is certainly no better reference to be found than *La Nouvelle Héloïse* for putting to the test the nearly unanimous conviction that the origins of romanticism coincide with the beginnings of a predominantly symbolical diction.

Interpreters of Rousseau's epistolary novel have had no difficulty in pointing out the close correspondence between inner states of the soul and the outward aspect of nature, especially in passages such as the Meillerie episode in the fourth part of the novel.[31] In this letter, St. Preux revisits, in the company of the now-married Julie, the deserted region on the northern bank of the lake from which he had, in earlier days, written the letter that sealed their destiny. Rousseau stresses that the *lieu solitaire* he describes is like a wild desert *"sauvage et désert; mais plein de ces sortes de beautés qui ne plaisent qu'aux âmes sensibles et paraissent horribles aux autres* [savage and deserted; but full of those kinds of beauty which please only sensitive souls and horrify everyone else]."[32] A polemical reference to current taste is certainly present here, and such passages can be cited to illustrate the transition from the eighteenth-century, idyllic landscape that we still find in Girardin to the somber, tormented scenes that are soon to predominate in Macpherson. But this polemic of taste is superficial, for Rousseau's concerns are clearly entirely different. It is true that the intimate analogy between scenery and emotion serves as a basis for some of the dramatic and poetic effects of the passage: the sensuous passion, reawakened by memory and threatening to disturb a precarious tranquillity, is conveyed by the contrasting effects of light and setting which give the passage its dramatic power. The analogism of

28. See note 25 above.
29. Robert Mauzi, *L'Idée du bonheur dans la littérature et la pensée française du XVIIIe siècle* (Paris: A. Colin, 1960).
30. *Ibid.*, p. 10.
31. J. J. Rousseau, *Julie ou la Nouvelle Héloïse*, pt. 4, letter 17, in *Oeuvres complètes*, B. Gagnebin and Marcel Raymond, eds. (Paris: Gallimard [Bibliotèque de la Pléiade], 1961), 2: 514ff.
32. *Ibid.*, p. 518.

the style and the sensuous intensity of the passion are closely related. But this should not blind us to the explicit thematic function of the letter, which is one of temptation and near-fatal relapse into former error, openly and explicitly condemned, without any trace of ambiguity, in the larger context of Rousseau's novel.

In this respect, the reference to the Meillerie landscape as a wilderness is particularly revealing, especially when contrasted with other landscapes in the novel that are not emblematic of error, but of the virtue associated with the figure of Julie. This is the case for the central emblem of the novel, the garden that Julie has created on the Wolmar estate as a place of refuge. On the allegorical level the garden functions as the landscape representative of the "beautiful soul." Our question is whether this garden, the Elysium described at length in the eleventh letter of the fourth part of the novel, is based on the same kind of subject/object relationship that was thematically and stylistically present in the Meillerie episode.

A brief consideration of Rousseau's sources for the passage is enlightening. The main non-literary source has been all too strongly emphasized by Mornet in his critical edition of the novel:[33] Rousseau derives several of the exterior aspects of his garden from the so-called *jardins anglais,* which, well before him, were being preferred to the geometrical abstraction of the classical French gardens. The excessive symmetry of Le Nôtre, writes Rousseau, echoing a commonplace of sophisticated taste at the time, is *"ennemie de la nature et de la variété* [enemy of nature and variety]."[34] But this "natural" look of the garden is by no means the main theme of the passage. From the beginning we are told that the natural aspect of the site is in fact the result of extreme artifice, that in this bower of bliss, contrary to the tradition of the *topos,* we are entirely in the realm of art and not that of nature. "Il est vrai," Rousseau has Julie say, "que la nature a tout fait [dans ce jardin] mais sous ma direction, et il n'y a rien là que je n'aie ordonné [It is true that nature has made everything in this garden —but only under my direction, and there is nothing there that I have not ordered]."[35] The statement should at least alert us to the literary sources of the gardens of the passage that Mornet, preoccupied as he was with the outward history of taste, was led to neglect.

33. *La Nouvelle Héloïse,* Daniel Mornet, ed. (Paris: 1925), Introduction, 1: 67–74, and notes, 3: 223–47.
34. Rousseau, p. 483.
35. *Ibid.,* p. 472.

Confining ourselves to the explicit literary allusions that can be found in the text, the reference to *"une Ile déserte . . . (où) je n'aperçois aucuns pas d'hommes* [a deserted island . . . where I saw no one else]."[36] points directly toward Rousseau's favorite contemporary novel, the only one considered suitable for Emile's education, Defoe's *Robinson Crusoe,* whereas the allusion to the *Roman de la rose* in the pages immediately preceding the letter on Julie's Elysium[37] is equally revealing. The combination of *Robinson Crusoe* with the *Roman de la rose* may not look very promising at first sight, but it has, in fact, considerable hidden possibilities. The fact that the medieval romance, re-issued in 1735 and widely read in Rousseau's time,[38] had given the novel its subtitle of *"La Nouvelle Héloïse"* is well known, but its influence is manifest in many other ways as well. The close similarity between Julie's garden and the love garden of Deduit, which appears in the first part of Guillaume de Lorris' poem, is obvious. There is hardly a detail of Rousseau's description that does not find its counterpart in the medieval text: the self-enclosed, isolated space of the *"asile"*; the special privilege reserved to the happy few who possess a key that unlocks the gate; the traditional enumeration of natural attributes—a catalogue of the various flowers, trees, fruits, perfumes, and, above all, of the birds, culminating in the description of their song.[39] Most revealing of all is the emphasis on water, on fountains and pools that, in *Julie* as in the *Roman de la rose,* are controlled not by nature but by the ingenuity of the inhabitants.[40] Far from being an observed scene or the expression of a personal *état d'âme,* it is clear that Rousseau has deliberately taken all the details of his setting from the medieval literary source, one of the best-known versions of the traditional *topos* of the erotic garden.

In linguistic terms, we have something very different, then, from the descriptive and metaphorical language that, from Chateaubriand on, will predominate in French romantic diction. Rousseau does not even pretend to be observing. The language is purely figural, not

---

36. *Ibid.,* p. 479.
37. "Richesse ne fait pas riche, dit le Roman de la Rose," quoted in letter 10 of pt. 4, *ibid.,* p. 466 and n.
38. *Ibid.,* p. 1606, n. 2. I have consulted a copy of the Lenglet du Fresnoy edition which, at first sight, offers no variants that are immediately relevant to our question.
39. Guillaume de Lorris and Jean de Meun, *Le Roman de la rose,* Félix Lecoy, ed. (Paris: Champion, 1965), vol. 1, esp. 11. 499ff., 629ff., 1345ff.
40. *Ibid.,* ll. 1385ff.

based on perception, less still on an experienced dialectic between nature and consciousness. Julie's claim of domination and control over nature *("il n'y a rien là que je n'aie ordonné")* may well be considered as the fitting emblem for a language that submits the outside world entirely to its own purposes, contrary to what happens in the Meillerie episode, where the language fuses together the parallel movements of nature and of passion.

In the first part of the *Roman de la rose,* however, the use of figural language in no way conflicts with the exalted treatment of erotic themes; quite to the contrary, the erotic aspects of the allegory hardly need to be stressed. But in *La Nouvelle Héloïse* the emphasis on an ethic of renunciation conveys a moral climate that differs entirely from the moralizing sections of the medieval romance. Rousseau's theme of renunciation is far from being one-sided and is certainly not to be equated with a puritanical denial of the world of the senses. Nevertheless, it is in the use of allegorical diction rather than of the language of correspondences that the medieval and eighteenth-century sources converge. Recent studies of Defoe, such as G. A. Starr's *Defoe and Spiritual Autobiography*[41] and Paul Hunter's *The Reluctant Pilgrim,*[42] have reversed the trend to see in Defoe one of the inventors of a modern "realistic" idiom and have rediscovered the importance of the puritanical, religious element to which Rousseau responded. Paul Hunter has strongly emphasized the stylistic importance of this element, which led Defoe to make an allegorical rather than a metaphorical and descriptive use of nature. Thus Defoe's gardens, far from being realistic natural settings, are stylized emblems, quite similar in structure and detail to the gardens of the *Roman de la rose.* But they serve primarily a redemptive, ethical function. Defoe's garden, writes Paul Hunter, "is not . . . a prelapsarian paradise but rather an earthly paradise *in posse,* for Crusoe is postlapsarian man who has to toil to cultivate his land into full abundance."[43] The same stress on hardship, toil, and virtue is present in Julie's garden, relating the scene closely to the Protestant allegorical tradition of which the English version, culminating in Bunyan, reached Rousseau through a variety of sources, including

41. G. A. Starr, *Defoe and Spiritual Autobiography* (Princeton, N.J.: Princeton University Press, 1965).
42. J. Paul Hunter, *The Reluctant Pilgrim: Defoe's Emblematic Method and Quest in Robinson Crusoe* (Baltimore: Johns Hopkins University Press, 1966).
43. *Ibid.,* p. 172.

Defoe. The stylistic likeness of the sources supersedes all further differences between them; the tension arises not between the two distant literary sources, the one erotic, the other puritanical, but between the allegorical language of a scene such as Julie's Elysium and the symbolic language of passages such as the Meillerie episode. The moral contrast between these two worlds epitomizes the dramatic conflict of the novel. This conflict is ultimately resolved in the triumph of a controlled and lucid renunciation of the values associated with a cult of the moment, and this renunciation establishes the priority of an allegorical over a symbolic diction. The novel could not exist without the simultaneous presence of both metaphorical modes, nor could it reach its conclusion without the implied choice in favor of allegory over symbol.

Subsequent interpreters of *La Nouvelle Héloïse* have, in general, ignored the presence of allegorical elements in shaping the diction of the novel, and it is only recently that one begins to realize how false the image of Rousseau as a primitivist or as a naturalist actually is. These false interpretations, very revealing in their own right, resist correction with a remarkable tenacity, thereby indicating how deeply this correction conflicts with the widespread *"idées reçues"* on the nature and the origins of European romanticism.

For, if the dialectic between subject and object does not designate the main romantic experience, but only one passing moment in a dialectic, and a negative moment at that, since it represents a temptation that has to be overcome, then the entire historical and philosophical pattern changes a great deal. Similar allegorizing tendencies, though often in a very different form, are present not only in Rousseau but in all European literature between 1760 and 1800. Far from being a mannerism inherited from the exterior aspects of the baroque and the rococo, they appear at the most original and profound moments in the works, when an authentic voice becomes audible. The historians of English romanticism have been forced, by the nature of things, to mention allegory, although it is often a problem of secondary importance. Wimsatt has to encounter it in dealing with Blake; he quotes two brief poems by Blake, entitled "To Spring" and "To Summer," and comments: "Blake's starting point . . . is the opposite of Wordsworth's and Byron's, not the landscape but a spirit personified or allegorized. Nevertheless, this spirit as it approaches the 'western isle' takes on certain distinctly terrestrial hues. . . . These early romantic poets are examples of the Biblical, classical, and Renaissance tradition of allegory as it approaches the romantic condition of landscape naturalism—as Spring and Summer descend into the landscape and are fused with it."[44] Rather than such a continuous development from allegory to romantic naturalism, the example of Rousseau shows that we are dealing instead with the rediscovery of an allegorical tradition beyond the sensualistic analogism of the eighteenth century. This rediscovery, far from being spontaneous and easy, implies instead the discontinuity of a renunciation, even of a sacrifice. Taking for his starting point the descriptive poem of the eighteenth century, Abrams can speak with more historical precision. After having stressed the thematic resemblance between the romantic lyric and the metaphysical poem of the seventeenth century, he writes: "There is a very conspicuous and significant difference between the Romantic lyric and the seventeenth-century meditation on created nature. . . . [In the seventeenth century] the 'composition of place' was not a specific locality, nor did it need to be present to the eyes of the speaker, but was a typical scene or object, usually called up . . . before 'the eyes of the imagination' in order to set off and guide the thought by means of correspondences whose interpretation was firmly controlled by an inherited typology."[45] The distinction between seventeenth- and late eighteenth-century poetry is made in terms of the determining role played by the geographical *place* as establishing the link between the language of the poem and the empirical experience of the reader. However, in observing the development of even as geographically concrete a poet as Wordsworth, the significance of the locale can extend so far as to include a meaning that is no longer circumscribed by the literal horizon of a given place. The meaning of the site is often made problematic by a sequence of spatial ambiguities, to such an extent that one ends up no longer at a specific place but with a mere name whose geographical significance has become almost meaningless. Raising the question of the geographical locale of a given metaphorical object (in this case, a river), Wordsworth writes: "The spirit of the answer [as to the whereabouts of the river] through the word might be a certain stream, accompanied perhaps with an image gathered from a Map, or from a real object in nature—these might have been the latter, but the spirit of the answer must have been, as inevitably—a receptacle without bounds or dimensions;—nothing less than infinity."[46] Passages in Wordsworth such as the crossing of the Alps or the

---

44. Wimsatt, p. 113.
45. Abrams, p. 556.
46. W. Wordsworth, "Essay upon Epitaphs," in *The Poetical Works* (Oxford, 1949), 4:446.

ascent of Mount Snowden, or texts less sublime in character, such as the sequence of poems on the river Duddon, can no longer be classified with the locodescriptive poem of the eighteenth century. In the terminology proposed by Abrams, passages of this kind no longer depend on the choice of a specific locale, but are controlled by "a traditional and inherited typology," exactly as in the case of the poems from the sixteenth and seventeenth centuries—with this distinction, however, that the typology is no longer the same and that the poet, sometimes after long and difficult inner struggle, had to renounce the seductiveness and the poetic resources of a symbolical diction.

Whether it occurs in the form of an ethical conflict, as in *La Nouvelle Héloïse*, or as an allegorization of the geographical site, as in Wordsworth, the prevalence of allegory always corresponds to the unveiling of an authentically temporal destiny. This unveiling takes place in a subject that has sought refuge against the impact of time in a natural world to which, in truth, it bears no resemblance. The secularized thought of the pre-romantic period no longer allows a transcendance of the antimonies between the created world and the act of creation by means of a positive recourse to the notion of divine will; the failure of the attempt to conceive of a language that would be symbolical as well as allegorical, the suppression, in the allegory, of the analogical and anagogical levels, is one of the ways in which this impossibility becomes manifest. In the world of the symbol it would be possible for the image to coincide with the substance, since the substance and its representation do not differ in their being but only in their extension: they are part and whole of the same set of categories. Their relationship is one of simultaneity, which, in truth, is spatial in kind, and in which the intervention of time is merely a matter of contingency, whereas, in the world of allegory, time is the originary constitutive category. The relationship between the allegorical sign and its meaning *(signifié)* is not decreed by dogma; in the instances we have seen in Rousseau and in Wordsworth, this is not at all the case. We have, instead, a relationship between signs in which the reference to their respective meanings has become of secondary importance. But this relationship between signs necessarily contains a constitutive temporal element; it remains necessary, if there is to be allegory, that the allegorical sign refer to another sign that precedes it. The meaning constituted by the allegorical sign can then consist only in the *repetition* (in the Kierkegaardian sense of the term) of a previous sign with which it can never coincide, since it is of the essence of this previous sign to be pure anteriority. The secularized allegory of the early romantics thus necessarily contains the negative moment which in Rousseau is that of renunciation, in Wordsworth that of the loss of self in death or in error.

Whereas the symbol postulates the possibility of an identity or identification, allegory designates primarily a distance in relation to its own origin, and, renouncing the nostalgia and the desire to coincide, it establishes its language in the void of this temporal difference. In so doing, it prevents the self from an illusory identification with the non-self, which is now fully, though painfully, recognized as a non-self. It is this painful knowledge that we perceive at the moments when early romantic literature finds its true voice. It is ironically revealing that this voice is so rarely recognized for what it really is and that the literary movement in which it appears has repeatedly been called a primitive naturalism or a mystified solipsism. The authors with whom we are dealing had often gone out of their way to designate their theological and philosophical sources: too little attention has been paid to the complex and controlled set of literary allusions which, in *La Nouvelle Héloïse,* established the link between Rousseau and his Augustinian sources, mostly by way of Petrarch.

We are led, in conclusion, to a historical scheme that differs entirely from the customary picture. The dialectical relationship between subject and object is no longer the central statement of romantic thought, but this dialectic is now located entirely in the temporal relationships that exist within a system of allegorical signs. It becomes a conflict between a conception of the self seen in its authentically temporal predicament and a defensive strategy that tries to hide from this negative self-knowledge. On the level of language the asserted superiority of the symbol over allegory, so frequent during the nineteenth century, is one of the forms taken by this tenacious self-mystification. Wide areas of European literature of the nineteenth and twentieth centuries appear as regressive with regards to the truths that come to light in the last quarter of the eighteenth century. For the lucidity of the pre-romantic writers does not persist. It does not take long for a symbolic conception of metaphorical language to establish itself everywhere, despite the ambiguities that persist in aesthetic theory and poetic practice. But this symbolical style will never be allowed to exist in serenity; since it is a veil thrown over a light one no longer wishes to perceive, it will never be able to gain an entirely good poetic conscience. . . .

HAYDEN WHITE

It seems that theory is obliged to make Kant's point again and again, or Tennyson's more euphonious version of it: ". . . we cannot know,/ For knowledge is of things we see." De Man reminds us that we are exiled in language, in phenomena, that no mediate thing can know the immediate immediately. Hayden White makes his disturbing point—though he himself is undisturbed by it—in the field of historiography. Put simply, the problem is this: as a historian, one has data and one has coherence of data. Where does the coherence of the data come from? Does it come from the data or from the perceptual apparatus of the historian? What if, when the historian finds the truth, he merely spins out a narrative—a story which he was programmed, genetically or socially, to tell —regardless of the nature of the data? We humans are submerged, as Nietzsche says in "On Truth and Lie," in illusions and dream images; our eyes glide on the surface of things; our feelings lead nowhere to the truth; we play a "game of blindman's bluff on the backs of things."* Consciousness is "tropic"; it interprets according to what it understands. Understanding makes the unfamiliar familiar. For example, when Plato wants to prove the existence of the soul after death in the *Phaedo,* he speaks of sleeping and waking, assuming a reciprocity in nature that may in fact not hold at all. When the student chooses as a metaphor for marriage the process of driving an automobile, she commits herself to certain ideological assumptions of authority and enforced passivity, especially when she predicts a crackup when more than one pair of hands is on the wheel.

The patterns of organization discovered everywhere by White, including in authors who reject methodology and emphasize concrete historical reality, correspond to the "master tropes" of Kenneth Burke: metaphor, metonymy, synecdoche, and irony. White sees this pattern in Piaget's account of a child's cognitive development. First, the child lacks any sense of distinction between self and other. The world of objects is an extension of the child's own body. This stage is called "metaphoric" by White and is the same as the "symbolic" in de Man, who considers the stage "regressive" in an adult, whether poet or philosopher. White refuses to privilege as primitive or sophisticated one stage over another. No metaphor is ever completely erroneous, he says. In fact, he considers reversion to the metaphoric stage desirable for shattering the "Egyptian rigidity" of later stages. He identifies this metaphoric stage with poetry and claims it is "every bit as authoritative as logic itself." In the second stage, Piaget's child understands contiguity, the body becoming one

The Portable Nietzsche, ed. and trans. by Walter Kaufmann (New York: Viking Press, 1954) 43.

object adjacent to others. The third stage is marked by classification projects. Objects are parts of wholes, elements of a totality. This is the stage of preadolescent logic. The fourth stage allows reflection on reflection; thought is no longer dependent upon the "physical manipulability" of objects. These stages are typical both of Freud's rhetoric of the unconscious and E. P. Thompson's growth to consciousness of the English working class.

Whether this tropic pattern is subjectively imposed or empirically discovered by Piaget, Freud, Thompson, Foucault, or White himself seems not to matter.† The crucial point is its universality. These tropes are the ways we see things. Yet to cut himself loose from Structuralism, White closes with a gesture which resurrects ethics from the exercise of will. The unforgivable thing is not to believe in will, for without it, the moral implications of one's favored mode of rationality are repressed. One should be conscious of the model one uses to organize entities of consciousness. Whether this unrelenting self-awareness does not commit one, after all, to de Man's allegorical mode, White does not admit here, though he can hardly be unconscious of the fact.

Tropology, Discourse, and the Modes of Human Consciousness
1978

hen we seek to make sense of such problematical topics as human nature, culture, society, and history, we never say precisely what we wish to say or mean precisely what we say. Our discourse always tends to slip away from our data towards the structures of consciousness with which we are trying to grasp them; or, what amounts to the same thing, the data always resist the coherency of the

†See White's account of Foucault in *Structuralism and Since,* ed. John Sturrock (Oxford: Oxford University Press, 1979) 81–115.

image which we are trying to fashion of them.[1] Moreover, in topics such as these, there are always legitimate grounds for differences of opinion as to *what* they are, *how* they should be spoken about, and the *kinds* of knowledge we can have of them.

All genuine discourse takes account of these differences of opinion in the suggestion of doubt as to its own authority which it systematically displays on its very surface. This is especially the case when it is a matter of trying to *mark out* what appears to be a new area of human experience for preliminary analysis, *define* its contours, *identify* the elements in its field, and *discern* the kinds of relationships that obtain among them. It is here that discourse itself must establish the adequacy of the language used in analyzing the field to the objects that appear to occupy it. And discourse effects this adequation by a *pre*figurative move that is more tropical than logical.

The essays in this collection deal one way or another with the tropical element in all discourse, whether of the realistic or the more imaginative kind. This element is, I believe, inexpungeable from discourse in the human sciences, however realistic they may aspire to be. Tropic is the shadow from which all realistic discourse tries to flee. This flight, however, is futile; for tropics is the process by which all discourse *constitutes* the objects which it pretends only to describe realistically and to analyze objectively. How tropes function in the discourses of the human sciences is the subject of these essays, and that is why I have entitled them as I have done.

The word *tropic* derives from *tropikos, tropos,* which in Classical Greek meant "turn" and in Koiné "way" or "manner." It comes into modern Indo-European languages by way of *tropus,* which in Classical Latin meant "metaphor" or "figure of speech" and in Late Latin, especially as applied to music theory, "mood" or "measure." All of these meanings, sedimented in the early English word *trope,* capture the force of the concept that modern English intends by the word *style,* a concept that is especially apt for the consideration of that form of verbal composition which, in order to distinguish it from logical

1. The disparity between speech, *lexis,* or mode of utterance, on the one side, and meaning, on the other, is of course a fundamental tenet of modern Structuralist and post-Structuralist theories of the text, arising from the notion of the arbitrariness of the union of signifier and signified in the sign, as postulated by Saussure. The literature is immense, but see Frederic Jameson, *The Prison-House of Language: A Critical Account of Structuralism and Russian Formalism* (Princeton, 1972), chap. 1; Jonathan Culler, *Structuralist Poetics: Structuralism, Linguistics, and the Study of Literature* (Ithaca, 1975), pt. 1; and Terence Hawkes, *Structuralism and Semiotics* (Berkeley and Los Angeles, 1977), chap. 2.

demonstration on the one side and from pure fiction on the other, we call by the name *discourse*.

For rhetoricians, grammarians, and language theorists, tropes are deviations from literal, conventional, or "proper" language use, swerves in locution sanctioned neither by custom nor logic.[2] Tropes generate figures of speech or thought by their variation from what is "normally" expected, and by the associations they establish between concepts normally felt not to be related or to be related in ways different from that suggested in the trope used. If, as Harold Bloom has suggested,[3] a trope can be seen as the linguistic equivalent of a psychological mechanism of defense (a defense against literal meaning in discourse, in the way that repression, regression, projection, and so forth are defenses against the apprehension of death in the psyche), it is always not only a deviation *from* one possible, proper meaning, but also a deviation *towards* another meaning, conception, or ideal of what is right and proper *and true* "in reality." Thus considered, troping is both a movement *from* one notion of the way things are related *to* another notion, and a connection between things so that they can be expressed in a language that takes account of the possibility of their being expressed otherwise. Discourse is the genre in which the effort to earn this right of expression, with full credit to the possibility that things might be expressed otherwise, is preemininent. And troping is the soul of discourse, therefore, the mechanism without which discourse cannot do its work or achieve its end. This is why we can agree with Bloom's contention that "all interpretation depends upon the antithetical relation between meanings, and not on the supposed relation between a text and its meaning."[4]

2. The literature on tropes is as great as, if not greater than, that on the theory of the sign—and growing daily at a frantic pace, without as yet, however, giving any sign of a general consensus as to their classification. For general surveys of the state of the question, see "Recherches rhétoriques," *Communications* (publication of the École pratique des hautes études—Centre d'études des communications de masses) 16 (1970); "Frontières de la rhétorique," *Littérature,* 18 (May 1975); "Rhétorique et herméneutique," *Poétique* 23 (1975). Systematic studies of tropes, informed by modern linguistic theories are Heinrich Lausberg, *Elemente der literarischen Rhetorik* (Munich, 1967); J. DuBois et al., *Rhétorique générale* (Paris, 1970); and Chaim Perelman and L. Olbrechts-Tyteca, *The New Rhetoric: A Treatise on Argumentation,* trans. John Wilkinson and Purcell Weaver (Notre Dame and London, 1969). One should also mention the works of Kenneth Burke, Gérard Genette, Roland Barthes, Umberto Eco, and Tzvetan Todorov.

3. Harold Bloom, *A Map of Misreading* (New York, 1975), p. 91.

4. Ibid., p. 76.

To be sure, Bloom is concerned with poetic texts, and especially with modern (Romantic and post-Romantic) lyric poetry, so that his notion of interpretation as the explication of the "antithetical relation between meanings" within a single text is less shocking than any similar claim made for discursive prose texts would be. And yet we are faced with the ineluctable fact that even in the most chaste discursive prose, texts intended to represent "things as they are" without rhetorical adornment or poetic imagery, there is always a failure of intention. Every mimetic text can be shown to have left something out of the description of its object or to have put something into it that is inessential to what *some* reader, with more or less authority, will regard as an adequate description. On analysis, every mimesis can be shown to be distorted and can serve, therefore, as an occasion for yet another description of the same phenomenon, one claiming to be more realistic, more "faithful to the facts."[5]

So too, any prose description of any phenomenon can be shown on analysis to contain at least one move or transition in the sequence of descriptive utterances that violates a canon of logical consistency. How could it be otherwise, when even the model of the syllogism itself displays clear evidence of troping? The move from the major premise (All men are mortal) to the *choice* of the datum to serve as the minor (Socrates is a man) is itself a tropological move, a "swerve" from the universal to the particular which logic cannot preside over, since it is logic itself that is being served by this move.[6] Every *applied* syllogism contains an enthymemic element, this element consisting of nothing but the *decision* to move from the plane of universal propositions (themselves extended synecdoches) to that of singular existential statements (these being extended metonymies). And if this is true even of the classical syllogism, how much more true must it be of those pseudosyllogisms and chains of pseudosyllogisms which make up mimetic-analytic prose discourse, or the sort found in history, philosophy, literary criticism, and the human sciences in general?

The conventional technique for assessing the validity of prose discourses—such as, let us say, Machiavelli's or Locke's political

5. Whence the possibility of a work like Erich Auerbach's *Mimesis: The Representation of Reality in Western Literature,* trans. Willard Trask (New York, 1957), which charts changes in the conception of the "real" and in the styles deemed most appropriate for its representation, from Homer to Joyce.
6. Here I follow G. W. F. Hegel, *Logic,* trans. William Wallace (Oxford, 1975), §§ 181–90, pp. 244–54.

tracts, Rousseau's essay on inequality, Ranke's histories, or Freud's ethnological speculations—is to check them, first, for their fidelity to the facts of the subject being discussed and, then, for their adherence to the criteria of logical consistency as represented by the classical syllogism. This critical technique manifestly flies in the face of the practice of discourse, if not some theory of it, because the discourse is intended to *constitute* the ground whereon to decide *what shall count as a fact* in the matters under consideration and to determine *what mode of comprehension* is best suited to the understanding of the facts thus constituted. The etymology of the word *discourse,* derived from Latin *discurrere,* suggests a movement "back and forth" or a "running to and fro." This movement, discursive practice shows us, may be as much prelogical or antilogical as it is dialectical. As antilogical, its aim would be to deconstruct a conceptualization of a given area of experience which has become hardened into a hypostasis that blocks fresh perception or denies, in the interest of formalization, what our will or emotions tell us ought not be the case in a given department of life. As prelogical, its aim is to mark out an area of experience for subsequent analysis by a thought guided by logic.

A discourse moves "to and fro" between received encodations of experience and the clutter of phenomena which refuses incorporation into conventionalized notions of "reality," "truth," or "possibility." It also moves "back and forth" (like a shuttle?)[7] between alternative ways of encoding this reality, some of which may be provided by the traditions of discourse prevailing in a given domain of inquiry and others of which may be idiolects of the author, the authority of which he is seeking to establish. Discourse, in a word, is quintessentially a *mediative* enterprise. As such, it is both interpretive and preinterpretive; it is always as much *about* the nature of interpretation itself as it is *about* the subject matter which is the manifest occasion of its own elaboration.

This twofold nature of discourse is sometimes referred to as dialectical. But apart from being fraught with ideological associations of a specific sort, the term *dialectical* too often suggests a transcendental subject or narrative ego which stands above the contending interpretations of reality and arbitrates between them. Let me offer another term to suggest how I conceive the dynamic movement of a discourse: *diatactical.* This notion has the merit of suggesting a

7. See Geoffrey Hartman, "The Voice of the Shuttle: Language from the Point of View of Literature," in *Beyond Formalism* (New York and London, 1970), pp. 337–55.

somewhat different kind of relationship between the discourse, its putative subject matter, and contending interpretations of the latter. It does not suggest that discourses about reality can be classified as hypotactical (conceptually overdetermined), on the one side, and paratactical (conceptually underdetermined), on the other, with the discourse itself occupying the middle ground (of properly syntactical thought) that everyone is seeking. On the contrary, discourse, if it is genuine discourse—that is to say, as *self*-critical as it is critical of others—will radically challenge the notion of the syntactical middle ground itself. It throws all "tactical" rules into doubt, including those originally governing its own formation. Precisely because it is aporetic, or ironic, with respect to its own adequacy, discourse cannot be governed by logic alone.[8] Because it is always slipping the grasp of logic, constantly asking if logic is adequate to capture the essence of its subject matter, discourse always tends toward metadiscursive reflexiveness. This is why every discourse is always as much about discourse itself as it is about the objects that make up its subject matter.

Considered as a genre, then, discourse must be analyzed on three levels: that of the description (mimesis) of the "data" found in the field of inquiry being invested or marked out for analysis; that of the argument or narrative (diegesis), running alongside of or interspersed with the descriptive materials;[9] and that on which the combination of these previous two levels is effected (diataxis). The rules which crystallize on this last, or diatactical, level of discourse determine possible objects of discourse, the ways in which description and argument are to be combined, the phases through which the discourse must pass in the process of earning its right of closure, and the modality of the metalogic used to link up the conclusion of the discourse with its inaugurating gestures. As thus envisaged, a discourse is itself a kind of model of the processes of consciousness by which a given area of experience, originally apprehended as simply a field of phenomena demanding understanding, is assimilated by analogy to those areas of experience felt to be *already* understood as to *their* essential natures.

Understanding is a process of rendering the unfamiliar, or the

---

8. Umberto Eco, *A Theory of Semiotics* (Bloomington and London, 1976), pp. 276–86. See also Paul de Man, *Blindness and Insight: Essays in the Rhetoric of Contemporary Criticism* (New York, 1971), pp. 102–41.

9. Gérard Genette, "Boundaries of Narrative," *New Literary History* 8, no. 1 (Autumn 1976): 1–13.

"uncanny" in Freud's sense of that term,[10] familiar; of removing it from the domain of things felt to be "exotic" and unclassified into one or another domain of experience encoded adequately enough to be felt to be humanly useful, nonthreatening, or simply known by association. This process of understanding can only be tropological in nature, for what is involved in the rendering of the unfamiliar into the familiar is a troping that is generally figurative. It follows, I think, that this process of understanding proceeds by the exploitation of the principal modalities of figuration, identified in post-Renaissance rhetorical theory as the "master tropes" (Kenneth Burke's phrase) of metaphor, metonymy, synecdoche, and irony.[11] Moreover, there appears to be operative in this process an archetypal pattern for tropologically construing fields of experience requiring understanding which follows the sequence of modes indicated by the list of master tropes as given.

The archetypal plot of discursive formations appears to require that the narrative "I" of the discourse move from an original metaphorical characterization of a domain of experience, through metonymic deconstructions of its elements, to synecdochic representations of the relations between its superficial attributes and its presumed essence, to, finally, a representation of whatever contrasts or oppositions can legitimately be discerned in the totalities identified in the third phase of discursive representation. Vico suggested such a pattern of moves in his analysis of the "Poetic Logic" which underlay consciousness's efforts to "make" a world adequate to the satisfaction of the felt needs of human beings, in prerational cognitive processes.[12] And he further suggested that this diataxis of discourse not only mirrored the processes of consciousness but in fact underlay and informed all efforts of human beings to endow their world with meaning. Hegel appears to have held the same view, if I read him correctly, and Marx certainly did, as my analysis of his discourse on "The Forms of Value" in the opening book of *Capital* demonstrates.[13]

Considerations such as these suggest that discourse itself, as a

10. Sigmund Freud, "The Uncanny," in *On Creativity and the Unconscious* (New York, 1958), pp. 122–61.
11. See Kenneth Burke, *A Grammar of Motives* (Berkeley and Los Angeles, 1969), app. D, pp. 503–17.
12. Giambattista Vico, *The New Science*, trans. Thomas Goddard Bergin and Max Harold Fisch (Ithaca, 1968), §§ 400ff., pp. 127ff.
13. Hayden White, *Metahistory: The Historical Imagination in Nineteenth-Century Europe* (Baltimore, 1973), pp. 287ff.

product of consciousness's efforts to come to terms with problematical domains of experience, serves as a model of the metalogical
operations by which consciousness, in general cultural praxis, effects
such comings to terms with its milieux, social or natural as the case
may be. The move from a metaphorical apprehension of a "strange"
and "threatening" reality to a metonymic dispersion of its elements
into the contiguities of the series is not logical. There is no rule to tell
us when our original, metaphorical constitution of a domain of
experience as a possible object of inquiry is complete and when we
should proceed to a consideration of the elements which, construed
in their particularity, simply as parts of an as yet unidentified whole,
occupy the domain in question. This shift in modality of construal, or
as I have called it in *Metahistory,* modality of *pre*figuration, is tropical
in nature.[14] Nor are the other shifts in descriptive modes logically
determined (unless, as I suggested above, logic itself is merely a
formalization of tropical strategies).[15]

Once I have dispersed the elements of a given domain across a
time series or spatial field, I can either remain satisfied with what
appears to be a final analytical act, or I can proceed to "integrate"
these elements, by assigning them to different orders, classes, genera,
species, and so on—which is to say, hypotactically order them such
that their status either as essences or merely as attributes of these
essences can be established. This having been done, I can then either
remain content with the discernment of such patterns of integration,
in the way that the idealist in philosophy and the organicist in natural
science will do; or I can "turn" once more, to a consideration of the
extent to which this taxonomic operation fails to take account of
certain features of the elements thus classified and, an even more
sophisticated move, try to determine the extent to which my own
taxonomic system is as much a product of my own need to organize
reality in this way rather than in some other as it is of the objective
reality of the elements previously identified.

This fourth move, from a synecdochic characterization of the field
under scrutiny to ironic reflection on the inadequacy of the characterization with respect to the elements which resist inclusion in the
hypotactically ordered totality, or to that self-reflexivity on the constructivist nature of the ordering principle itself, is not logically

14. Ibid., pp. 30ff.
15. Tzvetan Todorov, "On Linguistic Symbolism," *New Literary History* 6, no. 1
    (Autumn 1974): 111–34.

determined either. Such shifts seem to correspond to those "gestalt switches," or "restructurations" of the perceptual field which Piaget has identified in the development of the child's cognitive powers as it moves from its "sensorimotor" through its "representational" and its "operational" phases, to the attainment of "rational" understanding of the nature of classification in general. For Piaget's formulation, it is not logic, but a combination of ontogenetic capabilities, on the one side, and the operations of capacities of assimilation of and accommodation to the external world, on the other, which effects these (tropological) restructurations.[16] For tropological these restructurations certainly are, both in the spontaneity of their successive onsets and the modalities of relationship between the child and its "reality" which the modes of cognition identified presuppose even in Piaget's characterization of them.

In fact, Piaget's studies of the cognitive development of the child provide us with some insight into the relationship between a tropical mode of prefiguring experience, on the one side, and the kind of cognitive control which each mode makes possible, on the other. If his experimentally derived concepts of the phases through which the child passes in its cognitive development are valid, then the ontogenetic basis of figurative consciousness is considerably illuminated. Vico considered "poetic logic"to be the modes of cognition not only of poets, but of children and primitive peoples as well, as of course did Rousseau, Hegel, and Nietzsche.[17] But neither Vico nor the other thinkers mentioned set these prefigurative modes of cognition over against rational modes by way of opposition; on the contrary, they all consider tropes and figures the foundation on which rational knowledge of the world was erected, so much so that for Vico and Hegel especially, rational or scientific knowledge was little more than the truth yielded by reflection in the prefigurative modes raised to the level of abstract concepts and submitted to criticism for logical consistency, coherency, and so on. Not even Rousseau and Nietzsche —who set the feelings and the will, respectively, over against the reason by way of antitheses—were interested in forcing a choice

16. Jean Piaget, *The Child and Reality: Problems of Genetic Psychology,* trans. Arnold Rosin (New York, 1973), p. 18. Hereafter cited in the text by page number.
17. Vico, *The New Science,* pp. 127ff.; J. J. Rousseau, "Essay on the Origin of Languages," in *On the Origin of Language: Two Essays by Jean-Jacques Rousseau and Johann Gottfried Herder,* trans. John H. Moran and Alexander Gode (New York, 1966), pp. 11–13; and Friedrich Nietzsche, *Genealogy of Morals,* trans. Francis Golffing (New York, 1956), pp. 177–84.

between the poetic modes of cognition and the rational or scientific ones. On the contrary, they were interested in their integration within a notion of the total human capacity to make sense of the world, and to make *a sense* of it, moreover, that would not fault the powers of either *poiesis* or *noesis* unduly.

Although he would not appreciate being put in this line of thinking, Jean Piaget demonstrates the same kind of continuity between an early naturally "metaphoric" phase in the child's mode of relating to the world and the kind of "ironic" manipulation of alternative modes of classifying and manipulating phenomena attained to by the "rational" adult. At the earliest, sensorimotor phase, he tells us, the infant lives in an apprehension of a world of objects "all centered on the body proper" but lacking any "coordination with each other" (p. 15). But if they lack coordination with each other, they are existentially coordinated in infantile consciousness as homogenous extensions of the child's own body. We cannot, of course, speak of the infant's *thinking* metaphorically, in the mode of similitude; but we are more than justified in speaking of the child's living of the experience of similitude, one in which the distinction between self and other, container and contained, is utterly lacking. "Thus," Piaget says of this sensorimotor stage, lasting for the first year and a half of the average child's life, "there are egocentric spaces, we might say, not coordinated, and not including the body itself as an element in a container" (ibid.). But if we do not wish to call this "existence in the mode of metaphor," or even of similitude (since the latter term, in order to be meaningful, would have to presuppose the apprehension of difference), the break or shift to the second stage, by its occurrence and the mode of cognition which it makes possible, permits us to liken the transition effected to that of a "troping" from metaphorical to metonymic consciousness.

Piaget calls this shift a veritable "Copernican Revolution," in which there crystallizes

> a notion of a general space which encompasses all of these individual varieties of [egocentric] spaces, including all objects which have become solid and permanent, *with the body itself as an object among others,* [and] the *displacements* coordinated and capable of being deduced and anticipated in relation to the displacements proper. (Pp. 15–16)

In other words, the child has undergone a "turn" in its development, from a condition in which it (all unconsciously, we must suppose) makes no distinction between itself and other objects or among objects except insofar as they relate to itself. At eighteen months or thereabouts, therefore, we see a "total decentration in relation to the original egocentric space." This decentration (or displacement) is a necessary condition for what Piaget calls "the symbolical function," the most important aspect of which is speech. Only because of the possibility of apprehending relationships of contiguity is this process of symbolization, and *a fortiori*, of thought itself, rendered possible. Prior to the "Copernican Revolution," there is no apprehension of contiguous relationships; there is only the timeless, spaceless experience of the Same. With the onset of a consciousness of contiguity —what we would call metonymic capability—a radical tranformation is effected without which the "group of displacements" necessary for symbolization, speech, and thought would be impossible (p. 16).

Then again, at about the age of seven, Piaget argues, another "fundamental turning point is noted in the child's development. He becomes capable of a certain logic; he becomes capable of coordinating operations in the sense of reversibility, in the sense of the total system." This is the stage of what Piaget calls preadolescent logic, which "is not based on verbal statements but only on the objects themselves" (p. 21). This will be, he says, a logic of classifications,

> because objects can be collected all together or in classifications; or else it will be a logic of relations because objects can be materially counted by manipulating them. This will thus be a logic of classifications, relations, and numbers, and not yet a logic of propositions. . . . It is a logic in the sense that the operations are coordinated, grouped in whole systems which have their laws in terms of *totalities*. And we must very strongly insist on the necessity of these *whole structures* for the development of thought. (Pp. 20–21).

What Piaget has discovered, if he is right, is the genetic basis of the trope of synecdoche, that figure of rhetoric or poetic which constitutes objects as parts of wholes or gathers entities together as elements of a totality sharing the same essential natures. This operation in the child of age seven to twelve is still prelogical in a strict sense, inasmuch as it depends upon the physical manipulability of the objects being classified; it is not an operation which normally can be carried out in thought alone.

With the onset of adolescence, however, this latter operation becomes possible:

The child not only becomes capable of reasoning and deduct-
ing on manipulable objects, like sticks to arrange, numbers of
objects to collect, etc., but he also becomes capable of logic and
deductive reasoning on theories and propositions . . . a whole
new set of specific operations are superimposed on the preceding ones and this can be called the logic of propositions. (P. 24)

Note, however, what is presupposed as the bases for the enactment of
these new operations. There is, first of all, the *dissociation* of thought
from its possible objects, a capacity to reflect on reflection itself, what
Collingwood called "second order consciousness," or "thought
about thought."[18] Piaget calls the product of this dissociation the
"combinatory" *(combinatoire)*: "Until now everything was done
gradually by a series of interlockings; whereas the combinatory
connects any element with any other. Here then is a new characteristic based on a kind of *classification of all the classifications* or
seriation of all the seriations" (p. 24). In addition, it produces a
mental system that can stand over against the random order or
apprehended disorder of experience and serve as a check on both
perception and mental operations of the earlier kinds, which, by their
nature, remain inadequate to the praxis of the social and material
worlds: "The logic of propositions will suppose, moreover, the
combination in a unique system of the different groupings which
until now were based either on reciprocity or on inversion, on the
different forms of reversibility" (pp. 24–25). The crystallization of
these capacities in the young adult child gives him the power of a
thought that is not only conscious but also *self*-conscious, not only
critical of the *operations* of the earlier stages of consciousness
(metaphorical, metonymic, and synecdochic) but critical also of the
structures of those operations. We may say then that, with the onset of
adult consciousness, the child becomes not only capable of logic, as
Piaget stresses, but also of irony—the capacity not only to say things
about the world in a particular way but also to say things about it in
alternative ways—and of reflecting on this capacity of thought (or
language; it does not matter, since Piaget, at this stage, conflates the
two) to say one thing and mean another or to mean one thing and say
it in a host of alternative, even mutually exclusive or illogical ways.

If Piaget regards logical thought as the highest kind of thought,

---

18. R. G. Collingwood, *The Idea of History* (New York, 1956), pp. 1–3; see also Louis
   O. Mink, *Mind, History, and Dialectic: The Philosophy of R. G. Collingwood*
   (Bloomington and London, 1969), pp. 82–92.

making it the end stage toward which the whole cognitive development of the individual tends, it would follow that earlier modes of
cognition, representing the earlier stages, would constitute inferior
forms of thought. But Piaget does not suggest this line of argument.
On the contrary, he stresses that in the process of development, a
given mode of cognition is not so much obliterated as preserved,
transcended, and assimilated to the mode that succeeds it in the
ontogenetic process. It would be possible to imagine, then, that in
those situations in which we might wish to break the hold of a given
chain of logical reasoning, in order to resist the implications to be
derived by deduction from it or to reconsider the adequacy of the
major or minor premises of a given hypothetico-deductive exercise,
we might consider reversion (or regression?) to a more "primitive"
mode of cognition as represented by the earlier, prelogical stages in
the process of development. Such a move would represent a
metalogical "turn" against logic itself in the interest of resituating
consciousness with respect to its environment, of redefining the
distinction between self and environment or of reconceptualizing the
relation between self and other in specifically nonlogical, more nearly
imaginative ways.

To be sure, an unconscious or unintended lapse into a prelogical
mode of comprehending reality would merely be an error or, more
correctly, a regression, similar to those lapses philosophers condemn
when they find a metaphor being taken literally. But such lapses,
when undertaken in the interest of bringing logical thinking itself
under criticism and questioning either its presuppositions, its structure, or its adequacy to an existentially satisfying relationship to
reality, would be poetry, what Hegel defined as the conscious use of
metaphor to release us from the tyranny of conceptual overdeterminations and what Nietzsche personified as the Dionysiac breaking of
the forms of individuation which an unopposed Apollonian consciousness would harden into "Egyptian rigidity."[19] Logic cannot
preside over this rupture with itself, for it has no ground on which to
arbitrate between the claims of contending logical systems, much less
between the kinds of knowledge that we derive from logical operations, on the one side, and, dislogical or analogical operations on the
other. Metaphorical consciousness may be a primitive form of know-

19. G. W. F. Hegel, *The Philosophy of Fine Art*, trans. F. P. B. Osmaston (London,
1920), 4:243–4; Friedrich Nietzsche, *The Birth of Tragedy*, trans. Francis Golffing
(New York, 1956), pp. 22, 51, 65.

ing in the ontogenesis of human consciousness in its passage from infancy to maturity, but insofar as it is the fundamental mode of poetic apprehension in general, it is a mode of situating language with respect to the world every bit as authoritative as logic itself.

Above all, what we might mean by discourse is clarified by the opposition of metaphoric to ironic consciousness suggested by Piaget's theory of the ontogenetic pattern of cognitive development in the child. Insofar as the four phases in the development of the child are concerned, the kind of "logic" which appears in the fourth phase is as primitive, when judged against the standards of formal logicians, as the "metaphorical" consciousness of the infant seems to be when judged against the sophisticated manipulation of metaphors characteristic of the mature poet. Yet, the one phase is neither more "human" nor more "natural" than the other. And discourse itself, the verbal operation by which the questing consciousness situates its own efforts to bring a problematical domain of experience under cognitive control, can be defined as a movement through *all* of the structures of relating self to other which remain implicit as different ways of knowing in the fully matured consciousness.

What Piaget fails to note, but what the linguistic-rhetorical and poetic theory of tropes shows, are the relations of affinity and opposition which exist among the four modes of cognition identified as successive stages in this theory of the child's development. Piaget sees a sequence of stages, with each stage crystallizing, superimposing itself on, and succeeding that preceeding it. At the same time, he insists on the radical *break* between the first, or egocentric, phase and the second, decentrated phase. "In other words, at eighteen months, it is no exaggeration to speak of a Copernican revolution (in the Kantian sense of the term). Here there is a complete return, a total decentration in relation to the original egocentric space" (p. 16). During the former phase, of course, the child acquires language, the capacity to symbolize; but this acquisition is prepared for by the operations of the sensorimotor phase, such that what the child acquires in the succeeding symbolizing phase is already present in the praxis of the originary stage.

Piaget is puzzled by the fact that logical operations do not appear simultaneously with the appearance of speech and the symbolical function. His reflection on this puzzle turns upon the concept of "interiorization." "Why," he asks, "must we wait eight years to acquire the invariant of substance and more so for the other notions instead of their appearing the moment there is a symbolical function, that is, the possibility of thought and not simply material action?" And his answer is: "For the basic reason that the actions that have allowed for certain results on the ground of material effectivity cannot be *interiorized* any further in an immediate manner, and that it is a matter of *relearning on the level of thought* what *has already been learned on the level of action.*" And he goes on to conclude: "Actually, this interiorization is a new structuration; it is not simply a translation but a *restructuration* with a lag which takes a considerable time" (pp. 17–18).

What we have here, I would suggest, is Piaget's rediscovery of a principle of cognitive creativity analogous to, if not originating in the traditional, post-Renaissance theory of tropes. To be sure, Piaget is concerned with phases of a developmental process that stretches along a synchronic spectrum (and is elaborated along a diachronic series) extending from a condition that can hardly be called consciousness at all to one of high self-consciousness. This process he explains in terms of the precognitive operations by which the organism achieves assimilation of external objects to itself or accommodation to them where assimilation fails. These are, in the originary phases at least, preeminently practical operations which, as it were, either activate conceptual schemata implicitly present in the child's consciousness at birth or create them through an adequation of the organism to the conditions of existence in the world. In any event, such schemata—templates, so to speak, of the modes of construing relationships—are not thought to have their origin in speech, since the first modality precedes the appearance of speech in the child; nor in some natural logic possessed by the child, since logical thought does not appear along with the advent of speech. But what Piaget's theories do suggest is that the tropes of figuration, metaphor, metonymy, synecdoche, and irony, which are used in conscious processes of poiesis and discourse formation, are grounded, in some way, in the psychogenetic endowment of the child, the bases of which appear sequentially in the fourfold phasal development which Piaget calls sensorimotor, representational, operational, and logical.

Of course, the thought arises that Piaget has not *found* these phases at all, but has *imposed* them upon his experimentally derived data (or framed the experiments in such a way as to permit their characterization in precisely this way) by some kind of projection of his own sense of the nature of the tropes of figuration. If the evolution of human cognitive capacity actually prefigures the archetypal form of discourse itself, or if discourse is a recapitulation of the process of cognitive development similar to the way that the child comes to a comprehension not only of his "reality" but of the relation between reality and his consciousness, then it hardly matters whether Piaget imposed these forms on the data or not. His genius would have been revealed in the ways that he applied an archetype of discourse, the process by which we all make sense of reality and, in the best instances, take account of our efforts to make such sense, to the evolutionary process of cognitive growth in the child.

I have shown in *Metahistory,* and in a number of the essays contained in this book,[20] how specific analysts of processes of consciousness seem to project the fourfold pattern of tropes onto them, in order to emplot them, and to chart the growth from what might be called naive (or metaphorical) apprehensions of reality to self-reflective (ironic) comprehensions of it. This pattern of emplotment is analyzed, I think, as the "logic" of *poiesis* by Vico and Nietzsche and as the logic of *noesis* by Hegel and Marx. If Piaget has provided an ontogenetic base for this pattern, he adds another, more positivistic confirmation of its archetypal nature.

The ubiquity of this pattern of tropological prefiguration, especially as used as the key to an understanding of the Western discourse about consciousness, inevitably raises the question of its status as a psychological phenomenon. If it appeared universally as an analytical or representational model for discourse, we might seek to credit it as a genuine "law" of discourse. But, of course, I do not claim for it the status of a law of discourse, even of the discourse about consciousness (since there are plenty of discourses in which the pattern does not fully appear in the form suggested), but only the status of a model which recurs persistently in modern discourses about human consciousness. I claim for it only the force of a convention in the discourse about consciousness and, secondarily, the discourse about discourse itself, in the modern Western cultural tradition. And, moreover, the force of a convention that has for the most part not been recognized as such by the various reinventors of it within the tradition of the discourse on consciousness since the early nineteenth century. Piaget is only the latest in a long line of researchers, empirical *and* idealistic, who have rediscovered or reinvented the fourfold schema of tropes as a model of the modes of mental association characteristic of human consciousness whether considered as a structure or a process. Freud too may be listed among these

20. Chapters 1, 5, 8, 9, 11, and 12.

reinventors or rediscoverers of the tropological structure of consciousness, as the famous Chapter VI, "The Dreamwork," in *The Interpretation of Dreams,* amply shows. In this work, Freud provides the basis for belief in the operation of tropological schemata of figuration on the level of the Unconscious; and his work may be taken as complementary to that of Piaget, whose primary concern was to analyze the process by which conscious and self-conscious troping is achieved.

In the analysis of the dreamwork, Freud pays little attention to the diachronic development of that form of poiesis called dreaming; and he does not actually concern himself overly much with the phases passed through in the composition of a dream. At least, he does not concern himself with it in the way that Harold Bloom does in his discussion of the phasal development of such conscious compositions as lyric poems. Freud was no doubt aware that conscious, or "waking" discourse is phasally developed; for that ironic trope which he called secondary revision is constantly operative in conscious poiesis as a dominant trope, insofar as any discourse must be seen as evolving under the aegis of the psychological defense called rationalization.[21] There is a suggestion of a certain diachronic dimension in the dreamwork, to be sure, inasmuch as secondary revision would seem to require some prior operation of condensation, displacement, or representation, the other mechanisms identified by Freud, in order for it to become activated; secondary revision needs some "matter" on which to work, and this matter is provided by the other mechanisms of the dreamwork. But this is relatively unimportant to his purpose, which is to provide an analytical method for deconstructing completed dreams and disclosing the latent "dream thoughts" that lurk within their interior as their true, as against their manifest, "contents."

I am interested here, obviously, in the mechanisms which Freud identifies as effecting the mediations between the manifest dream contents and the latent dream thoughts. These seem to correspond, as Jakobson has suggested,[22] to the tropes systematized as the classes

21. Freud, *The Interpretation of Dreams,* trans. James Strachey (New York, 1965), pp. 526–44.

22. Roman Jakobson, "Two Types of Language and Two Types of Aphasic Disturbance," in Roman Jakobson and Morris Halle, *Fundamentals of Language* (The Hague and Paris, 1971), p. 95. Cf. Emile Benveniste, "Remarks on the Function of Language in Freudian Theory," in *Problems in General Linguistics,* trans. Mary Elizabeth Meek (Coral Gables, 1971), pp. 65–75.

of figuration in modern rhetorical theory (a theory with which, incidentally, insofar as it classifies figures into the four tropes of metaphor, metonymy, synecdoche, and irony, Freud would have been acquainted, as a component of the educational cursus of gymnasia and colleges of his time). His "discovery" of the processes of "condensation," "displacement," "representation," and "secondary revision" might seem to be undermined by the suggestion that he had only rediscovered in, or unconsciously imposed upon, the psychodynamics of dreaming, transformative models already explicated fully, and in much the same terms as those used by Freud, as the tropes of rhetoric.

But we do not detract from the originality of Freud's enterprise by our discovery that his dreamwork mechanisms correspond almost point by point with the structures of the tropes, first of all, because Freud himself explicitly compares the mechanisms of the dreamwork with those of poiesis and even uses the terminology of figuration to describe these processes;[23] secondly, because the scope of Freud's enterprise is sufficiently great to allow his borrowing from one domain of cultural analysis to apply its principles to a limited aspect of that enterprise without in the least detracting from the stature of his total achievement; and third, because it *was* a stroke of genius to identify the processes of the dreamwork with those processes of waking consciousness which are more imaginative than ratiocinative. More importantly, however, for anyone interested in the theory of discourse in general and in the discourse about consciousness specifically, Freud's patient analysis of the mechanisms of the dreamwork provides insight into the operations of waking thought which lie between and seek consciously to mediate between the imaginative and the ratiocinative faculties, which is to say, operations of discourse itself. If Freud has correctly identified, in his own terms, the fourfold nature of the processes operative in the dreamwork, he has provided considerable insight into the same processes as they operate in discourse, mediating between perception and conceptualization, description and argument, mimesis and diegesis—or whatever other dichotomous terms we wish to use to indicate the mixture of poetic and noetic levels of consciousness between which the discourse itself seeks to mediate in the interests of "understanding."

I will not spell out the correspondence between the four mecha-

---

23. See Freud, *Interpretation of Dreams,* pp. 374–84.

nisms of the dreamwork, as Freud describes them, and the four master tropes of figuration. This correspondence is by no means perfect, as Todorov has demonstrated very clearly,[24] but it is close enough to permit us to view Freud's analysis of the mediations between the dream thoughts and the dream contents as a key to the understanding of the mechanisms which, in waking consciousness, permit us to move in the other direction, i.e., from poetic figurations of reality to noetic comprehensions of it. Or, to put it in terms of theory of discourse, once we recognize Freud's notion of the mechanisms of the dreamwork as psychological equivalents of what tropes are in language and transformational patterns are in conceptual thought, we have a way of relating mimetic and diegetic elements in every representation of reality, whether of the sleeping or the waking consciousness.

I have shown how Marx anticipated the discovery of these transformational patterns in his analysis of the Forms of Value in *Capital* and how such tropical structures served him as a way of marking the stages in a diachronic process, such as the events in France between 1848 and 1851, in *The Eighteenth Brumaire of Louis Bonaparte*.[25] But this latter aspect of the theory of tropes—i.e., their function as signs of stages in the evolution of consciousness—can be spelled out more concretely, perhaps, if applied to the work of a historian somewhat more "empirical" in method than Marx is supposed to have been or at least one who claims to be concerned quintessentially with "concrete historical reality" rather than with "methodology." I refer to the work of E. P. Thompson, *The Making of the English Working Class,* a book praised by scholars of many different ideological orientations for its mastery of factual detail, general openness of plan, and explicit rejection of methodology and abstract theory. Thompson's work is as much about the development of working-class consciousness over a finite time span as it is about the events, personalities, and institutions which manifest that development in concrete forms; and as such, it provides another test either of the ubiquity of the tropological model for the emplotting of stages in the development of (here, a group) consciousness or (if it is granted that Thompson has, as it were, found, rather than imposed his categories)

24. See Tzvetan Todorov, "La Rhétorique de Freud," in *Théories du symbole* (Paris, 1977), pp. 303, 315–16.
25. White, *Metahistory,* pp. 320–27.

a test of the reality of these categories as the types of the modes of consciousness through which groups actually pass in a finite movement from a naive to an ironic condition in their evolution.

At the outset of his discourse, Thompson defines explicitly what he means by the term *class;* it is not a thing or entity for him, but rather a "relationship." He tells us that "class happens when some men . . . feel and articulate the identity of their interests as between themselves, and as against other men whose interests are different from (and usually opposed to) theirs."[26] He then goes on to remark: "We can see a *logic* in the responses of similar occupational groups undergoing similar experiences, but we cannot predict any *law.*" And yet the phases into which Thompson divides the evolution of working-class consciousness in his book are predictable enough, not as to the times in which the specific phases took shape, but in both the content of the different phases (considered as structures of consciousness) and the specific sequence of their elaboration. Not surprisingly, this determination of the phases and their structures conforms to that which Marx spelled out in both his study of consciousness's modes of construing the relationships between commodities and his analysis of the phases through which socialist consciousness was supposed to have passed, given in the appendix to the *Communist Manifesto.*[27] This is not to suggest that Thompson is to be taken less seriously because he imposed *a* pattern on his subject matter; for it is impossible to imagine his having done anything else. As a matter of fact, the book and the tropological theory of consciousness both gain in stature from the fact that he apparently *discovered* the phases in question. The *historical* authority of his book is increased by the care and attention to detail with which he determined the specific chronology of the phases in the sequence.

Thompson takes issue with vulgar Marxists on the one side and equally vulgar positivistic sociologists on the other for their abstractionist tendencies. He claims to be a realist of a sort: "I am convinced that we cannot understand class unless we see it as a social and cultural formation, arising from processes which can only be studied as they work themselves out over a considerable historical period" (p. 11). Here is the well-known gesture towards concreteness and "real

---

26. E. P. Thompson, *The Making of the English Working Class* (New York, 1963), pp. 9–10. Hereafter cited in the text by page number.
27. Karl Marx and Frederick Engels, "Manifesto of the Communist Party," *The Marx-Engels Reader,* ed. Robert C. Tucker (New York, 1972), pp. 353–60.

historical contexts" that we are accustomed to find in opponents of methodology and abstract theorizing, especially of the down-to-earth, British variety.

But no sooner has Thompson pilloried Smelser and Dahrendorf than, in the very next sentence, he writes: "This [his own] book can be seen as a biography of the English working class from its adolescence until its early manhood" (ibid.), as if biography were an unproblematical genre and the categories of adolescence and early manhood were not culturally determined metaphors treated as "concrete" realities. And then, when Thompson goes on to offer an outline of his history, he conceptualizes its phases in ways which, if predictive of no law of history, fulfill perfectly the conditions of the predictability of the composition of discourses such as his own. The four-phase movement is explicitly embraced, and interestingly enough, as a pattern that is constructed rather than simply found:

> The book is written in this way. In Part One I consider the continuing popular traditions in the 18th century which influenced the crucial Jacobin agitation of the 1790s. In Part Two I move from subjective to objective influences—the experiences of groups of workers during the Industrial Revolution which seem to me to be of especial significance. I also attempt an estimate of the character of the new industrial work-discipline, and the bearing upon this of the Methodist Church. In Part III I pick up the story of plebian Radicalism and carry it through Luddism to the heroic age at the close of the Napoleonic Wars. Finally, I discuss some aspects of political theory and of the consciousness of class in the 1820 and 1830s. (P. 12)

Why these divisions in the discourse? Thompson insists that he is not providing a "consecutive narrative," but only a "group of studies, on related themes" (ibid.). But the title, with its prominent featuring of the gerund "making," suggests the activist, constructivist nature both of the subject being dealt with and of the discourse about this subject, while the parts of the discourse delineated in the preface suggest the "logic" of tropological organization.

Part I, entitled "The Liberty Tree," with its concentration on "popular traditions," obviously has to do with only a vaguely apprehended class existence; it is working-class consciousness awakening to itself, as the Hegelian would say, but grasping its particularity only in general terms, the kind of consciousness we would call metaphorical, in which working people apprehend their differences from the wealthy and sense their similarity to one another, but are unable to organize themselves except in terms of the general desire for an elusive "liberty." Part II, entitled "The Curse of Adam," is a long discourse, in which the different forms of working-class existence, determined by the variety of kinds of work in the industrial land-scape, crystallize into distinctive kinds, the whole having nothing more than the elements of a series. The mode of class consciousness described in this section is metonymic, corresponding to the model of the Extended Form of Value explicated by Marx in the discourse on the Forms of Value in *Capital*.[28] "The working people were forced into political and social apartheid during the [Napoleonic Wars]," Thompson tells us; ". . . the people were subjected simultaneously to an intensification of two intolerable forms of relationship: those of economic exploitation and of political oppression" (pp. 198–99). The whole period being dealt with is one in which "we feel the general pressure of long hours of unsatisfying labour under severe discipline for alien purposes" (pp. 445–46). This, Thompson says in the conclusion of the section, "was at the source of that 'ugliness' which, D. H. Lawrence wrote, 'betrayed the spirit of man in the nineteenth century'. After all other impressions fade, this one re-mains: together with that of the loss of any felt cohesion in the community, save that which the working people, in antagonism to their labour and to their masters, built for themselves" (p. 447).

Part III, entitled "The Working Class Presence," marks a new stage in the growth of class consciousness, the actual crystallization of a distinctively "working-class" spirit among the laborers. In the face of oppression and force used to destroy them, especially at Peterloo in 1819, the workers achieved a new sense of unity or identity of the parts with the whole—what we would call synecdochic conscious-ness and what Marx, in his study of the Forms of Value, labelled the "Generalized Form."[29] Only at this stage are we permitted, Thompson instructs us, to speak of "working people's consciousness of their interests and of their predicament *as a class.*" Working people

> learned to see their own lives as part of a general history of conflict between the loosely defined 'industrious classes' on the one hand and the unreformed House of Commons on the other. From 1830 onwards [therefore] a more clearly-defined class

28. Karl Marx, *Capital,* trans. Eden Paul and Cedar Paul (London, 1962), 1: 34–37; cf. White, *Metahistory,* pp. 290–96.
29. Thompson, *The English Working Class,* p. 711; cf. Marx, *Capital,* 1: 37–42.

consciousness, in the customary Marxist sense, was maturing, in which working people were aware of continuing both old and new battles on their own. (P. 712)

This clears the way for the last section of the book, which is not a separate part but only a chapter, dealing with political theory and aspects of class consciousness manifested in the literary and intellectual culture of the 1820s and 1830s.

The account of the fourth phase is shot through with melancholy, product of a perception of an ironic situation, since it marks not only the ascent of *class* consciousness to *self*-consciousness but also and at the same time the fatal fracturing of the working-class movement itself. We may call this stage that of irony, for what is involved here was the simultaneous emergence and debilitation of the two ideals which might have given the working-class movement a radical future: internationalism, on one hand, and industrial syndicalism, on the other. But, Thompson remarks, closing his work on a note of melancholy, "This vision was lost, almost as soon as it had been found, in the terrible defeats of 1834 and 1835" (p. 830). The specific gain was a kind of class resiliency and pride in working-class membership, but these tended to isolate workers from their masters as much as contribute to their organization for the attainment of modest, trade union reforms. On the surface of society, Romantics and Radical craftsmen continued to debate their views on the nature of labor, profit, and production; but they both failed and, moreover, contributed to a schism among intellectuals over the nature of work which has persisted to the present day, creating two cultures in which, after Blake, "no mind could be at home in both" (p. 832). Whence the irony with which Thompson himself ends his great book: "In the failure of the two traditions to come to a point of junction, something was lost. How much we cannot be sure, for we are among the losers." And whence also the forgivable sentimentality with which he adds: "Yet the working people should not be seen only as the lost myriads of eternity. They had also nourished, for fifty years, and with incomparable fortitude, the Liberty Tree. We may thank them for these years of heroic culture" (ibid.).

I have lingered on this tropological unpacking of the structure of Thompson's discourse because, unlike Piaget and Freud in their analyses of consciousness, Thompson claims to be proceeding with primary attention to "concrete historical reality," rather than by means of the application of a "method." Moreover, although he was concerned with human consciousness, he was concerned with it as a social-group, rather than as an individual, phenomenon. If we honor his claim to have derived his categories for discriminating among different phases in the development of this group's consciousness from an *empirical consideration* of the evidence (as many have honored him), then some kind of empirical confirmation of the operation of tropological modes in group consciousness has been achieved. If we hold that he has *imposed* these modes on the general range of phenomena which he studied, as a means of characterizing it in a purely hypothetical way, so as merely to block out the larger structures of its representation in his discourse about it, then we must ask why so subtle an interpreter of "data" hit upon this tropological pattern for organizing his discourse, rather than some other?

If, however, we agree that the structure of any sophisticated, i.e., self-conscious and self-critical, discourse mirrors or replicates the phases through which consciousness itself must pass in *its* progress from a naive (metaphorical) to a self-critical (ironic) comprehension of itself, then the necessity of a choice between the alternative judgments listed above is dissolved. It is a mark of Thompson's own high degree of discursive self-consciousness that he found the pattern of development in the "making", of the consciousness of the English working class which was operative in his own "making" of his discourse. The pattern which Thompson discerned in the history of English working-class consciousness was perhaps as much imposed upon his data as it was found in them, but the issue here surely is not whether some pattern was imposed, but the tact exhibited in the choice of the pattern used to give order to the process being represented. This tact is manifested in his choice, planned or intuitive, of a pattern long associated with the analysis of processes of consciousness in rhetoric and poetics, dialectic, and, as we have shown, experimental psychology and psychoanalysis alike. Where else should Thompson have turned for a model of a process of consciousness, especially one whose phases and their modalities of structuration had to be construed as products of some combination of theory and practice, conscious and unconscious processes of (self) creation?

If Thompson has not consciously applied the theory of the tropes to his representation of the history of his subject, he has divined or reinvented this theory in the composition of his own discourse. We would not wish to say that his phases are to be equated with those discerned by Piaget in the development of the child's cognitive powers or by Freud in the mediations effected between the manifest and latent levels of the dream in his analysis of the dreamwork. These seem to be analogous structures, rather than replications of a common theoretical model implicitly held by three analysts of three different kinds of subject matter. But the fact that these three analogous structures appear in the work of thinkers so different in the way they construe the problems of representation and analysis, the aims they set for their discourses, and their consciously held conceptions of the structure of consciousness itself—this fact seems to constitute sufficient reason for treating the theory of tropology as a valuable model of discourse, if not of consciousness in general.

Now, the question that must arise at this point in our own discourse is this: why privilege the linguistic theory of tropes as the common term of these various theories of different kinds of consciousness, rather than treat the tropes as linguistic expressions of the modes of consciousness themselves? Why not say "condensation," "displacement," "representation," and "secondary revision," as Freud did; "sensorimotor," "representational," "operational," and "logical," as Piaget did; "Elementary," "Extended," "Generalized," and "Absurd," as Marx did; or, for that matter, use the fourfold terminology that Hegel did in his analysis of the modes of consciousness?[30] The first answer to these questions must be that, insofar as we are concerned with discourse, we are concerned with what are, after all, verbal artifacts; and that, therefore, a terminology derived from the study of verbal artifacts could, on the face of it, claim priority for our purposes on this occasion. But the second answer is that, insofar as we are concerned with structures of consciousness, we are acquainted with those structures only as they are manifested in discourse. Consciousness in its active, creative aspects, as against its passive, reflexive aspects (as manifested in the operations of Piaget's child at the sensorimotor stage, for example), is most directly apprehendable in discourse and, moreover, in discourse guided by formulable intentions, goals, or aims of *understanding.* This understanding is not, we suppose, an affective state that crystallizes spontaneously on the threshold of consciousness without some minimally conscious effort of *will to know.* This will to know does not, in turn, take shape out of some confrontation between a consciousness utterly without intention and the environment it occupies. It must take shape out of some awareness of difference between alternative figurations of reality in images held in memory and fashioned, perhaps out of responses to

---

30. Hegel's four-stage plan is analyzed in *Metahistory*, pp. 123–31. See the schematic representation of the stages of world history given in Hegel, *Philosophy of Right*, trans. T. M. Knox (Oxford, 1965), §§ 352–56, pp. 219–23.

contradictory desires or emotional investments, into complex structures, vague apprehensions of the forms that reality *should* take even if it fails to assume those forms *(especially* if it fails to assume those forms) in existentially vital situations.

Understanding, I presume, following Hegel, Nietzsche, and Freud, is a process by which memory images are assigned names or linked up with words, or ordered sounds, so as to be combined with other memory images similarly linked with words in the form of propositions—probably of the form "This *is* that."[31] It hardly matters at this level of understanding what two terms are placed on the opposite sides of the copula. The result may be, when viewed from the perspective of a later and more sophisticated system of propositions, only error; but as Bacon said, when it is a matter of seeking knowledge of the world, an erroneous hypothesis is better than none at all. It at least provides the basis for any intended action, a praxis in which the adequacy of the proposition to the world of which it speaks can be tested. But more importantly, such primitive propositions, erroneous or not, are also and more basically metaphors, without which our transition from a state of ignorance to one of practical understanding would be unthinkable. And precisely because every thing in the world and every experience of it can be likened to any other thing or experience by analogy or similitude (because as elements of the one reality they do share some attribute, if only being itself), then there is a sense in which no metaphor is completely erroneous. The basis of their unity, expressed in the copula of identity, may not be known or even conceivable to a given intelligence, but even the most shocking metaphorical transfer, the most paradoxical catachresis, the most contradictory oxymoron, like the most banal pun, gains its effect as an illumination, if not of reality, then of the relationship between words and things, which also is an aspect of reality, by its production of such "errors." The tropoligical theory of discourse gives us understanding of the existential continuity between error and truth, ignorance and understanding, or to put it another way, imagination and thought. For too long the relationship between these pairs has been conceived as an opposition. The

31. Hegel, *Philosophy of Mind,* trans. William Wallace (Oxford, 1971), §§ 451–68, pp. 201–28; Freud, *The Ego and the Id,* trans. Joan Riviere (New York, 1962), pp. 10–15; and Nietzsche, "On Truth and Falsity in Their Ultramoral Sense," in *Early Greek Philosophy and Other Essays,* trans. Maximilian A. Mügge, vol. 2 of *The Complete Works of Friedrich Nietzsche,* ed. Oscar Levy (New York, 1924), pp. 179ff.

tropological theory of discourse helps us understand how speech mediates between these supposed oppositions, just as discourse itself mediates between our apprehension of those aspects of experience still "strange" to us and those aspects of it which we "understand" because we have found an order of words adequate to its domestication.

Finally, the tropological theory of discourse could provide us with a way of classifying different kinds of discourses by reference to the linguistic modes that predominate in them rather than by reference to supposed "contents" which are always identified differently by different interpreters. And this would be as true of our attempts to classify various types of "practical" discourse, such as those discourses about social phenomena (madness, suicide, sexuality, war, politics, economics), as it would be of similar attempts to classify types of "formal" discourse (such as plays, novels, poems, and so on).

For example, Durkheim's justly famous analysis of the types of suicide can be shown to be, among other things, a hypostatization of the modes of relationship presupposed in the tropological model of possible conceptualizations of relations of (individual) parts to the (social) wholes of which they are members.[32] So too Lukács's exceedingly suggestive and fruitful typology of the modern novel, each type identified by the mode of relationship predominating between the protagonist and his social milieu, would have been improved and refined by attention to the linguistic aspect of his examples.[33] But Lukács, for all of his professed Hegelianism at the time of the composition of his book and his professed Marxism at the time of his repudiation of it, thought that he could specify a content for novels without paying much attention to the linguistic container in which they came embodied. And this belief in the transparency of language, its purely reflective, rather than constitutive nature, also blinded Durkheim to the extent to which his types had been as much created by his own descriptions of his data as they had been explicated from the data by statistical correlations and their analysis. For that matter, we might add that statistical representations are little more than projections of data construed in the mode of metonymy,

32. Emile Durkheim, *Suicide: A Study in Sociology*, trans. John A. Spaulding and George Simpson, ed. George Simpson (New York, 1966), p. 276, n. 25 and pp. 277–94.
33. Georg Lukács, *The Theory of the Novel: A Historico-Philosophical Essay on the Forms of Great Epic Literature*, trans. Anna Bostock (Cambridge, Mass., 1971), pp. 97ff.

the validity of which as contributions to our understanding of reality extend only as far as the elements of the structures represented in them are in fact related by contiguity alone. Insofar as they are not so related, other language protocols, governed by other tropes, are required for an explication of their natures adequate to the human capacity to *understand* anything. And the same can be said of the synecdochic mode of representation favored by Lukács in his analysis of the principal types of the modern novel.

But why, we must ask, should we wish such a typology of discourses? First, because the beginning of all understanding is classification, and a classification of discourses based on tropology, rather than on presumed contents or manifest (but inevitably flawed) logics, would provide a way of apprehending the possible structure of relationships between these two aspects of a text, rather than denying the adequacy of the one because the other was inadequately achieved. Secondly, if discourse is our most direct manifestation of consciousness seeking understanding, occupying that middle ground between the awakening of a general interest in a domain of experience and the attainment of some comprehension of it, then a typology of the modes of discourse would provide entry into a typology of the modes of understanding. This being achieved, it might become possible to provide protocols for translating between alternative modes which, because they are taken for granted either as natural or as established truth, had hardened into ideologies. Next, such a typology of the modes of understanding might permit us to mediate between contending ideologues, each of whom regards his own position as scientific and that of his opponent as mere ideology or "false consciousness." Finally, a typology of the modes of understanding might permit us to advance the notion of what Lukács defined as the relationship between "possible class consciousness" and "false class consciousness." This would entail surrender by the Marxist theorists of their claim to see "objectively" the "reality" which their opponents always apprehend in a "distorted" way. For we would recognize that it is not a matter of choosing between objectivity and distortion, but rather between different strategies for constituting "reality" in thought so as to deal with it in different ways, each of which has its own ethical implications.

The essays in this book all, in one way or another, examine the problem of the relationships among description, analysis, and ethics in the human sciences. It will be immediately apparent that this division of the human faculties is Kantian. I will not apologize for this

Kantian element in my thought, but I do not think that modern psychology, anthropology, or philosophy has improved upon it. Moreover, when it is a matter of speaking about human consciousness, we have no absolute theory to guide us; everything is under contention. It therefore becomes a matter of choice as to which model we should use to mark out, and constitute entries into, the problem of consciousness in general. Such choices should be self-conscious rather than unconscious ones, and they should be made with a full understanding of the kind of human nature to the constitution of which they will contribute if they are taken as valid. Kant's distinctions among the emotions, the will, and the reason are not very popular in this, an age which has lost its belief in the will and represses its sense of the moral implications of the mode of rationality that it favors. But the moral implications of the human sciences will never be perceived until the faculty of the will is reinstated in theory.

In the past, I have been accused of radical skepticism, even pessimism, regarding the possibility of the achievement of real knowledge in the human sciences. This was the response of some critics to the first essay reprinted in this collection, "The Burden of History," as well as to *Metahistory,* which grew out of my efforts to deal with the issues raised in that essay. I trust that the bulk of these essays will relieve me of those charges, at least in part. I have never denied that knowledge of history, culture, and society was possible; I have only denied that a scientific knowledge, of the sort actually attained in the study of physical nature, was possible. But I have tried to show that, even if we cannot achieve a properly scientific knowledge of human nature, we can achieve another kind of knowledge about it, the kind of knowledge which literature and art in general give us in easily recognizable examples. Only a willful, tyrannical intelligence could believe that the only kind of knowledge we can aspire to is that represented by the physical sciences. My aim has been to show that we do not have to choose between art and science, that indeed we cannot do so in practice, if we hope to continue to speak about culture as against nature—and, moreover, speak about it in ways that are responsible to all the various dimensions of our specifically *human* being.

GEOFFREY HARTMAN

The essay reprinted here by Geoffrey Hartman is entertaining not just because it is written with his usual elegance and wit, but also because it provides some essential cultural background for the hostility often shown in Anglo-Saxon contexts for critical theory. It is amusing to note that Hartman uses Anglo-Saxon criticism's best features—charm and conversational accessibility—against it. His conclusions, however, are not kind, though perhaps they are not as libellous as Émile Cioran's more outrageous evaluation: "Thanks to the conformism and enlightened stupidity of her citizens," he says, England "has not produced a single anarchist."* Hartman's word is "prissy," also rather below the belt.

England, says Hartman, has developed a "conversational," logocentric criticism in part because of the eighteenth-century development of the coffeehouse, where the literati gathered socially to test their theories. What can be said in such a civilized setting limits the fine distinctions, not to mention subordinate clauses, typical of theories forged in places where solitary anguish and analytical concentration are possible. The conversational or "friendship" style has been further reinforced, then, by the tutorial system of teaching that is typical of the English university. The system, says Hartman, limits inwardness and encourages conformity. Good prose is chatty prose. But chattiness is journalistic, designed to assimilate the difficult and defang the frightening. The price of conviviality is the sacrifice of the challenging, the blunting of the cutting edge, the reduction of that "totality," which, precisely because of its breathtaking difficulty, is fascinating in its own right. Moreover, the conversational style is just as coercive and monologic as any Teutonic soliloquy, though the English style conceals its tyrannies behind a veil of charm.

---

*E. M. Cioran, "Russia and the Virus of Liberty," trans. Richard Howard, *Southern Humanities Review* (Fall 1986) 309.

Tea and Totality: The Demand of Theory on Critical Style

1984

I n almost every order of discourse there has been a call at one time or another for a higher seriousness. We are asked to pursue "some graver subject" or a more exacting style. The call may come, as in Milton or Keats, from within the poet's sense of a vocation spurred on by exemplary forebears: the reputed career of Vergil, for example, who left the oaten pipe of pastoral and playful song for the pursuit of didactic verse in his farmer's manual *The Georgics,* which is climaxed in turn by the trumpets stern of his epic *Aeneid* that deals with a warrior become culture-bearer. This call for a higher style or a graver subject has also burdened philosophy. However diverse their mode, in Husserl, Heidegger, and Wittgenstein the ideal of rigor besets what with a phrase from Spenser's proem to the *Faerie Queene* we may term their "afflicted style."

It is not otherwise in literary criticism. Grave it certainly is, and didactic, so that the formalist or playful thinker who does not justify his enterprise by appealing to theory or science is not considered worthwhile. The real terror we have experienced, and are still experiencing, produces a pressure on our purposes that is itself not unterroristic. "A theory of culture," George Steiner writes in *Bluebeard's Castle* (1971), "an analysis of our present circumstances, which do not have at their pivot a consideration of the modes of terror that brought on the death, through war, starvation, and deliberate massacre, of some seventy million human beings in Europe and Russia, between the start of the first World War and the end of the second, seems to me irresponsible."

But as we read this appeal, from a book that asks with anguish why

TEA AND TOTALITY: THE DEMAND OF THEORY ON CRITICAL STYLE   by Geoffrey Hartman from *After Strange Texts,* eds. Greg Jay and David Miller. University of Alabama Press 1985. Copyright © 1984 by Geoffrey Hartman, reprinted by generous permission. Footnotes have been omitted.

European high culture could not stem Nazi barbarism, we wonder how far even a relevant "theory" would take us. It would remain an interpretation; it would raise the further question of how interpretations acquire the force to change anything. The sincere thinker, moreover, need not be the effective one: men and women of conscience may unwittingly trivialize a subject by becoming obsessed about it. At a time when the air is as full of strident sounds as it was once of fairy folk, the question of what kind of seriousness our discipline may claim, or what sort of style might best convey it, is more troublesome than ever. The purpose of literary commentary cannot be simply its amplifying the cliches of our predicament.

Some question of style has always existed. Literature, we are told, should please or move as well as teach. Rhetoric has forensic and religious roots, however cognitively developed. Our culture depends on formalized arts of verbal exchange, which have their rules and limits, as in an adversarial court system and a parliamentary mode of debate; and they determine what is evidence rather than what is truth. They may even put obstacles in the way of those who think they know the truth, for we don't live with each other in an unmediated relation but in a strongly rhetoricized world where verbal and stylistic choices must constantly be made.

Yet just as logic tries to escape or purify rhetoric, so literary criticism too has tried to control words or else recall them to their directest, most referential function. It may seem strange to admit that the literary critic is often no friendlier to imaginative literature than the logician. In this self-deputized censor, the critic, there is love –hate rather than friendship; and recently this passionate engagement has tended to sort itself out in a schizoid way. The drift toward the extreme in modern art is so strong that it is not, on the whole, resisted. The resistance comes, rather, when a critic breaches the ramparts of decorum and modifies the language of literary criticism itself.

For that language has remained as unpretentious as possible. Critics, after all, should be critical, and fend off inflated rhetoric, faked authority, and indigest foreignness. Suspicious of their love for literature, they are even more suspicious of the literary element in themselves. They are sober people who shield themselves from contamination by the hygiene of their practice. Their tone is nicely aggressive and their nasty conservatism is great fun, after the fact —however pernicious and parochial it may have been in its own time.

How many know of Stuart Sherman's attack on Mencken in a book called *Americans?* His essay is entitled "Mr. Mencken, the *Jeune Fille* and the New Spirit in Letters"; and the *jeune fille* clearly plays the same role for Sherman as the young corruptible student does for Denis Donoghue, who worries about creative critics inciting their disciples to dithyrambs instead of dissertations. Here is one of Sherman's sallies:

> The *jeune fille* . . . feels within herself . . . an exhilarating chaos, a fluent welter. . . . She revels in the English paradoxes and mountebanks, the Scandinavian misanthropes, the German egomaniacs, and, above all, in the later Russian novelists, crazy with war, taxes, anarchy, vodka, and German philosophy. . . . Lured by a primitive instinct to the sound of animals roving, she ventures a curious foot in the fringes of the Dreiserian wilderness vast and drear; and barbaric impulses in her blood answer the wail of the forest. . . . Imagine a thousand *jeunes filles* thus wistful, and you have the conditions ready for the advent of a new critic. At this point enters at a hard gallop, spattered with mud, H. L. Mencken high in oath. . . . He leaps from the saddle with sabre flashing, stables his horse in the church, shoots the priest, hangs the professors, exiles the Academy, burns the library and the university, and, amid the smoking ashes, erects a new school of criticism on modern German principles.

Sherman has some reason to be apprehensive of the Germanizing spirit in literary studies: unfortunately even his name sounded as if a German were pronouncing "German." He wanted to save America from the Saxon in Anglo-Saxon. What a paradox that the *jeune fille* would not prefer the delicacy of the French tradition which has named her type to the Carlylese coarseness of Mencken. Sherman intends the *jeune fille* to read Sainte-Beuve rather than Nietzsche, though he concludes that Mencken's style, "hard, pointed, forcible, cocksure" might substitute for a stiff freshman course in rhetoric and remove the softer forms of "slush" and "pishposh" from her mind.

It is, clearly, not only Mencken's macho manners (Sherman's are nothing to boast of) which cause the offense. As today, there is a struggle going on to define the American spirit in its true independence. There is, further, a struggle over what democracy means in education. Finally, there is a near-physical disgust at German philosophizing as an idiom that could infect our entire verbal constitution. How would Sherman react, now that even philosophers in the Romance languages have succumbed to the Germanizing style?

Sartre, Lévi-Strauss, Lacan, Foucault, Derrida, Kristeva, Althusser —where may delicacy and true aesthetic feeling be found? You will notice that I have been dealing with prejudices about style rather than with particular philosophical issues. Critics in the Anglo-American tradition are arbiters of taste, not developers of ideas. Their type of judiciousness, moreover, is almost always linked to a strong sense for the vernacular: more precisely, to the idealization of the vernacular as an organic medium, a language of nature that communicates ideas without the noise or elaboration of extraverted theory. In fact, to argue too much about what is deeply English or American means one has to acknowledge the outside; and being inside—an insider—is what counts. Perhaps this assumption of inwardness can be laid to every nationalism. Acculturated, one secretes one's culture. Yet unselfconsciousness or antiselfconsciousness, however attractive it may be, is surely a limitation rather than expansion of the critical spirit. In the Anglophile tradition, the critical spirit, as it approaches Mencken's gallop, is suspected of being a modern form of enthusiasm as dangerous as the dogmatic spirit it displaced.

This suspicion of the critical spirit reaches an English high in the most influential of modern arbiters: T. S. Eliot. Such pronouncements, especially, as "From Poe to Valéry" and *Notes towards the Definition of Culture* are urbane exercises to limit criticism in the name of culture. It is symptomatic that the epigraph on the title page of *Notes* is taken from the *OED* and reads: "DEFINITION: 1. The setting of bounds; limitation (rare)—1483." Back to 1483, then? This finicky scrutiny of words, which communicates itself even to strong epigones like Trilling (just as Heidegger's etymological virtuosity turns up in Derrida) causes Eliot to say that rescuing the word *culture* is "the extreme of my ambition."

Let me now come to the extreme of *my* ambition. It is to understand what happened to English criticism in the period of roughly 1920 to 1950, when a "teatotalling" style developed in academic circles despite so many marvelous and often idiosyncratic talents, from Eliot himself to Richards, Empson, Leavis, and (in America) Trilling.

Now what happened is, in a sense, that nothing happened. An order of discourse strove hard to remain a discourse of order. The happening was all on the side of art and literature; and the courage of the critic lay in acknowledging the newness or forwardness of modernist experiments. Compared to his own *Waste Land,* Eliot's essays are prissy. Compared to the novels of Lawrence, Leavis's revaluations are cultic gestures, precise elliptical movements charged with significance for the one who has truly read. Criticism is asked to exhibit an ideal decorum, to show that despite the stress of class antagonism, national disunity, and fragmentation, concepts of order are still possible.

In adopting this demeanor English commentators followed an ingrained tradition. They took no solace from the notion of a science or a theory of literature: that was the Continental way, leading from Dilthey to Lukács, and then increasingly to reflections inspired by Marxism and structuralism. The English classical writer, even when the stakes were high, wished to please rather than teach, and to remind rather than instruct. This critical tradition, keeping its distance from sacred but also from learned commentary, sought to purify the reader's taste and the national language, and so addressed itself to peers or friends—in short, to a class of equally cultured people.

Indeed, the highest recommendation of such criticism was the artfulness of its accommodation. Richards's *The Philosophy of Rhetoric* is as careful of its audience as Ruskin's *Sesame and Lilies.* It is not philosophy as Lukács, Adorno, Heidegger, or Benjamin practiced it, who can leave ordinary language behind or beat it into surprising shapes. I emphasize these writers in German not because they had no choice but precisely because they did have a choice: namely, German classical prose as it culminated in Goethe, and still provided Freud with a style that made his science accessible.

The "friendship style" (as I tend to name this accommodated and classical prose) has political as well as sentimental ramifications. Writers in the later eighteenth century can talk of a "republic of letters," and Keats of a "freemasonry of spirits." Indeed, in Matthew Arnold the idea of culture moves to oppose the idea of class: culture, he said, exists to do away with classes. Even if the audience addressed in the friendship style may be as provisional and uncertain as Addison's and Steele's was when they published *The Spectator,* the guiding fiction is that all the members of this society correspond on equal footing. They are "lettered"; and in terms of style there is an attempt to erase from their demeanor the "patronage style," that is, a vacillation between exaggerated modesty and extreme gravity, between presenting oneself as "all too mean" and all too manic. The friendship style cancels the disparity between the social class of the writer and his transcendent subject-matter or ambition.

Criticism, then, treads lightly: its prose can be savage, but only when affronted by pedantry or the self-inflated nonsense of other writers. From the time of the neoclassical movement in seventeenth-century France, it was a form of good conversation, a discourse among equals. This speak-easy quality still joins *The Spectator* to *The New York Review of Books,* which is notorious for using Anglos. Only in Germany, and then after Hegel—when an attempt is made to separate the *Geisteswissenschaften* ("moral" or "human" sciences) from the natural sciences—is literary criticism burdened by ideas of *Bildung* and *Aufbau,* as if it had at once to anticipate and survive "absolute spirit." (So Dilthey's Berlin Academy lectures of 1905–1910, coinciding with Lukács literary prentice years, were entitled "Der Aufbau der geschichtlichen Welt in den Geisteswissenschaften" [The construction of the historical world in the human sciences].) Yet even after the First World War, when Lukács published his *Theory of the Novel* (1920), then *History and Class Consciousness* (1923) —works whose emphasis on "totality" may be said to have inaugurated the philosophical type of criticism that was to dominate France as well as Germany—even in that postwar decade the radical editor A. R. Orage (*The New Age*) would caution Herbert Read in words that reflect the decorum of Anglo-French criticism, whose pattern-book was Sainte-Beuve's *Causeries.* "Not articles," Orage advises Read, "but causeries." "Beware of the valueless business that insists on *essay* in place of causerie. 'Everything divine runs on light feet.' "

If we take the position, itself a literary one, that how we say it is as important as what we say, then the contrast that developed between English and Continental types of discourse should not be disregarded. There is no need, of course, to insist that one style must be used for every situation; and there may well be a mingling of tones, sometimes uneasy, in the best critics. But the contrast between "tea" and "totality" is too striking to be evaded by mere habits of tolerance.

Let me recapitulate my argument so far. The great virtue of the English, Basil de Selincourt said in the 1920s, is their unconsciousness; and Goethe remarked of Byron: "All Englishmen are as such devoid of inwardness [*eigentliche Reflexion*]; distraction and party spirit do not allow them to achieve a quiet development. But they are imposing as a practical people." I do not quote these statements to malign a critical tradition but to point out a paradox in it that should make us wary of its practical emphasis. So deliberate an unconsciousness tends to quiet the real unconscious. It does so, Goethe suggests, by diverting the mind from spiritual to practical matters. And when we think of the contemporary situation in America, who will cast the first stone? Talent is taking refuge in business schools, law schools, and computer science; and *eigentliche Reflexion,* even when it appears, as in certain types of philosophic criticism, is denounced as navel-gazing or mandarinism.

The dominance of review essay and expository article reflects in a general way the self-delimitation of practical criticism in America and England. Though these forms of commentary serve primary texts, they now claim to teach rather than preach. And to teach as unselfconsciously as possible. "Culture is the one thing that we cannot deliberately aim at," Eliot remarks in his *Notes* on culture. The intrusion of large questions involving religion or philosophy puts the exegete at risk; not because such questions are unimportant but because they are so very important. The practical is defined as the teachable rather than as "lived religion" (Eliot) or the *Umwelt* of "birth-death-existence-decision-communication with others." Paul Ricoeur, author of this rather Germanic sentence, associates "preaching" with such a "totality" as it informs every effort to articulate what we know. Preaching, he emphasizes, invades all good teaching; and teaching that claims to be method rather than discourse—that claims to be a purely objective mode of questioning or communication —has not understood anything about theory, or the domain of preunderstanding.

My own purpose is more modest than to rethink the relation of teaching and preaching, although it seems obvious enough that great preaching did not reject ordinary language, but through the mode of parable, for example, or Swift's "attacking play" (C. J. Rawson) produced a strange intersection of ordinary and extraordinary conversation. My purpose is to reconstruct historically the provenance and character of the classical style in criticism, which has now become the teatotalling style. With a book like Denis Donoghue's *Ferocious Alphabets* we are, in terms of argument, not far from Maugham's summing up of the tradition he embodies. "To like good prose is an affair of good manners. It is, unlike verse, a civil art." To understand why alternate and challenging styles have developed in the last thirty years one must first value an older prose that was, at once, classic and journalistic.

I begin by stating the obvious: a battle of styles as well as books broke out in the seventeenth century, from which there came the clarified expository and journalistic medium we relish today. The Royal Society in England as well as the French Academy played an important role in the spread of this purified style; in America too it gradually took hold against the "fantastic school" represented by such forceful theological writers as Cotton Mather. Mather intended to humble the understanding, to make it aware of its "imbecility" by a contagious parody of impotent speculative maneuvers adorned with puns and quibbles. In Mather it is sometimes hard to tell whether his display of learning and parascientific knowledge is a genuine attempt to "solve the phenomena" by elevating the mind toward the wonders and riddles of the universe (that "totality" which mere tea-drinkers can never taste) or whether it is not a subversive manifestation of fallible wit in even the most splendid of bookworms. Whatever the truth, Mather knew his style was questionable, and in his handbook for the ministry, the *Manuductio* published in 1726, he defends himself as follows:

> There has been a great deal of ado about a STYLE; So much that I must offer you my Sentiments upon it. There is a *Way of Writing* wherein the author endeavours, that the Reader may have *something to the Purpose* in every Paragraph. There is not only a *Vigour* sensible in every *Sentence* but the Paragraph is embellished with *Profitable References,* even to something beyond what is *directly spoken.* . . . The Writer pretends not unto *Reading,* yet he could not have writ as he does if he had not *Read* very much in his Time; and his Composures are not only a *Cloth of Gold,* but also stuck with as many *Jewels,* as the Gown of a Russian Embassador. This *Way of Writing* has been decried by many, and is at this Day more than ever so. . . . But, however *Fashion* and *Humour* may prevail, they must not think that the Club at their *Coffee-House* is, *All the World.* . . . After all, Every Man will have his own Style, which will distinguish him as much as his *Gate* [gait].

It was indeed the coffeehouses mentioned by Mather that played a certain role in producing the new, chastened prose; and except for the exigencies of alliteration, I might have entitled the present essay "Coffee and Totality." In the sober yet convivial atmosphere of the coffeehouses news and gossip were exchanged, and the *literati* conversed on equal footing. As Socrates brought philosophy down from the heavens into the marketplace, so Addison and Steele insinuated it into these bourgeois places of leisure, less exclusive than clubs yet probably as effective in transacting business in a casual setting. I am no sociologist, however, and do not want to ascribe too much to either tea or coffee. Yet in the pleasant spirit of generalization, adapted from the English sphere, one might say it was in these sociable places that "theories" were tested, that the conversational habit became the opium of the intellectual, and a lucid, unpedantic form of prose developed. It is in this era, too, that the English tradition modifies both the scientific and the French demand for a univocal and universal language by appealing to the mingled force of a middle or epistolary style. More exactly, by appealing to the symbiosis, rather than clash, of learned and vernacular traditions, a symbiosis that had previously characterized English poetry, even if the results were as different as Spenser and Shakespeare. The mingled style develops into the ideal of unaffected conversation, in which something is held in reserve and solicits reader or listener. It intends to provoke a reply rather than to dazzle, and it subordinates ingeniousness to the *ingenium* of natural wit. Such an ideal naturalizes rather than banishes Latinity, or seeks an equivalent in English to the philosophic ease of Plato's Greek. "It is straight from Plato's lips, as if in natural conversation," Pater will write, "that the language came in which the mind has ever since been discoursing with itself, in that inward dialogue which is the 'active principle' of the dialectic method" (*Plato and Platonism,* 1896).

The triumph of modern English, though not quite yet of modern American, is anticipated by this ideal of criticism as an extended conversation, civilizing difficult ideas without falling back into gossip or opinionation. That criticism as a causerie may have had its origin in French circles of the seventeenth century, that it was formalized and even patented by Sainte-Beuve (so much so that Proust, closer to Pater, wrote an *Against Sainte-Beuve*), does not make it less attractive to the British. It is true that many intermediary developments should be taken into account, such as the nervy style of Hazlitt; and that even in recent times the grip of the causerie has not gone unchallenged. Many writers between 1920 and 1950 try to make criticism more professional. They feel its dandyish or donnish character, and they signal a return to the vernacularist movement in Puritan England, which intended to "ratifie and settle" English as the national language. "It is more facil," George Snell wrote in 1649, "by the eie of reason, to see through the *Medium,* and light of the English tongue; then by the more obscure light of anie forreign language . . . to learn unknown arts and terms" (quoted in R. F. Jones, *The Triumph of the English Language*). Yet both in journalism and in the university the following basic features of genteel criticism kept their hold.

It should be neither utilitarian as in business, nor abstract as in pure science, nor highly specialized as in scholarship. These types of discourse are allowed in only when dressed down, reduced to a witty gentility first attributed to the "honest man" (*honnête homme*) in seventeenth-century French culture—a person, that is, whose rank or profession could not be discerned when he talked in polite society. "Honest" here means *not* relying on privilege, *not* imposing on a potential peer group because of rank or social standing or expertise. When a cultured person writes or converses, you cannot tell his profession or background because, as La Rochefoucauld said, "il ne se pique de rien." Or, to quote from the definition of the *honnête homme* given by the *Dictionary* of the French Academy: "un galant homme, homme de bonne conversation, de bonne compagnie," that is, "a courteous man, a good conversationalist and interesting to be with."

Certainly an appealing ideal, for today we are even less able to talk in a nonspecialized manner. The art of conversation has not improved. But if it has not, perhaps the older ideal was the wrong way of democratizing discourse or limiting pedantry and snobbery. Without the conversational style (still practiced in Oxbridge tutorials) our situation might be worse; yet it must be said that those who presently uphold the art of criticism as conversation too often stifle intellectual exchange. The conversational decorum has become a defensive mystique for which "dialectic" and even "dialogue" (in Plato's or Gadamer's or Bakhtin's strong sense) are threatening words.

In Pater the conversational ideal is the last refuge of a neoclassical decorum striving to maintain the mask of a unified sensibility. Yet it is merely a mask. Pater holds onto the beautiful soul, the *schöne Seele*. It is time to try something else.

What might that be? It is hardly surprising that English studies should resist the influx of a French *discours* heavily indebted to post-Hegelian German philosophy. Tea and totality don't mix. Something should eventually grow from within the English tradition, even if the pressure comes from without. Richards and Empson certainly made a beginning; and criticism did become more principled, more aware of the complex structure of assigning meaning and making a literary judgment. But the problem of style remained, that is, of communicating in colloquial form the theory or methodology developed. Today George Steiner and Frank Kermode are the only successful translators of technical or speculative ideas into an idiom familiar to the university don brought up "before the flood." Yet it might be said that they are superb reviewers rather than originative thinkers: their vocation is the Arnoldian diffusion of ideas and not a radical revision or extension of knowledge.

We seem to have reached an impasse. What alternatives are there to the conversational style if we grant its necessity as a pedagogical rather than social matter? Yet this shift of perspective, however slight, indicates that such a style is useful rather than ideal, and no more "natural" than other kinds. We know, moreover, that pedagogical tools can become merely tools: "instrumental reason," as the Frankfurt School calls it, may affect language by homogenizing it. The critic who uses the conversational style because of its propriety may actually be doing a disservice to language. However difficult Blackmur, Burke, Heidegger, or Derrida may be, there is less entropy in them than in those who translate, with the best intentions, hazardous ideas or expressions into ordinary speech. Kermode's translative skill is great; one admires how rebarbative concepts from German hermeneutics or French semiotics steal into the English idiom, but something has leaked away.

We have accepted difficulty in art, but in criticism there is still a wish to "solve the phenomena." The irony and intricacy of art were fully described, not resolved, by the New Criticism; nevertheless, a sort of pedagogical illusion arose that codified the language of explication and exempted it from the very analysis it so carefully applied to art. It is not surprising, therefore, to find that Paul de Man's *Blindness and Insight* (1971) is subtitled "Essays in the Rhetoric of Contemporary Criticism." In the aggressively modern thinkers he takes up, de Man was concerned to show traces of a "Hellenic" ideal of embodiment which continued to privilege categories of presence and plenitude. What was passed over, according to de Man, was the "temporal labyrinth of interpretation" with its purely negative kind of totality (Sartre had coined the phrase *totalité détotalisé*). But now, some ten to twenty years later—de Man's essays were all written in the sixties—the situation has changed. It is no longer a pseudoclassical notion of *paidea* that needs scrutiny but a para-Marxist and utopian notion of pedagogy.

I mean by that a "dream of communication" that looks not only toward the transparence of the text or the undistorted transmission of messages from sender (writer) to receiver (reader) but also toward a social system that is supposed to create that language-possibility instead of merely enforcing it. Yet everything we have learned from politics or pragmatics has put the dream of communication in doubt. It is an ever-receding horizon like Hegel's end-state, where subject and substance, real and rational, concrete and universal coincide. That end-state remains a *topos noetos,* a heaven in the form of a horizon, a glimpse of totality that converts every end into a means and so proves to be the moving principle it sought to arrest. Every style (stile) is also a Gate, to pun with Mather; but a style is at once open and closed.

Developments in criticism since about 1920 show that language can be analyzed more closely than was deemed possible, but not purified by prescriptions arising from the analysis. The intimate alliance of writing with "difference" we find in Derrida, and such typical assertions that "language is the *rupture* with totality itself . . . primarily the caesura makes meaning emerge," are symptomatic of a cautious attitude toward both theory and the dream of communication. "The theory of the Text," Barthes has said, "can coincide only with a practise of writing." We are now as aware of our language condition as of the condition of our language.

Derrida is important also because he exposes the privilege accorded to voice in the form of the conversational style as it aspires to Pater's "inward dialogue." Derrida's deconstruction, of course, does not aim at a historical style but at the dream of communication which that style, as the proprium of all styles, underwrites. The columns of *Glas* are cut by the arbitrary "justification" of the margins and the edginess of pages that interrupt, like a caesura, the words. *Glas* becomes a stylish reprisal against style—that word whose *y grecque* was hellenized into it during the Renaissance. Derrida rescues style from its confusion with Greek *stulos,* column, and so recovers its link both with stiletto, a pointed weapon, and *stiglus* or *stigma* that emphasize cutting, pointing, branding. Style is, in fact, short for *vertere stilum,* or turning the incising stylus to its blunt side, which was used to erase the impression made on waxed tablets; writing stylishly is thus to erase what is written and write over it. The term "verse" takes up the other half of that phrase, as in Wordsworth's "the turnings intricate of verse"—although the metaphor accrues overtones of the turning earth, the turning of the plough, and so forth. Style is what cannot stand still.

I want to conclude with a few remarks on a philosopher's recent attempt to introduce the conversational style once more. This attempt is a valiant throwback to the Age of Hume, when the conversationalists had won out, at least in prose. Yet philosophy remained under the imperative of not entirely forsaking the quest for a universal and immutable discourse. It honored the conversational mode for its virtues of social accommodation. It was philosophy for the salon. But subversively so, if we recall that it led to such strange conversation as *La Philosophie dans le Boudoir,* which put nature out of countenance. The contemporary post-Wittgensteinian attempt to revive the conversational ethos and to use it as a critique of fundamentalist perspectives in philosophy is of course that of Richard Rorty.

Rorty's *Philosophy and the Mirror of Nature* examines three modern thinkers who have had an immense influence on both professional and nonprofessional philosophers. The careers of Wittgenstein, Heidegger, and Dewey are taken to be exemplary: each began with a project to make philosophy "foundational," that is, to discover a basis for distinguishing truth from falsity, science from speculation, and verifiable representation from mere appearance. Each of the three breaks free of this project (labelled "epistemological" and "Kantian") so that their work becomes therapeutic rather than constructive, or as Rorty also likes to say "edifying" (in the secular sense of the adjective, that conveys the German idea of *Bildung*) rather than systematic. Indeed they warn us against the very temptations acceded to in their earlier, scientific phase.

Rorty ends with a section entitled "Philosophy in the Conversation of Mankind," alluding to Michael Oakeshott's well-known "The Voice of Poetry in the Conversation of Mankind," published in *Rationalism and Politics* (1975). He latches onto the idea of "conversation," which suggests an alternative to the rigorous terminology and analytic pretensions of epistemological inquiry. Contemporary issues in philosophy, he writes, are "events in a certain stage of conversation —a conversation which once knew nothing of these issues and may know nothing of them again." And he distinguishes between treating philosophy as a "voice in a conversation" on the one hand, and treating it "as a subject, a *Fach,* a field of professional inquiry," on the other. This denial of a special field to philosophers has an attractive Emersonian ring, and of course brings Plato back as our most edifying thinker. Yet Rorty stops short of exalting even Plato, mainly because "the conversation Plato began has been enlarged by more voices than Plato would have dreamed possible."

This conclusion is surprisingly close to what recent literary critics have wished for. They take back from philosophy what is their own; they are tired of being treated as camp followers of this or that movement in philosophy. When the privilege accorded to science spills over into philosophy, literary culture is considered a dilution of ideas originated by stronger heads, a crude and subjective application of those ideas. Literary critics are then deemed parasitic not only vis-à-vis creative poem or novel but also vis-à-vis exact philosophy. Their very attempt to think independently, intensely, theoretically, is denounced—often by other literary critics. They are said to be big with the "arrogance of theory" and accused of emulating a discipline that should be kept out of the fair fields of literary study. "Whereas a generation ago," we read in a recent issue of *Novel,* "fine American literary journals would devote complete issues to a Hardy, Yeats, Faulkner, or G. M. Hopkins, current journals devote whole issues to French professors"; and the complainant goes on to charge that it was Northrop Frye's insistence on criticism as a systematic subject that allowed the "pod-people, so many of them dropouts from technical philosophy, or linguistics, or the half-science of sociology, into the fair fields of Anglo-American literary study."

However comforting it is to have a philosopher like Rorty on one's side, and to have him appreciate the recognitive as well as cognitive function of words, a hard question must be put. Can Rorty's position do more than redress the balance between philosophy and literary studies by demystifying the scientistic streak in modern thought? Can it disclose also something substantive in literary study itself, as the distance between philosophical discourse and literary commentary is lessened by viewing both as "conversation"?

The term "conversation" is a metaphor. It slides over the question of style. Should we really name something "conversation" when it is written? There is "dialogue," of course; but Rorty's concept does not wish to be dependent on a formal or stylized exchange between persons. Perhaps he would say that all writing is internalized conversation, a select polyphony of voices. The problem is not adequately treated from a literary point of view; nor entirely from a philosophical point of view. Is Rorty arguing that thinking is possible in idiomatic language without special terms or neologisms? Or is he saying that noncolloquial language also, even when it seems harsh and abstract, as so often in Kant and Husserl—in all such Teuton-Titans—is figurative or inventive despite itself? Does he not, in fact, challenge *two* assumptions: (1) that technical terms (which diverge from so-called ordinary language) are necessary for rigorous thinking, but also (2) that ordinary language—vernacular, conversational—is more inventive or figurative than the language of abstruse, systematic thought?

To these challenges there may not be a resolution. What is important is the recognition aroused in us by contemporary philosophers like Rorty and Stanley Cavell that no order of discourse or institutional way of writing has a monopoly either on rigor or invention. Philosophy remains a "conversation" with unexpected turns that cannot all be predicted, though they can later be integrated by subtle adjustments or shifts in the way we think.

At the very moment, then, that Rorty seeks to deliver philosophy from pretentiousness (both metaphysical and epistemological), literary study is seeking to deliver itself from the ideal he propagates: *conversation*.

In fact, the gentility of literary dons and the avoidance of theory are on the increase, because science has invaded literary studies too, and the older ideal is becoming, in reaction, more defensive. Many otherwise intelligent critics turn into bulldogs of understatement as they try and preserve an elegance, however mouldy, and a casualness, however fake. In Christopher Ricks, for example, a word-chopping, ordinary-language type of analysis is directed against all who attempt theory, as if the big words were naughty words we had to be shamed out of, and as if any inventive, elaborated schematism were a sin against the English sentence.

What is appealing about Rorty's position is how little difference there is between him and Pater in *Plato and Platonism* (1893). Pater did not wish to distinguish sharply between dialogue and dialectic; the same holds today for Hans-Georg Gadamer (an "edifying" rather than "systematic" philosopher, according to Rorty). Yet however attractive this Hellenic ideal may be, the results have often been dismaying. An Anglicized version of Greek *paidea* (tutorials pretending to be dialogue) has now become an unthinking attack on theory and is in danger of returning literary study to a supercilious kind of lexical inquisition that undoes everything we have learned from the large-hearted stylistics of a Leo Spitzer, an Erich Auerbach, and others.

Yet it is also clear that to take back from philosophy what is ours cannot mean a method that applies specific philosophical ideas to literature. What does Heidegger really tell us about William Carlos Williams or Paul Ricoeur about Yeats? Or Derrida about Melville? Such mixing it up may have its uses, of course. We write by assimilating what we read: we could therefore read philosophy as a sister-art; and philosophy, in turn, could consider literature as something better than time out for conversation. "Literature" here should be understood to include essays, and also larger scholarly structures in context: Spitzer in the context of German philology and the making of dictionaries; Auerbach in the context of Marxism and socioeconomic philosophies; Frye in that of anthropology and the ecumenical unifying of all fables; Empson in that of English, abdicating its political supremacy as a culture yet asserting itself as a "moral science" by constructing a new language-centered ethos.

As we pursue this institutional analysis the thorny issue of whether we need an abnormal or special terminology (a metalanguage) becomes moot. Either we shall give up the idea that there is *one* correct way of talking about literature (in a terminology that is "logical" rather than "literary"), or we shall realize that all commentary is as much metacommentary (Fredric Jameson's term) as metacommentary or theory remains context-bound commentary. The real issue that will come forward is how skeptical we should be about *cultural translation.* Can the affairs of one culture (so dependent on a different text-milieu and not only on a different language) be understood by thinkers situated in another culture, even when the latter is a relative? (It may be easier to understand a culture when the distance is great enough to prevent easy rapprochement, or what translators call "false friends.") A creative skepticism about the crossover from culture to culture seems to me the right attitude. We need a "negative capability" that does not deny speculative criticism but engages with the highly mediated status of cultural and verbal facts. The basic question then is about the nature of understanding, and what sort of responsive style might articulate this understanding. Is a conversation between cultures possible? Or is such a conversation, as between persons, always mixed with imposition? Though we talk about "dialogue" and "keeping lines of communication open," it is hard to think of a conversation that is not forcefully interspersed with moments of appropriation and expropriation. The ruses of language, the cunning of reasonableness, the sheer display of intellect or personality enter an unpredictable equation. The perfect English style, Orage said, will charm by its power; yet power and charm are precisely what the resistant thinker would like to keep separate.

EDWARD SAID

Edward Said has been included among the Heideggerians and Deconstructors not because he would be honored to be, but because his Orientalism project bears inevitable resemblances in strategies and procedures to the "destruction" of received ideas—that is, the resistance to the ideology-producing institutions that prevent us from seeing things from a less complacent point of view. That Said evokes cheers from audiences when he claims still to believe in "facts" does not mean that he is unaware of the equivocal status of all representations, none of which is so objective that it transcends everyone's language, culture, or political ambiance.* Nevertheless, some good work can be done simply by being aware of the ideology of representation. At issue in this case is a binary distinction as clear as Bataille's head/toe pair or Derrida's voice/writing opposition. The new distinction is that between the Occident and the Orient. We find it deeply embedded in Greek literature. The modest piety of the Greek—his rationality—is time and again contrasted by Herodotus with the maniacal irrationality of an Asiatic like Xerxes. Milton can refer to Satan as "Sultan" of the fallen angels and invoke crazed hoards of dark devils swinging scimitars and pouring down among innocent, well-ordered communities. It is very easy to reactivate this mythology, as we saw during the Iran hostage episode, covered by Said in his book *Covering Islam* (1981). The mythology is transmitted by our very culture, by the texts we have written, by the words we use. As Said says, these images we take for truth are "poetic," produced perhaps by the predilection of a bilaterally symmetrical creature for clear-cut oppositions. Herodotus tells us in his *Histories:* "All the Indian tribes I have mentioned copulate in the open like cattle; their skins are all of the same colour, much like Ethiopians'. Their semen is not white like other peoples', but black like their own skins. . . ."†

Orientalism is the stereotype of the Eastern Other produced by the normal functioning of Western discourse. Orientalism is also now a well-funded academic institution which produces such stereotypes intentionally: the Orientalist ". . . neither tries nor wants to unsettle already firm convictions." The Orientalist's job is to speak for the unarticulate Other, to tell us what this Other thinks and wants. Said is the startlingly articulate, indefatigable, but increasingly melancholy voice of the heretofore silenced. Perhaps his most moving book, *After the Last*

*Edward Said, *Orientalism* (New York: Random House, 1978) 272.
†Herodotus, *The Histories,* trans. Aubrey de Selincourt (Harmondsworth: Penguin, 1968) 217.

Sky (1986), with photographs by Jean Mohr of entirely unidealized Palestinian lives, is the positive counterpart of *Orientalism's* negative critique.

Orientalizing the Oriental

1978

S trictly speaking, Orientalism is a field of learned study. In the Christian West, Orientalism is considered to have commenced its formal existence with the decision of the Church Council of Vienne in 1312 to establish a series of chairs in "Arabic, Greek, Hebrew, and Syriac at Paris, Oxford, Bologna, Avignon, and Salamanca." Yet any account of Orientalism would have to consider not only the professional Orientalist and his work but also the very notion of a field of study based on a geographical, cultural, linguistic, and ethnic unit called the Orient. Fields, of course, are made. They acquire coherence and integrity in time because scholars devote themselves in different ways to what seems to be a commonly agreed-upon subject matter. Yet it goes without saying that a field of study is rarely as simply defined as even its most committed partisans—usually scholars, professors, experts, and the like—claim it is. Besides, a field can change so entirely, in even the most traditional disciplines like philology, history, or theology, as to make an all-purpose definition of subject matter almost impossible. This is certainly true of Orientalism, for some interesting reasons.

To speak of scholarly specialization as a geographical "field" is, in the case of Orientalism, fairly revealing since no one is likely to imagine a field symmetrical to it called Occidentalism. Already the special, perhaps even eccentric attitude of Orientalism becomes apparent. For although many learned disciplines imply a position taken towards, say, *human* material (a historian deals with the human past from a special vantage point in the present), there is no real analogy for taking a fixed, more or less total geographical position towards a wide variety of social, linguistic, political, and historical realities. A classicist, a Romance specialist, even an Americanist focuses on a relatively modest portion of the world, not on a full half of it. But Orientalism is a field with considerable geographical ambition. And since Orientalists have traditionally occupied themselves with things Oriental (a specialist in Islamic law, no less than an expert in Chinese dialects or in Indian religions, is considered an Orientalist by people who call themselves Orientalists), we must learn to accept enormous, indiscriminate size plus an almost infinite capacity for subdivision as one of the chief characteristics of Orientalism—one that is evidenced in its confusing amalgam of imperial vagueness and precise detail.

All of this describes Orientalism as an academic discipline. The "ism" in Orientalism serves to insist on the distinction of this discipline from every other kind. The rule in its historical development as an academic discipline has been its increasing scope, not its greater selectiveness. Renaissance Orientalists like Erpenius and Guillaume Postel were primarily specialists in the languages of the Biblical provinces, although Postel boasted that he could get across Asia as far as China without needing an interpreter. By and large, until the mid-eighteenth-century Orientalists were Biblical scholars, students of the Semitic languages, Islamic specialists, or, because the Jesuits had opened up the new study of China, Sinologists. The whole middle expanse of Asia was not academically conquered for Orientalism until, during the later eighteenth century, Anquetil-Duperron and Sir William Jones were able intelligibly to reveal the extraordinary riches of Avestan and Sanskrit. By the middle of the nineteenth century Orientalism was as vast a treasure-house of learning as one could imagine. There are two excellent indices of this new, triumphant eclecticism. One is the encyclopedic description of Orientalism roughly from 1765 to 1850 given by Raymond Schwab in his *La Renaissance orientale*. Quite aside from the scientific discoveries of things Oriental made by learned professionals during this period in Europe, there was the virtual epidemic of Orientalia affecting every major poet, essayist, and philosopher of the period. Schwab's notion is that "Oriental" identifies an amateur or professional enthusiasm for everything Asiatic, which was wonderfully synonymous with the exotic, the mysterious, the profound, the seminal; this is a later transposition eastwards of a similar enthusiasm in Europe for Greek and Latin antiquity during the High Renaissance. In 1829 Victor Hugo put this change in directions as follows: "Au siècle de Louis XIV on était helléniste, maintenant on est orientaliste." A nineteenth-century Orientalist was therefore either a scholar (a Sinologist, an Islamicist, an Indo-Europeanist) or a gifted enthusiast (Hugo in *Les Orientales*, Goethe in the *Westöstlicher Diwan*), or both (Richard Burton, Edward Lane, Friedrich Schlegel).

The second index of how inclusive Orientalism had become since the Council of Vienne is to be found in nineteenth-century chronicles of the field itself. The most thorough of its kind is Jules Mohl's *Vingt-sept Ans d'histoire des études orientales*, a two-volume logbook of everything of note that took place in Orientalism between 1840 and 1867. Mohl was the secretary of the Société asiatique in Paris, and for something more than the first half of the nineteenth century, Paris was the capital of the Orientalist world (and, according to Walter Benjamin, of the nineteenth century). Mohl's position in the Société could not have been more central to the field of Orientalism. There is scarcely anything done by a European scholar touching Asia during those twenty-seven years that Mohl does not enter under "études orientales." His entries of course concern publications, but the range of published material of interest to Orientalist scholars is awesome. Arabic, innumerable Indian dialects, Hebrew, Pehlevi, Assyrian, Babylonian, Mongolian, Chinese, Burmese, Mesopotamian, Javanese: the list of philological works considered Orientalist is almost uncountable. Moreover, Orientalist studies apparently cover everything from the editing and translation of texts to numismatic, anthropological, archaeological, sociological, economic, historical, literary, and cultural studies in every known Asiatic and North African civilization, ancient and modern. Gustave Dugat's *Histoire des orientalistes de l'Europe du XIIe au XIXe siècle* (1868–1870) is a selective history of major figures, but the range represented is no less immense than Mohl's.

Such eclecticism as this had its blind spots, nevertheless. Academic Orientalists for the most part were interested in the classical period of whatever language or society it was that they studied. Not until quite late in the century, with the single major exception of Napoleon's Institut d'Égypte, was much attention given to the academic study of the modern, or actual, Orient. Moreover, the Orient studied was a textual universe by and large; the impact of the Orient was made through books and manuscripts, not, as in the impress of Greece on the Renaissance, through mimetic artifacts like sculpture and pottery. Even the rapport between an Orientalist and the Orient was textual, so much so that it is reported of some of the early-nineteenth-century German Orientalists that their first view of an eight-armed Indian statue cured them completely of their Orientalist taste. When a learned Orientalist traveled in the country of his specialization, it was always with unshakable abstract maxims about the "civilization" he had studied; rarely were Orientalists interested in anything except proving the validity of these musty "truths" by applying them, without great success, to uncomprehending, hence degenerate, natives. Finally, the very power and scope of Orientalism produced not only a fair amount of exact positive knowledge about the Orient but also a kind of second-order knowledge—lurking in such places as the "Oriental" tale, the mythology of the mysterious East, notions of Asian inscrutability—with a life of its own, what V. G. Kiernan has aptly called "Europe's collective day-dream of the Orient." One happy result of this is that an estimable number of important writers during the nineteenth century were Oriental enthusiasts: It is perfectly correct, I think, to speak of a genre of Orientalist writing as exemplified in the works of Hugo, Goethe, Nerval, Flaubert, Fitzgerald, and the like. What inevitably goes with such work, however, is a kind of free-floating mythology of the Orient, an Orient that derives not only from contemporary attitudes and popular prejudices but also from what Vico called the conceit of nations and of scholars. I have already alluded to the political uses of such material as it has turned up in the twentieth century.

Today an Orientalist is less likely to call himself an Orientalist than he was almost any time up to World War II. Yet the designation is still useful, as when universities maintain programs or departments in Oriental languages or Oriental civilizations. There is an Oriental "faculty" at Oxford, and a department of Oriental studies at Princeton. As recently as 1959, the British government empowered a commission "to review developments in the Universities in the fields of Oriental, Slavonic, East European and African studies . . . and to consider, and advise on, proposals for future development." The Hayter Report, as it was called when it appeared in 1961, seemed untroubled by the broad designation of the word *Oriental,* which it found serviceably employed in American universities as well. For even the greatest name in modern Anglo-American Islamic studies, H. A. R. Gibb, preferred to call himself an Orientalist rather than an Arabist. Gibb himself, classicist that he was, could use the ugly neologism "area study" for Orientalism as a way of showing that area studies and Orientalism after all were interchangeable geographical titles. But this, I think, ingenuously belies a much more interesting relationship between knowledge and geography. I should like to consider that relationship briefly.

Despite the distraction of a great many vague desires, impulses, and images, the mind seems persistently to formulate what Claude Lévi-Strauss has called a science of the concrete. A primitive tribe, for example, assigns a definite place, function, and significance to every leafy species in its immediate environment. Many of these grasses and flowers have no practical use; but the point Lévi-Strauss makes is that mind requires order, and order is achieved by discriminating and taking note of everything, placing everything of which the mind is aware in a secure, refindable place, therefore giving things some role to play in the economy of objects and identities that make up an environment. This kind of rudimentary classification has a logic to it, but the rules of the logic by which a green fern in one society is a symbol of grace and in another is considered maleficent are neither predictably rational nor universal. There is always a measure of the purely arbitrary in the way the distinctions between things are seen. And with these distinctions go values whose history, if one could unearth it completely, would probably show the same measure of arbitrariness. This is evident enough in the case of fashion. Why do wigs, lace collars, and high buckled shoes appear, then disappear, over a period of decades? Some of the answer has to do with utility and some with the inherent beauty of the fashion. But if we agree that all things in history, like history itself, are made by men, then we will appreciate how possible it is for many objects or places or times to be assigned roles and given meanings that acquire objective validity only *after* the assignments are made. This is especially true of relatively uncommon things, like foreigners, mutants, or "abnormal" behavior.

It is perfectly possible to argue that some distinctive objects are made by the mind, and that these objects, while appearing to exist objectively, have only a fictional reality. A group of people living on a few acres of land will set up boundaries between their land and its immediate surroundings and the territory beyond, which they call "the land of the barbarians." In other words, this universal practice of designating in one's mind a familiar space which is "ours" and an unfamiliar space beyond "ours" which is "theirs" is a way of making geographical distinctions that *can be* entirely arbitrary. I use the word "arbitrary" here because imaginative geography of the "our land –barbarian land" variety does not require that the barbarians acknowledge the distinction. It is enough for "us" to set up these boundaries in our own minds; "they" become "they" accordingly, and both their territory and their mentality are designated as different from "ours." To a certain extent modern and primitive societies seem thus to derive a sense of their identities negatively. A fifth-century Athenian was very likely to feel himself to be nonbarbarian as much as he positively felt himself to be Athenian. The geographic boundaries accompany the social, ethnic, and cultural ones in expected ways. Yet often the sense in which someone feels himself to be not-foreign is based on a very unrigorous idea of what is "out there," beyond one's own territory. All kinds of suppositions, associations, and fictions appear to crowd the unfamiliar space outside one's own.

The French philosopher Gaston Bachelard once wrote an analysis of what he called the poetics of space. The inside of a house, he said, acquires a sense of intimacy, secrecy, security, real or imagined, because of the experiences that come to seem appropriate for it. The objective space of a house—its corners, corridors, cellar, rooms—is far less important than what poetically it is endowed with, which is usually a quality with an imaginative or figurative value we can name and feel: thus a house may be haunted, or homelike, or prisonlike, or magical. So space acquires emotional and even rational sense by a kind of poetic process, whereby the vacant or anonymous reaches of distance are converted into meaning for us here. The same process occurs when we deal with time. Much of what we associate with or even know about such periods as "long ago" or "the beginning" or "at the end of time" is poetic—made up. For a historian of Middle Kingdom Egypt, "long ago" will have a very clear sort of meaning, but even this meaning does not totally dissipate the imaginative, quasi-fictional quality one senses lurking in a time very different and distant from our own. For there is no doubt that imaginative geography and history help the mind to intensify its own sense of itself by dramatizing the distance and difference between what is close to it and what is far away. This is no less true of the feelings we often have that we would have been more "at home" in the sixteenth century or in Tahiti.

Yet there is no use in pretending that all we know about time and space, or rather history and geography, is more than anything else imaginative. There are such things as positive history and positive geography which in Europe and the United States have impressive achievements to point to. Scholars now do know more about the world, its past and present, than they did, for example, in Gibbon's time. Yet this is not to say that they know all there is to know, nor, more important, is it to say that what they know has effectively dispelled the imaginative geographical and historical knowledge I have been considering. We need not decide here whether this kind of imaginative knowledge infuses history and geography, or whether in some way it overrides them. Let us just say for the time being that it is there as something *more* than what appears to be merely positive knowledge.

Almost from earliest times in Europe the Orient was something more than what was empirically known about it. At least until the early eighteenth century, as R. W. Southern has so elegantly shown, European understanding of one kind of Oriental culture, the Islamic, was ignorant but complex. For certain associations with the East —not quite ignorant, not quite informed—always seem to have gathered around the notion of an Orient. Consider first the demarcation between Orient and West. It already seems bold by the time of the *Iliad.* Two of the most profoundly influential qualities associated with the East appear in Aeschylus's *The Persians,* the earliest Athenian play extant, and in *The Bacchae* of Euripides, the very last one extant. Aeschylus portrays the sense of disaster overcoming the Persians when they learn that their armies, led by King Xerxes, have been destroyed by the Greeks. The chorus sings the following ode:

> Now all Asia's land
> Moans in emptiness.
> Xerxes led forth, oh oh!
> Xerxes destroyed, woe woe!
> Xerxes' plans have all miscarried
> In ships of the sea.
> Why did Darius then
> Bring no harm to his men
> When he led them into battle,
> That beloved leader of men from Susa?

What matters here is that Asia speaks through and by virtue of the European imagination, which is depicted as victorious over Asia, that hostile "other" world beyond the seas. To Asia are given the feelings of emptiness, loss, and disaster that seem thereafter to reward Oriental challenges to the West; and also, the lament that in some glorious past Asia fared better, was itself victorious over Europe.

In *The Bacchae,* perhaps the most Asiatic of all the Attic dramas, Dionysus is explicitly connected with his Asian origins and with the strangely threatening excesses of Oriental mysteries. Pentheus, king of Thebes, is destroyed by his mother, Agave, and her fellow bacchantes. Having defied Dionysus by not recognizing either his power or his divinity, Pentheus is thus horribly punished, and the play ends with a general recognition of the eccentric god's terrible power. Modern commentators on *The Bacchae* have not failed to note the play's extraordinary range of intellectual and aesthetic effects; but there has been no escaping the additional historical detail that Euripides "was surely affected by the new aspect that the Dionysiac cults must have assumed in the light of the foreign ecstatic religions of Bendis, Cybele, Sabazius, Adonis, and Isis, which were introduced from Asia Minor and the Levant and swept through Piraeus and Athens during the frustrating and increasingly irrational years of the Peloponnesian War."

The two aspects of the Orient that set it off from the West in this pair of plays will remain essential motifs of European imaginative geography. A line is drawn between two continents. Europe is powerful and articulate; Asia is defeated and distant. Aeschylus *represents* Asia, makes her speak in the person of the aged Persian queen, Xerxes' mother. It is Europe that articulates the Orient; this articulation is the prerogative, not of a puppet master, but of a genuine creator, whose life-giving power represents, animates, constitutes the otherwise silent and dangerous space beyond familiar boundaries. There is an analogy between Aeschylus's orchestra, which contains the Asiatic world as the playwright conceives it, and the learned envelope of Orientalist scholarship, which also will hold in the vast, amorphous Asiatic sprawl for sometimes sympathetic but always dominating scrutiny. Secondly, there is the motif of the Orient as insinuating danger. Rationality is undermined by Eastern excesses, those mysteriously attractive opposites to what seem to be normal values. The difference separating East from West is symbolized by the sternness with which, at first, Pentheus rejects the hysterical bacchantes. When later he himself becomes a bacchant, he is destroyed not so much for having given in to Dionysus as for having incorrectly assessed Dionysus's menace in the first place. The lesson that Euripides intends is dramatized by the presence in the play of Cadmus and Tiresias, knowledgeable older men who realize that "sovereignty" alone does not rule men; there is such a thing as judgment, they say, which means sizing up correctly the force of alien powers and expertly coming to terms with them. Hereafter Oriental mysteries will be taken seriously, not least because they challenge the rational Western mind to new exercises of its enduring ambition and power.

But one big division, as between West and Orient, leads to other smaller ones, especially as the normal enterprises of civilization provoke such outgoing activities as travel, conquest, new experiences. In classical Greece and Rome geographers, historians, public figures like Caesar, orators, and poets added to the fund of taxonomic lore separating races, regions, nations, and minds from each other; much of that was self-serving, and existed to prove that Romans and Greeks were superior to other kinds of people. But concern with the Orient had its own tradition of classification and hierarchy. From at least the second century B.C. on, it was lost on no traveler or eastward-looking and ambitious Western potentate that Herodotus —historian, traveler, inexhaustibly curious chronicler—and Alexander—king warrior, scientific conqueror—had been in the Orient before. The Orient was therefore subdivided into realms previously known, visited, conquered, by Herodotus and Alexander as well as their epigones, and those realms not previously known, visited, conquered. Christianity completed the setting up of main intra-Oriental spheres: there was a Near Orient and a Far Orient, a familiar Orient, which René Grousset calls "l'empire du Levant," and a novel Orient. The Orient therefore alternated in the mind's geography between being an Old World to which one returned, as to Eden or Paradise, there to set up a new version of the old, and being a wholly new place to which one came as Columbus came to America, in order to set up a New World (although, ironically, Columbus himself thought that he discovered a new part of the Old World). Certainly neither of these Orients was purely one thing or the other: it is their vacillations, their tempting suggestiveness, their capacity for entertaining and confusing the mind, that are interesting.

Consider how the Orient, and in particular the Near Orient, became known in the West as its great complementary opposite since antiquity. There were the Bible and the rise of Christianity; there were travelers like Marco Polo who charted the trade routes and patterned a regulated system of commercial exchange, and after him Lodovico di Varthema and Pietro della Valle; there were fabulists like Mandeville; there were the redoubtable conquering Eastern movements, principally Islam, of course; there were the militant pilgrims, chiefly the Crusaders. Altogether an internally structured archive is built up from the literature that belongs to these experiences. Out of this comes a restricted number of typical encapsulations: the journey, the history, the fable, the stereotype, the polemical confrontation. These are the lenses through which the Orient is experienced, and they shape the language, perception, and form of the encounter between East and West. What gives the immense number of encounters some unity, however, is the vacillation I was speaking about earlier. Something patently foreign and distant acquires, for one reason or another, a status more rather than less familiar. One tends to stop judging things either as completely novel or as completely well known; a new median category emerges, a category that allows one to see new things, things seen for the first time, as versions of a previously known thing. In essence such a category is not so much a way of receiving new information as it is a method of controlling what seems to be a threat to some established view of things. If the mind must suddenly deal with what it takes to be a radically new form of life—as Islam appeared to Europe in the early Middle Ages—the response on the whole is conservative and defensive. Islam is judged to be a fraudulent new version of some previous experience, in this case Christianity. The threat is muted, familiar values impose themselves, and in the end the mind reduces the pressure upon it by accommodating things to itself as either "original" or "repetitious." Islam thereafter is "handled": its novelty and its suggestiveness are brought under control so that relatively nuanced discriminations are now made that would have been impossible had the raw novelty of Islam been left unattended. The Orient at large, therefore, vacillates between the West's contempt for what is familiar and its shivers of delight in—or fear of—novelty.

Yet where Islam was concerned, European fear, if not always respect, was in order. After Mohammed's death in 632, the military and later the cultural and religious hegemony of Islam grew enormously. First Persia, Syria, and Egypt, then Turkey, then North Africa fell to the Muslim armies; in the eighth and ninth centuries Spain, Sicily, and parts of France were conquered. By the thirteenth and fourteenth centuries Islam ruled as far east as India, Indonesia, and

China. And to this extraordinary assault Europe could respond with very little except fear and a kind of awe. Christian authors witnessing the Islamic conquests had scant interest in the learning, high culture, and frequent magnificence of the Muslims, who were, as Gibbon said, "coeval with the darkest and most slothful period of European annals." (But with some satisfaction he added, "since the sum of science has risen in the West, it should seem that the Oriental studies have languished and declined." What Christians typically felt about the Eastern armies was that they had "all the appearance of a swarm of bees, but with a heavy hand . . . they devastated everything": so wrote Erchembert, a cleric in Monte Cassino in the eleventh century.

Not for nothing did Islam come to symbolize terror, devastation, the demonic, hordes of hated barbarians. For Europe, Islam was a lasting trauma. Until the end of the seventeenth century the "Ottoman peril" lurked alongside Europe to represent for the whole of Christian civilization a constant danger, and in time European civilization incorporated that peril and its lore, its great events, figures, virtues, and vices, as something woven into the fabric of life. In Renaissance England alone, as Samuel Chew recounts in his classic study *The Crescent and the Rose,* "a man of average education and intelligence" had at his fingertips, and could watch on the London stage, a relatively large number of detailed events in the history of Ottoman Islam and its encroachments upon Christian Europe. The point is that what remained current about Islam was some necessarily diminished version of those great dangerous forces that it symbolized for Europe. Like Walter Scott's Saracens, the European representation of the Muslim, Ottoman, or Arab was always a way of controlling the redoubtable Orient, and to a certain extent the same is true of the methods of contemporary learned Orientalists, whose subject is not so much the East itself as the East made known, and therefore less fearsome, to the Western reading public.

There is nothing especially controversial or reprehensible about such domestications of the exotic; they take place between all cultures, certainly, and between all men. My point, however, is to emphasize the truth that the Orientalist, as much as anyone in the European West who thought about or experienced the Orient, performed this kind of mental operation. But what is more important still is the limited vocabulary and imagery that impose themselves as a consequence. The reception of Islam in the West is a perfect case in point, and has been admirably studied by Norman Daniel. One constraint acting upon Christian thinkers who tried to understand

Islam was an analogical one; since Christ is the basis of Christian faith, it was assumed—quite incorrectly—that Mohammed was to Islam as Christ was to Christianity. Hence the polemic name "Mohammedanism" given to Islam, and the automatic epithet "imposter" applied to Mohammed. Out of such and many other misconceptions "there formed a circle which was never broken by imaginative exteriorisation. . . . The Christian concept of Islam was integral and self-sufficient." Islam became an image—the word is Daniel's but it seems to me to have remarkable implications for Orientalism in general—whose function was not so much to represent Islam in itself as to represent it for the medieval Christian.

> The invariable tendency to neglect what the Qur'an meant, or what Muslims thought it meant, or what Muslims thought or did in any given circumstances, necessarily implies that Qur'anic and other Islamic doctrine was presented in a form that would convince Christians; and more and more extravagant forms would stand a chance of acceptance as the distance of the writers and public from the Islamic border increased. It was with very great reluctance that what Muslims said Muslims believed was accepted as what they did believe. There was a Christian picture in which the details (even under the pressure of facts) were abandoned as little as possible, and in which the general outline was never abandoned. There were shades of difference, but only with a common framework. All the corrections that were made in the interests of an increasing accuracy were only a defence of what had newly been realised to be vulnerable, a shoring up of a weakened structure. Christian opinion was an erection which could not be demolished, even to be rebuilt.

This rigorous Christian picture of Islam was intensified in innumerable ways, including—during the Middle Ages and early Renaissance—a large variety of poetry, learned controversy, and popular superstition. By this time the Near Orient had been all but incorporated in the common world-picture of Latin Christianity—as in the *Chanson de Roland* the worship of Saracens is portrayed as embracing Mahomet *and* Apollo. By the middle of the fifteenth century, as R. W. Southern has brilliantly shown, it became apparent to serious European thinkers "that something would have to be done about Islam," which had turned the situation around somewhat by itself arriving militarily in Eastern Europe. Southern recounts a dramatic episode between 1450 and 1460 when four learned men, John of Segovia, Nicholas of Cusa, Jean Germain, and Aeneas Silvius (Pius II), attempted to deal with Islam through *contraferentia,* or "conference." The idea was John of Segovia's: it was to have been a staged conference with Islam in which Christians attempted the wholesale conversion of Muslims. "He saw the conference as an instrument with a political as well as a strictly religious function, and in words which will strike a chord in modern breasts he exclaimed that even if it were to last ten years it would be less expensive and less damaging than war." There was no agreement between the four men, but the episode is crucial for having been a fairly sophisticated attempt—part of a general European attempt from Bede to Luther—to put a representative Orient in front of Europe, to *stage* the Orient and Europe together in some coherent way, the idea being for Christians to make it clear to Muslims that Islam was just a misguided version of Christianity. Southern's conclusion follows:

> Most conspicuous to us is the inability of any of these systems of thought [European Christian] to provide a fully satisfying explanation of the phenomenon they had set out to explain [Islam]—still less to influence the course of practical events in a decisive way. At a practical level, events never turned out either so well or so ill as the most intelligent observers predicted; and it is perhaps worth noticing that they never turned out better than when the best judges confidently expected a happy ending. Was there any progress [in Christian knowledge of Islam]? I must express my conviction that there was. Even if the solution of the problem remained obstinately hidden from sight, the statement of the problem became more complex, more rational, and more related to experience. . . . The scholars who labored at the problem of Islam in the Middle Ages failed to find the solution they sought and desired; but they developed habits of mind and powers of comprehension which, in other men and in other fields, may yet deserve success.

The best part of Southern's analysis, here and elsewhere in his brief history of Western views of Islam, is his demonstration that it is finally Western ignorance which becomes more refined and complex, not some body of positive Western knowledge which increases in size and accuracy. For fictions have their own logic and their own dialectic of growth or decline. Onto the character of Mohammed in the Middle Ages was heaped a bundle of attributes that corresponded to the "character of the [twelfth-century] prophets of the 'Free Spirit' who did actually arise in Europe, and claim credence and collect followers." Similarly, since Mohammed was viewed as the disseminator of a false Revelation, he became as well the epitome of lechery, debauchery, sodomy, and a whole battery of assorted treacheries, all of which derived "logically" from his doctrinal impostures. Thus the Orient acquired representatives, so to speak, and representations, each one more concrete, more internally congruent with some Western exigency, than the ones that preceded it. It is as if, having once settled on the Orient as a locale suitable for incarnating the infinite in a finite shape, Europe could not stop the practice; the Orient and the Oriental, Arab, Islamic, Indian, Chinese, or whatever, become repetitious pseudo-incarnations of some great original (Christ, Europe, the West) they were supposed to have been imitating. Only the source of these rather narcissistic Western ideas about the Orient changed in time, not their character. Thus we will find it commonly believed in the twelfth and thirteenth centuries that Arabia was "on the fringe of the Christian world, a natural asylum for heretical outlaws," and that Mohammed was a cunning apostate, whereas in the twentieth century an Orientalist scholar, an erudite specialist, will be the one to point out how Islam is really no more than second-order Arian heresy.[1]

Our initial description of Orientalism as a learned field now acquires a new concreteness. A field is often an enclosed space. The idea of representation is a theatrical one: the Orient is the stage on which the whole East is confined. On this stage will appear figures whose role it is to represent the larger whole from which they emanate. The Orient then seems to be, not an unlimited extension beyond the familiar European world, but rather a closed field, a theatrical stage affixed to Europe. An Orientalist is but the particular specialist in knowledge for which Europe at large is responsible, in the way that an audience is historically and culturally responsible for (and responsive to) dramas technically put together by the dramatist. In the depths of this Oriental stage stands a prodigious cultural repertoire whose individual items evoke a fabulously rich world: the Sphinx, Cleopatra, Eden, Troy, Sodom and Gomorrah, Astarte, Isis and Osiris, Sheba, Babylon, the Genii, the Magi, Nineveh, Prester John, Mahomet, and dozens more; settings, in some cases names only, half-imagined, half-known; monsters, devils, heroes; terrors, pleasures, desires. The European imagination was nourished extensively from this repertoire: between the Middle Ages and the eighteenth century such major authors as Ariosto, Milton, Marlowe, Tasso, Shakespeare, Cervantes, and the authors of the *Chanson de Roland*

---

1. D. B. MacDonald, "Whither Islam," *Muslim World,* XXIII (January 1933), 2.

and the *Poema del Cid* drew on the Orient's riches for their productions, in ways that sharpened the outlines of imagery, ideas, and figures populating it. In addition, a great deal of what was considered learned Orientalist scholarship in Europe pressed ideological myths into service, even as knowledge seemed genuinely to be advancing.

A celebrated instance of how dramatic form and learned imagery come together in the Orientalist theater is Barthélemy d'Herbelot's *Bibliothèque orientale,* published posthumously in 1697, with a preface by Antoine Galland. The introduction of the recent *Cambridge History of Islam* considers the *Bibliothèque,* along with George Sale's preliminary discourse to his translation of the Koran (1734) and Simon Ockley's *History of the Saracens* (1708, 1718), to be "highly important" in widening "the new understanding of Islam" and conveying it "to a less academic readership." This inadequately describes d'Herbelot's work, which was not restricted to Islam as Sale's and Ockley's were. With the exception of Johann H. Hottinger's *Historia Orientalis,* which appeared in 1651, the *Bibliothèque* remained the standard reference work in Europe until the early nineteenth century. Its scope was truly epochal. Galland, who was the first European translator of *The Thousand and One Nights* and an Arabist of note, contrasted d'Herbelot's achievement with every prior one by noting the prodigious range of his enterprise. D'Herbelot read a great number of works, Galland said, in Arabic, Persian, and Turkish, with the result that he was able to find out about matters hitherto concealed from Europeans. After first composing a dictionary of these three Oriental languages, d'Herbelot went on to study Oriental history, theology, geography, science, and art, in both their fabulous and their truthful varieties. Thereafter he decided to compose two works, one a *bibliothèque,* or "library," an alphabetically arranged dictionary, the second a *florilège,* or anthology. Only the first part was completed.

Galland's account of the *Bibliothèque* stated that "orientale" was planned to include principally the Levant, although—Galland says admiringly—the time period covered did not begin only with the creation of Adam and end with the "temps où nous sommes": d'Herbelot went even further back, to a time described as "plus haut" in fabulous histories—to the long period of the pre-Adamite Solimans. As Galland's description proceeds, we learn that the *Bibliothèque* was like "any other" history of the world, for what it attempted was a complete compendium of the knowledge available on such matters as the Creation, the Deluge, the destruction of Babel, and so forth—with the difference that d'Herbelot's sources were Oriental. He divided history into two types, sacred and profane (the Jews and Christians in the first, the Muslims in the second), and two periods, pre- and postdiluvian. Thus d'Herbelot was able to discuss such widely divergent histories as the Mogul, the Tartar, the Turkish, and the Slavonic; he took in as well all the provinces of the Muslim Empire, from the Extreme Orient to the Pillars of Hercules, with their customs, rituals, traditions, commentaries, dynasties, palaces, rivers, and flora. Such a work, even though it included some attention to "la doctrine perverse de Mahomet, qui a causé si grands dommages au Christianisme," was more capaciously thorough than any work before it. Galland concluded his "Discours" by assuring the reader at length that d'Herbelot's *Bibliothèque* was uniquely "utile et agréable"; other Orientalists, like Postel, Scaliger, Golius, Pockoke, and Erpenius, produced Orientalist studies that were too narrowly grammatical, lexicographical, geographical, or the like. Only d'Herbelot was able to write a work capable of convincing European readers that the study of Oriental culture was more than just thankless and fruitless: only d'Herbelot, according to Galland, attempted to form in the minds of his readers a sufficiently ample idea of what it meant to know and study the Orient, an idea that would both fill the mind and satisfy one's great, previously conceived expectations.

In such efforts as d'Herbelot's, Europe discovered its capacities for encompassing and Orientalizing the Orient. A certain sense of superiority appears here and there in what Galland had to say about his and d'Herbelot's *materia orientalia;* as in the work of seventeenth-century geographers like Raphael du Mans, Europeans could perceive that the Orient was being outstripped and outdated by Western science. But what becomes evident is not only the advantage of a Western perspective: there is also the triumphant technique for taking the immense fecundity of the Orient and making it systematically, even alphabetically, knowable by Western laymen. When Galland said of d'Herbelot that he satisfied one's expectations he meant, I think, that the *Bibliothèque* did not attempt to revise commonly received ideas about the Orient. For what the Orientalist does is to *confirm* the Orient in his readers' eyes; he neither tries nor wants to unsettle already firm convictions. All the *Bibliothèque orientale* did was represent the Orient more fully and more clearly; what may have been a loose collection of randomly acquired facts concerning vaguely Levantine history, Biblical imagery, Islamic culture, place names, and so on were transformed into a rational Oriental panorama, from A to Z. Under the entry for Mohammed, d'Herbelot first supplied all of the Prophet's given names, then proceeded to confirm Mohammed's ideological and doctrinal value as follows:

> C'est le fameux imposteur Mahomet, Auteur et Fondateur d'une hérésie, qui a pris le nom de religion, que nous appellons Mahometane. *Voyez* le titre d'Eslam.
> Les Interprètes de l'Alcoran et autres Docteurs de la Loy Musulmane ou Mahometane ont appliqué à ce faux prophète tous les éloges, que les Ariens, Paulitiens ou Paulianistes & autres Hérétiques ont attribué à Jésus-Christ, en lui ôtant sa Divinité. . . .

> (This is the famous imposter Mahomet, Author and Founder of a heresy, which has taken on the name of religion, which we call Mohammedan. See entry under *Islam*.
> The interpreters of the Alcoran and other Doctors of Muslim or Mohammedan Law have applied to this false prophet all the praises which the Arians, Paulicians or Paulianists, and other Heretics have attributed to Jesus Christ, while stripping him of his Divinity. . . .)

"Mohammedan" is the relevant (and insulting) European designation; "Islam," which happens to be the correct Muslim name, is relegated to another entry. The "heresy . . . which we call Mohammedan" is "caught" as the imitation of a Christian imitation of true religion. Then, in the long historical account of Mohammed's life, d'Herbelot can turn to more or less straight narrative. But it is the *placing* of Mohammed that counts in the *Bibliothèque.* The dangers of free-wheeling heresy are removed when it is transformed into ideologically explicit matter for an alphabetical item. Mohammed no longer roams the Eastern world as a threatening, immoral debauchee; he sits quietly on his (admittedly prominent) portion of the Orientalist stage. He is given a genealogy, an explanation, even a development, all of which are subsumed under the simple statements that prevent him from straying elsewhere.

Such "images" of the Orient as this are images in that they represent or stand for a very large entity, otherwise impossibly diffuse, which they enable one to grasp or see. They are also *characters,* related to such types as the braggarts, misers, or gluttons produced by Theophrastus, La Bruyère, or Selden. Perhaps it is not exactly correct to say that one *sees* such characters as the *miles gloriosus* or Mahomet the imposter, since the discursive confinement of a character is supposed at best to let one apprehend a generic type without difficulty or ambiguity. D'Herbelot's character of Mahomet is an *image,* however, because the false prophet is part of a general theatrical representation called *orientale* whose totality is contained in the *Bibliothèque.*

The didactic quality of the Orientalist representation cannot be detached from the rest of the performance. In a learned work like the *Bibliothèque orientale,* which was the result of systematic study and research, the author imposes a disciplinary order upon the material he has worked on; in addition, he wants it made clear to the reader that what the printed page delivers is an ordered, disciplined judgment of the material. What is thus conveyed by the *Bibliothèque* is an idea of Orientalism's power and effectiveness, which everywhere remind the reader that henceforth in order to get at the Orient he must pass through the learned grids and codes provided by the Orientalist. Not only is the Orient accommodated to the moral exigencies of Western Christianity; it is also circumscribed by a series of attitudes and judgments that send the Western mind, not first to Oriental sources for correction and verification, but rather to other Orientalist works. The Orientalist stage, as I have been calling it, becomes a system of moral and epistemological rigor. As a discipline representing institutionalized Western knowledge of the Orient, Orientalism thus comes to exert a three-way force, on the Orient, on the Orientalist, and on the Western "consumer" of Orientalism. It would be wrong, I think, to underestimate the strength of the three-way relationship thus established. For the Orient ("out there" towards the East) is corrected, even penalized, for lying outside the boundaries of European society, "our" world; the Orient is thus *Orientalized,* a process that not only marks the Orient as the province of the Orientalist but also forces the uninitiated Western reader to accept Orientalist codifications (like d'Herbelot's alphabetized *Bibliothèque*) as the *true* Orient. Truth, in short, becomes a function of learned judgment, not of the material itself, which in time seems to owe even its existence to the Orientalist.

This whole didactic process is neither difficult to understand nor difficult to explain. One ought again to remember that all cultures impose corrections upon raw reality, changing it from free-floating objects into units of knowledge. The problem is not that conversion takes place. It is perfectly natural for the human mind to resist the assault on it of untreated strangeness; therefore cultures have always been inclined to impose complete transformations on other cultures, receiving these other cultures not as they are but as, for the benefit of the receiver, they ought to be. To the Westerner, however, the Oriental was always *like* some aspect of the West; to some of the German Romantics, for example, Indian religion was essentially an Oriental version of Germano-Christian pantheism. Yet the Orientalist makes it his work to be always converting the Orient from something into something else: he does this for himself, for the sake of his culture, in some cases for what he believes is the sake of the Oriental. This process of conversion is a disciplined one: it is taught, it has its own societies, periodicals, traditions, vocabulary, rhetoric, all in basic ways connected to and supplied by the prevailing cultural and political norms of the West. And, as I shall demonstrate, it tends to become more rather than less total in what it tries to do, so much so that as one surveys Orientalism in the nineteenth and twentieth centuries the overriding impression is of Orientalism's insensitive schematization of the entire Orient.

How early this schematization began is clear from the examples I have given of Western representations of the Orient in classical Greece. How strongly articulated were later representations building on the earlier ones, how inordinately careful their schematization, how dramatically effective their placing in Western imaginative geography, can be illustrated if we turn now to Dante's *Inferno*. Dante's achievement in *The Divine Comedy* was to have seamlessly combined the realistic portrayal of mundane reality with a universal and eternal system of Christian values. What Dante the pilgrim sees as he walks through the Inferno, Purgatorio, and Paradiso is a unique vision of judgment. Paolo and Francesca, for instance, are seen as eternally confined to hell for their sins, yet they are seen as enacting, indeed living, the very characters and actions that put them where they will be for eternity. Thus each of the figures in Dante's vision not only represents himself but is also a typical representation of his character and the fate meted out to him.

"Maometto"—Mohammed—turns up in canto 28 of the *Inferno*. He is located in the eighth of the nine circles of Hell, in the ninth of the ten Bolgias of Malebolge, a circle of gloomy ditches surrounding Satan's stronghold in Hell. Thus before Dante reaches Mohammed, he passes through circles containing people whose sins are of a lesser order: the lustful, the avaricious, the gluttonous, the heretics, the wrathful, the suicidal, the blasphemous. After Mohammed there are only the falsifiers and the treacherous (who include Judas, Brutus, and Cassius) before one arrives at the very bottom of Hell, which is where Satan himself is to be found. Mohammed thus belongs to a rigid hierarchy of evils, in the category of what Dante calls *seminator di scandalo e di scisma*. Mohammed's punishment, which is also his eternal fate, is a peculiarly disgusting one: he is endlessly being cleft in two from his chin to his anus like, Dante says, a cask whose staves are ripped apart. Dante's verse at this point spares the reader none of the eschatological detail that so vivid a punishment entails: Mohammed's entrails and his excrement are described with unflinching accuracy. Mohammed explains his punishment to Dante, pointing as well to Ali, who precedes him in the line of sinners whom the attendant devil is splitting in two; he also asks Dante to warn one Fra Dolcino, a renegade priest whose sect advocated community of women and goods and who was accused of having a mistress, of what will be in store for him. It will not have been lost on the reader that Dante saw a parallel between Dolcino's and Mohammed's revolting sensuality, and also between their pretensions to theological eminence.

But this is not all that Dante has to say about Islam. Earlier in the *Inferno,* a small group of Muslims turns up. Avicenna, Averroës, and Saladin are among those virtuous heathens who, along with Hector, Aeneas, Abraham, Socrates, Plato, and Aristotle, are confined to the first circle of the Inferno, there to suffer a minimal (and even honorable) punishment for not having had the benefit of Christian revelation. Dante, of course, admires their great virtues and accomplishments, but because they were not Christians he must condemn them, however lightly, to Hell. Eternity is a great leveler of distinctions, it is true, but the special anachronisms and anomalies of putting pre-Christian luminaries in the same category of "heathen" damnation with post-Christian Muslims does not trouble Dante. Even though the Koran specifies Jesus as a prophet, Dante chooses to consider the great Muslim philosophers and king as having been fundamentally ignorant of Christianity. That they can also inhabit the same distinguished level as the heroes and sages of classical antiquity is an ahistorical vision similar to Raphael's in his fresco *The School of Athens,* in which Averroës rubs elbows on the academy floor with Socrates and Plato (similar to Fénelon's *Dialogues des morts* [1700– 1718], where a discussion takes place between Socrates and Confucius).

The discriminations and refinements of Dante's poetic grasp of Islam are an instance of the schematic, almost cosmological inevitability with which Islam and its designated representatives are creatures of Western geographical, historical, and above all, moral apprehension. Empirical data about the Orient or about any of its parts count for very little; what matters and is decisive is what I have been calling the Orientalist vision, a vision by no means confined to the professional scholar, but rather the common possession of all who have thought about the Orient in the West. Dante's powers as a poet intensify, make more rather than less representative, these perspectives on the Orient. Mohammed, Saladin, Averroës, and Avicenna are fixed in a visionary cosmology—fixed, laid out, boxed in, imprisoned, without much regard for anything except their "function" and the patterns they realize on the stage on which they appear. Isaiah Berlin has described the effect of such attitudes in the following way:

> In [such a] . . . cosmology the world of men (and, in some versions, the entire universe) is a single, all-inclusive hierarchy; so that to explain why each object in it is as, and where, and when it is, and does what it does, is *eo ipso* to say what its goal is, how far it successfully fulfills it, and what are the relations of coordination and subordination between the goals of the various goal-pursuing entities in the harmonious pyramid which they collectively form. If this is a true picture of reality, then historical explanation, like every other form of explanation, must consist, above all, in the attribution of individuals, groups, nations, species, each to its own proper place in the universal pattern. To know the "cosmic" place of a thing or a person is to say what it is and what it does, and at the same time why it should be and do as it is and does. Hence to be and to have value, to exist and to have a function (and to fulfill it more or less successfully) are one and the same. The pattern, and it alone, brings into being and causes to pass away and confers purpose, that is to say, value and meaning, on all there is. To understand is to perceive patterns. . . . The more inevitable an event or an action or a character can be exhibited as being, the better it has been understood, the profounder the researcher's insight, the nearer we are to the one ultimate truth.
> This attitude is profoundly anti-empirical.

And so, indeed, is the Orientalist attitude in general. It shares with magic and with mythology the self-containing, self-reinforcing character of a closed system, in which objects are what they are *because* they are what they are, for once, for all time, for ontological reasons that no empirical material can either dislodge or alter. The European encounter with the Orient, and specifically with Islam, strengthened this system of representing the Orient and, as has been suggested by Henri Pirenne, turned Islam into the very epitome of an outsider against which the whole of European civilization from the Middle Ages on was founded. The decline of the Roman Empire as a result of the barbarian invasions had the paradoxical effect of incorporating barbarian ways into Roman and Mediterranean culture, Romania; whereas, Pirenne argues, the consequence of the Islamic invasions beginning in the seventh century was to move the center of European culture away from the Mediterranean, which was then an Arab province, and towards the North. "Germanism began to play its part in history. Hitherto the Roman tradition had been uninterrupted. Now an original Romano–Germanic civilization was about to develop." Europe was shut in on itself: the Orient, when it was not merely a place in which one traded, was culturally, intellectually, spiritually *outside* Europe and European civilization, which, in Pirenne's words, became "one great Christian community, coterminous with the *ecclesia. . . .* The Occident was now living its own life." In Dante's poem, in the work of Peter the Venerable and other Cluniac Orientalists, in the writings of the Christian polemicists against Islam from Guibert of Nogent and Bede to Roger Bacon, William of Tripoli, Burchard of Mount Syon, and Luther, in the *Poema del Cid,* in the *Chanson de Roland,* and in Shakespeare's *Othello* (that "abuser of the world"), the Orient and Islam are always represented as outsiders having a special role to play *inside* Europe.

Imaginative geography, from the vivid portraits to be found in the *Inferno* to the prosaic niches of d'Herbelot's *Bibliothèque orientale,* legitimates a vocabulary, a universe of representative discourse peculiar to the discussion and understanding of Islam and of the Orient. What this discourse considers to be a fact—that Mohammed is an imposter, for example—is a component of the discourse, a statement the discourse compels one to make whenever the name Mohammed occurs. Underlying all the different units of Orientalist discourse—by which I mean simply the vocabulary employed whenever the Orient is spoken or written about—is a set of representative figures, or tropes. These figures are to the actual Orient—or Islam, which is my main concern here—as stylized costumes are to characters in a play; they are like, for example, the cross that Everyman will carry, or the particolored costume worn by Harlequin in a *commedia dell'arte* play. In other words, we need not look for correspondence between the language used to depict the Orient and the Orient itself, not so much because the language is inaccurate but because it is not even trying to be accurate. What it is trying to do, as Dante tried to do in the *Inferno*, is at one and the same time to characterize the Orient as alien and to incorporate it schematically on a theatrical stage whose audience, manager, and actors are *for* Europe, and only for Europe. Hence the vacillation between the familiar and the alien; Mohammed is always the imposter (familiar, because he pretends to be like the Jesus we know) and always the Oriental (alien, because although he is in some ways "like" Jesus, he is after all not like him).

Rather than listing all the figures of speech associated with the Orient—its strangeness, its difference, its exotic sensuousness, and so forth—we can generalize about them as they were handed down through the Renaissance. They are all declarative and self-evident; the tense they employ is the timeless eternal; they convey an impression of repetition and strength; they are always symmetrical to, and yet diametrically inferior to, a European equivalent, which is sometimes specified, sometimes not. For all these functions it is frequently enough to use the simple copula *is*. Thus, Mohammed *is* an imposter, the very phrase canonized in d'Herbelot's *Bibliothèque* and dramatized in a sense by Dante. No background need be given; the evidence necessary to convict Mohammed is contained in the "is." One does not qualify the phrase, neither does it seem necessary to say that Mohammed *was* an imposter, nor need one consider for a moment that it may not be necessary to repeat the statement. It *is* repeated, he *is* an imposter, and each time one says it, he becomes more of an imposter and the author of the statement gains a little more authority in having declared it. Thus Humphrey Prideaux's famous seventeenth-century biography of Mohammed is subtitled *The True Nature of Imposture*. Finally, of course, such categories as imposter (or Oriental, for that matter) imply, indeed require, an opposite that is neither fraudulently something else nor endlessly in need of explicit identification. And that opposite is "Occidental," or in Mohammed's case, Jesus.

Philosophically, then, the kind of language, thought, and vision that I have been calling Orientalism very generally is a form of radical realism; anyone employing Orientalism, which is the habit for dealing with questions, objects, qualities, and regions deemed Oriental, will designate, name, point to, fix what he is talking or thinking about with a word or phrase, which then is considered either to have acquired, or more simply to be, reality. Rhetorically speaking, Orientalism is absolutely anatomical and enumerative: to use its vocabulary is to engage in the particularizing and dividing of things Oriental into manageable parts. Psychologically, Orientalism is a form of paranoia, knowledge of another kind, say, from ordinary historical knowledge. These are a few of the results, I think, of imaginative geography and of the dramatic boundaries it draws. . . .

PART THREE

MARXISM

V. N. VOLOSHINOV

In their 1986 Translators' Preface to *Marxism and the Philosophy of Language,* Ladislav Matejka and I. R. Titunik call attention to some of the mysteries surrounding the authorship of the work. It was published in Russian in 1929, the same year as Mikhail Bakhtin's *Problems of Dostoevsky's Poetics.* Voloshinov's work was not well-received by the Soviet authorities—Bakhtin's was. In 1973, Voloshinov's book was translated into English. That same year Bakhtin turned 75 years old, and during his birthday celebration in the Soviet Union, a prominent Soviet linguist, V. V. Ivanov, announced that Bakhtin was the actual author of Voloshinov's book, and that there were witnesses to this fact. Voloshinov, who had disappeared without a trace during the Stalin purges of the 1930s, was not one of them. Bakhtin did not deny Ivanov's announcement, nor did he confirm it. However, he did refuse to sign the copyright transfer of the book to his name before he died. For that reason and others, Matejka and Titunik retained Voloshinov's name for the 1986 Harvard edition of their translation.

This book is an interesting alternative to Saussurian linguistics, which, with its notion of the arbitrary sign (that is, language as a self-enclosed system with no necessary connection to material things), provided the basis for French Structuralism's "textual" reality. Saussure devalued the individual speech act *(parole)* and exalted the linguistic system as a whole *(langue). Langue* is the system which gradually penetrates us as children and determines how we think and what we see in the world. It seems at times that language speaks through us, that we do not use language to speak but rather it uses us, that we are zombies of discourse. Voloshinov takes up Saussure's "abstract objectivism" in Part II, Chapter 1 of his book. He complains that Saussure's model is mathematical and Cartesian, that his system ignores both the relationship of sign to reality and the relationship of sign to the individual, who, some say, originated the sign in his private creativity. Instead, for Saussure, the relationship is of sign to other signs. Voloshinov also takes issue in the chapter reprinted here with romantic subjectivists, the "Vosslerites," who overemphasize the individual speaker's inner world as the source of all value. This way of thinking tends to see expression as a deformation of "the purity of the inner element." All creativity is within. Between the extremes of abstract objectivism and romantic subjectivism stands Voloshinov. The speech act—the sign—is a bridge between the speaker and the community. For example, my word does in part belong to me. It also belongs in part to the social context, the presence of a real or implied addressee, who receives the expression. The organizing center of expression is, in any case, outside the speaker. Outside the social context there is no inside, no consciousness at all. The content of the psyche is purely sociological in character. Our inner world is deepened by the increased potentialities of our expression, and expression is wholly a product of complex social interaction. The sign, therefore, is material, as is consciousness; and every book written is written collectively.

Social Interaction and the Bridge of Words

1929

Translated by Ladislav Matejka and I. R. Titunik

The second trend of thought in the philosophy of language was associated, as we saw, with rationalism and neoclassicism. The first trend—individualistic subjectivism—is associated with *romanticism.* Romanticism, to a considerable degree, was a reaction against the alien word and the categories of thought promoted by the alien word. More particularly and more immediately, romanticism was a reaction against the last resurgences of the cultural power of the alien word—the epochs of the Renaissance and neoclassicism. The romanticists were the first philologists of native language, the first to attempt a radical restructuring of linguistic thought. Their restructuring was based on experience with native language as the medium through which consciousness and ideas are generated. True, the romanticists remained philologists in the strict sense of the word. It was, of course, beyond their power to restructure a mode of thinking about language that had taken shape and had been sustained over the course of centuries. Nevertheless, new categories were introduced into that thinking, and these new categories were precisely what gave the first trend its specific characteristics. Symptomatically, even recent repre-

SOCIAL INTERACTION AND THE BRIDGE OF WORDS by V. N. Voloshinov from *Marxism and the Philosophy of Language,* trans. Ladislav Matejka and I. R. Titunik, specifically from "Verbal Interaction, Part II, Chapter 3. Reprinted by permission of Academic Press, Inc. Copyright © 1973 by Seminar Press, Inc.

sentatives of individualistic subjectivism have been specialists in modern languages, chiefly the Romance languages (Vossler, Leo Spitzer, Lorch, *et al.*).

However, individualistic subjectivism also took the monologic utterance as the ultimate reality and the point of departure for its thinking about language. To be sure, it did not approach the monologic utterance from the viewpoint of the passively understanding philologist but, rather, approached it from within, from the viewpoint of the person speaking and expressing himself.

What does the monologic utterance amount to, then, in the view of individualistic subjectivism? We have seen that it is a purely individual act, the expression of an individual consciousness, its ambitions, intentions, creative impulses, tastes, and so on. The category of expression for individualistic subjectivism is the highest and broadest category under which the speech act—the utterance—may be subsumed.

But what is expression?

Its simplest, rough definition is: something which, having in some way taken shape and definition in the psyche of an individual, is outwardly objectified for others with the help of external signs of some kind.

Thus there are two elements in expression: that inner something which is *expressible,* and its *outward objectification* for others (or possibly for oneself). Any theory of expression, however complex or subtle a form it may take, inevitably presupposes these two elements —the whole event of expression is played out between them. Consequently, any theory of expression inevitably presupposes that the expressible is something that can somehow take shape and exist apart from expression; that it exists first in one form and then switches to another form. This would have to be the case; otherwise, if the expressible were to exist from the very start in the form of expression, with quantitative transition between the two elements (in the sense of clarification, differentiation, and the like), the whole theory of expression would collapse. The theory of expression inevitably presupposes a certain dualism between the inner and outer elements and the explicit primacy of the former, since each act of objectification (expression) goes from inside out. Its sources are within. Not for nothing were idealistic and spiritualistic grounds the only grounds on which the theory of individualistic subjectivism and all theories of expression in general arose. Everything of real importance lies within; the outer element can take on real importance only by becoming a vessel for the inner, by becoming expression of spirit. To be sure, by becoming external, by expressing itself outwardly, the inner element does undergo alteration. After all, it must gain control of outer material that possesses a validity of its own apart from the inner element. In this process of gaining control, of mastering outer material and making it over into a compliant medium of expression, the experiential, expressible element itself undergoes alteration and is forced to make a certain compromise. Therefore, idealistic grounds, the grounds on which all theories of expression have been established, also contain provision for the radical negation of expression as something that deforms the purity of the inner element.[1] In any case, all the creative and organizing forces of expression are within. Everything outer is merely passive material for manipulation by the inner element. Expression is formed basically within and then merely shifts to the outside. The understanding, interpretation, and explanation of an ideological phenomenon, it would follow from this argument, must also be directed inward; it must traverse a route the reverse of that for expression. Starting from outward objectification, the explanation must work down into its inner, organizing bases. That is how individualistic subjectivism understands expression.

The theory of expression underlying the first trend of thought in philosophy of language is fundamentally untenable.

The experiential, expressible element and its outward objectification are created, as we know, out of one and the same material. After all, there is no such thing as experience outside of embodiment in signs. Consequently, the very notion of a fundamental, qualitative difference between the inner and the outer element is invalid to begin with. Furthermore, the location of the organizing and formative center is not within (i.e., not in the material of inner signs) but outside. It is not experience that organizes expression, but the other way around—*expression organizes experience.* Expression is what first gives experience its form and specificity of direction.

Indeed, from whichever aspect we consider it, expression-utterance is determined by the actual conditions of the given utterance—above all, by its *immediate social situation.*

---

1. "Spoken thought is a lie" (Tjutčev); "Oh, if one could speak from the soul without words" (Fet). These statements are extremely typical of idealistic romanticism.

Utterance, as we know, is constructed between two socially organized persons, and in the absence of a real addressee, an addressee is presupposed in the person, so to speak, of a normal representative of the social group to which the speaker belongs. The *word is oriented toward an addressee,* toward *who* that addressee might be: a fellow-member or not of the same social group, of higher or lower standing (the addressee's hierarchical status), someone connected with the speaker by close social ties (father, brother, husband, and so on) or not. There can be no such thing as an abstract addressee, a man unto himself, so to speak. With such a person, we would indeed have no language in common, literally and figuratively. Even though we sometimes have pretensions to experiencing and saying things *urbi et orbi,* actually, of course, we envision this "world at large" through the prism of the concrete social milieu surrounding us. In the majority of cases, we presuppose a certain typical and stabilized *social purview* toward which the ideological creativity of our own social group and time is oriented, i.e., we assume as our addressee a contemporary of our literature, our science, our moral and legal codes.

Each person's inner world and thought has its stabilized *social audience* that comprises the environment in which reasons, motives, values, and so on are fashioned. The more cultured a person, the more closely his inner audience will approximate the normal audience of ideological creativity; but, in any case, specific class and specific era are limits that the ideal of addressee cannot go beyond.

Orientation of the word toward the addressee has an extremely high significance. In point of fact, *word is a two-sided act.* It is determined equally by *whose* word it is and *for whom* it is meant. As word, it is precisely *the product of the reciprocal relationship between speaker and listener, addresser and addressee.* Each and every word expresses the "one" in relation to the "other." I give myself verbal shape from another's point of view, ultimately, from the point of view of the community to which I belong. A word is a bridge thrown between myself and another. If one end of the bridge depends on me, then the other depends on my addressee. A word is territory shared by both addresser and addressee, by the speaker and his interlocutor.

But what does being the speaker mean? Even if a word is not entirely his, constituting, as it were, the border zone between himself and his addressee—still, it does in part belong to him.

There is one instance of the situation wherein the speaker is the undoubted possessor of the word and to which, in this instance, he has full rights. This instance is the physiological act of implementing the word. But insofar as the act is taken in purely physiological terms, the category of possession does not apply.

If, instead of the physiological act of implementing sound, we take the implementation of word as sign, then the question of proprietorship becomes extremely complicated. Aside from the fact that word as sign is a borrowing on the speaker's part from the social stock of available signs, the very individual manipulation of this social sign in a concrete utterance is wholly determined by social relations. The stylistic individualization of an utterance that the Vosslerites speak about represents a reflection of social interrelationships that constitute the atmosphere in which an utterance is formed. *The immediate social situation and the broader social milieu wholly determine —and determine from within, so to speak—the structure of an utterance.*

Indeed, take whatever kind of utterance we will, even the kind of utterance that is not a referential message (communication in the narrow sense) but the verbal expression of some need—for instance, hunger—we may be certain that it is socially oriented in its entirety. Above all, it is determined immediately and directly by the participants of the speech event, both explicit and implicit participants, in connection with a specific situation. That situation shapes the utterance, dictating that it sound one way and not another—like a demand or request, insistence on one's rights or a plea for mercy, in a style flowery or plain, in a confident or hesitant manner, and so on.

The immediate social situation and its immediate social participants determine the "occasional" form and style of an utterance. The deeper layers of its structure are determined by more sustained and more basic social connections with which the speaker is in contact.

Even if we were to take an utterance still in process of generation "in the soul," it would not change the essence of the matter, since the structure of experience is just as social as is the structure of its outward objectification. The degree to which an experience is perceptible, distinct, and formulated is directly proportional to the degree to which it is socially oriented.

In fact, not even the simplest, dimmest apprehension of a feeling —say, the feeling of hunger not outwardly expressed—can dispense with some kind of ideological form. Any apprehension, after all, must have inner speech, inner intonation and the rudiments of inner style:

one can apprehend one's hunger apologetically, irritably, angrily, indignantly, etc. We have indicated, of course, only the grosser, more egregious directions that inner intonation may take; actually, there is an extremely subtle and complex set of possibilities for intoning an experience. Outward expression in most cases only continues and makes more distinct the direction already taken by inner speech and the intonation already embedded in it.

Which way the intoning of the inner sensation of hunger will go depends upon the hungry person's general social standing as well as upon the immediate circumstances of the experience. These are, after all, the circumstances that determine in what evaluative context, within what social purview, the experience of hunger will be apprehended. The immediate social context will determine possible addressees, friends or foes, toward whom the consciousness and the experience of hunger will be oriented: whether it will involve dissatisfaction with cruel Nature, with oneself, with society, with a specific group within society, with a specific person, and so on. Of course, various degrees of perceptibility, distinctiveness, and differentiation in the social orientation of an experience are possible; but without some kind of evaluative social orientation there is no experience. Even the cry of a nursing infant is "oriented" toward its mother. There is the possibility that the experience of hunger may take on political coloring, in which case its structure will be determined along the lines of a potential political appeal or a reason for political agitation. It may be apprehended as a form of protest, and so on.

With regard to the potential (and sometimes even distinctly sensed) addressee, a distinction can be made between two poles, two extremes between which an experience can be apprehended and ideologically structured, tending now toward the one, now toward the other. Let us label these two extremes the *"I-experience"* and the *"we-experience."*

The "I-experience" actually tends toward extermination: the nearer it approaches its extreme limit, the more it loses its ideological structuredness and, hence, its apprehensible quality, reverting to the physiological reaction of the animal. In its course toward this extreme, the experience relinquishes all its potentialities, all outcroppings of social orientation, and, therefore, also loses its verbal delineation. Single experiences or whole groups of experiences can approach this extreme, relinquishing, in doing so, their ideological clarity and structuredness and testifying to the inability of the consciousness to strike social roots.[2]

The "we-experience" is not by any means a nebulous herd experience; it is differentiated. Moreover, ideological differentiation, the growth of consciousness, is in direct proportion to the firmness and reliability of the social orientation. The stronger, the more organized, the more differentiated the collective in which an individual orients himself, the more vivid and complex his inner world will be.

The "we-experience" allows of different degrees and different types of ideological structuring.

Let us suppose a case where hunger is apprehended by one of a disparate set of hungry persons whose hunger is a matter of chance (the man down on his luck, the beggar, or the like). The experience of such a declassé loner will be colored in some specific way and will gravitate toward certain particular ideological forms with a range potentially quite broad: humility, shame, enviousness, and other evaluative tones will color his experience. The ideological forms along the lines of which the experience would develop would be either the individualistic protest of a vagabond or repentant, mystical resignation.

Let us now suppose a case in which the hungry person belongs to a collective where hunger is not haphazard and does bear a collective character—but the collective of these hungry people is not itself tightly bound together by material ties, each of its members experiencing hunger on his own. This is the situation most peasants are in. Hunger is experienced "at large," but under conditions of material disparateness, in the absence of a unifying economic coalition, each person suffers hunger in the small, enclosed world of his own individual economy. Such a collective lacks the unitary material frame necessary for united action. A resigned but unashamed and undemeaning apprehension of one's hunger will be the rule under such conditions—"everyone bears it, you must bear it, too." Here grounds are furnished for the development of the philosophical and religious systems of the nonresistor or fatalist type (early Christianity, Tolstoyanism).

---

2. On the possibility of a set of human sexual experiences falling out of social context with concomitant loss of verbal cognizance, see our book, *Frejdizm* [Freudianism] (1927), pp. 135–136.

A completely different experience of hunger applies to a member of an objectively and materially aligned and united collective (a regiment of solders; workers in their association within the walls of a factory; hired hands on a large-scale, capitalist farm; finally, a whole class once it has matured to the point of "class unto itself"). The experience of hunger this time will be marked predominantly by overtones of active and self-confident protest with no basis for humble and submissive intonation. These are the most favorable grounds for an experience to achieve ideological clarity and structuredness.[3]

All these types of expression, each with its basic intonations, come rife with corresponding terms and corresponding forms of possible utterances. The social situation in all cases determines which term, which metaphor, and which form may develop in an utterance expressing hunger out of the particular intonational bearings of the experience.

A special kind of character marks the individualistic *self-experience*. It does not belong to the "I-experience" in the strict sense of the term as defined above. The individualistic experience is fully differentiated and structured. Individualism is a special ideological form of the "we-experience" of the bourgeois class (there is also an analogous type of individualistic self-experience for the feudal aristocratic class). The individualistic type of experience derives from a steadfast and confident social orientation. Individualistic confidence in oneself, one's sense of personal value, is drawn not from within, not from the depths of one's personality, but from the outside world. It is the ideological interpretation of one's social recognizance and tenability by rights, and of the objective security and tenability provided by the whole social order, of one's individual livelihood. The structure of the conscious, individual personality is just as social a structure as is the collective type of experience. It is a particular kind of interpretation, projected into the individual soul, of a complex and sustained socioeconomic situation. But there resides in this type of individualistic "we-experience," and also in the very order to which it corre-

---

3. Interesting material about expressions of hunger can be found in Leo Spitzer's books, *Italienische Kriegsgefangenenbriefe* and *Die Umschreibungen des Begriffes Hunger*. The basic concern in these studies is the adaptability of word and image to the conditions of an exceptional situation. The author does not, however, operate with a genuine sociological approach.

sponds, an inner contradication that sooner or later will demolish its ideological structuredness.

An analogous structure is presented in solitary self-experience ("the ability and strength to stand alone in one's rectitude"), a type cultivated by Romain Rolland and, to some extent, by Tolstoj. The pride involved in this solitude also depends upon "we." It is a variant of the "we-experience" characteristic of the modern-day West European intelligentsia. Tolstoj's remarks about there being different kinds of thinking—"for oneself" and "for the public"—merely juxtapose two different conceptions of "public." Tolstoj's "for oneself" actually signifies only another social conception of addressee peculiar to himself. There is no such thing as thinking outside orientation toward possible expression and, hence, outside the social orientation of that expression and of the thinking involved.

Thus the personality of the speaker, taken from within, so to speak, turns out to be wholly a product of social interrelations. Not only its outward expression but also its inner experience are social territory. Consequently, the whole route between inner experience (the "expressible") and its outward objectification (the "utterance") lies entirely across social territory. When an experience reaches the stage of actualization in a full-fledged utterance, its social orientation acquires added complexity by focusing on the immediate social circumstances of discourse and, above all, upon actual addressees.

Our analysis casts a new light upon the problem of consciousness and ideology that we examined earlier.

Outside objectification, outside embodiment in some particular material (the material of gesture, inner word, outcry), *consciousness is a fiction.* It is an improper ideological construct created by way of abstraction from the concrete facts of social expression. But consciousness as organized, material expression (in the ideological material of word, a sign, drawing, colors, musical sound, etc.) —consciousness, so conceived, is an objective fact and a tremendous social force. To be sure, this kind of consciousness is not a supraexistential phenomenon and cannot determine the constitution of existence. It itself is part of existence and one of its forces, and for that reason it possesses efficacy and plays a role in the arena of existence. Consciousness, while still inside a conscious person's head as inner-word embryo of expression, is as yet too tiny a piece of existence, and the scope of its activity is also as yet too small. But once it passes through all the stages of social objectification and enters into the power system of science, art, ethics, or law, it becomes a real force, capable even of exerting in turn an influence on the economic bases of social life. To be sure, this force of consciousness is incarnated in specific social organizations, geared into steadfast ideological modes of expression (science, art, and so on), but even in the original, vague form of glimmering thought and experience, it had already constituted a social event on a small scale and was not an inner act on the part of the individual.

From the very start experience is set toward fully actualized outward expression and, from the very start, tends in that direction. The expression of an experience may be realized or it may be held back, inhibited. In the latter case, the experience is inhibited expression (we shall not go into the extremely complex problem of the causes and conditions of inhibition). Realized expression, in its turn, exerts a powerful, reverse influence on experience: it begins to tie inner life together, giving it more definite and lasting expression.

This reverse influence by structured and stabilized expression on experience (i.e., inner expression) has tremendous importance and must always be taken into account. The claim can be made that it is a matter *not so much of expression accommodating itself to our inner world but rather of our inner world accommodating itself to the potentialities of our expression, its possible routes and directions.*

To distinguish it from the established systems of ideology—the systems of art, ethics, law, etc.—we shall use the term *behavioral ideology* for the whole aggregate of life experiences and the outward expressions directly connected with it. Behavioral ideology is that atmosphere of unsystematized and unfixed inner and outer speech which endows our every instance of behavior and action and our every "conscious" state with meaning. Considering the sociological nature of the structure of expression and experience, we may say that behavioral ideology in our conception corresponds basically to what is termed "social psychology" in Marxist literature. In the present context, we should prefer to avoid the word "psychology," since we are concerned exclusively with the content of the psyche and the consciousness. That content is ideological through and through, determined not by individual, organismic (biological or physiological) factors, but by factors of a purely sociological character. The individual, organismic factor is completely irrelevant to an understanding of the basic creative and living lineaments of the content of consciousness.

The established ideological systems of social ethics, science, art, and religion are crystallizations of behavioral ideology, and these crystallizations, in turn, exert a powerful influence back upon behavioral ideology, normally setting its tone. At the same time, however, these already formalized ideological products constantly maintain the most vital organic contact with behavioral ideology and draw sustenance from it; otherwise, without that contact, they would be dead, just as any literary work or cognitive idea is dead without living, evaluative perception of it. Now, this ideological perception, for which alone any ideological piece of work can and does exist, is carried out in the language of behavioral ideology. Behavioral ideology draws the work into some particular social situation. The work combines with the whole content of the consciousness of those who perceive it and derives its apperceptive values only in the context of that consciousness. It is interpreted in the spirit of the particular content of consciousness (the consciousness of the perceiver) and is illuminated by it anew. This is what constitutes the vitality of an ideological production. In each period of its historical existence, a work must enter into close association with the changing behavioral ideology, become permeated with it, and draw new sustenance from it. Only to the degree that a work can enter into that kind of integral, organic association with the behavioral ideology of a given period is it viable for that period (and of course, for a given social group). Outside its connection with behavioral ideology it ceases to exist, since it ceases to be experienced as something ideologically meaningful.

We must distinguish several different strata in behavioral ideology. These strata are defined by the social scale on which experience and expression are measured, or by the social forces with respect to which they must directly orient themselves.

The purview in which an experience or expression comes into being may, as we know, vary in scope. The world of an experience may be narrow and dim; its social orientation may be haphazard and ephemeral and characteristic only for some adventitious and loose coalition of a small number of persons. Of course, even these erratic experiences are ideological and sociological, but their position lies on the borders of the normal and the pathological. Such an experience will remain an isolated fact in the psychological life of the person exposed to it. It will not take firm root and will not receive differentiated and full-fledged expression; indeed, if it lacks a socially grounded and stable audience, where could it possibly find bases for its differentiation and finalization? Even less likely would such an adventitious experience be set down, in writing or even more so in print. Experiences of that kind, experiences born of a momentary and accidental state of affairs, have, of course, no chance of further social impact or efficacy.

The lowest, most fluid, and quickly changing stratum of behavioral ideology consists of experiences of that kind. To this stratum, consequently, belong all those vague and undeveloped experiences, thoughts, and idle, accidental words that flash across our minds. They are all of them cases of miscarriages of social orientations, novels without heroes, performances without audiences. They lack any sort of logic or unity. The sociological regulatedness in these ideological scraps is extremely difficult to detect. In this lowest stratum of behavioral ideology only statistical regularity is detectable; given a huge quantity of products of this sort, the outlines of socioeconomic regulatedness could be revealed. Needless to say, it would be a practical impossibility to descry in any one such accidental experience or expression its socioeconomic premises.

The upper strata of behavioral ideology, the ones directly linked with ideological systems, are more vital, more serious and bear a creative character. Compared to an established ideology, they are a great deal more mobile and sensitive: they convey changes in the socioeconomic basis more quickly and more vividly. Here, precisely, is where those creative energies build up through whose agency partial or radical restructuring of ideological systems comes about. Newly emerging social forces find ideological expression and take shape first in these upper strata of behavioral ideology before they can succeed in dominating the arena of some organized, official ideology. Of course, in the process of this struggle, in the process of their gradual infiltration into ideological organizations (the press, literature, and science), these new currents in behavioral ideology, no matter how revolutionary they may be, undergo the influence of the established ideological systems and, to some extent, incorporate forms, ideological practices, and approaches already in stock.

What usually is called "creative individuality" is nothing but the expression of a particular person's basic, firmly grounded, and consistent line of social orientation. This concerns primarily the uppermost, fully structured strata of inner speech (behavioral ideology), each of whose terms and intonations have gone through the stage of expression and have, so to speak, passed the test of expression. Thus what is involved here are words, intonations, and inner-word gestures that have undergone the experience of outward expression on a more or less ample social scale and have acquired, as it were, a high social polish and lustre by the effect of reactions and responses, resistance or support, on the part of the social audience.

In the lower strata of behavioral ideology, the biological-biographical factor does, of course, play a crucial role, but its importance constantly diminishes as the utterance penetrates more deeply into an ideological system. Consequently, while bio-biographical explanations are of some value in the lower strata of experience and expression (utterance), their role in the upper strata is extremely modest. Here the objective sociological method takes full command.

So, then, the theory of expression underlying individualistic subjectivism must be rejected. *The organizing center of any utterance, of any experience, is not within but outside—in the social milieu surrounding the individual being.* Only the inarticulate cry of an animal is really organized from inside the physiological apparatus of an individual creature. Such a cry lacks any positive ideological factor vis-à-vis the physiological reaction. Yet, even the most primitive human utterance produced by the individual organism is, from the point of view of its content, import, and meaning, organized outside the organism, in the extraorganismic conditions of the social milieu. Utterance as such is wholly a product of social interaction, both of the immediate sort as determined by the circumstances of the discourse, and of the more general kind, as determined by the whole aggregate of conditions under which any given community of speakers operates.

The individual utterance *(parole),* despite the contentions of abstract objectivism, is by no means an individual fact not susceptible to sociological analysis by virtue of its individuality. Indeed, if this were so, neither the sum total of these individual acts nor any abstract features common to all such individual acts (the "normatively identical forms") could possibly engender a social product.

Individualistic subjectivism is *correct* in that individual utterances *are* what constitute the actual, concrete reality of language, and in that they *do have* creative value in language.

But individualistic subjectivism is *wrong* in ignoring and failing to understand the social nature of the utterance and in attempting to derive the utterance from the speaker's inner world as an expression of that inner world. The structure of the utterance and of the very experience being expressed is a *social structure.* The stylistic shaping of an utterance is shaping of a social kind, and the very verbal stream of utterances, which is what the reality of language actually amounts to, is a social stream. Each drop of that stream is social and the entire dynamics of its generation is social.

Individualistic subjectivism is also completely *correct* in that linguistic form and its ideological impletion are *not* severable. Each and every word is ideological and each and every application of language involves ideological change. But individualistic subjectivism is *wrong* insofar as it also derives this ideological impletion of the word from the conditions of the individual psyche.

Individualistic subjectivism is *wrong* in taking the monologic utterance, just as abstract objectivism does, as its basic point of departure. Certain Vosslerites, it is true, have begun to consider the problem of dialogue and so to approach a more correct understanding of verbal interaction. Highly symptomatic in this regard is one of Leo Spitzer's books—his *Italienische Umgangssprache* (Leipzig, 1922), a book that attempts to analyze the forms of Italian conversational language in close connection with the conditions of discourse and above all with the issue of the addressee.[4] However, Leo Spitzer utilizes a *descriptive psychological* method. He does not draw from his analysis the fundamentally sociological conclusions it suggests. For the Vosslerites, therefore, the monologic utterance still remains the basic reality.

The problem of verbal interaction has been posed clearly and distinctly by Otto Dietrich.[5] He proceeds by way of subjecting to criticism the theory of utterance as expression. For him, the basic function of language is not expression but *communication* (in the strict sense), and this leads him to consider the role of the addressee. The minimal condition for a linguistic manifestation is, according to Dietrich, *twofold* (speaker and listener). However, Dietrich shares assumptions of a general psychological type with individualistic subjectivism. Dietrich's investigations likewise lack any determinate sociological basis.

Now we are in a position to answer the question we posed at the

---

4. In this respect, the very organization of the book is symptomatic. The book divides into four main chapters. Their titles are as follows: I. *Eröffnungsformen des Gesprächs.* II. *Sprecher und Hörer;* A. *Höflichkeit (Rücksicht auf den Partner).* B. *Sparsamkeit und Verschwendung im Ausdruck;* C. *Ineinandergreifen von Rede und Gegenrede.* III. *Sprecher und Situation.* IV. *Der Abschluss des Gesprächs.* Spitzer's predecessor in the study of conversational language under conditions of real-life discourse was Hermann Wunderlich. See his book, *Unsere Umgangssprache* (1894).

5. See *Die Probleme der Sprachpsychologie* (1914).

end of the first chapter of this section of our study. *The actual reality of language-speech is not the abstract system of linguistic forms, not the isolated monologic utterance, and not the psychophysiological act of its implementation, but the social event of verbal interaction implemented in an utterance or utterances.*

Thus, verbal interaction is the basic reality of language.

Dialogue, in the narrow sense of the word, is, of course, only one of the forms—a very important form, to be sure—of verbal interaction. But dialogue can also be understood in a broader sense, meaning not only direct, face-to-face, vocalized verbal communication between persons, but also verbal communication of any type whatsoever. A book, i.e., a *verbal performance in print,* is also an element of verbal communication. It is something discussable in actual, real-life dialogue, but aside from that, it is calculated for active perception, involving attentive reading and inner responsiveness, and for organized, *printed* reaction in the various forms devised by the particular sphere of verbal communication in question (book reviews, critical surveys, defining influence on subsequent works, and so on). Moreover, a verbal performance of this kind also inevitably orients itself with respect to previous performances in the same sphere, both those by the same author and those by other authors. It inevitably takes its point of departure from some particular state of affairs involving a scientific problem or a literary style. Thus the printed verbal performance engages, as it were, in ideological colloquy of large scale: it responds to something, objects to something, affirms something, anticipates possible responses and objections, seeks support, and so on.

Any utterance, no matter how weighty and complete in and of itself, *is only a moment in the continuous process of verbal communication.* But that continuous verbal communication is, in turn, itself only a moment in the continuous, all-inclusive, generative process of a given social collective. An important problem arises in this regard: the study of the connection between concrete verbal interaction and the extraverbal situation—both the immediate situation and, through it, the broader situation. The forms this connection takes are different, and different factors in a situation may, in association with this or that form, take on different meanings (for instance, these connections differ with the different factors of situation in literary or in scientific communication). *Verbal communication can never be understood and explained outside of this connection with a concrete situation.* Verbal intercourse is inextricably interwoven with communication of other types, all stemming from the common ground of production communication. It goes without saying that word cannot be divorced from this eternally generative, unified process of communication. In its concrete connection with a situation, verbal communication is always accompanied by social acts of a nonverbal character (the performance of labor, the symbolic acts of a ritual, a ceremony, etc.), and is often only an accessory to these acts, merely carrying out an auxiliary role. *Language acquires life and historically evolves precisely here, in concrete verbal communication, and not in the abstract linguistic system of language forms, nor in the individual psyche of speakers.*

From what has been established, it follows that the methodologically based order of study of language ought to be: (1) the forms and types of verbal interaction in connection with their concrete conditions; (2) forms of particular utterances, of particular speech performances, as elements of a closely linked interaction—i.e., the genres of speech performance in human behavior and ideological creativity as determined by verbal interaction; (3) a reexamination, on this new basis, of language forms in their usual linguistic presentation.

This is the order that the actual generative process of language follows: *social intercourse is generated* (stemming from the basis); *in it verbal communication and interaction are generated; and in the latter, forms of speech performances are generated; finally, this generative process is reflected in the change of language forms.*

One thing that emerges from all that has been said is the extreme importance of the problem of the forms of an utterance *as a whole.* We have already pointed out that contemporary linguistics lacks any approach to the utterance itself. Its analysis goes no further than the elements that constitute an utterance. Meanwhile, utterances are the real units that make up the stream of language-speech. What is necessary in order to study the forms of this real unit is precisely that it not be isolated from the historical stream of utterances. As a whole entity, the utterance is implemented only in the stream of verbal intercourse. The whole is, after all, defined by its boundaries, and these boundaries run along the line of contact between a given utterance and the extraverbal and verbal (i.e., made up of other utterances) milieu.

The first and last words, the beginning and end points of real-life utterance—that is what already constitutes the problem of the whole. The process of speech, broadly understood as the process of inner and outer verbal life, goes on continuously. It knows neither beginning nor end. The outwardly actualized utterance is an island rising from the boundless sea of inner speech; the dimensions and forms of this island are determined by the particular *situation* of the utterance and its *audience.* Situation and audience make inner speech undergo actualization into some kind of specific outer expression that is directly included into an unverbalized behavioral context and in that context is amplified by actions, behavior, or verbal responses of other participants of the utterance. The full-fledged question, exclamation, command, request—these are the most typical forms of wholes in behavioral utterances. All of them (especially the command and request) require an extraverbal complement and, indeed, an extraverbal commencement. The very type of structure these little behavioral *genres* will achieve is determined by the effect of its coming up against the extraverbal milieu and against another word (i.e., the words of other people). Thus, the form a command will take is determined by the obstacles it may encounter, the degree of submissiveness expected, and so on. The structure of the genre in these instances will be in accord with the accidental and unique features of behavioral situations. Only when social custom and circumstances have fixed and stabilized certain forms in behavioral interchange to some appreciable degree, can one speak of specific types of structure in genres of behavioral speech. So, for instance, an entirely special type of structure has been worked out for the genre of the light and casual causerie of the drawing room where everyone "feels at home" and where the basic differentiation within the gathering (the audience) is that between men and women. Here we find devised special forms of insinuation, half-sayings, allusions to little tales of an intentionally nonserious character, and so on. A different type of structure is worked out in the case of conversation between husband and wife, brother and sister, etc. In the case where a random assortment of people gathers—while waiting in a line or conducting some business—statements and exchanges of words will start and finish and be constructed in another, completely different way. Village sewing circles, urban carouses, workers' lunchtime chats, etc., will all have their own types. Each situation, fixed and sustained by social custom, commands a particular kind of organization of audience and, hence, a particular repertoire of little behavioral genres. The behavioral genre fits everywhere into the channel of social intercourse assigned to it and functions as an ideological reflection of its type, structure, goal, and social composition. The behavioral genre is a fact of the social milieu: of holiday, leisure time, and of social contact in the parlor, the workshop, etc. It meshes with that milieu and is delimited and defined by it in all its internal aspects.

The production processes of labor and the processes of commerce know different forms for constructing utterances.

As for the forms of ideological intercourse in the strict sense of the term—forms for political speeches, political acts, laws, regulations, manifestos, and so forth; and forms for poetic utterances, scientific treatises, etc.—these have been the object of special investigation in rhetoric and poetics, but, as we have seen, these investigations have been completely divorced from the problem of language on the one hand, and from the problem of social intercourse on the other.[6] Productive analysis of the forms of the whole of utterances as the real units in the stream of speech is possible only on a basis that regards the individual utterance as a purely sociological phenomenon. Marxist philosophy of language should and must stand squarely on the utterance as the real phenomenon of language-speech and as a socioideological structure.

Now that we have outlined the sociological structure of the utterance, let us return to the two trends in philosophical linguistic thought and make a final summing up.

R. Šor, a Moscow linguist and an adherent of the second trend of thought in philosophy of language, ends a brief sketch of the contemporary state of linguistics with the following words:

> "Language is not an artifact *(ergon)* but a natural and congeni-
> tal activity of mankind"—so claimed the romanticist linguistics
> of the 19th century. Theoretical linguistics of modern times
> claims otherwise: "Language is not individual activity *(energiea)*
> but a cultural-historical legacy of mankind *(ergon)*.[7]

This conclusion is amazing in its bias and one-sidedness. On the factual side, it is completely untrue. Modern theoretical linguistics includes, after all, the Vossler school, one of Germany's most powerful movements in contemporary linguistic thought. It is impermissible to identify modern linguistics with only one of its trends.

From the theoretical point of view, both the thesis and the

6. On the topic of disjuncture of a literary work of art with conditions of artistic communication and the resulting inertness of the work, see our study, "Slovo v žizni i slovo v poèzii" [Word in Life and Word in Poetry], *Zvezda,* **6** (1926).
7. R. Šor, "Krizis sovremennoj linvistiki" [The Crisis in Contemporary Linguistics], *Jafetičeskij sbornik,* **V** (1927), p. 71.

antithesis made up by Šor must equally be rejected, since they are equally inadequate to the real nature of language.

Let us conclude the argument with an attempt to formulate our own point of view in the following set of propositions:

1. *Language as a stable system of normatively identical forms is merely a scientific abstraction,* productive only in connection with certain particular practical and theoretical goals. This abstraction is not adequate to the concrete reality of language.
2. *Language is a continuous generative process implemented in the social–verbal interaction of speakers.*
3. *The laws of the generative process of language are not at all the laws of individual psychology, but neither can they be divorced from the activity of speakers.* The laws of language generation are *sociological* laws.
4. *Linguistic creativity does not coincide with artistic creativity nor with any other type of specialized ideological creativity. But, at the same time, linguistic creativity cannot be understood apart from the ideological meanings and values that fill it.* The generative process of language, as is true of any historical generative process, can be perceived as blind mechanical necessity, but it can also become "free necessity" once it has reached the position of a conscious and desired necessity.
5. *The structure of the utterance is a purely sociological structure.* The utterance, as such, obtains between speakers. The individual speech act (in the strict sense of the word "individual") is *contradictio in adjecto.*

MIKHAIL BAKHTIN

We may already know all that we are going to know about the Leningrad communes, where Mikhail Bakhtin and his wife lived between 1926–29 with several other couples, artists, and theorists in an attempt to produce a collective revision of culture according to Marxism.* These were years when nothing seemed impossible to Russian intellectuals. All human experience was to be synthesized. Bolshevism was to link up with Christianity, patriotism with internationalism, community spirit with individual freedom, social progress with prayer. Love for one's fellow men and women would propel the subject beyond self-centeredness to the other. Materiality and all joys of the flesh were just as important as the spiritual world, but bourgeois possessiveness and greed would give way to a dialogical spirit of mutual stimulation and sharing. There are those who say Bakhtin, in this spirit of collectivity, "gave" books to members of his circle to publish under their names. Others feel that this notion of "giving" something already completed and whole misconstrues the nonproprietary nature of the creative exchange that obtained in that setting on the Finnish Gulf.

Soon after Bakhtin's book on Dostoevsky appeared in 1929, Bakhtin left the Leningrad area. He spent six years beyond the Urals in Kustanai, a city in Kazakhstan. His friends Medvedev and Voloshinov were "repressed" in the 1930s and died. Bakhtin lost a leg to osteomyelitis in 1938. He then spent the war years near Moscow teaching in secondary schools. When he retired from teaching in 1961, his work began to be reissued. From a footnote in the 1963 edition of the Dostoevsky book, we learn that he wrote his book on Rabelais, from which "Laughter and Freedom" is taken, in 1940.† It did not appear in Russian until 1965.

The thesis of *Rabelais and His World* is that literary history tends to transmit only the official culture of the ruling classes to subsequent ages, that is, in this official version of events, ". . . we do not hear the voice of the people."** The essential nature of this popular voice is laughter. The

---

*M. M. Bakhtin and P. M. Medvedev, *The Formal Method in Literary Scholarship,* trans. Albert J. Wehrle. Foreword by Wlad Godzich (Cambridge and London: Harvard University Press, 1985; Russian, 1928). See the "Introduction," xv ff.

† The title for this selection from the *Rabelais* text is adopted from Maynard Solomon's excellent anthology, *Marxism and Art* (Detroit: Wayne State University Press, 1979) 295 ff., where it also appears.

**Mikhail Bakhtin, *Rabelais and His World,* trans. Helene Iswolsky (Cambridge and London: MIT Press, 1968) 474. To make too rigid a distinction between the official and popular is probably misleading, since the medieval upper classes also participated in the popular festivities. See Richard Berrong, *Rabelais and Bakhtin* (Lincoln: University of Nebraska Press, 1986) 14.

popular is entirely distinct from the empowered, "monolithically serious" ecclesiastical, political establishment, which, at a certain point in the gradual rigidification of class structure, banished laughter to the non-official and the low (6). One of the sources of the laughable is the body. To rehabilitate the ludicrous is to celebrate the functions of the body. Carnival and Rabelais do precisely that. During Carnival, hierarchies are overturned, the serious mocked, the grotesque made visible, and, for a time, the people enter". . . the utopian realm of community, freedom, equality, and abundance" (9). Laughter becomes the revolutionary principle *par excellence*, used by Rabelais and Renaissance popular culture to shatter the dark ceremonials of the Gothic Age (439). Nor would it be wrong to read into this critique of Rabelais' time an allegory of the monolithic rigidity of Stalinism, called into question by the populist, anarchic tendencies of Russian folk culture.‡

Laughter and Freedom
1940

Translated by Helene Iswolsky

edieval laughter is directed at the same object as medieval seriousness. Not only does laughter make no exception for the upper stratum, but indeed it is usually directed toward it. Furthermore, it is directed not at one part only, but at the whole. One might say that it builds its own world versus the official world, its own church versus the official church, its own state versus the official state. Laughter celebrates its masses, professes its faith, celebrates marriages and funerals, writes its epitaphs, elects kings and bishops. Even the smallest medieval parody is always built as part of a whole comic world.

This universal character of laughter was most clearly and consist-

LAUGHTER AND FREEDOM   by Mikhail Bakhtin from *Rabelais and His World*, trans. Helene Iswolsky, pp. 88–94. Copyright © 1968 MIT Press. Reprinted by permission of MIT Press.

‡Katerina Clark and Michael Holquist, *Mikhail Bakhtin* (Cambridge, MA, and London, England: Harvard University Press, 1984) 315.

ently brought out in the carnival rituals and spectacles and in the parodies they presented. But universality appears as well in all the other forms of medieval culture of humor: in the comic elements of church dramas, in the comic *dits* (fairy tales) and *débats* (debates), in animal epics, *fabliaux* and *Schwänke*.[1] The main traits of laughter and of the lower stratum remain identical in all these genres.

It can be said that medieval culture of humor which accompanied the feasts was a "satyric" drama, a fourth drama, after the "tragic trilogy" of official Christian cult and theology to which it corresponded but was at the same time in opposition. Like the antique "satyric" drama, so also the medieval culture of laughter was the drama of bodily life (copulation, birth, growth, eating, drinking, defecation). But of course it was not the drama of an individual body or of a private material way of life; it was the drama of the great generic body of the people, and for this generic body birth and death are not an absolute beginning and end but merely elements of continuous growth and renewal. The great body of satyric drama cannot be separated from the world; it is perfused with cosmic elements and with the earth which swallows up and gives birth.

Next to the universality of medieval laughter we must stress another striking peculiarity: its indissoluble and essential relation to freedom. We have seen that this laughter was absolutely unofficial but nevertheless legalized. The rights of the fool's cap were as inviolable as those of the *pileus* (the clown's headgear of the Roman Saturnalias).

This freedom of laughter was, of course, relative; its sphere was at times wider and at times narrower, but it was never entirely suspended. As we have seen, free laughter was related to feasts and was to a certain extent limited by the time allotted to feast days. It coincided with the permission for meat, fat, and sexual intercourse. This festive liberation of laughter and body was in sharp contrast with the stringencies of Lent which had preceded or were to follow.

The feast was a temporary suspension of the entire official system with all its prohibitions and hierarchic barriers. For a short time life came out of its usual, legalized and consecrated furrows and entered the sphere of utopian freedom. The very brevity of this freedom

---

1. True, such manifestations already express at times the specific limitations of early bourgeois culture; in those cases the material bodily principle becomes petty and degenerate to a certain extent.

increased its fantastic nature and utopian radicalism, born in the festive atmosphere of images. The atmosphere of ephemeral freedom reigned in the public square as well as at the intimate feast in the home. The antique tradition of free, often improper, but at the same time philosophical table talk had been revived at the time of the Renaissance; it converged with the local tradition of festive meals which had common roots in folklore.[2] This tradition of table talk was continued during the following centuries. We find similar traditions of bacchic prandial songs which combine universalism (problems of life and death) with the material bodily element (wine, food, carnal love), with awareness of the time element (youth, old age, the ephemeral nature of life, the changes of fortune); they express a peculiar utopian strain, the brotherhood of fellow-drinkers and of all men, the triumph of affluence, and the victory of reason.

The comic rituals of the feast of fools, the feast of the ass, and the various comic processions and ceremonies of other feasts enjoyed a certain legality. The diableries were legalized and the devils were allowed to run about freely in the streets and in the suburbs a few days before the show and to create a demonic and unbridled atmosphere. Entertainments in the marketplace were also legalized as well as carnival. Of course, this legalization was forced, incomplete, led to struggles and new prohibitions. During the entire medieval period the Church and state were obliged to make concessions, large or small, to satisfy the marketplace. Throughout the year there were small scattered islands of time, strictly limited by the dates of feasts, when the world was permitted to emerge from the official routine but exclusively under the camouflage of laughter. Barriers were raised, provided there was nothing but laughter.

Besides universalism and freedom, the third important trait of laughter was its relation to the people's unofficial truth.

2. Up to the second part of the sixteenth century, the literature of free talk (with prevailing material bodily themes) was characteristic. The following were table, recreational, or promenading talks: Noël du Fail, "Rustic and Facetious Talks" *(Propos rustiques et facétieux)*, 1547, and Entrapel's "Tales and New Discourses" *(Contes et nouveaux discours d'Entrapel)*, 1585; Jacques Tahureau, *Dialogues,* 1562; Nicolas de Chaulières, "Morning Talks" (Matinées), 1585, and "Postprandial Talks" (Les Après-diners); Guillaume Boucher, "After Supper Talks" (Soirées), 1584–1597. "How To Succeed in Life" by Béroalde de Verville, 1612, also belongs to this category. All these works represent the special type of carnivalized dialogue and reflect to a greater or lesser extent Rabelais' influence.

The serious aspects of class culture are official and authoritarian; they are combined with violence, prohibitions, limitations and always contain an element of fear and of intimidation. These elements prevailed in the Middle Ages. Laughter, on the contrary, overcomes fear, for it knows no inhibitions, no limitations. Its idiom is never used by violence and authority.

It was the victory of laughter over fear that most impressed medieval man. It was not only a victory over mystic terror of God, but also a victory over the awe inspired by the forces of nature, and most of all over the oppression and guilt related to all that was consecrated and forbidden ("mana" and "taboo"). It was the defeat of divine and human power, of authoritarian commandments and prohibitions, of death and punishment after death, hell and all that is more terrifying than the earth itself. Through this victory laughter clarified man's consciousness and gave him a new outlook on life. This truth was ephemeral; it was followed by the fears and oppressions of everyday life, but from these brief moments another unofficial truth emerged, truth about the world and man which prepared the new Renaissance consciousness.

The acute awareness of victory over fear is an essential element of medieval laughter. This feeling is expressed in a number of characteristic medieval comic images. We always find in them the defeat of fear presented in a droll and monstrous form, the symbols of power and violence turned inside out, the comic images of death and bodies gaily rent asunder. All that was terrifying becomes grotesque. We have already mentioned that one of the indispensable accessories of carnival was the set called "hell." This "hell" was solemnly burned at the peak of the festivities. This grotesque image cannot be understood without appreciating the defeat of fear. The people play with terror and laugh at it; the awesome becomes a "comic monster."

Neither can this grotesque image be understood if oversimplified and interpreted in the spirit of abstract rationalism. It is impossible to determine where the defeat of fear will end and where joyous recreation will begin. Carnival's hell represents the earth which swallows up and gives birth, it is often transformed into a cornucopia; the monster, death, becomes pregnant. Various deformities, such as protruding bellies, enormous noses, or humps, are symptoms of pregnancy or of procreative power. Victory over fear is not its abstract elimination; it is a simultaneous uncrowning and renewal, a gay transformation. Hell has burst and has poured forth abundance.

We have said that medieval laughter defeated something which was more terrifying than the earth itself. All unearthly objects were transformed into earth, the mother which swallows up in order to give birth to something larger that has been improved. There can be nothing terrifying on earth, just as there can be nothing frightening in a mother's body, with the nipples that are made to suckle, with the genital organ and the warm blood. The earthly element of terror is the womb, the bodily grave, but it flowers with delight and a new life.

However, medieval laughter is not a subjective, individual and biological consciousness of the uninterrupted flow of time. It is the social consciousness of all the people. Man experiences this flow of time in the festive marketplace, in the carnival crowd, as he comes into contact with other bodies of varying age and social caste. He is aware of being a member of a continually growing and renewed people. This is why festive folk laughter presents an element of victory not only over supernatural awe, over the sacred, over death; it also means the defeat of power, of earthly kings, of the earthly upper classes, of all that oppresses and restricts.[3]

Medieval laughter, when it triumphed over the fear inspired by the mystery of the world and by power, boldly unveiled the truth about both. It resisted praise, flattery, hypocrisy. This laughing truth, expressed in curses and abusive words, degraded power. The medieval clown was also the herald of this truth.

3. Profound thoughts concerning the functions of laughter in the history of culture were expressed by Herzen (though he was not acquainted with the laughing Middle Ages): "laughter contains something revolutionary . . . Voltaire's laughter was more destructive than Rousseau's weeping." (Works in nine volumes, Goslitizdat, Moscow, 1956. Vol. 3, p. 92.) And elsewhere: "Laughter is no matter for joking, and we shall not give up our right to it. In the antique world, the public roared with laughter on Olympus and upon earth while listening to Aristophanes and his comedies, and roared with laughter up to Lucian. Humanity ceased to laugh from the fourth century on; it did nothing but weep, and heavy chains fell on the mind amidst moans and pangs of remorse. As soon as the fever of fanaticism subsided, men began to laugh once more. It would be extremely interesting to write the history of laughter. In church, in the palace, on parade, facing the department head, the police officer, the German administrator, nobody laughs. The serfs are deprived of the right to smile in the presence of the landowners. *Only equals may laugh.* If inferiors are permitted to laugh in front of their superiors, and if they cannot suppress their hilarity, this would mean farewell to respect. To make men smile at the god Apis is to deprive him of his sacred rank and to transform him into a common bull." (A. I. Herzen, *On Art*, published by "Art," Goslitizdat, Moscow, 1954, p. 223.)

In his article devoted to Rabelais, Veselovsky characterized as follows the clown's social meaning:

> In the Middle Ages, the clown is the lawless herald of the objectively abstract truth. At a time when all life was built within the conventional frameworks of caste, prerogative, scholastic science and hierarchy, truth was localized according to these frameworks; it was relatively feudal, scholastic, etc., drawing its strength from its given milieu; thus truth was a mere result of the rights it could practically exercise. Feudal truth was the right to oppress the slave, to despise his work, to go to war, to hunt in the peasants' fields. . . . Scholastic truth was the right to possess exclusive knowledge outside of which nothing made sense; therefore knowledge had to be defended against everything that could obscure it. . . . All general human truth, not adapted to the caste, to an established profession, i.e., to determined rights, was excluded. It was not taken into consideration, it was despised, dragged to the stake on the slightest suspicion. It was only tolerated in a harmless form, arousing laughter, without any pretense at any serious role. Thus was the clown's social meaning determined.[4]

Veselovsky gives a correct definition of feudal truth. He is also right to assert that the clown was the herald of another, nonfeudal, nonofficial truth. But this nonofficial truth can hardly be determined as "objectively abstract." Furthermore, Veselovsky sees the clown as isolated from all the mighty culture of medieval humor. He, therefore, considers laughter an external defensive form of this "objective abstract truth," a defense of human value in general, which the clown proclaimed using this external form. If there had been no repressions, no stake, truth would have cast off the clown's attire; it could have spoken in serious tones. Such an interpretation of medieval laughter appears incorrect in our mind.

No doubt laughter was in part an external defensive form of truth. It was legalized, it enjoyed privileges, it liberated, to a certain extent, from censorship, oppression, and from the stake. This element should not be underestimated. But it would be inadmissible to reduce the entire meaning of laughter to this aspect alone. Laughter is essentially not an external but an interior form of truth; it cannot be transformed into seriousness without destroying and distorting the very contents

4. See A. N. Veselovsky. "Collected Articles," Goslitizdat, Leningrad, 1939, pp. 441–442.

of the truth which it unveils. Laughter liberates not only from external censorship but first of all from the great interior censor; it liberates from the fear that developed in man during thousands of years; fear of the sacred, of prohibitions, of the past, of power. It unveils the material bodily principle in its true meaning. Laughter opened men's eyes on that which is new, on the future. This is why it not only permitted the expression of an antifeudal, popular truth; it helped to uncover this truth and to give it an internal form. And this form was achieved and defended during thousands of years in its very depths and in its popular-festive images. Laughter showed the world anew in its gayest and most sober aspects. Its external privileges are intimately linked with interior forces; they are a recognition of the rights of those forces. This is why laughter could never become an instrument to oppress and blind the people. It always remained a free weapon in their hands. . . .

GEORG LUKÁCS

To say that Georg Lukács is a proponent of a reflection theory of art can be misleading if one understands by "reflection," "imitation," or "mimesis" anything very slavish, that is, to be merely a "copying function."* In his long essay "Art and Objective Truth" (1954), Lukács considers photographic correspondence with reality incorrect, even subjective.† On the other hand, a novel like *Père Goriot,* whose realism for Lukács is exemplary, can portray events which are in a sense "scarcely credible" (49–50). The crucial thing for art to do is to penetrate to the inner nature of the period it represents, selecting details that are illustrative of the total dynamic context of history. He quotes Aristotle with approval, saying that art is more universal than history in precisely the sense that history is too obsessed with surface detail to ascend to typicality (45–46). Lukács situates the ideal aesthetic approach between mechanistic materialism (Diderot and Zola) and philosophical idealism (Schiller), though Lukács is clearly more sympathetic to the latter than to the former. Schiller's method is to attempt to realize harmony by annihilating the material side of things.‡ However, annihilating the material side by attempting subjectively and aesthetically to realize the beautiful and harmonious is doomed to failure; instead, it is necessary to *reform* the economic developments that insist on the specialization and division of labor and hence give rise to the psychic disharmony in the first place. In other words, German idealism provides an evasion of life's ugliness, not a solution to it.

The notion of the dissociated sensibility appeared in Schiller before it appeared in Eliot's essay on "The Metaphysical Poets" (1921).** There was a time, it seems, when the heart and the mind were not at odds. For Schiller, Hegel, and Lukács, this was the era of the Greeks. "The Ideal of the Harmonious Man in Bourgeois Aesthetics" (1938) is a history of the loss of this harmony as reflected in literature. It is also a critique of the various attempts made in literature to recapture the harmony or to destroy the notion altogether, as Lukács says that Nietzsche does, in

---

* See Hans Robert Jauss, *Toward an Aesthetic of Reception,* trans. Timothy Bahti (Minneapolis: University of Minnesota Press, 1982) 11. "Marxist aesthetics . . . believed it must legitimate itself with a theory of copying."
† George Lukács, *Writer and Critic and Other Essays,* trans. Arthur Kahn (London: Merlin Press, 1970) 43.
‡ Friedrich Schiller, *On the Aesthetic Education of Man,* trans. Reginald Snell (New York: Ungar, 1965) 106.
**In Schiller see the *Aesthetic Education,* letter 5; it is also a key concept in *On Naive and Sentimental Poetry* (1795–96).

order to prepare the way for Fascist antihumanism. Against the objection that the idealized ancient Greek political structure allowed psychic wholeness only to those who were freed from physical labor by slaves, Lukács would presumably have responded that anachronistic morality is inappropriate, that "right can never be higher than the economic structure of society and its cultural development conditioned thereby."† Slavery was quite an advance in its time, even for the slaves, who had been faced, as prisoners of war, with the possibility of being killed and eaten.

The Ideal of the Harmonious Man in Bourgeois Aesthetics

1938

Translated by Arthur D. Kahn

I f we are to attempt a serious examination of the question indicated in our title, we cannot direct our attention to the theory and practice of those who make "an art of living" in the contemporary stage of imperialism. The aspiration towards harmony of man's accomplishments as against his potential is never quite extinguished. The bleaker and emptier life becomes under capitalism, the more intense is the yearning after beauty. But this yearning for harmony under imperialism too often takes the form of a craven retreat or a faint-hearted withdrawal before the contradictory problems thrown up by life. By seeking inner harmony men cut themselves off from society's struggles. Such "harmony" is illusory and superficial; it vanishes at any serious contact with reality.

The great thinkers and artists who have championed this aspiration for harmony have always recognized that harmony for the individual

THE IDEAL OF THE HARMONIOUS MAN IN BOURGEOIS AESTHETICS   by Georg Lukács from *Writer and Critic, and Other Essays,* ed. and trans. Arthur D. Kahn. Reprinted by permission of The Merlin Press, copyright © 1970.

† Karl Marx, "Critique of the Gotha Program," in *The Marx-Engels Reader,* ed. Robert Tucker (New York: Norton, 1978) 531. See also Friedrich Engels, *Anti-Dühring* (Moscow: Foreign Languages Publishing House, 1959) 249.

presupposes his harmonious integration into his environment, into his society. The philosophical advocates of the integrated man from the Renaissance through Winckelmann to Hegel not only admired the Greeks for realizing this ideal but also recognized that the basis for the harmonious development of the individual in Classical Greece lay in the social and political structure of ancient democracy. That they more or less ignored the fact that this democracy was based on slavery is another matter.

Hegel has this to say about Greek harmony: "The Greeks, as far as their immediate reality was concerned, lived happily in the midst of a self-conscious subjective freedom and a self-conscious moral order." And expatiating upon this thought, Hegel contrasted Greek democracy both with oriental despotism, under which the individual had no rights, and with modern society with its fully fledged social division of labour. "In Greek moral life, the individual enjoyed independence and freedom without being isolated from the interests of the state. In accordance with the basic principle of Greek life, the universal morality existed in an undisturbed harmony with the abstract subjective and objective freedom of the individual, and . . . there never was a question of a dichotomy between political principles and personal morality. The rare sensitivity, intellectuality and spirituality in this felicitous harmony permeates all the works in which the Greeks expressed their freedom and in which the essence of their freedom is exposed."

It was left to Marx to disclose the economic and social basis of that unique flourishing of human culture, of the harmonious fulfilment of the individual personality among the free citizens of the Greek democracies. He also explained the rational core to the unappeasable longing of mankind's finest spirits for this harmony, which has never been regained. Because of Marx we understand why this period of the "normal childhood" in man's development can never return.

But the longing to recapture this harmony has persisted since the Renaissance among the most progressive intellectuals. The revival of Classical thought, poetry and art during the Renaissance has admittedly visible causes in the class struggles of the time. Unquestionably, too, the study of Classical constitutions and of the civil wars from the Renaissance to Robespierre provided all bourgeois and democratic revolutionaries with powerful weapons in their struggle against feudalism and absolute monarchy. Whatever illusions accompanied these struggles were heroic illusions which sought to restore Classical democracy on the basis of a capitalist economy. And there is no doubt that it was precisely these heroic illusions which were necessary to sweep away the rubble of the Middle Ages.

But beyond all this, the revival of antiquity both during and after the Renaissance is distinguished by a (self-contradictory) tendency which points, sometimes more and sometimes less, beyond the bourgeois horizon. With turbulent enthusiasm and brilliant versatility of talent, scarcely imaginable today, the great men of the Renaissance strove to develop all the productive forces of society. Their lofty aim was to shatter the narrow localized restrictions of medieval social life and to create a social order in which all human capacities and potentialities would be liberated for an understanding of nature for the benefit of mankind. And these great men recognized that the development of the productive forces meant simultaneously the development of man's own productive capacities. The mastery of nature by free men in a free society—such was the Renaissance ideal of the harmonious man. Engels said of this great progressive human revolution: "The men who established the modern hegemony of the bourgeoisie were anything but narrow bourgeois." Engels perceived, however, that such an impressive, many-sided development of individual capacities, of even the most outstanding men, was possible only while capitalism was still undeveloped: "The heroes of that time had not yet been enslaved in the specialized division of labour whose crippling one-sidedness we so often encounter in their successors."

With the development of the productive forces of capitalism, the subjugation inherent in the capitalist division of labour became more pronounced. By the manufacturing stage, the worker had already become a narrow specialist in a single operation, and the state apparatus had already begun to transform its civil servants into mindless and soulless bureaucrats.

The leading thinkers of the Enlightenment fought against the vestiges of the Middle Ages with even greater passion than the men of the Renaissance; as honest thinkers who hid nothing from themselves they saw symptoms of the contradictions within the emerging forces of production, within the very progress for which they were vanguard fighters. Thus Ferguson "denounced" (as Marx noted) the capitalist division of labour which grew before his eyes: "Many occupations demand in fact no intellectual capacity. They succeed best when there is complete suppression of feeling and thought; and ignorance is the mother of industry as well as of superstition." He predicted pessimistically that if the trend continued "we will create a nation of helots and have no free citizens any more".

With Ferguson as with all the important men of the Enlightenment, this harsh criticism of the capitalist division of labour accompanies (though is not directly related to) a keen championing of the development of productive forces and the elimination of all social obstacles to continued progress. Thus these men exhibit the dichotomy, basic to our discussion, that continues in modern bourgeois thought regarding society, a dichotomy in all significant modern aesthetics and in all serious thought about harmony in life and art. It is a road full of contradictions which the leading eighteenth and nineteenth century thinkers seek between two equally false yet socially necessary extremes.

The one extreme is the glorification of the capitalist mode of developing the means of production—for a long time, indeed, the only possible mode—and concomitantly an apologetic evasion of the enslavement and fragmentation of the individual and of the horrifying ugliness of life which inevitably and increasingly accompanies this development. The other false extreme is to ignore the progressive character of this development because of its shocking human consequences—to escape from the present into the past, from the present of meaningless work in which a man has become a mere appendage to the machine back to the Middle Ages, when the varied labour of the craftsman could "reach a certain limited artistic awareness" (Marx), when a man still enjoyed a "comfortable bondage relationship" (Marx) to his work. These extremes are apologetics, on the one hand, and romantic reaction, on the other.

The great poets and aestheticians of the Enlightenment and of the first half of the nineteenth century did not succumb to this dilemma. But neither were they capable of resolving the contradictions in capitalist society. Undaunted by the conditions that confined them, they exhibited greatness and brilliance in maintaining an unrelenting critique of bourgeois society without abandoning their affirmation of progress. As a result, these antithetical attitudes are to be found side-by-side in the works of the men of the Enlightenment.

The poets and thinkers of German Classicism, whose major activity followed the French Revolution, seek various utopian solutions. Their criticism of the capitalist division of labour is no less incisive than that of the men of the Enlightenment. They, too, stress ever more sharply the fragmentation of the individual. Goethe's Wilhelm Meister poses these questions: "What use is it to manufacture good iron when inside I am full of slag? What good is it to put an estate in order if I am never at one with myself?" And he perceives that this disharmony is a product of bourgeois society. He says: "A bourgeois can make profit and with some difficulty even develop his mind; but he will lose his individuality, do what he will. He may not ask: 'What are you? but only what do you have? what ability, what understanding, what knowledge, how great a fortune? He has to exploit individual aptitudes in order to put them to use, and it is taken for granted that he may not enjoy an inner harmonious development, for he must neglect everything that cannot be put to use.'"

The great poets and thinkers of German Classicism sought in art for the harmonious integration of the individual and the beauty accompanying it. Active after the French Revolution, they had lost the heroic illusions of the Enlightenment. They did not, however, give up the struggle for harmony in the individual and for its artistic expression. As a result, they assigned to questions of aesthetic practice an excessive and often an exaggeratedly idealistic significance. They saw artistic harmony not only as a reflection and expression of the harmonious individual but also as the chief means of overcoming subjectively the fragmentation and distortion resulting from the capitalist division of labour. This approach resulted in their abandoning all practical attempts at overcoming in life itself the absence of harmony under capitalism. Their concepts of harmony in man and of beauty are divorced and alienated from life. Schiller sings of beauty with such a view:

> Piercing even unto Beauty's sphere,
> In the dust still lingers here
> Gravitation, with the world it sways,
> Not from out the mass, with labour wrung,
> Light and graceful, as from nothing sprung,
> Stands the image to the ravish'd gaze.
> Mute is ev'ry struggle, ev'ry doubt,
> In the uncertain glow of victory;
> While each witness hence is driven out
> Of frail man's necessity.[1]

1. Aber dringt bis in der Schönheit Sphäre
   Und im Staube bleibt die Schwere
   Mit dem Stoff, den sie beherrscht, zurück.

Here the idealistic side of classical philosophy and poetry is clearly exemplified. There is idealism, too, in the rigid opposition which Schiller makes between aesthetic activity and ordinary work. With astute historical insight, he finds the origin of man's aesthetic activity in his surplus energy. His resultant "play" theory is directed toward the elimination of the division within man under the capitalist division of labour. With this theory he campaigns for the total, many-sided and developed human personality, yet only sees this development as happening outside the labour process of his time: "For . . . man plays only when he is human in the fullest sense of the word, and he is only fully human when he plays."

The idealism in such theories is clear. It is necessary, however, to recognize that the idealism of these great German classicists was the inevitable product of their social situation. It is precisely because they neither wish to disguise the inhumanity of capitalism nor make concessions to the reactionary and romantic critique, being in no way able to foresee the displacement of capitalism by socialism, that they are forced to seek these solutions in order to preserve the ideal of the integrated man.

This aesthetic utopia does not merely avoid dealing with actual labour as it exists but also seeks utopian solutions in a general social sense. Goethe and Schiller believed that small groups could achieve the ideal of the integrated individual among themselves and provide nuclei for a general diffusion of this ideal—rather after the model of Fourier, who hoped that from the establishment of a phalanstery a gradual transformation of all society to socialism, as he understood it, might be achieved. The educational philosophy in *Wilhelm Meister* is based on a theory of this kind; similar

---

Nicht der Masse qualvoll abgerungen,
Schlank und leicht, wie aus dem Nichts, gesprungen,
Steht das Bild vor dem entzückten Blick,
Alle Zweifel, alle Kämpfe schweigen
In des Sieges hoher Sicherheit;
Ausgestossen hat es jeden Zeugen
Menschlicher Bedürftigkeit.

From "The Ideal and Life", translated by Edgar A. Bowring, *The Poems of Schiller*, London, 1910, p. 189.

utopianism is echoed in Schiller's "On the Aesthetic Education of Man".

Insofar as fragmentation and its cure were sought primarily within the individual, the problem of the fragmentation of sensibility and intellect was emphasized. Clearly, once again, the importance of this position is closely related to philosophic idealism. It is also clear, however, that there did exist, objectively, a fundamental problem in the fragmentation of the individual through the capitalist division of labour. The specialized, forced cultivation of certain individual capacities under this division of labour set the remaining qualities and passions "free" to atrophy or to run riot. In tackling this aspect of the question, Goethe and Schiller were raising the important question of whether it is possible to bring the human passions into harmony.

Some decades later this question was to become crucial to Fourier's utopian socialism. Fourier started with the premise that there is no human emotion that is intrinsically evil. An emotion becomes evil only as a consequence of the anarchy and inhumanity of the capitalist division of labour. Thus Fourier carries his criticism far beyond that of the Enlighteners or the German Classicists, making it a critique of the basic objective problems of the social division of labour; for example, the separation of town and country. The socialism of his utopian dream, with all its social constructs, aimed primarily at developing the abilities and sensibilities latent in every man and at promoting within the harmonious co-operative effort of varied personalities under socialism the integration of the capacities within each individual as well.

Fourier's great contemporaries, Hegel and Balzac, experienced the contradictions emerging from the capitalist division of labour at a more advanced stage than Goethe and Schiller during the period of their collaboration. The note of elegiac resignation which echoed through all the utopian dreams of Goethe and Schiller now predominates. Both the great thinker and the great realist see the inhumanity of capitalist society, that all the harmony within man, his every creative expression, is being ruthlessly crushed. For Hegel the aesthetic harmony in Greek life and after has been irretrievably lost: the "World Spirit" has moved beyond the sphere of the aesthetic and hastens to other goals. The dominion of prose has been established over mankind. And Balzac portrays with what cruel relentlessness capitalist society generates discord and ugliness in every manifestation of human existence, how all human aspirations toward a beautiful and harmonious existence are inexorably crushed by society. Balzac does include episodes in which "islands" of harmonious personalities appear; these are, however, no longer nuclei for a utopian renewal of the world but just exceptional instances of fortunate individuals rescued by chance from under the iron heel of capitalism.

Thus the heroic struggle for the integrated man of the bourgeois revolutionary period terminates in elegiac mourning; for the conditions for developing man's capacities into a harmonious integration have been irretrievably lost. Only where the critique of capitalism evolves into a prescience of socialism does this atmosphere of elegiac mourning, characteristic of the utopian dreamers who founded socialism, disappear.

With the destruction of the heroic illusions of the revolutionary period and the illusions of a possible revival of ancient democracy, there is an accompanying loss of appreciation of the classical experience in bourgeois art and aesthetics. The purely formal "harmony" that takes the place of the classical conception bears little relationship to life, whether of the past or the present; it is "academic", without content, an expression of a smug and complacent evasion of the ugliness of life.

The leading artists and thinkers of the period of bourgeois decline became increasingly dissatisfied with this banal academicism. There are fundamental social and artistic grounds for their renunciation of the ideals of classical harmony. The serious realists seek to depict the social life of their day with uncompromising verisimilitude and thus reject any pretence of harmony in life and of beauty in human personality.

But what lies behind this rejection and how does it manifest itself? Academicism can indeed reduce beauty and harmony to matters of no importance or treat them as mere questions of form, but by their very nature beauty and harmony cannot be matters of indifference to mankind. Concepts of beauty and harmony seem empty only because capitalist society denies them any realization in life. The dream of harmony can be realized and be effective in art only when occasioned by genuinely serious, progressive tendencies in actual life.

Such a dream of human harmony is diametrically opposed to that envisaged by the academician, who, though supposedly the perpetuator of the classics, actually proposes a fraudulent substitute, a false and empty pseudo-harmony. His flight from the ugliness and inhumanity of capitalist life is nothing but a capitulation without struggle.

This is not the only form of artistic capitulation before the fundamental hostility towards art and before the growing barbarism. Leading artists, dedicated fighters against their times, passionate defenders of progress also capitulate—without wishing to, indeed without knowing it—and do so as artists in the face of the philistinism of their time.

In this situation the social and humanist content of the "old-fashioned" concepts of beauty and harmony continue to exert a powerful influence extending far beyond literature and art. In their dedication to truth great realists of the period of mature capitalism like Balzac had to reject any representation of beauty in life or of the integrated personality. To be faithful realists they could only depict disharmonious, shattered lives, lives in which the beautiful and noble in man is inexorably crushed, worse, lives inwardly warped, corrupted and brutalized. The conclusion at which they must arrive is that capitalist society is a vast cemetery for integrity and human capacity, that under capitalism, as Balzac notes with pungent irony, men become either bank clerks or swindlers, that is, either exploited dupes or scoundrels.

This courageous condemnation is what distinguishes genuine realism from apologetic academicism, which seeks escape from life's discord. The creative artist may follow one of two courses in his denunciation of capitalist society. Either he can depict the mere result of this human disintegration or he can, in addition, portray the fine, and noble human energies destroyed in the struggle to resist. Superficially, the distinction seems to be of a purely literary artistic kind. And indeed the analogy with the political and the social opposition to capitalist and imperialist barbarism does not hold mechanically. There is a whole group of seemingly left-wing writers who accept the degradation and destruction of the individual under capitalism as fact; they are indignant and express their indignation in their art; they expose the horror, but they do not depict the human nobility in the resistance to this horror. There are others who do not proclaim their political and social convictions so obviously in their own rebellion but who nevertheless describe with passionate vividness the daily, even hourly, resistance which mankind maintains against the crippling capitalist environment in defence of human integrity. In this uneven battle the individual is doomed if he relies solely on his own powers; he can maintain resistance only as a participant in the opposition movement destined to secure the final victory of humanism in society, economically, politically, socially and culturally.

In this regard Maxim Gorki is the foremost figure in contemporary world literature since his works depict with superb artistry this association of the individual and the popular movements. The horror of life under capitalism has probably never been so accurately exposed or painted in such bleak colours; yet the result is quite different from that in the works of most of his contemporaries, including leading writers of our time, for Gorki never presents the destruction under capitalism as an accomplished fact. He shows what is being destroyed and how, in what kind of struggle, the destruction is taking place. He reveals the beauty, the innate drive to harmony and to the unfolding of the varied but repressed, distorted and misdirected potentialities even in the worst of humanity. The fact that the vital aspiration toward beauty and harmony is crushed before our eyes is what makes his condemnation so resounding, what gives it an echo that can be heard everywhere.

Furthermore, Gorki points to a concrete solution in his work, that is, he shows how the revolutionary labour movement, the popular revolt, awakens an individual, matures him, encourages his inner life to bloom and imbues him with awareness, power and sensitivity. Gorki does not counterpose one social system to another or one ideology to another, but presents the emergent new kind of human being through whom the reader can experience directly and con-cretely the content of the new life.

Thus a principle of artistic representation turns into a political and social principle. None of Gorki's contemporaries reveals either the revulsion against the old or enthusiasm for the new with as much passion as Gorki. This revulsion and enthusiasm and certainty of victory—embodied in living people—exemplifies what has just been discussed: no artistic capitulation to capitalism! Gorki achieves a coincidence of the artistic and the political, a unity that is neither automatic nor mechanical. A writer only a trifle less consequent ideologically and artistically in his radicalism might attempt swifter, more direct effects and fall into lifeless propaganda and provide a dead, fetishized picture of life.

Capitalist antipathy to art is not one-dimensional; every dedicated artist must—consciously or not—end up as an enemy of capitalism in his attempt to create richly investigated characters. He may consider himself "uncommitted", he may seek refuge in scepticism, he may even claim to be conservative. But unless, profoundly confused about social and intellectual issues, he embraces a romantic reaction against progress, his revolt will emerge clearly in his work.

In the defence of repressed human values and of frustrated humanity, Anatole France is more radical and decisive than Emile Zola, the early Sinclair Lewis than Upton Sinclair, Thomas Mann than Dos Passos. It is no accident that the leading realists of our time have succeeded in obtaining a popular audience because their revolt is profound, for they really detest the destruction they see about them and do not merely dress up slogans in a formalist literature. Romain Rolland pursued this course most resolutely. Progressive writers must give careful consideration to the approaches followed by Heinrich and Thomas Mann and many others, too, in this regard. The revolt of the leading realists is the most significant development in the art of the bourgeois world today. This revolt has produced important art in a period most unfavourable to art, a period of a general decline in bourgeois culture. How aware each of the outstanding exponents of this genuine realism is in his association with the great humanist tradition is not decisive. With Romain Rolland or Thomas Mann the association is conscious and of importance. What is decisive is the objective relationship to, the objective continuation of, the fundamental humanist view, a continuation adapted, of course, to the special conditions of the day, in opposition to capitalist culture, a culture which every artist of integrity must reject.

There is another road, however, one which many writers, by no means insignificant in literature or in the general cultural life, have taken. They reject without compromise all ideals of beauty and harmony as "out-of-date"; they take people and society "as they are", or rather as they usually appear in ordinary life under capitalism. And in a depiction of such a given world, the categories of the old aesthetics do indeed lose meaning. Not because they are out-of-date! (We have seen how pertinent and valid they are when adapted to changed conditions by the leading realist of our time.) But they have lost all meaning since capitalism is destroying their social and individual base day by day; and these writers set out to represent a world destroyed and not the battle against the destruction, not a dynamic process but a lifeless result. The consequence is that they reject beauty and harmony and produce a mere chronicle of the "iron age".

Such has been the general course in this development. Writers have produced intellectual quintessences, local colour studies —presenting the primary material with which a dynamic re-creation of the world should start. They sketch characters and lives, arranged as in a chronicle, and expose the most obvious aspects of the destruction of the individual in capitalist society. The readers feel no impelling compassion for the characters or their experiences since the authors have presented only the consequences or nearly completed results of the destructive process. The readers cannot experience what was destroyed in this process nor appreciate at all the consequences of a continuation of such a process in the view of the author, for the author provides them with nothing but an abstract ideological programme.

Needless to add, this is not the only current in literature, nor is it ever to be found in absolute purity, for there is scarcely a true writer—no matter what his political philosophy—who rejects beauty altogether. Beauty, however, becomes something extraneous, something essentially alien to their subject matter and even antithetical to it. Flaubert turns beauty into a mere formal quality in rhetoric or picturesque diction; beauty is a quality to be imposed artificially on subject matter that is inherently unbeautiful. Baudelaire carries this alienation of beauty from life and the antipathy of life to beauty to the point of transforming beauty into a thing in itself—exotic, demonic, and vampire-like.

In the profound pessimism of their art and ideologies, leading writers reflect capitalism's hostility to art and the general ugliness of life under capitalism. Artists and thinkers become increasingly overwhelmed by the bleakness of life in the age of imperialism. Though they represent the inhumanity of capitalism with ever-greater intensity, they no longer manifest a rebellious fury but exhibit a conscious or unconscious respect for its "monumentality". The Greek ideal of beauty disappears and is replaced by a modern orientalism or a modernized glorification of the Gothic or the baroque. Nietzsche completes the ideological transformation by pronouncing the harmonious man of Greece a myth and by transfiguring Greece and the Renaissance "realistically" into civilizations of "monumental inhumanity and bestiality". Fascism inherits these decadent tendencies of bourgeois development and adapts them to its own demogogic purposes, using them to provide an ideological rationale for its prisons and torture chambers.

The power and vitality of anti-fascist literature lies in its reawakened humanism. The Hitlerites knew what they were doing when they set as the principal task for their "Professor for Political Pedagogy", Alfred Baeumler, the struggle against classical humanism. Imbued with a humanistic spirit and a humanistic revolt, the works of Anatole France, Romain Rolland, Thomas and Heinrich Mann and of all the outstanding anti-fascist writers represent a literature of which we can be proud, a literature which will in the future bear witness to artistic integrity in our time. This is a literature "against the stream", fighting the barbarous reactionary attitudes and deeds of our day, maintaining a courageous and effective resistance to the attempts to annihilate great art and defending the great realist tradition against the dominant current that is the inevitable reflection of contemporary capitalist society.

How far the individual anti-fascist writers consider themselves or profess to be the inheritors and perpetuators of the classical tradition is not decisive; what is important is that they are in fact carrying on the best traditions of mankind.

WALTER BENJAMIN

The two most widely read essays by Walter Benjamin are "The Work of Art in the Age of Mechanical Reproduction" and "The Storyteller," both dating from 1936.* They adopt opposite, if not incompatible, strategies with regard to the effacement of traditional values and forms in art by modern technological developments. The "Mechanical Reproduction" essay emphasizes the positive side of lost tradition; the "Storyteller" essay remains unmistakably nostalgic. According to the first, advances in reproducibility have served not only to bring the art treasures of distant places to be viewed simultaneously by an unlimited number of people, but these advances have, at the same time, reduced the cultic authority of the original upon which the reproductions are based. One might imagine that Benjamin, as the son of a successful Berlin antiquarian art dealer and a collector himself, would regret the evaporation of art's auratic atmosphere—that magical religious mystery compounded of a work's singularity, as well as its organic connection with a certain landscape and the historical tradition in which it is embedded. Instead, he identifies art's cultic associations as filled with undesirable and outmoded attitudes: an iconicity serving as a receptacle for alienated human adoration. Marx had written in *Capital* about commodities which are valued beyond their actual use value because they contain, in a veiled way, all the social and economic relations between human beings. The commodity "fetish" presents a worker's labor, the economic status of the company that employs him, the salary of its president, and such, as a property of the object produced.† Value is thus alienated here in a way similar to Benjamin's auratic icon, which received all the hysterical adoration that should, if justice were done, go to the human image, "the human form divine," as Blake would say. The removal of the aura from art is the first step in redirecting alienated revolutionary energies of men toward their proper goal.

The futuristic character of the "aura" essay is reversed in "The Storyteller" in a manner reminiscent at times of William Morris' medievalism. The story, or tale, is rooted in communal life (the trade structure of the Middle Ages) by the oral institutions of the resident master craftsman and the traveling journeyman. The craftsman knew all the local lore, and the other brought news from afar. They offered something useful to the listener, moral advice or some proverbial focus. Their tales did not

*Walter Benjamin, *Illuminations,* trans. Harry Zohn (New York: Schocken, 1969).
†*Marxism and Art,* ed. Maynard Solomon (Detroit: Wayne State University Press, 1979) 545–47. Karl Marx, *Capital,* Vol. 1, tr. Ben Fowkes (New York: Vintage, 1977) 163 ff.

exhaust themselves in the telling but were eternally fascinating. They were patiently crafted, lovingly shaped. They implied companionship and a universally acknowledged vision of life's significance, including shared experience of death. This world is lost now. We return silent from our greatest adventures. Hospitals separate us from the dying. We have no counsel to offer others. The novel, dependent on mechanical printing, has replaced the tale. It is consumed in isolation, in the desperation and perplexity of the solitary bourgeois reader looking for the meaning of life. But the novel has no wisdom to impart. It is the genre, as Lukács said, of transcendental homelessness. The instantaneous dissemination of global information has eradicated the need for storytellers, who were once the main source of the marvelous. And the entertainment technologies have eradicated sacred boredom, "the dream bird that hatches the egg of experience." There is no more weaving and spinning to engender the self-forgetfulness necessary for the story to impress itself deeply and permanently on the mind.

The advantage of a dialectical habit of mind is that what seems to be a fruitless longing for a sublated mode of production can be converted, not only to criticism of present inadequacies, but also can be said to contain the seeds of a higher community, one more appropriate for an as yet inconceivable, rational society.‡‡

‡‡Fredric Jameson, *Marxism and Form* (Princeton: Princeton University Press, 1971) 82.

The Storyteller: Reflections on the Works of Nikolai Leskov

1936

Translated by Harry Zohn

I

Familiar though his name may be to us, the storyteller in his living immediacy is by no means a present force. He has already become something remote from us and something that is getting even more distant. To present someone like Leskov as a storyteller does not mean bringing him closer to us but, rather, increasing our distance from him. Viewed from a certain distance, the great, simple outlines which define the storyteller stand out in him, or rather, they become visible in him, just as in a rock a human head or an animal's body may appear to an observer at the proper distance and angle of vision. This distance and this angle of vision are prescribed for us by an experience which we may have almost every day. It teaches us that the art of storytelling is coming to an end. Less and less frequently do we encounter people with the ability to tell a tale properly. More and more often there is embarrassment all around when the wish to hear a story is expressed. It is as if something that seemed inalienable to us, the securest among our possessions, were taken from us: the ability to exchange experiences.

One reason for this phenomenon is obvious: experience has fallen in value. And it looks as if it is continuing to fall into bottomlessness. Every glance at a newspaper demonstrates that it has reached a new low, that our picture, not only of the external world but of the moral world as well, overnight has undergone changes which were never thought possible. With the [First] World War a process began to become apparent which has not halted since then. Was it not noticeable at the end of the war that men returned from the battlefield grown silent—not richer, but poorer in communicable experience? What ten years later was poured out in the flood of war books was anything but experience that goes from mouth to mouth. And there was nothing remarkable about that. For never has experience been contradicted more thoroughly than strategic experience by tactical warfare, economic experience by inflation, bodily experience by mechanical warfare, moral experience by those in power. A generation that had gone to school on a horse-drawn streetcar now stood under the open sky in a countryside in which nothing remained unchanged but the clouds, and beneath these clouds, in a field of force of destructive torrents and explosions, was the tiny, fragile human body.

II

Experience which is passed on from mouth to mouth is the source from which all storytellers have drawn. And among those who have written down the tales, it is the great ones whose written version differs least from the speech of the many nameless storytellers. Incidentally, among the last named there are two groups which, to be sure, overlap in many ways. And the figure of the storyteller gets its full corporeality only for the one who can picture them both. "When someone goes on a trip, he has something to tell about," goes the German saying, and people imagine the storyteller as someone who has come from afar. But they enjoy no less listening to the man who has stayed at home, making an honest living, and who knows the local tales and traditions. If one wants to picture these two groups through their archaic representatives, one is embodied in the resident tiller of the soil, and the other in the trading seaman. Indeed, each sphere of life has, as it were, produced its own tribe of storytellers. Each of these tribes preserves some of its characteristics centuries later. Thus, among nineteenth-century German storytellers, writers like Hebel and Gotthelf stem from the first tribe, writers like Sealsfield and Gerstäcker from the second. With these tribes, however, as stated above, it is only a matter of basic types. The actual extension of the realm of storytelling in its full historical breadth is inconceivable without the most intimate interpenetration of these two archaic types. Such an interpenetration was achieved particularly by the Middle Ages in their trade structure. The resident master craftsman and the traveling journeymen worked together in the same rooms; and every master had been a traveling journeyman before he settled down in his home town or somewhere else. If peasants and seamen were past masters of storytelling, the artisan class was its university. In it was combined the lore of faraway places, such as a much-traveled man brings home, with the lore of the past, as it best reveals itself to natives of a place.

III

Leskov was at home in distant places as well as distant times. He was a member of the Greek Orthodox Church, a man with genuine religious interests. But he was a no less sincere opponent of ecclesiastic bureaucracy. Since he was not able to get along any better with secular officialdom, the official positions he held were not of long duration. Of all his posts, the one he held for a long time as Russian representative of a big English firm was presumably the most useful one for his writing. For this firm he traveled through Russia, and these trips advanced his worldly wisdom as much as they did his knowledge of conditions in Russia. In this way he had an opportunity of becoming acquainted with the organization of the sects in the country. This left its mark on his works of fiction. In the Russian legends Leskov saw allies in his fight against Orthodox bureaucracy. There are a number of his legendary tales whose focus is a righteous man, seldom an ascetic, usually a simple, active man who becomes a saint apparently in the most natural way in the world. Mystical exaltation is not Leskov's forte. Even though he occasionally liked to indulge in the miraculous, even in piousness he prefers to stick with a sturdy nature. He sees the prototype in the man who finds his way about the world without getting too deeply involved with it.

He displayed a corresponding attitude in worldly matters. It is in keeping with this that he began to write late, at the age of twenty-nine. That was after his commercial travels. His first printed work was entitled "Why Are Books Expensive in Kiev?" A number of other writings about the working class, alcoholism, police doctors, and unemployed salesmen are precursors of his works of fiction.

IV

An orientation toward practical interests is characteristic of many born storytellers. More pronouncedly than in Leskov this trait can be recognized, for example, in Gotthelf, who gave his peasants agricultural advice; it is found in Nodier, who concerned himself with the perils of gas light; and Hebel, who slipped bits of scientific instruction for his readers into his *Schatzkästlein,* is in this line as well. All this points to the nature of every real story. It contains, openly or covertly, something useful. The usefulness may, in one case, consist in a moral; in another, in some practical advice; in a third, in a proverb or maxim. In every case the storyteller is a man who has counsel for his readers. But if today "having counsel" is beginning to have an old-fashioned ring, this is because the communicability of experience is decreasing. In consequence we have no counsel either for ourselves or for others. After all, counsel is less an answer to a question than a proposal concerning the continuation of a story which is just unfolding. To seek this counsel one would first have to be able to tell the story. (Quite apart from the fact that a man is receptive to counsel only to the extent that he allows his situation to speak.) Counsel woven into the fabric of real life is wisdom. The art of storytelling is reaching its end because the epic side of truth, wisdom, is dying out. This, however, is a process that has been going on for a long time. And nothing would be more fatuous than to want to see in it merely a "symptom of decay," let alone a "modern" symptom. It is, rather, only a concomitant symptom of the secular productive forces of history, a concomitant that has quite gradually removed narrative from the realm of living speech and at the same time is making it possible to see a new beauty in what is vanishing.

V

The earliest symptom of a process whose end is the decline of storytelling is the rise of the novel at the beginning of modern times. What distinguishes the novel from the story (and from the epic in the narrower sense) is its essential dependence on the book. The dissemination of the novel became possible only with the invention of printing. What can be handed on orally, the wealth of the epic, is of a different kind from what constitutes the stock in trade of the novel.

What differentiates the novel from all other forms of prose literature —the fairy tale, the legend, .even the novella—is that it neither comes from oral tradition nor goes into it. This distinguishes it from storytelling in particular. The storyteller takes what he tells from experience—his own or that reported by others. And he in turn makes it the experience of those who are listening to his tale. The novelist has isolated himself. The birthplace of the novel is the solitary individual, who is no longer able to express himself by giving examples of his most important concerns, is himself uncounseled, and cannot counsel others. To write a novel means to carry the incommensurable to extremes in the representation of human life. In the midst of life's fullness, and through the representation of this fullness, the novel gives evidence of the profound perplexity of the living. Even the first great book of the genre, *Don Quixote,* teaches how the spiritual greatness, the boldness, the helpfulness of one of the noblest of men, Don Quixote, are completely devoid of counsel and do not contain the slightest scintilla of wisdom. If now and then, in the course of the centuries, efforts have been made—most effectively, perhaps, in *Wilhelm Meisters Wanderjahre*—to implant instruction in the novel, these attempts have always amounted to a modification of the novel form. The *Bildungsroman,* on the other hand, does not deviate in any way from the basic structure of the novel. By integrating the social process with the development of a person, it bestows the most frangible justification on the order determining it. The legitimacy it provides stands in direct opposition to reality. Particularly in the *Bildungsroman,* it is this inadequacy that is actualized.

VI

One must imagine the transformation of epic forms occurring in rhythms comparable to those of the change that has come over the earth's surface in the course of thousands of centuries. Hardly any other forms of human communication have taken shape more slowly, been lost more slowly. It took the novel, whose beginnings go back to antiquity, hundreds of years before it encountered in the evolving middle class those elements which were favorable to its flowering. With the appearance of these elements, storytelling began quite slowly to recede into the archaic; in many ways, it is true, it took hold of the new material, but it was not really determined by it. On the other hand, we recognize that with the full control of the middle class, which has the press as one of its most important instruments in fully developed capitalism, there emerges a form of communication which, no matter how far back its origin may lie, never before influenced the epic form in a decisive way. But now it does exert such an influence. And it turns out that it confronts storytelling as no less of a stranger than did the novel, but in a more menacing way, and that it also brings about a crisis in the novel. This new form of communication is information.

Villemessant, the founder of *Le Figaro,* characterized the nature of information in a famous formulation. "To my readers," he used to say, "an attic fire in the Latin Quarter is more important than a revolution in Madrid." This makes strikingly clear that it is no longer intelligence coming from afar, but the information which supplies a handle for what is nearest that gets the readiest hearing. The intelligence that came from afar—whether the spatial kind from foreign countries or the temporal kind of tradition—possessed an authority which gave it validity, even when it was not subject to verification. Information, however, lays claim to prompt verifiability. The prime requirement is that it appear "understandable in itself." Often it is no more exact than the intelligence of earlier centuries was. But while the latter was inclined to borrow from the miraculous, it is indispensable for information to sound plausible. Because of this it proves incompatible with the spirit of storytelling. If the art of storytelling has become rare, the dissemination of information has had a decisive share in this state of affairs.

Every morning brings us the news of the globe, and yet we are poor in noteworthy stories. This is because no event any longer comes to us without already being shot through with explanation. In other words, by now almost nothing that happens benefits storytelling; almost everything benefits information. Actually, it is half the art of storytelling to keep a story free from explanation as one reproduces it. Leskov is a master at this (compare pieces like "The Deception" and "The White Eagle"). The most extraordinary things, marvelous things, are related with the greatest accuracy, but the psychological connection of the events is not forced on the reader. It is left up to him to interpret things the way he understands them, and thus the narrative achieves an amplitude that information lacks.

VII

Leskov was grounded in the classics. The first storyteller of the Greeks was Herodotus. In the fourteenth chapter of the third book of his *Histories* there is a story from which much can be learned. It deals with Psammenitus.

When the Egyptian king Psammenitus had been beaten and captured by the Persian king Cambyses, Cambyses was bent on humbling his prisoner. He gave orders to place Psammenitus on the road along which the Persian triumphal procession was to pass. And he further arranged that the prisoner should see his daughter pass by as a maid going to the well with her pitcher. While all the Egyptians were lamenting and bewailing this spectacle, Psammenitus stood alone, mute and motionless, his eyes fixed on the ground; and when presently he saw his son, who was being taken along in the procession to be executed, he likewise remained unmoved. But when afterwards he recognized one of his servants, an old, impoverished man, in the ranks of the prisoners, he beat his fists against his head and gave all the signs of deepest mourning.

From this story it may be seen what the nature of true storytelling is. The value of information does not survive the moment in which it was new. It lives only at that moment; it has to surrender to it completely and explain itself to it without losing any time. A story is different. It does not expend itself. It preserves and concentrates its strength and is capable of releasing it even after a long time. Thus Montaigne referred to this Egyptian king and asked himself why he mourned only when he caught sight of his servant. Montaigne answers: "Since he was already overfull of grief, it took only the smallest increase for it to burst through its dams." Thus Montaigne. But one could also say: The king is not moved by the fate of those of royal blood, for it is his own fate. Or: We are moved by much on the stage that does not move us in real life; to the king, this servant is only an actor. Or: Great grief is pent up and breaks forth only with relaxation. Seeing this servant was the relaxation. Herodotus offers no explanations. His report is the driest. That is why this story from ancient Egypt is still capable after thousands of years of arousing astonishment and thoughtfulness. It resembles the seeds of grain which have lain for centuries in the chambers of the pyramids shut up air-tight and have retained their germinative power to this day.

VIII

There is nothing that commends a story to memory more effectively than that chaste compactness which precludes psychological analysis. And the more natural the process by which the storyteller forgoes psychological shading, the greater becomes the story's claim to a place in the memory of the listener, the more completely is it integrated into his own experience, the greater will be his inclination to repeat it to someone else someday, sooner or later. This process of assimilation, which takes place in depth, requires a state of relaxation which is becoming rarer and rarer. If sleep is the apogee of physical relaxation, boredom is the apogee of mental relaxation. Boredom is the dream bird that hatches the egg of experience. A rustling in the leaves drives him away. His nesting places—the activities that are intimately associated with boredom—are already extinct in the cities and are declining in the country as well. With this the gift for listening is lost and the community of listeners disappears. For storytelling is always the art of repeating stories, and this art is lost when the stories are no longer retained. It is lost because there is no more weaving and spinning to go on while they are being listened to. The more self-forgetful the listener is, the more deeply is what he listens to impressed upon his memory. When the rhythm of work has seized him, he listens to the tales in such a way that the gift of retelling them comes to him all by itself. This, then, is the nature of the web in which the gift of storytelling is cradled. This is how today it is becoming unraveled at all its ends after being woven thousands of years ago in the ambience of the oldest forms of craftsmanship.

IX

The storytelling that thrives for a long time in the milieu of work—the rural, the maritime, and the urban—is itself an artisan form of communication, as it were. It does not aim to convey the pure essence of the thing, like information or a report. It sinks the thing into the life of the storyteller, in order to bring it out of him again. Thus traces of the storyteller cling to the story the way the handprints of the potter cling to the clay vessel. Storytellers tend to begin their story with a presentation of the circumstances in which they themselves have learned what is to follow, unless they simply pass it off as their own experience. Leskov begins his "Deception" with the description of a train trip on which he supposedly heard from a fellow passenger the events which he then goes on to relate; or he thinks of Dostoevsky's funeral, where he sets his acquaintance with the heroine of his story "À Propos of the Kreutzer Sonata"; or he evokes a gathering of a reading circle in which we are told the events that he reproduces for us in his "Interesting Men." Thus his tracks are frequently evident in his narratives, if not as those of the one who experienced it, then as those of the one who reports it.

This craftsmanship, storytelling, was actually regarded as a craft by Leskov himself. "Writing," he says in one of his letters, "is to me no liberal art, but a craft." It cannot come as a surprise that he felt bonds with craftsmanship, but faced industrial technology as a stranger. Tolstoy, who must have understood this, occasionally touches this nerve of Leskov's storytelling talent when he calls him the first man "who pointed out the inadequacy of economic progress. . . . It is strange that Dostoevsky is so widely read. . . . But I simply cannot comprehend why Leskov is not read. He is a truthful writer." In his artful and high-spirited story "The Steel Flea," which is midway between legend and farce, Leskov glorifies native craftsmanship through the silversmiths of Tula. Their masterpiece, the steel flea, is seen by Peter the Great and convinces him that the Russians need not be ashamed before the English.

The intellectual picture of the atmosphere of craftsmanship from which the storyteller comes has perhaps never been sketched in such a significant way as by Paul Valéry. "He speaks of the perfect things in nature, flawless pearls, full-bodied, matured wines, truly developed creatures, and calls them 'the precious product of a long chain of causes similar to one another.'" The accumulation of such causes has its temporal limit only at perfection. "This patient process of Nature," Valéry continues, "was once imitated by men. Miniatures, ivory carvings, elaborated to the point of greatest perfection, stones that are perfect in polish and engraving, lacquer work or paintings in which a series of thin, transparent layers are placed one on top of the other—all these products of sustained, sacrificing effort are vanishing, and the time is past in which time did not matter. Modern man no longer works at what cannot be abbreviated."

In point of fact, he has succeeded in abbreviating even storytelling. We have witnessed the evolution of the "short story," which has removed itself from oral tradition and no longer permits that slow piling one on top of the other of thin, transparent layers which constitutes the most appropriate picture of the way in which the perfect narrative is revealed through the layers of a variety of retellings.

X

Valéry concludes his observations with this sentence: "It is almost as if the decline of the idea of eternity coincided with the increasing aversion to sustained effort." The idea of eternity has ever had its strongest source in death. If this idea declines, so we reason, the face of death must have changed. It turns out that this change is identical with the one that has diminished the communicability of experience to the same extent as the art of storytelling has declined.

It has been observable for a number of centuries how in the general consciousness the thought of death has declined in omnipresence and vividness. In its last stages this process is accelerated. And in the course of the nineteenth century bourgeois society has, by means of hygienic and social, private and public institutions, realized a secondary effect which may have been its subconscious main purpose: to make it possible for people to avoid the sight of the dying. Dying was once a public process in the life of the individual and a most exemplary one; think of the medieval pictures in which the deathbed has turned into a throne toward which the people press through the wide-open doors of the death house. In the course of modern times dying has been pushed further and further out of the perceptual world of the living. There used to be no house, hardly a room, in which someone had not once died. (The Middle Ages also felt spatially what makes that inscription on a sun dial of Ibiza, *Ultima multis* [the last day for many], significant as the temper of the times.) Today people live in rooms that have never been touched by death, dry dwellers of eternity, and when their end approaches they are stowed away in sanatoria or hospitals by their heirs. It is, however, characteristic that not only a man's knowledge or wisdom, but above all his real life—and this is the stuff that stories are made of—first assumes transmissible form at the moment of his death. Just as a sequence of images is set in motion inside a man as his life comes to an end—unfolding the views of himself under which he has encountered himself without being aware of it—suddenly in his expressions and looks the unforgettable emerges and imparts to everything that concerned him that authority which even the poorest wretch in dying possesses for the living around him. This authority is at the very source of the story.

XI

Death is the sanction of everything that the storyteller can tell. He has borrowed his authority from death. In other words, it is natural history to which his stories refer back. This is expressed in exemplary form in one of the most beautiful stories we have by the incomparable Johann Peter Hebel. It is found in the *Schatzkästlein des rheinischen Hausfreundes,* is entitled "Unexpected Reunion," and begins with the betrothal of a young lad who works in the mines of Falun. On the eve of his wedding he dies a miner's death at the bottom of his tunnel. His bride keeps faith with him after his death, and she lives long enough to become a wizened old woman; one day a body is brought up from the abandoned tunnel which, saturated with iron vitriol, has escaped decay, and she recognizes her betrothed. After this reunion she too is called away by death. When Hebel, in the course of this story, was confronted with the necessity of making this long period of years graphic, he did so in the following sentences: "In the meantime the city of Lisbon was destroyed by an earthquake, and the Seven Years' War came and went, and Emperor Francis I died, and the Jesuit Order was abolished, and Poland was partitioned, and Empress Maria Theresa died, and Struensee was executed. America became independent, and the united French and Spanish forces were unable to capture Gibraltar. The Turks locked up General Stein in the Veteraner Cave in Hungary, and Emperor Joseph died also. King Gustavus of Sweden conquered Russian Finland, and the French Revolution and the long war began, and Emperor Leopold II went to his grave too. Napoleon captured Prussia, and the English bombarded Copenhagen, and the peasants sowed and harvested. The millers ground, the smiths hammered, and the miners dug for veins of ore in their underground workshops. But when in 1809 the miners at Falun. . . ."

Never has a storyteller embedded his report deeper in natural history than Hebel manages to do in this chronology. Read it carefully. Death appears in it with the same regularity as the Reaper does in the processions that pass around the cathedral clock at noon.

XII

Any examination of a given epic form is concerned with the relationship of this form to historiography. In fact, one may go even further and raise the question whether historiography does not constitute the common ground of all forms of the epic. Then written history would be in the same relationship to the epic forms as white light is to the colors of the spectrum. However this may be, among all forms of the epic there is not one whose incidence in the pure, colorless light of written history is more certain than the chronicle. And in the broad spectrum of the chronicle the ways in which a story can be told are graduated like shadings of one and the same color. The chronicler is the history-teller. If we think back to the passage from Hebel, which has the tone of a chronicle throughout, it will take no effort to gauge the difference between the writer of history, the historian, and the teller of it, the chronicler. The historian is bound to explain in one way or another the happenings with which he deals; under no circumstances can he content himself with displaying them as models of the course of the world. But this is precisely what the chronicler does, especially in his classical representatives, the chroniclers of the Middle Ages, the precursors of the historians of today. By basing their historical tales on a divine plan of salvation—an inscrutable one—they have from the very start lifted the burden of demonstrable explanation from their own shoulders. Its place is taken by interpretation, which is not concerned with an accurate concatenation of definite events, but with the way these are embedded in the great inscrutable course of the world.

Whether this course is eschatologically determined or is a natural one makes no difference. In the storyteller the chronicler is preserved in changed form, secularized, as it were. Leskov is among those whose work displays this with particular clarity. Both the chronicler with his eschatological orientation and the storyteller with his profane outlook are so represented in his works that in a number of his stories it can hardly be decided whether the web in which they appear is the golden fabric of a religious view of the course of things, or the multicolored fabric of a wordly view.

Consider the story "The Alexandrite," which transports the reader into "that old time when the stones in the womb of the earth and the planets at celestial heights were still concerned with the fate of men, and not today when both in the heavens and beneath the earth everything has grown indifferent to the fates of the sons of men and no voice speaks to them from anywhere, let alone does their bidding. None of the undiscovered planets play any part in horoscopes any more, and there are a lot of new stones, all measured and weighed and examined for their specific weight and their density, but they no longer proclaim anything to us, nor do they bring us any benefit. Their time for speaking with men is past."

As is evident, it is hardly possible unambiguously to characterize the course of the world that is illustrated in this story of Leskov's. Is it determined eschatologically or naturalistically? The only certain thing is that in its very nature it is by definition outside all real historical categories. Leskov tells us that the epoch in which man could believe himself to be in harmony with nature has expired. Schiller called this epoch in the history of the world the period of naïve poetry. The storyteller keeps faith with it, and his eyes do not stray from that dial in front of which there moves the procession of creatures of which, depending on circumstances, Death is either the leader or the last wretched straggler.

XIII

It has seldom been realized that the listener's naïve relationship to the storyteller is controlled by his interest in retaining what he is told. The cardinal point for the unaffected listener is to assure himself of the possibility of reproducing the story. Memory is the epic faculty *par excellence*. Only by virtue of a comprehensive memory can epic writing absorb the course of events on the one hand and, with the passing of these, make its peace with the power of death on the other. It is not surprising that to a simple man of the people, such as Leskov once invented, the Czar, the head of the sphere in which his stories take place, has the most encyclopedic memory at his command. "Our Emperor," he says, "and his entire family have indeed a most astonishing memory."

Mnemosyne, the rememberer, was the Muse of the epic art among the Greeks. This name takes the observer back to a parting of the ways in world history. For if the record kept by memory —historiography—constitutes the creative matrix of the various epic forms (as great prose is the creative matrix of the various metrical forms), its oldest form, the epic, by virtue of being a kind of common denominator includes the story and the novel. When in the course of centuries the novel began to emerge from the womb of the epic, it turned out that in the novel the element of the epic mind that is derived from the Muse—that is, memory—manifests itself in a form quite different from the way it manifests itself in the story.

Memory creates the chain of tradition which passes a happening on from generation to generation. It is the Muse-derived element of the epic art in a broader sense and encompasses its varieties. In the first place among these is the one practiced by the storyteller. It starts the web which all stories together form in the end. One ties on to the next, as the great storytellers, particularly the Oriental ones, have always readily shown. In each of them there is a Scheherazade who thinks of a fresh story whenever her tale comes to a stop. This is epic remembrance and the Muse-inspired element of the narrative. But this should be set against another principle, also a Muse-derived element in a narrower sense, which as an element of the novel in its earliest form—that is, in the epic—lies concealed, still undifferenti-ated from the similarly derived element of the story. It can, at any rate, occasionally be divined in the epics, particularly at moments of solemnity in the Homeric epics, as in the invocations to the Muse at their beginning. What announces itself in these passages is the perpetuating remembrance of the novelist as contrasted with the short-lived reminiscences of the storyteller. The first is dedicated to *one* hero, *one* odyssey, *one* battle; the second, to *many* diffuse occurrences. It is, in other words, *remembrance* which, as the Muse-derived element of the novel, is added to reminiscence, the corresponding element of the story, the unity of their origin in memory having disappeared with the decline of the epic.

XIV

"No one," Pascal once said, "dies so poor that he does not leave something behind." Surely it is the same with memories too —although these do not always find an heir. The novelist takes charge of this bequest, and seldom without profound melancholy. For what Arnold Bennett says about a dead woman in one of his novels—that she had had almost nothing in the way of real life—is usually true of the sum total of the estate which the novelist administers. Regarding this aspect of the matter we owe the most important elucidation to Georg Lukács, who sees in the novel "the form of transcendental homelessness." According to Lukáçs, the novel is at the same time the only art form which includes time among its constitutive principles.

"Time," he says in his *Theory of the Novel,* "can become constitutive only when connection with the transcendental home has been lost. Only in the novel are meaning and life, and thus the essential and the temporal, separated; one can almost say that the whole inner action of a novel is nothing else but a struggle against the power of time. . . . And from this . . . arise the genuinely epic experiences of time: hope and memory. . . . Only in the novel . . . does there occur a creative memory which transfixes the object and transforms it. . . . The duality of inwardness and outside world can here be overcome for the subject 'only' when he sees the . . . unity of his entire life . . . out of the past lifestream which is compressed in memory. . . . The insight which grasps this unity . . . becomes the divinatory-intuitive grasping of the unattained and therefore inexpressible meaning of life."

The "meaning of life" is really the center about which the novel moves. But the quest for it is no more than the initial expression of perplexity with which its reader sees himself living this written life. Here "meaning of life"—there "moral of the story": with these slogans novel and story confront each other, and from them the totally different historical co-ordinates of these art forms may be discerned. If *Don Quixote* is the earliest perfect specimen of the novel, its latest exemplar is perhaps the *Éducation sentimentale.*

In the final words of the last-named novel, the meaning which the bourgeois age found in its behavior at the beginning of its decline has settled like sediment in the cup of life. Frédéric and Deslauriers, the boyhood friends, think back to their youthful friendship. This little incident then occurred: one day they showed up in the bordello of their home town, stealthily and timidly, doing nothing but presenting the *patronne* with a bouquet of flowers which they had picked in their own gardens. "This story was still discussed three years later. And now they told it to each other in detail, each supplementing the recollection of the other. 'That may have been,' said Frédéric when they had finished, 'the finest thing in our lives.' 'Yes, you may be right,' said Deslauriers, 'that was perhaps the finest thing in our lives.' "

With such an insight the novel reaches an end which is more proper to it, in a stricter sense, than to any story. Actually there is no story for which the question as to how it continued would not be legitimate. The novelist, on the other hand, cannot hope to take the smallest step beyond that limit at which he invites the reader to a divinatory realization of the meaning of life by writing "Finis."

XV

A man listening to a story is in the company of the storyteller; even a man reading one shares this companionship. The reader of a novel, however, is isolated, more so than any other reader. (For even the reader of a poem is ready to utter the words, for the benefit of the listener.) In this solitude of his, the reader of a novel seizes upon his material more jealously than anyone else. He is ready to make it completely his own, to devour it, as it were. Indeed, he destroys, he swallows up the material as the fire devours logs in the fireplace. The suspense which permeates the novel is very much like the draft which stimulates the flame in the fireplace and enlivens its play.

It is a dry material on which the burning interest of the reader feeds. "A man who dies at the age of thirty-five," said Moritz Heimann once, "is at every point of his life a man who dies at the age of thirty-five." Nothing is more dubious than this sentence—but for the sole reason that the tense is wrong. A man—so says the truth that was meant here—who died at thirty-five will appear to *remembrance* at every point in his life as a man who dies at the age of thirty-five. In other words, the statement that makes no sense for real life becomes indisputable for remembered life. The nature of the character in a novel cannot be presented any better than is done in this statement, which says that the "meaning" of his life is revealed only in his death. But the reader of a novel actually does look for human beings from whom he derives the "meaning of life." Therefore he must, no matter what, know in advance that he will share their experience of death: if need be their figurative death—the end of the novel—but preferably their actual one. How do the characters make him understand that death is already waiting for them—a very definite death and at a very definite place? That is the question which feeds the reader's consuming interest in the events of the novel.

The novel is significant, therefore, not because it presents someone else's fate to us, perhaps didactically, but because this stranger's fate by virtue of the flame which consumes it yields us the warmth which we never draw from our own fate. What draws the reader to the novel is the hope of warming his shivering life with a death he reads about.

XVI

"Leskov," writes Gorky, "is the writer most deeply rooted in the people, and is completely untouched by any foreign influences." A great storyteller will always be rooted in the people, primarily in a milieu of craftsmen. But just as this includes the rural, the maritime, and the urban elements in the many stages of their economic and technical development, there are many gradations in the concepts in which their store of experience comes down to us. (To say nothing of the by no means insignificant share which traders had in the art of storytelling; their task was less to increase its didactic content than to refine the tricks with which the attention of the listener was captured. They have left deep traces in the narrative cycle of *The Arabian Nights.*) In short, despite the primary role which storytelling plays in the household of humanity, the concepts through which the yield of the stories may be garnered are manifold. What may most readily be put in religious terms in Leskov seems almost automatically to fall into place in the pedagogical perspectives of the Enlightenment in Hebel, appears as hermetic tradition in Poe, finds a last refuge in Kipling in the life of British seamen and colonial soldiers. All great storytellers have in common the freedom with which they move up and down the rungs of their experience as on a ladder. A ladder extending downward to the interior of the earth and disappearing into the clouds is the image for a collective experience to which even the deepest shock of every individual experience, death, constitutes no impediment or barrier.

"And they lived happily ever after," says the fairy tale. The fairy tale, which to this day is the first tutor of children because it was once the first tutor of mankind, secretly lives on in the story. The first true storyteller is, and will continue to be, the teller of fairy tales. Whenever good counsel was at a premium, the fairy tale had it, and where the need was greatest, its aid was nearest. This need was the need created by the myth. The fairy tale tells us of the earliest arrangements that mankind made to shake off the nightmare which the myth had placed upon its chest. In the figure of the fool it shows us how mankind "acts dumb" toward the myth; in the figure of the youngest brother it shows us how one's chances increase as the mythical primitive times are left behind; in the figure of the man who sets out to learn what fear is, it shows us that the things we are afraid of can be seen through; in the figure of the wiseacre it shows us that the questions posed by the myth are simple-minded, like the riddle of the Sphinx; in the shape of the animals which come to the aid of the child in the fairy tale it shows that nature not only is subservient to the myth, but much prefers to be aligned with man. The wisest thing—so the fairy tale taught mankind in olden times, and teaches children to this day—is to meet the forces of the mythical world with cunning and with high spirits. (This is how the fairy tale polarizes *Mut*, courage, dividing it dialectically into *Untermut*, that is, cunning, and *Übermut*, high spirits.) The liberating magic which the fairy tale has at its disposal does not bring nature into play in a mythical way, but points to its complicity with liberated man. A mature man feels this complicity only occasionally, that is, when he is happy; but the child first meets it in fairy tales, and it makes him happy.

XVII

Few storytellers have displayed so profound a kinship with the spirit of the fairy tale as did Leskov. This involves tendencies that were promoted by the dogmas of the Greek Orthodox Church. As is well known, Origen's speculation about *apokatastasis*—the entry of all souls into Paradise—which was rejected by the Roman Church plays a significant part in these dogmas. Leskov was very much influenced by Origen and planned to translate his work *On First Principles.* In keeping with Russian folk belief he interpreted the Resurrection less as a transfiguration than as a disenchantment, in a sense akin to the fairy tale. Such an interpretation of Origen is at the bottom of "The Enchanted Pilgrim." In this, as in many other tales by Leskov, a hybrid between fairy tale and legend is involved, not unlike that hybrid which Ernst Bloch mentions in a connection in which he utilizes our distinction between myth and fairy tale in his fashion.

"A hybrid between fairy tale and legend," he says, "contains figuratively mythical elements, mythical elements whose effect is certainly captivating and static, and yet not outside man. In the legend there are Taoist figures, especially very old ones, which are 'mythical' in this sense. For instance, the couple Philemon and Baucis: magically escaped though in natural repose. And surely there is a similar relationship between fairy tale and legend in the Taoist climate of Gotthelf, which, to be sure, is on a much lower level. At certain points it divorces the legend from the locality of the spell, rescues the flame of life, the specifically human flame of life, calmly burning, within as without."

"Magically escaped" are the beings that lead the procession of Leskov's creations: the righteous ones. Pavlin, Figura, the toupée artiste, the bear keeper, the helpful sentry—all of them embodiments of wisdom, kindness, comfort the world, crowd about the storyteller. They are unmistakably suffused with the *imago* of his mother.

This is how Leskov describes her: "She was so thoroughly good that she was not capable of harming any man, nor even an animal. She ate neither meat nor fish, because she had such pity for living creatures. Sometimes my father used to reproach her with this. But she answered: 'I have raisèd the little animals myself, they are like my children to me. I can't eat my own children, can I?' She would not eat meat at a neighbor's house either. 'I have seen them alive,' she would say; 'they are my acquaintances. I can't eat my acquaintances, can I?' "

The righteous man is the advocate for created things and at the same time he is their highest embodiment. In Leskov he has a maternal touch which is occasionally intensified into the mythical (and thus, to be sure, endangers the purity of the fairy tale). Typical of this is the protagonist of his story "Kotin the Provider and Platonida." This figure, a peasant named Pisonski, is a hermaphrodite. For twelve years his mother raised him as a girl. His male and female organs mature simultaneously, and his bisexuality "becomes the symbol of God incarnate."

In Leskov's view, the pinnacle of creation has been attained with this, and at the same time he presumably sees it as a bridge established between this world and the other. For these earthily powerful, maternal male figures which again and again claim Leskov's skill as a storyteller have been removed from obedience to the sexual drive in the bloom of their strength. They do not, however, really embody an ascetic ideal; rather, the continence of these righteous men has so little privative character that it becomes the elemental counterpoise to uncontrolled lust which the storyteller has personified in *Lady Macbeth of Mzensk*. If the range between a Pavlin and this merchant's wife covers the breadth of the world of created beings, in the hierarchy of his characters Leskov has no less plumbed its depth.

XVIII

The hierarchy of the world of created things, which has its apex in the righteous man, reaches down into the abyss of the inanimate by many gradations. In this connection one particular has to be noted. This whole created world speaks not so much with the human voice as with what could be called "the voice of Nature" in the title of one of Leskov's most significant stories.

This story deals with the petty official Philip Philipovich who leaves no stone unturned to get the chance to have as his house guest a field marshal passing through his little town. He manages to do so. The guest, who is at first surprised at the clerk's urgent invitation, gradually comes to believe that he recognizes in him someone he must have met previously. But who is he? He cannot remember. The strange thing is that the host, for his part, is not willing to reveal his identity. Instead, he puts off the high personage from day to day, saying that the "voice of Nature" will not fail to speak distinctly to him one day. This goes on until finally the guest, shortly before continuing on his journey, must grant the host's public request to let the "voice of Nature" resound. Thereupon the host's wife withdraws. She "returned with a big, brightly polished, copper hunting horn which she gave to her husband. He took the horn, put it to his lips, and was at the same instant as though transformed. Hardly had he inflated his cheeks and produced a tone as powerful as the rolling of thunder when the field marshal cried: 'Stop, I've got it now, brother. This makes me recognize you at once! You are the bugler from the regiment of jaegers, and because you were so honest I sent you to keep an eye on a crooked supplies supervisor.' 'That's it, Your Excellency,' answered the host. 'I didn't want to remind you of this myself, but wanted to let the voice of Nature speak.' "

The way the profundity of this story is hidden beneath its silliness conveys an idea of Leskov's magnificent humor. This humor is confirmed in the same story in an even more cryptic way. We have heard that because of his honesty the official was assigned to watch a crooked supplies supervisor. This is what we are told at the end, in the recognition scene. At the very beginning of the story, however, we learn the following about the host: "All the inhabitants of the town were acquainted with the man, and they knew that he did not hold a high office, for he was neither a state official nor a military man, but a little supervisor at the tiny supply depot, where together with the rats he chewed on the state rusks and boot soles, and in the course of time had chewed himself together a nice little frame house." It is evident that this story reflects the traditional sympathy which storytellers have for rascals and crooks. All the literature of farce bears witness to it. Nor is it denied on the heights of art; of all

Hebel's characters, the Brassenheim Miller, Tinder Frieder, and Red Dieter have been his most faithful companions. And yet for Hebel, too, the righteous man has the main role in the *theatrum mundi*. But because no one is actually up to this role, it keeps changing hands. Now it is the tramp, now the haggling Jewish peddler, now the man of limited intelligence who steps in to play this part. In every single case it is a guest performance, a moral improvisation. Hebel is a casuist. He will not for anything take a stand with any principle, but he does not reject it either, for any principle can at some time become the instrument of the righteous man. Compare this with Leskov's attitude. "I realize," he writes in his story "À Propos of the Kreutzer Sonata," "that my thinking is based much more on a practical view of life than on abstract philosophy or lofty morality; but I am nevertheless used to thinking the way I do." To be sure, the moral catastrophes that appear in Leskov's world are to the moral incidents in Hebel's world as the great, silent flowing of the Volga is to the babbling, rushing little millstream. Among Leskov's historical tales there are several in which passions are at work as destructively as the wrath of Achilles or the hatred of Hagen. It is astonishing how fearfully the world can darken for this author and with what majesty evil can raise its scepter. Leskov has evidently known moods—and this is probably one of the few characteristics he shares with Dostoevsky—in which he was close to antinomian ethics. The elemental natures in his *Tales from Olden Times* go to the limit in their ruthless passion. But it is precisely the mystics who have been inclined to see this limit as the point at which utter depravity turns into saintliness.

XIX

The lower Leskov descends on the scale of created things the more obviously does his way of viewing things approach the mystical. Actually, as will be shown, there is much evidence that in this, too, a characteristic is revealed which is inherent in the nature of the storyteller. To be sure, only a few have ventured into the depths of inanimate nature, and in modern narrative literature there is not much in which the voice of the anonymous storyteller, who was prior to all literature, resounds so clearly as it does in Leskov's story "The Alexandrite." It deals with a semiprecious stone, the chrysoberyl. The mineral is the lowest stratum of created things. For the storyteller, however, it is directly joined to the highest. To him it is granted to see in this chrysoberyl a natural prophecy of petrified, lifeless nature concerning the historical world in which he himself lives. This world is the world of Alexander II. The storyteller—or rather, the man to whom he attributes his own knowledge—is a gem engraver named Wenzel who has achieved the greatest conceivable skill in his art. One can juxtapose him with the silversmiths of Tula and say that—in the spirit of Leskov—the perfect artisan has access to the innermost chamber of the realm of created things. He is an incarnation of the devout. We are told of this gem cutter: "He suddenly squeezed my hand on which was the ring with the alexandrite, which is known to sparkle red in artificial light, and cried: 'Look, here it is, the prophetic Russian stone! O crafty Siberian. It was always green as hope and only toward evening was it suffused with blood. It was that way from the beginning of the world, but it concealed itself for a long time, lay hidden in the earth, and permitted itself to be found only on the day when Czar Alexander was declared of age, when a great sorcerer had come to Siberia to find the stone, a magician. . . . ' 'What nonsense are you talking,' I interrupted him; 'this stone wasn't found by a magician at all, it was a scholar named Nordenskjöld!' 'A magician! I tell you, a magician!' screamed Wenzel in a loud voice. 'Just look; what a stone! A green morning is in it and a bloody evening. . . . This is fate, the fate of noble Czar Alexander!' With these words old Wenzel turned to the wall, propped his head on his elbows, and . . . began to sob."

One can hardly come any closer to the meaning of this significant story than by some words which Paul Valéry wrote in a very remote context. "Artistic observation," he says in reflections on a woman artist whose work consisted in the silk embroidery of figures, "can attain an almost mystical depth. The objects on which it falls lose their names. Light and shade form very particular systems, present very individual questions which depend upon no knowledge and are derived from no practice, but get their existence and value exclusively from a certain accord of the soul, the eye, and the hand of someone who was born to perceive them and evoke them in his own inner self."

With these words, soul, eye, and hand are brought into connection. Interacting with one another, they determine a practice. We are no longer familiar with this practice. The role of the hand in production has become more modest, and the place it filled in storytelling lies waste. (After all, storytelling, in its sensory aspect, is by no means a job for the voice alone. Rather, in genuine storytelling the hand plays a part which supports what is expressed in a hundred ways with its gestures trained by work.) That old co-ordination of the soul, the eye, and the hand which emerges in Valéry's words is that of the artisan which we encounter wherever the art of storytelling is at home. In fact, one can go on and ask oneself whether the relationship of the storyteller to his material, human life, is not in itself a craftsman's relationship, whether it is not his very task to fashion the raw material of experience, his own and that of others, in a solid, useful, and unique way. It is a kind of procedure which may perhaps most adequately be exemplified by the proverb if one thinks of it as an ideogram of a story. A proverb, one might say, is a ruin which stands on the site of an old story and in which a moral twines about a happening like ivy around a wall.

Seen in this way, the storyteller joins the ranks of the teachers and sages. He has counsel—not for a few situations, as the proverb does, but for many, like the sage. For it is granted to him to reach back to a whole lifetime (a life, incidentally, that comprises not only his own experience but no little of the experience of others; what the storyteller knows from hearsay is added to his own). His gift is the ability to relate his life; his distinction, to be able to tell his entire life. The storyteller: he is the man who could let the wick of his life be consumed completely by the gentle flame of his story. This is the basis of the incomparable aura about the storyteller, in Leskov as in Hauff, in Poe as in Stevenson. The storyteller is the figure in which the righteous man encounters himself.

THEODOR ADORNO

The death of Adorno has already, like the rose-thorn death of Rilke, attained mythic status. He was slain, so goes the legend, in Frankfurt, by bare-breasted Maenads of the New Left, who in April 1969 charged his podium and covered him with flowers and erotic caresses while he was trying to deliver a lecture. During his retreat from the auditorium, the students pursued him with jeers that "as an institution" he was dead.* In actual fact, he did die on a vacation in Switzerland four months after the incident, his *Aesthetic Theory* unfinished. His interest in aesthetic matters was indeed one of the reasons for the quarrel with the student movement of that time. He repeatedly insisted that art be disengaged from overt political action. He disapproved of Brecht and Sartre because they insisted on engagement (130). Partisanship or tendentiousness in art was one of the many sources of his disagreements with Lukács.† He had refused to change the topic of a June 1967 talk (on Goethe's classicism) in the wake of a Berlin student's death at the hands of the police (Jay:154). The point here is not at all that art has no connection to society or that art has no political content. If one wants to find politics in art one must look in esoteric places, in Kafka, Celan, or Beckett; politics is never so present as in those places which seem politically dead.‡ Only in the aesthetic is there any hope at all. In art there is the level of sensuous receptivity, a respect for the object, which qualifies the will to power of the conceptual and theoretical over nature. Art worthy of the name, moreover, de-aestheticizes itself, "expresses the idea of harmony nega-tively,"** makes it clear that a mere aesthetic reconciliation of contradic-tions, a harmony of form and content, is insufficient, and, in a sense, unreal "semblance." But this unreality of art knows itself to be unreal, and that is precisely its utopian moment. "Semblance is a promise of nonsemblance." In *Aesthetic Theory,* Adorno says further: "Figuratively speaking, art undoes the enduring injustice that society perpetrates against the individual. This attempted restitution aborts because art cannot achieve substantial change unless change is present as a

*Martin Jay, *Adorno* (Cambridge: Harvard University Press, 1984) 55.
† Georg Lukács, *Writer and Critic,* trans. Arthur Kahn (London: Merlin Press, 1971) 29.
‡ *Aesthetics and Politics: Debates Between Bloch, Lukács, Brecht, Benjamin, Adorno,* ed. *New Left Review,* afterword by Fredric Jameson (London, 1977) 194. Quoted in Jay, 130.
**Theodor Adorno, *Prisms,* trans. Samuel and Shierry Weber (London: Neville Spearman, 1967) 32. See Martin Jay, *The Dialectical Imagination* (Boston: Little, Brown, 1973) 179.

concrete possibility in society itself" (422). Those who were present in 1969 know that these are rather subtle points for the spirit of those days. The great danger posed even to high art, certainly to beauty, by the culture industry is that even the auratic can be torn from its context and sold as entertainment, as any other high resolution "sensuous stimuli."† But the power of blackness, the horror of the ugly, resist the culture industry's efforts to absorb them into the sauce of comfort, *kitsch,* which it pours over our lives everywhere we go. Muzak will not make use of Schönberg. The "culinary" cannot corrupt what is inedible. Adorno thus makes a case for the most troubling works of modernism. In Adorno's article on Kafka in *Prisms,* he says approvingly, Kafka's "sentences cry out for interpretation, and none will permit it" (246).

Black as an Ideal

▲ 1970 ▼

Translated by C. Lenhardt

I f works of art are to survive in the context of extremity and darkness, which is social reality, and if they are to avoid being sold as mere comfort, they have to assimilate themselves to that reality. Radical art today is the same as dark art: its background colour is black. Much of contemporary art is irrelevant because it does not take note of this fact, continuing instead to take a childish delight in bright colours. The ideal of blackness is, in substantive terms, one of the most profound impulses of abstract art. It may well be that the naive tinkering with sound and colours that is current now is a response to the impoverishment wrought by the ideal of blackness. It may also be

BLACK AS AN IDEAL by Theodor Adorno from *Aesthetic Theory,* pp. 58–60, trans. C. Lenhardt, eds. Gretel Adorno and Rolf Tiedemann. Reprinted by permission of Routledge & Kegan Paul. Copyright © 1984.

†Theodor Adorno, *Aesthetic Theory,* trans. C. Lenhardt, eds. Gretel Adorno and Rolf Tiedemann (London and New York: Routledge and Kegan Paul, 1984) 430.

that one day art will be able to invalidate that ideal without committing an act of treachery. Brecht may have had an inkling of this when he put down these verses: 'What an age is this anyway where/A conversation about trees is almost a crime/Because it entails being silent about so many misdeeds?'[1] By being voluntarily poor itself, art indicts the unnecessary poverty of society. By the same token, art indicts asceticism, which is not a suitable norm for art. Along with the impoverishment of means brought on by the ideal of the black, if not by functionalist matter-of-factness, we also notice an impoverishment of the creations of poetry, painting and music themselves. On the verge of silence, the most advanced forms of art have sensed the force of this tendency.

One has to be downright naive to think that art can restore to the world the fragrance it has lost, according to a line by Baudelaire.[2] Baudelaire's insight is apt to fuel the scepticism as to whether or not art is still possible even though it does not send art crashing down. Already during the early romantic period, an artist like Schubert, who later was to become the darling of affirmative ideologues of culture, had his doubts about whether or not there is such a thing as cheerful art. The injustice inherent in all cheerful art, especially in the form of entertainment, is an injustice against the stored-up and speechless suffering of the dead. All the same, black art has certain features which, if hypostatized, would perpetuate our historical despair. Therefore, as long as there is hope for change, these features may be regarded as ephemeral, too.

The old but battle-scarred hedonism in aesthetics has recently zeroed in on what it claims to be a perverse implication of the ideal of blackness, namely the notion that the dark aspects of art ought to yield something approximating pleasure, as is the case with black humour in the context of surrealism. Actually, the ideal of darkness does no more and no less than postulate that art properly understood finds happiness in nothing except its ability to stand its ground. This happiness illuminates the sensuous phenomenon from the inside. Just as in internally consistent works of art spirit penetrates even the most impermeable phenomena, redeeming them sensuously, as it

---

1. Bertolt Brecht, 'An die Nachgeborenen', in *Gesammelte Werke* (Frankfurt 1967), vol. 9, p. 723.
2. Charles Baudelaire, *Oeuvres complètes* (Paris 1961), p. 72: 'Le printemps adorable a perdu son odeur', and, one might add, its colour too.

were, so blackness too—the antithesis of the fraudulent sensuality of culture's façade—has a sensual appeal. There is more pleasure in dissonance than in consonance—a thought that metes out justice to hedonism, measure for measure.[3] The discordant moment, dynamically honed to a point and clearly set off from the homogeneous mass of affirmative elements, becomes a stimulus of pleasure in itself. And it is this stimulus together with the disgust with feeble-minded affirmation that ushers modern art into a no-man's land, which is a plenipotentiary of a world made habitable. This aspect of modernism has been realized for the first time in Arnold Schönberg's *Pierrot Lunaire,* where the imaginary essence of details and a dissonant totality are combined into one. Negation can pass over into pleasure but not into positivity.

On the Concept of Ugliness
▲ 1970 ▼

I t is a platitude to say that art is not co-extensive with the concept of the beautiful but needs the ugly as a negation through which to actualize itself. This insight does not imply as a corollary that the category of ugliness has to be abolished. Quite the opposite: ugliness persists as a canon of prohibitions—one that no longer interdicts transgressions of general rules but does debar violations of internal consistency. Such a canon has its universality exclusively in the primacy of particularity, stipulating as it does that there ought not to be anything but the specific. The taboo on ugliness has been transformed into a taboo on crude shapelessness and lack of structure. In art itself, dissonance is the technical term for what ordinary

ON THE CONCEPT OF UGLINESS   by Theodor Adorno from *Aesthetic Theory,* pp. 68–72, trans. C. Lenhardt, eds. Gretel Adorno and Rolf Tiedemann. Reprinted by permission of Routledge & Kegan Paul. Copyright © 1984.

3. Interpolating 'Gerechtigkeit' after the words 'Mass für Mass'.—Tr.

language and aesthetics call ugliness. Ugliness, no matter what exactly it may be, is supposed to be a moment of art, actually or potentially. This was first postulated by Karl Rosenkranz, a disciple of Hegel, who wrote a book entitled *The Aesthetics of the Ugly*.[1] Archaic art and traditional art since the emergence of fauns and sileni in the visual arts during Hellenism abound in the portrayal of subjects considered ugly. In modernism, the significance of this element grew to such proportions that it has assumed a qualitatively new and different function. According to traditional aesthetics, the ugly conflicts with the law of form that dominates a work; therefore it has to be integrated so as to confirm the primacy of form and of subjective freedom as against the material. Thus the ugly subject matter, it is said, becomes in some higher sense beautiful because it has a function in an overall pictorial composition or because it helps produce a dynamic equilibrium. This is in line with one of the motifs of Hegel's aesthetics, where beauty is not the resultant equilibrium *per se* but always the latter together with the tensions that produced it. Harmony which tries to disown the tensions that came to rest in it becomes false, disturbing, even dissonant. In short, it is 'harmonistic'.

The harmonistic view of the ugly has gone bankrupt in modern art. The ugly has undergone a change in kind. The repulsive focus on anatomical details in Rimbaud and Gottfried Benn, the physical repugnance in Beckett and the scatological tendencies in modern drama have nothing whatever to do with the rustic uncouthness of seventeenth-century Dutch paintings. The anal pleasure and the self-satisfaction of art at being able to incorporate that pleasure have given way to a situation where the law of form surrenders to ugliness, the point being that the concept of the ugly, just like that of the beautiful, is dynamic through and through, defying definition and invalidating traditional aesthetics which, no matter how indirectly, takes these categories for granted.

A statement to the effect that something 'is just plain ugly'—say, a landscape despoiled by an industrial complex or a distorted face in a painting—may be a spontaneous response to such phenomena, but it does not have the self-evident validity it claims to have. It does not explain why this impression of ugliness emanates from technology and industrial landscapes—an impression, incidentally, that is unlikely to disappear with the emergence of 'aesthetically sound functional forms' (Adolf Loos) in the designing of factories and so on.

1. Karl Rosenkranz, *Aesthetik des Hässlichen* (Königsberg 1853).

The impression of ugliness stems from the principle of violent destruction that is at work when human purposes are posited in opposition to nature's own purposes. In technology the repression of nature is not reflected through the medium of artistic portrayal but presents itself immediately and starkly to the observer. Putting an end to this state of affairs would require a reorientation of technical forces of production such that they are rationalized in terms not only of human intentions but also of nature's claim to articulate itself in however mediated a fashion. After the abolition of scarcity, any further expansion of productive forces should occur in a dimension that is different from the quantitative growth of production. There are intimations of this in functional buildings that have been adapted to forms and lines in the surrounding landscape; or in old architecture where the raw materials for buildings were taken from the surrounding area, as is the case with many castles and chateaux. What is called 'culture landscape' in German captures the possibilities of such beauty. Today such motifs might be taken up in a deliberate, rational manner in order to close some of the wounds that rationality has inflicted on nature. In naively condemning the ugliness of a landscape torn up by industry, the bourgeois mind zeroes in on the appearance of the domination of nature at the precise juncture where nature shows man a façade of irrepressibility. That bourgeois condemnation therefore is part of the ideology of domination. This kind of ugliness will vanish only when the relation between man and nature throws off its repressive character, which is a continuation rather than an antecedent of the repression of man. Chances for such a change lie in the pacification of technology, not in the idea of setting up enclaves in a world ravished by technology.

In art there is nothing ugly *per se*. All that is ugly has its function in some specific work of art. What is more, all that is ugly can discard its ugliness, once art is free of the attitude of culinary hedonism.

Looking at the other end of the historical spectrum, i.e. at the origin of the concept of ugliness, we find further proof of the thesis that the ugly is indeed a historical and mediated category. It probably originated contemporaneously with the passage from archaic to post-archaic art and it has marked the eternal recurrence of the archaic ever since. That is why it is intimately tied up with the general dialectic of enlightenment, of which art is a part. The archaic ugliness of primitive cult masks and painted faces was a substantive imitation of fear, diffused in the form of repentance. As the mythical fear grew weaker and as subjectivity grew correspondingly stronger, the ugly traits in archaic art became the target of a taboo (whereas originally they had served as a vehicle for enforcing taboos). Their ugliness did not disclose itself until the idea of reconciliation was born in the wake of the formation of the subject and its nascent sense of freedom. But for all that, the old bogies did not fade away in the future. History did not redeem the promise of freedom. Instead, the subject as the agent of unfreedom has perpetuated the mythical spell, rebelling against it and submitting to it at the same time. The empirical basis for Nietzsche's dictum that all good things were once terrible things and for Schelling's insight that at the beginning of time there was horror may well be the history of art.

In due time the displaced and forever recurrent mythical content became sublimated into imagination and form. Beauty, too, is a historical product, not some pure beginning as in Platonic philosophy. It too came about at some distant historical point in the context of a general turning away from the dreaded mythical powers, which in retrospect came to be viewed as ugly. Beauty is a spell on a spell, tainted by the legacy of that spell. The ambiguity of ugliness results from the fact that the subject subsumes under the abstract and formal category of subjectivity all that it has found wanting, from polymorphous sexuality to mutilating repression and death. What keeps recurring is the antithetical other without which art would not be what its concept implies. Appropriated through negation, the ugly as antithesis of the beautiful gnaws away at the affirmative spiritualization of art. In art history the concept of the beautiful then can be said to have been absorbed into the dialectic of the ugly. In this connection, the phenomenon of kitsch or sugary trash is the beautiful minus its ugly counterpart. Therefore, kitsch, purified beauty, becomes subject to an aesthetic taboo that in the name of beauty pronounces kitsch to be ugly.

Only formal definitions can be given of the concept of the ugly and of its positive correlate, beauty. This is closely linked with the process of enlightenment that is inherent in art. The more art becomes permeated by subjectivity, the more hostile it becomes to all that is objectively given, and the more subjective reason grows into an exclusively formal principle and aesthetic rule.[2] This tendency to be

---

2. Cf. M. Horkheimer and T. W. Adorno, *Dialectics of Enlightenment* (New York 1972), *passim*.

faithful to the laws of subjectivity alone, without regard to an objective other, retains its ability to satisfy:[3] unperturbed by the other, subjectivity unconsciously gains satisfaction from itself, that is, from the feeling of power. At this point, where aesthetics is rid of all crude materiality, satisfaction coincides with the appreciation of mathematical relations in the artistic object, the best known examples being the golden section in the visual arts and the fixed overtone relations among consonant musical sounds. Appropriate for such an aesthetics of satisfaction would be the paradoxical subtitle Max Frisch gave to his play on the theme of Don Juan: *The Love of Geometry*. The price art pays for wanting to rise above the powers of nature—only to perpetuate these powers in the form of domination over nature and human beings—that price is its formalistic approach to the ugly and the beautiful. Kantian aesthetics is a case in point. Its formalistic classicism sullies the very beauty the concept of which it glorifies. Its most exemplary works have something violent about them in that they seek to arrange and 'compose' every detail. By imposing its harmony from outside, classical art flouts the truth of that harmony. Where harmony is made to govern in this manner it has no validity. Reconciliation as violence, aesthetic formalism, and antagonistic reality form a triad.

In trying to define what the content of the ugly and the beautiful is, one need not dismiss formalism entirely and abruptly. It is important that the formal aspect of this dichotomy counterbalances a merely substantive differentiation, thus preventing any attempt to want to correct the inherent abstractness of beauty by giving undue weight to the level of content.

---

3 'Sein Wohlgefälliges'. Cf. the earlier discussion on Kant and 'disinterested satisfaction'.—Tr.

ERNST BLOCH

For Theodor Adorno, hope persists somehow in an otherwise unrelenting cultural pessimism; for Ernst Bloch, optimism and the omnipresence of hope is the predominant impression. Not only does Bloch see utopian stirrings in the *horror vacui,* which is where one would expect Adorno to find it; he also is able dialectically to convert elements of popular culture of which Adorno would be highly suspicious. The happy end is a lie, to be sure, a kind of narcotic for the capitalist culture industry, which fills its cinema and magazines with rosy conclusions to keep alive the notion of upward mobility in a context wherein upward mobility is increasingly unlikely. If the status quo is thus stabilized and the little man blames himself for his impoverished life, then the community pillars are free to plunder at will. On the other hand, there is a sense in which this art is more than the ideology of the ruling class. It is only vulgar Marxism (Zhdanovism) that would say the whole of popular culture is a swindle. The cynic is far more dangerous and paralytic in his influence on the future than the dreamer. The cynic fails to see that soaring above a sugary musical, a dance party, circus act, or sports event is a genuine "surplus," a "plus" that never decays once the age and its cultural productions have fallen to dust.* In fact, one could say that only this utopian element never fails, never grows old, never disappoints —precisely because it has never been (91). That it is of the status of the "not yet" is nothing against it. Reality or "crawling empiricism" can never refute the utopian, only rectify it (91). Such dreams will persist as long as the "absolute *Umsonst"* (in vain) has not triumphed. Meanwhile, we must continue to dream *forward* and refuse to make peace with what is by living in those dotted lines of extension that lead away from where we are toward those "utopian margins which surround actuality with real and objective possibility" (96). We must move toward the final state when there is genuine happiness and pleasure for everyone, when nature is historicized, man naturalized, and all predicates, all possibilities, have become one with their subjects. Until that truly happy moment, unfortunately, "S is not yet P."†

---

*Ernst Bloch, *A Philosophy of the Future,* trans. John Cumming (New York: Herder and Herder, 1970) 95. From *Tübinger Einleitung in die Philosophie,* Vol. 1 (Frankfurt: Suhrkamp, 1963).

†Leszek Kolakowski, *Main Currents of Marxism,* trans. P. S. Falla (Oxford and New York: Oxford University Press, 1978). See Vol. 3, p. 422. The formula which Bloch claimed as a one-sentence summary of his philosophy is to be found in his doctoral thesis on Rickert, *Kritische Erörterungen über Rickert und das Problem der modernen Erkenntnistheorie* (1909).

Happy End, Seen Through and Yet Still Defended
1954

Translated by Neville Plaice, Stephen Plaice, and Paul Knight

> I'd like to dance a Can-Can,
> As brazen as Pompadour,
> For we Parisian lasses can
> Think only l'amour, l'amour.
>
> *Offenbach, Paris Life*

The salesman also has hours when he leans on a sugar barrel and is lost in sweet daydreams. Then it's like a twenty-five pound load on his heart to think that he's been chained to the shop like a watch-dog to its kennel ever since he was a boy. If your knowledge of the world's confined to what you've picked up from shoddy chap-books with half their pages missing, if you only know the sunset from an attic window, and the evening glow merely from what customers tell you, then you feel an emptiness inside which all the oil-kegs of the south and all the herring-kegs of the north can't fill, a blandness which all the mace in India can't season.

> *Nestroy, On the Razzle*

We know only too well men want to be deceived. But this not only because stupid people are in the majority. But because men, born to pleasure, have none, because they are crying out for pleasure. This at first even makes clever people one-track and simple at times, they are taken in by glitter, and it is not even necessary for the glitter to promise gold, here it can be enough that it glitters. We learn by our mistakes, but soon the obsession is at work again and hopes that this time it will not be deceived. It keeps itself fresh for the emergency and does not want to miss it; meanwhile however, new children with unburnt fingers are always growing up, new deceivers are always hooking into a weakness which could also be a strength. For this obsession still has a weakness for happiness, for laughing ultimately, and it is not of the beaten-up opinion that anything better could seldom follow. The exploiting of weakness need not come about through swindlers, on a small or large scale. Glossing over is sought after everywhere, bad books are full of it. But, characteristically, the sugar increases towards the end, it rises or rises up so to speak. Life is dubious, but on balance it should be worth it. Even the man who has otherwise learnt by experience is thus impressed by all's well that ends well.

There is a lot to be said for condemning outright the illusion at the end. When we consider the disaster which it has sown and sows today, in increasing fashion. Where work no longer gives any pleasure at all, art is forced to be good fun, merry swindle, tacked-on happy end. This keeps hold of the listeners; at the end of the Fascist national community[1] or of the American way of life everyone will get something, and indeed without the least thing having to be changed in existing reality. The cinema-goers and the readers of magazine stories catch sight of rosy red upward paths, as if they were the norm in present society, and only chance has blocked them for the chance viewer. Indeed, the happy end becomes all the more unavoidable in capitalist terms, the smaller the chances of moving upwards have become in the society that exists today, the less hope the latter can offer. In addition there is the 'moral' dosage of the good outcome; because not everyone becomes rich and happy, there is not enough sugar for this even in the magazine world. Rather, a bank account is only reserved for the virtuous, and misery for the wicked, and only for them; thus one of the most brazen inversions of the real situation takes place. The Rich Man Hotel is occupied everywhere by good people; but the many bad things, hunger, slums, prisons, which the ruling society cannot abolish and cannot even deny, are expediently allotted to the morally bad. These are the old Sunday sermons of crafty edification which have now become complete hypocrisy and part of the cosmetic industry too. 'If money', says Marx, 'comes into

1. 'Volksgemeinschaft': a National Socialist expression.

the world with natural bloodstains on one cheek, then capital does so from head to toe, bleeding and dripping with filth at every pore'; thus it needs, all the more, the longer it goes on, a mask for the outcome, happiness of honesty at the outcome. The happy end is however not only a lie, it has also become shallower than at any other time, it confines itself to the smile of the car and perfume advertisements. Well-groomed gentlemen and ladies show the high-life of a declining society, without sweetness of life being compressed into this end as in the Rococo. The happiness of bourgeois wealth has itself become as crass as it is empty, its happiness borders in reality more on the void than the dead themselves. Nevertheless, this lying, prescribed happy end deceives millions for whom it replaces the church's empty promises of the other world, and it is prescribed only for the sake of deception. With imagination that is always newly warmed up the poor devil who builds himself up in golden dreams is supposed to remain in the belief that these dreams are certainly fulfillable in capitalism, at least in capitalism plus patience and a little time to wait. But for the little man there is no stock-market killing, every rosy red ends for him as Black Friday. There are very sophisticated capitalist fireworks, not only in an optical respect, against which the socialist world can hardly compete. But after all the snakes of lightning and boxes of stars, de luxe Venetian bombs and the Queen of the Night, there follows the violent thunder-flash bomb and that is the highlight and the conclusion of the matter. Everything capitalism stages with happy end, business like never before, Greater Germany,[2] America first, even keep smiling, leads into death. In the most uninspired way the beautiful in the world of the whitewashed graves becomes the beginning of the terrible.

And yet this is only one side of illusion, which is itself false. An unmistakable drive is working in the direction of the good end, it is not only confined to gullibility. The fact that deceivers make use of this drive disproves it au fond almost as little as the 'socialist' Hitler disproved socialism. The deceivability of the happy end drive merely says something against the state of its reason; this, however, is as teachable as it is improvable. The deception represents the good end as if it were attainable in an unchanged Today of society or even the Today itself. But just because knowledge destroys rotten optimism, it does not also destroy urgent hope for a good end. For this hope is too indestructibly grounded in the human drive for happiness, and it has

2. A National Socialist concept.

always been too clearly a motor of history. It has been so as expectation and incitement of a positively visible goal, for which it is important to fight and which sends a Forwards into barrenly continuing time. More than once the fiction of a happy end, when it seized the will, when the will had learnt both through mistakes and in fact through hope as well, and when reality did not stand in too harsh contradiction to it, reformed a bit of the world; that is: an initial fiction was made real. Sometimes even, when there was great belief, a paradox succeeded: the victory of the urgent over the mighty enemy, of the cheerful over the nasty probable. If the will-content of the goal is missing, then even the good probable is left undone; if the goal remains, however, then even the improbable can be done or at least made more probable for later. Not even the breaking of the chain at its weakest link succeeded and succeeds, if the breakers do not have the Positivum: anti-chain wholly in mind. Men reduce themselves when their purpose is reduced, whereas when it is great and cheerful it makes itself unavoidable in a world which only still has the choice between swamp or energetic new construction before it.

So it never befits the colour red to be voluntarily timid. Every barrier, when it is felt as such, is at the same time crossed. For just coming up against it presupposes a movement which goes beyond it and contains this in embryo. This is the most simple dialectical At-the-same-time in the objective factor, primarily when it completes and activates the consciousness of the barrier. Then consciousness reaches the other side in a mediated way, enters into the struggle for the happy end, which already senses itself, almost announces itself in the dissatisfaction with what is available. The discontented person then sees all at once how bad capitalist conditions are and how urgently the socialist beginnings need him, how good their consequence can and will be. This makes the barrier into a rung, assuming that the other side, the happiness of the goal, always remains present on the path. And the indispensable insight, unalterable, into the economic laws attests that these laws have, as recognized and used laws, the stuff in them to lead to a good end. Thus socialism does not need to borrow from other colours, customs, powers, as though its own colour were not sufficient. It does not need to do this above all when these colours or frames lie so much on this side of the crossed barrier and have already supported such very different things that they cannot easily, nor unequivocally be re-functioned. Socialism, which possesses and keeps its path to the happy end as its own, is precisely also as a cultural inheritance a socialism through its own creative power, its own fullness-goal, without plush, without intellectual timidity. The nouveau riche bourgeoisie of the second half of the previous century did not get by with its own material; so it cultivated finery and substitutes with bows, little covers, masked houses and pictures, uncomprehended ornaments, palatial façades, historicisms; and the substitutes really looked the part. This is all miles away from socialism, which never ploughs with a strange team, which unmasks and aesthetically condemns masquerade and swankiness with social criticism. 'Gründerzeiten' are foreign bodies here, particularly noticeable in socialism; it finds no path to the cultural inheritance which goes through the parlour either. Politically the revolutionary proletariat never borders on the petite bourgeoisie, how should it do so culturally? In reality this kind of thing is never practised either; because a practice which has no realistic theory behind it and in its favour, would not be one, is impossible in socialism. Indeed, socialism does not incorporate the genuine cultural inheritance either in such a way that it begins with it and then continues to build on it as if it were a finished first floor so to speak. Instead, the drive to build is moral here for the first time in the history of civilization, is the building of a world without exploitation and its ideology. Furthermore, neither bareness nor epigonism characterize this work, but the matching colours red and gold, manifestly a splendidly bold match. However, already contained in the red is the gold that brings affinity to the best from tradition and forms its classical material—as growing substance, not as previous local form. Therefore: fresh air and great breadth belong to this outcome, as the one in which no plush happy end hangs any more and none from the laurel-scheme of historicism. There are enough merry trading centres on the stream to the true happy end; for this flows solely through socialism. As observed above, every barrier, if it is felt as such, is already crossed. But equally: no barrier is actively crossed without the intended goal drifting ahead in genuine images and concepts and transposing us into such significant conditions.

See the outcome of things as friendly, that is then not always foolish or stupid. The stupid drive to a good end can become a clever one, passive belief a knowledgeable and summoning one. To this extent we can proceed to the defence of the old merry farewell celebration, for it invites us, partly, to eat, not only to contemplate. And this wanting to eat has sometimes first made us sensitive to the block which—in the shape of the existing society—forces itself between the idea and the pleasure-banquet. Whereas people who do not believe at all in a happy end impede changing the world almost as much as the sweet swindlers, the marriage-swindlers, the charlatans of apotheosis. Unconditional pessimism therefore promotes the business of reaction not much less than artificially conditioned optimism; the latter is nevertheless not so stupid that it does not believe in anything at all. It does not immortalize the trudging of the little life, does not give humanity the face of a chloroformed gravestone. It does not give the world the deathly sad background in front of which it is not worth doing anything at all. In contrast to a pessimism which itself belongs to rottenness and may serve it, a tested optimism, when the scales fall from its eyes, does not deny the goal-belief in general; on the contrary, what matters now is to find the right one and to prove it. For this reason there is more possible pleasure in the idea of a converted Nazi than from all the cynics and nihilists. That is why the most dogged enemy of socialism is not only, as is understandable, great capital, but equally the load of indifference, hopelessness; otherwise great capital would stand alone. Otherwise there would not in fact be, despite all mistakes in propaganda, the delays until socialism ignites in the massive majority whose interests belong to it, without it knowing. Thus pessimism is paralysis per se, whereas even the most rotten optimism can still be the stupefaction from which there is an awakening. Even the contentment with the minimum for existence so long as it is there, the shortsightedness in the daily struggle for bread and the miserable triumphs in this struggle ultimately stem from the disbelief in the goal; the first thing is therefore to break into this. It is no coincidence that capitalism has striven to spread, apart from the false happy end, its own genuine nihilism. Because this is the stronger danger and, in contrast to the happy end, cannot be corrected at all, except through its own demise. The truth is its demise, as expropriating and as liberating truth, towards a humanity which is finally socially possible. So truth then, sweeping clean, an instruction to build, is in no way grieving or ice. On the contrary, its attitude is, becomes, remains critical-militant optimism, and this orientates itself in the Become always towards the Not-Yet-Become, towards viable possibilities of the light. It creates the readiness, which is uninterrupted and informed of tendency, to risk the intervention into what has not yet been achieved. As long as no absolute In-Vain (triumph of evil) has appeared, then the happy end of the right direction and path is not only our pleasure, but our duty. Where the dead bury their dead, grieving may rightly take place and failure may be the existential condition. Where snobs participated as traitors in the revolution until it broke out, all that is left to pray may in fact be: Give us this day our daily illusion. Where the capitalist sum no longer works out anywhere, the bankrupt may in fact be forced to pour and spread a blot over the ledger of the whole of existence, so that the world in general looks coal-black and no inspector will call the nightmaker to account. All this is an even worse deception than that of the radiant façades which can no longer be kept up. The work against this, with which history continues, indeed has been continuing for a long time, leads to the matter which could be good, not as abyss, but as mountain into the future. Mankind and the world carry enough good future; no plan is itself good without this fundamental belief within it.

RAYMOND WILLIAMS

Fredric Jameson insists that nostalgia is permissible for a Marxist if it is a "conscious" nostalgia designed to provide "remorseless dissatisfaction with the present on the grounds of some remembered plenitude. . . ."* This kind of permissible nostalgia is supposedly present in Benjamin's reflections on "The Storyteller." For Ernst Bloch, on the other hand, the tendency for religion, philosophy, indeed, the whole history of human thought has been to look to the past, to what has been, so that even attempts at thinking of a final state of perfection have simply involved "only a repetition of what was in the beginning—something already fulfilled, which has meanwhile become lost or alienated."† Psychoanalysis is a particularly grievous example of this backward-looking negation of the future, and Carl Jung, the "psychoanalytical Fascist," is the worst of the lot (431). Raymond Williams in his book *The Country and the City* (1973) shows how art, particularly pastoral poetry, has exploited nostalgia, not only to provide financial support for the artist through flattery of rural landowners, but also to repress the contribution, indeed the very memory of an entire class of agrarian laborers, whose "brief and aching lives" never appear in those tributes to the lofty values, the Edenic perfection of the great country houses. It is an excellent example of the artist as ideologue, who uses beauty to acquire patronage and in doing so promotes a certain property arrangement, which in the 18th century was in the process of consolidating one-quarter of arable land in England in the hands of 400 families.‡ Williams' book depends on a relationship between history and art that does not always redound to the benefit of art. If other media had not preserved faint, factual accounts of the lives of the people whose labor made the great rural estates flourish, we would not be inclined to bring them to mind at all—the poet having had no incentive to notice them.

In the selection reprinted here, Williams examines the ubiquity of the nostalgic pastoral mechanism. He makes two points: that the "organic community of old England" sought by every generation was never there or was there only as a displacement of the poet's childhood; and that the comfortable plangency of any obsession with what has been makes what *is* that much more likely to persist.

* Fredric Jameson, *Marxism and Form* (Princeton, NJ: Princeton University Press, 1971) 82.
† Leszek Kolakowski, *Main Currents of Marxism,* Vol. 3, trans. P. S. Falla (Oxford and New York: Oxford University Press, 1978) 430.
‡ Raymond Williams, *Politics and Letters. Interviews with New Left Review* (London: New Left Books, 1979) 303 ff. Raymond Williams, *The Country and the City* (New York, Oxford University Press, 1973) 60.

The Nostalgic Escalator

▲ 1973 ▼

T he initial problem is one of perspective. A few years ago I was sent a book for review: a country book, in a familiar idiom, that I would normally have enjoyed reading. But there in front of the experience was a formula:

> A way of life that has come down to us from the days of Virgil has suddenly ended.

In detail, certainly, this was curious. From Virgil? Here? A way of country life?

But in outline, of course, the position was familiar. As it is put in a memorable sentence, in the same book:

> A whole culture that had preserved its continuity from earliest times had now received its quietus.

It had happened, it seemed, in the last fifty years: say since the First World War. But this raised a problem. I remembered a sentence in a critically influential book: Leavis and Thompson's *Culture and Environment,* published in 1932. The 'organic community' of 'Old England' had disappeared; 'the change is very recent indeed'. This view was primarily based on the books of George Sturt, which appeared between 1907 and 1923. In *Change in the Village,* published in 1911, Sturt wrote of the rural England 'that is dying out now'. Just back, we can see, over the last hill.

But then what seemed like an escalator began to move. Sturt traced this ending to two periods: enclosure after 1861 and residential

THE NOSTALGIC ESCALATOR   from *The Country and the City* by Raymond Williams. The original title of the selection is "A Problem of Perspective." Copyright © 1973 by Raymond Williams. Reprinted by permission of Oxford University Press.

settlement after 1900. Yet this at once takes us into the period of Thomas Hardy's novels, written between 1871 and 1896 and referring back to rural England since the 1830s. And had not critics insisted that it was here, in Hardy, that we found the record of the great climacteric change in rural life: the disturbance and destruction of what one writer has called the 'timeless rhythm of agriculture and the seasons'? And that was also the period of Richard Jefferies, looking back from the 1870s to the 'old Hodge', and saying that there had been more change in rural England in the previous half-century —that is, since the 1820s—than in any previous time. And wasn't George Eliot, in *Mill on the Floss* (1860) and in *Felix Holt* (1866), looking back, similarly, to the old rural England of the 1820s and early 1830s?

But now the escalator was moving without pause. For the 1820s and 1830s were the last years of Cobbett, directly in touch with the rural England of his time but looking back to the happier country, the old England of his boyhood, during the 1770s and 1780s. Thomas Bewick, in his *Memoir,* written during the 1820s, was recalling the happier village of his own boyhood, in the 1770s. The decisive change, both men argued, had happened during their lifetimes. John Clare, in 1809, was also looking back—

Oh, happy Eden of those golden years

—to what seems, on internal evidence, to be the 1790s, though he wrote also, in another retrospect on a vanishing rural order, of the 'far-fled pasture, long evanish'd scene'.

Yet still the escalator moved. For the years of Cobbett's and of Bewick's boyhood were the years of Crabbe's *The Village* (1783)

No longer truth, though shown in verse, disdain,
But own the Village Life a life of pain

and of Goldsmith's *The Deserted Village* (1769)

E'en now, methinks, as pondering here I stand
I see the rural virtues leave the land.

And by ordinary arithmetic, in the memory of Sweet Auburn—

loveliest village of the plain,
Where health and plenty cheer'd the labouring swain,

> Where smiling spring its earliest visit paid,
> And parting summer's lingering blooms delay'd;
> Dear lovely bowers of innocence and ease,
> Seats of my youth, when every sport could please

—back we would go again, over the next hill, to the 1750s.

It is clear, of course, as this journey in time is taken, that something more than ordinary arithmetic and something more, evidently, than ordinary history, is in question. Against sentimental and intellectualised accounts of an unlocalised 'Old England', we need, evidently, the sharpest scepticism. But some at least of these witnesses were writing from direct experience. What we have to inquire into is not, in these cases, historical error, but historical perspective. Indeed the fact of what I have called the escalator may be an important clue to the real history, but only when we begin to see the regularity of its pattern.

It is worth, perhaps, getting on the escalator again, since all we have done so far is to move 'Old England' and its timeless agricultural rhythms back from the early twentieth century to the middle of the eighteenth century. When we remember 'our mature, settled eighteenth century', we may not, after all, have made very much difference to the ordinary accounts. Shall we then go back to Philip Massinger, in the early 1620s, in *The City Madam* and *A New Way to Pay Old Debts?* Here the new commercialism is breaking the old landed settlement and its virtues. Here is the enclosing and engrossing Sir Giles Overreach. Here is the corruption of an older rural civilisation:

> Your father was
> An honest country farmer, goodman Humble,
> By his neighbours ne'er called Master. Did your pride
> Descend from him?

We can't say, but we can go on back to Bastard's *Chrestoleros,* in 1598, where the same complaints are being made, or, if we are asked to assume that the disturbance occurred at the turn of the century, to Thomas More's *Utopia,* in 1516, where another old order is being destroyed:

> For looke in what partes of the realme doth growe the fynest and
> therfore dearest woll, there noblemen and gentlemen, yea and
> certeyn abbottes, holy men no doubt, not contenting them selfes
> with the yearely revenues and profytes, that were wont to grow to
> theyr forefathers and predecessours of their landes, nor beynge

content that they live in rest and pleasure nothinge profiting, yea
much noyinge the weale publique, leave no ground for tillage,
thei inclose all into pastures; thei throw doune houses; they
plucke downe townes, and leave nothing standynge, but only the
churche to be made a shepehouse. And as though you lost no
small quantity of grounds by forestes, chases, laundes and
parkes, those good holy men turne all dwellinge places and all
glebeland into desolation and wildernes.

Except that then, of course, we find ourselves referred back to the
settled Middle Ages, an organic society if ever there was one. To the
1370s, for example, when Langland's Piers Plowman sees the dissatisfaction of the labourers, who will not eat yesterday's vegetables but
must have fresh meat, who blame God and curse the King, but who
used not to complain when Hunger made the Statutes. Must we go
beyond the Black Death to the beginning of the Game Laws, or to the
time of Magna Carta, when Innocent III writes:

the serf serves; terrified with threats, wearied by corvees, afflicted
with blows, despoiled of his possessions?

Or shall we find the timeless rhythm in Domesday, when four men
out of five are villeins, bordars, cotters or slaves? Or in a free Saxon
world before what was later seen as the Norman rape and yoke? In a
Celtic world, before the Saxons came up the rivers? In an Iberian
world, before the Celts came, with their gilded barbarism? Where
indeed shall we go, before the escalator stops?

One answer, of course, is Eden, and we shall have to look at that
well-remembered garden again. But first we must get off the escalator,
and consider its general movement.

Is it anything more than a well-known habit of using the past, the
'good old days', as a stick to beat the present? It is clearly something
of that, but there are still difficulties. The apparent resting places, the
successive Old Englands to which we are confidently referred but
which then start to move and recede, have some actual significance,
when they are looked at in their own terms. Of course we notice their
location in the childhoods of their authors, and this must be relevant.
Nostalgia, it can be said, is universal and persistent; only other men's
nostalgias offend. A memory of childhood can be said, persuasively,
to have some permanent significance. But again, what seemed a
single escalator, a perpetual recession into history, turns out, on
reflection, to be a more complicated movement: Old England,
settlement, the rural virtues—all these, in fact, mean different things

at different times, and quite different values are being brought to question. We shall need precise analysis of each kind of retrospect, as it comes. We shall see successive stages of the criticism which the retrospect supports: religious, humanist, political, cultural. Each of these stages is worth examination in itself. And then, within each of these questions, but returning us finally to a formidable and central question, there is a different consideration.

The witnesses we have summoned raise questions of historical fact and perspective, but they raise questions, also, of literary fact and perspective. The things they are saying are not all in the same mode. They range, as facts, from a speech in a play and a passage in a novel to an argument in an essay and a note in a journal. When the facts are poems, they are also, and perhaps crucially, poems of different kinds. We can only analyse these important structures of feeling if we make, from the beginning, these critical discriminations. And then the first problem of definition, a persistent problem of form, is the question of pastoral, of what is known as pastoral.

FREDRIC JAMESON

When Fredric Jameson says that the Beatles are to the Talking Heads as Le Corbusier is to John Portman, as Van Gogh is to Andy Warhol, and as Marlon Brando is to William Hurt, it is obvious that the theoretical divisions between high-art and mass entertainment sacred to Theodor Adorno have begun to break down. That is, one would not expect Adorno to place the Beatles and Van Gogh on the same side of a binary division. Not that Adorno's theoretical practice never touched on popular entertainment: he did write on jazz, films, television, and cartoons but usually to condemn them, thundering like a Jeremiah against abominable appetites. In obligating himself to process all aspects of cultural production without exception and without elitist prejudice, Jameson has recently gone more in the direction of Bloch's encyclopedic omnivorousness than Adorno's astringent asceticism. Jameson's recent and most widely discussed work has been on the subject of postmodernism. Several essays have appeared, his most "definitive" being the long study in the *New Left Review* 146 (1984). The shorter essay, reprinted here from *New German Critique* 33 (1984), touches on some of the same considerations, although analysis of examples remains necessarily abbreviated.

For Jameson the "privileged terrain" of the debates on postmodernism concerns architecture. Old High Modernists—Mies van der Rohe, Gropius, and others—had dreamed of transforming social life by transforming space. They created majestic, monumental glass boxes which would rise fastidiously up and out of the undistinguished, tasteless American landscape. The inadvertent result was an authoritarian degradation of the city's microfabric that surrounded the new buildings. The postmodern hotels of John Portman, on the other hand, are not as forbidding; they do not repudiate the surrounding neighborhoods with sumptuous, operatic entryways. Instead, they are popular buildings that entice the yokels to watch, openmouthed, the soaring Japanese lantern elevators, to picnic beside the lakes and fountains, and to lose themselves in delicious jungles with enormous squawking red and yellow parrots. Losing one's bearings in general seems to be the intended effect here. Clients never know where they are; they can never find again the store where they saw a choice piece of merchandise and failed to buy it. For Jameson, the loss of coordinates has parallels both in other art forms (for example, Language Poetry, Duane Hanson's simulacra, John Cage's music, pastiche replacing parody) and in society at large (the hallucinatory intensity of drug trips, the dispersion of multinational capital, the decentered ego). The computer is the great sublime figure of the new era of capital; its complexity is beyond the capacity of any normal mind. Jameson refuses to allow moralizing judgments about the end of Modernism (in which one still had one's bearings and knew up from down, even if one was gazing enviously into the abyss with Conrad's Kurtz). The beginning of the postmodern world, Jameson says, may contain seeds of a new communality—a new internationalism. Even if from one point of view postmodernism is catastrophic, history has a way of converting horror into its opposite. Indeed, there is no other way of proceeding, the dialectic being beyond good and evil. And here Jameson has at least the part-time support of both Marx and Engels, as the most cursory examination of *Anti-Dühring* or the 1867 Preface to *Capital* will show.*

The Politics of Theory: Ideological Positions in the Postmodernism Debate

1984

The problem of postmodernism—how its fundamental characteristics are to be described, whether it even exists in the first place, whether the very *concept* is of any use, or is, on the contrary, a mystification—this problem is at one and the same time an aesthetic and a political one. The various positions which can logically be taken on it, whatever terms they are couched in, can always be shown to articulate visions of history, in which the evaluation of the social moment in which we live today is the object of an essentially political affirmation or repudiation. Indeed, the very enabling premise of the debate turns on an initial, strategic, presupposition about our social system: to grant some historic originality to a postmodernist culture is also implicitly to affirm some radical structural difference between what is sometimes called consumer society and earlier moments of the capitalism from which it emerged.

THE POLITICS OF THEORY: IDEOLOGICAL POSITIONS IN THE POSTMODERNISM DEBATE   by Fredric Jameson. Reprinted by kind permission of *New German Critique* and David Bathrick. The article appeared in Fall 1984, number 33.

*Friedrich Engels, *Anti-Dühring* (Moscow: Foreign Languages Publishing House, 1959) 130–31; 253–54. Karl Marx, *Capital,* Vol. 1, trans. Ben Fowkes (New York: Vintage, 1977) 92; 301; 381.

The various logical possibilities, however, are necessarily linked with the taking of a position on that other issue inscribed in the very designation "postmodernism" itself, namely, the evaluation of what must now be called high or classical modernism itself. Indeed, when we make some initial inventory of the varied cultural artifacts that might plausibly be characterized as postmodern, the temptation is strong to seek the "family resemblance" of such heterogeneous styles and products, not in themselves, but in some common high modernist impulse and aesthetic against which they all, in one way or another, stand in reaction.

The seemingly irreducible variety of the postmodern can be observed fully as problematically within the individual media (of arts) as between them: what affinities, besides some overall generational reaction, to establish between the elaborate false sentences and syntactic mimesis of John Ashbery and the much simpler talk poetry that began to emerge in the early 1960s in protest against the New Critical aesthetic of complex, ironic style? Both register, no doubt, but in very different ways indeed, the institutionalization of high modernism in this same period, the shift from an oppositional to a hegemonic position of the classics of modernism, the latter's conquest of the university, the museum, the art gallery network and the foundations, the assimilation, in other words, of the various high modernisms, into the "canon" and the subsequent attenuation of everything in them felt by our grandparents to be shocking, scandalous, ugly, dissonant, immoral and antisocial.

The same heterogeneity can be detected in the visual arts, between the inaugural reaction against the last high modernist school in painting—Abstract Expressionism—in the work of Andy Warhol and so-called pop art, and such quite distinct aesthetics as those of conceptual art, photorealism and the current New Figuration or neo-Expressionism. It can be witnessed in film, not merely between experimental and commercial production, but also within the former itself, where Godard's "break" with the classical filmic modernism of the great "auteurs" (Hitchcock, Bergman, Fellini, Kurasawa) generates a series of stylistic reactions against itself in the 1970s, and is also accompanied by a rich new development of experimental video (a new medium inspired by, but significantly and structurally distinct from, experimental film). In music also, the inaugural moment of John Cage now seems far enough from such later syntheses of classical and popular styles in composers like Phil Glass and Terry Riley, as well as from punk and New Wave rock of the type of The

Clash, The Talking Heads and The Gang of Four, themselves significantly distinct from disco or glitter rock. (In film or in rock, however,
a certain historical logic can be reintroduced by the hypothesis that
such newer media recapitulate the evolutionary stages or breaks
between realism, modernism and postmodernism, in a compressed
time span, such that the Beatles and the Stones occupy the high
modernist moment embodied by the "auteurs" of 1950s and 1960s art
films.)

In narrative proper, the dominant conception of a dissolution of
linear narrative, a repudiation of representation, and a "revolutionary" break with the (repressive) ideology of storytelling generally,
does not seem adequate to encapsulate such very different work as
that of Burroughs, but also of Pynchon and Ishmael Reed; of Beckett,
but also of the French *nouveau roman* and its own sequels, and of
the "non-fiction novel" as well, and the New Narrative. Meanwhile, a
significantly distinct aesthetic has seemed to emerge both in commercial film and in the novel with the production of what may be called
nostalgia art (or *la mode rétro*).

But it is evidently architecture which is the privileged terrain of
struggle of postmodernism and the most strategic field in which this
concept has been debated and its consequences explored. Nowhere
else has the "death of modernism" been felt so intensely, or
pronounced more stridently; nowhere else have the theoretical and
practical stakes in the debate been articulated more programmatical-
ly. Of a burgeoning literature on the subject, Robert Venturi's
Learning from Las Vegas (1971), a series of discussions by Christopher Jencks, and Pier Paolo Portoghesi's Biennale presentation, *After
Modern Architecture,* may be cited as usefully illuminating the
central issues in the attack on the architectural high modernism of
the International Style (Le Corbusier, Wright, Mies): namely, the
bankruptcy of the monumental (buildings which, as Venturi puts it,
are really *sculptures*), the failure of its protopolitical or Utopian
program (the transformation of all of social life by way of the
transformation of space), its elitism including the authoritarianism of
the charismatic leader, and finally its virtual destruction of the older
city fabric by a proliferation of glass boxes and of high rises that,
disjoining themselves from their immediate contexts, turn these last
into the degraded public space of an urban no-man's-land.

Still, architectural postmodernism is itself no unified or monolithic
period style, but spans a whole gamut of allusions to styles of the past,
such that within it can be distinguished a baroque postmodernism,

(say, Michael Graves), a rococo postmodernism (Charles Moore or Venturi), a classical and a neoclassical postmodernism (Rossi and De Porzemparc respectively), and perhaps even a Mannerist and a Romantic variety, not to speak of a High Modernist postmodernism itself. This complacent play of historical allusion and stylistic pastiche (termed "historicism" in the architectural literature) is a central feature of postmodernism more generally.

Yet the architectural debates have the merit of making the political resonance of these seemingly aesthetic issues inescapable, and allowing it to be detectable in the sometimes more coded or veiled discussion in the other arts. On the whole, four general positions on postmodernism may be disengaged from the variety of recent pronouncements on the subject; yet even this relatively neat scheme or *combinatoire* is further complicated by one's impression that each of these possibilities is susceptible of either a politically progressive or a politically reactionary expression (speaking now from a Marxist or more generally left perspective).

One can, for example, salute the arrival of postmodernism from an essentially anti-modernist standpoint.[1] A somewhat earlier generation of theorists (most notably Ihab Hassan) seems already to have done something like this when they dealt with the postmodernist aesthetic in terms of a more properly post-structuralist thematics (the *Tel quel* attack on the ideology of representation, the Heideggerian or Derridean "end of Western metaphysics"): here what is often not yet called postmodernism (see the Utopian prophecy at the end of Foucault's *The Order of Things*) is saluted as the coming of a whole new way of thinking and being in the world. But since Hassan's celebration also includes a number of the more extreme monuments of high modernism (Joyce, Mallarmé), this would be a relatively more ambiguous stance, were it not for the accompanying celebration of a new information high technology which marks the affinity between such evocations and the political thesis of a properly *postindustrial society.*

All of which is largely disambiguated in Tom Wolfe's *From Bauhaus to Our House,* an otherwise undistinguished book report on the recent architectural debates by a writer whose own New Journalism itself constitutes one of the varieties of postmodernism. What is interesting and symptomatic about this book is however the absence

---

1. The following analysis does not seem to me applicable to the work of the *boundary two* group, who early on appropriated the term "postmodernism" in the rather different sense of a critique of establishment "modernist" thought.

of any Utopian celebration of the postmodern and—far more strikingly—the passionate hatred of the Modern that breathes through the otherwise obligatory camp sarcasm of the rhetoric; and this is not a new, but a dated and archaic passion. It is as though the original horror of the first middle class spectators of the very emergence of the Modern itself—the first Corbusiers, as white as the first freshly built cathedrals of the 12th century, the first scandalous Picasso heads, with two eyes on one profile like a flounder, the stunning "obscurity" of the first editions of *Ulysses* or *The Waste Land:* as though this disgust of the original philistines, Spiessbürger, bourgeois or Main Street Babbitry, had suddenly come back to life, infusing the newer critiques of modernism with an ideologically very different spirit, whose effect is on the whole to reawaken in the reader an equally archaic sympathy with the protopolitical, Utopian, anti-middle-class impulses of a now extinct high modernism itself. Wolfe's diatribe thus offers a stunning example of the way in which a reasoned and contemporary, theoretical repudiation of the modern —much of whose progressive force springs from a new sense of the urban and a now considerable experience of the destruction of older forms of communal and urban life in the name of a high modernist orthodoxy—can be handily reappropriated and pressed into the service of an explicitly reactionary cultural politics.

These positions—anti-modern, pro-postmodern—then find their opposite number and structural inversion in a group of counterstatements whose aim is to discredit the shoddiness and irresponsibility of the postmodern in general by way of a reaffirmation of the authentic impulse of a high modernist tradition still considered to be alive and vital. Hilton Kramer's twin manifestoes in the inaugural issue of his new journal, *The New Criterion,* articulate these views with force, contrasting the moral responsibility of the "masterpieces" and monuments of classical modernism with the fundamental irresponsibility and superficiality of a postmodernism associated with camp and with the "facetiousness" of which the Wolfe style is a ripe and obvious example.

What is more paradoxical is that politically Wolfe and Kramer have much in common; and there would seem to be a certain inconsistency in the way in which Kramer must seek to eradicate from the "high seriousness" of the classics of the modern their fundamentally anti-middle-class stance and the protopolitical passion which informs the repudiation, by the great modernists, of Victorian taboos and family life, of commodification, and of the increasing asphyxiation of a desacralizing capitalism, from Ibsen to Lawrence, from Van Gogh to Jackson Pollock. Kramer's ingenious attempt to assimilate this ostensibly anti-bourgeois stance of the great modernists to a "loyal opposition" secretly nourished, by way of foundations and grants, by the bourgeoisie itself—while most unconvincing indeed—is surely itself enabled by the contradictions of the cultural politics of modernism proper, whose negations depend on the persistence of what they repudiate and entertain—when they do not, very rarely indeed (as in Brecht), attain some genuine political self-consciousness—a symbiotic relationship with capital.

It is, however, easier to understand Kramer's move here when the political project of *The New Criterion* is clarified: for the mission of the journal is clearly to eradicate the 1960s and what remains of that legacy, to consign that whole period to the kind of oblivion which the 1950s was able to devise for the 1930s, or the 1920s for the rich political culture of the pre-World-War-I era. *The New Criterion* therefore inscribes itself in the effort, on-going and at work everywhere today, to construct some new conservative cultural counter-revolution, whose terms range from the aesthetic to the ultimate defense of the family and of religion. It is therefore paradoxical that this essentially political project should explicitly deplore the omnipresence of politics in contemporary culture—an infection largely spread during the 1960s, but which Kramer holds responsible for the moral imbecility of the postmodernism of our own period.

The problem with the operation—an obviously indispensible one from the conservative viewpoint—is that for whatever reason its paper-money rhetoric does not seem to have been backed by the solid gold of state power, as was the case with McCarthyism or in the period of the Palmer raids. The failure of the Vietnam War seems, at least for the moment, to have made the naked exercise of repressive power impossible,[2] and endowed the 1960s with a persistence in collective memory and experience which it was not given to the traditions of the 1930s or the pre-World-War-I period to know. Kramer's "cultural revolution" therefore tends most often to lapse into a feebler and sentimental nostalgia for the 1950s and the Eisenhower era.

It will not be surprising, in the light of what has been shown for an

2. Written in spring, 1982.

earlier set of positions on modernism and postmodernism, that in spite of the openly conservative ideology of this second evaluation of the contemporary cultural scene, the latter can also be appropriated for what is surely a far more progressive line on the subject. We are indebted to Jürgen Habermas[3] for this dramatic reversal and rearticulation of what remains the affirmation of the supreme value of the Modern and the repudiation of the theory, as well as the practice, of postmodernism. For Habermas, however, the view of postmodernism consists very centrally in its politically reactionary function, as the attempt everywhere to discredit a modernist impulse Habermas himself associates with the bourgeois Enlightenment and with the latter's still universalizing and Utopian spirit. With Adorno himself, Habermas seeks to rescue and to recommemorate what both see as the essentially negative, critical and Utopian power of the great high modernisms. On the other hand, his attempts to associate these last with the spirit of the 18th century Enlightenment marks a decisive break indeed with Adorno and Horkheimer's somber *Dialectic of Enlightenment,* in which the scientific ethos of the *philosophes* is dramatized as a misguided will to power and domination over nature, and their own desacralizing program as the first stage in the development of a sheerly instrumentalizing world view which will lead straight to Auschwitz. This very striking divergence can be accounted for by Habermas' own vision of history, which seeks to maintain the promise of "liberalism" and the essentially Utopian content of the first, universalizing bourgeois ideology (equality, civil rights, humanitarianism, free speech and open media) over against the failure of those ideals to be realized in the development of capital itself.

As for the aesthetic terms of the debate, however, it will not be adequate to respond to Habermas' resuscitation of the modern by some mere empirical certification of the latter's extinction. We need to take into account the possibility that the national situation in which Habermas thinks and writes is rather different from our own: McCarthyism and repression are, for one thing, realities in the Federal Republic today, and the intellectual intimidation of the Left and the silencing of a left culture (largely associated, by the West German right, with "terrorism") has been on the whole a far more successful

3. See his "Modernity—An Incomplete Project," in Hal Foster, ed., *The Anti-Aesthetic* (Port Townsend, Washington: Bay Press, 1983), pp. 3–15. The essay was first published in *New German Critique,* 22 (Winter 1981), 3–14, under the different title "Modernity versus Postmodernity."

operation than elsewhere in the West.[4] The triumph of a new McCarthyism and of the culture of the Spiessbürger and the philistine suggests the possibility that in this particular national situation Habermas may well be right, and the older forms of high modernism may still retain something of the subversive power which they have lost elsewhere. In that case, a postmodernism which seeks to enfeeble and to undermine that power may well also merit his ideological diagnosis in a local way, even though the assessment remains ungeneralizable.

Both of the previous positions—antimodern/propostmodern, and promodern/antipostmodern—are characterized by an acceptance of the new term which is tantamount to an agreement on the fundamental nature of some decisive "break" between the modern and the postmodern moments, however these last are evaluated. There remain, however, two final logical possibilities both of which depend on the repudiation of any conception of such a historical break and which therefore, implicitly or explicitly, call into question the usefulness of the very category of postmodernism. As for the works associated with the latter, they will then be assimilated back into classical modernism proper, so that the "postmodern" becomes little more than the form taken by the authentically modern in our own period, and a mere dialectical intensification of the old modernist impulse towards innovation. (I must here omit yet another series of debates, largely academic, in which the very continuity of modernism as it is here reaffirmed is itself called into question by some vaster sense of the profound continuity of Romanticism itself, from the late 18th century on, of which both the modern and the postmodern will be seen as mere organic stages.)

The two final positions on the subject thus logically prove to be a positive and negative assessment respectively of a postmodernism now assimilated back into the high modernist tradition. Jean-Francois Lyotard[5] thus proposes that his own vital commitment to the new and the emergent, to a contemporary or postcontemporary cultural production now widely characterized as "postmodern," be grasped as

4. The specific politics associated with the "Greens" would seem to constitute a reaction to this situation, rather than an exception from it.
5. See "Answering the Questions: What Is Postmodernism?" in J.-F. Lyotard, *The Postmodern Condition* (Minneapolis: University of Minnesota Press, 1984), pp. 71–82; the book itself focusses primarily on science and epistemology rather than on culture.

part and parcel of a reaffirmation of the authentic older high modernisms very much in Adorno's spirit. The ingenious twist or swerve in his own proposal involves the proposition that something called "postmodernism" does not *follow* high modernism proper, as the latter's waste product, but rather very precisely *precedes* and prepares it, so that the contemporary postmodernisms all around us may be seen as the promise of the return and the reinvention, the triumphant reappearance, of some new high modernism endowed with all its older power and with fresh life. This is a prophetic stance, whose analyses turn on the anti-representational thrust of modernism and postmodernism; Lyotard's aesthetic positions, however, cannot be adequately evaluated in aesthetic terms, since what informs them is an essentially social and political conception of a new social system beyond classical capitalism (our old friend, "postindustrial society"): the vision of a regenerated modernism is in that sense inseparable from a certain prophetic faith in the possibilities and the promise of the new society itself in full emergence.

The negative inversion of this position will then clearly involve an ideological repudiation of modernism of a type which might conceivably range from Lukács' older analysis of modernist forms as the replication of the reification of capitalist social life all the way to some of the more articulated critiques of high modernism of the present day. What distinguishes this final position from the antimodernisms already outlined above is, however, that it does not speak from the security of an affirmation of some new postmodernist culture, but rather sees even the latter itself as a mere degeneration of the already stigmatized impulses of high modernism proper. This particular position, perhaps the bleakest of all and the most implacably negative, can be vividly confronted in the works of the Venetian architecture historian Manfredo Tafuri, whose extensive analyses[6] constitute a powerful indictment of what we have termed the "protopolitical" impulses in high modernism (the "Utopian" substitution of cultural politics for politics proper, the vocation to transform the world by transforming its forms, space or language). Tafuri is however no less harsh in his anatomy of the negative, demystifying, "critical" vocation of the various modernisms, whose function he reads as a kind of

---

6. See in particular *Architecture and Utopia* (Cambridge: MIT Press, 1976) and *Modern Architecture*, with Francesco Dal Co (New York: Abrams, 1979); and also my "Architecture and the Critique of Ideology," in *ReVisions: Papers in Architectural Theory and Criticism*, 1–1 (Winter, 1984).

Hegelian "ruse of History," whereby the instrumentalizing and desacralizing tendencies of capital itself are ultimately realized through just such demolition work by the thinkers and artists of the modern movement. Their "anticapitalism" therefore ends up laying the basis for the "total" bureaucratic organization and control of late capitalism, and it is only logical that Tafuri should conclude by positing the impossibility of any radical transformation of culture before a radical transformation of social relations themselves.

The political ambivalence demonstrated in the earlier two positions seems to me to be maintained here, but *within* the positions of both of these very complex thinkers. Unlike many of the previously mentioned theorists, Tafuri and Lyotard are both explicitly political figures, with an overt commitment to the values of an older revolutionary tradition. It is clear, for example, that Lyotard's embattled endorsement of the supreme value of aesthetic innovation is to be understood as the figure for a certain kind of revolutionary stance; while Tafuri's whole conceptual framework is largely consistent with the classical Marxist tradition. Yet both are also, implicitly, and more openly at certain strategic moments, rewritable in terms of a post-arxism which at length becomes indistinguishable from anti-Marxism proper. Lyotard has for example, very frequently sought to distinguish his "revolutionary" aesthetic from the older ideals of political revolution, which he sees as either being Stalinist, or as archaic and incompatible with the conditions of the new postindustrial social order; while Tafuri's apocalyptic notion of the total social revolution implies a conception of the "total system" of capitalism which, in a period of depolitization and reaction, is only too fatally destined for the kind of discouragement which has so often led Marxists to a renunciation of the political altogether (Adorno and Merleau-Ponty come to mind, along with many of the ex-Trotskyists of the 1930s and 1940s and the ex-Maoists of the 1960s and 1970s).

The combination scheme outlined above can now be schematically represented as follows; the plus and minus signs designating the politically progressive or reactionary functions of the positions in question (see p. 380.)

With these remarks we come full circle and may now return to the more positive potential political content of the first position in question, and in particular to the question of a certain *populist* impulse in postmodernism which it has been the merit of Charles Jencks (but also of Venturi and others) to have underscored—a question which will also allow us to deal a little more adequately with

	ANTI-MODERNIST	PRO-MODERNIST
PRO-POSTMODERNIST	Wolfe − Jencks +	Lyotard { ±
ANTI-POSTMODERNIST	Tafuri { ∓	Kramer − Habermas +

the absolute pessimism of Tafuri's Marxism itself. What must first be observed, however, is that most of the political positions which we have found to inform what is most often conducted as an aesthetic debate are in reality moralizing ones, which seek to develop final judgments on the phenomenon of postmodernism, whether the latter is stigmatized as corrupt or on the other hand saluted as a culturally and aesthetically healthy and positive form of innovation. But a genuinely historical and dialectical analysis of such phenomena —particularly when it is a matter of a present of time and of history in which we ourselves exist and struggle—cannot afford the impoverished luxury of such absolute moralizing judgments: the dialectic is "beyond good and evil" in the sense of some easy taking of sides, whence the glacial and inhuman spirit of its historical vision (something that already disturbed contemporaries about Hegel's original system). The point is that we are *within* the culture of postmodernism to the point where its facile repudiation is as impossible as any equally facile celebration of it is complacent and corrupt. Ideological judgment on postmodernism today necessarily implies, one would think, a judgment on ourselves as well as on the artifacts in question; nor can an entire historical period, such as our own, be grasped in any adequate way by means of global moral judgments or their somewhat degraded equivalent, pop-psychological diagnosis (such as those of Lasch's *Culture of Narcissism*). On the classical Marxian view, the seeds of the future already exist within the present and must be conceptually disengaged from it, both through analysis and through political praxis (the workers of the Paris Commune, Marx once remarked in a striking phrase, *"have no ideals to realize"*; they merely sought to disengage emergent forms of new social relations from the older capitalist social relations in which the former had already. begun to stir). In place of the temptation either to denounce the complacencies of postmodernism as some final symptom of decadence, or to salute the new forms as the harbingers of a new technological and technocratic Utopia, it seems more appropriate to assess the new cultural production within the working hypothesis of a general modification of culture itself within the social restructuration of late capitalism as a system.[7]

As for emergence, however, Jencks' assertion that postmodern architecture distinguishes itself from that of high modernism through its populist priorities,[8] may serve as the starting point for some more general discussion. What is meant, in the specifically architectural context, is that where the now more classical high modernist space of a Corbusier or a Wright sought to differentiate itself radically from the fallen city fabric in which it appears—its forms thus dependent on an act of radical disjunction from its spatial context (the great *pilotis* dramatizing separation from the ground and safeguarding the *Novum* of the new space)—postmodernist buildings on the contrary celebrate their insertion into the heterogeneous fabric of the commercial strip and the motel and fast-food landscape of the post-superhighway American city. Meanwhile a play of allusion and formal echoes ("historicism") secure the kinship of these new art buildings with the surrounding commercial icons and spaces, thereby renouncing the high modernist claim to radical difference and innovation.

Whether this undoubtedly significant feature of the newer architecture is to be characterized as *populist* must remain an open question: since it would seem essential to distinguish the emergent forms of a new commercial culture—beginning with advertisements and spreading on to formal *packaging* of all kinds, from products to buildings and not excluding artistic commodities such as television shows (the "logo") and bestsellers and films—from the older kinds of folk and genuinely "popular" culture which flourished when the

---

7. I have tried to do this in "Postmodernism, Or, The Cultural Logic of Late Capitalism," *New Left Review,* 146 (July-August, 1984), 53–92; my contribution to *The Anti-Aesthetic,* op. cit., is a fragment of this definitive version.
8. See, for example, Charles Jencks, *Late-Modern Architecture* (New York: Rizzoli, 1980); Jencks here however shifts his usage of the term from the designation for a cultural dominant or period style to the name for one aesthetic movement among others.

older social classes of a peasantry and an urban *artisanat* still existed
and which, from the mid-19th century on, have gradually been
colonized and extinguished by commodification and the market
system.

What can at least be admitted is the more universal presence of this
particular feature, which appears more unambiguously in the other
arts as an effacement of the older distinction between high and
so-called mass culture, a distinction on which modernism depended
for its specificity, its Utopian function consisting at least in part in the
securing of a realm of authentic experience over against the surrounding environment of philistinism, of schlock and kitsch, of
commodification and of Reader's Digest culture. Indeed, it can be
argued that the emergence of high modernism is itself contempora-
neous with the first great expansion of a recognizable mass culture
(Zola may be taken as the marker for the last coexistence of the art
novel and the bestseller to be within a single text).

It is now this constitutive differentiation which seems on the point
of disappearing: we have already mentioned the way in which, in
music, after Schönberg and even after Cage, the two antithetical
traditions of the "classical" and the "popular" once again begin to
merge. In a more general way, it seems clear that the artists of the
"postmodern" period have been fascinated precisely by the whole
new object world, not merely of the Las Vegas strip, but also of the
late show and the grade-B Hollywood film, of so-called paraliterature
with its airport paperback categories of the gothic and the romance,
the popular biography, the murder mystery and the science-fiction or
fantasy novel (in such a way that the older generic categories
discredited by modernism seem on the point of living an unexpected
reappearance). In the visual arts, the renewal of photography as a
significant medium in its own right and also as the "plane of
substance" in pop art or photorealism is a crucial symptom of the
same process. At any rate, it becomes minimally obvious that the
newer artists no longer "quote" the materials, the fragments and
motifs, of a mass or popular culture, as Joyce (and Flaubert) began to
do, or Mahler; they somehow incorporate them to the point where
many of our older critical and evaluative categories (founded precisely on the radical differentiation of modernist and mass culture) no
longer seem functional.

But if this is the case, then it seems at least possible that what wears
the mask and makes the gestures of "populism" in the various
postmodernist apologias and manifestoes is in reality a mere reflex

and symptom of a (to be sure momentous) cultural mutation, in which what used to be stigmatized as mass or commercial culture is now received into the precincts of a new and enlarged cultural realm. In any case, one would expect a term drawn from the typology of political ideologies to undergo basic semantic readjustments when its initial referent (that Popular-front class coalition of workers, peasants and petty bourgeois generally called "the people") has disappeared.

Perhaps, however, this is not so new a story after all: one remembers, indeed, Freud's delight at discovering an obscure tribal culture, which alone among the multitudinous traditions of dream-analysis on the earth had managed to hit on the notion that all dreams had hidden sexual meanings—except for sexual dreams, which meant something else! So also it would seem in the postmodernist debate, and the depoliticized bureaucratic society to which it corresponds, where all seemingly cultural positions turn out to be symbolic forms of political moralizing, except for the single overtly political note, which suggests a slippage from politics back into culture again. I have the feeling that the only adequate way out of this vicious circle, besides praxis itself, is a historical and dialectical view which seeks to grasp the present as History.

PART
FOUR

HERMENEUTICS AND
RECEPTION THEORY

HANS-GEORG GADAMER

While Deconstruction emerges from the revolutionary, iconoclastic side of Heidegger, that is, from his "destructive" method of analysis, Reception Theory, at least in its recent German phase, derives from the central focus of Heidegger's *Being and Time*. This focus is historicity as the essential fact of human being. In earlier forms of hermeneutics (the art of interpretation as methodology of Hermes, bringer of divine messages) precisely this central fact of time had been forgotten, says Gadamer. What the interpreter seemed to forget was to factor in his own historical standpoint. He had been under the illusion that he could establish an interpretation that put an end to doubt once and for all. The obsession with that which can not be doubted derives from Cartesianism, a philosophy that Gadamer, following Heidegger, finds guilty of establishing this erroneous ahistorical objectivism in the first place.* Objectivity is the icon before which science worships, at least until Thomas Kuhn's *The Structure of Scientific Revolutions* (1962) made the claim that scientific research proceeds by interpretive models and prejudices, which change unaccountably over time, making room for new discoveries. In literary hermeneutics, too, understanding is perspectival. There is no aperspectival understanding. *Verstehen* (understanding) and *Auslegung* (interpretation) are the same act. There is no one correct interpretation of a text (358). Nor can one simply dream of approaching interpretive work free of prejudice, presuppositions, and tradition. Descartes had thought reason/ authority and reason/tradition were incompatible (246–50). But it is precisely tradition that permits us to understand anything at all. We are never free of it; to repudiate it is impossible. We are our history. It is always part of us. To reject tradition, prejudice, and presupposition is to jerk the rug out from under our own reason. Voices of the past echo throughout every historical consciousness (252). Hence, Schleiermacher is silly to believe that to understand a work of art properly, the theorist must cross the gulfs of time and reestablish the world, the mind of the artist, and the historical situation in which the work was originally at home. When such a context is reconstructed, it is still not the original context. Time has moved on since then. What is recovered is dead. Hegel understood better that works from the past are "fruits torn from the tree," that the historical spirit does not just seek to restore the past but also to conduct a "thoughtful mediation with contemporary life." What is there as meaning is meaning *for us*.

*Martin Heidegger, *Being and Time,* trans. John Macquarrie and Edward Robinson (New York and Evanston: Harper and Row, 1962) 46; 194–5. Hans-Georg Gadamer, *Truth and Method,* trans. Garrett Barden and John Cumming (New York: Continuum, 1975) 211, 248. Subsequent page numbers refer to Gadamer.

Schleiermacher, Hegel, and the Hermeneutical Task
▲ 1960 ▼

Translated by Garrett Barden and John Cumming

T he classical discipline concerned with the art of understanding texts is hermeneutics. If my argument is correct, however, then the real problem of hermeneutics is quite different from its common acceptance. It points in the same direction in which my criticism of the aesthetic consciousness has moved the problem of aesthetics. In fact, hermeneutics would then have to be understood in so comprehensive a sense as to embrace the whole sphere of art and its complex of questions. Every work of art, not only literature, must be understood like any other text that requires understanding, and this kind of understanding has to be acquired. This gives to the hermeneutical consciousness a comprehensive breadth that surpasses even that of the aesthetic consciousness. Aesthetics has to be absorbed into hermeneutics. This statement not only reveals the extent of the problem, but is substantially accurate. Conversely, hermeneutics must be so determined as a whole that it does justice to the experience of art. Understanding must be conceived as a part of the process of the coming into being of meaning, in which the significance of all statements—those of art and those of everything else that has been transmitted—is formed and made complete.

In the nineteenth century, the old theological and literary ancillary discipline of hermeneutics was developed into a system which made it the basis of all the human sciences. It wholly transcended its original pragmatic purpose of making it possible, or easier, to understand literary texts. It is not only the literary tradition that is estranged and in need of new and more appropriate assimilation, but all that no longer expresses itself in and through its own world—that is, everything that is handed down, whether art or the other spiritual creations of the past, law, religion, philosophy and so forth—is estranged from its original meaning and depends, for its unlocking and communicating, on that spirit that we, like the Greeks, name Hermes: the messenger of the gods. It is to the development of historical consciousness that hermeneutics owes its central function within the human sciences. But we may ask whether the whole range of the problem that it poses can be properly grasped on the basis of the premises of historical consciousness.

Work in this field hitherto, defined primarily by Wilhelm Dilthey's hermeneutical grounding of the human sciences[1] and by his research into the origins of hermeneutics,[2] determined in its way the dimensions of the hermeneutical problem. Today's task could be to free ourselves from the dominant influence of Dilthey's approach to the question, and the prejudices of the discipline that he founded: namely Geistesgeschichte (cultural history).

To give a preliminary indication of what is involved and to combine the systematic result of my argument so far with the new extension of the problem, let us consider first the hermeneutical task set by the phenomenon of art. However clearly I showed that aesthetic differentiation was an abstraction that could not cancel and transcend the attachment of the work of art to its world, it remains irrefutable that art is never simply past, but is able to cross the gulf of time by virtue of its own meaningful presence. Hence art offers, in both ways, an excellent example of understanding. Even though it is no mere object of historical consciousness, understanding it always includes historical mediation. What, then, is the task of hermeneutics in relation to it?

Schleiermacher and Hegel suggest two very different ways of answering this question. They might be described as reconstruction and integration. The primary point for Schleiermacher as for Hegel is the consciousness of loss and estrangement in relation to tradition, which rouses them to hermeneutical reflection. Nevertheless, they define the task of hermeneutics very differently.

1. O. F. Bollnow, *Dilthey*, 1936
2. *Gesammelte Schriften* VII, p 281

Schleiermacher (whose theory of hermeneutics will be considered later) is wholly concerned to reproduce in the understanding the original purpose of a work. For art and literature which are transmitted to us from the past are wrenched from the context of their original world. As my analysis revealed, this is true of all art, including literature, but it is seen with particular clarity in the case of plastic art. Schleiermacher says that it is no longer the natural and primary thing 'when works of art come into general commerce. Part of the intelligibility of each one derives from its original purpose. Hence the work of art loses something of its significance if it is torn from its original context, unless this happens to be historically preserved.' He even says: 'Hence a work of art, too, is really rooted in its own soil. It loses its meaning when it is wrenched from this environment and enters into general commerce; it is like something that has been saved from the fire but still bears the marks of the burning upon it'.[3]

Surely, then, the work of art enjoys its true significance only where it originally belongs? Is to grasp its significance, then, to re-establish, in a sense, this original world? If it is acknowledged that the work of art is not a timeless object of aesthetic experience, but belongs to a world that endorses it with its significance, it would follow that the true significance of the work of art can be understood only in terms of its origin and genesis within that world. Hence all the various means of historical reconstruction, the re-establishment of the 'world' to which it belongs, the re-establishment of the original situation about which the creative artist was writing, performance in the original style, and so on, can claim to reveal the true meaning of a work of art and guard against misunderstanding and false reproduction. This is, in fact, Schleiermacher's conception and the tacit premise of his entire hermeneutics. According to Schleiermacher, historical knowledge opens the way towards replacing what is lost and re-establishing tradition, inasmuch as it brings back the circumstances of the situation and restores it 'as it was'. The work of hermeneutics seeks to rediscover the point of contact in the mind of

3. The early form of the problem of knowledge which we find in classical antiquity with, say, Democritus and which the neo-Kantian historians also read into Plato, was on another basis. The discussion of the problem of knowledge, which began with Democritus, ended in fact with the Sceptics (cf Paul Natorp, *Studien zum Erkenntnisproblem im Altertum* (1892) and my paper 'Antike Atomtheorie', *Zeitschrift für die ges. Naturwissenschaften, 1935.*

the artist which will open up fully the significance of a work of art, just as in the case of texts it seeks to reproduce the writer's original words.

The reconstruction of the conditions in which a work that has come down to us from the past fulfilled its original purpose is undoubtedly an important aid to its understanding. But it may be asked whether what is then obtained is really what we look for as the meaning of the work of art, and whether it is correct to see understanding as a second creation, the reproduction of the original production. Ultimately, this view of hermeneutics is as foolish as all restitution and restoration of past life. The reconstruction of the original circumstances, like all restoration, is a pointless undertaking in view of the historicity of our being. What is reconstructed, a life brought back from the lost past, is not the original. In its continuance in an estranged state it acquires only a secondary, cultural, existence. The recent tendency to take works of art out of a museum and put them back in the place for which they were originally intended, or to restore architectural monuments to their original form, merely confirms this judgment. Even the painting taken from the museum and replaced in the church, or the building restored to its original condition are not what they once were—they become simply tourist attractions. Similarly, a hermeneutics that regarded understanding as the reconstruction of the original would be no more than the recovery of a dead meaning.

Hegel, in contrast, indicates another possibility of balancing out the profit and loss of the hermeneutical enterprise. He shows his clear grasp of the futility of restoration when he writes of the decline of the classical world and its religion of art that the works of the Muses 'are now what they are for us—beautiful fruits torn from the tree. A friendly fate presents them to us as a girl might offer those fruits. We have not the real life of their being—the tree that bore them, the earth and elements, the climate that determined their substance, the seasonal changes that governed their growth. Nor does fate give us, with those works of art, their world, the spring and summer of the ethical life in which they bloomed and ripened, but only the veiled memory of this reality'.[4] And he calls the relationship of posterity to those works of art that have been handed down an

4. P. Duhem, *Etudes sur Léonard de Vinci*, 3 vols, Paris, 1955; *Le système du monde*, x.

'external activity' that 'wipes spots of rain or dust from this fruit and instead of the internal elements of the surrounding, productive and lifegiving reality of the ethical world substitutes the elaborate structure of the dead elements of its external existence, of language, of its historical features and so forth. And this not in order to live within that reality but merely to represent it within oneself'.[5]

What Hegel is describing here is precisely what is involved in Schleiermacher's demand for historical preservation except that with Hegel there is a negative emphasis. The search for those circumstances which would add to the significance of works of art cannot succeed in reproducing them. They remain fruit torn from the tree. To place them in their historical context does not give one a living relationship with them but rather one of mere imaginative representation. Hegel does not deny the legitimacy of taking up an historical attitude towards the art of the past. On the contrary, he affirms the principle of art-historical research—but this, like any 'historical' relation, is, in Hegel's eyes, an external activity.

The authentic task of the thinking mind in relation to history, including the history of art, is not, according to Hegel, an external one inasmuch as the mind would see itself represented in history in a higher way. Developing his image of the girl who offers the fruit torn from the tree, he writes: 'But as the girl who presents the plucked fruit is more than Nature that presented it in the first place with all its conditions and elements—trees, air, light and so on—in so far as she combines all these in a higher way in the light of self-consciousness in her eyes and in her gestures, so also is the spirit of destiny which gives us these works of art, greater than the ethical life and reality of a particular people, for it is the interior recollection of the still external spirit manifest in them. It is the spirit of tragic fate that gathers all these individual gods and attributes of substance within one Pantheon, into its spirit conscious of itself as spirit'.

Here Hegel goes beyond the entire dimension in which Schleiermacher conceived the problem of understanding. Hegel raises it to the level at which he has established philosophy as the highest form of absolute Mind. That self-consciousness of spirit that, as the text has it, comprehends the truth of art within itself in a higher way, culminates in the absolute knowledge of philosophy. For Hegel, then, it is philosophy, the historical self-penetration of spirit, that

5. Cf H. Rickert's book of the same name, *Der Gegenstand der Erkenntnis.*

carries out the hermeneutical task. It is the most extreme counter-position to the self-forgetfulness of historical consciousness. For it, the historical attitude of imaginative representation is changed into a thinking attitude towards the past. Here Hegel states a definite truth, inasmuch as the essential nature of the historical spirit does not consist in the restoration of the past, but in thoughtful mediation with contemporary life. Hegel is right when he does not conceive of such thoughtful mediation as an external and supplementary relationship, but places it on the same level as the truth of art itself. In this way he wholly transcends Schleiermacher's idea of hermeneutics. The question of the truth of art forces us, too, to undertake a critique of both aesthetic and historical consciousness, inasmuch as we are enquiring into the truth that manifests itself in art and history.

HANS ROBERT JAUSS

The new literary history devised at the University of Constance in the late 1960s and early 1970s explicitly evoked Gadamer. This new form adapted the historicity of understanding by rejecting older (biographical and positivistic) forms of literary history. At times these adaptations seem infelicitous, as when Jauss raises the possibility of "objectifying" the horizon of expectation of a past era, while criticizing any interpreter who thinks he can bracket (ignore) his own historical standpoint, speak from a purely objective point of view, or present an unmediated version of the past.* On the other hand, if radical historicity is adopted, what happens to the significance of a literary history written during a given historical period after the preoccupations of that period have decayed and given way to new interests? The sacrifice of timeless significance to historical dynamism, change, and the eternal novelty of future response seems theoretically to guarantee the eventual obsolescence of everyone's critical exertions.† This question of aesthetic obsolescence is taken up by Stanley Fish in the "Demonstration vs. Persuasion" essay (1980) in this book.

The subject of the following essay "History of Art and Pragmatic History" (1970, published 1973) explores the extent to which history is of the same order artistically as fiction. Also explored is the extent to which art's central interest—the beautiful—is subject to the undertow of time, that is, to history. The subject, then, is the art of history and the historicality of art. Jauss' treatment of the poetics of history is instructive for those who assume that the topic was first raised in the wake of Deconstruction by Hayden White. In fact, it was a central concern of the Prussian historian Johann Gustav Droysen, a contemporary of Edgar Allen Poe and the hero of Jauss' essay here. Droysen's course at the University of Berlin was called "Encyclopedia and Methodology of History" and was taught eighteen times beginning in 1857. The course outline published in 1858 for Droysen's students, *Grundriss der Historik,* was partially translated by E. Benjamin Andrews in 1897 and titled *Outline of the Principles of History.* The *Outline* is beginning to be more widely available now in English and has been anthologized most recently in *The Hermeneutics Reader,* ed. Kurt Mueller-Vollmer (New York: Continuum, 1985).

---

*Hans Robert Jauss, "Literary History as a Challenge to Literary Theory," in *Toward an Aesthetics of Reception,* trans. Timothy Bahti. Introduction by Paul de Man (Minneapolis: University of Minnesota Press, 1982). Compare sections VII and IX.
† Robert Holub, *Reception Theory: A Critical Introduction* (London and New York: Methuen, 1984) 65.

Droysen makes what should be an obvious point: the connections between artists and their works made by art historicans are quite different from the connections actually experienced at the time by the artists themselves. Similarly, Droysen criticizes the dogma of the objective fact and, with it, both the notion of scientific history and the kind of art history that slavishly imitates the methods of scientific history. No fact can speak for itself. As Jauss says, with regard to the ahistorical errors of other theorists like Heidegger, Gadamer, and Curtius, tradition is not self-activating: "Even classical models are present only where they are responded to. . . ." Droysen's specific critique is against Leopold von Ranke, whose histories had for Droysen about the same truth value as the historical novels of Walter Scott. In fact, whenever the past is presented as a narrative, there is lying, whether intentional or not. *Poesis* employs three great illusions: that of completed process, of the definitive beginning and end, and of the objective picture of the past. Droysen implies that narrative can be completely transcended. Jauss doubts that it can be. But Jauss does say that Droysen's recommendations for a truer history are good ones and can be met. His recommendations are for the admission of limited perspective: the historian must not repress his own situatedness in time and social context; he must leave open the historical horizon, since, until time stops, no historical process can have been completed. Interestingly for Jauss, these developments are precisely the narrative innovations of Flaubert, who "systematically dismantled the teleology of the epic story" by allowing the future's open horizon to erupt into the story of the past, by breaking narrative omniscience through localized perspectives, and by troubling completeness by always leaving unexplained details scattered about.

The rest of the essay consists of, at times, quite sensitive distinctions between Jauss' own position and that of the competing theories of his time, especially Marxism and Structuralism. With regard to Marxism, he shows here more appreciation for its possibilities than he showed in his earlier "Challenge" essay (1967), where Marxism was convicted of a crude reflection theory. French Structuralism, as represented by Lévi-Strauss, rejects history as a fall from blissful savage participation in the logico-natural order toward the ontic distraction of technology; it tends to view art paralyzingly, as the repetition of a few simple formulae. Jauss, on the other hand, emphasizes dynamism, innovation, and emancipation in art: a great work is one which evokes, then violates, the aesthetic expectations (the horizon) of its time. He has positive things to say about Prague Structuralism, which sees artistic structure as activated by art's reception and thus occupies a proper position between the extreme aesthetic dogmatism of Gadamer, with his eternally valid classical models, and the extreme relativistic subjectivism of Barthes.

History of Art and Pragmatic History

1973

Translated by David Henry Wilson

I

At first sight, history in the realm of the arts presents two contradictory views. With the first, it would appear that the history of architecture, music, or poetry is more consistent and more coherent than that of society. The chronological sequence of works of art is more closely connected than a chain of political events, and the more gradual transformations of style are easier to follow than the transformations of social history. Valéry once said that the difference between art history and social history was that in the former the products were "filles visibles les unes des autres [visibly related daughters]," whereas in the latter "chaque enfant semble avoir mille pères et réciproquement [each child seems to have a thousand fathers, and vice versa]."[1] One might conclude from this that the claim "man makes his history himself" is most strongly borne out in the realm of the arts.

With the second view, the paradigms of art historiography, in their pre-scientific and then again in their positivistic phase,[2] show that this

HISTORY OF ART AND PRAGMATIC HISTORY   by Hans Robert Jauss, trans. by David H. Wilson, from *New Perspectives in German Literary Criticism, A Collection of Essays,* ed. by Richard E. Amacher and Victor Lange. Copyright © 1979 by Princeton University Press. Excerpt, pp. 432–64, reprinted with permission of Princeton University Press.

1. "Letter to André Lebey," Sept., 1906, *Œuvres II* (Paris, 1960), p. 1543; also S. Kracauer, in *Die nicht mehr schönen Künste,* ed. H. R. Jauss (Munich, 1968), *Poetik und Hermeneutik,* III, p. 123.
2. Concerning the change of paradigm in the history of science, see Th. S. Kuhn, *Die Struktur wissenschaftlicher Revolutionen* (Frankfurt, 1967), and H. R. Jauss, "Paradigmawechsel in der Literaturwissenschaft," in *Linguistische Berichte,* I (1969), pp. 44–56.

greater consistency of detail is purchased at the price of an overall inconsistency as regards the links between art *genres* as well as their relation to the general historical and social process. Before it turned to tracing the history of style, art history had always taken the form of artists' biographies, which were linked only through chronological order. The literary historiography of the humanists also began with "stories," i.e., biographies of writers, in the order of their dates of death, sometimes divided up into categories of authors.[3] The model was Plutarch's *Lives,* which also established the pattern of "parallels." This form of integration, which until the end of the eighteenth century underlay the response to classical art and the dispute over its exemplariness, belonged specifically to the first stage of the "histories of art appreciation."[4] For the literary form of "parallels" presupposes the idea of perfection as a criterion that transcends time, even when authors or works extend it to "genres" of art or to national "golden ages." The historical appearance of art splits up into a variety of different elemental courses, each of which is directed towards its own "point of perfection" and, through esthetic norms, can be compared with earlier histories or "forerunners." The appearance of all histories in the arts can then be joined together again in the composite historical picture of a periodic recurrence of the golden age—a picture that is typical of humanistic historiography, and also of Voltaire's social history.[5]

A second stage of the "histories" came about through *Historism* (overestimation of historical singularity) in its positivistic phase. The principle of explaining a work of art by the sum of its historical conditions meant that, with every work, study had to start right from scratch, so that the "beginnings" could be ascertained from its sources, and the determinant factors of time and environment could be extracted from the author's life. The question of sources, which inevitably leads to the question of sources of sources, loses its way in "histories" just as completely as that of the link between life and work. Thus the sequent link between one work and the next is lost in a historical vacuum, which would be obvious

---

3. P. Brockmeier, *Darstellungen der französischen Literaturgeschichte von Claude Fauchet bis Laharpe* (Berlin, 1963).
4. See H. R. Jauss, *Literaturgeschichte als Provokation* (Frankfurt, 1970), pp. 35 ff.
5. See H. R. Jauss, *Ästhetische Normen und geschichtliche Reflexion in der Querelle des Anciens et des Modernes* (Munich, 1964), pp. 23–33.

simply from the chronological order if it were not concealed by the vague generalization of "currents" or "schools," or bridged by an external nexus, borrowed from pragmatic history—first and foremost, that of nationhood. As against that, the question may justifiably be asked whether art history can in fact do anything else but borrow its overall coherence from pragmatic history.

Between the first and second stages of the "histories" lies the historism of the Enlightenment, in which art history played a not insignificant part. The epochal turning point at which singular history, together with the newly founded *philosophie de l'histoire,* won the battle against plural histories,[6] began at the start of the eighteenth century through perceptions made in the study of art. The dispute that flared up again at the height of French classicism concerning the exemplariness of classical art, brought both sides—the *Anciens* and the *Modernes*—ultimately to the same conclusion, which was that ancient and modern art in the long run could not be measured against the same standard of perfection *(Beau absolu),* because each epoch had its own customs, its own tastes, and therefore its own ideas of beauty *(Beau relatif).* The discovery of the historical element of beauty, and the historical perception of art that it initiated, led up to the historism of the Enlightenment.[7] In the eighteenth century, this process resulted in an increasing emphasis on the time element of both art history and philosophical history, which since Fénelon's *Projet d'un traité sur l'histoire* (1714) had deliberately utilized the unifying means and classical norms of the epic in order to legitimize its superiority over the merely factual ruler-and-state type of history.[8]

Winckelmann's *Geschichte der Kunst des Altertums* (1764) is the first landmark of the new historiography of art, which was made possible through the historicizing of Antiquity, and was set on its way by the abandoning of comparative description in the form of "parallels." In turning away from the traditional "history of artists,"

---

6. R. Koselleck, "Historia magistra vitae," in: *Natur und Geschichte, Karl Löwith zum 70. Geburtstag* (Stuttgart, 1968), pp. 196–219.

7. See thesis quoted in note 5.

8. See *Nachahmung und Illusion,* ed. H. R. Jauss (Munich, 1964), *Poetik und Hermeneutik,* I, p. 191.

Winckelmann sets the new "history of art" the task of "teaching the origin, the growth, the change and the decline of the same, together with the different styles of nations, times, and artists."[9] Art history, as Winckelmann inaugurated it, does not need to borrow its overall coherence from pragmatic history, as it can claim a greater consistency of its own: "The arts . . . , like all inventions, began with necessity; afterwards one sought for beauty, and finally there followed the superfluous: these are the three outstanding stages of art."[10] As against the course of events in pragmatic history, the sequence of works in the art of Antiquity is distinguished by a complete and therefore normative course: in the realm of the arts, the historical element can complete itself naturally. Friedrich Schlegel, who carried this principle over to poetry, looked for and found in Greek poetry "a complete natural history of art and of taste," in the course of which "even the incompleteness of the earlier stages and the degeneration of the later" could take on exemplary significance.[11] Herder's critique of Winckelmann can, in this context, be interpreted as an attempt logically to extend the time element of art history to "the whole sequence of times,"[12] and to assert the historical universality of beauty, as against the singularized art of the Greeks which had nevertheless been raised to the level of a norm.[13] Poetry "as a tool or as an artistic product and flower of civilization and humanity" reveals through its history something that "could only be brought about progressively in the great course of times and nations."[14] And here the point is reached at which art history and social history enter into a relationship that raises a new question: whether the history of art, which is usually regarded as a dependent "poor relation" of general history, might not once have been the head of the family, and might not once more become a paradigm of historical knowledge.

9. *Geschichte der Kunst des Altertums* (1764), ed. W. Senff (Weimar, 1964), p. 7.
10. *Ibid.*, p. 21.
11. *Über das Studium der griechischen Poesie*, ed. P. Hankamer (Godesberg, 1947), p. 153.
12. *Briefe zur Beförderung der Humanität*, 7th and 8th collections, ed. Suphan (Berlin, 1883), XVIII, p. 57.
13. See H.–D. Weber, *Fr. Schlegels "Transzendentalpoesie" und das Verhältnis von Kritik und Dichtung im 18. Jahrhundert* (Munich, 1973), pp. 88–101.
14. This is the basic principle behind the history of modern poetry, with which Herder, in letters 81–107, along with Schiller and F. Schlegel (1796–1797), again takes up the questions of the *Querelle des Anciens et des Modernes;* see work quoted in note 4, pp. 72–74.

II

The decay of the traditional form of literary history, shaped in the nineteenth century and now drained of all scholarly exemplariness, makes it almost impossible for us to realize the high rank that was enjoyed by art history at its birth, with the formation of historical perception in the thought of the Enlightenment, in the philosophy of history of the German Idealists, and at the beginning of historism. With the turning away from traditional histories, chronicles, and accounts of rulers, states and wars, the history of the arts seemed like a paradigm of the new form of history, which—above all—could claim a philosophical interest: "Tous les peuples ont produit des héros et des politiques: tous les peuples ont éprové des révolutions: toutes les histoires sont presque égales pour qui ne veut mettre que des faits dans sa mémoire. Mais quiconque pense, et, ce qui est encore plus rare, quiconque a du goût, ne compte que quatre siécles dans l'histoire de monde [Every nation has produced heroes and politicians; every nation has experienced revolutions; all histories are nearly the same for those who want only to stuff their memory with facts. But anyone who thinks, and, what is even more rare, anyone who has taste, will recognize only four ages in world history]."[15] Pragmatic histories are of monotonous uniformity; only through the perfection of the arts can the human spirit rise to its own particular greatness and leave behind works that engage not only the memory, but also thought and taste. Thus Voltaire justifies the new undertaking of his *Siècle de Louis XIV* (1751). Voltaire's change-over to the "philosophy of history" was followed by Winckelmann and Herder's founding of the history of art and literature. They made the same claims, and made their criticisms of traditional political and war history no less clearly.

Before his famous works, Winckelmann wrote down *Gedanken vom mündlichen Vortrag der neuern allgemeinen Geschichte* (1754), in order to distinguish "what is truly useful in history" from the "nice and beautiful." He sets himself apart from "our pragmatic scribes" and from the "diverse general histories," demands "great examples" and "decisive studies," sets up a canon: "Of scholars and artists, general history immortalizes only inventors, not copyists; only originals, not collectors: a Galileo, Huygens and Newton, not a Viviani, not a Hopital . . . ," and thus follows the basic principle: "Everything

15. Voltaire, *Le siècle de Louis XIV,* Intr.

subordinate belongs to specialist history."[16] The new demands of
Winckelmann's *Geschichte der Kunst des Altertums* (1764) denigrate
not only the previous "History of Artists," but also the chronological
presentation of previous history. The history of art is to be "no mere
narration of chronology and changes within it," but history and
system all in one; it is to bring out the complete "essence of art" and
the idea of beauty throughout its historical development.[17]

For Herder, too, the advantages of a history of the poetry of times
and nations were clear. This can be seen from the panoramic
presentation of current poetry with which, in his "Humanitäts-
Briefen" of 1796, he refers to the historical-philosophical problem of
the *Querelle:* "In this gallery of different ways of thinking, aspirations
and desires, we certainly get to know periods and nations more
deeply than on the deceptive, dreary route of their political and war
history. In the latter we seldom see more of a people than how it let
itself be governed and killed; in the former we learn how it thought,
what it hoped and wished for, how it enjoyed itself, and how it was
led by its teachers or its inclinations."[18] The history of the arts
becomes a medium through which the historical individuation of the
human spirit is presented throughout the course of times and nations.
Thus the ideality of the Greeks, which Winckelmann had still
maintained, is pushed back into its historical setting, the normative
element of perfection carried over to the diversity of individual
beauty, and the world-historical study of poetry related to a conception of history that has no further need of any immanent teleology[19]
and yet again promises the *esthete* a coherent whole. Those aspects of
a natural history of art that are still to be found in Herder—the

16. The fragment, dating from 1754, is quoted from *J. Winckelmanns sämtliche
    Werke,* ed. J. Eiselein (Donaueschingen), XII, pp. iii-xv; see also Fontius,
    Winckelmann und die französische Aufklärung (Berlin, 1968), *Sitz.-Ber. d. dt.
    Akad. d. Wsch. zu Berlin,* Cat. for language, literature and art, 1968, I, to whom I
    am obliged for the reference.
17. P. 7.
18. Ed. Suphan, XVIII, p. 137.
19. In his presentation of modern poetry, 1796, Herder still holds fast to a "telos" of
    history, insofar as he asks, at the outset: "What is the law of this change? Does it
    change for the better or for the worse?" (p. 6), and at the end, concludes from a
    comparison of periods: *"tendimus in Arcadiam, tendimus!* To the land of
    simplicity, truth and morals goes our path" (p. 140). As regards the esthete
    (XXXII, p. 63) or *poetic philologist* (XXXII, p. 83) that one must be, in order to
    risk oneself on the ocean of historical observations, see Weber (note 13), p. 110.

imagery of growth and old age, the cyclic completion of every culture, and the "classical" as the "highest of its (respective) kind"—bring into view the coherence of art history in the traditional way as conditioned by the outcome of the *Querelle*. The path-finding approach with which Herder outstripped this immanent teleology and also the progress theory of the arts, arose out of his return to the tradition of biblical hermeneutics. Herder—as Weber showed —developed a theory of beauty which once more asserted its historical universality against the relativism of national and epochal individualities: the beautiful, which is no longer something metaphysically definable or essentially imitable, can be reassembled through the hermeneutic critical process as the "supra-historical" quintessence of historical manifestations, taking on an eidetic form for the expert or the critic.[20] Thus history exposes itself to "esthetic study as a spiritual continuity in a sense different from that of the literalness of facts."[21]

We shall be looking later at the question of whether the historian of fully developed historism owes something to Herder's *Ästhetiker* and whether in fact the hermeneutic science of history of the nineteenth century had a latent paradigm in the *poetic heuristics*[22] of art history. The course which literary and art history followed in the nineteenth century can be characterized through the progressive reduction of all claims to advance a unique insight of their own. Under historicism, which entailed the historical study of ancient and modern art as a new paradigm of historical experience, art history handed over lock, stock, and barrel its legitimation as a medium for esthetic, philosophical or hermeneutic reflection. The new history of national literatures, however, became an ideal counterpart to political history, and claimed to develop, through the context of all literary appearances, the idea of how national individuality could attain its identity, from quasi-mythical beginnings to the fulfillment of national classicism.

Positivism did gradually reduce this ideological orientation through a greater emphasis on science, but this merely left research into literary history without *any* particular framework. What Herder said of the old annalistic literary history can again be applied to the positivistic, which is a mere imitation of the external linking of events

20. Note 13, p. 123.
21. *Ibid.,* p. 119.
22. Ed. Suphan, I, pp. 441–44.

in pragmatic history: it "steps through nations and times with the quiet tread of a miller's mule."[23] The modern theory of literary science, dating from the First World War, lays emphasis on stylistic, formalistic, and structuralistic methods, and in turning away from positivism has also turned away from literary history. Now the literary historian tends to keep quiet when the discussion is on problems of the science of history and historical hermeneutics. But even today the history of literature can still awaken that same interest it took on in the ideas of the Enlightenment and the period of Idealism, if only the appearance and function of literature in history are liberated from the rigid conventions and false causalities of literary history, and the historicity of literary works is put in its right perspective against the positivistic idea of knowledge and the traditionalist idea of art.

III

The scientifically sanctioned form of literary history is conceivably the worst medium through which to display the historicity of literature. It covers up the paradox of all art history, which Droysen touched on when he explained why the past reality of historic facts and their posterior interpretation are different, as for instance with pictures in an art-gallery: "Art history establishes a connection between them which, in themselves, they do not have, for which they are not painted, and from which there arises a sequence, a continuity, under the influence of which the painters of these pictures stood without being aware of it."[24]

Representing the "objective facts" of literary history are data of works, authors, trends, and periods. But even when their chronology can be fully confirmed, their interconnection, as seen in retrospect by the literary historian, is quite different from that "which once in its present [time] had a thousand other connections than those which concern us historically."[25] The retrospectively established, "actual" connection of literary "facts" captures neither the continuity in which a past work arose, nor that in which the contemporary reader or historian recognizes its meaning and importance. What has been

23. Ed. Suphan, II, p. 112.
24. *Historik: Vorlesung über Enzyklopädie und Methodologie der Geschichte,* ed. R. Hübner (Munich, 1967), p. 35.
25. *Ibid.,* p. 34.

the "event" of a literary work cannot be directly gauged from the facts listed by literary history. The question, left open by Droysen, as to how one is to extract from the sequence of works that continuity in which works are first created and received, can be answered only when one realizes that the analogy between "literary facts" and "historical facts" is an epiphenomenon.[26] This analogy, positivistic in origin, debases the historicity of the work of art and at the same time the interconnection of literary works. As a literary fact, or intersecting point of definable factors, the literary work forfeits its historically concrete appearance. This latter has its basis in the form and meaning created by the author, realized by his readers, and to be realized by them over and over again. When literary history adopted the paradigm of positivistic history, reducing the experience of literature to causal links between work and work or author and author, the historical communication between author, work, and reader disappeared behind an hypostatized succession of monographs, which only retained the name of history.[27]

Behind the appearances of literary history, however, there is basically no objective link between work and work that is not brought about by the creating and receiving subjects of literature.[28] It is this intersubjective communication that separates the historicity of literature from the factual objectivity of pragmatic history. But this difference narrows if one follows Droysen's critique of the dogma of "objective facts," and accepts that diffuse events are only "understood and combined through the interpretation (of them) as a coherent process, as a complex of cause and effect, of aim and fulfillment, in short as A Fact," and that these same events can also be interpreted differently from "the point of view of the new fact" or from the later standpoint of the observer.[29] In this way Droysen gave back to the historical fact its basic character as an event, which like the work of art is an open field as far as interpretation is concerned. For it is not only the "right of historical study" but also an equally primary right of esthetic interpretation, to view works or "facts in the light of the significance they have gained through their effects."[30] And

26. Droysen himself was caught up in the idea that in the history of art or literature "the sought-for, objective facts lie directly in front of us" (*ibid.,* p. 96).
27. See the critique of literary history by R. Barthes, *Literatur oder Geschichte* (Frankfurt, 1969), p. 12
28. See *op. cit.* in note 4, pp. 171–73 (Thesis VI).
29. *Historik,* pp. 133, 167.
30. *Ibid.,* p. 91.

so the analogy that constitutes the link between art history and pragmatic history lies in the character both of the work of art and of the historical fact as an event—a character which in both cases was levelled out by positivism's objectivist idea of knowledge.

The problem of the connections and structural interactions of art history and pragmatic history is one that needs to be looked at again. On the one hand, one must infer, from Droysen's critique of the objectivism of the Historical School, that there may have been unacknowledged fictional narrative forms and esthetic categories of the history of style which made possible this classical form of historiography. And, on the other hand, one must ask whether Droysen's idea of "the event," which includes the consequences of things as well as the standpoint of the retrospective observer, does not itself presuppose the paradigm of the past work of art and its undefined meaning.

IV

"The science of history is not an encyclopaedia of historical sciences, or a philosophy (or theology) of history, or a physics of the historical world, or—least of all—a poetics for historiography. It must set itself the task of being an organon of historical thought and research."[31] Droysen's science of history is, in its approach, hermeneutic. This makes it hard for it to give the lie to the expectation that it will merely be a "poetics for historiography," like Gervinus' *Grundzüge der Historik* (1837). The fact that it also implies a philosophy (the continuity of progressive historical *work*) and a theology of history (the highest aim of a *theodicy*) is less harmful to its claims to independence than the suspicion that history is an art, and therefore cannot be raised to the rank of a science. For the method of investigating sources—the "physics of the historical world"—could not suffice to assure history of this rank. Despite its triumphs—as Droysen ironically points out—people hailed "as the greatest historian of our time the man who, in his presentation (of history), was closest to the novels of Walter Scott" (p. 322). Droysen's polemic against Ranke and the objectivity ideal of historism is aimed principally at exposing the

31. Droysen, *Historik*, § 16 (henceforth quoted only with page number or §).

illusions that accompany the apparently objective narration of traditional facts.

The first is the illusion of the completed process. Although every historian knows that our knowledge of history must always remain incomplete, the prevailing form of the narrative creates "the illusion, and wants to create it, that we are faced with a complete process of historical things, a finished chain of events, motives and purposes" (p. 144). The historical narrative uses the law of fiction, that even disparate elements of a story come closer and closer together for the reader, and ultimately combine in a picture of the whole; if this esthetic effect is to be avoided and the imagination prevented from closing the gaps, then special preventive measures are required which, paradoxically, are more common to modern artistic prose than to historiography.

The second is the illusion of the first beginning and the definitive end. Here, with a sagacity rare for his time, Droysen uncovered and denounced the "false doctrine of the so-called organic development in history" (p. 152): "It is completely beyond the scope of historical research to get to a point that would be . . . the beginning, the sudden origin" (p. 150). It is untrue of history "that all conditions for the later are present in the earlier" (p. 141), and it is equally untrue that things in history have as definite a conclusion as Ranke makes out in his history of the period of the Reformation—for "what has become bears in itself all elements of new unrest" (p. 298). When the historical narrative proceeds genetically and tries to explain things from the standpoint of their origin, it once more falls back upon a law of fiction—namely, the Aristotelian definition of the poetic fiction, which must have a beginning, a middle, and an end: a beginning that does not originate out of something else, and an end that can be followed by nothing.

The third illusion is that of an objective picture of the past. Whoever believes with Ranke that the historian need only disregard his partialist self and cause his present to be forgotten (p. 306), in order to capture an undistorted past, is as little able to guarantee the truth of the resultant "pictures from the past or illustrations of what is long since lost" as are "poets and novelists" (p. 27). Even if a past could be "established in the full breadth of its former present" (p. 27), in the past things themselves there would still not be that "criterion for the important and characteristic" which can only be gained by reflecting on the standpoint from which the whole variety of phenomena can be viewed as a (relative) whole. "Only the thoughtless is objective,"[32] for: "Here the 'facts' only seem to be speaking, alone, exclusive, 'objective.' They would be dumb without the narrator, who makes them speak" (§91).

The epic fictions of the completed process, of the first beginning and the definitive end, and of the self-presenting past, are the consequences of what Droysen showed to be the illusion of Romantic historism, according to which the historian need only repeat the pure facts as extracted from his sources, "and the resultant illusion of handed-down facts then passed off as history" (§360). The flourishing historiography of the nineteenth century, which sought to disavow the artistic character of history writing in order to gain recognition as a science, devolved on a fictionalization of its subject matter to the extent that it followed the principle that the historian must efface himself for history to be able to tell its own story. The poetics involved in this is no different from that of the contemporary peak of literature—the historical novel. However, it is not enough to characterize this new poetics of historical narrative just by the material revelation and poetic, anecdotal animation of the past with which Sir Walter Scott's novels satisfied the historically curious. The fact that Scott was able to bully scientific historiography into an individualized presentation of the past such as history had never been capable of before, was also due to a principle of form.

What so impressed A. Thierry, Barante, and other historians of the Twenties, in Scott's novels, was not only the suggestive power of historical color and detail, the individual physiognomy of a past epoch, and the perspective enabling historical events to be followed through persons instead of the usual impersonal actions. It was also, above all, the new form of the "drama"—one of Scott's major claims to fame—by which his contemporaries meant not so much the dramatic plot-weaving as the still unfamiliar dramatic form of the narrative: as the narrator of the historical novel remains completely in the background, the story can unfold itself like a play, giving the reader the illusion that he himself is present at the drama of the persons involved. This also means that the reader is put in the position of being able to make his own judgments and draw his own moral conclusions—which had previously always been denied him by argumentative historians like Hume or Robertson.[33] These analo-

32. Variant in manuscript print of 1858.
33. A. Thierry: *Sur les trois grandes méthodes historiques en usage depuis le seizième*

gies between the poetics of the historical novel and the ideal of objectivity sought by contemporary historiography speak for themselves.[34] In both cases we have a narrator who is explicitly withdrawn, but implicitly present, all the time communicating and passing judgment—this situation arising out of the illusion of an unmediated presentation of the past. Even more than the novelist Scott, who could delegate his narrative functions to his characters—or hide them through perspectives—the historian Ranke continually reveals himself through a *posteriori* viewpoints and esthetic classifications which could have played no part in the lives of those who actually experienced the historical event. The fact that he defiantly cuts the thread joining the period "as it actually was" with that "which resulted from it" becomes painfully obvious whenever a judgment, selection, motivation, or linking of events presupposes the hindsight of the historian, and whenever the impression has to be conveyed that a view made possible only by this hindsight and by the aftereffects of the event in question was a pattern inherent in that original event. In Ranke's historiography, these inconsistencies are concealed by the illusion of a completed process—and this in a manner no longer reminiscent of Scott's handling of historical plots, but of the stylistic approach to the sequential continuity of events evinced by the form of art history.

V

We shall now illustrate the thesis that Ranke's historiography is determined by esthetic categories that fall in with the latent paradigm of the history of style, by analyzing the period of the English War as presented in Ranke's *Französische Geschichte* (Chap. I, 3;

siècle (1820); De Barante, *Préface de l'Histoire des Ducs de Bourgogne* (1824), and the anonymous article: "De la nouvelle école historique" (1828); quoted from K. Massmann, *Die Rezeption des historischen Romans von Sir Walter Scott in Frankreich von 1816 bis 1832*, Diss. Konstanz, 1969, esp. p. 118.

34. The fact that there was here a "parallelism of intention . . . which justifies the assertion that the historical novel of the Scott type . . . was capable of fulfilling the programme of the eighteenth-century Scottish school of history more completely than it could itself" is also shown by E. Wolff, "Zwei Versionen des historischen Romans: Scotts 'Waverley' und Thackerays 'Henry Esmond,'" in *Lebende Antike, Symposium für R. Sühnel*, ed. H. Meller and H.-J. Zimmermann (Berlin, 1967), pp. 348–369 (esp. 357).

1852–1861).[35] History of style, in the form created by Winckelmann, has the following characteristics: turning point through the introduction of something new (change of style);[36] division into phases (e.g., the four phases of Greek art: older style, high, beautiful, and the style of imitators); the completeness of periods (styles have clear beginnings and a definite end, sealed off by the success of the new).

In Ranke's presentation, the period of the English War starts off in several respects with a radical change to something new. Louis IX, the "original of all religious kings," is succeeded by a king from the same Capetian stock, but "a character of a different kind"—Philip the Fair, a believer in the specifically modern doctrine of power politics (p. 78). He was the first that "with ruthless ambition" dared to "violate" the frontiers to the German Empire maintained by his predecessors—a fact concerning which Ranke has this comment to make: "he knew, or felt, that he was in league with the nature of things" (pp. 78–79). This sentence is a perfect example of a narrative statement (henceforth to be abbreviated n.s.), possible only in retrospect, which the narrator Ranke obviously passes off ("or felt") as coming from the person of Philip. The change to the new is then thematized in the dispute with Pope Boniface VIII, the breaking off of crusade politics, and the destruction of the Order of the Temple. In the latter case, Ranke does not even attempt to test the truth of the accusations against the Templars, his reason being that "it is enough for us to take note of the change in ideas" (p. 79). And so the border between the old and the new can be defined in its full, epoch-making significance: "The age that had been enlivened by the ideas of general Christendom, was over (n.s.); the goods from which the profits were to be used in the reconquering of Jerusalem, were collected up and used in the service of the kingdom. . . . Through his (Philip's) whole being there blew already the sharp breeze of modern history (n.s., p. 80)." Historical processes of such a general kind as Ranke had in mind do not, in reality, take over one from the other at a single frontier between old ("was over") and new ("blew already"), but they merge into one another at a variety of levels and

35. Ed. O. Vossler (Stuttgart, 1954), pp. 78–95 (henceforth quoted only with page numbers).
36. The beginnings of a new style are, according to K. Badt (see note 87) "often not tentative or imperfect, but—like Athene out of the head of Zeus—the new style stands complete before us, perhaps a little coarse, but nevertheless fully and characteristically developed" (p. 139).

crossing-points, sometimes delayed, sometimes premature. Ranke's presentation, which is highly effective from the points of view of narrative and perspective, brushes aside the heterogeneity and gives this new impulse a function that one can only call esthetic, for here the "change in ideas," like the creation of a new style, proceeds as a sort of event from a definite beginning, and at a stroke changes the whole outlook of the world.

Ranke has stylized the political starting point of this epoch in a manner that betrays him: "But scarcely had this standpoint been adopted of a ruthless, isolated policy oriented only towards a furtherance of the State of France, when there occurred an event through which the country was plunged into a general confusion and thrown back completely upon itself" (n.s., pp. 80, 81). With this temporal vagueness ("but scarcely had . . . when there occurred") Ranke surreptitiously introduces a teleology which continues to show itself in the linking and phasing of events right up to the formulation of an end result: "The world was astonished to see not only French flags flying in Normandy, but also the English retreating from the hundred-year possession of Aquitania. They kept nothing except Calais. Perhaps as great a piece of good fortune for the conquered as for the conquerors, for the nations had to separate, if each of them (was to) develop in accordance with its own instincts" (n.s., p. 95). Just like the unfolding of a new style, then, the history of the new epoch also has its purpose, in the light of which all individual contingencies become meaningful and their connection clear —"Clear" as the sequence of works representing a particular style, sharing in every change in that style, and revealing only the sort of changes that can be included in a description of that style.

With Ranke's narrative style, the heterogeneous is often absorbed into the general course of things by means of temporal phasing and harmonizing. Heterogeneous elements of an event are brought in as it were in stages ("for centuries" . . . "long since" . . . "finally" . . . p. 79), then to be plunged into their main development with the "now" of a vital moment ("And this great faction now made contact with the struggle over the succession" [p. 83]). Or the main action might bring to the fore a long hidden, heterogeneous event through a highly significant "completely," so that it may thus be incorporated into the general process. Thus, for instance, the new power of the cities is first "prepared in secret," then "supported by all those elements working in the depths," and finally released "completely" by the English War (p. 82). The temporal sequence implied in "completely," in the typical "now" (which not infrequently has the meaning of "at this very moment"), or in the combination "already . . . but" (p. 86), leaves matters of chronology very vague where often it would be difficult to be precise or precision would destroy the harmonious flow, and it creates out of the contingency of events a continuity of significant moments.

This very idealized time sequence, like the history of a style, describes a steady upward and downward movement, except that here the curve runs in the opposite direction, as Ranke follows the line of the decline and subsequent rise of royal power. Corresponding to the culminating-point of a style history is the moment at which all the heterogeneous trends are homogenized: "Meanwhile, however, the English War had broken out again, and there came a moment at which all these questions, however little they originally had in common, merged into one another" (p. 88). The ideality of this moment is again betrayed by the fact that it is obviously not identical with any of the events of this phase (Agincourt, Treaty of Troyes, Henry V's entry into Paris), but rather symbolized the lowest ebb of the French crown. The upward movement begins with a reference to a higher need: "But his (the Dauphin's) sword . . . alone would scarcely have saved him; first he had to separate himself from the (. . .) union of the Armagnacs (. . .) if he really wanted to be King of France" (p. 89). Once again the "great and saving moment," which the narrator Ranke dwells on for some time (p. 90), does not coincide with any concrete event. The description of the upward movement homogenizes the events and changes that strengthen the monarchy, and leaves the defeated opposition nothing but its dying moments of decline. And so the idea concealed in the event, but brought out by the narrator as the decisive impulse behind the transition, can be fulfilled by the historical outcome already described—the idea of a new monarchical order, together with which is inaugurated a new idea of the nation "developed in accordance with its own instincts" (p. 95). But the historian, who describes the cut-and-dried historical individuality of this epoch with such apparent objectivity, still owes us the reasons for his interpretation and narrative perspective, which betray themselves in his *parti pris* for the consolidation of the "fixed order" of the monarchy (p. 94) and against the repressed ideas of the towns and estates movement.

VI

While the principle behind Ranke's presentation of history refers back to the latent paradigm of the history of style, Droysen's critique of the narrative presentation and the resultant artistic nature of "objective" historiography presupposes a hermeneutics that arose from the historical approach to art. Droysen tries to shatter the "conventional view (. . .) that the only type of historical presentation is the narrative" (p. 254) through the distinction of non-narrative forms of presentation (the "examining," the "didactic," the "discursive") and also through the attempt to draw a borderline between "artistic" and "historical" narrative. His statement that the artistic creation is "a totality, something complete in itself" (p. 285) is aimed at the historical novel ("a picture, a photograph of that which once was," p. 285), and applies equally to the history of the past and to the historical representation of respective epochs by historicism. Underlying this is Droysen's main arguement: "That which was, does not interest us because it was, but because in a certain sense it still is, in that it is still effective because it stands in the total context of things which we call the historical, i.e., moral world, the moral cosmos" (p. 275). The narrative form of historical presentation, according to Droysen, can escape the suspicion of being artistic fiction only if, as a mimesis of development, it includes and reflects "our interpretation of important events from this standpoint" (p. 285). But this presentation of history—according to Droysen the only "historically" legitimate one—has its precedent in the hermeneutic process of experiencing and readapting the art of the past. The meaning of a work of art, too, is extracted only during the progressive process of its reception; it is not a mystic whole that can reveal itself totally on its first showing.[37] The art of the past, just like history, does not interest merely because it was, but because "in a certain sense it still is" and invites one to new adaptations.

Droysen's argument against the narrative technique leaves unanswered the question of how the classical narrative form of history can be cut out, and how the contrasting didactic form of presentation can

---

37. See Droysen, p. 285, and also A. C. Danto, *Analytical Philosophy of History* (Cambridge, 1965), who overlooks the fact that the difference between the "whole" of a work of art, and the never completed "whole of history" only exists so long as one does not consider the work of art in the historical dimension of its reception.

be brought in—"in order to use the whole wealth of the past for the enlightenment of our present and for our deeper understanding of it" (p. 275). Droysen seems to have overlooked the fact that the new task "of showing the development of this present and of its thought content" (p. 275), like any "mimesis of development," cannot be performed linguistically without a narrative link—in other words, without the form of a "story." This also applies to the individual event if, as Droysen maintains, a historical fact as an event—just like a work of art—is constituted by the range of its possible meanings and can therefore be made concrete only through the interpretation of later observers or performers. Droysen's new definition of the historical fact—"What happens is understood and put together only by interpretation as a coherent event . . . in short, as A Fact" (pp. 133–34) —necessarily implies narration if the diffuse event of the past is to be grasped as a totality in the light of its present meaning. In this context, narrative is to be understood primarily as a basic category of historical perception, and only secondarily as a form of historical presentation. The different modes of narrative presentation have, throughout history, been subject to a process consisting of various phases and degrees of literariness and "anti-literariness." Droysen's polemic against the "artistically" closed narrative form of historism again implies an "anti-literary" form of presentation—with a limited perspective, aware of its own location, and a horizon that is left open; and, paradoxically, the poetics of modern literature offers paradigms for such a presentation.

This interweaving of poetics and history reappears in A. C. Danto's analytical philosophy of history. Danto's premise is: "our knowledge of the past is significantly limited by our ignorance of the future" (p. 16); he bases narrative logic on the posteriority of its statements: "[they] give descriptions of events under which those events could not have been witnessed" (p. 61); historical explanation presupposes "conceptual evidence" (p. 119)[38] and narrative ("A narrative describes and explains at once" [p. 141]); it should not try to reproduce the past, but with the aid of the past "organize present experience"

38. This preconception, which Danto seeks to explain as a "social inheritance" (pp. 224, 242), like his general attempt to establish a relative legitimacy for the historical, would be easier to grasp through Droysen's idea of analogies of historical experience. See *Historik,* p. 159: "Whatever is given in the nature of the thing, we have learnt from our experience and knowledge elsewhere of analogous situations—as the sculptor, restoring an old torso, has this basic analogy in the constant form of the human body."

(p. 79). All this is directly in line with Droysen's approach to history, though Danto makes no reference to it. Poetics comes onto the scene when Danto deals with the role of narrative in historical explanation and seeks an equivalent to the unprovable "historical laws" (Chaps. x-xi). He claims to find it in "temporal wholes," which first of all he explains by referring to the historical variability of literary forms (p. 226), and then traces back to definitions (pp. 233 ff.) that are basically just a rehash of the classical, Aristotelian norms of epic fiction. But if the narrative as a form of historical explanation is to keep open the possibility of further narrative statements about the same event (p. 167), the closed horizon of the classical narrative form must be surmounted and the contingency of history made to prevail against the epic tendency of the "story."

"A story is an account, I shall say an explanation, of how the change from beginning to end took place" (p. 234): this corresponds to the Aristotelian definition of the story (*Poetics,* 1450 b)—all the more so as Danto had already substituted "change," in the sense of the tragic dénouement (1450 a; 1452 a) for the mere event as the actual subject of historical explanation (p. 233). In this way Danto falls into the illusion, already uncovered by Droysen, of the first beginning and the definitive end; it immediately gets him into trouble when he observes —but swiftly dismisses as a mere problem of causality—that the "change of things" might be the middle of a history that stretches as far back as it does forwards (p. 240). His thesis "that we are in fact referring to a change when we demand an explanation of some event" (p. 246) also narrows the idea of an event to a homogeneous change, and ignores the fact that in an event not only the change from before to after, but also the aftereffects and the retrospective importance for the observer or for the acting person need to be explained. Danto believes he can achieve homogeneity through what seems to him to be the obvious condition that the historical narrative requires a never-changing subject, and should include only details or episodes that will serve the cause of explanation (p. 250). But this is precisely how Aristotle defined the epic unity of the story (1451 a), at the same time drawing attention to the superiority of fiction—which is concerned with the possible or the general—over history, which can deal only with the factual and the particular (1451 b). If narrative logic, which here is still completely confined to the closed circle of classical poetics, is to fit in with the contingency of history, it could follow the paradigm of the modern novel: since Flaubert, this has systematically dismantled the teleology of the epic story, and developed new narrative techniques in order to incorporate the open horizon of the future into the story of the past, to replace the omniscient narrator by localized perspectives, and to destroy the illusion of completeness through unexpected and unexplained details.

Narrative as a basic form of historical perception and explanation can be viewed throughout in accordance with Danto's analogy to the basic form of literary genres and their historical appearance. Only one must then refute the substantialist misconception that in a history of genres the multiplicity of historical variants is countered by an invariable form which, as "historic law" subsumes every possible historical form of a genre.[39] The history of artistic genres in fact reveals the existence of forms that are possessed of no greater generality than that which shows itself in the change of their historical appearance.[40] What Droysen said of the individuality of nations also applies to the literary form or artistic genre as an historical unit: "they change to the extent that they have history, and they have history to the extent that they change" (p. 198). This sentence refers back to the basic view of history in Droysen's *Historik,* the "continuity of progressive historical work" (p. 29), or—in Droysen's interpretation—the ἐπίδοσις εἰς αὑτό [a growth into its real self], through which according to Aristotle (*De an,* II, 5.7) the species of man differs from that of animals, which can only reproduce *as* species. It is obvious that the history of art, as regards the historical appearance of its forms, fulfills in a very distinct manner Droysen's idea of a continuity "in which everything earlier extends and supplements itself through the later" (p. 12). If it is inherent in the idea of "historical work" that "with every new and individual appearance it creates a newness and an addition" (p. 9), then artistic productions correspond to this idea more than other manifestations of historical life which, in the framework of continuing institutions, change more slowly and not always in such a way that every change "creates a newness and an addition" as the work of art in fact can with every new and individual appearance. The analogy between the historical event and the past work of art, which Droysen's *Historik* presupposes, therefore extends even further. The history of art,

---

39. The metric scheme alone is not enough to determine the generic form of a sonnet, as Danto, p. 256, obviously assumes.
40. See H. R. Jauss, "Littérature médiévale et théorie des genres," in *Poétique, revue de théorie et d'analyse littéraires* (1970), pp. 79–101 (esp. p. 92).

through its manner of progression in time, and the study of art, through its continuous mediation of past and present art, can become a paradigm for a history that is to show the "development of this present" (p. 275). But art history can take on this function only if it itself overcomes the organon-type principle of style history, and thus liberates itself from traditionalism and its metaphysics of supra-temporal beauty. Droysen was already pointing the way when he tried to bring the histories of individual arts back into the "progression" of historical work, and when he spurred on the art history of his day, which was "still only in its beginning," with the words: "The idea of beauty will progress in the same measure as the acknowledged beauty of ideas" (p. 230).

VII

The conception of a history of art that is to be based on the historical functions of production, communication, and reception, and is to take part in the process of continuous mediation of past and present art, requires the critical abandonment of two contrasting positions. First, it defies historical objectivism, which remains a convenient paradigm ensuring the normal progress of philological research, but in the realm of literature can achieve only an apparent precision, which in the exemplary disciplines of natural and social science scarcely earns it any respect. It also challenges the philological metaphysics of tradition and with this the classicism of a view of fiction that disregards the historicity of art, in order to confer on "great fiction" its own relation to truth—"timeless present" or "self-sufficient presence"[41]—and a more substantial, organic history —"tradition" or "the authority of the traditional."[42]

Traditionalism, which holds fast to the "eternal store" and guaranteed classicality of "masterpieces" and so creates for itself the

41. M. Heidegger, "Der Ursprung des Kunstwerks," in *Holzwege*, Frankfurt, 1950, p. 18; also the corresponding definition of *classical* in H. G. Gadamer, *Wahrheit und Methode* (Tübingen, 1960), p. 272: ". . . a consciousness of permanence, of the unlosable meaning independent of all temporal circumstances . . . a kind of timeless present, which means contemporaneousness for every present"; or E. R. Curtius, *Europäische Literatur und lateinisches Mittelalter* (Bern, 1948), p. 23: "The 'timeless present' which is an essential element of literature, means that the literature of the past can always remain effective in any present."
42. H. G. Gadamer, pp. 261 seq.: *Die Rehabilitierung von Autorität und Tradition.*

spectacle of a *Sonntagsstrasse der Literaturgeschichte* (Sunday street of literary history),[43] can appeal to a secular experience of the fine arts. For, as Droysen remarks in his *Historik* (1857): "No-one before Aristotle thought that dramatic poetry might have a history; until about the middle of our century it did not occur to anybody to talk of a history of music."[44] The fact that the timelessly beautiful is also subject to historical experience because of historical influences, elements of which will remain in the work of art, and because of the open horizon of its meaning, which becomes apparent in the never-ending process of interpretation, and the fact that the fine arts also have a history, to the extent that they do change in this way—these facts are a comparatively recent discovery, which the triumph of historism could not make self-evident. What Droysen's contemporary Baudelaire provocatively formulated in 1859 as a "théorie rationnelle et historique du beau," illustrated with the outrageous example of clothing fashions, and contrasted with the low-brow bourgeois taste for the "immortal,"[45] has continually been regarded ever since the *Querelle des Anciens et des Modernes* as a new challenge to the classical interpretation of art by the enlightened or historical consciousness.

The conception of tradition which this idea of art goes back to is—according to Theodor W. Adorno—carried over from natural, spontaneous situations (the link between generations, traditions of crafts and trades) to the realm of the mind.[46] This carrying over endows what is past with an authoritative orientation, and sets the creations of the mind into a substantial continuity which supports and harmonizes history, at the cost of suppressing the contrary, the revolutionary, the unsuccessful.[47] In accordance with the transmission image *(tradere)*, the process of historical action here turns into a

---

43. W. Krauss, *Literaturgeschichte als geschichtlicher Auftrag*, in: *Sinn und Form 2* (1950), p. 113.
44. P. 138.
45. In: *Le Peintre de la vie moderne* (Paris, 1951), pp. 873–76.
46. "Thesen über Tradition," in *Insel Almanach auf das Jahr 1966*, pp. 21–33.
47. See Adorno, p. 29: "(Here) one meets with the true theme of the recollection of tradition, which brings together all that has remained by the wayside, the neglected, the defeated, under the name of the out-of-date. There the living element of tradition seeks refuge, and not in the store of works that are to defy time"; and see especially S. Kracauer, whose philosophy of history in *History: The Last Things Before the Last* (New York, 1969) vindicates in many respects the demand "to undo the injurious work of tradition" (p. 7).

self-activating movement of imperishable substances or into the sequent effect of original norms. To put it as briefly as possible: "In truth history does not belong to us, but we belong to it."[48]

In the sphere of art, the changing of the historical praxis of human creativity into self-sufficient recurrence of shaping historical entities reveals itself in the hypostatized metaphor of the *after-life of Antiquity*. This stands for an historiographic model which, in the humanist's credo, has its counterpart as "imitation of the ancient" and, in the course of history, witnesses nothing but the continual alternation of decline and return to classical models and lasting values. But tradition cannot transmit itself by itself. It presupposes a response whenever an "effect" of something past is recognizable in the present. Even classical models are present only where they are responded to: if tradition is to be understood as the historical process of artistic praxis, this latter must be understood as a movement that begins with the recipient, takes up and brings along what is past, and translates or "transmits" it into the present, thus setting it in the new light of present meaning.

Along with the illusion of self-activating tradition, esthetic dogmatism also falls into discredit—the belief in an "objective" meaning, which is revealed once and for all in the original work, and which an interpreter can restore at any time, provided he sets aside his own historical position and places himself, without any prejudices, back into the original intention of the work. But the form and meaning of a tradition-building work are not the unchangeable dimensions or appearances of an esthetic object, independent of perception in time and history: its potential of meaning only becomes progressively visible and definable in the subsequent changes of esthetic experience, and dialogically so in the interaction between the literary work and the literary public. The tradition-forming potential of a classic work can only be seen by its contemporaries within the horizon of its first "materialization."[49] Only as the horizon changes and expands with each subsequent historical materialization, do responses to the work legitimize particular possibilities of understanding, imitation, transformation, and continuation—in short, structures of exemplariness that condition the process of literary tradition-forming.

---

48. Gadamer, p. 261.
49. Concerning the term *"Konkretisation"* (materialization), which I have taken over from F. Vodička, see below.

If one wishes to give the name "tradition" to this discontinuous process of an active, normative, and changing reproduction of what is past in the sphere of art, then one must do away with the Platonic idea of art and with the substantialist conception of history as an "event of tradition." The receiving consciousness certainly stands among traditions that precondition its way of understanding, but, just as certainly, the traditional cannot be fitted out with predicates and a life of its own, for without the active participation of the receiving mind, these are simply not conceivable. It is therefore a substantialist relapse in the historical hermeneutics of H. G. Gadamer when —obviously indulging a predilection for the classics—he expects of the traditional text per se (regardless of whether it is a work of art or a historical document) "that it asks a question of the interpreter. Interpretation . . . always contains a basic reference to the question that has been asked of one. To understand a text means to understand a question."[50] But a past text cannot, of its own accord, across the ages, ask us or later generations a question that the interpreter would not first have to uncover or reformulate for us, proceeding from the answer which the text hands down or appears to contain. Literary tradition is a dialectic of question and answer which is always kept going—though this is often not admitted—from the present interest. A past text does not survive in historical tradition, thanks to old questions that would have been preserved by tradition and could be asked in an identical way for all times including our own. For the question whether an old or allegedly timeless question still—or once more—concerns us, while innumerable other questions leave us indifferent, is decided first and foremost by an interest that arises out of the present situation, critically opposes it, or maintains it.

W. Benjamin, in his critique of historism, reaches an analogous conception of historical tradition: "To put into operation experience with history—which for every present is an original experience—is the task of historical materialism. It turns to a consciousness of the present, which shatters the continuum of history."[51] Why this task should fall to the historical materialist alone is not made clear by this essay. For, after all, a historical materialist must presumably believe in a "real historical continuity" if, with Benjamin, he declares his allegiance to the ideas expressed in Engels' letter to Mehring (14 July

50. *Wahrheit und Methode, loc. cit.* pp. 351–55.
51. "Edward Fuchs, der Sammler und Historiker," in *Angelus Novus* (Frankfurt, 1966), p. 304.

1893). Anyone who, with Engels, wishes to proclaim the apparent triumph of thought as "intellectual reflections of changed economic fact," cannot also impute to the conscious mind the achievement of "shattering the continuum of history." According to materialist dogma, he cannot apply any consciousness to the present that is not previously conditioned by changed economic facts in the midst of the real, historical continuity which, paradoxically, that consciousness is meant to shatter. The famous "tiger leap into the past" *(Geschichtsphilosophische Thesen,* XIV) completely brushes aside historical materialism: Benjamin's anti-traditionalist theory of reception superseded it in the Fuchs essay before he himself realized it.

VIII

The classical idea of art as the history of creative spirits and timeless masterpieces, together with its positivistic distortion in the form of innumerable histories of "Man and Work," has since the Fifties been the subject of critical examination conducted in the name of the "structural method." In Anglo-American criticism this proceeded from Northrop Frye's theory of archetypal literature, and in French from Claude Lévi-Strauss; it aimed at a predominantly elitist idea of culture and art, contrasted this with a new interest in primitive art, folklore, and sub-literature, and demanded a methodical approach starting with the individual work and finishing with literature as a system.[52] For Frye, literature is an "order of words," not a "piled aggregate of works": "Total literary history gives us a glimpse of the possibility of seeing literature as a complication of a relatively restricted and simple group of formulas that can be studied in primitive culture."[53] Archetypes or "communicable symbols" mediate between the structure of primitive myths and the forms or figures of later art and literature. The historical dimension of literature withdraws behind the omnipresence or transferability of these symbols, which obviously change gradually, with literary means of expression from myth to mimesis; it reemerges only when, at the last moment, Frye attributes to the myth an emancipatory function regarding ritual,

52. See the detailed critique by G. Hartman, "Toward Literary History," in *Daedalus* (Spring, 1970), pp. 355–83; also C. Segre, *I segni e la critica* (Turin, 1969), who also subjects the claims of semasiological literary theory to well-argued criticism.
53. Northrop Frye, *Anatomy of Criticism* (New York, 1967), pp. 16 seq.

so that—like Matthew Arnold—he can set art the task of removing class barriers, enabling it to participate "in the vision of the goal of social effort, the idea of complete and classless society."[54]

The gulf between structure and event, between synchronous system and history, becomes absolute in Lévi-Strauss, who searches behind the myths for nothing but the structure in depth of the closed synchronous system of a functional logic. The latent Rousseauism of this theory is apparent in the chapter "Du mythe au roman" from *L'Origine des manières de table.*[55] When the structural analysis of the Indian myths, which in one breath are awarded and refused "liberté d'invention nous pouvons au moins démontrer la nécessité de cette liberté [we can at least demonstrate the necessity of this freedom],[104] throws up a historical process such as the development from myth to novel, this process appears as an incontrovertible degradation in the general *"débâcle"* of history (pp. 105–106). In this downward movement of the real through the symbolic to the imaginary, the structures of contrast decline into those of repetition. Lévi-Strauss is reminded here of the "serial," which also draws its life from the denatured repetition of original works and, like the "mythe à tiroir [episodic myth]," is subject to a short periodicty and the same "contraintes formelles [formal constraints]." But this new version of the old theory of the "decayed matter of culture" (or here, "matter of Nature") is contradicted by the fact that in the nineteenth century the serial novel was not the "état dernier de la dégradation du genre romanesque [last state of degradation of the novelistic mode]" but, on the contrary, the starting point for the great, "original" novel of the Balzac and Dostoyevsky type—not to mention the fact that the *Mystères de Paris* kind of novel developed a new mythology of city life that cannot be fitted in with the idea of a decline in the "exténuation du mythe [exhaustion of myth]." Ultimately Lévi-Strauss's theory of a decline itself surreptitiously takes on the nature of a new myth, when in the moral outcome of the serial novel he claims to find an equivalent to the closed structure of the myth, "par lequel une société qui se livre à l'histoire croit pouvoir remplacer l'ordre logico-naturel qu'elle a abandonné, à moins qu'elle-même n'ait été abandonée par lui [by which a society which gives itself to history believes to be able to replace

54. P. 348.
55. Paris, 1968 (*Mythologiques,* III), pp. 69–106.

the logico-natural order it has abandoned—unless society was not abandoned by the logico-natural order]"(p.106). History as the deviation of society from Nature, personified in the "ordre logico-naturel," if one were not to assume that Nature herself (comparable to Heidegger's "Kehre") has turned away from Man: with this, Heidegger's myth of "Seinsvergessenheit" (oblivion of existence) is given a worthy, panstructuralistic companion-piece!

For Lévi-Strauss every work of art is completely explicable through its function within the secondary system of reference of society; every act of speech is reduced to a combinatory element in a primary system of signs; all meaning and individuation merges into an anonymous, subjectless system, establishing the priority of a spontaneous natural order over any historical process. And so we may assume, with Paul Ricoeur, that the paradigm of anthropological structuralism will only be productive for the methodology of the study of art and literature if, along with the results of structural analysis, the latter takes up and regains what the former seeks dogmatically to exclude: "une production dialectique, qui fasse advenir le système comme acte et la structure comme événement [a dialectical production, which makes the system occur as an act and the structure as an event]."[56]

An approach to bridging the gap between structure and event is already to be distinguished in the literary theory of Roland Barthes, who in France paved the way for criticism of the "Lansonist system" of university literary history, and was the first to show what structural analysis of a literary work could really achieve. His Racine interpretation penetrates behind the historical explanation and naive psychology of literary creation, and establishes a kind of structural anthropology of classical tragedy. The archaic system of characters is transplanted into a surprisingly rich context of functions, a context which extends from the three dimensions of topography right up to metaphysics and the inverted redemption theology of the Racinian hero, and which stimulates and expands one's historical understanding.[57] The question left open in L'homme racinien as to what

---

56. "La structure, le mot, l'événement," in: *Esprit*, 35 (1967) pp. 801–21, esp. 808; special attention should be paid to this fundamental critique, which develops hermeneutic approaches to the problem of overcoming structural dogmatism.

57. *Sur Racine* (Paris, 1963), see esp. p. 17: "Les trois espaces extérieurs: mort, fuite, événement" and p. 54: "La faute (La théologie racinienne est une rédemption inversée: c'est l'homme qui rachète Dieu)", p. 55.

literature meant to Racine and his contemporaries is, for Barthes, one of those problems that literary history can solve only through a radical conversion "analogous to that which made possible the transition from the chronicles of kings to genuine history." For literary history can only "deal on the level of literary functions (production, communication, consumption), and not on that of the individuals who have exercised these functions."[58] From a scientific point of view, literary history would accordingly be sociologically possible only as a history of the literary institution, while the other side of literature—the individual connection between author and work, between work and meaning—would be left to the subjectivity of criticism, of which Barthes can, quite rightly, make the demand that it confess to its preconceptions if it wants to prove its historical legitimacy.[59] But this raises the question whether the thus legitimized subjectivity or series of interpretations of a work is not itself again "institutionalized" through history, forming a system in its historical sequence. The question also arises as to how one is to conceive the structure of a work which, in opposition to the structuralistic axiom of completeness, remains open to an interpretation that in principle is incapable of completeness and, indeed, takes on its specific character as art through this very openness and dependence on individual response.

Barthes has not asked the first of these questions, but his answer to the second is equally exasperating for the dogmatists of Positivism and of Structuralism.[60] "Ecrire, c'est ébranler le sens du monde, y disposer une interrogation indirecte, à laquelle l'écrivain, par un dernier suspens, s'abstient de répondre. La réponse, c'est chacun de nous qui la donne, y apportant son histoire, son langage, sa liberté; mais comme histoire, langage et liberté changent infiniment, la réponse du monde à l'écrivain est infinie: on ne cesse jamais de répondre à ce qui a été écrit hors de toute réponse: affirmés, puis mis en rivalité, puis remplacés, les sens passent, la question demeure[61]

---

58. *Ibid.*, p. 156.
59. *Literatur oder Geschichte*, pp. 34–35.
60. See statements of R. Picard and C. Lévi-Strauss, quoted by G. Schiwy, *Der französische Strukturalismus* (Hamburg, 1969), p. 67 and p. 71 respectively.
61. *Sur Racine* (Paris, ²1963), p. 11; cf. *Literatur oder Geschichte:* "In literature, which is an order of connotation, there is no *pure* question; a question is always nothing but its own scattered answer, which is split up in fragments, between which the meaning springs up and at the same time escapes." This new accentuation of the problem in itself implies what Barthes did not see—the answer nature of the text, which is the prime connecting-point for its reception.

[To write is to disturb the meaning of the world, to pose an indirect question, which the writer, by an ultimate abstinence, refuses to answer. It is we who give the answer, each of us bringing to it our own history, language, and liberty; but since history, language, and liberty are infinitely variable, the world's response to the writer is infinite: there is no end to answering what has been written once and for all: affirmed, then disputed, then replaced—the meanings pass, the question remains]." Here the open structure of the literary work is observed in the open relation between meaning, question, and answer, but the cost of this is a yawning gap of subjective arbitrariness between the past work and its progressive interpretation—a gap that can be bridged only by the historical mediation of question and answer. For the implicit question, which in fact is what first awakens our present interest in the past work, can be obtained only through the answer that the esthetic object, in its present materialization, holds or seems to hold ready for us. Literary works differ from purely historical documents precisely because they do more than simply document a particular time, and remain "speaking" to the extent that they attempt to solve problems of form or content, and so extend far beyond the silent relics of the past.[62]

If the literary text is taken primarily as an answer, or if the later reader is primarily seeking an answer in it, this by no means implies that the author himself has formulated an explicit answer in his work. The answering nature of the text, which provides the historical link between the past work and its later interpretation, is a modality of its structure—seen already from the viewpoint of its reception; it is not an invariable value within the work itself. The answer or meaning expected by the later reader can have been ambivalent or have remained altogether indeterminate in the original work. The degree of indeterminacy can—as W. Iser has shown—actually determine the degree of esthetic effectiveness and hence the artistic character of a work.[63] But even the extreme case of an open-structured fictional text, with its quantity of indeterminacy calculated to stimulate the imagination of the active reader, reveals how every fresh response links up

---

62. Hence the greater resistance of art to time—that "paradoxical nature" of the work, unexplained by R. Barthes: "it is a sign for history, and at the same time resistance against it" (p. 13).

63. *Die Appellstruktur der Texte: Unbestimmtheit als Wirkungsbedingung literarischer Prosa* (Konstanz, 1970) *Konstanzer Universitätsreden*, ed. G. Hess, vol. XXVIII.

with an expected or supposed meaning, the fulfillment or non-fulfillment of which calls forth the implicit question and so sets in motion the new process of understanding. This process emerges most clearly in the history of the interpretation of great works, when the new interpreter is no longer satisfied with the conventionally accepted answer or interpretation, and looks for a new answer to the implied or "posthumous" question. The open, indeterminate structure makes a new interpretation possible, whereas on the other hand the historical communication of question and answer limits the mere arbitrariness of interpretation.

It makes no difference whether the conventionally accepted answer of a text has been given explicitly, ambivalently, or indeterminately by the author himself; or whether it is an interpretation of the work that first arose at its reception—the question implied in the answer presented by the work of art—a question which, according to Barthes, each present must answer in its own way—is now set within a changed horizon of esthetic experience, and so is no longer asked as it was originally by the past text, but is the result of interaction between present and past.[64] The question, which enables the past work of art to affect us still or anew, has to be implicit because it presupposes the active mind's testing the conventional answer, finding it convincing or otherwise, discarding it or putting it in a new light so that the question implied first and now for us may be revealed. In the historical tradition of art, a past work survives not through eternal questions, or through permanent answers, but through the more or less dynamic interrelationship between question and answer, between problem and solution, which can stimulate a new understanding and can allow the resumption of the dialogue between present and past.

Analysis of the tradition-forming dialectic of question and answer in the history of literature and art is a task which literary criticism has scarcely even begun. It goes beyond the semiotic conception of a new science of literature, which Barthes sees in an all too narrow framework: "It cannot be a science of contents (which can only be

64. This interaction has been described by H. G. Gadamer as a "fusion of horizons: *(Horizontverschmelzung)*, pp. 289 seq., 356. In my opinion, this description, with which I concur, does not necessarily give rise to the reversal of the relationship between question and answer which Gadamer (pp. 351–56) brings about in order to ensure the precedence of the "event of tradition" over understanding as "a productive procedure" (p. 280).

suckled by historical science proper), but a science of the conditions of contents, i.e., of forms: what will concern it is the variations of meaning applied and to a certain extent applicable to the works."[65] However, the constantly renewed interpretation is more than an answer left to the discretion of the interpreter, for literary tradition is more than just a variable series of subjective projections or "fulfilled meanings" over a mere matrix or "empty meaning" of works, "which bears all of those."[66] It is not only the formal constitution and variability of the meanings applicable to works that can be described in accordance with the linguistic rules of the symbol. The content, the sequence of interpretations as they have appeared historically —this, too, has a logic: that of question and answer, through which the accepted interpretations can be described as a tradition-forming coherence; it also has a counterpart to the language or "literature competence"[67] that is a prerequisite for all transformations: the initial meaning or problem structure of the work, which is its "a priori" content, conditioning all subsequent interpretations, and providing the first instance against which all these must prove themselves. And so there is no reason why the science of literature should not also be a science of contents. And indeed it will have to be, because the science of history cannot relieve it of the task of closing the gap which Barthes, through his formal rigorism, has widened between author and reader, reader and critic, critic and historian, and furthermore between the functions of literature (production, communication, reception).[68] A new science of literature will cease to be a mere auxiliary to history at the moment when it uses the privilege of its still "speaking" sources, and their communication of response and tradition, to attempt the move away from the old "history of development" and towards a new "history of structure"—a move which the science of history is also concerned with making.

---

65. *Kritik und Wahrheit* (Frankfurt, 1967), p. 68.
66. *Ibid.,* p. 68.
67. *Ibid.,* p. 70.
68. *Ibid.,* pp. 88–91. In *Literatur oder Geschichte,* the programmatic "literary history without individuals" is understood as a history of the literary institution; the mediation between production, communication, and reception remains quite open, and in the end R. Barthes has to confess that the result of this reduction is "simply history," and so no longer specific to the historicity of art (pp. 22–23).

IX

How can the history of art and literature contribute towards closing the gap between structural method and historical hermeneutics? This problem is common nowadays to various approaches to a theory of literature which—like my own attempt[69]—regard as necessary the destruction of literary history in its old monographic or "epic" tradition, in order to arouse a new interest in the history and historicity of literature. This is especially true of the French *Nouvelle Critique* and Prague Structuralism,[70] whose standpoint we must examine here, at least as it is represented in a few pioneer works.

One representative advocate of the *Nouvelle Critique* is G. Genette. In his programmatic essay *Structuralisme et critique littéraire* (1966),[71] he shows different ways in which literary criticism could use structural description, and theory of style could integrate already current analyses of immanent structures in a structural synthesis. The contrast between intersubjective or hermeneutic analysis and structural analysis would not require literature to be divided into two separate spheres of mythographic or sub-literature, on the one hand, and artistic literature, in the exegetic tradition, on the other—as Ricoeur suggested, in his critique of Lévi-Strauss.[72] For the two methods could expose complementary meanings of the same text: "à propos d'une même oeuvre, la critique herméneutique parlerait le langage de la reprise du sens et de la récréation intérieure, et la

---

69. *Literaturgeschichte als Provokation der Literaturwissenschaft* (Konstanz, 1967).
70. For my account of this, I am indebted to Jurij Striedter and the Research Group for the Structural Study of Language and Literature at the University of Constance, who have prepared a detailed presentation and a German edition of the most important texts of Prague Structuralism for the series *Theorie und Geschichte der Literatur und der Schönen Künste,* published by W. P. Fink, Munich, and have allowed me to quote from their translation of F. Vodička's book *Struktura vývoje* (published in the meantime: *Die Structure der literarischen Einbildung,* intro. by J. Striedter, Munich, 1976). The semiotic structuralism of Soviet literary study does not yet appear to be concerned with the problem of a structural history of literature so much as with structural analysis of literary genres. See K. Eimermacher, "Entwicklung, Charakter und Probleme des sowjetischen Strukturalismus in der Literaturwissenschaft," in *Sprache im technischen Zeitalter,* 30 (1969), pp. 126–57. Of prime importance are the writings of Jurij Lotman: *Lekcii po struktural' noj poetike* (Tartu, 1964), repr. Providence, Rhode Island, 1968.
71. In the collection of essays *Figures* (Paris, 1966), pp. 145–70.
72. "Structure et herméneutique," in: *Esprit* 31 (1963), pp. 596–627; continued with: "La structure, le mot, l'événement." in: *Esprit* 35 (1967), pp. 801–21.

critique structurale celui de la parole distante et da la reconstruction intelligible [with regard to the same work, hermeneutic criticism could speak the language of the resumption of meaning and of internal recreation, and structural criticism that of distant speech and of intelligible reconstruction]."[73] Thematic criticism, which until now has been concerned almost exclusively with the individual works of authors, would have to relate these to a collective topic of literature, dependent on the attitude, taste and wishes—in short, the "expectation of the public."[74] Literary production and consumption would act in the same way as *parole* and *langue;* and so it must also be possible to formulate the literary history of a system in a series of synchronous sections, and to translate the mere sequence of autonomous, mutually "influencing" works into a structural history of literature and its functions.[75]

J. Starobinski, on the other hand, with his new definition of literary criticism *(La relation critique,* 1968), proceeds from the belief that structuralism in its strict form is applicable only to literatures that represent a "regulated play in a regulated society."[76] The moment literature questions the given order of institutions and traditions, oversteps the closed limits of the surrounding society with its sanctioned literature, and thus opens up the dimension of history in a culture, the result is that the synchronous structure of a society and the appearance of its literature as an event no longer belong to the homogeneous texture of the same logos: "la plupart des grandes oeuvres modernes ne déclarent leur relation au monde que sur le mode du refus, de l'opposition, de la contestation [most of the great modern works declare their relation to the world only under the sign of refusal, of opposition, of contestation]."[77] The task of a new criticism will be to bring this "relation différentielle" back into the structural context of literature. This does not only require that thematic criticism opens the closed hermeneutic circle between

73. P. 161.
74. *Ibid.,* pp. 162–64.
75. *Ibid.,* p. 167: "L'idée structuraliste, ici, c'est de suivre la littérature dans son évolution globale en pratiquant des coupes synchroniques à diverses étapes, et en comparant les tableaux entre eux. . . . C'est dans le changement continuel de fonction que se manifeste la vraie vie des éléments de l'oeuvre littéraire."
76. In *Quatre conférences sur la "Nouvelle Critique"* (Turin, Società editrice internazionale, 1968), p. 38.
77. *Ibid.,* p. 39.

work and interpreter (trajet textuel) onto the work's path to the world of its readers (trajet intentionnel); it also requires that critical understanding should not frustrate the differential or "transgressive" function of the work: if history continually cancels out the protest element and the exceptionality of literature, absorbing it as a paradigm of the next order, the critic must fight against this levelling out of works in the line of tradition, and must hold fast to the differences,[78] thus emphasizing the discontinuity of literature in the history of society.

Furthest from the dogma of the irreconcilability of structural and historical analysis is probably Prague structuralism. Here approaches of formalistic literary theory have been developed into a structural esthetics, which seeks to comprehend the literary work with categories of esthetic perception and then to describe the perceived gestalt of the esthetic object diachronically, in its "concretizations" conditioned by response. The pioneer work of J. Mukařovský has been continued, particularly by F. Vodička, to form a theory of literary history that is based on the esthetics of response.[79] In his book *Struktura vývoje* (1969), he sees the main task of literary history in the context of the polarity between the literary work and reality, which is to be materialized and historically described according to the manner of its perception, i.e., the dynamic connections between the work and the literary public.[80] This requires, on the one hand, the reconstruction of the "literary norm," i.e., the "totality of literary postulates" and the hierarchy of literary values of a given period, and, on the other, the ascertainment of the literary structure through the "concretization" of literary works, i.e., through the concrete gestalt that they have assumed in the perception of the public of the time. Prague structuralism therefore sees the structure of a work as a

---

78. *Ibid.*, p. 39: "Les grandes oeuvres rebelles sont ainsi trahies, elles sont—par le commentaire et la glose—exorcisées, rendues acceptables et versées au patrimoine commun. . . . Mais la compréhension critique ne vise pas à l'assimilation du dissemblable. Elle ne serait pas compréhension si elle ne comprenait pas la différence en tant que différence."

79. The most important writings of J. Mukařovský are to be found in "Chapters from Czech Poetry," *Kapitoly z české poetiky* (Prague, 1948), 3 vols., and *Studie z estetiky* (Studies from Aesthetics) (Prague, 1966).

80. The book *Struktura vývoje* (Structure of Development), published in Prague in 1969, takes up two older works: *Konkretizace literárního díla* (Materialization of the Literary Work, 1941), and *Literární historie, její problemy a úkoly* (Literary History, Its Problems and Tasks, 1942); see note 70.

component part of the broader structure of literary history, and sees the latter as a process arising out of the dynamic tension between work and norm, between the historic sequence of literary works and the sequence of changing norms or attitudes of the public: "Between them there is always a certain parallelism, for both creations—the creation of norms and the creation of a new literary reality—proceed from a common base: from the literary tradition that they overcome."[81] This presupposes that esthetic values, like the "essence" of works of art, only reveal their different forms through a process and are not permanent factors in themselves. The literary work —according to Mukařovský's bold new version of the social character of art—is offered not as a structure that is independent of its reception, but simply as an "esthetic object," which can therefore be described only in accordance with the succession of its concretizations.

By *concretization,* Vodička means the picture of the work in the consciousness of those "for whom the work is an esthetic object."[82] With this idea, Prague structuralism has taken up and historicized an approach of R. Ingarden's phenomenological esthetics. According to the latter, the work, in the polyphonic harmony of its qualities, still had the character of a structure independent of temporal changes in the literary norm; but Vodička disputes the idea that the esthetic values of a work could be given complete expression through an optimal concretization: "As soon as the work is divided up on its absorption into new contexts (changed state of the language, different literary postulates, changed social structure, new system of spiritual and practical values etc.), one can feel the esthetic effect of precisely those qualities of a work which earlier . . . were not felt as esthetically effective."[83] Only the reception, i.e., the historical life of the work in literature, reveals its structure, in an open series of aspects, through the active interrelationships between the literary work and the literary public. With this theory, Prague structuralism has gained a position for the esthetics of reception which relieves it of the twin problems of esthetic dogmatism and extreme subjectivism: "Dogmatism found eternal, unchangeable values in the work, or interpreted the history of responses as a way to the ultimate, correct perception. Extreme subjectivism, on the other hand, saw in all

81. *Struktura vývoje,* p. 35.
82. P. 199.
83. P. 41.

responses proof of individual perception and ideas, and sought only in exceptional cases to overcome this subjectivism through a temporal determination."[84] Vodička's theory of reception links up with the methodological principle that the materialization legitimated by a literary public—which itself can become a norm for other works—is to be distinguished from merely subjective forms of materialization which do not enter any current tradition as a value judgment: "The object of cognition cannot be all materializations possible with regard to the individual attitude of the reader, but only those which show a confrontation between the structure of the work and the structure of the norms currently valid."[85] Thus the critic who records and publishes a new materialization joins the author and the reader as someone with his own particular function within the "literary community," whose constitution as "literary public" is only one of several perspectives that can offer this theory of a structural literary history as a shot in the arm to the methodologically stagnating sociology of literature.

X

A theory that sets out to destroy the substantialist idea of tradition, and to replace it with a functional idea of history, is bound to be open to the charge of one-sidedness precisely in this sphere of art and literature. Whoever abandons the latent Platonism of the philological method, dismisses as illusory the eternal essence of the work of art and the timeless standpoint of its observer, and begins to regard the history of art as a process of production and reception, in which not identical functions but dialogic structures of question and answer mediate between past and present—such a person must run the risk of missing a specific experience of art that is obviously in opposition to its historicity. Art historiography that follows the principle of the open structure and the never completable interpretation of works, in accordance with the process of productive understanding and critical reinterpretation, is concerned primarily with the intellectual and emancipatory function of art.[86] Is it not, then, bound to ignore the

84. P. 196.
85. P. 206.
86. This objection is raised by M. Wehrli in his address: *Literatur und Geschichte, Jahresbericht der Universität Zürich* (1969–1970), p. 6.

social and, in the narrower sense, esthetic character of art—its critical, communicative, and socially influential function and those achievements which the active and the suffering man experiences as impulses of ecstasy, pleasure, and play, and withal as impulses that remove him from his historical existence and his social situation?

It cannot be disputed that the emancipatory and socially formative function of art represents only one side of its historical role in the process of human history. The other side is revealed in the fact that works of art are "directed against the course of time, against disappearance and transience," because they seek to immortalize, i.e., "to confer on the objects of life the dignity of immortalization."[87] And so, according to Kurt Badt, art history also has the task of showing "what art has been able to present of human perfection, for instance even in suffering (Grünewald's *Christus*)."[88] However, recognizing the supratemporal character of this glorifying and immortalizing function does not mean contrasting the historicity of art with the timeless essence of an absolute beauty that has manifested itself only in the immortality of the work. The glorified immortality of the work of art is something that has been created *against* transience and within history itself.[89] The history of art incorporates the historical appearance of works and their immortality as the result of esthetic activities of mankind. If, with Karel Kosík, we understand the dialectics of history as a process in which history "contains both the historicity that is transient, sinks into the past and *does not* return, and historical character, the formation of the immortal—i.e., the self-forming and self-creating"[90]—then the history of art is distinguished from other spheres of historical reality by the fact that in it the formation of the immortal is not only visibly carried out through the production of works, but also through reception, by its constant reenactment of the enduring features of works which long since have been committed to the past.

The history of art maintains this special status even if one concurs with the Marxist literary theory that art and literature cannot claim

87 K. Badt, *Wissenschaftslehre der Kunstgeschichte* (p. 160). This is a yet unpublished work, which the author has kindly allowed me to quote from; it also proceeds from a consideration of Droysen's *Historik*, in order to establish a new methodological basis for the history of the fine arts (published in the meantime, Cologne, 1971).
88. *Ibid.*, p. 190.
89. Here I am following K. Kosík, *Die Dialektik des Konkreten* (Frankfurt, 1967), esp. the chapter: "Historismus und Historizismus," pp. 133–49.
90. *Ibid.*, p. 143.

any history of their own, but only become historical insofar as they participate in the general process of historical praxis. The history of art keeps its special position within pragmatic history to the extent that, through the medium of perception and by means of interpretation, it can consciously bring out the historical capacity of "totalization, in which human praxis incorporates impulses from the past and animates them through this very integration."[91] Totalization, in the sense of "a process of production and reproduction, animation and rejuvenation,"[92] is presented in exemplary form by the history of art. For here—as T. S. Eliot pointed out—it is not only the authentically new work that revises our view of all past works. Here the past work, too, which has the appearance of immortal beauty and—according to Malraux—embodies art as a counter to fate, needs the productive work of understanding in order to be taken out of the imaginary museum and appropriated by the interpretative eye of the present. And here, too, ultimately, art historiography can win back its disputed legitimation insofar as it seeks out and describes the canons and contexts of works, rejuvenating the great wealth of human experience preserved in past art, and making it accessible to the perception of the present age.

91. *Ibid.*, p. 148.
92. *Ibid.*

WOLFGANG ISER

The reading theory of Wolfgang Iser, Jauss' colleague at the University of Constance, coincides at several points with Jauss' own. Both are addicted to the notion that good art will not give us what we want or expect but will evoke certain expectations, then violate them. If art did not do that, we would be bored, and boredom is to be avoided at all costs. Later, however, Iser explains that if these expectations are not violated, if there are not disturbing inconsistencies as we read, then illusion takes over. Uninterrupted illusion is to be found in escapist literature—women's magazines and brash detective stories—the general affect of which, however, is surely enjoyment, however trivial, not boredom. That Iser is bored by such works suggests he is not the reader "intended" by those texts. The sophisticated reader, then, must be given something to do as he reads. The text must not solve every problem for him. The text should consequently leave some "gaps" in the telling of its story. This gives the reader room to be creative in his or her own right. This creativity is a variable that accounts for a multiplicity of readings. The same reader at different times can have different experiences with the same text, indeed, should be expected to have them. Good art stretches our sense of the familiar, the "repertoire" (Jauss' "horizon"), and demands reorientation. This process "reflects" the process by which we gain experience. If, however, we cannot leave behind our preconceptions, the attitudes that shape our personalities, we cannot properly be penetrated by the text. Iser's predilection for phenomenology evinces itself in the closing treatment of Georges Poulet, who describes the reading experience as an act of self-oblivion so profound that the reader is thinking the thoughts of the author—and this to such an extent that the "I" of the reader is no longer the reader at all but someone else. Iser denies that we need go this far. For him we are not possessed so much as mildly schizophrenic when we read. The alien self and the real self never completely sever diplomatic ties.

The Reading Process: A Phenomenological Approach

1972

Translated with David Henry Wilson

I

The phenomenological theory of art lays full stress on the idea that, in considering a literary work, one must take into account not only the actual text but also, and in equal measure, the actions involved in responding to that text. Thus Roman Ingarden confronts the structure of the literary text with the ways in which it can be *konkretisiert* (realized).[1] The text as such offers different "schematised views"[2] through which the subject matter of the work can come to light, but the actual bringing to light is an action of *Konkretisation*. If this is so, then the literary work has two poles, which we might call the artistic and the esthetic: the artistic refers to the text created by the author, and the esthetic to the realization accomplished by the reader. From this polarity it follows that the literary work cannot be completely identical with the text, or with the realization of the text, but in fact must lie halfway between the two. The work is more than the text, for the text only takes on life when it is realized, and furthermore the realization is by no means independent of the individual disposition of the reader—though this in turn is acted upon by the different patterns of the text. The convergence of text and reader brings the literary work into existence, and this conver-

THE READING PROCESS: A PHENOMENOLOGICAL APPROACH, by Wolfgang Iser from *The Implied Reader,* trans. with David Henry Wilson. English translation copyright © 1974 Johns Hopkins University Press. Reprinted by permission of Johns Hopkins University Press.

1. Cf. Roman Ingarden, *Vom Erkennen des literarischen Kunstwerks* (Tübingen, 1968), pp. 49 ff.
2. For a detailed discussion of this term see Roman Ingarden, *Das literarische Kunstwerk* (Tübingen, 1960), pp. 270 ff.

gence can never be precisely pinpointed, but must always remain virtual, as it is not to be identified either with the reality of the text or with the individual disposition of the reader. It is the virtuality of the work that gives rise to its dynamic nature, and this in turn is the precondition for the effects that the work calls forth. As the reader uses the various perspectives offered him by the text in order to relate the patterns and the "schematised views" to one another, he sets the work in motion, and this very process results ultimately in the awakening of responses within himself. Thus, reading causes the literary work to unfold its inherently dynamic character. That this is no new discovery is apparent from references made even in the early days of the novel. Laurence Sterne remarks in *Tristram Shandy:* ". . . no author, who understands the just boundaries of decorum and good-breeding, would presume to think all: The truest respect which you can pay to the reader's understanding, is to halve this matter amicably, and leave him something to imagine, in his turn, as well as yourself. For my own part, I am eternally paying him compliments of this kind, and do all that lies in my power to keep his imagination as busy as my own."[3] Sterne's conception of a literary text is that it is something like an arena in which reader and author participate in a game of the imagination. If the reader were given the whole story, and there were nothing left for him to do, then his imagination would never enter the field, the result would be the boredom which inevitably arises when everything is laid out cut and dried before us. A literary text must therefore be conceived in such a way that it will engage the reader's imagination in the task of working things out for himself, for reading is only a pleasure when it is active and creative. In this process of creativity, the text may either not go far enough, or may go too far, so we may say that boredom and overstrain form the boundaries beyond which the reader will leave the field of play.

The extent to which the 'unwritten' part of a text stimulates the reader's creative participation is brought out by an observation of Virginia Woolf's in her study of *Jane Austen:*

> Jane Austen is thus a mistress of much deeper emotion than appears upon the surface. She stimulates us to supply what is not there. What she offers is, apparently, a trifle, yet is composed of something that expands in the reader's mind and endows with

3. Laurence Sterne, *Tristram Shandy* (London, 1956), II, 11:79.

the most enduring form of life scenes which are outwardly trivial. Always the stress is laid upon character. . . . The turns and twists of the dialogue keep us on the tenterhooks of suspense. Our attention is half upon the present moment, half upon the future. . . . Here, indeed, in this unfinished and in the main inferior story, are all the elements of Jane Austen's greatness.[4]

The unwritten aspects of apparently trivial scenes and the unspoken dialogue within the "turns and twists" not only draw the reader into the action but also lead him to shade in the many outlines suggested by the given situations, so that these take on a reality of their own. But as the reader's imagination animates these 'outlines,' they in turn will influence the effect of the written part of the text. Thus begins a whole dynamic process: the written text imposes certain limits on its unwritten implications in order to prevent these from becoming too blurred and hazy, but at the same time these implications, worked out by the reader's imagination, set the given situation against a background which endows it with far greater significance than it might have seemed to possess on its own. In this way, trivial scenes suddenly take on the shape of an "enduring form of life." What constitutes this form is never named, let alone explained in the text, although in fact it is the end product of the interaction between text and reader.

II

The question now arises as to how far such a process can be adequately described. For this purpose a phenomenological analysis recommends itself, especially since the somewhat sparse observations hitherto made of the psychology of reading tend mainly to be psychoanalytical, and so are restricted to the illustration of predetermined ideas concerning the unconscious. We shall, however, take a closer look later at some worth-while psychological observations.

As a starting point for a phenomenological analysis we might examine the way in which sequent sentences act upon one another. This is of especial importance in literary texts in view of the fact that they do not correspond to any objective reality outside themselves. The world presented by literary texts is constructed out of what

4. Virginia Woolf, *The Common Reader,* First Series (London, 1957), p. 174.

Ingarden has called *intentionale Satzkorrelate* (intentional sentence correlatives):

> Sentences link up in different ways to form more complex units of meaning that reveal a very varied structure giving rise to such entities as a short story, a novel, a dialogue, a drama, a scientific theory. . . . In the final analysis, there arises a particular world, with component parts determined in this way or that, and with all the variations that may occur within these parts—all this as a purely intentional correlative of a complex of sentences. If this complex finally forms a literary work, I call the whole sum of sequent intentional sentence correlatives the 'world presented' in the work.[5]

This world, however, does not pass before the reader's eyes like a film. The sentences are "component parts" insofar as they make statements, claims, or observations, or convey information, and so establish various perspectives in the text. But they remain only "component parts"—they are not the sum total of the text itself. For the intentional correlatives disclose subtle connections which individually are less concrete than the statements, claims, and observations, even though these only take on their real meaningfulness through the interaction of their correlatives.

How is one to conceive the connection between the correlatives? It marks those points at which the reader is able to 'climb aboard' the text. He has to accept certain given perspectives, but in doing so he inevitably causes them to interact. When Ingarden speaks of intentional sentence correlatives in literature, the statements made or information conveyed in the sentence are already in a certain sense qualified: the sentence does not consist solely of a statement—which, after all, would be absurd, as one can only make statements about things that exist—but aims at something beyond what it actually says. This is true of all sentences in literary works, and it is through the interaction of these sentences that their common aim is fulfilled. This is what gives them their own special quality in literary texts. In their capacity as statements, observations, purveyors of information, etc., they are always indications of something that is to come, the structure of which is foreshadowed by their specific content.

They set in motion a process out of which emerges the actual content of the text itself. In describing man's inner consciousness of

5. Ingarden, *Vom Erkennen des literarischen Kunstwerks,* p. 29.

time, Husserl once remarked: "Every originally constructive process is inspired by pre-intentions, which construct and collect the seed of what is to come, as such, and bring it to fruition."[6] For this bringing to fruition, the literary text needs the reader's imagination, which gives shape to the interaction of correlatives foreshadowed in structure by the sequence of the sentences. Husserl's observation draws our attention to a point that plays a not insignificant part in the process of reading. The individual sentences not only work together to shade in what is to come; they also form an expectation in this regard. Husserl calls this expectation "preintentions." As this structure is characteristic of *all* sentence correlatives, the interaction of these correlatives will not be a fulfillment of the expectation so much as a continual modification of it.

For this reason, expectations are scarcely ever fulfilled in truly literary texts. If they were, then such texts would be confined to the individualization of a given expectation, and one would inevitably ask what such an intention was supposed to achieve. Strangely enough, we feel that any confirmative effect—such as we implicitly demand of expository texts, as we refer to the objects they are meant to present—is a defect in a literary text. For the more a text individualizes or confirms an expectation it has initially aroused, the more aware we become of its didactic purpose, so that at best we can only accept or reject the thesis forced upon us. More often than not, the very clarity of such texts will make us want to free ourselves from their clutches. But generally the sentence correlatives of literary texts do not develop in this rigid way, for the expectations they evoke tend to encroach on one another in such a manner that they are continually modified as one reads. One might simplify by saying that each intentional sentence correlative opens up a particular horizon, which is modified, if not completely changed, by succeeding sentences. While these expectations arouse interest in what is to come, the subsequent modification of them will also have a retrospective effect on what has already been read. This may now take on a different significance from that which it had at the moment of reading.

Whatever we have read sinks into our memory and is foreshortened. It may later be evoked again and set against a different background with the result that the reader is enabled to develop hitherto unforeseeable connections. The memory evoked, however,

---

6. Edmund Husserl, *Zur Phänomenologie des inneren Zeitbewusstseins, Gesammelte Werke* (The Hague, 1966), 10:52.

can never reassume its original shape, for this would mean that memory and perception were identical, which is manifestly not so. The new background brings to light new aspects of what we had committed to memory; conversely these, in turn, shed their light on the new background, thus arousing more complex anticipations. Thus, the reader, in establishing these interrelations between past, present and future, actually causes the text to reveal its potential multiplicity of connections. These connections are the product of the reader's mind working on the raw material of the text, though they are not the text itself—for this consists just of sentences, statements, information, etc.

This is why the reader often feels involved in events which, at the time of reading, seem real to him, even though in fact they are very far from his own reality. The fact that completely different readers can be differently affected by the 'reality' of a particular text is ample evidence of the degree to which literary texts transform reading into a creative process that is far above mere perception of what is written. The literary text activates our own faculties, enabling us to recreate the world it presents. The product of this creative activity is what we might call the virtual dimension of the text, which endows it with its reality. This virtual dimension is not the text itself, nor is it the imagination of the reader: it is the coming together of text and imagination.

As we have seen, the activity of reading can be characterized as a sort of kaleidoscope of perspectives, preintentions, recollections. Every sentence contains a preview of the next and forms a kind of viewfinder for what is to come; and this in turn changes the 'preview' and so becomes a 'viewfinder' for what has been read. This whole process represents the fulfillment of the potential, unexpressed reality of the text, but it is to be seen only as a framework for a great variety of means by which the virtual dimension may be brought into being. The process of anticipation and retrospection itself does not by any means develop in a smooth flow. Ingarden has already drawn attention to this fact and ascribes a quite remarkable significance to it:

> Once we are immersed in the flow of *Satzdenken* (sentence-thought), we are ready, after completing the thought of one sentence, to think out the 'continuation,' also in the form of a sentence—and that is, in the form of a sentence that connects up with the sentence we have just thought through. In this way the process of reading goes effortlessly forward. But if by chance the following sentence has no tangible connection whatever with

the sentence we have just thought through, there then comes a blockage in the stream of thought. This hiatus is linked with a more or less active surprise, or with indignation. This blockage must be overcome if the reading is to flow once more.[7]

The hiatus that blocks the flow of sentences is, in Ingarden's eyes, the product of chance, and is to be regarded as a flaw; this is typical of his adherence to the classical idea of art. If one regards the sentence sequence as a continual flow, this implies that the anticipation aroused by one sentence will generally be realized by the next, and the frustration of one's expectations will arouse feelings of exasperation. And yet literary texts are full of unexpected twists and turns, and frustration of expectations. Even in the simplest story there is bound to be some kind of blockage, if only because no tale can ever be told in its entirety. Indeed, it is only through inevitable omissions that a story gains its dynamism. Thus whenever the flow is interrupted and we are led off in unexpected directions, the opportunity is given to us to bring into play our own faculty for establishing connections—for filling in the gaps left by the text itself.[8]

These gaps have a different effect on the process of anticipation and retrospection, and thus on the 'gestalt' of the virtual dimension, for they may be filled in different ways. For this reason, one text is potentially capable of several different realizations, and no reading can ever exhaust the full potential, for each individual reader will fill in the gaps in his own way, thereby excluding the various other possibilities; as he reads, he will make his own decision as to how the gap is to be filled. In this very act the dynamics of reading are revealed. By making his decision he implicitly acknowledges the inexhaustibility of the text; at the same time it is this very inexhaustibility that forces him to make his decision. With 'traditional' texts this process was more or less unconscious, but modern texts frequently exploit it quite deliberately. They are often so fragmentary that one's attention is almost exclusively occupied with the search for connections between the fragments; the object of this is not to complicate the 'spectrum' of connections, so much as to make us aware of the nature of our own capacity for providing links. In such cases, the text

7. Ingarden, *Vom Erkennen des literarischen Kunstwerks,* p. 32.
8. For a more detailed discussion of the function of "gaps" in literary texts see Wolfgang Iser, "Indeterminacy and the Reader's Response in Prose Fiction," *Aspects of Narrative* (English Institute Essays), ed. J. Hillis Miller (New York, 1971), pp. 1–45.

refers back directly to our own preconceptions—which are revealed by the act of interpretation that is a basic element of the reading process. With all literary texts, then, we may say that the reading process is selective, and the potential text is infinitely richer than any of its individual realizations. This is borne out by the fact that a second reading of a piece of literature often produces a different impression from the first. The reasons for this may lie in the reader's own change of circumstances, still, the text must be such as to allow this variation. On a second reading familiar occurrences now tend to appear in a new light and seem to be at times corrected, at times enriched.

In every text there is a potential time sequence which the reader must inevitably realize, as it is impossible to absorb even a short text in a single moment. Thus the reading process always involves viewing the text through a perspective that is continually on the move, linking up the different phases, and so constructing what we have called the virtual dimension. This dimension, of course, varies all the time we are reading. However, when we have finished the text, and read it again, clearly our extra knowledge will result in a different time sequence; we shall tend to establish connections by referring to our awareness of what is to come, and so certain aspects of the text will assume a significance we did not attach to them on a first reading, while others will recede into the background. It is a common enough experience for a person to say that on a second reading he noticed things he had missed when he read the book for the first time, but this is scarcely surprising in view of the fact that the second time he is looking at the text from a different perspective. The time sequence that he realized on his first reading cannot possibly be repeated on a second reading, and this unrepeatability is bound to result in modifications of his reading experience. This is not to say that the second reading is 'truer' than the first—they are, quite simply, different: the reader establishes the virtual dimension of the text by realizing a new time sequence. Thus even on repeated viewings a text allows and, indeed, induces innovative reading.

In whatever way, and under whatever circumstances the reader may link the different phases of the text together, it will always be the process of anticipation and retrospection that leads to the formation of the virtual dimension, which in turn transforms the text into an experience for the reader. The way in which this experience comes about through a process of continual modification is closely akin to the way in which we gather experience in life. And thus the 'reality' of the reading experience can illuminate basic patterns of real experience:

> We have the experience of a world, not understood as a system of relations which wholly determine each event, but as an open totality the synthesis of which is inexhaustible. . . . From the moment that experience—that is, the opening on to our *de facto* world—is recognized as the beginning of knowledge, there is no longer any way of distinguishing a level of *a priori* truths and one of factual ones, what the world must necessarily be and what it actually is.[9]

The manner in which the reader experiences the text will reflect his own disposition, and in this respect the literary text acts as a kind of mirror; but at the same time, the reality which this process helps to create is one that will be *different* from his own (since, normally, we tend to be bored by texts that present us with things we already know perfectly well ourselves). Thus we have the apparently paradoxical situation in which the reader is forced to reveal aspects of himself in order to experience a reality which is different from his own. The impact this reality makes on him will depend largely on the extent to which he himself actively provides the unwritten part of the text, and yet in supplying all the missing links, he must think in terms of experiences different from his own; indeed, it is only by leaving behind the familiar world of his own experience that the reader can truly participate in the adventure the literary text offers him.

III

We have seen that, during the process of reading, there is an active interweaving of anticipation and retrospection, which on a second reading may turn into a kind of advance retrospection. The impressions that arise as a result of this process will vary from individual to individual, but only within the limits imposed by the written as opposed to the unwritten text. In the same way, two people gazing at the night sky may both be looking at the same collection of stars, but one will see the image of a plough, and the other will make out a dipper. The 'stars' in a literary text are fixed; the lines that join them

9. M. Merleau-Ponty, *Phenomenology of Perception,* trans. Colin Smith (New York, 1962), pp. 219, 221.

are variable. The author of the text may, of course, exert plenty of influence on the reader's imagination—he has the whole panoply of narrative techniques at his disposal—but no author worth his salt will ever attempt to set the *whole* picture before his reader's eyes. If he does, he will very quickly lose his reader, for it is only by activating the reader's imagination that the author can hope to involve him and so realize the intentions of his text.

Gilbert Ryle, in his analysis of imagination, asks: "How can a person fancy that he sees something, without realizing that he is not seeing it?" He answers as follows:

> Seeing Helvellyn [the name of a mountain] in one's mind's eye does not entail, what seeing Helvellyn and seeing snapshots of Helvellyn entail, the having of visual sensations. It does involve the thought of having a view of Helvellyn and it is therefore a more sophisticated operation than that of having a view of Helvellyn. It is one utilization among others of the knowledge of how Helvellyn should look, or, in one sense of the verb, it is thinking how it should look. The expectations which are fulfilled in the recognition at sight of Helvellyn are not indeed fulfilled in picturing it, but the picturing of it is something like a rehearsal of getting them fulfilled. So far from picturing involving the having of faint sensations, or wraiths of sensations, it involves missing just what one would be due to get, if one were seeing the mountain.[10]

If one sees the mountain, then of course one can no longer imagine it, and so the act of picturing the mountain presupposes its absence. Similarly, with a literary text we can only picture things which are not there; the written part of the text gives us the knowledge, but it is the unwritten part that gives us the opportunity to picture things; indeed without the elements of indeterminacy, the gaps in the text, we should not be able to use our imagination.[11]

The truth of this observation is borne out by the experience many people have on seeing, for instance, the film of a novel. While reading *Tom Jones,* they may never have had a clear conception of what the hero actually looks like, but on seeing the film, some may say, "That's not how I imagined him." The point here is that the reader of *Tom Jones* is able to visualize the hero virtually for himself, and so his

---

10. Gilbert Ryle, *The Concept of Mind* (Harmondsworth, 1968), p. 255.
11. Cf. Iser, "Indeterminacy," pp. 11 ff., 42 ff.

imagination senses the vast number of possibilities; the moment these possibilities are narrowed down to one complete and immutable picture, the imagination is put out of action, and we feel we have somehow been cheated. This may perhaps be an oversimplification of the process, but it does illustrate plainly the vital richness of potential that arises out of the fact that the hero in the novel must be pictured and cannot be seen. With the novel the reader must use his imagination to synthesize the information given him, and so his perception is simultaneously richer and more private; with the film he is confined merely to physical perception, and so whatever he remembers of the world he had pictured is brutally cancelled out.

IV

The 'picturing' that is done by our imagination is only one of the activities through which we form the 'gestalt' of a literary text. We have already discussed the process of anticipation and retrospection, and to this we must add the process of grouping together all the different aspects of a text to form the consistency that the reader will always be in search of. While expectations may be continually modified, and images continually expanded, the reader will still strive, even if unconsciously, to fit everything together in a consistent pattern. "In the reading of images, as in the hearing of speech, it is always hard to distinguish what is given to us from what we supplement in the process of projection which is triggered off by recognition . . . it is the guess of the beholder that tests the medley of forms and colours for coherent meaning, crystallizing it into shape when a consistent interpretation has been found."[12] By grouping together the written parts of the text, we enable them to interact, we observe the direction in which they are leading us, and we project onto them the consistency which we, as readers, require. This 'gestalt' must inevitably be colored by our own characteristic selection process. For it is not given by the text itself; it arises from the meeting between the written text and the individual mind of the reader with its own particular history of experience, its own consciousness, its own outlook. The 'gestalt' is not the true meaning of the text; at best it is a configurative meaning; ". . . comprehension is

12. E. H. Gombrich, *Art and Illusion* (London, 1962), p. 204.

an individual act of seeing-things-together, and only that."[13] With a literary text such comprehension is inseparable from the reader's expectations, and where we have expectations, there too we have one of the most potent weapons in the writer's armory—illusion.

Whenever "consistent reading suggests itself . . . illusion takes over."[14] Illusion, says Northrop Frye, is "fixed or definable, and reality is best understood as its negation."[15] The 'gestalt' of a text normally takes on (or, rather, is given) this fixed or definable outline, as this is essential to our own understanding, but on the other hand, if reading were to consist of nothing but an uninterrupted building up of illusions, it would be a suspect, if not downright dangerous, process: instead of bringing us into contact with reality, it would wean us away from realities. Of course, there is an element of 'escapism' in all literature, resulting from this very creation of illusion, but there are some texts which offer nothing but a harmonious world, purified of all contradiction and deliberately excluding anything that might disturb the illusion once established, and these are the texts that we generally do not like to classify as literary. Women's magazines and the brasher forms of the detective story might be cited as examples.

However, even if an overdose of illusion may lead to triviality, this does not mean that the process of illusion-building should ideally be dispensed with altogether. On the contrary, even in texts that appear to resist the formation of illusion, thus drawing our attention to the cause of this resistance, we still need the abiding illusion that the resistance itself is the consistent pattern underlying the text. This is especially true of modern texts, in which it is the very precision of the written details which increases the proportion of indeterminacy; one detail appears to contradict another, and so simultaneously stimulates and frustrates our desire to 'picture,' thus continually causing our imposed 'gestalt' of the text to disintegrate. Without the formation of illusions, the unfamiliar world of the text would remain unfamiliar; through the illusions, the experience offered by the text becomes accessible to us, for it is only the illusion, on its different levels of consistency, that makes the experience 'readable.' If we cannot find (or impose) this consistency, sooner or later we will put the text

13. Louis O. Mink, "History and Fiction as Modes of Comprehension," *New Literary History* I (1970):553.
14. Gombrich, *Art and Illusion*, p. 278.
15. Northrop Frye, *Anatomy of Criticism* (New York, 1967), pp. 169 f.

down. The process is virtually hermeneutic. The text provokes certain expectations which in turn we project onto the text in such a way that we reduce the polysemantic possibilities to a single interpretation in keeping with the expectations aroused, thus extracting an individual, configurative meaning. The polysemantic nature of the text and the illusion-making of the reader are opposed factors. If the illusion were complete, the polysemantic nature would vanish; if the polysemantic nature were all-powerful, the illusion would be totally destroyed. Both extremes are conceivable, but in the individual literary text we always find some form of balance between the two conflicting tendencies. The formation of illusions, therefore, can never be total, but it is this very incompleteness that in fact gives it its productive value.

With regard to the experience of reading, Walter Pater once observed: "For to the grave reader words too are grave; and the ornamental word, the figure, the accessory form or colour or reference, is rarely content to die to thought precisely at the right moment, but will inevitably linger awhile, stirring a long 'brainwave' behind it of perhaps quite alien associations."[16] Even while the reader is seeking a consistent pattern in the text, he is also uncovering other impulses which cannot be immediately integrated or will even resist final integration. Thus the semantic possibilities of the text will always remain far richer than any configurative meaning formed while reading. But this impression is, of course, only to be gained through reading the text. Thus the configurative meaning can be nothing but a *pars pro toto* fulfillment of the text, and yet this fulfillment gives rise to the very richness which it seeks to restrict, and indeed in some modern texts, our awareness of this richness takes precedence over any configurative meaning.

This fact has several consequences which, for the purpose of analysis, may be dealt with separately, though in the reading process they will all be working together. As we have seen, a consistent, configurative meaning is essential for the apprehension of an unfamiliar experience, which through the process of illusion-building we can incorporate in our own imaginative world. At the same time, this consistency conflicts with the many other possibilities of fulfillment it seeks to exclude, with the result that the configurative meaning is

16. Walter Pater, *Appreciations* (London, 1920), p. 18.

always accompanied by "alien associations" that do not fit in with the illusions formed. The first consequence, then, is the fact that in forming our illusions, we also produce at the same time a latent disturbance of these illusions. Strangely enough, this also applies to texts in which our expectations are actually fulfilled—though one would have thought that the fulfillment of expectations would help to complete the illusion. "Illusion wears off once the expectation is stepped up; we take it for granted and want more."[17]

The experiments in gestalt psychology referred to by Gombrich in *Art and Illusion* make one thing clear: ". . . though we may be intellectually aware of the fact that any given experience *must* be an illusion, we cannot, strictly speaking, watch ourselves having an illusion."[18] Now, if illusion were not a transitory state, this would mean that we could be, as it were, permanently caught up in it. And if reading were exclusively a matter of producing illusion—necessary though this is for the understanding of an unfamiliar experience—we should run the risk of falling victim to a gross deception. But it is precisely during our reading that the transitory nature of the illusion is revealed to the full.

As the formation of illusions is constantly accompanied by "alien associations" which cannot be made consistent with the illusions, the reader constantly has to lift the restrictions he places on the 'meaning' of the text. Since it is he who builds the illusions; he oscillates between involvement in and observation of those illusions; he opens himself to the unfamiliar world without being imprisoned in it. Through this process the reader moves into the presence of the fictional world and so experiences the realities of the text as they happen.

In the oscillation between consistency and "alien associations," between involvement in and observation of the illusion, the reader is bound to conduct his own balancing operation, and it is this that forms the esthetic experience offered by the literary text. However, if the reader were to achieve a balance, obviously he would then no longer be engaged in the process of establishing and disrupting consistency. And since it is this very process that gives rise to the balancing operation, we may say that the inherent nonachievement of balance is a prerequisite for the very dynamism of the operation. In

17. Gombrich, *Art and Illusion*, p. 54.
18. Ibid., p. 5.

seeking the balance we inevitably have to start out with certain expectations, the shattering of which is integral to the esthetic experience.

> Furthermore, to say merely that "our expectations are satisfied" is to be guilty of another serious ambiguity. At first sight such a statement seems to deny the obvious fact that much of our enjoyment is derived from surprises, from betrayals of our expectations. The solution to this paradox is to find some ground for a distinction between "surprise" and "frustration." Roughly, the distinction can be made in terms of the effects which the two kinds of experiences have upon us. Frustration blocks or checks activity. It necessitates new orientation for our activity, if we are to escape the *cul de sac.* Consequently, we abandon the frustrating object and return to blind impulse activity. On the other hand, surprise merely causes a temporary cessation of the exploratory phase of the experience, and a recourse to intense contemplation and scrutiny. In the latter phase the surprising elements are seen in their connection with what has gone before, with the whole drift of the experience, and the enjoyment of these values is then extremely intense. Finally, it appears that there must always be some degree of novelty or surprise in all these values if there is to be a progressive specification of the direction of the total act . . . and any aesthetic experience tends to exhibit a continuous interplay between "deductive" and "inductive" operations.[19]

It is this interplay between "deduction" and "induction" that gives rise to the configurative meaning of the text, and not the individual expectations, surprises, or frustrations arising from the different perspectives. Since this interplay obviously does not take place in the text itself, but can only come into being through the process of reading, we may conclude that this process formulates something that is unformulated in the text and yet represents its 'intention.' Thus, by reading we uncover the unformulated part of the text, and this very indeterminacy is the force that drives us to work out a configurative meaning while at the same time giving us the necessary degree of freedom to do so.

As we work out a consistent pattern in the text, we will find our 'interpretation' threatened, as it were, by the presence of other

19. B. Ritchie, "The Formal Structure of the Aesthetic Object," in *The Problems of Aesthetics,* ed. Eliseo Vivas and Murray Krieger (New York, 1965), pp. 230 f.

possibilities of 'interpretation,' and so there arise new areas of indeterminacy (though we may only be dimly aware of them, if at all, as we are continually making 'decisions' which will exclude them). In the course of a novel, for instance, we sometimes find that characters, events, and backgrounds seem to change their significance; what really happens is that the other 'possibilities' begin to emerge more strongly, so that we become more directly aware of them. Indeed, it is this very shifting of perspectives that makes us feel that a novel is much more 'true-to-life.' Since it is we ourselves who establish the levels of interpretation and switch from one to another as we conduct our balancing operation, we ourselves impart to the text the dynamic lifelikeness which, in turn, enables us to absorb an unfamiliar experience into our personal world.

As we read, we oscillate to a greater or lesser degree between the building and the breaking of illusions. In a process of trial and error, we organize and reorganize the various data offered us by the text. These are the given factors, the fixed points on which we base our 'interpretation,' trying to fit them together in the way we think the author meant them to be fitted. "For to perceive, a beholder must *create* his own experience. And his creation must include relations comparable to those which the original producer underwent. They are not the same in any literal sense. But with the perceiver, as with the artist, there must be an ordering of the elements of the whole that is in form, although not in details, the same as the process of organization the creator of the work consciously experienced. Without an act of recreation the object is not perceived as a work of art."[20]

The act of recreation is not a smooth or continuous process, but one which, in its essence, relies on *interruptions* of the flow to render it efficacious. We look forward, we look back, we decide, we change our decisions, we form expectations, we are shocked by their nonfulfillment, we question, we muse, we accept, we reject; this is the dynamic process of recreation. This process is steered by two main structural components within the text: first, a repertoire of familiar literary patterns and recurrent literary themes, together with allusions to familiar social and historical contexts; second, techniques or strategies used to set the familiar against the unfamiliar. Elements of the repertoire are continually backgrounded or foregrounded with a resultant strategic overmagnification, trivialization,

20. John Dewey, *Art as Experience* (New York, 1958), p. 54.

or even annihilation of the allusion. This defamiliarization of what the reader thought he recognized is bound to create a tension that will intensify his expectations as well as his distrust of those expectations. Similarly, we may be confronted by narrative techniques that establish links between things we find difficult to connect, so that we are forced to reconsider data we at first held to be perfectly straightforward. One need only mention the very simple trick, so often employed by novelists, whereby the author himself takes part in the narrative, thus establishing perspectives which would not have arisen out of the mere narration of the events described. Wayne Booth once called this the technique of the "unreliable narrator,"[21] to show the extent to which a literary device can counter expectations arising out of the literary text. The figure of the narrator may act in permanent opposition to the impressions we might otherwise form. The question then arises as to whether this strategy, opposing the formation of illusions, may be integrated into a consistent pattern, lying, as it were, a level deeper than our original impressions. We may find that our narrator, by opposing us, in fact turns us against him and thereby strengthens the illusion he appears to be out to destroy; alternatively, we may be so much in doubt that we begin to question all the processes that lead us to make interpretative decisions. Whatever the cause may be, we will find ourselves subjected to this same interplay of illusion-forming and illusion-breaking that makes reading essentially a recreative process.

We might take, as a simple illustration of this complex process, the incident in Joyce's *Ulysses* in which Bloom's cigar alludes to Ulysses's spear. The context (Bloom's cigar) summons up a particular element of the repertoire (Ulysses's spear); the narrative technique relates them to one another as if they were identical. How are we to 'organize' these divergent elements, which, through the very fact that they are put together, separate one element so clearly from the other? What are the prospects here for a consistent pattern? We might say that it is ironic—at least that is how many renowned Joyce readers have understood it.[22] In this case, irony would be the form of organization that integrates the material. But if this is so, what is the object of the irony? Ulysses's spear, or Bloom's cigar? The uncertainty

---

21. Cf. Wayne C. Booth, *The Rhetoric of Fiction* (Chicago, 1963), pp. 211 ff., 339 ff.
22. Richard Ellmann, "Ulysses. The Divine Nobody," in *Twelve Original Essays on Great English Novels,* ed. Charles Shapiro (Detroit, 1960), p. 247, classified this particular allusion as "mock-heroic."

surrounding this simple question already puts a strain on the consistency we have established and, indeed, begins to puncture it, especially when other problems make themselves felt as regards the remarkable conjunction of spear and cigar. Various alternatives come to mind, but the variety alone is sufficient to leave one with the impression that the consistent pattern has been shattered. And even if, after all, one can still believe that irony holds the key to the mystery, this irony must be of a very strange nature; for the formulated text does not merely mean the opposite of what has been formulated. It may even mean something that cannot be formulated at all. The moment we try to impose a consistent pattern on the text, discrepancies are bound to arise. These are, as it were, the reverse side of the interpretative coin, an involuntary product of the process that creates discrepancies by trying to avoid them. And it is their very presence that draws us into the text, compelling us to conduct a creative examination not only of the text but also of ourselves.

This entanglement of the reader is, of course, vital to any kind of text, but in the literary text we have the strange situation that the reader cannot know what his participation actually entails. We know that we share in certain experiences, but we do not know what happens to us in the course of this process. This is why, when we have been particularly impressed by a book, we feel the need to talk about it; we do not want to get away from it by talking about it—we simply want to understand more clearly what it is in which we have been entangled. We have undergone an experience, and now we want to know consciously *what* we have experienced. Perhaps this is the prime usefulness of literary criticism—it helps to make conscious those aspects of the text which would otherwise remain concealed in the subconscious; it satisfies (or helps to satisfy) our desire to talk about what we have read.

The efficacy of a literary text is brought about by the apparent evocation and subsequent negation of the familiar. What at first seemed to be an affirmation of our assumptions leads to our own rejection of them, thus tending to prepare us for a re-orientation. And it is only when we have outstripped our preconceptions and left the shelter of the familiar that we are in a position to gather new experiences. As the literary text involves the reader in the formation of illusion and the simultaneous formation of the means whereby the illusion is punctured, reading reflects the process by which we gain experience. Once the reader is entangled, his own preconceptions are continually overtaken, so that the text becomes his 'present' while his own ideas fade into the 'past;' as soon as this happens he is open to the immediate experience of the text, which was impossible so long as his preconceptions were his 'present.'

V

In our analysis of the reading process so far, we have observed three important aspects that form the basis of the relationship between reader and text: the process of anticipation and retrospection, the consequent unfolding of the text as a living event, and the resultant impression of life-likeness.

Any 'living event' must, to a greater or lesser degree, remain open. In reading, this obliges the reader to seek continually for consistency, because only then can he close up situations and comprehend the unfamiliar. But consistency-building is itself a living process in which one is constantly forced to make selective decisions—and these decisions in their turn give a reality to the possibilities which they exclude, insofar as they may take effect as a latent disturbance of the consistency established. This is what causes the reader to be entangled in the text-'gestalt' that he himself has produced.

Through this entanglement the reader is bound to open himself up to the workings of the text and so leave behind his own preconceptions. This gives him the chance to have an experience in the way George Bernard Shaw once described it: "You have learnt something. That always feels at first as if you had lost something."[23] Reading reflects the structure of experience to the extent that we must suspend the ideas and attitudes that shape our own personality before we can experience the unfamiliar world of the literary text. But during this process, something happens to us.

This 'something' needs to be looked at in detail, especially as the incorporation of the unfamiliar into our own range of experience has been to a certain extent obscured by an idea very common in literary discussion: namely, that the process of absorbing the unfamiliar is labeled as the *identification* of the reader with what he reads. Often the term 'identification' is used as if it were an explanation, whereas in actual fact it is nothing more than a description. What is normally

23. G. B. Shaw, *Major Barbara* (London, 1964), p. 316.

meant by 'identification' is the establishment of affinities between oneself and someone outside oneself—a familiar ground on which we are able to experience the unfamiliar. The author's aim, though, is to convey the experience and, above all, an attitude toward that experience. Consequently, 'identification' is not an end in itself, but a strategem by means of which the author stimulates attitudes in the reader.

This of course is not to deny that there does arise a form of participation as one reads; one is certainly drawn into the text in such a way that one has the feeling that there is no distance between oneself and the events described. This involvement is well summed up by the reaction of a critic to reading Charlotte Brontë's *Jane Eyre:* "We took up *Jane Eyre* one winter's evening, somewhat piqued at the extravagant commendations we had heard, and sternly resolved to be as critical as Croker. But as we read on we forgot both commendations and criticism, identified ourselves with Jane in all her troubles, and finally married Mr. Rochester about four in the morning."[24] The question is how and why did the critic identify himself with Jane?

In order to understand this 'experience,' it is well worth considering Georges Poulet's observations on the reading process. He says that books only take on their full existence in the reader.[25] It is true that they consist of ideas thought out by someone else, but in reading the reader becomes the subject that does the thinking. Thus there disappears the subject-object division that otherwise is a prerequisite for all knowledge and all observation, and the removal of this division puts reading in an apparently unique position as regards the possible absorption of new experiences. This may well be the reason why relations with the world of the literary text have so often been misinterpreted as identification. From the idea that in reading we must think the thoughts of someone else, Poulet draws the following conclusion: "Whatever I think is a part of *my* mental world. And yet here I am thinking a thought which manifestly belongs to another mental world, which is being thought in me just as though I did not exist. Already the notion is inconceivable and seems even more so if I reflect that, since every thought must have a subject to think it, this *thought* which is alien to me and yet in me, must also have in me a

---

24. William George Clark, *Fraser's* (December, 1849): 692, quoted by Kathleen Tillotson, *Novels of the Eighteen-Forties* (Oxford, 1961), pp. 19 f.
25. Cf. Georges Poulet, "Phenomenology of Reading," *New Literary History* I (1969):54.

subject which is alien to me. . . . Whenever I read, I mentally pronounce an *I*, and yet the *I* which I pronounce is not myself."[26]

But for Poulet this idea is only part of the story. The strange subject that thinks the strange thought in the reader indicates the potential presence of the author, whose ideas can be 'internalized' by the reader: "Such is the characteristic condition of every work which I summon back into existence by placing my consciousness at its disposal. I give it not only existence, but awareness of existence."[27] This would mean that consciousness forms the point at which author and reader converge, and at the same time it would result in the cessation of the temporary self-alienation that occurs to the reader when his consciousness brings to life the ideas formulated by the author. This process gives rise to a form of communication which, however, according to Poulet, is dependent on two conditions: the life-story of the author must be shut out of the work and the individual disposition of the reader must be shut out of the act of reading. Only then can the thoughts of the author take place subjectively in the reader, who thinks what he is not. It follows that the work itself must be thought of as a consciousness, because only in this way is there an adequate basis for the author-reader relationship —a relationship that can only come about through the negation of the author's own lifestory and the reader's own disposition. This conclusion is actually drawn by Poulet when he describes the work as the self-presentation or materialization of consciousness: "And so I ought not to hesitate to recognize that so long as it is animated by this vital inbreathing inspired by the act of reading, a work of literature becomes (at the expense of the reader whose own life it suspends) a sort of human being, that it is a mind conscious of itself and constituting itself in me as the subject of its own objects."[28] Even though it is difficult to follow such a substantialist conception of the consciousness that constitutes itself in the literary work, there are, nevertheless, certain points in Poulet's argument that are worth holding onto. But they should be developed along somewhat different lines.

If reading removes the subject-object division that constitutes all perception, it follows that the reader will be 'occupied' by the

26. Ibid., p. 56.
27. Ibid., p. 59.
28. Ibid.

thoughts of the author, and these in their turn will cause the drawing of new 'boundaries.' Text and reader no longer confront each other as object and subject, but instead the 'division' takes place within the reader himself. In thinking the thoughts of another, his own individuality temporarily recedes into the background, since it is supplanted by these alien thoughts, which now become the theme on which his attention is focussed. As we read, there occurs an artificial division of our personality, because we take as a theme for ourselves something that we are not. Consequently when reading we operate on different levels. For although we may be thinking the thoughts of someone else, what we are will not disappear completely—it will merely remain a more or less powerful virtual force. Thus, in reading there are these two levels—the alien 'me' and the real, virtual 'me'—which are never completely cut off from each other. Indeed, we can only make someone else's thoughts into an absorbing theme for ourselves, provided the virtual background of our own personality can adapt to it. Every text we read draws a different boundary within our personality, so that the virtual background (the real 'me') will take on a different form, according to the theme of the text concerned. This is inevitable, if only for the fact that the relationship between alien theme and virtual background is what makes it possible for the unfamiliar to be understood.

In this context there is a revealing remark made by D. W. Harding, arguing against the idea of identification with what is read: "What is sometimes called wish-fulfillment in novels and plays can . . . more plausibly be described as wish-formulation or the definition of desires. The cultural levels at which it works may vary widely; the process is the same. . . . It seems nearer the truth . . . to say that fictions contribute to defining the reader's or spectator's values, and perhaps stimulating his desires, rather than to suppose that they gratify desire by some mechanism of vicarious experience."[29] In the act of reading, having to think something that we have not yet experienced does not mean only being in a position to conceive or even understand it; it also means that such acts of conception are possible and successful to the degree that they lead to something being formulated in us. For someone else's thoughts can only take a form in our consciousness if, in the process, our unformulated faculty for deciphering those thoughts is brought into play—a faculty which,

29. D. W. Harding, "Psychological Processes in the Reading of Fiction," in *Aesthetics in the Modern World,* ed. Harold Osborne (London, 1968), pp. 313 f.

in the act of deciphering, also formulates itself. Now since this formulation is carried out on terms set by someone else, whose thoughts are the theme of our reading, it follows that the formulation of our faculty for deciphering cannot be along our own lines of orientation.

Herein lies the dialectical structure of reading. The need to decipher gives us the chance to formulate our own deciphering capacity—i.e., we bring to the fore an element of our being of which we are not directly conscious. The production of the meaning of literary texts—which we discussed in connection with forming the 'gestalt' of the text—does not merely entail the discovery of the unformulated, which can then be taken over by the active imagination of the reader; it also entails the possibility that we may formulate ourselves and so discover what had previously seemed to elude our consciousness. These are the ways in which reading literature gives us the chance to formulate the unformulated.

STANLEY FISH

It is tempting to compare Stanley Fish's current position in literary criticism with that of Richard Rorty's in philosophy.* Rorty is trying to do what he says Wittgenstein and Heidegger did—to work out "honorable terms on which philosophy might surrender to poetry" (11). This would mean giving up the correspondence theory of language for a self-expression theory. The correspondence theory is positivistic and teleological and assumes that every succeeding generation is getting closer to finding a way of expressing "truth," to which language more or less adequately corresponds. It is this search for "truth," the traditional obsession of philosophy, that Rorty says we must abandon now. Instead of a reality "out there," each new philosophy expresses "just one more human project, just one more set of metaphors, . . . one more redescription of things to be filed alongside all the others" (14). For demonstration we now substitute dialectic; for correspondence we substitute coherence; for discovery we substitute self-creation. Whether our language corresponds to anything out there is irrelevant now. Rorty quotes William James' account of his own blindness when he discovered a site in the Appalachians that had once been virgin forest and was now a hideous muddy ulcer with tree stumps, a log cabin, and a pigpen. To the people in the cabin, however, the site was a profound personal victory, an occasion for pride and the cultivation of crops. James claimed to feel chastised when he understood this version of things. Freud's work, for Rorty, was designed to open us up to similar examples of alternative visions —"private poems of the pervert, sadist, and lunatic: as richly textured and 'redolent of moral memories' as our own life" (14).

Fish's plea for persuasion over demonstration in literary criticism seems to parallel Rorty's substitution of coherence over correspondence. However, where Fish differs with Rorty is in the relative humility of the participants: or to put it another way, in Fish's double attitude toward "truth." When we hold certain beliefs we have no doubt about their truth. We know for certain they are true, while we are holding them. And if someone points out to us that we have held quite different beliefs and that consequently we should be skeptical about the finality of our current ones, we are incapable of such skepticism. One's perspective is accessible to doubt only when one no longer holds it. At that point one holds a new position which can be doubted by others but not by oneself. When

* Richard Rorty, "The Contingency of Language," *London Review of Books* (17 April 1986) 3–6; "The Contingency of Selfhood," *London Review of Books* (8 May 1986) 11–15.

we change our beliefs we will feel we have made progress. We will feel closer to the truth than we were. Progress is, however, only an illusion generated by the passion with which we occupy our new position. There have been 400 years of readers of a given Shakespeare sonnet. A sonnet is only 14 lines. If what Fish says about "truth' is not true, how can we explain that after so much time we are still writing about that sonnet, that we still don't "have it right" in our commentaries?

So for Fish we believe and do not believe in "truth." In practice we do. In theory, how can we? Our main task as critics is to displace other versions of "truth." Our discourse is our will to power which we disguise as "truth" to ourselves. The stakes are higher in this version of things than in the old demonstration model, because we are playing for all the marbles, not just producing a humble fact to add to the shelf of other facts about a shining miracle of expression (a poem), the glory of which we as humble critics could never approach. The shining miracle does not shine, does not even exist until we turn to it. What this "it" is apart from our versions of it, Fish does not know nor does he particularly care.

Demonstration vs. Persuasion: Two Models of Critical Activity

1980

By asserting, as I did at the close of my last lecture, that interpretation is the only game in town, I may have seemed only to confirm the fears of those who argue for the necessity of determinate meaning: for, one might say, if interpretation covers the field, there is nothing to constrain its activities and no way to prevent, or even to recognize, its irresponsible exercise. But this is to think of interpretation as something external to the center it supposedly threatens, whereas I have been arguing that interpretation is constitutive of the center—of what will count as a fact, as a text, as a piece of evidence, as a reasonable argument—and thus defines its own limits and boundaries. The mistake is to think of interpretation as an activity in need of constraints, when in fact interpretation is a *structure* of constraints. The field interpretation covers comes complete with its own internal set of rules and regulations, its list of prescribed activities which is also, and at the same time, a list of activities that are proscribed. That is, within a set of interpretive assumptions, to know what you can do is, *ipso facto,* to know what you can't do; indeed, you can't know one without the other; they come together in a diacritical package, indissolubly wed. So that while irresponsible behavior certainly exists (in that one can always recognize it), it exists not as a threat to the system but as a component within it, as much defining responsible behavior as responsible behavior defines it.

That is why the fear of interpretation that is anarchic or totally relativistic will never be realized; for in the event that a fringe or off-the-wall interpretation makes its way into the center, it will merely take its place in a new realignment in which *other* interpretations will occupy the position of being off-the-wall. That is, off-the-wallness is not a property of interpretations that have been judged inaccurate with respect to a free-standing text but a property of an interpretive system within whose confines the text is continually being established and reestablished. It is not a pure but a relational category; an off-the-wall interpretation is simply one that exits in a reciprocally defining relationship with interpretations that are on the wall (you know it by what it is not, and you know what it is not by it); and since the stipulation of what is and is not off the wall is a matter of dispute (the system is precisely a mechanism for the endless negotiation of what will be authorized or nonauthorized) there is always the possibility, and indeed the certainty, that the shape of the stipulation will change. What is not a possibility, however, is that there be *only* off-the-wall interpretation (that "anything goes") because the category only has meaning by virtue of its binary opposite, which is, of course, no less dependent on it. The conclusion is paradoxical, but only superficially so: there is no such thing as an off-the-wall interpretation if by that one means an interpretation that has nothing to do with the text; and yet there is always an off-the-wall interpretation if by that one means an interpretation constitutive of the boundaries within which the text can emerge.

The further conclusion is that off-the-wallness is not inimical to the system but essential to it and to its operation. The production and perception of off-the-wall interpretations is no less a learned and conventional activity than the production and perception of interpretations that are judged to be acceptable. They are, in fact, the same activities enabled by the same set of inforce assumptions about what one can say and not say as a certified member of a community. It is, in short, no easier to disrupt the game (by throwing a monkey wrench into it), than it is to get away from it (by performing independently of it), and for the same reasons. One cannot disrupt the game because any interpretation one puts forward, no matter how "absurd," will already be *in* the game (otherwise one could not even conceive of it as an interpretation); and one cannot get away from the game because anything one does (any account of a text one offers) will be possible and recognizable only within the conditions the game has established.

It is because one can neither disrupt the game nor get away from it that there is never a rupture in the practice of literary criticism. Changes are always produced and perceived within the rules of the game, that is, within its stipulations as to what counts as a successful performance, what claims can be made, what procedures will validate or disconfirm them; and even when some of these stipulations are challenged, others must still be in place in order for the challenge to be recognized. Continuity in the practice of literary criticism is assured not despite but because of the absence of a text that is independent of interpretation. Indeed, from the perspective I have been developing, the fear of discontinuity is an incoherent one. The irony is that discontinuity is only a danger within the model erected to guard against it; for only if there is a free-standing text is there the possibility of moving away from it. But in the system I have been describing any movement away from the text is simultaneously a movement toward it, that is, toward its reappearance as an extension of whatever interpretation has come to the fore.

It could be objected that the continuity I have demonstrated is purchased at its own price, the price of an even greater incoherence attaching to the rationale for engaging in the activity at all; for if changes are to be explained with reference to the conventions of criticism rather than to the ideal of more accurately presenting an independent text, then their succession is pointless, and there is no reason, except for the opportunities made available by the conventions, to argue for one interpretation rather than another. Criticism thus becomes a supremely cynical activity in which one urges a point of view only because it is likely to win points or because it is as yet unsponsored by anyone else. In this view, while all developments are related and therefore not random, in the absence of any extrainstitutional goal such as the progressive clarification of the text, they are empty. Not only is such a view disturbing but it seems counterintuitive given the very real sense we all have, both as critics and teachers, of advancing toward a clearer sight of our object. Jonathan Culler speaks for all of us when he declares that "often one feels that one has indeed been shown the way to a fuller understanding of literature," and, as he points out, "the time and effort devoted to literary education by generations of students and teachers creates a strong presumption that there is something to be learned, and teachers do not hesitate to judge their pupils' progress toward a general literary competence."[1] Of all the objections to the denial of determinate meaning, this is the most powerful because it trades on the fear, as Culler expresses it, "that the whole institution of literary education is but a gigantic confidence trick." That is to say, if we really believe that a text has no determinate meaning, then how can we presume to judge our students' approximations of it, and, for that matter, how can we presume to teach them anything at all? The question is the one posed by E. D. Hirsch in 1967—"On what ground does [the teacher of literature] claim that his 'reading' is more valid than that of any pupil?"—and common sense as well as professional self-respect are on the side of asserting that the ground must be something other than the accidental fact of a teacher's classroom authority.

The issue is not simply the basis of the confidence we ask our students to have in us but the basis of the confidence we might have in ourselves. How can someone who believes that the force and persuasiveness of an interpretation depends on institutional circumstances (rather than any normative standard of correctness), and that those circumstances are continually changing, argue with conviction for the interpretation he happens to hold at the present time? The answer is that the general or metacritical belief (to which I am trying to persuade you in these lectures) does not in any way affect the belief or set of beliefs (about the nature of literature, the proper mode of critical inquiry, the forms of literary evidence, and so on) which yields the interpretation that now seems to you (or me) to be inescapable and obvious. I may, in some sense, *know* that my present reading of *Paradise Lost* follows from assumptions that I did not always hold and may not hold in a year or so, but that "knowledge"

1. *Structuralist Poetics* (Ithaca: Cornell University Press, 1975), p. 121.

does not prevent me from knowing that my present reading of *Paradise Lost* is the correct one. This is because the reservation with which I might offer my reading amounts to no more than saying "of course I may someday change my mind," but the fact that my mind may someday be other than it now is does not alter the fact that it *is* what it now is; no more than the qualifying "as far as I know" with which someone might preface an assertion means that he doesn't know what he knows—he may someday know something different, and when he does, that something will *then* be as far as he knows and he will know it no less firmly than what he knows today. An awareness that one's perspective is limited does not make the facts yielded by that perspective seem any less real; and when that perspective has given way to another, a new set of facts will occupy the position of the real ones.

Now one might think that someone whose mind had been changed many times would at some point begin to doubt the evidence of his sense, for, after all, "this too may pass," and "what I see today I may not see tomorrow." But doubting is not something one does outside the assumptions that enable one's consciousness; rather doubting, like any other mental activity, is something that one does *within* a set of assumptions that cannot at the same time be the object of doubt. That is to say, one does not doubt in a vacuum but from a perspective, and that perspective is itself immune to doubt until it has been replaced by another which will then be similarly immune. The project of radical doubt can never outrun the necessity of being situated; in order to doubt *everything*, including the ground one stands on, one must stand somewhere else, and that somewhere else will then be the ground on which one stands. This infinite regress could be halted only if one could stand free of any ground whatsoever, if the mind could divest itself of all prejudices and presuppositions and start, in the Cartesian manner, from scratch; but then of course you would have nothing to start *with* and anything with which you *did* start (even "I think, therefore I am") would be a prejudice or a presupposition. To put the matter in a slightly different way: radical skepticism is a possibility only if the mind exists independently of its furnishing, of the categories of understanding that inform it; but if, as I have been arguing, the mind is constituted by those categories, there is no possibility of achieving the distance from them that would make them available to a skeptical inquiry. In short, one cannot, properly speaking, *be* a skeptic, and one cannot be a skeptic for the same reason that one cannot be a relativist, because one cannot achieve the distance from his own beliefs and assumptions that would result in their being no more authoritative *for him* than the beliefs and assumptions held by others or the beliefs and assumptions he himself used to hold. The conclusion is tautological but inescapable: one believes what one believes, and one does so without reservation. The reservation inherent in the general position I have been arguing—that one's beliefs and therefore one's assumptions are always subject to change—has no real force, since until a change occurs the interpretation that seems self-evident to me will continue to seem so, no matter how many previous changes I can recall.

This does not mean that one is always a prisoner of his present perspective. It is always possible to entertain beliefs and opinions other than one's own; but that is precisely how they will be seen, as beliefs and opinions *other than one's own,* and therefore as beliefs and opinions that are false, or mistaken, or partial, or immature, or absurd. That is why a revolution in one's beliefs will always feel like a progress, even though, from the outside, it will have the appearance merely of a change. If one believes what one believes, then one believes that what one believes is *true,* and conversely, one believes that what one doesn't believe is not true, even if that is something one believed a moment ago. We can't help thinking that our present views are sounder than those we used to have or those professed by others. Not only does one's current position stand in a privileged relation to positions previously held, but previously held positions will always have the status of false or imperfect steps, of wrongly taken directions, of clouded or deflected perceptions. In other words, the idea of progress is inevitable, not, however, because there *is* a progress in the sense of a clearer and clearer sight of an independent object but because the *feeling* of having progressed is an inevitable consequence of the firmness with which we hold our beliefs, or, to be more precise, of the firmness with which our beliefs hold us.[2]

That firmness does not preclude a certain nostalgia for the beliefs

2. To the objection that this condemns everyone to a state of mass delusion I would answer, "mass delusion in relation to what?" Presumably, in relation to a truth independent of anyone's particular set of beliefs; but if there is no one (with the exception of God) who occupies a position independent of belief, no one, that is, who is not a particular, situated, one, then the objection loses its force because the notion "mass delusion" has no operational validity.

we used to hold; the sense of progress that attends belief is not always a comfortable one. Quite often we find it inconvenient to believe the things we currently believe, but we find too that it is impossible not to believe them. The recent history of formal linguistics provides a nice example. Whatever judgment history will finally make on the "Chomsky revolution," there can be no doubt of its effects on the practitioners of the discipline. The promise, held out by the generative model, that linguistic behavior could be reduced to a set of abstract formal rules with built-in recursive functions united linguists in a sustained and exhilarating search for those rules. Not only did success seem just around the corner but the generality of the model (it seemed to offer no less than a picture of the operations of the human mind) was such that it recommended itself to a succession of neighboring and not so neighboring disciplines—anthropology, philosophy, sociology, psychology, educational theory, literary criticism. Suddenly in each of these fields one heard the increasingly familiar talk of transformations, deep and surface structures, the distinction between competence and performance, and so on. Linguistics, which had occupied a position in the intellectual world not unlike that of Classics—well thought of but little attended to—suddenly found itself at the center of discussion and debate. In the late sixties, however, a group of Chomsky's best students mounted a disquieting and finally successful challenge to the model within whose assumptions researchers were working by pointing to data that could not be accommodated within those assumptions. In a classic instance of a Kuhnian paradigm shift, the now orthodox Chomskians (defending what they called, significantly, the "standard theory") responded by either ignoring the data, or consigning them to the wastebasket of "performance," or declaring them to be assimilable within the standard model given a few minor revisions or refinements (here a key phrase was "notational variant"). In time, however, the weight of the unassimilable data proved too much for the model, and it more or less collapsed, taking with it much of the euphoria and optimism that had energized the field for a brief but glorious period. The workers in the field (or at least many of them) were in the position of no longer being able to believe in something they would have liked to believe in.

One sees this clearly, for example, in the opening paragraph of Barbara Partee's survey, in 1971, of linguistic metatheory:

> It was much easier to teach a course in syntax in 1965 or 1966 than it is now. In 1965 we had Chomsky's *Aspects* model, and if

one didn't pay too much attention to disquieting things like Lakoff's thesis and Postal's underground *Linguistic anarchy notes,* one could present a pretty clear picture of syntax with a well understood phonological component tacked on one end and a not-yet-worked-out imaginable semantic component tacked on the other end. There were plenty of unsolved problems to work on, but the *paradigm* (in Kuhn's sense) seemed clear. But now we're in a situation where there is no theory which is both worked out in a substantial and presentable form and compatible with all the data considered important.[3]

In the face of this situation, Professor Partee finds herself still teaching the *Aspects* model, but only as an "elegant solution" to some syntactic problems; she spends most of her time, she reports, showing her students the "data which doesn't seem amenable to treatment in the framework at all" (p. 652). This is not what she would like to do, but what she *has* to do. "I'm by now sure," she declares regretfully, "that the Katz-Postal-*Aspects* model can't work, and I consider that a great pity" (p. 675). Pity or not, she can't help herself. No matter how convenient it would be if she still believed in the *Aspects* model —convenient for her teaching, for her research, for her confidence in the very future of the discipline—she can only believe what she believes. That is, she can't *will* a belief in the *Aspects* model any more than she can will a disbelief in the arguments that persuaded her that it was unworkable. (Willing, like doubting, is an action of the mind, and like doubting, it cannot be performed outside the beliefs that are the mind's furniture.)

In literary studies the analogous situation would be one in which a critic or teacher felt compelled (against his wishes, if not his will) to give up an interpretation because it no longer seemed as self-evident as it once did. I myself am now precisely in that position with respect to Spenser's *Shepheardes Calender.* For more than fifteen years I have taught the *Calender* as a serious exploration of pastoral attitudes and possibilities, as a sequence more or less preliminary to Milton's "Lycidas"; but recently I have been persuaded to a different idea of pastoral, one less serious (in the sense of solemn) and more informed by a spirit of play and playful inquiry. As a result when I now look at the *Calender,* I no longer see what I used to see and things that I never saw before now seem obvious and indisputable.

3. "Linguistic Metatheory," in *A Survey of Linguistic Science,* ed. W. Dingwall (College Park: University of Maryland Press, 1971), p. 651.

Moreover, my sense of which eclogues are central, and in what ways, has changed entirely so that I am now (self-) deprived of some of the set pieces with which I used to adorn my teaching. Instead, I spend most of my time talking about eclogues to which I had previously paid no attention at all, and fielding questions that sound disconcertingly like objections from my former self.

Of course everyone will have had similar experiences, and they will all point to the same conclusion: not only does one believe what one believes but one *teaches* what one believes even if it would be easier and safer and more immediately satisfying to teach something else. No one ever tells a class that he will not teach the interpretation he believes in because he thinks that the interpretation he used to believe in is better. If he thought that his former interpretation was better, he would still believe in it, because to believe in an interpretation is to think that it is better. And since you will always believe in something, there will always be something to teach, and you will teach that something with all the confidence and enthusiasm that attends belief, even if you know, as I do, that the belief which gives you that something, and gives it to you so firmly, may change. The question sometimes put to me—"If what you are saying is true, what is the point of teaching or arguing for anything?"—misses *my* point, which is not that there is no perspective within which one may proceed confidently but that one is always and already proceeding within just such a perspective because one is always and already proceeding within a structure of beliefs. The fact that a standard of truth is never available independently of a set of beliefs does not mean that we can never know for certain what is true but that we *always* know for certain what is true (because we are always in the grip of some belief or other), even though what we certainly know may change if and when our beliefs change. Until they do, however, we will argue *from* their perspective and *for* their perspective, telling our students and readers what it is that we certainly see and trying to alter their perceptions so that, in time, they will come to see it too.

In short, we try to persuade others to our beliefs because if they believe what we believe, they will, as a consequence of those beliefs, see what we see; and the facts to which we point in order to support our interpretations will be as obvious to them as they are to us. Indeed, this is the whole of critical activity, an attempt on the part of one party to alter the beliefs of another so that the evidence cited by the first will be seen *as* evidence by the second. In the more familiar model of critical activity (codified in the dogma and practices of New

Criticism) the procedure is exactly the reverse: evidence available apart from any particular belief is brought in to judge between competing beliefs, or, as we call them in literary studies, interpretations. This is a model derived from an analogy to the procedures of logic and scientific inquiry, and basically it is a model of *demonstration* in which interpretations are either confirmed or disconfirmed by facts that are independently specified. The model I have been arguing for, on the other hand, is a model of *persuasion* in which the facts that one cites are available only because an interpretation (at least in its general and broad outlines) has already been assumed. In the first model critical activity is controlled by free-standing objects in relation to which its accounts are either adequate or inadequate; in the other model critical activity is constitutive of its object. In one model the self must be purged of its prejudices and presuppositions so as to see clearly a text that is independent of them; in the other, prejudicial or perspectival perception is all there is, and the question is from which of a number of equally interested perspectives will the text be constituted. In one model change is (at least ideally) progressive, a movement toward a more accurate account of a fixed and stable entity; in the other, change occurs when one perspective dislodges another and brings with it entities that had not before been available.

Obviously the stakes are much higher in a persuasion than in a demonstration model, since they include nothing less than the very conditions under which the game, in all of its moves (description, evaluation, validation, and so on), will be played. That is why Jonathan Culler is only half right when he says that "the possibility of bringing someone to see that a particular interpretation is a good one assumes shared points of departure and common notions of how to read" (p. 28). Culler is right to insist that notions of correctness and acceptability are institution-specific and that knowledge of these "shared points of departure" is a prerequisite of what he calls "literary competence." But he is wrong to imply (as he does here and elsewhere) that literary competence is an unchanging set of rules or operations to which critics must submit in order to be recognized as players in the game. Culler's model of critical activity is one that will hold for the majority of critical performances; for it is certainly true that most of the articles we read and write do little more than confirm or extend assumptions that are already in place. But the activity that is most highly valued by the institution (even if it is often resisted) is more radically innovative. The greatest rewards of our profession are reserved for those who challenge the assumptions within which ordinary practices go on, not so much in order to eliminate the category of the ordinary but in order to redefine it and reshape its configurations. This act of challenging and redefining can occur at any number of levels: one can seek to overturn the interpretation of a single work, or recharacterize the entire canon of an important author, or argue for an entirely new realignment of genres, or question the notion of genre itself, or even propose a new definition of literature and a new account of its function in the world. At any of these levels one will necessarily begin, as Culler says, "with shared points of departure and common notions of how to read," but the goal of the performance will be the refashioning of those very notions and the establishments of new points of departure. That is why, as I said, the stakes in a persuasion model are so high. In a demonstration model our task is to be adequate to the description of objects that exist independently of our activities; we may fail or we may succeed, but whatever we do the objects of our attention will retain their ontological separateness and still be what they were before we approached them. In a model of persuasion, however, our activities are directly constitutive of those objects, and of the terms in which they can be described, and of the standards by which they can be evaluated. The responsibilities of the critic under this model are very great indeed, for rather than being merely a player in the game, he is a maker and unmaker of its rules.

That does not, however, mean that he (or you or I) is ever without rules or texts or standards or "shared points of departure and common notions of how to read." It has been my strategy in these lectures to demonstrate how little we lose by acknowledging that it is persuasion and not demonstration that we practice. We have everything that we always had—texts, standards, norms, criteria of judgment, critical histories, and so on. We can convince others that they are wrong, argue that one interpretation is better than another, cite evidence in support of the interpretations we prefer; it is just that we do all those things within a set of institutional assumptions that can themselves become the objects of dispute. This in turn means that while we still have all the things we had before (texts, standards, norms, criteria of judgment), we do not always have them in the same form. Rather than a loss, however, this is a gain, because it provides us with a principled account of change and allows us to explain to ourselves and to others why, if a Shakespeare sonnet is only 14 lines long, we haven't been able to get it right after four hundred years.

It also allows us to make sense of the history of literary criticism, which under the old model can only be the record of the rather dismal performances of men—like Sidney, Dryden, Pope, Coleridge, Arnold—who simply did not understand literature and literary values as well as we do. Now we can regard those performances not as unsuccessful attempts to approximate our own but as extensions of a literary culture whose assumptions were not inferior but merely different. That is, once we give up the essentialist notions that inform a demonstration model—the notion that literature is a monolith and that there is a single set of operations by which its characteristics are discovered and evaluated—we are free to consider the various forms the literary institution has taken and to uncover the interpretative strategies by which its canons have been produced and understood. But perhaps the greatest gain that falls to us under a persuasion model is a greatly enhanced sense of the importance of our activities. (In certain quarters of course, where the critical ideal is one of self-effacement, this will be perceived to be the greatest danger.) No longer is the critic the humble servant of texts whose glories exist independently of anything he might do; it is what he does, within the constraints embedded in the literary institution, that brings texts into being and makes them available for analysis and appreciation. The practice of literary criticism is not something one must apologize for; it is absolutely essential not only to the maintenance of, but to the very production of, the objects of its attention.

Two questions remain and they are both concerned with what the poststructuralists would term "the status of my own discourse." I have been saying that all arguments are made within assumptions and presuppositions that are themselves subject to challenge and change. Well, isn't that also an argument, and one therefore that is no more securely based than the arguments it seeks to dislodge? The answer, of course, is yes; but the answer is also "so what?" According to the position presented here, no one can claim privilege for the point of view he holds and therefore everyone is obliged to practice the art of persuasion. This includes me, and persuasion is the art that I have been trying to practice here. I have not merely presented my position; I have been arguing for it, and I have been arguing for it in a way that can serve as an example (not necessarily a successful one) of how one must proceed if one operates within a model of persuasion. The first thing that one must do is not assume that he is preaching to the converted. That means that whatever the point of view you wish to establish, you will have to establish it in the face of anticipated objections. In general, people resist what you have to say when it seems to them to have undesirable or even disastrous consequences. With respect to what I have been saying, those consequences include the absence of any standards by which one could determine error, the impossibility of preferring one interpretation to another, an inability to explain the mechanisms by which interpretations are accepted and rejected, or the source of the feeling we all have of progressing, and so on. It has been my strategy to speak to these fears, one by one, and to remove them by showing that dire consequences do not follow from the position I espouse and that in fact it is only within that position that one can account for the phenomena my opponents wish to preserve. In short, I have been trying to persuade you to believe what I believe because it is in your own best interests as *you* understand them. (Notice that the determination of what would count as being persuasive is a function of what is understood to be at stake. That is, the mechanisms of persuasion, like everything else, are context-specific; what will be persuasive in any argument depends on what the parties have agreed to in advance; there must be some shared assumption about what is important and necessary and undesirable, for if there were not, neither party could make a point that would be recognized by the other as telling.)

Of course there is always the possibility that it could happen the other way around: you could persuade me that everything I want to preserve depends on a position other than the one I hold, and if you did that, your position would then be mine and I would believe what you believe; but until that happens I will argue for my position with all the confidence that attends belief even though I know that under certain conditions at some time in the future I might believe something else. Another way to put this is to say that the fact that I am subject to the same challenge I have put to my predecessors is not a weakness in my position but a restatement of it. The idea of a position that was invulnerable to challenge makes sense only if you believe in the possibility of a position innocent of assumptions; this of course is exactly what I do not believe and therefore the fact that my assumptions are capable of being dislodged does not refute my argument but confirms it, because it is an extension of it.

The final question concerns the practical consequences of that argument. Since it is primarily a literary argument, one wonders what implications it has for the practice of literary criticism. The answer is, none whatsoever. That is, it does not follow from what I have been saying that you should go out and do literary criticism in a certain way or refrain from doing it in other ways. The reason for this is that the position I have been presenting is not one that you (or anyone else) could live by. Its thesis is that whatever seems to you to be obvious and inescapable is only so within some institutional or conventional structure, and that means that you can never operate outside some such structure, even if you are persuaded by the thesis. As soon as you descend from theoretical reasoning about your assumptions, you will once again inhabit them and you will inhabit them without any reservations whatsoever; so that when you are called on to talk about Milton or Wordsworth or Yeats, you will do so from within whatever beliefs you held about these authors. The fear that one consequence of this position might be that you would be unable to do practical criticism depends on the possibility of your not believing anything at all about them; but it is impossible even to think about them independently of some or other belief, and so long as you can think about them, there is no danger of your being without something to say or without the confidence to say it. That is why this is not a position you can live by, because to live by it you would have to be forever analyzing beliefs, without ever being committed to any, and that is not a position any of us can occupy. It is, however, a position that we are all living *out*, as one set of firmly held beliefs gives way to another, bringing with them an endless succession of practical activities that we are always able to perform.

I can imagine someone saying at this point that if your argument will have no effect on the way I read and teach poetry, why should I be interested in it? What does it matter? There are two answers to this question. The first is to point out that the question itself assumes that in order for something to be interesting, it must directly affect our everyday experience of poetry; and that assumption is in turn attached to a certain antitheoretical bias built into the ideology of New Criticism. In other words, the fact that a thesis has no consequences for practical criticism is damning only from a parochial point of view and it is that point of view I have been challenging. The other answer to the question is institutional, as it must be. The elaboration of this position is something that matters because the issues it takes up are considered central to the institution's concerns. The status of the text, the source of interpretive authority, the relationship between subjectivity and objectivity, the limits of interpretation—these are topics that have been discussed again and again; they are basic topics, and anyone who is able to advance the discussion of them will automatically be accorded a hearing and be a candidate for the profession's highest rewards. One incontestable piece of evidence in support of this assertion is the fact that I have been here speaking to you for an entire week, and that you have been listening; and for that, and for very much more, I thank you.

That last has the ring of a concluding sentence, but before we adjourn I must remember to tell you the end of the story with which this series of lectures began. You will recall that my colleague was finally able to recognize his student as one of my victims and to hear her question ("Is there a text in this class?") as an inquiry into his theoretical beliefs and therefore as an inquiry into the nature of the standards and accepted practices that would be in force in his classroom. I have deliberately withheld his final reply because if I had reported it earlier you might have heard in it a ringing defense of determinate meaning as something available independently of social and institutional circumstances. But if I have been at all persuasive, you will now be able to hear it as a testimony to the power of social and institutional circumstances to establish norms of behavior not despite, but because of, the absence of transcendental norms. He said: "Yes, there *is* a text in this class; what's more, it has meanings; and I am going to tell you what they are."

PART FIVE

PSYCHOANALYSIS AND MYTH CRITICISM

SIGMUND FREUD

The best-known statement by Freud on creative writing is a mixture of admiration and condescension.* Even if we "laymen" knew how creative writers are able to make such a powerful impression on us, this knowledge would never help make creative writers out of us, says Freud, ingenuously including himself among the laymen. At the same time, Freud connects creative writing to the wish-fulfillment fantasies of childhood —playing and pretending. Everyone fantasizes, but adults are ashamed to admit the fact, since a happy person never has occasion to fantasize. Novelists are able to sell their fantasies to us because they are able to remove the private nature of the fantasy, which then appears to us as our own. It is also a fact, Freud says, that fantasies are "the immediate mental precursors" of mental illness, of neurosis or psychosis. It is as a clinician that he has been able to learn so much about fantasies and their even more "shameful" nocturnal counterparts, dreams. If fantasies represent wishes we can't admit to others, dreams represent wishes we can't admit to ourselves. The conscious mind needs to be asleep for them to emerge at all. When they do, they are disguised. Freud learned how to read the disguises of dreams. The "dream-work" is the repertory of techniques that the unconscious mind uses in its dark masquerades. These techniques constitute a rhetoric which Freud elaborates at length in Chapter VI of *The Interpretation of Dreams* (1900). A compact version of this rhetoric appears in *Introductory Lectures on Psychoanalysis* (1916), Lecture XI.

The "poet" of sleep employs four techniques. The first, condensation, ensures that many dream-thoughts are compressed into a brief, composite structure, the best illustration of which perhaps is the slip of the tongue: a biology professor is speaking of "experiments" (*Versuche*) regarding female genitalia but says "temptations" (*Versuchungen*) instead. The second, *displacement,* operates on the principle of adjacency: a man scolds a child for reaching into the dish with his fingers, though an adult sitting next to the child had done the same thing, causing the original annoyance. The third technique translates abstractions into images of things, since the unconscious has no way, besides similarity (*das Gleichwie*), to represent logical relations. For example, a *Dobostorte,* an Austrian cake of many layers, each coated with carmelized sugar and hard to cut through, represents an image of a mind impenetrable to analysis. "Regressive transformation" is the device that is the

*Sigmund Freud, "Creative Writers and Day-Dreaming," in *The Standard Edition of the Complete Psychological Works of Sigmund Freud,* rev. and ed. James Strachey (New York: Basic books, 1966). See Volume 9. The article dates from 1908.

source of so much "vulgar Freudianism," involving neckties, plows, muffs, and furrows. The fourth technique is secondary revision, the order superimposed on the dream-text by the patient who relates it to his analyst, obscuring its meaning further by "clearing it up." As Freud points out, these devices are not unrelated to discoveries in other fields, especially those in the "development of speech and thought." (See especially Roman Jakobson and Hayden White on the "master tropes.")

When Freud applies his interpretive methods to literature, he finds the author's "regressive revision" has, like the authors of dreams, obscured the very meaning in which the analyst is most interested. "The Theme of the Three Caskets" (1913), reprinted here, refers to the three-woman constellation which Freud finds not only in *The Merchant of Venice* and *King Lear* but in Cinderella, Apuleius' Psyche story, and the beauty contests of Paris. In the deep, rather *fin de siècle* drift of the three-woman story, psychoanalytically, whenever it appears, remains the three fates, the third of whom, the fairest, wisest, and most loyal, is Atropos, the goddess of death. In *King Lear,* imaginative activity has repressed the truth of the Moerae by effecting a wishful reversal. Lear is an old man, and old men are dying men. The silent daughter, Cordelia, the goddess of death, is Lear's true partner, the woman unto whom he must cleave, for whom he must renounce all others.

The Dream-Work[1]
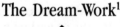
1916

Translated by James Strachey

LADIES AND GENTLEMEN,—When you have thoroughly grasped the dream-censorship and representation by symbols, you will not yet, it is true, have completely mastered the distortion in dreams, but you will nevertheless be in a position to understand most dreams. In

THE DREAM-WORK   reprinted from *Introductory Lectures on Psychoanalysis* by Sigmund Freud, trans. by James Strachey, by permission of W. W. Norton & Company, Inc. Copyright © 1966 by W. W. Norton & Company, Inc. Copyright © 1965, 1964, 1963 by James Strachey. Copyright 1920, 1935 by Edward L. Bernays.

1. [The whole of Chapter VI of *I. of D.* (over a third of the entire book) is devoted to the dream-work.]

doing so you will make use of both of the two complementary techniques: calling up ideas that occur to the dreamer till you have penetrated from the substitute to the genuine thing and, on the ground of your own knowledge, replacing the symbols by what they mean. Later on we shall discuss some uncertainties that arise in this connection.

We can now take up once more a task that we tried to carry out previously with inadequate means, when we were studying the relations between the elements of dreams and the genuine things they stood for. We laid down four main relations of the kind [Lect. VII]: the relation of a part to a whole, approximation or allusion, the symbolic relation and the plastic representation of words. We now propose to undertake the same thing on a larger scale, by comparing the manifest content of a dream *as a whole* with the latent dream as it is revealed by interpretation.

I hope you will never again confuse these two things with each other. If you reach that point, you will probably have gone further in understanding dreams than most readers of my *Interpretation of Dreams*. And let me remind you once again that the work which transforms the latent dream into the manifest one is called the *dream-work*. The work which proceeds in the contrary direction, which endeavours to arrive at the latent dream from the manifest one, is our *work of interpretation*. This work of interpretation seeks to undo the dream-work. The dreams of infantile type which we recognize as obvious fulfilments of wishes have nevertheless experienced some amount of dream-work—they have been transformed from a wish into an actual experience and also, as a rule, from thoughts into visual images. In their case there is no need for interpretation but only for undoing these two transformations. The additional dream-work that occurs in other dreams is called 'dream-distortion', and this has to be undone by our work of interpretation.

Having compared the interpretations of numerous dreams, I am in a position to give you a summary description of what the dream-work does with the material of the latent dream-thoughts. I beg you, however, not to try to understand too much of what I tell you. It will be a piece of description which should be listened to with quiet attention.

The first achievement of the dream-work is *condensation*.[2] By that

2. [Condensation is discussed, with numerous examples, in Section A of Chapter VI of *I. of D.*]

we understand the fact that the manifest dream has a smaller content than the latent one, and is thus an abbreviated translation of it. Condensation can on occasion be absent; as a rule it is present, and very often it is enormous. It is never changed into the reverse; that is to say, we never find that the manifest dream is greater in extent or content than the latent one. Condensation is brought about (1) by the total omission of certain latent elements, (2) by only a fragment of some complexes in the latent dream passing over into the manifest one and (3) by latent elements which have something in common being combined and fused into a single unity in the manifest dream.

If you prefer it, we can reserve the term 'condensation' for the last only of these processes. Its results are particularly easy to demonstrate. You will have no difficulty in recalling instances from your own dreams of different people being condensed into a single one. A composite figure of this kind may look like A perhaps, but may be dressed like B, may do something that we remember C doing, and at the same time we may know that he is D. This composite structure is of course emphasizing something that the four people have in common. It is possible, naturally, to make a composite structure out of things or places in the same way as out of people, provided that the various things and places have in common something which is emphasized by the latent dream. The process is like constructing a new and transitory concept which has this common element as its nucleus. The outcome of this superimposing of the separate elements that have been condensed together is as a rule a blurred and vague image, like what happens if you take several photographs on the same plate.[3]

The production of composite structures like these must be of great importance to the dream-work, since we can show that, where in the first instance the common elements necessary for them were missing, they are deliberately introduced—for instance, through the choice of the words by which a thought is expressed. We have already come across condensations and composite structures of this sort. They played a part in the production of some slips of the tongue. You will recall the young man who offered to *'begleitdigen'* [*'begleiten* (accompany)' + *'beleidigen* (insult)'] a lady. Moreover, there are

---

3. [Freud more than once compared the result of condensation with Francis Galton's 'composite photographs', e.g. Chapter IV of *I of D*.]

jokes of which the technique is based on a condensation like this.[4] But apart from these cases, it may be said that the process is something quite unusual and strange. It is true that counterparts to the construction of these composite figures are to be found in some creations of our imagination, which is ready to combine into a unity components of things that do not belong together in our experience —in the centaurs, for instance, and the fabulous beasts which appear in ancient mythology or in Böcklin's pictures. The 'creative' imagination, indeed, is quite incapable of *inventing* anything; it can only combine components that are strange to one another. But the remarkable thing about the procedure of the dream-work lies in what follows. The material offered to the dream-work consists of thoughts —a few of which may be objectionable and unacceptable, but which are correctly constructed and expressed. The dream-work puts these thoughts into another form, and it is a strange and incomprehensible fact that in making this translation (this rendering, as it were, into another script or language) these methods of merging or combining are brought into use. After all, a translation normally endeavours to preserve the distinctions made in the text and particularly to keep things that are similar separate. The dream-work, quite the contrary, tries to condense two different thoughts by seeking out (like a joke) an ambiguous word in which the two thoughts may come together. We need not try to understand this feature all at once, but it may become important for our appreciation of the dream-work.

But although condensation makes dreams obscure, it does not give one the impression of being an effect of the dream-censorship. It seems traceable rather to some mechanical or economic factor, but in any case the censorship profits by it.

The achievements of condensation can be quite extraordinary. It is sometimes possible by its help to combine two quite different latent trains of thought into one manifest dream, so that one can arrive at what appears to be a sufficient interpretation of a dream and yet in doing so can fail to notice a possible 'over-interpretation'.[5]

In regard to the connection between the latent and the manifest

---

4. [This technique is discussed, with many examples, in the first section of Chapter II of Freud's book on jokes (1905c), (Norton, 1960).]

5. [This is commented on at several points in *I. of D.*, e.g., near the end of Chapter VII, Section A. An example of such a second interpretation will be found in Chapter IV in *I. of D.*]

dream, condensation results also in no simple relation being left between the elements in the one and the other. A manifest element may correspond simultaneously to several latent ones, and, contrariwise, a latent element may play a part in several manifest ones—there is, as it were, a criss-cross relationship [Lect. VII]. In interpreting a dream, moreover, we find that the associations to a single manifest element need not emerge in succession: we must often wait till the whole dream has been interpreted.

Thus the dream-work carries out a very unusual kind of transcription of the dream-thoughts: it is not a word-for-word or a sign-for-sign translation; nor is it a selection made according to fixed rules—as though one were to reproduce only the consonants in a word and to leave out the vowels; nor is it what might be described as a representative selection—one element being invariably chosen to take the place of several; it is something different and far more complicated.

The second achievement of the dream-work is *displacement*.[6] Fortunately we have made some preliminary examination of this: for we know that it is entirely the work of the dream-censorship. It manifests itself in two ways: in the first, a latent element is replaced not by a component part of itself but by something more remote—that is, by an allusion; and in the second, the psychical accent is shifted from an important element on to another which is unimportant, so that the dream appears differently centred and strange.

Replacing something by an allusion to it is a process familiar in our waking thought as well, but there is a difference. In waking thought the allusion must be easily intelligible, and the substitute must be related in its subject-matter to the genuine thing it stands for. Jokes, too, often make use of allusion. They drop the precondition of there being an association in subject matter, and replace it by unusual external[7] associations such as similarity of sound, verbal ambiguity, and so on. But they retain the precondition of intelligibility: a joke would lose all its efficiency if the path back from the allusion to the

6. [Displacement is the subject of Section B of Chapter VI of *I. of D.,* but it comes up for discussion at a great many other places in the book.]

7. [An 'external' association is one that is based not on the *meaning* of the two associated words, but on superficial connections (such as similarity of sound) or purely accidental ones.]

genuine thing could not be followed easily.[8] The allusions employed for displacement in dreams have set themselves free from both of these restrictions. They are connected with the element they replace by the most external and remote relations and are therefore unintelligible; and when they are undone, their interpretation gives the impression of being a bad joke[9] or of an arbitrary and forced explanation dragged in by the hair of its head. For the dream-censorship only gains its end if it succeeds in making it impossible to find the path back from the allusion to the genuine thing.

Displacement of accent is unheard-of as a method of expressing thoughts. We sometimes make use of it in waking thought in order to produce a comic effect. I can perhaps call up the impression it produces of going astray if I recall an anecdote. There was a blacksmith in a village, who had committed a capital offense. The Court decided that the crime must be punished; but as the blacksmith was the only one in the village and was indispensable, and as on the other hand there were three tailors living there, one of *them* was hanged instead.[10]

The third achievement of the dream-work is psychologically the most interesting. It consists in transforming thoughts into visual images.[11] Let us keep it clear that this transformation does not affect *everything* in the dream-thoughts; some of them retain their form and appear as thoughts or knowledge in the manifest dream as well; nor are visual images the only form into which thoughts are transformed. Nevertheless they comprise the essence of the formation of dreams; this part of the dream-work is, as we already know, the second most regular one [Lect.VIII], and we have already made the acquaintance of the 'plastic' representation of words in the case of individual dream-elements [Lect. VII].

It is clear that this achievement is not an easy one. To form some

8. [An account of the 'allusion' technique of jokes with a number of examples appears in Section II of Chapter II of the book on jokes (1905c), (Norton, 1960). The necessity for their being easily intelligible is discussed ibid., 150.]
9. [This is further discussed on Lecture XV below.]
10. [This was a favourite anecdote of Freud's. He told it ten years earlier than this in his book on jokes (1905c), p. 206, and again eight years later in *The Ego and the Id* (1923b), (Norton, 1960), p. 45.]
11. [The main discussion of this is in Section C of Chapter VI of *I. of D.*]

idea of its difficulties, let us suppose that you have undertaken the task of replacing a political leading article in a newspaper by a series of illustrations. You will thus have been thrown back from alphabetic writing to picture writing. In so far as the article mentioned people and concrete objects you will replace them easily and perhaps even advantageously by pictures; but your difficulties will begin when you come to the representation of abstract words and of all those parts of speech which indicate relations between thoughts—such as particles, conjunctions and so on. In the case of abstract words you will be able to help yourselves out by means of a variety of devices. For instance, you will endeavour to give the text of the article a different wording, which may perhaps sound less usual but which will contain more components that are concrete and capable of being represented. You will then recall that most abstract words are 'watered-down' concrete ones, and you will for that reason hark back as often as possible to the original concrete meaning of such words. Thus you will be pleased to find that you can represent the 'possession' of an object by a real, physical sitting down on it.[12] And the dream-work does just the same thing. In such circumstances you will scarcely be able to expect very great accuracy from your representation: similarly, you will forgive the dream-work for replacing an element so hard to put into pictures as, for example, 'adultery' [*'Ehebruch'*, literally, 'breach of marriage'], by another breach—a broken leg *'Beinbruch'*].[13] And in this way you will succeed to some extent in

12. [The German word *'besitzen'* ('to possess') is more obviously connected with sitting than its English equivalent (*'sitzen'* = 'to sit'). An example of 'sitting down on' in a dream with the meaning of 'possession' occurred in one of the dreams of 'Little Hans'. See Section II of his case history (1909*b*), *Standard Ed.*, **10**, 37 and 39.]
13. While I am correcting the proofs of these pages chance has put into my hands a newspaper cutting which offers an unexpected confirmation of what I have written above:—

'DIVINE PUNISHMENT

'A Broken Arm for a Broken Marriage.

'Frau Anna M., wife of a militiaman, sued Frau Klementine K. for adultery. According to the statement of claim, Frau K. had carried on an illicit relationship with Karl M., while her own husband was at the front and was actually making her an allowance of 70 Kronen [about £3.10 or $17] a month. Frau K. had already received a considerable amount of money from the plaintiff's husband, while she and her child had to live in hunger and poverty. Fellow-soldiers of her husband had informed her that Frau K. had visited taverns with M. and had sat there drinking till far into the night. On one occasion the defendant had asked the

compensating for the clumsiness of the picture writing that is supposed to take the place of the alphabetic script.

For representing the parts of speech which indicate relations between thoughts—'because', 'therefore', 'however', etc.—you will have no similar aids at your disposal; those constituents of the text will be lost so far as translation into pictures goes. In the same way, the dream-work reduces the content of the dream-thoughts to its raw material of objects and activities. You will feel pleased if there is a possibility of in some way hinting, through the subtler details of the pictures, at certain relations not in themselves capable of being represented. And just so does the dream-work succeed in expressing some of the content of the latent dream-thoughts by peculiarities in the *form* of the manifest dream—by its clarity or obscurity, by its division into several pieces, and so on. The number of part-dreams into which a dream is divided usually corresponds to the number of main topics or groups of thoughts in the latent dream. A short introductory dream will often stand in the relation of a prelude to a following, more detailed, main dream or may give the motive for it[14]; a subordinate clause in the dream-thoughts will be replaced by the interpolation of a change of scene into the manifest dream, and so on. Thus the form of dreams is far from being without significance and itself calls for interpretation. When several dreams occur during the

---

plaintiff's husband in the presence of several other soldiers whether he would not get a divorce soon from "his old woman" and set up with her. Frau K.'s caretaker also reported that she had repeatedly seen the plaintiff's husband in the house most incompletely dressed.

'Before a court in the Leopoldstadt [district of Vienna] Frau K. yesterday denied knowing M., so that there could be no question of her having intimate relations with him.

'A witness, Albertine M., stated, however, that she had surprised Frau K. kissing the plaintiff's husband.

'At a previous hearing, M., under examination as a witness, had denied having intimate relations with the defendant. Yesterday the Judge received a letter in which the witness withdrew the statements he had made on the earlier occasion and admitted that he had had a love-affair with Frau K. up till the previous June. He had only denied his relations with the defendant at the former hearing because she had come to him before the hearing and begged him on her knees to save her and say nothing. "Today", the witness wrote, "I feel compelled to make a full confession to the Court, for I have broken my left arm and this seems to me to be a divine punishment for my wrong-doing."

'The Judge stated that the penal offence had lapsed under the statute of limitations. The plaintiff then withdrew her claim and the defendant was discharged.'

14. [This is discussed, with an example, in Section C of Chapter VI of *I. of D.*]

same night, they often have the same meaning and indicate that an attempt is being made to deal more and more efficiently with a stimulus of increasing insistence. In individual dreams a particularly difficult element may be represented by several symbols—by 'doublets'.[15]

If we make a series of comparisons between the dream-thoughts and the manifest dreams which replace them, we shall come upon all kinds of things for which we are unprepared: for instance, that nonsense and absurdity in dreams have their meaning. At this point, indeed, the contrast between the medical and the psycho-analytic view of dreams reaches a pitch of acuteness not met with elsewhere. According to the former, dreams are senseless because mental activity in dreams has abandoned all its powers of criticism; according to our view, on the contrary, dreams become senseless when a piece of criticism included in the dream-thoughts—a judgement that 'this is absurd'—has to be represented. The dream you are familiar with of the visit to the theatre ('three tickets for 1 florin 50') [Lect. VII] is a good example of this. The judgement it expressed was: 'it was absurd to marry so early.'[16]

Similarly, in the course of our work of interpretation we learn what it is that corresponds to the doubts and uncertainties which the dreamer so often expresses as to whether a particular element occurred in a dream, whether it was this or whether, on the contrary, it was something else. There is as a rule nothing in the latent dream-thoughts corresponding to these doubts and uncertainties; they are entirely due to the activity of the dream-censorship and are to be equated with an attempt at elimination which has not quite succeeded.[17]

Among the most surprising findings is the way in which the dream-work treats contraries that occur in the latent dream. We know already [Lect. XI] that conformities in the latent material are replaced by condensations in the manifest dream. Well, contraries are treated in the same way as conformities, and there is a special preference for

15. [In philology the term is used of two different words with the same etymology: e.g. 'fashion' and 'faction', both from the Latin 'factio'.]
16. [Absurdity in dreams is discussed in Section G of Chapter VI of *I. of D.*]
17. [Cf. Section A of Chapter VII in *I. of D.* Doubt as a symptom of obsessional neurosis is discussed in Lecture XVII.]

expressing them by the same manifest element. Thus an element in the manifest dream which is capable of having a contrary may equally well be expressing either itself or its contrary or both together: only the sense can decide which translation is to be chosen. This connects with the further fact that a representation of 'no'—or at any rate an unambiguous one—is not to be found in dreams.

A welcome analogy to this strange behaviour of the dream-work is provided for us in the development of language. Some philologists have maintained that in the most ancient languages contraries such as 'strong—weak', 'light—dark', 'big—small' are expressed by the same verbal roots. (What we term 'the antithetical meaning of primal words.') Thus in Ancient Egyptian *'ken'* originally meant 'strong' and 'weak'. In speaking, misunderstanding from the use of such ambivalent words was avoided by differences of intonation and by the accompanying gesture, and in writing, by the addition of what is termed a 'determinative'—a picture which is not itself intended to be spoken. For instance, *'ken'* meaning 'strong' was written with a picture of a little upright man after the alphabetic signs; when *'ken'* stood for 'weak', what followed was the picture of a man squatting down limply. It was only later, by means of slight modifications of the original homologous word, that two distinct representations were arrived at of the contraries included in it. Thus from *'ken'* 'strong —weak' were derived *'ken'* 'strong' and *'kan'* 'weak'. The remains of this ancient antithetical meaning seem to have been preserved not only in the latest developments of the oldest languages but also in far younger ones and even in some that are still living. Here is some evidence of this, derived from K. Abel (1884).[18]

In Latin, words that remained ambivalent in this way are *'altus'* ('high' and 'deep') and *'sacer'* ('sacred' and 'accursed').

As instances of modifications of the same root I may mention *'clamare'* ('to cry'), *'clam'* ('softly', 'quietly', 'secretly'); *'siccus'* ('dry'), *'succus'* ('juice'). And in German: *'Stimme'* ['voice'], *'stumm'* ['dumb'].

If we compare related languages, there are numerous examples. In English, 'to lock'; in German, *'Loch'* ['hole'] and *'Lücke'* ['gap']. In English, 'to cleave'; in German, *'kleben'* ['to stick'].

---

18. [Freud wrote a long review of Abel's monograph (1910c), from which much of what he says here is quoted in a condensed form. He returns to the subject in Lecture XV.]

The English word 'without' (which is really 'with—without') is used to-day for 'without' alone. 'With', in addition to its combining sense, originally had a removing one; this is still to be seen in the compounds 'withdraw' and 'withhold'. Similarly with the German *'wieder'* ['together with' and *'wider'* 'against'].

Another characteristic of the dream-work also has its counterpart in the development of language. In Ancient Egyptian, as well as in other, later languages, the order of the sounds in a word can be reversed, while keeping the same meaning. Examples of this in English and German are: *'Topf'* ['pot']—'pot'; 'boat'—'tub'; 'hurry' — *'Ruhe'* ['rest']; *'Balken'* ['beam']— *'Kloben'* ['log'] and 'club'; 'wait' — *'täuwen'* ['tarry']. Similarly in Latin and German: *'capere'*—packen' ['to seize']; *'ren'*—*'Niere'* ['kidney'].

Reversals like this, which occur here with individual words, take place in various ways in the dream-work. We already know reversal of meaning, replacement of something by its opposite [Lect. XI]. Besides this we find in dreams reversals of situation, of the relation between two people—a 'topsy-turvy' world. Quite often in dreams it is the hare that shoots the sportsman. Or again we find a reversal in the order of events, so that what precedes an event causally comes after it in the dream—like a theatrical production by a third-rate touring company, in which the hero falls down dead and the shot that killed him is not fired in the wings till afterwards. Or there are dreams where the whole order of the elements is reversed, so that to make sense in interpreting it we must take the last one first and the first one last. You will remember too from our study of dream-symbolism that going or falling into the water means the same as coming out of it—that is, giving birth or being born [Lect. X], and that climbing up a staircase or a ladder is the same thing as coming down it [Lect. X]. It is not hard to see the advantage that dream-distortion can derive from this freedom of representation.

These features of the dream-work may be described as *archaic*. They are equally characteristic of ancient systems of expression by speech and writing and they involve the same difficulties, which we shall have to discuss again later in a critical sense.[19]

And now a few more considerations. In the case of the dream-work it is clearly a matter of transforming the latent thoughts which are expressed in words into sensory images, mostly of a visual sort. Now

19. [See Lecture XIII below.]

our thoughts originally arose from sensory images of that kind: their first material and their preliminary stages were sense impressions, or, more properly, mnemic images of such impressions. Only later were words attached to them and the words in turn linked up into thoughts. The dream-work thus submits thoughts to a *regressive* treatment[20] and undoes their development; and in the course of the regression everything has to be dropped that had been added as a new acquisition in the course of the development of the mnemic images into thoughts.

Such then, it seems, is the dream-work. As compared with the processes we have come to know in it, interest in the manifest dream must pale into insignificance. But I will devote a few more remarks to the latter, since it is of it alone that we have immediate knowledge.

It is natural that we should lose some of our interest in the manifest dream. It is bound to be a matter of indifference to us whether it is well put together, or is broken up into a series of disconnected separate pictures. Even if it has an apparently sensible exterior, we know that this has only come about through dream-distortion and can have as little organic relation to the internal content of the dream as the façade of an Italian church has to its structure and plan. There are other occasions when this façade of the dream *has* its meaning, and reproduces an important component of the latent dream-thoughts with little or no distortion. But we cannot know this before we have submitted the dream to interpretation and have been able to form a judgement from it as to the amount of distortion that has taken place. A similar doubt arises when two elements in a dream appear to have been brought into a close relation to each other. This may give us a valuable hint that we may bring together what corresponds to these elements in the latent dream as well; but on other occasions we can convince ourselves that what belongs together in the dream-thoughts has been torn apart in the dream.

In general one must avoid seeking to explain one part of the manifest dream by another, as though the dream had been coherently conceived and was a logically arranged narrative. On the contrary, it is as a rule like a piece of breccia, composed of various fragments of rock held together by a binding medium, so that the designs that appear on it do not belong to the original rocks imbedded in it. And

20. [The subject of 'regression' is discussed at length in Lecture XXII.]

there is in fact one part of the dream-work, known as 'secondary revision',[21] whose business it is to make something whole and more or less coherent out of the first products of the dream-work. In the course of this, the material is arranged in what is often a completely misleading sense and, where it seems necessary, interpolations are made in it.

On the other hand, we must not over-estimate the dream-work and attribute too much to it. The achievements I have enumerated exhaust its activity; it can do no more than condense, displace, represent in plastic form and subject the whole to a secondary revision.[22] What appear in the dream as expressions of judgement, of criticism, of astonishment or of inference—none of these are achievements of the dream-work and they are very rarely expressions of afterthoughts about the dream; they are for the most part portions of the latent dream-thoughts which have passed over into the manifest dream with a greater or less amount of modification and adaptation to the context. Nor can the dream-work compose speeches. With a few assignable exceptions, speeches in dreams are copies and combinations of speeches which one has heard or spoken oneself on the day before the dream and which have been included in the latent thoughts either as material or as the instigator of the dream.[23] The dream-work is equally unable to carry out calculations. Such of them as appear in the manifest dream are mostly combinations of numbers, sham calculations which are quite senseless *quâ* calculations and are once again only copies of calculations in the latent dream-thoughts.[24] In these circumstances it is not to be wondered at that the interest which had turned to the dream-work soon tends to move away from it to the latent dream-thoughts, which are revealed, distorted to a greater or less degree, by the manifest dream. But there is no justification for carrying this shift of interest so far that, in looking at the matter theoretically, one replaces the dream entirely by the latent dream-thoughts and makes some assertion about the former which only applies to the latter. It is strange that the findings of psycho-analysis could be misused to bring about this confusion. One cannot give the name of 'dream' to anything other

21. [This is the subject of Section I of Chapter VI of *I. of D.*]
22. [Elsewhere Freud excluded secondary revision from the dreamwork, cf. 'An Evidential Dream' (1913*a*).]
23. [Cf. *I. of D.*, Last part of Section F of Chapter VI.]
24. [Cf. *I. of D.*, the discussion of calculations in dreams in Chapter VI (F).]

than the product of the dream-work—that is to say, the *form* into which the latent thoughts have been transmuted by the dream-work. [Cf. Lect. XIV.]

The dream-work is a process of quite a singular kind, of which the like has not yet become known in mental life. Condensations, displacements, regressive transformations of thoughts into images —such things are novelties whose discovery has already richly rewarded the labours of psycho-analysis. And you can see once more, from the parallels to the dream-work, the connections which have been revealed between psycho-analytic studies and other fields —especially those concerned in the development of speech and thought. You will only be able to form an idea of the further significance of these discoveries when you learn that the mechanism of dream-construction is the model of the manner in which neurotic symptoms arise.

I am also aware that we are not yet able to make a survey of the whole of the new acquisitions which these studies have brought to psychology. I will only point out the fresh proofs they have provided of the existence of unconscious mental acts—for this is what the latent dream-thoughts are—and what an unimaginably broad access to a knowledge of unconscious mental life we are promised by the interpretation of dreams.

But now the time has no doubt come for me to demonstrate to you from a variety of small examples of dreams what I have been preparing you for in the course of these remarks.

The Theme of the Three Caskets

1913

Translated by James Strachey

I

Two scenes from Shakespeare, one from a comedy and the other from a tragedy, have lately given me occasion for posing and solving a small problem.

The first of these scenes is the suitors' choice between the three caskets in *The Merchant of Venice*. The fair and wise Portia is bound at her father's bidding to take as her husband only that one of her suitors who chooses the right casket from among the three before him. The three caskets are of gold, silver and lead: the right casket is the one that contains her portrait. Two suitors have already departed unsuccessful: they have chosen gold and silver. Bassanio, the third, decides in favour of lead; thereby he wins the bride, whose affection was already his before the trial of fortune. Each of the suitors gives reasons for his choice in a speech in which he praises the metal he prefers and depreciates the other two. The most difficult task thus falls to the share of the fortunate third suitor; what he finds to say in glorification of lead as against gold and silver is little and has a forced ring. If in psycho-analytic practice we were confronted with such a speech, we should suspect that there were concealed motives behind the unsatisfying reasons produced.

Shakespeare did not himself invent this oracle of the choice of a casket; he took it from a tale in the *Gesta Romanorum*,[1] in which a girl

THE THEME OF THE THREE CASKETS from Collected Papers of Sigmund Freud, Volume 4. Authorized translation under the supervision of Joan Riviere. Published by Basic Books, Inc. by arrangement with the Hogarth Press Ltd and The Institute of Psycho-Analysis, London. Reprinted by permission of Basic Books, Inc., Publishers.

1. [A mediaeval collection of stories of unknown authorship.]

has to make the same choice to win the Emperor's son.[2] Here too the third metal, lead, is the bringer of fortune. It is not hard to guess that we have here an ancient theme, which requires to be interpreted, accounted for and traced back to its origin. A first conjecture as to the meaning of this choice between gold, silver and lead is quickly confirmed by a statement of Stucken's,[3] who has made a study of the same material over a wide field. He writes: 'The identity of Portia's three suitors is clear from their choice: the Prince of Morocco chooses the gold casket—he is the sun; the Prince of Arragon chooses the silver casket—he is the moon; Bassanio chooses the leaden casket—he is the star youth.' In support of this explanation he cites an episode from the Estonian folk-epic 'Kalewipoeg', in which the three suitors appear undisguisedly as the sun, moon and star youths (the last being 'the Pole-star's eldest boy') and once again the bride falls to the lot of the third.

Thus our little problem has led us to an astral myth! The only pity is that with this explanation we are not at the end of the matter. The question is not exhausted, for we do not share the belief of some investigators that myths were read in the heavens and brought down to earth; we are more inclined to judge with Otto Rank[4] that they were projected on to the heavens after having arisen elsewhere under purely human conditions. It is in this human content that our interest lies.

Let us look once more at our material. In the Estonian epic, just as in the tale from the *Gesta Romanorum,* the subject is a girl choosing between three suitors; in the scene from *The Merchant of Venice* the subject is apparently the same, but at the same time something appears in it that is in the nature of an inversion of the theme: a *man* chooses between three—caskets. If what we were concerned with were a dream, it would occur to us at once that caskets are also women, symbols of what is essential in woman, and therefore of a woman herself—like coffers, boxes, cases, baskets, and so on.[5] If we boldly assume that there are symbolic substitutions of the same kind in myths as well, then the casket scene in *The Merchant of Venice* really becomes the inversion we suspected. With a wave of the wand,

---

2. Brandes (1896).
3. Stucken (1907 655).
4. Rank (1909, 8 ff.).
5. [See *The Interpretation of Dreams* (1900a), *Standard Ed.,* **5,** 354.]

as though we were in a fairy tale, we have stripped the astral garment from our theme; and now we see that the theme is a human one, *a man's choice between three women.*

This same content, however, is to be found in another scene of Shakespeare's, in one of his most powerfully moving dramas; not the choice of a bride this time, yet linked by many hidden similarities to the choice of the casket in *The Merchant of Venice.* The old King Lear resolves to divide his kingdom while he is still alive among his three daughters, in proportion to the amount of love that each of them expresses for him. The two elder ones, Goneril and Regan, exhaust themselves in asseverations and laudations of their love for him; the third, Cordelia, refuses to do so. He should have recognized the unassuming, speechless love of his third daughter and rewarded it, but he does not recognize it. He disowns Cordelia, and divides the kingdom between the other two, to his own and the general ruin. Is not this once more the scene of a choice between three women, of whom the youngest is the best, the most excellent one?

There will at once occur to us other scenes from myths, fairy tales and literature, with the same situation as their content. The shepherd Paris has to choose between three goddesses, of whom he declares the third to be the most beautiful. Cinderella, again, is a youngest daughter, who is preferred by the prince to her two elder sisters. Psyche, in Apuleius's story, is the youngest and fairest of three sisters. Psyche is, on the one hand, revered as Aphrodite in human form; on the other, she is treated by that goddess as Cinderella was treated by her stepmother and is set the task of sorting a heap of mixed seeds, which she accomplishes with the help of small creatures (doves in the case of Cinderella, ants in the case of Psyche).[6] Anyone who cared to make a wider survey of the material would undoubtedly discover other versions of the same theme preserving the same essential features.

Let us be content with Cordelia, Aphrodite, Cinderella and Psyche. In all the stories the three women, of whom the third is the most excellent one, must surely be regarded as in some way alike if they are represented as sisters. (We must not be led astray by the fact that Lear's choice is between three *daughters;* this may mean nothing

---

6. I have to thank Dr. Otto Rank for calling my attention to these similarities. [Cf. a reference to this in Chapter XII of *Group Psychology* (1921*c*), *Standard Ed.,* **18,** 136.]

more than that he has to be represented as an old man. An old man cannot very well choose between three women in any other way. Thus they become his daughters.)

But who are these three sisters and why must the choice fall on the third? If we could answer this question, we should be in possession of the interpretation we are seeking. We have once already made use of an application of psycho-analytic technique, when we explained the three caskets symbolically as three women. If we have the courage to proceed in the same way, we shall be setting foot on a path which will lead us first to something unexpected and incomprehensible, but which will perhaps, by a devious route, bring us to a goal.

It must strike us that this excellent third woman has in several instances certain peculiar qualities besides her beauty. They are qualities that seem to be tending towards some kind of unity; we must certainly not expect to find them equally well marked in every example. Cordelia makes herself unrecognizable, inconspicuous like lead, she remains dumb, she 'loves and is silent'.[7] Cinderella hides so that she cannot be found. We may perhaps be allowed to equate concealment and dumbness. These would of course be only two instances out of the five we have picked out. But there is an intimation of the same thing to be found, curiously enough, in two other cases. We have decided to compare Cordelia, with her obstinate refusal, to lead. In Bassanio's short speech while he is choosing the casket, he says of lead (without in any way leading up to the remark):

'Thy paleness[8] moves me more than eloquence.'

That is to say: 'Thy plainness moves me more than the blatant nature of the other two.' Gold and silver are 'loud'; lead is dumb—in fact like Cordelia, who 'loves and is silent'.[9]

In the ancient Greek accounts of the Judgement of Paris, nothing is said of any such reticence on the part of Aphrodite. Each of the three goddesses speaks to the youth and tries to win him by promises. But, oddly enough, in a quite modern handling of the same scene this characteristic of the third one which has struck us makes its appearance again. In the libretto of Offenbach's *La Belle Hélène,* Paris, after

7. [From an aside of Cordelia's, Act I, Scene 1.]
8. 'Plainness' according to another reading.
9. In Schlegel's translation this allusion is quite lost; indeed, it is given the opposite meaning: 'Dein schlichtes Wesen spricht beredt mich an.' ['Thy plainness speaks to me with eloquence.']

telling of the solicitations of the other two goddesses, describes Aphrodite's behaviour in this competition for the beauty-prize:

> La troisième, ah! la troisième . . .
> La troisième ne dit rien.
> Elle eut le prix tout de même . . .[10]

If we decide to regard the pecularities of our 'third one' as concentrated in her 'dumbness', then psycho-analysis will tell us that in dreams dumbness is a common representation of death.[11]

More than ten years ago a highly intelligent man told me a dream which he wanted to use as evidence of the telepathic nature of dreams. In it he saw an absent friend from whom he had received no news for a very long time, and reproached him energetically for his silence. The friend made no reply. It afterwards turned out that he had met his death by suicide at about the time of the dream. Let us leave the problem of telepathy on one side:[12] there seems, however, not to be any doubt that here the dumbness in the dream represented death. Hiding and being unfindable—a thing which confronts the prince in the fairy tale of Cinderella three times, is another unmistakable symbol of death in dreams; so, too, is a marked pallor, of which the 'paleness' of the lead in one reading of Shakespeare's text is a reminder.[13] It would be very much easier for us to transpose these interpretations from the language of dreams to the mode of expression used in the myth that is now under consideration if we could make it seem probable that dumbness must be interpreted as a sign of being dead in productions other than dreams.

At this point I will single out the ninth story in Grimm's *Fairy Tales,* which bears the title 'The Twelve Brothers'.[14] A king and a queen have twelve children, all boys. The king declares that if the thirteenth child is a girl, the boys will have to die. In expectation of her birth he has twelve coffins made. With their mother's help the twelve sons take

---

10. [Literally: 'The third one, ah! the third one . . . the third one said nothing. She won the prize all the same.'—The quotation is from Act I, Scene 7, of Meilhac and Halévy's libretto. In the German version used by Freud 'the third one' *'blieb stumm'*—'remained dumb'.]

11. In Stekel's *Sprache des Traumes,* too, dumbness is mentioned among the 'death' symbols (1911a, 351). [Cf. *The Interpretation of Dreams* (1900a), *Standard Ed.,* **5,** 357.]

12. [Cf. Freud's later paper on 'Dreams and Telepathy' (1922a).]

13. Stekel (1911a), loc. cit.

14. ['Die zwölf Brüder.' Grimm, 1918, **1,** 42.]

refuge in a hidden wood, and swear death to any girl they may meet. A girl is born, grows up, and learns one day from her mother that she has had twelve brothers. She decides to seek them out, and in the wood she finds the youngest; he recognizes her, but is anxious to hide her on account of the brothers' oath. The sister says: 'I will gladly die, if by so doing I can save my twelve brothers.' The brothers welcome her affectionately, however, and she stays with them and looks after their house for them. In a little garden beside the house grow twelve lilies. The girl picks them and gives one to each brother. At that moment the brothers are changed into ravens, and disappear, together with the house and garden. (Ravens are spirit-birds; the killing of the twelve brothers by their sister is represented by the picking of the flowers, just as it is at the beginning of the story by the coffins and the disappearance of the brothers.) The girl, who is once more ready to save her brothers from death, is now told that as a condition she must be dumb for seven years, and not speak a single word. She submits to the test, which brings her herself into mortal danger. She herself, that is, dies for her brothers, as she promised to do before she met them. By remaining dumb she succeeds at last in setting the ravens free.

In the story of 'The Six Swans'[15] the brothers who are changed into birds are set free in exactly the same way—they are restored to life by their sister's dumbness. The girl has made a firm resolve to free her brothers, 'even if it should cost her her life'; and once again (being the wife of the king) she risks her own life because she refuses to give up her dumbness in order to defend herself against evil accusations.

It would certainly be possible to collect further evidence from fairy tales that dumbness is to be understood as representing death. These indications would lead us to conclude that the third one of the sisters between whom the choice is made is a dead woman. But she may be something else as well—namely, Death itself, the Goddess of Death. Thanks to a displacement that is far from infrequent, the qualities that a deity imparts to men are ascribed to the deity himself. Such a displacement will surprise us least of all in relation to the Goddess of Death, since in modern versions and representations, which these stories would thus be forestalling, Death itself is nothing other than a dead man.

But if the third of the sisters is the Goddess of Death, the sisters are

<hr/>

15. ['Die sechs Schwäne.' Grimm, 1918, **1**, 217. (No. 49.)]

known to us. They are the Fates, the Moerae, the Parcae or the Norns, the third of whom is called Atropos, the inexorable.

II

We will for the time being put aside the task of inserting the interpretation that we have found into our myth, and listen to what the mythologists have to teach us about the role and origin of the Fates.[16]

The earliest Greek mythology (in Homer) only knew a single *Moiρa*, personifying inevitable fate. The further development of this one Moera into a company of three (or less often two) sister-goddesses probably came about on the basis of other divine figures to which the Moerae were closely related—the Graces and the Horae [the Seasons].

The Horae were originally goddesses of the waters of the sky, dispensing rain and dew, and of the clouds from which rain falls; and, since the clouds were conceived of as something that has been spun, it came about that these goddesses were looked upon as spinners, an attribute that then became attached to the Moerae. In the sun-favoured Mediterranean lands it is the rain on which the fertility of the soil depends, and thus the Horae became vegetation goddesses. The beauty of flowers and the abundance of fruit was their doing, and they were accredited with a wealth of agreeable and charming traits. They became the divine representatives of the Seasons, and it is possibly owing to this connection that there were three of them, if the sacred nature of the number three is not a sufficient explanation. For the peoples of antiquity at first distinguished only three seasons: winter, spring and summer. Autumn was only added in late Graeco-Roman times, after which the Horae were often represented in art as four in number.

The Horae retained their relation to time. Later they presided over the times of day, as they did at first over the times of the year; and at last their name came to be merely a designation of the hours (*heure, ora*). The Norns of German mythology are akin to the Horae and the Moerae and exhibit this time-signification in their names.[17] It was

16. What follows is taken from Roscher's lexicon [1884–1937], under the relevant headings.
17. [Their names may be rendered: 'What was', 'What is', 'What shall be'.]

inevitable, however, that a deeper view should come to be taken of the essential nature of these deities, and that their essence should be transposed on to the regularity with which the seasons change. The Horae thus became the guardians of natural law and of the divine Order which causes the same thing to recur in Nature in an unalterable sequence.

This discovery of Nature reacted on the conception of human life. The nature-myth changed into a human myth: the weather-goddesses became goddesses of Fate. But this aspect of the Horae found expression only in the Moerae, who watch over the necessary ordering of human life as inexorably as do the Horae over the regular order of nature. The ineluctable severity of Law and its relation to death and dissolution, which had been avoided in the charming figures of the Horae, were now stamped upon the Moerae, as though men had only perceived the full seriousness of natural law when they had to submit their own selves to it.

The names of the three spinners, too, have been significantly explained by mythologists. Lachesis, the name of the second, seems to denote 'the accidental that is included in the regularity of destiny'[18]—or, as we should say, 'experience'; just as Atropos stands for 'the ineluctable'—Death. Clotho would then be left to mean the innate disposition with its fateful implications.

But now it is time to return to the theme which we are trying to interpret—the theme of the choice between three sisters. We shall be deeply disappointed to discover how unintelligible the situations under review become and what contradictions of their apparent content result, if we apply to them the interpretation that we have found. On our supposition the third of the sisters is the Goddess of Death, Death itself. But in the Judgement of Paris she is the Goddess of Love, in the tale of Apuleius she is someone comparable to the goddess for her beauty, in *The Merchant of Venice* she is the fairest and wisest of women, in *King Lear* she is the one loyal daughter. We may ask whether there can be a more complete contradiction. Perhaps, improbable though it may seem, there is a still more complete one lying close at hand. Indeed, there certainly is; since, whenever our theme occurs, the choice between the women is free, and yet it falls on death. For, after all, no one chooses death, and it is only by a fatality that one falls a victim to it.

However, contradictions of a certain kind—replacements by the

18. Roscher [ibid.], quoting Preller, ed. Robert (1894).

precise opposite—offer no serious difficulty to the work of analytic interpretation. We shall not appeal here to the fact that contraries are so often represented by one and the same element in the modes of expression used by the unconscious, as for instance in dreams.[19] But we shall remember that there are motive forces in mental life which bring about replacement by the opposite in the form of what is known as reaction-formation; and it is precisely in the revelation of such hidden forces as these that we look for the reward of this enquiry. The Moerae were created as a result of a discovery that warned man that he too is a part of nature and therefore subject to the immutable law of death. Something in man was bound to struggle against this subjection, for it is only with extreme unwillingness that he gives up his claim to an exceptional position. Man, as we know, makes use of his imaginative activity in order to satisfy the wishes that reality does not satisfy. So his imagination rebelled against the recognition of the truth embodied in the myth of the Moerae, and constructed instead the myth derived from it, in which the Goddess of Death was replaced by the Goddess of Love and by what was equivalent to her in human shape. The third of the sisters was no longer Death; she was the fairest, best, most desirable and most lovable of women. Nor was this substitution in any way technically difficult: it was prepared for by an ancient ambivalence, it was carried out along a primaeval line of connection which could not long have been forgotten. The Goddess of Love herself, who now took the place of the Goddess of Death, had once been identical with her. Even the Greek Aphrodite had not wholly relinquished her connection with the underworld, although she had long surrendered her chthonic role to other divine figures, to Persephone, or to the tri-form Artemis-Hecate. The great Mother-goddesses of the oriental peoples, however, all seem to have been both creators and destroyers—both goddesses of life and fertility and goddesses of death. Thus the replacement by a wishful opposite in our theme harks back to a primaeval identity.

The same consideration answers the question how the feature of a choice came into the myth of the three sisters. Here again there has been a wishful reversal. Choice stands in the place of necessity, of destiny. In this way man overcomes death, which he has recognized intellectually. No greater triumph of wish fulfilment is conceivable. A choice is made where in reality there is obedience to a compulsion;

19. [Cf. *The Interpretation of Dreams* (1900*a*), *Standard Ed.*, 4, 318.]

and what is chosen is not a figure of terror, but the fairest and most desirable of women.

On closer inspection we observe, to be sure, that the original myth is not so thoroughly distorted that traces of it do not show through and betray its presence. The free choice between the three sisters is, properly speaking, no free choice, for it must necessarily fall on the third if every kind of evil is not to come about, as it does in *King Lear.* The fairest and best of women, who has taken the place of the Death-goddess, has kept certain characteristics that border on the uncanny, so that from them we have been able to guess at what lies beneath.[20]

So far we have been following out the myth and its transformation, and it is to be hoped that we have correctly indicated the hidden causes of the transformation. We may now turn our interest to the way in which the dramatist has made use of the theme. We get an impression that a reduction of the theme to the original myth is being carried out in his work, so that we once more have a sense of the moving significance which had been weakened by the distortion. It is by means of this reduction of the distortion, this partial return to the original, that the dramatist achieves his more profound effect upon us.

To avoid misunderstandings, I should like to say that it is not my purpose to deny that King Lear's dramatic story is intended to inculcate two wise lessons: that one should not give up one's possessions and rights during one's lifetime, and that one must guard against accepting flattery at its face value. These and similar warnings are undoubtedly brought out by the play; but it seems to me quite impossible to explain the overpowering effect of *King Lear* from the impression that such a train of thought would produce, or to suppose

20. The Psyche of Apuleius's story has kept many traits that remind us of her relation with death. Her wedding is celebrated like a funeral, she has to descend into the underworld, and afterwards she sinks into a death-like sleep (Otto Rank).—On the significance of Psyche as goddess of the spring and as 'Bride of Death', cf. Zinzow (1881).—In another of Grimm's Tales ('The Goose-girl at the Fountain' ['Die Gänsehirtin am Brunnen', 1918, **2,** 300], No. 179) there is, as in 'Cinderella', an alternation between the beautiful and the ugly aspect of the third sister, in which one may no doubt see an indication of her double nature—before and after the substitution. This third daughter is repudiated by her father, after a test which is almost the same as the one in *King Lear.* Like her sisters, she has to declare how fond she is of their father, but can find no expression for her love but a comparison with salt. (Kindly communicated by Dr. Hanns Sachs.)

that the dramatist's personal motives did not go beyond the intention of teaching these lessons. It is suggested, too, that his purpose was to present the tragedy of ingratitude, the sting of which he may well have felt in his own heart, and that the effect of the play rests on the purely formal element of its artistic presentation; but this cannot, so it seems to me, take the place of the understanding brought to us by the explanation we have reached of the theme of the choice between the three sisters.

Lear is an old man. It is for this reason, as we have already said, that the three sisters appear as his daughters. The relationship of a father to his children, which might be a fruitful source of many dramatic situations, is not turned to further account in the play. But Lear is not only an old man: he is a dying man. In this way the extraordinary premiss of the division of his inheritance loses all its strangeness. But the doomed man is not willing to renounce the love of women; he insists on hearing how much he is loved. Let us now recall the moving final scene, one of the culminating points of tragedy in modern drama. Lear carries Cordelia's dead body on to the stage. Cordelia is Death. If we reverse the situation it becomes intelligible and familiar to us. She is the Death-goddess who, like the Valkyrie in German mythology, carries away the dead hero from the battlefield. Eternal wisdom, clothed in the primaeval myth, bids the old man renounce love, choose death and make friends with the necessity of dying.

The dramatist brings us nearer to the ancient theme by representing the man who makes the choice between the three sisters as aged and dying. The regressive revision which he has thus applied to the myth, distorted as it was by wishful transformation, allows us enough glimpses of its original meaning to enable us perhaps to reach as well a superficial allegorical interpretation of the three female figures in the theme. We might argue that what is represented here are the three inevitable relations that a man has with a woman—the woman who bears him, the woman who is his mate and the woman who destroys him; or that they are the three forms taken by the figure of the mother in the course of a man's life—the mother herself, the beloved one who is chosen after her pattern, and lastly the Mother Earth who receives him once more. But it is in vain that an old man yearns for the love of woman as he had it first from his mother; the third of the Fates alone, the silent Goddess of Death, will take him into her arms.

JACQUES LACAN

In her book on Lacan, Catherine Clément says that Lacan "perhaps has never *thought* anything else besides the mirror stage," that everything he has to say is already there *en germe.** What, then, seems to be there? Lacan's first paragraph of "The Mirror Stage," unmistakably, is an attack on the *cogito* of Cartesian tradition, that apparently self-present, self-transparent thinking process which persists after everything else has been subjected to doubt. What Descartes did not consider, however, was the fact that this pristine cogitation was contaminated already by the fact that it was speaking, contaminated by language, which had seeped in somehow from the outside.† Freud had said in his *Introductory Lectures* (XVIII) that his research provided the third great moment in the disorientation of man. Copernicus had shown that earth was not the center of the universe, and Darwin had said that man was not the privileged center of nature. The significance of Freud's work, finally, is that the ego is not master in its own house. Precisely this aspect of Freud had been forgotten, when after the Second World War psychoanalysis migrated to America and adapted—to its considerable financial advantage—a way of life alien to it—optimistic, naive, unreflecting, without the faintest notion of the death drive, without any sense at all of the dialectic at the heart of things.** Psychoanalysis became ego-centered in America, with the point of therapy being for the patient to adjust happily to the world as he or she found it. For Lacan no such adjustment is possible. There is no reconciliation of self with society or even of the self with itself. The reason for this permanent self-estrangement is the way the ego is formed. The mirror stage is an allegory for this process. Perhaps it is also something that literally happens. Before six months of age, a child has no clear sense of self, no sense of where its body begins or ends. There is a polymorphous melting together of its body and other objects. When the child sees its image in the mirror, it sees itself objectified and whole. It still *feels* turbulent animation, but its specular image is stable. This moment precipitates the primordial *I*, for Lacan. We discover the self, but when

---

*Catherine Clément, *The Lives and Legends of Jacques Lacan,* trans. Arthur Gold-hammer (New York: Columbia University Press, 1983) 100–101. Quoted in Jane Gallop, *Reading Lacan* (Ithaca and London: Cornell University Press, 1985) 77.

†William Richardson, "Lacan and the Subject of Psychoanalysis," in *Psychiatry and the Humanities* VI, *Interpreting Lacan* (New Haven and London: Yale University Press, 1983) 58–59.

**Stuart Schneiderman, *Jacques Lacan, The Death of an Intellectual Hero* (Cambridge and London: Harvard University Press, 1983) 157 ff.

we do, it is outside. No matter that the child is jubilant at first. Its joy will soon turn to anxiety as it projects itself into history, toward the future, and toward a specular ideal with which it will never coincide until its death collapses difference, the future is erased, and it becomes precisely what it has become. This rather Heideggerian scenario is the best one can do. The worst is to think the social self, that crumbling fortress formed by the order into which we are born, that name our family gives us, that role we play in the public world, is who we really are. Any point of view based on the autonomy of the ego—existentialism, for example—is deluded. The ego is a fiction, a misunderstanding. Lacan's practice, especially the maddening short session, was designed to stop the "secondary revision," the procrastination, the logical reordering by the ego of what the unconscious was trying to say (Schneiderman 129 ff.). For this reason Lacan is considered a surrealist among psychoanalysts, breaking the crust of reason beneath which the magma of primordial babble is seething. To read this primordial magmatic text, one must notice the unconscious disruptions of public language, puns, wordplay, metaphors —all the devices of the dream-work given to us by Freud. One reads against the grain of the public text. The ego is a logician. The "it," the unconscious, is a poet, repressed as we are colonized through language by our public role. The colonization is the moment of the Oedipus complex. While we are still in the jubilant polymorphic condition of the Imaginary, the mother belongs to us, responding to every movement, every desire, like our mirror image. We are all the mother desires, just as the mother is all we desire. That this notion of completion is erroneous we discover in the father's prohibition of incest, his law, his "no" (le Nom [Non] du Père). He represents the Symbolic Order. It tells us that we must abandon the narcissistic notion that we complete the mother's desire, are the "phallus" for her, as Lacan would say. Our desire constitutes the unconscious, which is the place where desire collects after it is deflected from its object into indefinite postponement. We must look elsewhere for what we've lost. But no subsequent object of our desire ever really is the object of our desire, hence "the centrifugal tendency of the genital drive in love life."* To read, for example, Madame Bovary in a Lacanian way, as Tony Tanner does, is to discover that the main character, Emma, is after all, not only an idle, foolish, and petulant woman, but also the very image of the tragic human project as it tries to name its desire, tries vainly to squeeze plenitude out of objects which can't provide it, until desire itself is stilled by a mouthful of arsenic.†

*Jacques Lacan, *Écrits,* trans. Alan Sheridan (New York and London: Norton, 1977) 290.

†Tony Tanner, *Adultery in the Novel* (Baltimore: Johns Hopkins University Press, 1979).

The Mirror Stage as Formative of the Function of the I as Revealed in Psychoanalytic Experience

1949

Translated by Alan Sheridan

The conception of the mirror stage that I introduced at our last congress, thirteen years ago, has since become more or less established in the practice of the French group. However, I think it worthwhile to bring it again to your attention, especially today, for the light it sheds on the formation of the *I* as we experience it in psychoanalysis. It is an experience that leads us to oppose any philosophy directly issuing from the *Cogito.*

Some of you may recall that this conception originated in a feature of human behaviour illuminated by a fact of comparative psychology. The child, at an age when he is for a time, however short, outdone by the chimpanzee in instrumental intelligence, can nevertheless already recognize as such his own image in a mirror. This recognition is indicated in the illuminative mimicry of the *Aha-Erlebnis,* which Köhler sees as the expression of situational apperception, an essential stage of the act of intelligence.

This act, far from exhausting itself, as in the case of the monkey, once the image has been mastered and found empty, immediately rebounds in the case of the child in a series of gestures in which he experiences in play the relation between the movements assumed in the image and the reflected environment, and between this virtual complex and the reality it reduplicates—the child's own body, and the persons and things, around him.

This event can take place, as we have known since Baldwin, from the age of six months, and its repetition has often made me reflect

THE MIRROR STAGE AS FORMATIVE OF THE FUNCTION OF THE I AS REVEALED IN PSYCHOANALYTIC EXPERIENCE   by Jacques Lacan from *Écrits, A Selection,* trans. Alan Sheridan. Reprinted with kind permission of Associated Book Publishers (U. K.) Ltd.

upon the startling spectacle of the infant in front of the mirror. Unable as yet to walk, or even to stand up, and held tightly as he is by some support, human or artificial (what, in France, we call a *'trotte-bébé'*), he nevertheless overcomes, in a flutter of jubilant activity, the obstructions of his support and, fixing his attitude in a slightly leaning-forward position, in order to hold it in his gaze, brings back an instantaneous aspect of the image.

For me, this activity retains the meaning I have given it up to the age of eighteen months. This meaning discloses a libidinal dynamism, which has hitherto remained problematic, as well as an ontological structure of the human world that accords with my reflections on paranoiac knowledge.

We have only to understand the mirror stage *as an identification,* in the full sense that analysis gives to the term: namely, the transformation that takes place in the subject when he assumes an image —whose predestination to this phase-effect is sufficiently indicated by the use, in analytic theory, of the ancient term *imago.*

This jubilant assumption of his specular image by the child at the *infans* stage, still sunk in his motor incapacity and nursling dependence, would seem to exhibit in an exemplary situation the symbolic matrix in which the *I* is precipitated in a primordial form, before it is objectified in the dialectic of identification with the other, and before language restores to it, in the universal, its function as subject.

This form would have to be called the Ideal-I,[1] if we wished to incorporate it into our usual register, in the sense that it will also be the source of secondary identifications, under which term I would place the functions of libidinal normalization. But the important point is that this form situates the agency of the ego, before its social determination, in a fictional direction, which will always remain irreducible for the individual alone, or rather, which will only rejoin the coming-into-being (*le devenir*) of the subject asymptotically, whatever the success of the dialectical syntheses by which he must resolve as *I* his discordance with his own reality.

The fact is that the total form of the body by which the subject anticipates in a mirage the maturation of his power is given to him only as *Gestalt,* that is to say, in an exteriority in which this form is certainly more constituent than constituted, but in which it appears

---

1. Throughout this article I leave in its peculiarity the translation I have adopted for Freud's *Ideal-Ich* [i.e., 'je-idéal'], without further comment, other than to say that I have not maintained it since.

to him above all in a contrasting size (*un relief de stature*) that fixes it and in a symmetry that inverts it, in contrast with the turbulent movements that the subject feels are animating him. Thus, this *Gestalt*—whose pregnancy should be regarded as bound up with the species, though its motor style remains scarcely recognizable—by these two aspects of its appearance, symbolizes the mental permanence of the *I*, at the same time as it prefigures its alienating destination; it is still pregnant with the correspondences that unite the *I* with the statue in which man projects himself, with the phantoms that dominate him, or with the automaton in which, in an ambiguous relation, the world of his own making tends to find completion.

Indeed, for the *imagos*—whose veiled faces it is our privilege to see in outline in our daily experience and in the penumbra of symbolic efficacity[2]—the mirror-image would seem to be the threshold of the visible world, if we go by the mirror disposition that the *imago of one's own body* presents in hallucinations or dreams, whether it concerns its individual features, or even its infirmities, or its object-projections; or if we observe the role of the mirror apparatus in the appearances of the *double,* in which psychical realities, however heterogeneous, are manifested.

That a *Gestalt* should be capable of formative effects in the organism is attested by a piece of biological experimentation that is itself so alien to the idea of psychical causality that it cannot bring itself to formulate its results in these terms. It nevertheless recognizes that it is a necessary condition for the maturation of the gonad of the female pigeon that it should see another member of its species, of either sex; so sufficient in itself is this condition that the desired effect may be obtained merely by placing the individual within reach of the field of reflection of a mirror. Similarly, in the case of the migratory locust, the transition within a generation from the solitary to the gregarious form can be obtained by exposing the individual, at a certain stage, to the exclusively visual action of a similar image, provided it is animated by movements of a style sufficiently close to that characteristic of the species. Such facts are inscribed in an order of homeomorphic identification that would itself fall within the larger question of the meaning of beauty as both formative and erogenic.

But the facts of mimicry are no less instructive when conceived as cases of heteromorphic identification, in as much as they raise the

---

2. Cf. Claude Lévi-Strauss, *Structural Anthropology,* Chapter X.

problem of the signification of space for the living organism
—psychological concepts hardly seem less appropriate for shedding
light on these matters than ridiculous attempts to reduce them to the
supposedly supreme law of adaptation. We have only to recall how
Roger Caillois (who was then very young, and still fresh from his
breach with the sociological school in which he was trained)
illuminated the subject by using the term *'legendary psychasthenia'*
to classify morphological mimicry as an obsession with space in its
derealizing effect.

I have myself shown in the social dialectic that structures human
knowledge as paranoiac[3] why human knowledge has greater autonomy than animal knowledge in relation to the field of force of desire,
but also why human knowledge is determined in that 'little reality'
(*ce peu de réalité*), which the Surrealists, in their restless way, saw as
its limitation. These reflections lead me to recognize in the spatial
captation manifested in the mirror-stage, even before the social
dialectic, the effect in man of an organic insufficiency in his natural
reality—in so far as any meaning can be given to the word 'nature'.

I am led, therefore, to regard the function of the mirror-stage as a
particular case of the function of the *imago*, which is to establish a
relation between the organism and its reality—or, as they say,
between the *Innenwelt* and the *Umwelt.*

In man, however, this relation to nature is altered by a certain
dehiscence at the heart of the organism, a primordial Discord
betrayed by the signs of uneasiness and motor unco-ordination of the
neo-natal months. The objective notion of the anatomical incompleteness of the pyramidal system and likewise the presence of
certain humoral residues of the maternal organism confirm the view I
have formulated as the fact of a real *specific prematurity of birth* in
man.

It is worth noting, incidentally, that this is a fact recognized as such
by embryologists, by the term *foetalization,* which determines the
prevalence of the so-called superior apparatus of the neurax, and
especially of the cortex, which psycho-surgical operations lead us to
regard as the intra-organic mirror.

This development is experienced as a temporal dialectic that
decisively projects the formation of the individual into history. The
mirror stage is a drama whose internal thrust is precipitated from
insufficiency to anticipation—and which manufactures for the sub-

3. Cf. 'Aggressivity in Psychoanalysis', p. 8 and *Écrits,* p. 180.

ject, caught up in the lure of spatial identification, the succession of phantasies that extends from a fragmented body-image to a form of its totality that I shall call orthopaedic—and, lastly, to the assumption of the armour of an alienating identity, which will mark with its rigid structure the subject's entire mental development. Thus, to break out of the circle of the *Innenwelt* into the *Umwelt* generates the inexhaustible quadrature of the ego's verifications.

This fragmented body—which term I have also introduced into our system of theoretical references—usually manifests itself in dreams when the movement of the analysis encounters a certain level of aggressive disintegration in the individual. It then appears in the form of disjointed limbs, or of those organs represented in exoscopy, growing wings and taking up arms for intestinal persecutions—the very same that the visionary Hieronymus Bosch has fixed, for all time, in painting, in their ascent from the fifteenth century to the imaginary zenith of modern man. But this form is even tangibly revealed at the organic level, in the lines of 'fragilization' that define the anatomy of phantasy, as exhibited in the schizoid and spasmodic symptoms of hysteria.

Correlatively, the formation of the *I* is symbolized in dreams by a fortress, or a stadium—its inner arena and enclosure, surrounded by marshes and rubbish-tips, dividing it into two opposed fields of contest where the subject flounders in quest of the lofty, remote inner castle whose form (sometimes juxtaposed in the same scenario) symbolizes the id in a quite startling way. Similarly, on the mental plane, we find realized the structures of fortified works, the metaphor of which arises spontaneously, as if issuing from the symptoms themselves, to designate the mechanisms of obsessional neurosis —inversion, isolation, reduplication, cancellation and displacement.

But if we were to build on these subjective givens alone—however little we free them from the condition of experience that makes us see them as partaking of the nature of a linguistic technique—our theoretical attempts would remain exposed to the charge of project-ing themselves into the unthinkable of an absolute subject. This is why I have sought in the present hypothesis, grounded in a conjunc-tion of objective data, the guiding grid for a *method of symbolic reduction.*

It establishes in the *defences of the ego* a genetic order, in accordance with the wish formulated by Miss Anna Freud, in the first part of her great work, and situates (as against a frequently expressed prejudice) hysterical repression and its returns at a more archaic stage than obsessional inversion and its isolating processes, and the latter in turn as preliminary to paranoic alienation, which dates from the deflection of the specular *I* into the social *I*.

This moment in which the mirror-stage comes to an end inaugurates, by the identification with the *imago* of the counterpart and the drama of primordial jealousy (so well brought out by the school of Charlotte Bühler in the phenomenon of infantile *transitivism*), the dialectic that will henceforth link the *I* to socially elaborated situations.

It is this moment that decisively tips the whole of human knowledge into mediatization through the desire of the other, constitutes its objects in an abstract equivalence by the co-operation of others, and turns the I into that apparatus for which every instinctual thrust constitutes a danger, even though it should correspond to a natural maturation—the very normalization of this maturation being henceforth dependent, in man, on a cultural mediation as exemplified, in the case of the sexual object, by the Oedipus complex.

In the light of this conception, the term primary narcissism, by which analytic doctrine designates the libidinal investment characteristic of that moment, reveals in those who invented it the most profound awareness of semantic latencies. But it also throws light on the dynamic opposition between this libido and the sexual libido, which the first analysts tried to define when they invoked destructive and, indeed, death instincts, in order to explain the evident connection between the narcissistic libido and the alienating function of the *I,* the aggressivity it releases in any relation to the other, even in a relation involving the most Samaritan of aid.

In fact, they were encountering that existential negativity whose reality is so vigorously proclaimed by the contemporary philosophy of being and nothingness.

But unfortunately that philosophy grasps negativity only within the limits of a self-sufficiency of consciousness, which, as one of its premises, links to the *méconnaissances* that constitute the ego, the illusion of autonomy to which it entrusts itself. This flight of fancy, for all that it draws, to an unusual extent, on borrowings from psychoanalytic experience, culminates in the pretention of providing an existential psychoanalysis.

At the culmination of the historical effort of a society to refuse to recognize that it has any function other than the utilitarian one, and in the anxiety of the individual confronting the 'concentrational'[4] form of the social bond that seems to arise to crown this effort, existentialism must be judged by the explanations it gives of the subjective impasses that have indeed resulted from it; a freedom that is never more authentic than when it is within the walls of a prison; a demand for commitment, expressing the impotence of a pure consciousness to master any situation; a voyeuristic-sadistic idealization of the sexual relation; a personality that realizes itself only in suicide; a consciousness of the other that can be satisfied only by Hegelian murder.

These propositions are opposed by all our experience, in so far as it teaches us not to regard the ego as centered on the *perception-consciousness system*, or as organized by the 'reality principle'—a principle that is the expression of a scientific prejudice most hostile to the dialectic of knowledge. Our experience shows that we should start instead from the *function of méconnaissance* that characterizes the ego in all its structures, so markedly articulated by Miss Anna Freud. For, if the *Verneinung* represents the patent form of that function, its effects will, for the most part, remain latent, so long as they are not illuminated by some light reflected on to the level of fatality, which is where the id manifests itself.

We can thus understand the inertia characteristic of the formations of the *I*, and find there the most extensive definition of neurosis—just as the captation of the subject by the situation gives us the most general formula for madness, not only the madness that lies behind the walls of asylums, but also the madness that deafens the world with its sound and fury.

The sufferings of neurosis and psychosis are for us a schooling in the passions of the soul, just as the beam of the psychoanalytic scales, when we calculate the tilt of its threat to entire communities, provides us with an indication of the deadening of the passions in society.

At this junction of nature and culture, so persistently examined by modern anthropology, psychoanalysis alone recognizes this knot of imaginary servitude that love must always undo again, or sever.

---

4. *'Concentrationnaire'*, an adjective coined after World War II (this article was written in 1949) to describe the life of the concentration-camp. In the hands of certain writers it became, by extension, applicable to many aspects of 'modern' life [Tr.].

For such a task, we place no trust in altruistic feeling, we who lay bare the aggressivity that underlies the activity of the philanthropist, the idealist, the pedagogue, and even the reformer.

In the recourse of subject to subject that we preserve, psychoanalysis may accompany the patient to the ecstatic limit of the *'Thou art that'*, in which is revealed to him the cipher of his mortal destiny, but it is not in our mere power as practitioners to bring him to that point where the real journey begins.

RENÉ GIRARD

The great danger to human communities is collective violence. It is a contagion, a plague, in the sense that it spreads from one person to another until it destroys the community. It spreads through imitation, as does sexual desire, which is closely connected to violence, not only because the biochemical changes are identical both in sexual excitement and violent aggression in general, but because both are associated with the shedding of blood, "such a very special juice," as Mephistopheles says in *Faust* (Ln. 1740).* Vengeance is the form mimetic violence takes, and unless there is some "braking mechanism" in the culture, everyone will become involved and order will collapse in an orgy of bloodletting. In the past, religion has provided this braking mechanism in the surrogate victim, someone who accepts all violence from all sides without returning it. In the surrogate, reciprocal violence becomes unanimous violence, exercised upon one victim whose fate purifies the community in one spasm of sacrifice. It is not necessary that he be the actual source of the "contagion"; it is only important that he is seen to be by the collectivity. His sacrifice allows him to become sacred; the scapegoat becomes the savior. ". . . All drama," says Girard, "is a mimetic reenactment of a scapegoat process." Sophocles' Oedipus plays are an example. Mere positivistic literary scholarship can never give us the faintest recognition of the true significance of drama, because the true significance is, in the end, religious. The secularization of western culture has made the necessary misunderstanding and metonymic displacement of unanimous victimage seem more rational by substituting the legal system for the scapegoat procedure. Supposedly independent and disinterested, the legal system applies vengeance directly to the guilty party in the name of society as a whole, thus limiting the spread of vengeance. With secularization, all is not well, but *not* because the judicial system is not really a disinterested entity. Demystification of the scapegoat mechanism obliterates the distinction between bad violence and purifying violence. There are still victims, to be sure, but they lose their sacredness. Now we merely hate them and kill them. We can't conceive of their transfiguration anymore, nor can they therefore as victims reconcile the community. Religion can protect only as long as its foundations are not visible. "To remove men's ignorance is only to risk exposing them to an even greater peril. The only barrier against human violence is raised on misconception" (135). One detects in Girard's apparent recommendation of

*René Girard, *Violence and the Sacred,* trans. Patrick Gregory (Baltimore and London: Johns Hopkins University Press, 1977) 33 ff.

the irrational a kinship with Bataille, that great acepalic who considered renewing the sense of community by an affirmation of frenzy and sacrifice.† In his case, though, and for Lacan as well, the enemy is the ego, reason, rigidity, and order. For Girard it is order that must be preserved by sacrifice. One surrogate victim is a small price to pay for the preservation of a well-ordered community.** Of course now that religious mechanisms have been exposed—albeit in part by Girard himself—there is nothing to do but renounce violence altogether, a rather suspicious solution, actually, for one who has explained that the murder of Abel by Cain took place precisely because Cain, unlike his gentle lamb-sacrificing brother, had no *other* sacrificial outlet (*Violence:*4).

The Plague in Literature and Myth

The plague is found everywhere in literature. It belongs to the epic with Homer, to tragedy with *Oedipus Rex,* to history with Thucydides, to the philosophical poem with Lucretius. The plague can serve as background to the short stories of Boccaccio's *Decameron;* there are fables about the plague, notably La Fontaine's "Les Animaux malades de la peste"; there are novels, such as Manzoni's *I Promessi Sposi* and Camus's *La Peste.* The theme spans the whole range of literary and even nonliterary genres, from pure fantasy to the most positive and scientific accounts. It is older than literature

THE PLAGUE IN LITERATURE AND MYTH   by René Girard from *To Double Business Bound: Essays on Literature, Mimesis, and Anthropology.* Copyright © 1978 by The Johns Hopkins University Press. Reprinted with permission of The Johns Hopkins University Press.
This essay first appeared in *Texas Studies in Literature and Language* 15 (Special Classics Issue 1974): 833–850.

†Georges Bataille, *Visions of Excess,* trans. Allan Stoekl (Minneapolis: University of Minnesota Press, 1985) 210, xx.
** "An Interview with René Girard," in *To Double Business Bound* (Baltimore and London: Johns Hopkins, 1978) 228.

—much older, really, since it is present in myth and ritual in the entire world.

The subject appears too vast for a brief exploration. Undoubtedly, a descriptive enumeration of literary and mythical plagues would be of little interest: there is a strange uniformity to the various treatments of the plague, not only literary and mythical but also scientific and nonscientific, of both past and present. Between the matter-of-fact, even statistical account of Defoe in his *Journal of the Plague Year* and the near hysteria of Artaud in *Le Théâtre et la peste,* the differences, at close range, turn out to be minor. It would be exaggerated to say that plague descriptions are all alike, but the similarities may well be more intriguing than the individual variations. The curious thing about these similarities is that they ultimately involve the very notion of the similar. The plague is universally presented as a process of undifferentiation, a destruction of specificities.

This destruction is often preceded by a reversal. The plague will turn the honest man into a thief, the virtuous man into a lecher, the prostitute into a saint. Friends murder and enemies embrace. Wealthy men are made poor by the ruin of their business. Riches are showered upon paupers who inherit in a few days the fortunes of many distant relatives. Social hierarchies are first transgressed, then abolished. Political and religious authorities collapse. The plague makes all accumulated knowledge and all categories of judgment invalid. It was traditionally believed that the plague attacked the strong and young in preference to the weak and old, the healthy rather than the chronically ill. Modern authorities do not believe that great epidemics really singled out any particular individuals or categories. The popular belief must have arisen from the fact that it is more surprising and shocking to see the death of the young and healthy than of the old and the sick. The scientific view, it must be noted, fits the eternal ethos of the plague just as well and better than the popular tradition. The distinctiveness of the plague is that it ultimately destroys all forms of distinctiveness. The plague overcomes all obstacles, disregards all frontiers. All life, finally, is turned into death, which is the supreme undifferentiation. Most written accounts insist monotonously on this leveling of differences. So does the medieval *danse macabre,* which, of course, is inspired by the plague.

This process of undifferentiation makes sense, obviously, and poses no special problem in the sociological sphere. The belief that a great plague epidemic can bring about a social collapse is not difficult to accept or irrational in any way; it can be based on positive observation. At the beginning of the modern age, when plague epidemics had not yet disappeared and the spirit of scientific investigation was already awakened, texts can be found that clearly distinguish the medical plague from its social consequences and yet continue to see a similarity. The French surgeon Ambroise Paré, for instance, writes:

> At the outbreak of the plague, even the highest authorities are likely to flee, so that the administration of justice is rendered impossible and no one can obtain his rights. General anarchy and confusion then set in and that is the worst evil by which the commonwealth can be assailed; *for that is the moment when the dissolute bring another and worse plague into the town.* [emphasis mine][1]

This sequence of events is perfectly positive and rational. The reverse sequence is no less so. A social upheaval can bring about conditions favorable to an outbreak of the plague. Historians still argue whether the Black Death was a cause or a consequence of the social upheavals in the fourteenth century.

Between the plague and social disorder there is a reciprocal affinity, but it does not completely explain the confusion of the two that prevails not only in innumerable myths but in a good number of literary plagues, from ancient times to contemporary culture. The Greek mythical plague not only kills men but provokes a total interruption of all cultural and natural activities; it causes the sterility of women and cattle and prevents the fields from yielding crops. In many parts of the world, the words we translate as "plague" can be viewed as a generic label for a variety of ills that affect the community as a whole and threaten or seem to threaten the very existence of social life. It may be inferred from various signs that interhuman tensions and disturbances often play the principal role.

In the passage just quoted, Paré separates what primitive thought unites—the medical and social components of the mythical plague. His language, however, is interesting. The social components are described as *another and worse plague.* Anarchy is a plague; in a sense, it is even more of a plague than the disease itself. The former unity is broken, and yet it is remembered and preserved in the stylistic effect of using the same word for two distinct and yet

---

1. Quoted in Johannes Nohl, ed., *The Black Death: A Chronicle of the Plague,* trans. C. H. Clarke (London: Unwin Books, 1961), p. 101.

curiously inseparable phenomena. The medical plague has become a metaphor for the social plague; it belongs to what we call literature.

Judging from the role of the plague in Western literature up to the present, this metaphor is endowed with an almost incredible vitality, in a world where the plague and epidemics in general have disappeared almost altogether.[2] Such vitality would be unthinkable, of course, if the social "plague" were not always with us, as fear or as reality, in some form or other. This fact is not enough, however, to account for the more obscure and persistent aspects of the metaphoric configuration as well as for what appears to be the real need it fulfills with a great many writers. Indeed, an analysis of significant texts reveals definite analogies between the plague, or rather all great epidemics, and the social phenomena, real or imagined, that are assimilated to them. One such text belongs to Dostoevski's *Crime and Punishment*. Raskolnikov has a dream during a grave illness that occurs just before his final change of heart, at the end of the novel. He dreams of a world-wide plague that affects people's relationship with each other. No specifically medical symptoms are mentioned. It is human interaction that breaks down, and the entire society gradually collapses.

> He dreamt that the whole world was condemned to a terrible new strange plague that had come to Europe from the depths of Asia. . . . Some new sorts of microbes were attacking the bodies of men, but these microbes were endowed with intelligence and will. Men attacked by them became at once mad and furious. But never had men considered themselves so intellectual and so completely in possession of the truth as these sufferers, never had they considered their decisions, their scientific conclusions, their moral convictions so infallible. Whole villages, whole towns and peoples went mad from the infection. All were excited and did not understand one another. Each thought that he alone had the truth and was wretched looking at the others, beat himself on the breast, wept, and wrung his hands. They did not know how to judge and could not agree what to consider evil and what good; they did not know whom to blame, whom to justify. Men killed each other in a sort of senseless spite. They gathered together in armies against one another, but even on the march the armies would begin attacking each other, the ranks

---

2. Concerning the symbolic significance of disease in modern literature, see Gian-Paolo Biasin, "From Anatomy to Criticism," *MLN* 86 (December 1971): 873–90.

would be broken and the soldiers would fall on each other, stabbing and cutting, biting and devouring each other. The alarm bell was ringing all day long in the towns; men rushed together, but why they were summoned and who was summoning them no one knew. The most ordinary trades were abandoned, because every one proposed his own ideas, his own improvements, and they could not agree. The land too was abandoned. Men met in groups, agreed on something, swore to keep together, but at once began on something quite different from what they had proposed. They accused one another, fought and killed each other. There were conflagrations and famine. All men and things were involved in destruction. The plague spread and moved further and further.[3]

The plague is a transparent metaphor for a certain reciprocal violence that spreads, literally, like the plague. The appropriateness of the metaphor comes, obviously, from this contagious character. The idea of contagiousness implies the presence of something harmful, which loses none of its virulence as it is rapidly transmitted from individual to individual. Such, of course, are bacteria in an epidemic; so is violence when it is *imitated,* either positively, whenever bad example makes the usual restraints inoperative, or negatively, when the efforts to stifle violence with violence achieve no more, ultimately, than an increase in the level of violence. Counterviolence turns out to be the same as violence. In cases of massive contamination, the victims are helpless, not necessarily because they remain passive but because whatever they do proves ineffective or makes the situation worse.

In order to appreciate Raskolnikov's dream, we must read it in the context of Dostoevski's entire work, of that self-defeating mixture of pride and humiliation characteristic of Raskolnikov and other Dostoevskian heroes. The victims of the plague seem to be possessed with the same desire as Raskolnikov. Each falls prey to the same megalomania and sees himself as the one and only superman: "Each thought that he alone had the truth and looked with contempt at the others."

This desire implies a contradiction; it aims at complete autonomy, at a near divine self-sufficiency, and yet it is *imitative.* The divinity this desire is trying to capture never fails, sooner or later, to appear as the divinity of someone else, as the exclusive privilege of a model after

---

3. Fedor Dostoevski, *Crime and Punishment,* trans. Constance Garnett (New York: Random House, 1945), pp. 528–29.

whom the hero must pattern not only his behavior but his very desires, insofar as these are directed toward objects. Raskolnikov worships Napoleon. The possessed imitate Stavrogin. The spirit of worship must combine with the spirit of hatred. To reveal the secret of this ambivalence, we need not turn to someone like Freud. There is no secret at all. To imitate the desires of someone else is to turn this someone else into a rival as well as a model. From the convergence of two or more desires on the same object, conflict must necessarily arise.

The mimetic nature of desire can account for the many contradictions in the Dostoevskian hero; this one principle can make his personality truly intelligible. Imitative desire necessarily generates its own living obstacles and comes to view this failure as a sign of the model's omnipotence, as convincing proof, in other words, that this model is the right one, that the door he keeps so tightly shut must be the door to heaven. Mimetic desire cannot keep its illusions alive without falling in love with its own disastrous consequences and focusing more and more on the violence of its rivals. The mimetic attraction of violence is a major topic of Dostoevskian art. Thus, violence becomes reciprocal. In the dream of the plague, the expressions "each other," "one another" recur constantly. The great Dostoevskian novels describe mimetic breakdowns of human relations that tend to spread further and further. The dream of the plague is nothing but the quintessential expression of the Dostoevskian crisis; and, as such, it must extend that crisis to the entire world, in truly apocalyptic fashion.

From Dostoevski, I would like to turn to another writer, Shakespeare, who appears very distant but is really very close in respect to the problem at hand. I want to compare the dream of the plague, a specific passage in *Crime and Punishment,* to a specific passage in a work of Shakespeare, the famous speech of Ulysses in *Troilus and Cressida,* a text that rests, in my view, on the same conception of a cultural crisis as the dream of the plague in Dostoevski.

First, it must be observed that *Troilus and Cressida* revolves entirely around a view of mimetic desire analogous if not identical to the one just detected in Dostoevski. The topic of the play is the decomposition of the Greek army stalled under the walls of Troy. Disorder begins at the top. Achilles imitates Agamemnon, both in the sense that he seriously aspires to his position (he wants to become the supreme ruler of the Greeks) and in the sense that he derisively mimics and parodies the commander-in-chief. Mimetic rivalry spreads from rank to rank and brings about a complete confusion:

> So every step
> Exampled by the first pace that is sick
> Of his superior, grows to an envious fever
> Of pale and bloodless emulation.
> [1.3.131–34]

These lines remind us of Raskolnikov's dream: "They gathered together in armies against one another, but even on the march the armies would begin attacking each other, the ranks would be broken and the soldiers would fall on each other."

Mimetic desire also dominates the two protagonists. No less than the political and the military, the erotic aspect of the play is an affair of worldly ambition, competitive and imitative in character. We would have to call Cressida "inauthentic" if we did not suspect that the ideal of autonomous desire by which she will be judged is itself a fruit of rampant imitation. The lovers are always open to the corruptive suggestion of spurious models or to the even worse advice of Pandarus. They are really nonheroes, always caught in a game of deception and vanity that is to real passion what the behavior of the army is to genuine military valor.

No individual or psychological approach can do justice to the scope of the phenomenon. That is why the high point of the play is that speech in which Ulysses describes a crisis so pervasive and acute that it goes beyond even the most radical notion of social crisis. The central concept, degree, from the Latin *gradus,* means a step, a measured distance, the necessary difference thanks to which two cultural objects, people, or institutions can be said to have a *being* of their own, an individual or categorical identity.

> Oh, when degree is shaked,
> Which is the ladder to all high designs,
> The enterprise is sick! How could communities,
> Degrees in schools and brotherhoods in cities,
> Peaceful commerce from dividable shores,
> The primogenitive and due of birth
> Prerogative of age, crowns, scepters, laurels,
> But by degree, stand in authentic place?
> Take but degree away, untune that string,
> And hark, what discord follows! Each thing meets

In mere oppugnancy. The bounded waters
Should lift their bosoms higher than the shores,
And make a sop of all this solid globe.
Strength should be the lord of imbecility,
And the rude son should strike his father dead.
Force should be right, or rather, right and wrong,
Between whose endless jar justice resides,
Should lose their names, and so should justice too.

[1.3.101–18]

The image of the untuned string clearly reveals that the cultural order is to be understood on the model of a melody, not as an aggregate, therefore, a mere collection of heterogeneous objects, but as a "totality" or, if we prefer, a "structure," a system of differences commanded by a single differentiating principle. Degree in the singular seems to define a purely social transcendence, almost in the sense of Durkheim, with the difference, however, that cultural systems in Shakespeare are always liable to collapse. It is with such a collapse, obviously, not with the systems themselves, that the tragic writer is preoccupied.

If mimetic desire has an object, it is degree itself; degree is vulnerable to criminal attempts from inside the structure. The thought appears irrational, but it is not. It does not mean that degree is something like an object that could be appropriated. It means exactly the opposite. If degree vanishes, becomes "vizarded" when it becomes an object of rivalry, it is precisely because it is really nothing but the absence of such rivalries in a cultural order that remains functional. The crisis, therefore, is a time of most frantic ambition that becomes more and more self-defeating. As these ambitions are mimetically multiplied, reciprocal violence grows and the differences dissolve; the "degrees" leading to the object and the object itself disintegrate. It is an ambition, therefore, that "by a pace goes backward / With a purpose it hath to climb."

As in Dostoevski's text, all constancy of purpose disappears, all useful activities are interrupted. The desire in each man to distinguish himself triggers instant imitation, multiplies sterile rivalries, produces conditions that make society unworkable through a growing uniformity. The process is one of undifferentiation that passes for extreme differentiation—false "individualism." Finally, even the most fundamental distinctions become impossible.

Shakespeare writes that "right and wrong . . . lose their names," and this is duplicated almost to the letter in Dostoevski: "They did not know how to judge and could not agree what to consider evil and what good; they did not know whom to blame, whom to justify."

In both texts, though more explicit in Shakespeare, the dominant idea is that regular human activities, however reciprocal their final results, can take place only on a basis of nonreciprocity. Constructive relationships of any type are differentiated. Ulysses certainly betrays a strong hierarchical and authoritarian bias. One should not conclude too hastily that the interest of his speech is thereby diminished. The concepts with which he operates, the very notion of the cultural order as a differential system susceptible of collapse, imply the essential *arbitrariness* of cultural differences.

When the difference goes, the relationship becomes violent and sterile as it becomes more symmetrical, as everything becomes more perfectly identical on both sides: *"Each thing meets in mere oppugnancy."* It is a relationship of doubles that emerges from the crisis. We would misunderstand this relationship if we interpreted it as a *coincidentia oppositorum,* in the tradition of philosophical idealism, or as a mere subjective reflection or hallucination, in the vein of psychological "narcissism," an approach adopted by Rank, for instance, in his essay on Don Juan and the double.

With Shakespeare, as earlier with the playwrights of classical antiquity, the relationship of doubles is perfectly real and concrete; it is the fundamental relationship of the tragic and comic antagonists. It is present among the four doubles of *A Comedy of Errors,* where it is almost identical to the relationship defined in *Troilus and Cressida* and dramatized in all of Shakespeare's plays. The fact that the doubles constantly run into each other in a desperate effort to part ways can be viewed either in a tragic or in a comic light. This is as true of Dostoevski as it is of Shakespeare. The relationship of conflictual symmetry and reciprocal fascination portrayed in the novels is fundamentally identical to what is attempted very early in the short story entitled *The Double.*

Thus, the speech of Ulysses closely parallels Raskolnikov's dream of the plague. In both these texts the authors find a way to conceptualize and generalize the same type of relationship that, in the rest of the work and in their other works, is developed in dramatic or novelistic form. The convergence of these two writers is particularly striking in view of their obvious differences of language, period, style, genre, etc. In order to be complete, the parallel should also include, on Shakespeare's side, the metaphor of the plague; and, of course, it does. In the passage quoted above, the idea of disease occurs repeatedly. Even though it does not play as prominent a role as in Raskolnikov's dream, the plague proper is not absent; it figures among the various and more or less natural disasters that accompany the crisis, as in a kind of mythical orchestration:

> What raging of the sea, shaking of the earth,
> What plagues and what portents, what mutiny
> Divert and crack, rend and deracinate
> The unity and married calm of states
> Quite from their fixture!

Looking back upon the preceding remarks, I must note that we are no longer dealing with a single theme, with the isolated plague, but with a thematic cluster that includes, besides the plague or, more generally, the theme of epidemic contamination, the dissolving of differences and the mimetic doubles. All these elements are present both in the text of Shakespeare and in the text of Dostoevski. I shall give more examples later, and they will show that this same thematic cluster almost never fails to gather around the plague in a great many texts that may appear to have very little in common. Some of the elements may be more emphasized than others; they may appear only in an embryonic form, but it is very rare when even one of them is completely missing.

First, however, I must complete the thematic cluster. Another element, which has not yet been mentioned, may be the most important of all, the *sacrificial* element. This sacrificial element can be limited to the assertion that all the death and suffering from the plague is not in vain, that the ordeal is necessary to purify and rejuvenate the society. Here is, for example, the conclusion of Raskolnikov's dream: "Only a few men could be saved in the whole world. They were a pure chosen people, destined to found a new race and a new life, to renew and purify the earth." Something very similar is present in Artaud's *Le Théâtre et la peste:* "The theater like the plague is a crisis which is resolved by death or cure. And the plague is a superior disease because it is a total crisis after which nothing remains except death or an extreme purification."[4] Death itself appears as the purifying agent, the death of all plague victims or a few, sometimes of a single chosen victim who seems to assume the plague in its entirety and whose death or expulsion cures the society, in the rituals of much of the world. Sacrifices and the so-called scapegoat rituals are prescribed when a community is stricken by "the plague" or other scourges. This thematic cluster is even more common in myth and ritual than in literature. In *Exodus,* for instance, we find the "ten plagues" of Egypt together with the incident of Moses stricken with leprosy and cured by Yahweh himself. The "ten plagues" are a worsening social breakdown, which also appears in the form of a destructive rivalry between Moses and the magicians of Egypt. Finally, there is a strong sacrificial theme in the death of the firstborn and the establishment of the passover ritual.

The sacrificial element is sometimes an invisible dimension, something like an atmosphere that pervades every theme but cannot be pinpointed as a theme; its status must be ascertained. An analysis not of the entire Oedipus myth, but of the mythical elements that appear in Sophocles' tragedy, *Oedipus the King,* may help shed some light upon that problem.

In the opening scenes of the tragedy, the city of Thebes is in the throes of a plague epidemic; the solution of the crisis becomes a test of power and prestige for the protagonists, Oedipus, Creon, and Tiresias. Each of these would-be doctors tries to place the blame on another, and they all turn into each other's doubles. Here, too, the tragic process is one with a worsening "crisis of degree," one with the plague itself, in other words. The tragic conflict and the plague are in the same metaphoric relationship as in Dostoevski or Shakespeare, except, of course, that this metaphoric character is less explicit, as if the task of uncovering the element of violence hidden behind the mythical plague were initiated by Sophocles but were less advanced than in the work of the two other writers.

In the light of these analyses, the tragic conflict of *Oedipus the King* amounts to nothing more and nothing less than a search for a scapegoat, triggered by the oracle, which says, "A murderer is in your midst; get rid of him and you will be rid of the plague." How could a single individual, even the worst offender, be responsible for whatev-

---

4. Antonin Artaud, *Le Théâtre et son double,* in *Oeuvres complètes* (Paris: Gallimard, 1964), 4: 38–39.

er social catastrophe may be at stake in the "plague"? Within the confines of the myth, however, not only is the significance of the strange medicine unquestioned, but its efficacy is actually verified. We must assume that the prescription works, that the discovery of the "culprit" cures the plague. The reciprocal witch hunt brings the crisis to a climax; then, the focusing of the guilt on Oedipus and his expulsion constitute a genuine resolution. The whole process is comparable to a "cathartic" purge.

A fascinating possibility arises. Even though the reasons adduced are quite mythical, the reality of the cure may be a fact. Behind the entire myth there could be a real crisis, concluded by the collective expulsion or death of a victim. In this case the oracle would be truthful in part. What is true is not that there is, as a "real culprit," a man who bears alone the entire responsibility for the plague. Such a man cannot exist, of course. The oracle is really talking about a victim who is "right," in the sense that against and around that victim everyone can unite. Oedipus may well be the right scapegoat in the sense that the accusation against him really "sticks" and restores the unity of the community. This restoration is tantamount to a "cure" if, as Sophocles himself appears to suggest, the plague is the same crisis as in Shakespeare or Dostoevski, a crisis of mimetic violence. The polarization of all fascination and hatred on a single victim leaves none for the other doubles and must automatically bring about their reconciliation.

How can the required unanimity be achieved if no one among the potential victims is likely to be either much more or much less guilty than anyone else? How can the mythical "guilt" become solidly fixed on a more or less random victim? The mimetic doubles are concretely alike; there is no difference between them. This means that at any time even the smallest incident, the most insignificant clue, can trigger a mimetic transfer against any double whatsoever. The positive effect of such a transfer, the end of the crisis, must necessarily be interpreted as a confirmation of the "oracle," as absolute proof that the "real culprit" has been identified. A faultless relationship of cause and effect appears to have been established.

The process just described implies that the random victim must be perceived as a "real culprit," missing before and now identified and punished. This random victim, in other words, will never be perceived as random; the "cure" would not be operative if its beneficiaries realized the randomness of the victim's selection.

All this goes without saying, and yet it needs very much to be said because the unperceived consequences of these facts may be decisive for the myth as a whole. I have just said that the entire responsibility for the crisis is collectively transferred upon the scapegoat. This transfer will not appear as such, of course. Instead of the truth, we will have the "crimes" of Oedipus, the "parricide and the incest" that are supposed to "contaminate" the entire city. These two crimes obviously signify the dissolving of even the most elemental cultural differences, those between father, mother, and child. The parricide and the incest represent the quintessence of the whole crisis, its most logical crystallization in the context of a scapegoating project, that is, of an attempt to make that crisis look like the responsibility of a single individual. Even today, these and similar accusations come to the fore when a pogrom is in the making, when a lynch mob goes on a rampage. The ideas of parricide and incest, and also infanticide, always crop up when cultural cohesion is threatened, when a society is in danger of disintegration. The nature of the crimes attributed to Oedipus should be enough to make us suspect that we are dealing with some kind of lynching process. And this suspicion has been present for many years; it has prompted many investigations. Unfortunately, scholars keep looking for a possible link that could be historically documented between the Oedipus myth and some particular scapegoat-type ritual. The results have been disappointing. The question of relating myth to ritual or ritual to myth is a circle that can be broken here by asking a more decisive question about the possible origin of both in a spontaneous lynching process that must necessarily remain invisible because of its very efficacy.

If the collective transfer is really effective, the victim will never appear as an explicit scapegoat, as an innocent destroyed by the blind passion of the crowd. This victim will pass for a real criminal, for the one guilty exception in a community now emptied of its violence. Oedipus is a scapegoat in the fullest sense *because he is never designated as such.* For the genuine recollection of the crisis, which allows for no differentiation whatever between the doubles, the two differentiated themes of the myth are substituted. The original elements are all there, but rearranged and transfigured in such a way as to destroy the reciprocity of the crisis and polarize all its violence on the wretched scapegoat, leaving everybody else a passive victim of that vague and undefined scourge called "the plague." A lynching viewed from the perspective of the lynchers will never become explicit as such. In order to apprehend the truth, we must carry out a radical critique that will see the mythical themes as systematic distortion of the former crisis.

The spontaneous scapegoat process now appears as the generative process of myth, the true *raison d'être* of its themes and notably of the plague, which must be viewed, I believe, as a mask for the crisis leading to the scapegoat process, not only in the Oedipus myth but in countless other myths of the entire world.

Oedipus, it will be said, is a religious hero as well as a villain. This is true, and it is no objection—far from it—to the genesis just outlined. The difference between the founding process of myth and the scapegoat processes we may know of and understand is that the first, being the more powerful, literally goes full circle from unanimous hatred to unanimous worship. The juxtaposition of the one and the other is intelligible. If the polarization of the crisis upon a single victim really effects a cure, this victim's guilt is confirmed, but his role as a savior is no less evident. That is why Oedipus and behind him the more remote but parallel figure of the god Apollo appear both as bringers of the plague and as benefactors. This is true of all primitive gods and other sacred figures associated with the mythical "plague." They are both the accursed divinities that curse with the plague and the blessed ones that heal. This duality, it must be noted, is present in all primitive forms of the "sacred."

I have already suggested that the present hypothesis bears also on ritual, that a sacrificial action or immolation is generally found, frequently interpreted as the reenactment of a divine murder supposed to be the decisive event in the foundation of the culture. In the preparatory stages of a ritual immolation, symmetrically arranged antagonists hold warlike dances or real and simulated battles. Familial and social hierarchies are reversed or suppressed. These and many other features may be interpreted as traces of some "crisis of degree" climaxed by its habitual resolution, the collective transfer on a single victim. We may suppose that ritual tries to reenact this entire process in order to recapture the unifying effect mentioned earlier. There are sound reasons to believe that this purpose is generally achieved. Being still unable to perceive the threat that internal violence constitutes for primitive society, we cannot recognize in ritual a relatively effective protection against that threat.

If the preceding and obviously too brief remarks are not unfounded,[5] the conjunction between the plague and sacrificial ritual, first in primitive religion and later in literature, becomes fully intelligible. Primitive societies constantly resort to ritual against anything they call the plague. That may comprise very diverse threats ranging from the crisis of mimetic violence and less acute forms of internal tensions and aggressions to purely exterior threats that have nothing to do with reciprocal violence, including, of course, real pathological epidemics, even the plague in the modern scientific sense.

Ritual tries to reproduce a process that has proved effective against one kind of "plague," the most terrible kind, the epidemic of reciprocal violence that never becomes explicit as such. It is my opinion that the scapegoat process, through religious myths, notably the myths of the plague, plays a major role in disguising and minimizing the danger its own potential for internal violence constitutes for a primitive community. This minimization must be viewed in turn as an integral part of the protection that myth and ritual provide against this same violence.

Certain lines of Sophocles and Euripides make it hard to believe that these writers did not have an intuition of collective mechanisms behind the myths they adapted, an intuition that is still incomplete, perhaps, but far superior to ours. These mechanisms are still well attested historically. In the Middle Ages, for instance, social catastrophes, notably the great plague epidemics, usually triggered persecutions against the Jews. Even though they have become less productive in terms of mythical lore, these mechanisms, quite obviously, are far from extinct.

We are now in a position to understand why the mythical plague is never present alone. It is part of a thematic cluster that includes various forms of undifferentiation and transgression, the mimetic doubles, and a sacrificial theme that may take the form of a scapegoat process. Earlier, I said that the plague, as a literary theme, is still alive today, in a world less and less threatened by real bacteri-

---

5. For a more complete exposition of the collective transfer and single victim process as mythical genesis, see René Girard, *La Violence et le sacré* (Paris: Grasset, 1972); René Girard, *Violence and the Sacred*, trans. Patrick Gregory (Baltimore: The Johns Hopkins University Press, 1977).

al epidemics. This fact looks less surprising now, as we come to realize that the properly medical aspects of the plague never were essential; in themselves, they always played a minor role, serving mostly as a disguise for an even more terrible threat that no science has ever been able to conquer. The threat is still very much with us, and it would be a mistake to consider the presence of the plague in literature as a matter of formal routine, as an example of a tradition that persists even though its object has vanished.

Not only the plague but the entire thematic cluster is alive, and its relevance to the current psychosociological predicament becomes evident as soon as specific examples are produced. The continued vitality of all these themes must correspond to a continued need to disguise as well as to suggest—the one and the other in varying degrees—a certain pervasive violence in our relationships.

I will give three examples, each so different from the other two and from the texts already mentioned, at least in terms of traditional literary values, that direct literary influence cannot account for the presence of the pattern. The first is Artaud's already mentioned *Le Théâtre et la peste*. Much of this text is devoted to a strange account of the medical and social effects not of a specific outbreak but of the plague in general. In a long pseudoclinical disquisition, Artaud rejects all attempts at making the transmission of the disease a scientifically determined phenomenon; he interprets the physiological process as a dissolution of organs, which may be a kind of melting away, a liquefaction of the body or, on the contrary, a desiccation and a pulverization. This loss of organic differentiation is medically mythical but esthetically powerful because it patterns the pathological symptoms on the breakdown of culture, producing an overwhelming impression of disintegration. The apocalyptic vision is quite close to Dostoevski's dream of the plague, but this time, in keeping with the destructive ethos of contemporary art, it is a cause for fierce jubilation.

At first glance it seems that, in spite of its intensity, the process of undifferentiation does not culminate in the doubles. The doubles are there, though—less explicit, to be sure, than in Dostoevski and Shakespeare but unmistakable nevertheless—notably in those passages that hint at a purely spiritual contamination, analogous to the mimetic *hubris* of the first two examples.

Other victims, without bubos, delirium, pain, or rash, examine themselves proudly in the mirror, in splendid health as they think and then fall dead with their shaving mugs in their hand, full of scorn for other victims.[6]

The proud self-examination is *hubristic* pride, reaching out for supreme mastery, even over the plague, immediately defeated, massively contradicted by the instant arrival of the disease. Still apparently intact, the victim dies, "full of scorn for the other victims." An unquenchable thirst to distinguish himself turns the apparently healthy man into a double of all other victims, his partners in violence and death. The mirror, everywhere, is an attribute to the doubles.

The sacrificial theme is there too: first, as earlier indicated, in the rejuvenation that the plague and its modern counterpart, the theater, are supposed to bring to a decadent world, but also in more subtle touches that may be limited, at least in one case, to one single word. At one point the author imagines some kind of surgical dissection performed on the victims not with just any knife but with a knife that, for no immediately apparent reason, is described as being made of obsidian. Anthropological literature knows of knives made of this material and used on human flesh, the Aztec sacrificial knives. In the context of my analyses, it is not excessive to suppose, perhaps, that the *couteau d'obsidienne,* in conjunction with the victims of the plague, was prompted by a reminiscence of human sacrifice.

The second example is the film work of Ingmar Bergman in which the plague, the dissolving of differences, the mimetic doubles, and the sacrificial scapegoat are recurrent themes. If one particular film should be mentioned in connection with the doubles, it is certainly *Persona.* Two characters only are constantly present, a nurse and her patient, a totally silent actress. The entire work is dedicated to the mimetic relationship of these two, never a communion, really, but the same violent dissolving of differences as elsewhere. Another film, *Shame,* makes the conjunction of the mimetic doubles and of a plaguelike contamination quite manifest. A senseless civil war is being fought between two perfectly undistinguishable parties. This absurd struggle of rival doubles gradually spreads into a general infection, a literal ocean of putrefaction. Here, as in many contemporary works, the old mythical plague literally merges with such positive threats as radioactive fallout and industrial pollution, both of which

6. Artaud, *Le Théâtre,* p. 29. My translation.

"function," of course, exactly like the plague and constitute disturb-ingly appropriate "metaphors" of individual and social relations in a state of extreme degradation.

One may single out *The Seventh Seal* as one film of Bergman in which the interplay of all the elements in the thematic cluster is quite spectacular. The mimetic doubles are there, and death is one of them. So is a real medieval plague with its cortege of flagellants. In the midst of all this comes the brief suggestion of a mob scene, a collective transfer against a very random and at the same time quite significant scapegoat, an actor, a mime, the very personification of mimesis.

The third example is both literary and cinematic. It is the famous short story by Thomas Mann, *Death in Venice,* which was made into a film by Luchino Visconti. My own comments are based on the short story, which remains, I believe, the more striking of the two in the present context.[7]

An older and famous writer, Aschenbach, goes to Venice for a rest. As he arrives, he notices another elderly man who clings desperately to a group of younger people. His modish attire and the rouge on his cheeks turn this pathetic figure into a monstrous mask of pseudo-youthfulness. Later, the protagonist will permit a hairdresser to paint his face and dye his hair, which makes of him the exact replica, the perfect double, of the grotesque vision encountered at the beginning.

In the meantime, at the hotel and on the beach, the artist has come under the spell of a Polish adolescent. The differences of age, language, and culture, as well as its homosexual character, make this silent attachment more than a mere transgression; it is really a destruction and a dissolution of the old man's entire life.

The sense of decay is heightened by the plague and the rumors of plague that are abroad in the city. The sacrificial theme is present, of course, first in the hero's dream of a primitive bacchanal during which animals are slaughtered and, no less decisively, in his sudden death the next morning, which seems a retribution for his surrender to the forces of cultural disintegration. The writer has become the very embodiment of the plague. He literally sides with the epidemic when he chooses not to inform the Polish family of its presence in

---

7. A paper on "The Plague in *Death in Venice,* " by Ruth Ellen Perlman, a student at SUNY at Buffalo (Spring 1972), first made me aware of the short story's relevance to the present investigation.

Venice, thus increasing their exposure to danger. He delights in the plague, and the plague will literally die with him since, as he dies, everybody is leaving Venice and the drama is resolved.

In these three contemporary examples the plague and associated themes are all present; the entire cluster is strikingly intact. It even has more thematic consistency than in Sophocles, Shakespeare, or Dostoevski. The plague is a less transparent metaphor in Thomas Mann and Artaud than in *Crime and Punishment, Troilus and Cressida,* and even *Oedipus the King.* This very opacity confers to the plague a great evocative and esthetic power. The doubles, too, appear in a light of romantic mystery, in contrast with the unadorned severity of the tragic rapport.

Such opacity, it must be noted, belongs to myth—distinguished, of course, from its tragic adaptations—as well as to modern literature. If we limited ourselves to these chronological or cultural extremes, which is what recent investigators tend to do, the conjunction between the plague, the doubles, and the sacrificial scapegoat would remain unintelligible. Many specialists, of course (for instance, the psychoanalysts), have all sorts of answers. Unfortunately, these ever ready answers shed no real light on the texts. As for the literary critics, they usually reject not only these superficial answers—which is good—but also the question itself—which cannot be good. In a misguided effort to protect the integrity of literature against all possible enemies, they refuse the open and equal dialogue between literature and anthropology they themselves should promote. We should not cut off literature from the vital concerns of our age. We should not divorce esthetic enjoyment from the power of intelligence, even from scientific investigation. We cannot simply "enjoy" the plague and be quiet, like old Aschenbach, I suppose, awaiting in pure esthetic bliss whatever fate may lie in store.

I find Shakespeare more bracing than Aschenbach. One reason is that he does not despair of the truth. If I had not turned to him earlier, I could not have made sense out of the thematic cluster. The brightest light available is still there. Shakespeare does not use the plague as verbal violence against an indifferent world. He is not interested in words as shields or weapons in the dubious battle of individual *ressentiment.* What concerns him most is the myth and the truth of his own language.

In these contemporary examples, the thematic elements of the cluster are juxtaposed a little like colors on the flat surface of a modern painting. It takes Shakespeare to realize that these themes are not really on a par, that they are not really even themes, and that it is a misnomer to call them so. The plague is less than theme, structure, or symbol, since it symbolizes desymbolization itself. The doubles, on the contrary, are more than a theme; they are the unperceived reciprocity of violence among men. They are essential to the understanding of sacrifice as a mitigation, a displacement, a substitution, and a metaphor of this same violence. The closer the writer gets to the fundamentals of that process, the more the plague and other metaphors become transparent. Sacrificial values disintegrate, disclosing their origin in the unifying and reconciling effect of a spontaneous scapegoat. If the scapegoat process described above is the resolution of the crisis and the source of mythical meaning, it must also be the end of tragedy and the restoration of degree. Shakespeare does not simply repeat; he reveals the entire process.

In *Romeo and Juliet,* for instance, it takes Shakespeare no more than six words to suggest the entire pattern of metaphoric and real interaction. The famous cry of the dying Mercutio, "A plague on both your houses," is not an idle wish. It is already fulfilled in the endlessly destructive rivalry of these same two houses, Montagues and Capulets, who turn each other into perfect doubles, thereby bringing the plague upon themselves. At the end of the play, the prince equates the death of the two lovers with the plague of their families: "See what a scourge is laid upon your hate." The two statements are really the same. Both are uttered *in extremis,* as a revelation of the truth: the first by a dying victim; the second as the last judgment of the sovereign authority, always a sacrificial figure in Shakespeare, and a potential scapegoat.

The death of the lovers is the entire plague, in the sense that it represents the climax of the scourge, the plague finally made visible and, as a consequence, exorcised by its very excess; the plague is both the disease and the cure. A sacrificial death brings about the end of the crisis and the reconciliation of the doubles. Talking to Capulet, Montague aptly calls the victims "poor sacrifices of our enmity."

Thus, a scapegoat mechanism is clearly defined as the solution to the tragic crisis, the catharsis inside the play that parallels the catharsis produced by that play, the catharsis twice announced and proposed to the spectators at the very opening, in an enigmatic little prologue that contains literally no other idea: Romeo and Juliet, we are told,

Do with their death bury their parents' strife.
The fearful passage of their death-marked love,
And the continuance of their parents' rage,
Which, but their children's end, naught could remove,
Is now the two hours' traffic of our stage.

[1.1.8–12]

The word *catharsis* originally refers to the purifying effect of a particular sacrifice. Shakespeare needs no etymology to see through Aristotelian estheticism and to reveal in the most concrete and *dramatic* fashion that all drama is a mimetic reenactment of a scapegoat process. In his tragedies, Shakespeare reproduces the cathartic mechanism of all tragedy; but he underlines it so forcefully that he lays it bare, so to speak, forcing us to ask questions that run counter to the cathartic effect, questions that would tear the entire dramatic structure asunder if they were seriously asked.

In his comedies, Shakespeare openly derides the sacrificial pattern. The Pyramus and Thisbe episode of *A Midsummer Night's Dream,* the play that comes immediately after *Romeo and Juliet,* parodies the cathartic system of this first play. He comes closer to a full revelation of the sacrificial values hidden behind the plague and other mythical or tragic metaphors than our contemporaries, including those like Artaud, whose frontal attacks against sacrificial values ultimately regress into the crudest forms of sacrifice. Contrary to what we believe, we may not be in a position to criticize Shakespeare. He may be the one who criticizes us. Rather than trying to judge him from above, from a necessarily superior "modern" viewpoint, we should try to recover some major intuitions of his that obviously escape us. We must have lost them somehow and somewhere, unless, of course, they have yet to be grasped.

HAROLD BLOOM

In Harold Bloom's dark revision of Freud, creativity is not just a matter of playful wish-fulfillment. It is the result of a profound illness, a psychic civil war, relentless, incurable anxiety, repression, denial, an unhealing narcissistic scar made by our first failure, as infants, in sexual love. It is the result of the catastrophe of consciousness itself, of the disaster of being born at all, of a birth simultaneous with the Fall. Lacan said that every ego is paranoid. Bloom agrees, if by "ego" is meant the source of "the most vital lyric poetry of the last three hundred years, and indeed of all literature that achieves the Sublime." Certainly Bloom's version is an American version of Freud (because ego-centered), but it is hardly curative or therapeutic in any comforting sense. Agonistic negation doesn't free anyone for blissful adjustment to his or her surroundings. It is simply what we have to do to stay alive, to keep that longing for the end of irritability, which Freud called the death-wish, from taking over completely. Bloom would agree with Lacan, it seems, if Lacan saw the Freudian legacy less as a source of healing than as a "science" of anxiety—a defense system which is at the same time a rhetorical system. For Bloom, as for Anna Freud, tropes are defenses. And Freud himself in *Die Endliche und die Unendliche Analyse* (1937) said that the defenses rise up in therapy to do combat with the healer. Recovery itself becomes the danger, because to recover is to accept the physician's authority, to accept "femininity" in this context, which appears to the patient as a reprise of castration. Bloom, it seems, would agree with the patient. Perhaps Freud does as well. Life is, in the end, negation and denial. There is even repression before there is anything to repress; our early dreams attempt to "master a stimulus retroactively by first developing the anxiety." What is the threat to which both creativity and erotic aggression are the response? The threat is the past. We are all Miltonic Satans arriving on the scene too late. Creation is in place. Our mothers already have a lover. The poem we want to write has been written. Not to take revenge in this intolerable situation is to be a "moldy fig." The sublime mode is always generated by Satanic (or Nietzschean) repression of anteriority, the Satanic comparison: is God's force indeed greater than my own? To clear a space for ourselves, we repress the anterior. But the anterior does not disappear. Negation accepts. Denial affirms. Repression remembers. It is no wonder then that when Satan's kingdom takes shape, the Trinity reappears, troped, transformed, and diabolic: Satan, the Author-Father; Sin, his daughter and his "darling," reigning at his right hand "voluptuous"; and Death, their begotten son, the Unholy Ghost (P.L. II.846 ff.).

Freud and the Sublime: A Catastrophe Theory of Creativity
▲ 1978 ▼

J acques Lacan argues that Freud "derived his inspiration, his ways of thinking and his technical weapons" from imaginative literature rather than from the sciences. On such a view, the precursors of Freud are not so much Charcot and Janet, Brücke and Helmholtz, Breuer and Fliess, but the rather more exalted company of Empedocles and Heraclitus, Plato and Goethe, Shakespeare and Schopenhauer. Lacan is the foremost advocate of a dialectical reading of Freud's text, a reading that takes into account those problematics of textual interpretation that stem from the philosophies of Hegel, Nietzsche and Heidegger, and from developments in differential linguistics. Such a reading, though it has attracted many intellectuals in English-speaking countries, is likely to remain rather alien to us, because of the strong empirical tradition in Anglo-American thought. Rather like Freud himself, whose distaste for and ignorance of the United States were quite invincible, Lacan and his followers distrust American pragmatism, which to them is merely irritability with theory. Attacks by French Freudians upon American psychoanalysis tend to stress issues of societal adjustment or else of a supposed American optimism concerning human nature. But I think that Lacan is wiser in his cultural vision of Freud than he is in his polemic against ego psychology, interpersonal psychoanalysis or any other American school. Freud's power *as a writer* made him the contemporary not so much of his rivals and disciples as of the strongest literary minds of our century. We read Freud not as we read Jung or Rank, Abraham or Ferenczi, but as we read Proust or Joyce, Valéry or Rilke or Stevens. A

FREUD AND THE SUBLIME: A CATASTROPHE THEORY OF CREATIVITY   from *Agon: Towards a Theory of Revisionism* by Harold Bloom, pp. 91–118. Copyright © 1982 by Oxford University Press, Inc. Reprinted by permission.

writer who achieves what once was called the Sublime will be susceptible to explication either upon an empirical *or* upon a dialectical basis.

The best brief account of Freud that I have read is by Richard Wollheim (1971), and Wollheim is an analytical philosopher, working in the tradition of Hume and of Wittgenstein. The Freud who emerges in Wollheim's pages bears very little resemblance to Lacan's Freud, yet I would hesitate to prefer either Wollheim's or Lacan's Freud, one to the other. There is no "true" or "correct" reading of Freud because Freud is so strong a writer that he *contains* every available mode of interpretation. In tribute to Lacan, I add that Lacan in particular has uncovered Freud as the greatest theorist we have of what I would call the necessity of misreading. Freud's text both exemplifies and explores certain limits of language, and therefore of literature, insofar as literature is a linguistic as well as a discursive mode. Freud is therefore as much the concern of literary criticism as he is of psychoanalysis. His intention was to found a science; instead he left as legacy a literary canon and a discipline of healing.

It remains one of the sorrows, both of psychoanalysis and of literary criticism, that as modes of interpretation they continue to be antithetical to one another. The classical essay on this antithesis is still Lionel Trilling's *Freud and Literature,* first published back in 1940, and subsequently revised in *The Liberal Imagination* (1950). Trilling demonstrated that neither Freud's notion of art's status nor Freud's use of analysis on works of art was acceptable to a literary critic, but nevertheless praised the Freudian psychology as being truly parallel to the workings of poetry. The sentence of Trilling's eloquent essay that always has lingered in my own memory is the one that presents Freud as a second Vico, as another great rhetorician of the psyche's twistings and turnings:

> In the eighteenth century Vico spoke of the metaphorical, imagistic language of the early stages of culture; it was left to Freud to discover how, in a scientific age, we still feel and think in figurative formations, and to create, what psychoanalysis is, a science of tropes, of metaphor and its variants, synecdoche and metonymy.

That psychoanalysis is a science of tropes is now an accepted commonplace in France, and even in America, but we do well to remember how prophetic Trilling was, since the *Discours de Rome* of Jacques Lacan dates from 1953. Current American thinkers in psychoanalysis like Marshall Edelson and Roy Schafer describe psychic defenses as fantasies, not mechanisms, and fantasies are always tropes, in which so-called "deep structures," like desires, become transformed into "surface structures," like symptoms. A fantasy of defense is thus, in language, the recursive process that traditional rhetoric named a trope or "turning," or even a "color," to use another old name for it. A psychoanalyst interpreting a symptom, dream or verbal slip and a literary critic interpreting a poem thus share the burden of having to become conceptual rhetoricians. But a common burden is proving to be no more of an authentic unifying link between psychoanalysts and critics than common burdens prove to be among common people, and the languages of psychoanalysis and of criticism continue to diverge and clash.

Partly this is due to a certain over-confidence on the part of writing psychoanalysts when they confront a literary text, as well as to a certain over-deference to psychoanalysis on the part of various critics. Psychoanalytic over-confidence, or courageous lack of wariness, is hardly untypical of the profession, as any critic can learn by conducting a seminar for any group of psychoanalysts. Since we can all agree that the interpretation of schizophrenia is a rather more desperately urgent matter than the interpretation of poetry, I am in no way inclined to sneer at psychoanalysts for their instinctive privileging of their own kinds of interpretation. A critical self-confidence, or what Nietzsche might have called a will-to-power over the text-of-life, is a working necessity for a psychoanalyst, who otherwise would cease to function. Like the shaman, the psychoanalyst cannot heal unless he himself is persuaded by his own rhetoric. But the writing psychoanalyst adopts, whether he knows it or not, a very different stance. As a writer he is neither more nor less privileged than any other writer. He cannot invoke the trope of the Unconscious as though he were doing more (or less) than the poet or critic does by invoking the trope of the Imagination, or than the theologian does by invoking the trope of the Divine. Most writing psychoanalysts privilege the realm of what Freud named as "the primary process." Since this privileging, or valorization, is at the center of any psychoanalytic account of creativity, I turn now to examine "primary process," which is Freud's most vital trope or fiction in his theory of the mind.

Freud formulated his distinction between the primary and secondary processes of the psyche in 1895, in his *Project for a Scientific Psychology,* best available in English since 1954 in *The Origins of Psychoanalysis* (ed. Bonaparte, A. Freud and Kris). In Freud's mapping of the mind, the primary process goes on in the system of the unconscious, while the secondary process characterizes the preconscious-conscious system. In the unconscious, energy is conceived as moving easily and without check from one idea to another, sometimes by displacement (dislocating) and sometimes by condensation (compression). This hypothesized energy of the psyche is supposed continually to reinvest all ideas associated with the fulfillment of unconscious desire, which is defined as a kind of primitive hallucination that totally satisfies, that gives a complete pleasure. Freud speaks of the primary process as being marked by a wandering-of-meaning, with meaning sometimes dislocated onto what ought to be an insignificant idea or image, and sometimes compressed upon a single idea or image at a crossing point between a number of ideas or images. In this constant condition of wandering, meaning becomes multiformly determined, or even over-determined, interestingly explained by Lacan as being like a palimpsest, with one meaning always written over another one. Dreaming is of course the principal Freudian evidence for the primary process, but wishing construed as a primitive phase of desiring may be closer to the link between the primary process and what could be called poetic thinking.

Wollheim calls the primary process "a primitive but perfectly coherent form of mental functioning." Freud expounded a version of the primary process in Chapter VII of his masterwork, *The Interpretation of Dreams* (1900), but his classic account of it is in the essay of 1911, *Formulations on the Two Principles of Mental Functioning*. There the primary process is spoken of as yielding to the secondary process when the person abandons the pleasure principle and yields to the reality principle, a surrender that postpones pleasure only in order to render its eventuality more certain.

The secondary process thus begins with a binding of psychic energy, which subsequently moves in a more systematic fashion. Investments in ideas and images are stabilized, with pleasure deferred, in order to make possible trial runs of thought as so many path-breakings towards a more constant pleasure. So described, the secondary process also has its links to the cognitive workings of poetry, as to all other cognitions whatsoever. The French Freudians, followers of Lacan, speak of the primary and secondary process as each having different laws of syntax, which is another way of describing these processes as two kinds of poetry or figuration, or two ways of "creativity," if one would have it so.

Anthony Wilden observes in his *System and Structure* (1972): "The concept of a primary process or system applies in both a synchronic and a diachronic sense to all systemic or structural theories." In Freudian theory, the necessity of postulating a primary process precludes any possibility of regarding the forms of that process as being other than abnormal or unconscious phenomena. The Lacanian psychoanalyst O. Mannoni concludes his study *Freud* (English translation 1971) by emphasizing the ultimate gap between primary process and secondary process as being the tragic, unalterable truth of the Freudian vision, since "what it reveals profoundly is a kind of original fracture in the way man is constituted, a split that opposes him to himself (and not to reality or society) and exposes him to the attacks of his unconscious."

In his book *On Art and the Mind* (1973), Wollheim usefully reminds us that the higher reaches of art "did not for Freud connect up with that other and far broader route by which wish and impulse assert themselves in our lives: Neurosis." Wollheim goes on to say that, in Freudian terms, we thus have no reason to think of art as showing any single or unitary motivation. Freud first had developed the trope or conceptual image of the unconscious in order to explain repression, but then had equated the unconscious with the primary process. In his final phase, Freud came to believe that the primary process played a positive role in the strengthening of the ego, by way of the fantasies or defenses of introjection and projection. Wollheim hints that Freud, if he had lived, might have investigated the role of art through such figures of identification, so as to equate art "with recovery or reparation on the path back to reality." Whether or not this surmise is correct, it is certainly very suggestive. We can join Wollheim's surmise to Jack Spector's careful conclusion in his *The Aesthetics of Freud* (1972) that Freud's contribution to the study of art is principally "his dramatic view of the mind in which a war, not of good and evil, but of ego, super-ego, and id forces occurs as a secular *psychomachia.*" Identification, through art, is clearly a crucial weapon in such a civil war of the psyche.

Yet it remains true, as Philip Rieff once noted, that Freud suggests very little that is positive about creativity as an intellectual process, and therefore explicit Freudian thought is necessarily antithetical to nearly any theory of the imagination. To quarry Freud for theories of creativity, we need to study Freud where he himself is most imaginative, as in his great phase that begins with *Beyond the Pleasure*

Principle (1920), continues with the essay *Negation* (1925) and then with *Inhibitions, Symptoms, and Anxiety* (1926, but called *The Problem of Anxiety* in its American edition), and that can be said to attain a climax in the essay *Analysis Terminable and Interminable* (1937). This is the Freud who establishes the priority of anxiety over its stimuli, and who both imagines the origins of consciousness as a catastrophe and then relates that catastrophe to repetition-compulsion, to the drive-towards-death, and to the defense of life as a drive towards agonistic achievement, an agon directed not only against death but against the achievements of anteriority, of others, and even of one's own earlier self.

Freud, as Rieff also has observed, held a catastrophe theory of the genealogy of drives, but *not* of the drive-towards-creativity. Nevertheless, the Freudian conceptual image of a catastrophe-creation of our instincts is perfectly applicable to our will-to-creativity, and both Otto Rank and more indirectly Sandor Ferenczi made many suggestions (largely unacceptable to Freud himself) that can help us to see what might serve as a Freudian theory of the imagination-as-catastrophe, and of art as an achieved anxiety in the agonistic struggle both to repeat and to defer the repetition of the catastrophe of creative origins.

Prior to any pleasure, including that of creativity, Freud posits the "narcissistic scar," accurately described by a British Freudian critic, Ann Wordsworth, as "the infant's tragic and inevitable first failure in sexual love." Parallel to this notion of the narcissistic scar is Freud's speculative discovery that there are early dreams whose purpose is not hallucinatory wish-fulfillment. Rather they are attempts to master a stimulus retroactively by first developing the anxiety. This is certainly a creation, though it is the *creation of an anxiety,* and so cannot be considered a sublimation of any kind. Freud's own circuitous path-breaking of thought connects this creation-of-an-anxiety to the function of repetition-compulsion, which turns out, in the boldest of all Freud's tropes, to be a regressive return to a death-instinct.

Freud would have rejected, I think, an attempt to relate this strain in his most speculative thinking to any theory of creativity, because for Freud a successful repression is a contradiction in terms. What I am suggesting is that any theory of artistic creation that wishes to use Freud must depart from the Freudian letter in order to develop the Freudian spirit, which in some sense is already the achievement of

Lacan and his school, though they have had no conspicuous success in speculating upon art. What the Lacanians *have* seen is that Freud's system, like Heidegger's, is a science of anxiety, which is what I suspect the art of belatedness, of the last several centuries, mostly is also. Freud, unlike Nietzsche, shared in the Romantics' legacy of over-idealizing art, of accepting an ill-defined trope of "the Imagination" as a kind of mythology of creation. But Freud, as much as Nietzsche (or Vico, before them both), provides the rational materials for demythologizing our pieties about artistic creation. Reading the later Freud teaches us that our instinctual life is agonistic and ultimately self-destructive and that our most authentic moments tend to be those of negation, contraction, and repression. Is it so unlikely that our creative drives are deeply contaminated by our instinctual origins?

Psychoanalytic explanations of "creativity" tend to discount or repress two particular aspects of the genealogy of aesthetics: first, that the creative or Sublime "moment" is a negative moment; second, that this moment tends to rise out of an encounter with someone else's prior moment of negation, which in turn goes back to an anterior moment, and so on. "Creativity" is thus always a mode of repetition *and* of memory and also of what Nietzsche called the will's revenge against time and against time's statement of: "It was." What links repetition and revenge is the psychic operation that Freud named "defense," and that he identified first with repression but later with a whole range of figurations, including identification. Freud's rhetoric of the psyche, as codified by Anna Freud in *The Ego and the Mechanisms of Defense* (1946), is as comprehensive a system of tropes as Western theory has devised. We can see now, because of Freud, that rhetoric always was more the art of defense than it was the art of persuasion, or rather that defense is always *prior* to persuasion. Trilling's pioneering observation that Freud's science shared with literature a reliance upon trope has proved to be wholly accurate. To clarify my argument, I need to return to Freud's trope of the unconscious and then to proceed from it to his concern with catastrophe as the origin of drive in his later works.

"Consciousness," as a word, goes back to a root meaning "to cut or split," and so to know something by separating out one thing from another. The unconscious (Freud's *das Unbewusste*) is a purely inferred division of the psyche, an inference necessarily based only upon the supposed effects that the unconscious has upon ways we think and act that can be *known,* that are available to consciousness. Because there are gaps or disjunctions to be accounted for in our thoughts and acts, various explanatory concepts of an unconscious have been available since ancient times, but the actual term first appears as the German *Unbewusste* in the later eighteenth century, to be popularized by Goethe and by Schelling. The English "unconscious" was popularized by Coleridge, whose theory of a poem as reconciling a natural outside with a human inside relied upon a formula that "the consciousness is so impressed on the unconscious as to appear in it." Freud acknowledged often that the poets had been there before him, as discoverers of the unconscious, but asserted his own discovery as being the scientific *use* of a concept of the unconscious. What he did not assert was his intense narrowing down of the traditional concept, for he separated out and away from it the attributes of creativity that poets and other speculators always had ascribed to it. Originality or invention are not mentioned by Freud as rising out of the unconscious.

There is no single concept of the unconscious in Freud, as any responsible reading of his work shows. This is because there are two Freudian topographies or maps of the mind, earlier and later (after 1920), and also because the unconscious is a dynamic concept. Freud distinguished his concept of the unconscious from that of his closest psychological percursor, Pierre Janet, by emphasizing his own vision of a civil war in the psyche, a dynamic conflict of opposing mental forces, conscious against unconscious. Not only the conflict was seen thus as being dynamic, but the unconscious peculiarly was characterized as dynamic in itself, requiring always a contending force to keep it from breaking through into consciousness.

In the first Freudian topography, the psyche is divided into Unconscious, Preconscious, and Conscious, while in the second the divisions are the rather different triad of id, ego, and super-ego. The Preconscious, descriptively considered, is unconscious, but can be made conscious, and so is severely divided from the Unconscious proper, in the perspective given either by a topographical or a dynamic view. But this earlier system proved simplistic to Freud himself, mostly because he came to believe that our lives began with all of the mind's contents in the unconscious. This finally eliminated Janet's conception that the unconscious was a wholly separate mode of consciousness, which was a survival of the ancient belief in a creative or inaugurating unconscious. Freud's new topology insisted upon the dynamics of relationship between an unknowable unconscious and consciousness by predicating three agencies or instances of personality: id, ego, super-ego. The effect of this new system was to devaluate the unconscious, or at least to demystify it still further.

In the second Freudian topography, "unconscious" tends to become merely a modifier, since all of the id and very significant parts of the ego and super-ego are viewed as being unconscious. Indeed, the second Freudian concept of the ego gives us an ego which is *mostly* unconscious, and so "behaves exactly like the repressed—that is, which produces powerful effects without itself being conscious and which requires special work before it can be made conscious," as Freud remarks in *The Ego and the Id*. Lacan has emphasized the unconscious element in the ego to such a degree that the Lacanian ego must be considered, despite its creator's protests, much more a revision of Freud than what ordinarily would be accounted an interpretation. With mordant eloquence, Lacan keeps assuring us that the ego, every ego, is essentially paranoid, which as Lacan knows *sounds* rather more like Pascal than it does like Freud. I think that this insistence is at once Lacan's strength and his weakness, for my knowledge of imaginative literature tells me that Lacan's conviction is certainly true if by the ego we mean the literary "I" as it appears in much of the most vital lyric poetry of the last three hundred years, and indeed in all literature that achieves the Sublime. But with the literary idea of "the Sublime" I come at last to the sequence of Freud's texts that I wish to examine, since the first of them is Freud's theory of the Sublime, his essay *The "Uncanny"* of 1919.

The text of *The "Uncanny"* is the threshold to the major phase of Freud's canon, which begins the next year with *Beyond the Pleasure Principle*. But quite aside from its crucial place in Freud's writings, the essay is of enormous importance to literary criticism because it is the only major contribution that the twentieth century has made to the aesthetics of the Sublime. It may seem curious to regard Freud as the culmination of a literary and philosophical tradition that held no particular interest for him, but I would correct my own statement by the modification, no *conscious* interest for him. The Sublime, as I read Freud, is one of his major *repressed* concerns, and this literary repression on his part is a clue to what I take to be a gap in his theory of repression.

I come now, belatedly, to the definition of "the Sublime," before considering Freud as the last great theorist of that mode. As a literary idea, the Sublime originally meant a style of "loftiness," that is of verbal power, of greatness or strength conceived agonistically, which is to say against all possible competition. But in the European Enlightenment, this literary idea was strangely transformed into a vision of the terror that could be perceived both in nature and in art, a terror uneasily allied with pleasurable sensations of augmented power, and even of narcissistic freedom, freedom in the shape of that wildness that Freud dubbed "the omnipotence of thought," the greatest of all narcissistic illusions.

Freud's essay begins with a curiously weak defensive attempt to separate his subject from the aesthetics of the Sublime, which he insists deals only "with feelings of a positive nature." This is so flatly untrue, and so blandly ignores the long philosophical tradition of the negative Sublime, that an alert reader ought to become very wary. A year later, in the opening paragraphs of *Beyond the Pleasure Principle,* Freud slyly assures his readers that "priority and originality are not among the aims that psycho-analytic work sets itself." One sentence later, he charmingly adds that he would be glad to accept any philosophical help he can get, but that none is available for a consideration of the meaning of pleasure and unpleasure. With evident generosity, he then acknowledges G. T. Fechner, and later makes a bow to the safely distant Plato as author of *The Symposium.* Very close to the end of *Beyond the Pleasure Principle,* there is a rather displaced reference to Schopenhauer, when Freud remarks that "we have unwittingly steered our course into the harbor of Schopenhauer's philosophy." The apogee of this evasiveness in regard to precursors comes where it should, in the marvelous essay of 1937, *Analysis Terminable and Interminable,* which we may learn to read as being Freud's elegiac *apologia* for his life's work. There the true precursor is unveiled as Empedocles, very safely remote at two and a half millennia. Perhaps psychoanalysis does not set priority and originality as aims in its *praxis,* but the first and most original of psychoanalysts certainly shared the influence-anxieties and defensive misprisions of all strong writers throughout history, and particularly in the last three centuries.

Anxieties when confronted with anterior powers are overtly the concerns of the essay on the "uncanny." E. T. A. Hoffmann's *The Sand-Man* provides Freud with his text, and for once Freud allows himself to be a very useful practical critic of an imaginative story. The repetition-compulsion, possibly imported backwards from *Beyond the Pleasure Principle* as work-in-progress, brilliantly is invoked to open up what is hidden in the story. Uncanniness is traced back to the narcissistic belief in "omnipotence of thought," which in aesthetic terms is necessarily the High Romantic faith in the power of the mind over the universe of the senses and of death. *Das Heimliche,* the homely or canny, is thus extended to its only apparent opposite, *das Unheimliche,* "for this uncanny is in reality nothing new or foreign, but something familiar and old-established in the mind that has been estranged only by the process of repression."

Freud weakens his extraordinary literary insight by the latter part of his essay, where he seeks to reduce the "uncanny" to either an infantile or a primitive survival in our psyche. His essay knows better, in its wonderful dialectical play on the *Unheimlich* as being subsumed by the larger or parental category of the *Heimlich.* Philip Rieff finely catches this interplay in his comment that the effect of Freud's writing is itself rather uncanny, and surely never more so than in this essay. Rieff sounds like Emerson or even like Longinus on the Sublime when he considers the condition of Freud's reader:

> The reader comes to a work with ambivalent motives, learning what he does not wish to know, or, what amounts to the same thing, believing he already knows and can accept as his own intellectual property what the author merely "articulates" or "expresses" for him. Of course, in this sense, everybody knows everything—or nobody could learn anything. . . .

Longinus had said that reading a sublime poet ". . . we come to believe we have created what we have only heard." Milton, strongest poet of the modern Sublime, stated this version of the reader's Sublime with an ultimate power, thus setting forth the principle upon which he himself read, in Book IV of his *Paradise Regained,* where his Christ tells Satan:

> . . . who reads
> Incessantly, and to his reading brings not
> A spirit and judgment equal or superior
> (And what he brings, what needs he elsewhere seek?),
> Uncertain and unsettled still remains. . . .

Pope followed Boileau in saying that Longinus "is himself the great Sublime he draws." Emerson, in his seminal essay *Self-Reliance,* culminated this theme of the reader's Sublime when he asserted that "in every work of genius we recognize our own rejected thoughts; they come back to us with a certain alienated majesty." The "majesty" is the true, high, breaking light, aura or lustre, of the Sublime, and this realization is at the repressed center of Freud's essay on the "uncanny." What Freud declined to see, at that moment, was the mode of conversion that alienated the "canny" into the "uncanny." His next major text, *Beyond the Pleasure Principle,* clearly exposes that mode as being catastrophe.

Lacan and his followers have centered upon *Beyond the Pleasure Principle* because the book has not lost the force of its shock value, even to Freudian analysts. My contention would be that this shock is itself the stigma of the Sublime, stemming from Freud's literary achievement here. The text's origin is itself shock or aura, the trauma that a neurotic's dreams attempt to master, *after the event.* "Drive" or "instinct" is suddenly seen by Freud as being catastrophic in its origins, and as being aimed, not at satisfaction, but at death. For the first time in his writing, Freud overtly assigns priority to the psyche's fantasizings over mere biology, though this valorization makes Freud uneasy. The pleasure principle produces the biological principle of constancy, and then is converted, through this principle, into a drive back to the constancy of death. Drive or instinct thus becomes a kind of defense, all but identified with repression. This troping of biology is so extreme, really so literary, that I find it more instructive to seek the aid of commentary here from a Humean empiricist like Wollheim than from Continental dialecticians like Lacan and Laplanche. Wollheim imperturbably finds no violation of empiricism or biology in the death-drive. He even reads "beyond," *jenseits,* as meaning only "inconsistent with" the pleasure principle, which is to remove from the word the transcendental or Sublime emphasis that Freud's usage gave to it. For Wollheim, the book is nothing more than the working through of the full implication of the major essay of 1914, *On Narcissism: An Introduction.* If we follow Wollheim's lead quite thoroughly here, we will emerge with conclusions that differ from his rather guarded remarks about the book in which Freud seems to have shocked himself rather more than he shocks Wollheim.

The greatest shock of *Beyond the Pleasure Principle* is that it ascribes the origin of all human drives to a catastrophe theory of creation (to which I would add: "of creativity"). This catastrophe theory is developed in *The Ego and the Id,* where the two major catastrophes, the drying up of ocean that cast life onto land and the Ice Age are said to be repeated psychosomatically in the way the latency period (roughly from the age of five until twelve) cuts a gap into sexual development. Rieff again is very useful when he says that the basis of catastrophe theory, whether in Freud or in Ferenczi's more drastic and even apocalyptic *Thalassa* (1921), "remains Freud's *Todestrieb,* the tendency of all organisms to strive toward a state of absence of irritability and finally 'the death-like repose of the inorganic world.'" I find it fascinating from a literary critical standpoint to note what I think has not been noted, that the essay on narcissism turns upon catastrophe theory also. Freud turns to poetry, here to Heine, in order to illustrate the psychogenesis of Eros, but the lines he quotes actually state a psychogenesis of creativity rather than of love:

> . . . whence does that necessity arise that urges our mental life to pass on beyond the limits of narcissism and to attach the libido to objects? The answer which would follow from our line of thought would once more be that we are so impelled when the cathexis of the ego with libido exceeds a certain degree. A strong egoism is a protection against disease, but in the last resort we must begin to love in order that we may not fall ill, and must fall ill if, in consequence of frustration, we cannot love. Somewhat after this fashion does Heine conceive of the psychogenesis of the creation:

> > Krankheit ist wohl der letzte Grund
> > Des ganzen Schöpferdrangs gewesen;
> > Erschaffend konnte ich genesen,
> > Erschaffend wurde ich gesund.

To paraphrase Heine loosely, illness is the ultimate ground of the drive to create, and so while creating the poet sustains relief, and by creating the poet becomes healthy. Freud transposes from the catastrophe of creativity to the catastrophe of falling in love, a transposition to which I will return in the final pages of this chapter.

Beyond the Pleasure Principle, like the essay on narcissism, is a discourse haunted by images (some of them repressed) of catastrophe. Indeed, what Freud verges upon showing is that to be human is a catastrophic condition. The coloring of this catastrophe, in Freud, is precisely Schopenhauerian rather than, say, Augustinian or Pascalian. It is as though, for Freud, the Creation and the Fall had been one and the same event. Freud holds back from this abyss of Gnosticism by reducing mythology to psychology, but since psychology and cosmology have been intimately related throughout human history, this reduction is not altogether persuasive. Though he wants to show us that the daemonic is "really" the compulsion to repeat, Freud tends rather to the "uncanny" demonstration that repetition-compulsion reveals many of us to be daemonic or else makes us daemonic. Again, Freud resorts to the poets for illustration, and again the example goes beyond the Freudian interpretation. Towards the close of section III of *Beyond the Pleasure Principle,* Freud looks for a supreme instance of "people all of whose human relationships have the same outcome" and he finds it in Tasso:

> The most moving poetic picture of a fate such as this is given by Tasso in his romantic epic *Gerusalemme Liberata.* Its hero, Tancred, unwittingly kills his beloved Clorinda in a duel while she is disguised in the armor of an enemy knight. After her burial he makes his way into a strange magic forest which strikes the Crusaders' army with terror. He slashes with his sword at a tall tree; but blood streams from the cut and the voice of Clorinda, whose soul is imprisoned in the tree, is heard complaining that he has wounded his beloved once again.

Freud cites this episode as evidence to support his assumption "that there really does exist in the mind a compulsion to repeat which overrides the pleasure principle." The repetition in Tasso is not just incremental, but rather is qualitative, in that the second wounding is "uncanny" or Sublime, and the first is merely accidental. Freud's citation is an allegory of Freud's own passage into the Sublime. When Freud writes (and the italics are his): *"It seems, then, that a drive is an urge inherent in organic life to restore an earlier state of things,"* then he slays his beloved trope of "drive" by disguising it in the armor of his enemy, mythology. But when he writes (and again the italics are his): *"the aim of all life is death,"* then he wounds his figuration of "drive" in a truly Sublime or "uncanny" fashion. In the qualitative leap from the drive to restore pure anteriority to the apothegm that life's purpose is death, Freud himself has abandoned the empirical for the daemonic. It is the literary authority of the daemonic rather than the analytical which makes plausible the further suggestion that

> . . . sadism is in fact a death instinct which, under the influence of the narcissistic libido, has been forced away from the ego. . . .

This language is impressive, and it seems to me equally against literary tact to accept it or reject it on any supposed biological basis.

Its true basis is that of an implicit catastrophe theory of meaning or interpretation, which is in no way weakened by being circular and therefore mythological. The repressed rhetorical formula of Freud's discourse in *Beyond the Pleasure Principle* can be stated thus: *literal meaning equals anteriority equals an earlier state of meaning equals an earlier state of things equals death equals literal meaning.* Only one escape is possible from such a formula, and it is a simpler formula: *Eros equals figurative meaning.* This is the dialectic that informs the proudest and most moving passage in *Beyond the Pleasure Principle,* which comprises two triumphant sentences *contra* Jung that were added to the text in 1921, in a Sublime afterthought:

> Our views have from the very first been *dualistic,* and today they are even more definitely dualistic than before—now that we describe the opposition as being, not between ego-instincts and sexual instincts, but between life instincts and death instincts. Jung's libido theory is on the contrary *monistic*; the fact that he has called his one instinctual force "libido" is bound to cause confusion, but need not affect us otherwise.

I would suggest that we read *dualistic* here as a trope for "figurative" and *monistic* as a trope for "literal." The opposition between life drives and death drives is not just a dialectic (though it *is* that) but is a great writer's Sublime interplay between figurative and literal meanings, whereas Jung is exposed as being what he truly was, a mere literalizer of anterior mythologies. What Freud proclaims here, in the accents of sublimity, is the power of his own mind over language, which in this context *is* the power that Hegelians or Lacanians legitimately could term "negative thinking."

I am pursuing Freud as prose-poet of the Sublime, but I would not concede that I am losing sight of Freud as analytical theorist. Certainly the next strong Freudian text is the incomparable *Inhibitions, Symptoms, and Anxiety* of 1926. But before considering that elegant and somber meditation, certainly the most illuminating analysis of anxiety our civilization has been offered, I turn briefly to Freud's essay on his dialectic, *Negation* (1925).

Freud's audacity here has been little noted, perhaps because he packs into fewer than five pages an idea that cuts a considerable gap into his theory of repression. The gap is wide enough so that such oxymorons as "a successful repression" and "an achieved anxiety," which are not possible in psychoanalysis, are made available to us as literary terms. Repressed images or thoughts, by Freudian definition, *cannot* make their way into consciousness, yet their content can, on condition that it is *denied*. Freud cheerfully splits head from heart in the apprehension of images:

> Negation is a way of taking account of what is repressed; indeed, it is actually a removal of the repression, though not, of course, an acceptance of what is repressed. It is to be seen how the intellectual function is here distinct from the affective process. Negation only assists in undoing *one* of the consequences of repression—namely, the fact that the subject-matter of the image in question is unable to enter consciousness. The result is a kind of intellectual acceptance of what is repressed, though in all essentials the repression persists. . . .

I would venture one definition of the literary Sublime (which to me seems always a negative Sublime) as being that mode in which the poet, while expressing previously repressed thought, desire, or emotion, is able to continue to defend himself against his own created image by disowning it, a defense of *un-naming* it rather than *naming* it. Freud's word *Verneinung* means both a grammatical negation and a psychic disavowal or denial, and so the linguistic and the psychoanalytical have a common origin here, as Lacan and his school have insisted. The ego and the poet-in-his-poem both proceed by a kind of "misconstruction," a defensive process that Lacan calls *méconnaissance* in psychoanalysis, and that I have called "misprision" in the study of poetic influence (a notion formulated before I had read Lacan, but which I was delighted to find supported in him). In his essay *Aggressivity in Psychoanalysis* Lacan usefully connects Freud's notion of a "negative" libido to the idea of Discord in Heraclitus. Freud himself brings his essay on *Verneinung* to a fascinating double conclusion. First, the issue of truth or falsehood in language is directly related to the defenses of introjection and projection; a true image thus would be introjected and a false one projected. Second, the defense of introjection is aligned to the Eros-drive of affirmation, "while negation, the derivative of expulsion, belongs to the instinct of destruction," the drive to death beyond the pleasure principle. I submit that what Freud has done here should have freed literary discussion from its persistent over-literalization of his idea of repression. Freud joins himself to the tradition of the Sublime, that is, of the strongest Western poetry, by showing us that negation allows poetry to free itself from the aphasias and hysterias of repression, *without* however freeing the poets themselves from the unhappier human consequences of repression. Negation is of *no* therapeutic value for the individual, but it *can* liberate him into the linguistic freedoms of poetry and thought.

I think that of all Freud's books, none matches the work on inhibitions, symptoms and anxiety in its potential importance for students of literature, for this is where the concept of defense is ultimately clarified. Wollheim says that Freud confused the issue of defense by the "overschematic" restriction of repression to a single species of defense, but this is one of the very rare instances where Wollheim seems to me misled or mistaken. Freud's revised account of anxiety *had* to distinguish between *relatively* nonrepressive and the more severely repressive defenses, and I only wish that both Freud and his daughter after him had been even more schematic in mapping out the defenses. We need a rhetoric of the psyche, and here the Lacanians have been a kind of disaster, with their simplistic over-reliance upon the metaphor/metonymy distinction. Freud's revised account of anxiety is precisely at one with the poetic Sublime, for anxiety is finally seen as a technique for mastering anteriority by *remembering* rather than *repeating* the past. By showing us that anxiety is a mode of expectation, closely resembling desire, Freud allows us to understand why poetry, which loves love, also seems to love anxiety. Literary and human romance both are exposed as being anxious quests that could not bear to be cured of their anxieties, even if such cures were possible. "An increase of excitation underlies anxiety," Freud tells us, and then he goes on to relate this increase to a repetition of the catastrophe of human birth, with its attendant trauma. Arguing against Otto Rank, who like Ferenczi had gone too far into the abysses of catastrophe-theory, Freud enunciated a principle that can help explain why the terror of the literary Sublime must and can give pleasure:

> Anxiety is an affective state which can of course be experienced only by the ego. The id cannot be afraid, as the ego can; it is not an organization, and cannot estimate situations of danger. On the contrary, it is of extremely frequent occurrence that processes are initiated or executed in the id which give the ego occasion to develop anxiety; as a matter of fact, the repressions which are probably the earliest are motivated, like the majority of all later ones, by such fear on the part of the ego of this or that process in the id. . . .

Freud's writing career was to conclude with the polemical assertion that "mysticism is the obscure self-perception of the realm outside the ego, of the id," which is a splendid farewell thrust at Jung, as we can see by substituting "Jung" for "the id" at the close of the sentence. The id perceiving the id is a parody of the Sublime, whereas the ego's earliest defense, its primal repression, is the true origin of the Sublime. Freud knew that "primal repression" was a necessary fiction, because without some initial fixation his story of the psyche could not begin. Laplanche and Pontalis, writing under Lacan's influence in their *The Language of Psychoanalysis,* find the basis of fixation

> in primal moments at which certain privileged ideas are indelibly inscribed in the unconscious, and at which the instinct itself becomes fixated to its psychical representative—perhaps by this very process constituting itself *qua* instinct.

If we withdrew that "perhaps," then we would return to the Freudian catastrophe-theory of the genesis of all drives, with fixation now being regarded as another originating catastrophe. How much clearer these hypotheses become if we transpose them into the realm of poetry! If fixation becomes the inscription in the unconscious of the privileged idea of a Sublime poet, or strong precursor, then the drive towards poetic expression originates in an agonistic repression, where the agon or contest is set against the pattern of the precursor's initial fixation upon an anterior figure. Freud's mature account of anxiety thus concludes itself upon an allegory of origins, in which the creation of an unconscious implicitly models itself upon poetic origins. There was repression, Freud insists, before there was anything to be repressed. This insistence is neither rational nor irrational; it is a figuration that knows its own status as figuration, without embarrassment.

My final text in Freud is *Analysis Terminable and Interminable.* The German title, *Die Endliche und die Unendliche Analyse,* might better be translated as "finite or indefinite analysis," which is Lacan's suggestion. Lacan amusingly violates the taboo of discussing how long the analytic session is to be when he asks:

> . . . how is this time to be measured? Is its measure to be that of what Alexander Koyré calls "the universe of precision"? Obviously we live in this universe, but its advent for man is relatively recent, since it goes back precisely to Huyghens' clock—in other words, to 1659—and the *malaise* of modern

man does not exactly indicate that this precision is in itself a liberating factor for him. Are we to say that this time, the time of the fall of heavy bodies, is in some way sacred in the sense that it corresponds to the time of the stars as they were fixed in eternity by God who, as Lichtenberg put it, winds up our sundials? . . .

I reflect, as I read Lacan's remarks, that it was just after Huyghens's clock that Milton began to compose *Paradise Lost,* in the early 1660's, and that Milton's poem is *the* instance of the modern Sublime. It is in *Paradise Lost* that temporality fully becomes identified with anxiety, which makes Milton's epic the most Freudian text ever written, far closer to the universe of psychoanalysis than such more frequently cited works, in Freudian contexts, as *Oedipus Tyrannus* and *Hamlet.* We should remember that before Freud used a Virgilian tag as epigraph for *The Interpretation of Dreams* (1908), he had selected a great Satanic utterance for his motto:

> Seest thou yon dreary plain, forlorn and wild,
> The seat of desolation, void of light,
> Save what the glimmering of these livid flames
> Casts pale and dreadful? Thither let us tend
> From off the tossing of these fiery waves,
> There rest, if any rest can harbour there,
> And reassembling our afflicted powers,
> Consult how we may henceforth most offend
> Our enemy, our own loss how repair,
> How overcome this dire calamity,
> What reinforcement we may gain from hope;
> If not, what resolution from despair.

This Sublime passage provides a true motto for all psychoanalysis, since "afflicted powers" meant "cast-down powers," or as Freud would have said, "repressed drives." But it would be an even apter epigraph for the essay on finite and indefinite analysis than it could have been for the much more hopeful *Interpretation of Dreams,* thirty years before. Freud begins his somber and beautiful late essay by brooding sardonically on the heretic Otto Rank's scheme for speeding up analysis in America. But this high humor gives way to the melancholy of considering every patient's deepest resistance to the analyst's influence, that "negative transference" in which the subject's anxiety-of-influence seeks a bulwark. As he reviews the main outlines of his theory, Freud emphasizes its *economic* aspects rather than the dynamic and topographical points of view. The *economic* modifies

any notion that drives have an energy that can be measured. To
estimate the magnitude of such excitation is to ask the classical,
agonistic question that *is* the Sublime, because the Sublime is always
a comparison of two forces or beings, in which the agon turns on the
answer to three queries: more? equal to? or less than? Satan confronting hell, the abyss, the new world, is still seeking to answer the
questions that he sets for himself in heaven, all of which turn upon
comparing God's force and his own. Oedipus confronting the
Sphinx, Hamlet facing the mystery of the dead father, and Freud
meditating upon repression are all in the same economic stance. I
would use this shared stance to re-define a question that psychoanalysis by its nature cannot answer. Since there is *no* biological warrant
for the Freudian concept of libido, what is the energy that Freud
invokes when he speaks from the economic point of view? Wollheim,
always faithful to empiricism, has only one comment upon the
economic theory of mind, and it is a very damaging observation:

> . . . though an economic theory allows one to relate the
> damming up of energy or frustration at one place in the psychic
> apparatus with discharge at another, it does not commit one to
> the view that, given frustration, energy will seek discharge along
> all possible channels indifferently. Indeed, if the system is of any
> complexity, an economic theory would be virtually uninforma-
> tive unless some measure of selectivity in discharge was
> postulated. . . .

But since Freud applied the economic stance to sexual drives
almost entirely, no measure of selectivity *could* be postulated. This
still leaves us with Freud's economic obsessions, and I suggest now
that their true model was literary, and not sexual. This would mean
that the "mechanisms of defense" are dependent for their formulaic
coherence upon the traditions of rhetoric, and not upon biology,
which is almost too easily demonstrable. It is hardly accidental that
Freud, in this late essay which is so much his *summa,* resorts to the
textual analogue when he seeks to distinguish repression from the
other defenses:

> Without pressing the analogy too closely we may say that
> repression is to the other methods of defense what the omission
> of words or passages is to the corruption of a text. . . . For quite a
> long time flight and an avoidance of a dangerous situation serve
> as expedients. . . . But one cannot flee from oneself and no flight
> avails against danger from within; hence the ego's defensive

mechanisms are condemned to falsify the inner perception, so that it transmits to us only an imperfect and travestied picture of our id. In its relations with the id the ego is paralysed by its restrictions or blinded by its errors. . . .

What is Freud's motive for this remarkably clear and eloquent recapitulation of his theory of repression and defense (which I take to be the center of his greatness)? The hidden figuration in his discourse here is his economics of the psyche, a trope which is allowed an overt exposure when he sadly observes that the energy necessary to keep such defenses going "proves a heavy burden on the psychical economy." If I were reading this essay on finite and indefinite analysis as I have learned to read Romantic poems, I would be on the watch for a blocking-agent in the poetic ego, a shadow that Blake called the Spectre and Shelley a daemon or *Alastor*. This shadow would be an anxiety narcissistically intoxicated with itself, an anxiety determined to go on being anxious, a drive towards destruction in love with the image of self-destruction. Freud, like the great poets of quest, has given all the premonitory signs of this Sublime terror determined to maintain itself, and again like the poets he suddenly makes the pattern quite explicit:

> The crux of the matter is that the mechanisms of defense against former dangers recur in analysis in the shape of *resistances* to cure. It follows that the ego treats recovery itself as a new danger.

Faced by the patient's breaking of the psychoanalytic compact, Freud broods darkly on the war between his true Sublime and the patient's false Sublime:

> Once more we realize the importance of the quantitative factor and once more we are reminded that analysis has only certain limited quantities of energy which it can employ to match against the hostile forces. And it does seem as if victory were really for the most part with the big battalions.

It is a true challenge to the interpreter of Freud's text to identify the economic stance here, for what is the source of *the energy of analysis,* however limited in quantity it may be? Empiricism, whether in Hume or in Wittgenstein, does not discourse on the measurement of its own libido. But if we take Freud as Sublime poet rather than empirical reasoner, if we see him as the peer of Milton rather than of Hume, of Proust rather than of the biologists, then we can speculate rather precisely about the origins of the psychoanalytical drive, about the nature of the powers made available by the discipline that one man was able to establish in so sublimely solitary a fashion. Vico teaches us that the Sublime or severe poet discovers the origin of his rhetorical drive, the catastrophe of his creative vocation, in *divination,* by which Vico meant both the process of foretelling dangers to the self's survival and the apotheosis of becoming a daemon or sort of god. What Vico calls "divination" is what Freud calls the primal instinct of Eros, or that "which strives to combine existing phenomena into ever greater unities." With moving simplicity, Freud then reduces this to the covenant between patient and analyst, which he calls "a love of truth." But, like all critical idealisms about poetry, this idealization of psychoanalysis is an error. No psychic economy (or indeed *any* economy) can be based upon "a love of truth." Drives depend upon fictions, because drives *are* fictions, and we want to know more about Freud's enabling fictions, which grant to him his Sublime "energy of analysis."

We can acquire this knowledge by a very close analysis of the final section of Freud's essay, a section not the less instructive for being so unacceptable to our particular moment in social and cultural history. The resistance to analytical cure, in both men and women, is identified by Freud with what he calls the "repudiation of femininity" *by both sexes,* the castration complex that informs the fantasy-life of everyone whatsoever: ". . . in both cases it is the attitude belonging to the sex opposite to the subject's own which succumbs to repression." This is followed by Freud's prophetic lament, with its allusion to the burden of Hebraic prophecy. Freud too sees himself as the *nabi* who speaks to the winds, to the winds only, for only the winds will listen:

> At no point in one's analytic work does one suffer more from the oppressive feeling that all one's efforts have been in vain and from the suspicion that one is "talking to the winds" than when one is trying to persuade a female patient to abandon her wish for a penis on the ground of its being unrealizable, or to convince a male patient that a passive attitude towards another man does not always signify castration and that in many relations in life it is indispensable. The rebellious over-compensation of the male produces one of the strongest transference-resistances. A man will not be subject to a father-substitute or owe him anything and he therefore refuses to accept his cure from the physician. . . .

It is again one of Lacan's services to have shown us that this is figurative discourse, even if Lacan's own figurative discourse becomes too baroque a commentary upon Freud's wisdom here. Freud prophesies to the winds because men and women cannot surrender their primal fantasies, which are their poor but desperately prideful myths of their own origins. We cannot let go of our three fundamental fantasies: the primal scene, which accounts for our existence; the seduction fantasy, which justifies our narcissism; and the castration complex, which explains to us the mystery of sexual differentiation. What the three fantasy-scenes share is the fiction of an originating catastrophe, and so a very close relation to the necessity for defense. The final barrier to Freud's heroic labor of healing, in Freud's own judgment, is the human imagination. The original wound in man cannot be healed, as it is in Hegel, by the same force that makes the wound.

Freud became a strong poet of the Sublime because he made the solitary crossing from a realm where effect is always traced to a cause, to a mode of discourse which asked instead the economic and agonistic questions of comparison. The question of how an emptiness came about was replaced by the question that asks: more, less, or equal to? which is the agonistic self-questioning of the Sublime. The attempt to give truer names to the rhetoric of human defense was replaced by the increasing refusal to name the vicissitudes of drive except by un-namings as old as those of Empedocles and Heraclitus. The ambition to make of psychoanalysis a wholly positive *praxis* yielded to a skeptical and ancient awareness of a rugged negativity that informed every individual fantasy.

Lacan and his school justly insist that psychoanalysis has contributed nothing to biology, despite Freud's wistful hopes that it could, and also that the life sciences inform psychoanalysis hardly at all, again in despite of Freud's eager scientism. Psychoanalysis is a varied therapeutic *praxis,* but it is a "science" only in the peculiar sense that literature, philosophy and religion are also *sciences of anxiety.* But this means that no single rhetoric or poetic will suffice for the study of psychoanalysis, any more than a particular critical method will unveil all that needs to be seen in literature. The "French way" of reading Freud, in Lacan, Derrida, Laplanche, and others, is no more a "right" reading than the way of the ego-psychologists Hartmann, Kris, Erikson, and others, which Lacan and his followers wrongly keep insisting is the only "American reading." In this conflict of strong misreadings, partisans of both ways evidently need to keep forgetting what the French at least ought to remember: strong texts become strong by mis-taking all texts anterior to them. Freud has more in common with Proust and Montaigne than with biological scientists, because his interpretations of life and death are mediated always by texts, first by the literary texts of others, and then by his own earlier texts, until at last the Sublime mediation of otherness begins to be performed by his text-in-process. In the *Essays* of Montaigne or Proust's vast novel, this ongoing mediation is clearer than it is in Freud's almost perpetual self-revision, because Freud wrote no definitive, single text; but the canon of Freud's writings shows an increasingly uneasy sense that he had become his own precursor, and that he had begun to defend himself against himself by deliberately audacious arrivals at final positions.

PART
SIX

FEMINISM

HÉLÈNE CIXOUS

With Derrida, Cixous shares both an Algerian-Jewish background and a subversive interest in binary habits of the mind. For Cixous, the presence of a pair (a couple) signals not only the patriarchy—male thought advances through oppositions—but hierarchy as well. Understanding is the "portentous power of the negative."* To put it another way, someone always has to win. One side of the binary must be in a defeated posture. It goes without saying that woman has the honor of being scripted for this role. Her part is played mostly on her back with her eyes closed, as she waits in the woods or in her enchanted castle for her prince to wake her up, at which point she will see only him, and he will see only adoration and gratitude. It is men, not women, says Cixous wickedly, who like to play with dolls. But it is not just a matter of retelling all the old stories, for example, of waking Sleeping Beauty up before the Prince arrives on the scene. The "text" into which woman finds she has been written is an extremely violent one. There is an overwhelming power holding things in their places. To understand this, one needs only to think of the male/female binary in terms of France/Algeria, white/black, rich/poor, smart/stupid, high/low, or clean/dirty. Perhaps it is the last of these oppositions which unleashes the most apoplectic rage. As Bataille knew, and as Cixous reminds us, the fear of the right side of the binary is the fear of death itself.† To such insane violence, she says, there was only one answer: "I have always wanted war." She means revolutionary movements, to be sure, but also texts of struggle, where at times one has to live, because there is simply nowhere else that does not replicate the status quo. Writing can dream and invent new worlds. It alone is the utopian space, where the Other begins to speak heretofore unheard things, where authorities are put to the sword, and where witches come in from their exile on the heaths to say how culture can be transformed, how sexuality can be unblocked from its cretinous organization around the phallus, how desire can proliferate, circulating openly beyond that paralyzing *ideé fixe* of the family. What will be speaking in this utopian, alogical, non-consequent text will be the previously silent organs and body of woman, no longer completely outside the

---

* G. W. F. Hegel, *The Phenomenology of Mind,* trans. J. B. Baillie (New York: Harper and Row, 1967) 93. The translation was originally published in 1910.
† Georges Bataille, "The Psychological Structure of Fascism," trans. Carl Lovitt in *Visions of Excess,* ed. Allan Stoekl (Minneapolis: University of Minnesota Press, 1985) 142–45.

male-dominated network of discourse. When we hear the "voice of the mother," all sovereignty, sadism, geometric rigidity, standing at attention, and states of erection will collapse in revolutionary effervescence and laughter.**

Sorties: Out and Out: Attacks/Ways Out/Forays

1975

Translated by Betsy Wing

Where is she?
Activity/passivity
Sun/Moon
Culture/Nature
Day/Night

Father/Mother
Head/Heart
Intelligible/Palpable
Logos/Pathos.
Form, convex, step, advance, semen, progress.
Matter, concave, ground—where steps are taken,
    holding- and dumping-ground.
Man
Woman
    Always the same metaphor: we follow it, it carries us, beneath all its figures, wherever discourse is organized. If we read or

SORTIES   by Hélène Cixous from *The Newly Born Woman*, trans. Betsy Wing. English translation by Minnesota University Press, 1986. In French, *La Jeune Née*, with Catherine Clément, Union Général d'Éditions, copyright © 1975. Reprinted with permission.

** Hélène Cixous, "Castration or Decapitation," trans. Annette Kuhn, in *Signs,* Vol. 7 (1981), No. 1: 51–55.

speak, the same thread or double braid is leading us throughout literature, philosophy, criticism, centuries of representation and reflection.
Thought has always worked through opposition,
Speaking/Writing
Parole/Écriture
High/Low
    Through dual, hierarchical oppositions. Superior/Inferior. Myths, legends, books. Philosophical systems. Everywhere (where) ordering intervenes, where a law organizes what is thinkable by oppositions (dual, irreconcilable; or sublatable, dialectical). And all these pairs of oppositions are *couples.* Does that mean something? Is the fact that Logocentrism subjects thought—all concepts, codes and values—to a binary system, related to "the" couple, man/woman?

Nature/History
Nature/Art
Nature/Mind
Passion/Action

    Theory of culture, theory of society, symbolic systems in general —art, religion, family, language—it is all developed while bringing the same schemes to light. And the movement whereby each opposition is set up to make sense is the movement through which the couple is destroyed. A universal battlefield. Each time, a war is let loose. Death is always at work.
Father/son   Relations of authority, privilege, force.
The Word/Writing   Relations: opposition, conflict, sublation, return.
Master/slave   Violence. Repression.
    We see that "victory" always comes down to the same thing: things get hierarchical. Organization by hierarchy makes all conceptual organization subject to man. Male privilege, shown in the opposition between *activity* and *passivity,* which he uses to sustain himself. Traditionally, the question of sexual difference is treated by coupling it with the opposition: activity/passivity.
    There are repercussions. Consulting the history of philosophy —since philosophical discourse both orders and reproduces all thought—one notices[1] that it is marked by an absolute *constant*

---

1. All Derrida's work traversing-detecting the history of philosophy is devoted to bringing this to light. In Plato, Hegel, and Nietzsche, the same process continues:

which orders values and which is precisely this opposition, activity/ passivity.

Moreover, woman is always associated with passivity in philosophy. Whenever it is a question of woman, when one examines kinship structures, when a family model is brought into play. In fact, as soon as the question of ontology raises its head, as soon as one asks oneself "what is it?," as soon as there is intended meaning. Intention: desire, authority—examine them and you are led right back . . . to the father. It is even possible not to notice that there is no place whatsoever for woman in the calculations. Ultimately the world of "being" can function while precluding the mother. No need for a mother, as long as there is some motherliness: and it is the father, then, who acts the part, who is the mother. Either woman is passive or she does not exist. What is left of her is unthinkable, unthought. Which certainly means that she is not thought, that she does not enter into the oppositions, that she does not make a couple with the father (who makes a couple with the son).

There is Mallarmé's tragic dream,[2] that father's lamentation on the mystery of paternity, that wrenches from the poet *the* mourning, the mourning of mournings, the death of the cherished son: this dream of marriage between father and son.—And there's no mother then. A man's dream when faced with death. Which always threatens him differently than it threatens a woman.

"a union
·a marriage, splendid   And dreams of filiation
—and with life   that is masculine, dreams
still in me   of God the father
I shall use it   issuing from himself
for . . .   in his son—and
so not mother then?"   no mother then

She does not exist, she can not-be; but there has to be something of her. He keeps, then, of the woman on whom he is no longer dependent, only this space, always virginal, as matter to be subjected to the desire he wishes to impart.

---

repression, repudiation, distancing of woman; a murder that is mixed up with history as the manifestation and representation of masculine power.

2. "For Anatole's Tomb" (Seuil, p. 138). This is the tomb in which Mallarmé keeps his son from death and watches over him as his mother.

And if we consult literary history, it is the same story. It all comes back to man—to *his* torment, his desire to be (at) the origin. Back to the father. There is an intrinsic connection between the philosophical and the literary (to the extent that it conveys meaning, literature is under the command of the philosophical) and the phallocentric. Philosophy is constructed on the premise of woman's abasement. Subordination of the feminine to the masculine order, which gives the appearance of being the condition for the machinery's functioning.

Now it has become rather urgent to question this solidarity between logocentrism and phallocentrism—bringing to light the fate dealt to woman, her burial—to threaten the stability of the masculine structure that passed itself off as eternal-natural, by conjuring up from femininity the reflections and hypotheses that are necessarily ruinous for the stronghold still in possession of authority. What would happen to logocentrism, to the great philosophical systems, to the order of the world in general if the rock upon which they founded this church should crumble?

If some fine day it suddenly came out that the logocentric plan had always, inadmissibly, been to create a foundation for (to found and fund) phallocentrism, to guarantee the masculine order a rationale equal to history itself.

So all the history, all the stories would be there to retell differently; the future would be incalculable; the historic forces would and will change hands and change body—another thought which is yet unthinkable—will transform the functioning of all society. We are living in an age where the conceptual foundation of an ancient culture is in the process of being undermined by millions of a species of mole (Topoi, ground mines) never known before.

When they wake up from among the dead, from among words, from among laws.

Once upon a time . . .

One cannot yet say of the following history "it's just a story." It's a tale still true today. Most women who have awakened remember having slept, *having been put to sleep.*

Once upon a time . . . once . . . and once again.

Beauties slept in their woods, waiting for princes to come and wake them up. In their beds, in their glass coffins, in their childhood forests like dead women. Beautiful, but passive; hence desirable: all mystery emanates from them. It is men who like to play dolls. As we have known since Pygmalion. Their old dream: to be god the mother.

The best mother, the second mother, the one who gives the second birth.

She sleeps, she is intact, eternal, absolutely powerless. He has no doubt that she has been waiting for him forever.

The secret of her beauty, kept for him: she has the perfection of something finished. Or not begun. However, she is breathing. Just enough life—and not too much. Then he will kiss her. So that when she opens her eyes she will see only *him;* him in place of everything, all-him.[3]

—This dream is so satisfying! Whose is it? What desire gets something out of it?

He leans over her . . . Cut. The tale is finished. Curtain. Once awake (him or her), it would be an entirely different story. Then there would be two people, perhaps. You never know with women. And the voluptuous simplicity of the preliminaries would no longer take place.

Harmony, desire, exploit, search—all these movements are preconditions—of woman's arrival. Preconditions, more precisely, of her *arising.* She is lying down, he stands up. She arises—end of the dream—what follows is sociocultural: he makes her lots of babies, she spends her youth in labor; from bed to bed, until the age at which the thing isn't "woman" for him anymore.

"Bridebed, childbed, bed of death": thus woman's trajectory is traced as she inscribes herself from bed to bed in Joyce's *Ulysses.* The voyage of Ulysses with Bloom standing constantly at the helm as he navigates Dublin. Walking, exploring. The voyage of Penelope—Everywoman: a bed of pain in which the mother is never done with dying, a hospital bed on which there is no end to Mrs. Purefoy's labor, the bed framing endless erotic daydreams, where Molly, wife and adulteress, voyages in her memories. She wanders, but lying down. In dream. Ruminates. Talks to herself. Woman's voyage: as a *body.* As if she were destined—in the distribution established by men (separated from the world where cultural exchanges are made and kept in the wings of the social stage when it is a case of History)—to be the nonsocial, nonpolitical, nonhuman half of the living structure. On nature's side of this structure, of course, tirelessly listening to what goes on inside—inside her

---

3. "She only awakens at love's touch and before that moment she is only a dream. But in this dream existence one can distinguish two stages: first love dreams of her, then she dreams of love." Thus Kierkegaard's *Seducer* dreams.

belly, inside her "house." In direct contact with her appetites, her affects.

And, whereas he takes (after a fashion) the risk and responsibility of being an agent, a bit of the public scene where transformations are played out, she represents indifference or resistance to this active tempo; she is the principle of consistency, always somehow the same, everyday and eternal.

Man's dream: I love her—absent, hence desirable, a dependent nonentity, hence adorable. Because she isn't there where she is. As long as she isn't where she is. How he looks at her then! When her eyes are closed, when he completely understands her, when he catches on and she is no more than this shape made for him: a body caught in his gaze.

Or woman's dream? It's only a dream. I am sleeping. If I weren't asleep, he wouldn't look for me, he wouldn't cross his good lands and my badlands to get to me. Above all, don't wake me up! What anguish! If I have to be entombed to attract him. And suppose he kissed me? How can I will this kiss? Am I willing?

What does she want? To sleep, perchance to dream, to be loved in a dream, to be approached, touched, almost, to almost come *(jouir)*. But not to come: or else she would wake up. But she came in a dream, once upon a time.

And once again upon a time, it is the same story repeating woman's destiny in love across the centuries with the cruel hoax of its plot. And each story, each myth says to her: "There is no place for your desire in our affairs of State." Love is threshold business. For us men, who are made to succeed, to climb the social ladder, temptation that encourages us, drives us, and feeds our ambitions is good. But carrying it out is dangerous. Desire must not disappear. You women represent the eternal threat, the anticulture for us. We don't stay in your houses; we are not going to remain in your beds. We wander. Entice us, get us worked up—that is what we want from you. Don't make us stretch out, soft and feminine, without a care for time or money. Your kind of love is death for us. A threshold affair:[4] it's all in the suspense, in what will soon be, always differed. On the other side is the fall: enslavement for the one and for the other, domestication, confinement in family and in social function.

---

4. The pleasure is preliminary, Freud says. This is a "truth" but only a partial one. It is a point of view, in fact, coming from and upheld by the masculine Imaginary, to the extent that the masculine Imaginary is shaped by the threat of castration.

By dint of reading this story-that-ends-well, she learns the paths that take her to the "loss" that is her fate. Turn around and he's gone! A kiss, and he goes. His desire, fragile and kept alive by lack, is maintained by absence: man pursues. As if he couldn't have what he has. Where is she, where is woman in all the spaces he surveys, in all the scenes he stages within the literary enclosure?

We know the answers and there are plenty: she is in the shadow. In the shadow he throws on her; the shadow she is.

Night to his day—that has forever been the fantasy. Black to his white. Shut out of his system's space, she is the repressed that ensures the system's functioning.

Kept at a distance so that he can enjoy the ambiguous advantages of the distance, so that she, who is distance and postponement, will keep alive the enigma, the dangerous delight of seduction, in suspense, in the role of "eloper," she is Helen, somehow "outside." But she cannot appropriate this "outside" (it is rare that she even wants it); it is his outside: outside on the condition that it not be entirely outside, the unfamiliar stranger that would escape him. So she stays inside a domesticated outside.

Eloper: carried away with herself and carried off from herself.

—Not only is she the portion of strangeness—*inside* his universe where she revives his restlessness and desire. Within his economy, she is the strangeness he likes to appropriate. Moreover, the "dark continent" trick has been pulled on her: she has been kept at a distance from herself, she has been made to see (= not-see) woman on the basis of what man wants to see of her, which is to say, almost nothing. She has been forbidden the possibility of the proud "inscription above my door" marking the threshold of The Gay Science. She could never have exclaimed:

> The house I live in is my own,
> I never copied anyone . . .

She has not been able to live in her "own" house, her very body. She can be incarcerated, slowed down appallingly and tricked into apartheid for too long a time—but still only for a time. One can teach her, as soon as she begins to speak, at the same time as she is taught her name, that hers is the dark region: because you are Africa, you are black. Your continent is dark. Dark is dangerous. You can't see anything in the dark, you are afraid. Don't move, you might fall.

Above all, don't go into the forest. And we have internalized this fear of the dark. Women haven't had eyes for themselves. They haven't gone exploring in their house. Their sex still frightens them. Their bodies, which they haven't dared enjoy, have been colonized. Woman is disgusted by woman and fears her.

They have committed the greatest crime against women: insidiously and violently, they have led them to hate women, to be their own enemies, to mobilize their immense power against themselves, to do the male's dirty work.

They have committed an antinarcissism in her! A narcissism that only loves itself if it makes itself loved for what is lacking! They have created the loathsome logic of antilove.

The "Dark Continent" is neither dark nor unexplorable: It is still unexplored only because we have been made to believe that it was too dark to be explored. Because they want to make us believe that what interests us is the white continent, with its monuments to Lack. And we believed. We have been frozen in our place between two terrifying myths: between the Medusa and the abyss. It would be enough to make half the world break out laughing, if it were not still going on. For the phallo-logocentric *aufhebung* is there, and it is militant, the reproducer of old schemes, anchored in the dogma of castration. They haven't changed a thing: they have theorized their desire as reality. Let them tremble, those priests; we are going to *show* them our *sexts!*

Too bad for them if they collapse on discovering that women aren't men, or that the mother doesn't have one. But doesn't this fear suit them fine? Wouldn't the worst thing be—isn't the worst thing that, really, woman is not castrated, that all one has to do is not listen to the sirens (because the sirens were men) for history to change its sense, its direction? All you have to do to see the Medusa is look her in the face: and she isn't deadly. She is beautiful and she laughs.

They say there are two things that cannot be represented: death and the female sex. Because they need femininity to be associated with death; they get a hard-on when you scare their pants off! For their own sake they need to be afraid of us. Look at the trembling Perseuses, with their advance, armor-clad in apotropes as they back toward us! Pretty backs. There's not a minute to lose. Let's get out of here.

They, the feminine ones, are coming back from far away, from forever, from "outside," from the heaths where witches stay alive;

from underneath, from the near side of "culture"; *from their child-hoods,* which men have so much trouble making women forget, and which they condemn to the *in-pace.* Walled in those little girls with their "bad-mannered" bodies. Preserved, safe from themselves and intact, on ice. Frigified. But the signs of unrest down there! How hard the sex cops have to work, always having to start over, to block women's threatening return. So many forces have been deployed on both sides that the struggle has been stuck for centuries, balanced in a shaky standstill.

We, coming early to culture, repressed and choked by it, our beautiful mouths stopped up with gags, pollen, and short breaths; we the labyrinths, we the ladders, we the trampled spaces; the stolen and the flights—we are "black" *and* we are beautiful.

A Woman's Coming to Writing:
Who
Invisible, foreign, secret, hidden, mysterious, black, forbidden
Am I . . .
Is this me, this no-body that is dressed up, wrapped in veils, carefully kept distant, pushed to the side of History and change, nullified, kept out of the way, on the edge of the stage, on the kitchen side, the bedside?
For you?
Is that me, a phantom doll, the cause of sufferings and wars, the pretext, "because of her beautiful eyes," for what men do, says Freud, for their divine illusions, their conquests, their havoc? Not for the sake of "me," of course. But for my "eyes," so that I will look at you, so that he will be looked at, so that he will see himself seen as he wants to be. Or as he fears he is not. Me, nobody, therefore, or else the mother that the Eternal Male always returns to when seeking admiration.

Men say that it is for her that the Greeks launched a thousand ships, destroyed, killed, waged a fabulous war for ten-times-ten years —among men! For the sake of her, yonder, the idol, carried off, hidden, lost. Because it is for-her and without-her that they live it up at the celebration of death that they call their life.
Murder of the Other:
I come, biographically, from a rebellion, from a violent and anguished direct refusal to accept what is happening on the stage on whose edge I find I am placed, as a result of the combined accidents

of History. I had this strange "luck": a couple of rolls of the dice, a meeting between two trajectories of the diaspora,[5] and, at the end of these routes of expulsion and dispersion that mark the functioning of western History through the displacements of Jews, I fall. —I am born—right in the middle of a scene that is the perfect example, the naked model, the raw idea of this very process: I learned to read, to write, to scream, and to vomit in Algeria. Today I know from experience that one cannot imagine what an Algerian French girl was; you have to have been it, to have gone through it. To have seen "Frenchmen" at the "height" of imperialist blindness, behaving in a country that was inhabited by humans as if it were peopled by nonbeings, born-slaves. I learned everything from this first spectacle: I saw how the white (French), superior, plutocratic, civilized world founded its power on the repression of populations who had suddenly become "invisible," like proletarians, immigrant workers, minorities who are not the right "color." Women.[6] Invisible as humans. But, of course, perceived as tools—dirty, stupid, lazy, underhanded, etc. Thanks to some annihilating dialectical magic. I saw that the great, noble, "advanced" countries established themselves by expelling what was "strange"; excluding it but not dismissing it; enslaving it. A commonplace gesture of History: there have to be *two* races—the masters and the slaves.

We know the implied irony in the master/slave dialectic: the *body* of what is strange must not disappear, but its force must be conquered and returned to the master. Both the appropriate and the inappropriate must exist: the clean, hence the dirty; the rich, hence the poor; etc.

5. My father, Sephardic—Spain—Morocco—Algeria—my mother, Ashkenazy—Austria—Hungary—Czechoslovakia (her father) and Spain (her mother) passing by chance through a Paris that was short-lived.

6. Women: at that time I wasn't thinking about them. At first, occupying the stage in a way that I could plainly see, the battle to death was the battle pitting colonial power against its victims. Beyond that I perceived that it was the imperialist result of capitalist structure and that it intensified the class struggle by deepening it and making it more monstrous and inhuman: the exploited were not even "workers" but, with racism's assistance, something worse—subhuman; and the universe could pretend to obey "natural" laws. War was on the horizon, partially concealed from me. I wasn't in France. I didn't see betrayal and collaboration with my own eyes. We were living under Vichy: I perceived its effects without knowing their causes. I had to guess why my father couldn't do his work, why I couldn't go to school, et cetera. And I had to guess why, as a little white girl informed me, "all Jews are liars."

So I am three or four years old and the first thing I see in the street is that the world is divided in half, organized hierarchically, and that it maintains this distribution through violence. I see that there are those who beg, who die of hunger, misery, and despair, and that there are offenders who die of wealth and pride, who stuff themselves, who crush and humiliate. Who kill. And who walk around in a stolen country as if they had had the eyes of their souls put out. Without seeing that the others are alive.

Already I know all about the "reality" that supports History's progress: everything throughout the centuries depends on the distinction between the Selfsame, the ownself (—what is mine, hence what is good) and that which limits it: so now what menaces my-own-good (good never being anything other than what is good-for-me) is the "other." What is the "Other"? If it is truly the "other," there is nothing to say; it cannot be theorized. The "other" escapes me. It is elsewhere, outside: absolutely other. It doesn't settle down. But in History, of course, what is called "other" is an alterity that does settle down, that falls into the dialectical circle. It is the other in a hierarchically organized relationship in which the same is what rules, names, defines, and assigns "its" other. With the dreadful simplicity that orders the movement Hegel erected as a system, society trots along before my eyes reproducing to perfection the mechanism of the death struggle: the reduction of a "person" to a "nobody" to the position of "other"—the inexorable plot of racism. There has to be some "other"—no master without a slave, no economico-political power without exploitation, no dominant class without cattle under the yoke, no "Frenchmen" without wogs, no Nazis without Jews, no property without exclusion—an exclusion that has its limits and is part of the dialectic. If there were no other, one would invent it. Besides, that is what masters do: they have their slaves made to order. Line for line. They assemble the machine and keep the alternator supplied so that it reproduces all the oppositions that make economy and thought run.

The paradox of otherness is that, of course, at no moment in History is it tolerated or possible as such. The other is there only to be reappropriated, recaptured, and destroyed as other. Even the exclusion is not an exclusion. Algeria was not France, but it was "French."

Me too. The routine "our ancestors, the Gauls" was pulled on me. But I was born in Algeria, and my ancestors lived in Spain, Morocco, Austria, Hungary, Czechoslovakia, Germany; my brothers by birth are Arab. So where are we in history? I side with those who are injured,

trespassed upon, colonized. I am (not) Arab. Who am I? I am "doing"
French history. I am a Jewish woman. In which ghetto was I penned
up during your wars and your revolutions? I want to fight. What is my
name? I want to change life. Who is this "I"? Where is my place? I am
looking. I search everywhere. I read, I ask. I begin to speak. Which
language is mine? French? German? Arabic? Who spoke for me
throughout the generations? It's my luck. What an accident! Being
born in Algeria, not in France, not in Germany; a little earlier and, like
some members of my family, I would not be writing today. I would
anonymiserate eternally from Auschwitz. Luck: if I had been born a
hundred years earlier, I told myself, I would have been part of the
Commune. How?—you? Where are my battles? my fellow soldiers?
What am I saying . . . the comrades, women, my companions-in-
arms?

I am looking everywhere. A daughter of chance. One year earlier. A
miracle. I know it; I hate it: I might never have been anything but
dead. Yesterday, what could I have been? Can I imagine my elsewhere?

—I live all of my childhood in this knowledge: several times I have
miraculously survived. In the previous generation, I would not have
existed. And I live in this rebellion: it is impossible for me to live, to
breathe, to eat in a world where my people don't breathe, don't eat,
are crushed and humiliated. My people: all those that I am, whose
same I am. History's condemned, the exiled, colonized, and burned.

> Yes, Algeria is unliveable. Not to mention France.
> Germany! Europe the accomplice! . . .

—There has to be somewhere else, I tell myself. And everyone
knows that to go somewhere else there are routes, signs, "maps"
—for an exploration, a trip.—That's what books are. Everyone knows
that a place exists which is not economically or politically indebted to
all the vileness and compromise. That is not obliged to reproduce the
system. That is writing. If there is a somewhere else that can escape
the infernal repetition, it lies in that direction, where *it* writes itself,
where *it* dreams, where *it* invents new worlds.

And that is where I go. I take books; I leave the real, colonial space;
I go away. Often I go read in a tree. Far from the ground and the shit. I
don't go and read just to read, to forget—No! Not to shut myself up in
some imaginary paradise. I am searching: somewhere there must be
people who are like me in their rebellion and in their hope. Because
I don't despair: if I myself shout in disgust, if I can't be alive without

being angry, there must be others like me. I don't know who, but when I am big, I'll find them and I'll join them, I don't yet know where. While waiting, I want to have only my true ancestors for company (and even at that I forgive the Gauls a great deal, thanks to their defeat; they, too, were alienated, deceived, enslaved, it's true) —my true allies, my true "race." Not this comical, repulsive species that exercises power in the place where I was born.

And naturally I focused on all the texts in which there is struggle. Warlike texts; rebellious texts. For a long time I read, I lived, in a territory made of spaces taken from all the countries to which I had access through fiction, an antiland (I can never say the word "patrie," "fatherland," even if it is provided with an "anti-") where distinctions of races, classes, and origins would not be put to use without someone's rebelling. Where there are people who are ready for anything—to live, to die for the sake of ideas that are right and *just*. And where it was not impossible or pathetic to be generous. I knew, I have always known, what I hated. I located the enemy and all his destructive figures: authority, repression, censorship, the unquenchable thirst for wealth and power. The ceaseless work of death—the constant of evil. But that couldn't last. Death had to be destroyed. I saw that reality, history, was a series of struggles, without which we would have long ago been dead. And in my mental voyage, I gave great importance to battlefields, conflicts, the confrontation between the forces of death and the forces of life, between wrong ideas and right ideas. Actually, I have always wanted war; I did not believe that changes would be made except through revolutionary movements. I saw the enormity of power every day. Nazism, colonialism, centuries of violent inequality, the massacre of peoples, religious wars. Only one answer—struggle. And without theorizing any of that, of course—I forged through the texts where there was struggle.

I questioned might—its use, its value; through a world of fiction and myths, I followed closely those who had it and who used it. I asked everywhere: where does your strength come from? What have you done with your power? What cause have you served? I watched the "masters" especially closely—the kings, chiefs, judges, leaders, all those who I thought could have changed society; and then the "heroes": that is to say, the persons endowed with an individual strength but without authority, those who were isolated, eccentric, the intruders: great, undaunted, sturdy beings, who were at odds with the Law.

I have not read the Bible: I took short cuts, I lingered with Saul and with David. The rise and fall of men spoiled by power.

I liked Hercules very much, because he did not put his muscles to work for death, until the day I began to discover he was not a revolutionary but a gullible policeman.

I fought the Trojan war my own way: on neither one side nor the other. I loathed the chiefs' stupid, petty, and sanctifying mentality. What did they serve? A narcissistic glory. What did they love? Their royal image. The masculine code, squared: not only the masculine value but the essence of virility as well, that is undisputed power. Now onto the stage comes the species of men-kings. Vile patterns. Villainous bosses. Wily. Guilty consciences. The Agamemnon type. I despised the species.

And I pushed ahead into all the mythical and historical times.

And what would I have been then? Who?—A question that didn't come to me until later. The day when suddenly I felt bad in every skin I had ever worn.

Indeed, in Homeric times I was Achilles. I know why. I was the antiking. And I was passion. I had fits of rage that made History difficult. I didn't give a damn for hierarchy, for command, and I know how to love. I greatly loved women and men. I knew the value of a unique person, the beauty, the sweetness. I didn't ask myself any petty questions, I was unaware of limits, I enjoyed my bisexuality without anxiety: that both kinds harmonized within me seemed perfectly natural to me. I never even thought it could be otherwise. Had I not lived among women for a long time? And among men I gave up nothing of the tender, feminine intensities. Prohibition didn't come near me. I was far above stupid superstitions, sterile divisions. And I always loved wholly: I adored Patroclus with all my might; as a woman I was his sister, his lover, his mother; as a man, his brother, his husband, and himself. And I knew better than any man how to love women because of having been their companion and their sister for so long. I loved and I loved love. I never went back on love.

But sometimes I was ashamed: I was afraid of being Ulysses, and wasn't I sometimes? As Achilles I was uncompromising. But when I changed weapons? When I used the weapons of the crafty one, the one who knew too much about mediocrity and human weakness and not enough about true unbending strength—? "Silence, exile and cunning" are the tools of the young man-artist with which Stephen Dedalus arms himself to organize his series of tactical retreats while he works out in "the smithy of his soul the uncreated conscience of his race." A help to a loner, of course. But I didn't like to catch myself being Ulysses, the artist of flight. The Winner: the one who was saved, the homecoming man! Always returning to himself—in spite of the most fantastic detours. The Loaner: loaning himself to women and never giving himself except to the ideal image of Ulysses, bringing his inalterable resistance home to his hot-shot little phallic rock, where, as the crowning act of the *nostos*—the return, which was so similar, I said to myself, to the Jewish fantasy (next year in Jerusalem) —he produced a remarkable show of force. I didn't analyze the bowshot, of course, but I did suspect it contained some "male" symbolic values that made it repugnant to me. How banal! To resist the Sirens, he ties himself up! to a mast! a little phallus and a big phallus too. . . . Later on Ulysses becomes a radical socialist. Noteworthy. I was bitter for a long time about having believed I was this resourceful man when I tried to get out of threatening situations by lying or subterfuge (which happened two or three times in my childhood). I was furious that I had been on the defensive. And, at that time, I didn't have the knowledge, the intellectual means that would have allowed me to understand and forgive myself. Thus from hero to hero went my armor, my sword, my shield.

Then the day comes—rather late for that matter—when I leave childhood. My anger is unmollified. The Algerian war approaches. Societies falter, I feel—the smell of my blood, too, is changing—a real war is coming, coming to a boil. And I quit being a child who is neuter, an angry bundle of nerves, a me seething with violent dreams, meditating widespread revenge, the overthrow of idols, the triumph of the oppressed.

No longer can I identify myself simply and directly with Samson or inhabit my glorious characters. My body is no longer innocently useful to my plans. (breasts) I am a woman.

Then everything gets complicated. I don't give up on war. That would be suicide: struggle is more necessary than ever. For in reality, the offense is also against me, as a woman, and the enemy is all over the place: not only are there class enemies, colonialists, racists, bourgeois, and antisemites against me—"men" are added to them. Or rather, the enemy becomes twice as formidable and more hated. But the worst of it is that among my brothers, in my own imaginary camp, some aggressors appear who are as narrow-minded, crude, and frightening as the ones confronting me. In some way I always knew, always saw this glaring, sexual brutishness surrounding me. But it never becomes intolerable to me until it hurts me as it passes through my own body and drags me into this spot of insoluble contradictions, impossible to overcome, this place I have never been able to get out of since: the friend is also the enemy. All women have lived that, are living it, as I continue to live it. "We" struggle together, yes, but, who is this "we"? A man and beside him a thing, somebody—(a woman: always in her parenthesis, always repressed or invalidated as a woman, tolerated as a nonwoman, "accepted"!)—someone you are not conscious of, unless she effaces herself, acts the man, speaks and thinks that way. For a woman, what I am saying is trite. It has often been said. It is that experience that launched the front line of the feminist struggle in the U.S. and in France: discovering discrimination, the fundamental unconscious masculine racism in places where, theoretically, it should not exist! A political irony: imagine fighting against racism with militants who *are* racist!

I, revolt, rages, where am I to stand? What is my place if I am a woman? I look for myself throughout the centuries and don't see myself anywhere. I know now that my fighters are masculine and that their value almost inevitably is limited: they are great in the eyes of men and for each other. But only on the condition that a woman not appear and make blind and grotesque tyrants of them, marred by all the flaws that I want them to be free of—exposing them to be miserly, inhuman, small, fearful . . .

Where to stand? Who to be? Who, in the long continuing episodes of their misfortune—woman's abundance always repaid by abandonment? Beginning Medea's story all over again, less and less violently, repeating more and more tenderly, sadly, the gift, the fervor, the passion, the alienation, the stunning discovery of the worst (which isn't death): that total love has been used by the loved one for his base ambitions. "The one who was everything for me, I know only too well, my husband has become the worst of men." (Euripides, *Medea*).

Vast—this procession of mistreated, deceived, devastated, rejected, patient women, dolls, cattle, cash. Stolen swarms. Exploited and plundered to such an extent. They give everything. That, doubtless, is their offense. For example—Ariadne, without calculating, without hesitating, but believing, taking everything as far as it goes, giving everything, renouncing all security—spending without a return—the anti-Ulysses—never looking back, knowing how to break off, how to leave, advancing into emptiness, into the unknown. But as for Theseus, he ties himself tightly to the line the woman holds fast to make him secure. While she, she takes her leap without a line. I read the *Life of Theseus* in Plutarch.

A model destiny! Two lines weave the elevation of man and the simultaneous debasement of woman. All the figures of a rise to power are inscribed in the route Theseus takes. The still unacknowledged son comes to be recognized by his father, Aegeus, who has won Medea as wife. (Here is an irony of history: with Medea, at the end of a career of successive exiles, once and for all the stage is cleared where the first version of male cultural organization will install itself!) Then the splendid moment in which the mystery of filiation is revealed: father and son recognize each other by the signs of their order, which are the sword (. . . and the sandals: for Theseus [his name recalls] is the one who was able to lift the boulder under which Aegeus stashed his sandals. What is a son? The man who can lift the rock . . . to tie on the inherited shoes).

Then a triumphant career is woven: the crossing of feminine bodies with the thread of a pitiless soul, and a huge territory is accumulated as he passes from woman to woman. Through Ariadne, Antiope, Hippolyta, Phaedra, hecatombs of numberless, loving women and amazons; with Theseus the last great flames die. And so on, down to Helen, abducted at the age of ten (this is how she got started or, rather, got "started.") At that point no more is known, because Theseus evaporates, at the end of the road of abduction and consummation/consumption . . . and he is still running. Moreover, after his father's death, he gathered the inhabitants of the whole province of Attica into one city and reduced them to a town body. Plutarch recounts that there were some in favor of submitting to Theseus's management and others who gave in anyhow, for fear of his strength. Centralization, destruction of all the little units of local administration: the birth of Athens. Afterward he lived happily, invented coins which he had hammered in the image of the Marathon bull, and had lots of money.

I could not have been Ariadne: it's all right that she gives herself out of love. But to whom? Theseus doesn't tremble, doesn't adore, doesn't desire; following his own destiny, he goes over bodies that are never even idealized. Every woman is a means. I see that clearly.

But I would have dared to be Dido. This is where I begin to suffer in a woman's place. Reading Virgil again, in the *Aeneid* (Books 3 and 4); one sees how the venerable Aeneas, who is destined to found a city, is kept from the feminine danger by the gods.

Less of a bastard than Jason, less "pure" in plain, brute *jouissance* than Theseus, more moral; there is always a god or a cause to excuse or explain Aeneas's skill at seeding and shaking off his women, dropping them. Act I, Exodus from Troy. Theseus is armed with his father on his shoulders and his son in his arms:

> for, my wife Creuse is taken away from me while I run, taking the wrong roads and straying from my usual direction. Did she stop as the result of any unfortunate fate, or did she take the wrong road, or did she succumb to fatigue? I don't know, but I have never seen her again. I didn't notice she was lost and didn't think about her until the moment at which we arrived at the burial mound, at the sacred habitation of ancient Ceres.

Second book:

> It was only there, when we were all together again that I saw that she alone was missing and had disappeared without her companions, her son or husband's knowing. Who then, both men and gods, did I not accuse in my distraction?

Horror! The venerable one looks all over and everywhere. Death herself comes to justify him before History.

> Then she spoke thus to me and took away my cares with these words "Why let yourself go on so in such an insane grief, oh my loving husband? These things don't happen unless the gods will them; and they do not allow you to take Creuse as your companion: a flourishing fortune, a kingdom, a royal wife are reserved for you; stop shedding tears for your darling Creuse. No I will not see the splendid homes of the Myrmidons and Dolops; I will not go, as a slave, to serve Greek women, I a Dardanadide and the daughter-in-law of divine Venus. The powerful mother of the gods keeps me on her shores. Farewell, and always love our common son.[7]

Act I. Theme: "a woman's slave?" No! Mercury who is sent by Jupiter intervenes in the name of the league of empire builders: so you are building a beautiful city for a woman and forgetting your kingdom and your own destiny? Thus pious Aeneas will be saved from shame. The next scenes would have been unbearable for him; grief, love, and Dido's beauty are mingled in heartrending songs, and Aeneas doubtless would have weakened. But "the fates are against it, and a god closes the hero's serene ears." He hurts, but he has his law,

---

7. *Aeneid* 1.4.320-65.

and that is what he espouses: and his law is clear, because, by dying, Creuse is giving him a sublime strength. The good love for man is his country, the fatherland. A masculine land to hand down from father to son. For Ascanias then . . .

In Dido's place. But I am not Dido. I cannot inhabit a victim, no matter how noble. I resist: detest a certain passivity, it promises death for me. So, who shall I be? I have gone back and forth in vain through the ages and through the stories within my reach, yet find no woman into whom I can slip. My sympathy, my tenderness, my sorrow, however, are all hers. But not me, not my life. I can never lay down my arms. Of course, Joan of Arc is someone; but for me, a Jew and suspicious of anything related to the Church and its ideological rule, she is totally uninhabitable. But otherwise I am with her—for her energy, her unique confidence, the stark simplicity of her action, her clear-cut relationship with men—and for her trial and her stake. But apart from her who I never was, there was nobody. For a long time I continued to be a sort of secret Achilles, profiting from his sexual ambiguity which permitted me mine. But you can't be Achilles every day. And I want to become a woman I can love. I want to meet women who love themselves, who are alive, who are not debased, overshadowed, wiped out. I read—now driven by the need to confirm whether or not there is, on the other side of the world, this relationship between beings that alone merits the name of love. For a springboard, there are some ideas—or rather, beliefs, premonitions —that I do not theorize and that stay more or less unconscious for quite a long time. Everywhere I see the battle for mastery that rages between classes, peoples, etc., reproducing itself on an individual scale. Is the system flawless? Impossible to bypass? On the basis of my desire, I imagine that other desires like mine exist. If my desire is possible, it means the system is already letting something else through. All the poets know that: whatever is thinkable is real, as William Blake suggests. And it's true. There have to be ways of relating that are completely different from the tradition ordained by the masculine economy. So, urgently and anxiously, I look for a scene in which a type of exchange would be produced that would be different, a kind of desire that wouldn't be in collusion with the old story of death. This desire would invent Love, it alone would not use the word love to cover up its opposite: one would not land right back in a dialectical destiny, still unsatisfied by the debasement of one by the other. On the contrary, there would have to be a recognition of each other, and this grateful acknowledgment would come about thanks to the intense and passionate work of knowing. Finally, each would take the risk of *other*, of difference, without feeling threatened by the existence of an otherness, rather, delighting to increase through the unknown that is there to discover, to respect, to favor, to cherish.

This love would not be trapped in contradictions and ambivalences entailing the murder of the other indefinitely. Nor would it be caught up again in the huge social machinery taking individuals back to the family model. It would not collapse in paradoxes of relationship to the other like the ones whose pitiless vicious circle Hegel based on the idea of *Physical Property*. . . .

JULIA KRISTEVA

"The desire to be a mother," says Julia Kristeva in her 1979 essay "Women's Time," ". . . has obviously not become a standard for the present generation."* The statement has the edge of understatement. And yet, for Kristeva, there is an increasing realization that the full complexity of the female experience is unknown to this tragic generation, which is so consumed with rage against the dominant order that they refuse to distinguish the role of mother from being anything other than a thrall and drudge. And it seems that they sacrifice a great deal more than themselves as they gain access to power—only to discover that they merely reinforce the order that had earlier enraged them (27). We have been made aware of the shortcomings of the male law institution and the legal and moral order dependent upon it. And if it has been recently troubled, it deserves to be. But what does "female right" entail? What can women do to provide an alternative ethic? The answer, when it obliquely appears at the end of "Women's Time," seems to be in some way religious, involving an end of anthropomorphism, by which she means a sublation—an end of feminism as well. Only a religious discourse, which seems at times to be aesthetic, would be able to support the new adventure of reconciling each person's "singularity" with his or her multiple possibilities of identification "with atoms . . . stretching from the family to the stars . . ." (34–35). That maternity is central to transcendence of this type might, in part, explain Kristeva's loving analysis, sublime in its own right, of the Virgin. The essay, published two years before "Women's Time," is reprinted here in its English version titled "Stabat Mater" (the reference is to "The Mother Was Standing," a 13th century Latin hymn often put to music). Such has been the power of this representation of the maternal that despite the permanent incompatibility of the sexes, it managed for centuries to calm anxiety and make community possible. The central point of maternity seems to be that it is outside the Symbolic Order, as it is referred to in France, outside linguistic expression, which carries the principles of social order. The maternal corresponds to the Unconscious in Lacan, representing that which is repressed by the subject's entry into history, linear time, and public purpose. Saints, mystics, and writers have always treated their experiences as "maternal," as an eruption of the nocturnal and uncanny. Karen Horney has written of male creativity as womb envy, and Kristeva suggests that woman might choose either maternity or psychoanalysis as

---

* For the English version see *Signs,* Vol. 7 (1981), No. 1: 30. The article was translated by Alice Jardine and Harry Blake.

a remedy for neurosis.† The heart of her essay, surely, is the remarkable passage in which Mary's anguish for her dead son is matched by the dying Pergolesi's musical contemplation of maternal love in his *Stabat Mater* (1736). The point is this interlocking self-transcendence of both male and female: the woman striving to share the "thoroughly masculine pain of the male," who, obsessed with death, "expires at each moment of ecstasy"; and the dying young man who, as the identity between thought and body is shattered, finds again that "spectrum of auditory, tactile, and visual memories that precede language," that fluidity of participation in the female before the ego has rigidified, before the carapace of the self is hardened. To know this moment again is to know love as a "fire of tongues," beside which every other love seems pathetic and pale. In it the love between mother and child—which the Father's law has jealously called incestuous—is sublimated and celebrated. It is this female experience which has yet to enter the Law and has often been seen in opposition to it (Sophocles' *Antigone*). Ethics based on this experience would be heretical ethics, "herethics," hence the title of the original composition in French, "Héréthique de l'amour." The short passages written in bold face are best described as personal and poetic; they should be read consecutively after the right hand columns in regular print.

Stabat Mater

▲ 1977

Translated by Arthur Goldhammer

THE PARADOX: MOTHER OR PRIMARY NARCISSISM

If, in speaking of a *woman,* it is impossible to say what she *is*—for to do so would risk abolishing her difference—might matters not stand

† Karen Horney, "The Distrust Between the Sexes," see *Die Ärztin* VII (1931) 5–12. Available in English in Lee A. Jacobus, *A World of Ideas* (New York: St. Martin's, 1986) 329–40.

differently with respect to the *mother*, motherhood being the sole function of the "other sex" to which we may confidently attribute existence? Yet here, too, we are caught in a paradox. To begin with, we live in a civilization in which the *consecrated* (religious or secular) representation of femininity is subsumed under maternity. Under close examination, however, this maternity turns out to be an adult (male and female) fantasy of a lost continent: what is involved, moreover, is not so much an idealized primitive mother as an idealization of the—unlocalizable—*relationship* between her and us, an idealization of primary narcissism. When feminists call for a new representation of femininity, they seem to identify maternity with this idealized misapprehension; and feminism, because it rejects this image and its abuses, sidesteps the real experience that this fantasy obscures. As a result, maternity is repudiated or denied by some avant-garde feminists, while its traditional representations are wittingly or unwittingly accepted by the "broad mass" of women and men.‡

FLASH—an instant of time or a timeless dream; atoms swollen beyond measure, atoms of a bond, a vision, a shiver, a still shapeless embryo, unnameable. Epiphanies. Photos of what is not yet visible and which language necessarily surveys from a very high altitude, allusively. Words always too remote, too abstract to capture the subterranean swarm of seconds, insinuating themselves into unimaginable places. Writing them down

Christianity is no doubt the most sophisticated symbolic construct in which femininity, to the extent that it figures therein —and it does so constantly—is confined within the limits of the *Maternal*.[1] By "maternal" I mean the ambivalent principle that derives on the one hand from the species and on the other hand from a catastrophe of identity which plunges the proper Name into that "unnameable" that somehow involves our imaginary representations of femininity, non-language, or the body. Thus, Christ, the Son of man, is in the

‡This essay first appeared, under the title "Héréthique de l'amour," in *Tel Quel*, no. 74 (Winter 1977). It was reprinted under the present title in Kristeva, *Histoires d'amour* (Paris: Denoël, 1983). This is the first English translation, very slightly shortened from the original.

1. For information about matters not covered here, see the two books that provided much of the basis for the reflections contained in this paper, Warner (1976) and Barande (1977).

tests an argument, as does love. What is love, for a woman, the same thing as writing. Laugh. Impossible. Flash on the unnameable, woven of abstractions to be torn apart. Let a body finally venture out of its shelter, expose itself in meaning beneath a veil of words. WORD FLESH. From one to the other, eternally, fragmented visions, metaphors of the invisible.

end "human" only through his mother: as if Christic or Christian humanism could not help being a form of maternalism (which is precisely the claim that has been made repeatedly, in a characteristically esoteric fashion, by certain secularizing tendencies within Christian humanism). Yet the humanity of the Virgin mother is not always evident, and we shall see later just how Mary is distinguished from the human race, for example by her freedom from sin. At the same time, however, mysticism, that most intense form of divine revelation, is vouchsafed only to those who take the "maternal" upon themselves. Saint Augustine, Saint Bernard, and Meister Eckhart, to name just three among many, assume the role of virgin spouse to the Father, and Bernard even receives drops of virginal milk on his lips. Comfortable in their relation to the maternal "continent," mystics use this comfort as a pedestal on which to erect their love of God; these "happy Schrebers," as Philippe Sollers calls them, thus shed a bizarre light on modernity's psychotic lesion, namely, the apparent incapacity of modern codes to make the maternal—i.e., primary narcissism —tractable. Rare and "literary" if always rather oriental, not to say tragic, are the mystics' contemporary counterparts: think of Henry Miller's claim to be pregnant or Artaud's imagining himself to be like "his girls" or "his mother." It is Christianity's Orthodox branch, through the golden tongue of John Chrysostom among others, that will consecrate this transitional function of the Maternal by referring to the Virgin as a "link," a "surrounding," or an "interval," thereby opening the way to more or less heretical attempts to identify the Virgin with the Holy Spirit.

Many civilizations have subsumed femininity under the Maternal, but Christianity in its own way developed this tendency to the full. The question is whether this was simply an appropriation of the Maternal by men and therefore, according to our working hypothesis, just a fantasy hiding the primary narcissism from view, or was it perhaps also the mechanism of enigmatic sublimation? This may have been masculine sublimation, but it was still sublimation, assuming that for Freud imagining Leonardo—and even for Leonardo himself—taming the Maternal—or primary narcissistic—economy is a necessary precondition of artistic or literary achievement.

Yet this approach leaves many questions unanswered, among them the following two. First, what is it about the representation of the Maternal in general, and about the Christian or virginal representation in particular, that enables it not only to calm social anxiety and supply what the male lacks, but also to satisfy a woman, in such a way that the community of the sexes is established beyond, and in spite of, their flagrant incompatibility and permanent state of war? Second, what is it about this representation that fails to take account of what a woman might say or want of the Maternal, so that when today women make their voices heard, the issues of conception and maternity are a major focus of discontent? Such protests go beyond sociopolitical issues and raise "civilization's discontents" to such a pitch that even Freud recoiled at the prospect: the discontent is somehow in the species itself.

A TRIUMPH OF THE UNCONSCIOUS IN MONOTHEISM

It seems that the epithet "virgin" applied to Mary was an error of translation: for the Semitic word denoting the social-legal status of an unmarried girl the translator substituted the Greek *parthenos,* which denotes a physiological and psychological fact, virginity. It is possible to read this as an instance of the Indo-European fascination (analyzed by Georges Dumezil) with the virgin daughter as repository of the father's power. It may also be interpreted as an ambivalent, and highly spiritualized, evocation of the underlying mother goddess and matriarchy, with which Greek culture and Jewish monotheism were locked in combat. Be that as it may, it remains true that Western Christendom orchestrated this "error of translation" by projecting its own fantasies on it, thereby producing one of the most potent imaginary constructs known to any civilization.

The history of the Christian cult of the Virgin is actually the history of the imposition of beliefs with pagan roots upon, and sometimes in opposition to, the official dogma of the Church. Admittedly, the Gospels acknowledge the existence of Mary. But they allude only in the most discreet way to the immaculate conception, say nothing at all about Mary's own history, and seldom depict her in the company of her son or in the scene surrounding his crucifixion. Thus we read, for example, in Matthew 1.20, that "the angel of the Lord appeared unto him in a dream, saying, Joseph, thou son of David, fear not to take unto thee Mary thy wife: for that which is conceived in her is of the Holy Ghost." And Luke 1.34 has Mary saying to the angel, "How shall this be, seeing I know not a man?" These texts open a path, narrow to be sure but quickly widened by apocryphal additions, that leads to the possibility of pregnancy without sex, wherein a woman preserved from penetration by a male conceives solely with the aid of a "third person" or, rather, non-person, the Spirit. On the rare occasions when the Mother of Jesus does appear in the Gospels, it is in order to signify the fact that the filial bond has to do not with the flesh but with the name; in other words, any trace of matrilinearity is explicitly disavowed, leaving only the symbolic tie between mother and son. Witness, for example, Luke 2.48–49: "And his mother said unto him, Son, why hast thou thus dealt with us? behold, thy father and I have sought thee sorrowing. And he said unto them, How is that ye sought me? wist ye not that I must be about my Father's business?" And John 2.3: "The mother of Jesus saith unto him, They have no wine. Jesus saith unto her, Woman, what have I to do with thee? mine hour is not yet come." Or again, John 19.26–27: "When Jesus therefore saw his mother, and the disciple standing by, whom he loved, he saith unto his mother, Woman, behold thy son! Then saith he to the disciple, Behold thy mother! And from that hour that disciple took her unto his own *home.*"

From this rather meager programmatic material an irresistible complex of images grew, essentially along three lines. The first involved attempts to establish an analogy between the Mother and the Son by developing the theme of the immaculate conception; by inventing a biography for Mary paralleling that of Jesus; and, by freeing Mary in this way from sin, freeing her also from death: Mary passes away in Dormition or Assumption. The second involved granting Mary letters of nobility, making use of a power which though exercised in the afterlife was nonetheless political, in that she was proclaimed queen, endowed with the attributes and paraphernalia of royalty, and simultaneously declared Mother of the divine institution on earth, the Church. Finally, the relationship to Mary and of Mary was revealed as the prototype of the love relationship; it consequently followed the development of those two fundamental subcategories of Western love, courtly love and love of the child, and thus became involved in the whole range of love-types from sublimation to asceticism and masochism.

NEITHER SEX NOR DEATH

The idea to model an imaginary life of Mary on that of Jesus seems to have come from the apocryphal literature. The story of Mary's miraculous or "immaculate" conception by Anne and Joachim after a long childless marriage, as well as the depiction of her as a pious young woman, first appears in apocryphal sources at the end of the first century. It may be found in its entirety in the Book of James as well as the Gospel according to pseudo-Matthew (which became the inspiration of Giotto's frescoes). The "facts" were cited by Clement of Alexandria and Origen but not officially recognized, and although the Eastern Orthodox church tolerated the stories without difficulty, they were not translated into Latin until the sixteenth century. The West was not slow, however, to glorify the life of Mary, using methods of its own, albeit still of Orthodox inspiration. The first Latin poem on Mary's birth, entitled "Maria," was the work of Hroswitha of Gandersheim (d. before 1002), a poet and playwright as well as a nun.

In the fourth century the notion of an immaculate conception was further developed and rationalized by grafting the Church Fathers' arguments for asceticism onto the spirit of the apocrypha. The logic of the case was simple: sexuality implies death and vice versa, so that it is impossible to escape the latter without shunning the former. A vigorous proponent of asceticism for both sexes was Saint John Chrysostom, who has the following to say in *On Virginity:* "For where there is death, there too is sexual coupling; and where there is no death, there is no sexual coupling either" (Warner 1976:52). Though combatted by Saint Augustine and Saint Thomas, Chrysostom was not without influence on Christian doctrine. Augustine, for example, condemned "concupiscence" *(epithumia)* and asserted that Mary's virginity was in fact merely a logical prerequisite for the chastity of Christ. The Orthodox church, which was doubtless the heir to a more violent matriarchy prevalent in the East, was bolder in emphasizing Mary's virginity. A contrast was drawn between Mary and Eve, life and death, as in Saint Jerome's *Twenty-second Letter:* "Death came through Eve, but life has come through Mary"; and Irenaeus wrote that through Mary "the guile of the serpent was overcome by the simplicity of the dove and we are set free from those chains by which we had been bound to death" (Warner 1976:54, 60). There were even some rather tortuous debates over the question whether Mary remained a virgin after giving birth: thus in A.D. 381 the Second Council of Constantinople, under the influence of Arianism, placed greater stress on Mary's role than did official dogma and proclaimed her perpetual virginity, and the council of A.D. 451 declared her *Aeiparthenos,* forever virgin. Once this position was established, it became possible to proclaim that Mary was not merely the Mother of man or Christ but the Mother of God, *Theotokos,* as the patriarch Nestor did, thus deifying her once and for all.

The strained eardrum wresting sound from the heedless silence. Wind in the grass, the cry of a gull in the distance, echoes of the waves, of sirens, of voices, or of nothing? Or his, my new-born child's, tears, syncopated spasm of the void. Now I hear nothing, but my eardrum continues to transmit this sonorous vertigo to my skull, to the roots of my hair. My body is no longer mine, it writhes, suffers, bleeds, catches cold, bites, slavers, coughs, breaks out in a rash, and laughs. Yet when his, my son's, joy returns, his smile cleanses only my eyes. But suffering, his suffering—that I feel inside; that never remains separate or alien but embraces me at once without a moment's respite. As if I had brought not a child but

The highly complex relationship between Christ and his Mother served as a matrix within which various other relations —God to mankind, man to woman, son to mother, etc. —took shape; this relationship soon gave rise to questions involving not only *causality* but also *time.* If Mary is prior to Christ, and if he, or at any rate his humanity, originates with her, then must she not too be immaculate? For otherwise a person conceived in sin and carrying sin within herself would have given birth to a God, and how could this be? Some apocryphal writers suggested with imprudent haste that Mary had indeed been conceived without sin, but the Fathers were more cautious. Saint Bernard refused to celebrate Saint Mary's conception by Saint Anne and in this way attempted to impede the assimilation of Mary's life to that of Christ. But it suffering into the world and it, suffering, refused to leave me, insisted on coming back, on haunting me, permanently. One does not bear children in pain, it's pain that one bears: the child is pain's representative and once delivered moves in for good. Obviously you can close your eyes, stop up your ears, teach courses, run errands, clean house, think about things, about ideas. But a mother is also marked by pain, she succumbs to it. "And you, one day a sword will pass through your soul."

was Duns Scotus who transformed this hesitation about promoting a mother goddess to a position within Christianity into a logical problem, in order to safeguard both the Great Mother and logic. He took the view that Mary's birth was a *praeredemptio,* based on an argument of congruity: if it is true that it is Christ alone who saves us by his redemption on the cross, then the Virgin who bore him can only be preserved from sin "recursively," as it were, from her own conception up to the moment of that redemption.

Pitting Franciscans against Dominicans, the battle that raged around the Virgin intensified on both sides, for and against, dogma versus clever logic, until finally, as is well known, the Counter Reformation overcame all resistance: from then on Catholics have venerated Mary in her own person. The Company of Jesus successfully concluded a process initiated by popular pressure filtered through patristic asceticism, and managed, without explicit hostility or blunt repudiation, to gain control of that aspect of the Maternal (in the sense I mentioned earlier) that was useful for establishing a certain equilibrium between the sexes. Oddly though inevitably, it was when this equilibrium was first seriously threatened in the nineteenth century that the Catholic Church, in 1854, gave the Immaculate Conception the status of dogma (thus showing itself to be more dialectical and more subtle than the Protestants, who were already engendering the first suffragettes). It is frequently suggested that the flourishing of feminism in the Protestant countries is due, among other things, to the fact that women there are allowed greater initiative in social life and ritual. But one wonders if it is not also due to Protestantism's *lacking* some necessary element of the Maternal which in Catholicism has been elaborated with the utmost sophistication by the Jesuits (and which again makes Catholicism very difficult to analyze).

That entity compounded of woman and God and given the name Mary was made complete by the avoidance of death. The fate of the Virgin Mary is more radiant even than that of her son: not having been crucified, she has no tomb and does not die, and therefore she has no need of resurrection. Mary does not die but rather—echoing Taoist and other oriental beliefs in which human bodies pass from one place to another in a never-ending cycle which is in itself an imitation of the process of childbirth—she passes over.

This transition is more passive in the east than in the west: the Orthodox Church holds to the doctrine of *Koimesis,* or Dormition, which in some iconographic representations has Mary becoming a little girl held in the arms of her son, who now becomes her Father; she thus passes from the role of Mother to that of Daughter, to the great pleasure of students of Freud's "Three Caskets."

Not only is Mary her son's *mother* and his *daughter,* she is also his *wife.* Thus she passes through all three women's stages in the most restricted of all possible kinship systems. Adapting the Song of Songs, Bernard of Clairvaux in 1135 glorified Mary in the role of beloved spouse. But long before that, Catherine of Alexandria (martyred in A.D. 307) imagined herself receiving the wedding ring from Christ aided by the Virgin; and later Catherine of Siena (d. 1380) entered into a mystical marriage with Christ. Was it the impact of Mary's role as Christ's beloved and spouse that was responsible for the rapid spread of Mariolatry in the West after Bernard and thanks to the Cistercians? *"Vergine Madre, figlia del tuo Figlio,"* exclaimed Dante, who perhaps best captures the combination of the three feminine roles—daughter-wife-mother—within a whole, where they lose their specific corporeal identities while retaining their psychological functions. The nexus of these three functions is the basis of immutable and atemporal spirituality: "the fixed term of an eternal design," as *The Divine Comedy* magisterially puts it.

By contrast, in the West, Mary's transition is more active: in the Assumption she rises body and soul to another world. Celebrated in Byzantium as early as the fourth century, the feast of the Assumption came to Gaul in the seventh century under the influence of the Eastern Church, but the earliest visions of the Virgin's assumption (all women's visions, and most notably that of Elisabeth of Schonan, d. 1164) date back no farther than the twelfth century. The Vatican did not declare the Assumption to be dogma until 1950—and even then (we may speculate) only to calm widespread anxieties over death in the aftermath of the most lethal of all wars.

FIGURE OF POWER

Turning now to the question of "power," an image of *Maria Regina* dating as far back as the sixth century can be found in Rome's Santa Maria Antiqua. It is interesting to observe that it is Mary, woman and mother, who takes it upon herself to represent the supreme terrestrial power. Christ is king, but it is neither Jesus nor his Father that one sees wearing crowns, diadems, sumptuous robes, and other external signs of abundant material wealth. The Virgin Mary became the center of this twisting of Christian idealism in the direction of opulence. When she later assumed the title of Our Lady, moreover, it was by analogy with the noble lady of the feudal court. The Church later became wary of Mary's role as repository of power and tried to put a halt to it, but it nevertheless persisted in popular and artistic imagery—witness Piero della Francesca's impressive painting *Madonna della Misericordia,* which was disavowed in its time by the Catholic authorities. Yet not only did the papacy venerate Christ's mother increasingly as it consolidated its power over the towns, it also openly identified the papal institution itself with the Virgin: Mary was officially proclaimed Queen by Pius XII in 1954 and *Mater Ecclesiae* in 1964.

EIA MATER, FONS AMORIS!

Ultimately, several fundamental features of western love converge in Mary. Initially, the cult of the Virgin, which assimilated Mary to Jesus and pushed asceticism to an extreme, seems to have contrasted sharply with courtly love for the noble lady, which constituted a social transgression but nothing of a physical or moral sin. Yet even in its carnal beginnings courtly love had this in common with Mariolatry, that both Mary and the Lady were focal points of men's aspirations and desires. Furthermore, by dint of uniqueness, by the exclusion of all other women, both were embodiments of an absolute authority that was all the more attractive because it seemed not to be subject to the severity of the father. This feminine power must have been experienced as power denied, all the more pleasant to seize because it was both archaic and secondary, an ersatz yet not less authoritarian form of the real power in the family and the city, a cunning double of the explicit phallic power. From the thirteenth century, helped by the establishment of ascetic forms of Christianity, and especially after

1328, when the Salic Laws—prohibiting inheritance by daughters —were promulgated, making the beloved lady quite vulnerable and tinging love for her with every shade of the impossible, the Marian tradition and the courtly tradition tended to merge. With Blanche of Castille (d. 1252), the Virgin explicitly became the focus of courtly love, combining the qualities of the desired woman and the holy mother in a totality as perfect as it was inaccessible. Enough to make any woman suffer and any man dream. And indeed one *Miracle of Our Lady* tells of a young man who abandons his fiancée for the Virgin after Mary reproaches him in a dream for having left her for an "earthly woman."

The smell of milk, dew-drenched greenery, sour and clear, a memory of wind, of air, of seaweed (as if a body lived without waste): it glides under my skin, not stopping at the mouth or nose but caressing my veins, and stripping the skin from the bones fills me like a balloon full of ozone and I plant my feet firmly on the ground in order to carry him, safe, stable, unprootable, while he dances in my neck, floats with my hair, looks right and left for a soft shoulder, "slips on the breast, swingles, silver vivid blossom of my belly" and finally flies up from my navel in his dream, borne by my hands. My son.

A night of vigil, fitful sleep, the child's gentleness, hot mercury in my arms, caress, tenderness, defenseless body, his or mine, sheltered, protected. Another wave

Meanwhile, alongside this ideal that no individual woman could possibly embody, the Virgin also served as a mooring point for the humanization of the West, and in particular for the humanization of love. It was again in the thirteenth century, with Saint Francis, that this tendency took shape, producing representations of Mary as a poor, modest, and humble woman as well as a tender, devoted mother. Pietro della Francesca's celebrated *Nativity*, now in London, which Simone de Beauvoir was too quick to see as a defeat for women because it depicts a mother kneeling before her newborn son, actually epitomizes the new cult of humanist sensibility. For the high spirituality that assimilated the Virgin to Christ, the painting substitutes an altogether human image of a mother of flesh and blood. Such maternal humility has inspired the most widespread of pious images and comes closer than early images to women's "real-

rises under my skin after he falls asleep—belly, thighs, legs: sleep of the muscles not the brain, sleep of the flesh. The watchful tongue tenderly remembers another abandonment, my own: decorated lead at the foot of the bed, a hollow, the sea. Childhood regained,recreated,dreamed-of peace, in sparks, flash of the cells, moments of laughter, a smile in the black of a dream, night, an opaque joy that holds me fast in my mother's bed and propels him, a son, a butterfly drinking dew from his hand, there, beside me in the night. Alone: she, I and he.

life" experience. Although it is to some degree tinged with female masochism, it also exhibits a compensating measure of gratification and ecstasy, in that the mother bows her head before her son but not without a boundless pride in the knowledge that she is also his wife and daughter. She knows that she is destined to that eternity (of spirit or species) of which every mother is subconsciously aware, and in relation to which the devotion, or even the sacrifice, of motherhood is but a ridiculously small price to pay. And that price is all the more easy to bear in that, compared with the love that binds mother to son, all other "human relationships" stand revealed as flagrant imitations. The Franciscan representation of the Mother adequately captured certain essential aspects of maternal psychology, thus not only bringing large numbers of worshipers into the churches but also extending the Marian cult to a remarkable degree, as is shown by the large numbers of churches that were dedicated to Our Lady. The humanization of Christianity through the cult of the Mother also led to a new interest in the humanity of the man-father: the celebration of family life brought Joseph to prominence in the fifteenth century.

WHAT BODY

Of the virginal body we are entitled only to the ear, the tears, and the breasts. That the female sexual organ has been transformed into an innocent shell which serves only to receive sound may ultimately contribute to an eroticization of hearing and the voice, not to say of understanding. But by the same token sexuality is reduced to a mere implication. The female sexual experience is therefore anchored in the universality of sound, since the spirit is *equally* given to all men, to all women. A woman has only two choices: either to experience herself in sex *hyperabstractly* (in an "immediately universal" way, as Hegel would say) so as to make herself worthy of divine grace and assimilation to the symbolic order, or else to experience herself as *different,* other, fallen (or, in Hegel's terms again, "immediately particular"). But she will not be able to achieve her complexity as a divided, heterogeneous being, a "fold-catastrophe"[2] of the "to-be" (or, in Hegel's terms, the "never singular").

The lover gone: now comes oblivion, but the pleasure of the sexes remains, and nothing is missing. No representation, sensation, memory. The brazier of vice. Later, forgetfulness returns, but now as a fall—of lead—gray, pale, opaque. Oblivion: a blinding, choking, yet tender mist. Like the fog that devours the park, swallowing its branches, wiping out the rusty new sun and clouding my eyes.

Absence, brazier, oblivion. Scansion of our loves.

Leaving, in place of the heart, a hunger. A spasm that spreads, that travels down the vessels to the ends of the breasts, to the tips of the fingers. It palpitates, bores a hole in the emptiness, erases it, and little by little takes up residence. My heart: an immense, beating wound. A thirst.

Anxious, guilty. The *Vaterkomplex* of Freud at the Acropolis? The impossibility

The virgin mother's ample blue gown will allow only the breast to be seen of the body underneath, while her face will gradually be covered with tears as the stiffness of the Byzantine icons is slowly overcome. Milk and tears are the signs *par excellence* of the *Mater dolorosa* who began invading the West in the eleventh century and reached a peak in the fourteenth. From then on she has never ceased to fill the Marian visions of all those, men and women (or frequently male child, female child) who suffer the anguish of some maternal frustration. That orality —the threshold of infantile regression—manifests itself in connection with the breast whereas the spasm that comes at eroticism's eclipse is associated with tears should not be allowed to obscure what milk and tears have in common: both are metaphors of non-language, of a "semiotic" that does not coincide with linguistic communication. The Mother and her attributes signifying suffering humanity thus become the symbol of a

2. The allusion is to René Thom's theory of catastrophes. (Translator's note.)

of existing without repeated legitimation (without books, map, family). Impossibility —depressing possibility—of "transgression."

Or of the repression in which *I* passes to the Other, what I desire from others.

Or this murmur of emptiness, this open wound in my heart which means that I exist only in purgatory. I desire the Law. And since it is not made for me alone, I run the risk of desiring outside the law. Then, the narcissism thus awakened that wants to be sex, wanders inflated. In the transport of the senses, I come up empty-handed. Nothing reassures because only the law makes permanent. Who calls this suffering ecstasy? It is the pleasure of the damned.

"return of the repressed" in monotheism. They reestablish the nonverbal and appear as a signifying modality closer to the so-called primary processes. Without them the complexity of the Holy Spirit would no doubt have been mutilated. Returning through the Virgin Mother, they instead found fertile soil in art —painting and music—of which the Virgin would of necessity become both patron and privileged object.

Thus we witness the emergence of the "virginal Maternal" function in the symbolic economy of the West: from the high Christic sublimation which she aspires to achieve and at times transcends, to the extralinquistic realms of the unnameable, the Virgin Mother occupies the vast territory that lies on either side of the parenthesis of language. She adds to the Christian Trinity, and to the Word which gives it its coherence, a heterogeneity that they subsume.

The ordering of the maternal libido is carried farthest in connection with the theme of death. The *Mater dolorosa* knows no male body except that of her dead son, and her only pathos (which is sharply distinguished from the sweet and somewhat absent serenity of the lactating Madonnas) comes from the tears she sheds over a corpse. Since resurrection lies in the offing, and since as the Mother of God she ought to know that it does, nothing justifies Mary's anguish at the foot of the cross unless it is the desire to feel in her own body what it is like for a man to be put to death, a fate spared her by her female role as source of life. Is the love of women who weep over the bodies of the dead a love as obscure as it is ancient, nourished by the same source as the aspiration of a woman whom nothing satisfies, namely, the desire to feel the thoroughly masculine pain of the male who, obsessed with the thought of death, expires at each moment of ecstasy? Still, Mary's suffering has nothing of tragic excess about it: joy and indeed a kind of triumph supplant her tears, as if the conviction that death does not exist were an unreasonable but unshakeable maternal certainty, upon which the principle of resurrection must have rested for support. The majestic figure of this woman twisted one way by desire for the male cadaver and the other by a denial of death—a twisting whose paranoid logic should not go unmentioned—is served up in magisterial fashion by the well-known *Stabat Mater*. All belief in resurrection is probably rooted in mythologies dominated by the mother goddess. True, Christianity found its vocation in the displacement of this biomaternal determinism by the postulate that immortality belongs primarily to the Name of the Father. But it could not achieve *its* symbolic revolution without drawing on the support of the feminine representation of biological immortality. Is it not the image of Mary braving death depicted in the many variations of the *Stabat Mater* which (in the text attributed to Jacopone da Todi) enraptures us even today in musical compositions from Palestrina to Pergolesi, Haydn, and Rossini?

Listen to the "baroquism" of the young Pergolesi (1710–1736) dying of tuberculosis while writing his immortal *Stabat Mater*. His musical invention, which, conveyed through Haydn, would be heard again in Mozart, is no doubt his only form of immortality. But when we hear the cry, *"Eia mater, fons amoris!"* ("Hail, mother, source of love"), referring to Mary confronting the death of her son, is it merely a residue of the baroque era? Man surmounts death, the unthinkable, by postulating instead—in the stead and place of thought as well as of death—maternal love. That love, of which divine love will be no more than a not always convincing derivative, is psychologically perhaps just a memory, prior to the primary identifications of the primitive shelter that guaranteed the survival of the newborn child. Logically in fact, that love is an unfurling of anguish at the very moment when the identity of thought and the living body breaks down. When the possibilities of communication are swept away, the last remaining rampart against death is the subtle spectrum of auditory, tactile, and visual memories that precede language and reemerge in its absence. Nothing could be more "normal" than that a maternal image should establish itself on the site of that tempered anguish known as love. No one is spared. Except perhaps the saint or the mystic, or the writer who, by force of language, can still manage nothing more than to demolish the fiction of the mother-as-love's-mainstay and to identify with love as it really is: *a fire of tongues*, an escape from representation. For the few who practice it, then, is modern art not a realization of maternal love—a veil over death, assuming death's very place and knowing that it does? A sublimated celebration of incest . . .

ALONE OF ALL HER SEX

Incommensurable, unlocalizable maternal body. First there is division, which precedes the pregnancy but is revealed by it, irrevocably imposed. . . . **Then another abyss opens between this body and the body that was inside it: the abyss that separates mother and child. What relationship is there between me or, more modestly, between my body and this internal graft, this crease inside, which with the cutting of the umbilical cord becomes another person, inaccessible? My body and . . . him. No relation. Nothing to do with one another. Nothing to do from the first gestures, cries, steps, well before *his* personality has made him my opposite: the child, *he* or *she*, is irremediably another. That "there is no relation between the sexes" (Lacan) is not much of a surprise in the face of this bolt of lightning**

Among the many art objects and archeological curiosities that Freud collected were innumerable statuettes of mother goddesses. Yet in the work of the founder of psychoanalysis this interest is alluded to only discreetly. It does come up in his study of Leonardo, where Freud considers artistic creation and homosexuality and in so doing discovers the influence of an archaic mother figure, which is thus seen in terms of its effects on man, and more particularly on the curious function he sometimes has: that of changing languages. Elsewhere, in analyzing changes that occurred in monotheism, Freud emphasizes the fact that Christianity, in opposition to the rigor of Judaism, reduced the gap between itself and pagan myth by incorporating a preconscious recognition of a maternal feminine. But one looks in vain to Freud's case studies for insight into mothers and their problems. It might seem as though maternity were a remedy for neurosis which *ipso facto* eliminated the that blinds me on the brink of the abyss between me and what was mine but is now irremediably alien. Try to imagine this abyss: dizzying visions. No identity lies therein. A mother's identity survives only thanks to the well-known fact that consciousness is lulled by habit, wherein a woman protects herself along the frontier that divides her body and makes an expatriate of her child. A kind of lucidity, however, might restore her, cut in two, one half alien to the other—fertile soil for delirium. But also, and for that very reason maternity along its borders destines us to experience a frenzied ecstasy to which by chance the nursling's laugh responds in the sunlit ocean's waters. What is the relationship between him and me? No relation, except that abundant laughter into which some sonorous, subtle, fluid identity collapses, gently carried by the waves.

From that time in my childhood, fragrant, warm and soft to the touch, I retain only a memory of space. Nothing of time. The smell of honey, the roundness of things, silk and velvet under

need for a woman to seek that other remedy, psychoanalysis. Or that in this area psychoanalysis deferred to religion. Broadly speaking, the only thing that Freud has to say about maternity is that the desire to have a child is a transformation of penis envy or anal compulsion, which led him to discover the equation child = penis = faeces. This discovery does indeed shed a good deal of light not only on male fantasies concerning childbirth, but also on female fantasies insofar as they conform to the male ones, which they largely do in their hysterical labyrinths. Still, about the complexities and difficulties of the maternal experience Freud has absolutely nothing to say, though it may interest students of his work to note that he reports his mother's efforts to prove to him one day, in the kitchen, that his body was not immortal but would eventually crumble like pastry dough, or to look closely at the bitter photographs of Frau Martha Freud, the wife, which tell a whole story without words. Thus Freud's successors were in effect left an entire dark continent to explore, and Jung was the first to plunge in with his whole panoply of esoteric notions, which is not to say that he did not succeed in calling attention to certain prominent features of the unconscious my fingers, on my cheeks. Mama. Almost nothing visual —a shadow that plunges into blackness, absorbs me or disappears in a few flashes of light. Almost no voice, in its placid presence. Except perhaps, from a later time, the sound of quarreling: her exasperation, her being fed up, her hatred. Never direct, always restrained, as if, though deserved by the stubborn child, the mother's hatred could not be received by the daughter, was not destined for her. A hatred without a recipient, or rather, whose recipient was no "ego" and which, troubled by this absence of receptivity, attenuated itself by irony or collapsed in remorse before its arrival. In some women this maternal aversion can work itself up to a delayed spasm, like a slow orgasm. Women no doubt reproduce between them the peculiar, forgotten forms of close combat in which they engaged with their mothers. Complicity in the non-said, connivance in the unsayable, the wink of an eye, the tone of voice, the

that not only have a bearing on maternity but still have not yielded to analytic rationality.[3]

Those interested in what maternity is for a woman will no doubt be able to shed new light on this obscure topic by listening, with greater attentiveness than in the past, to what today's mothers have to say not only about their economic difficulties but also, and despite the legacy of guilt left by overly existentialist approaches to feminism, about malaise, insomnia, joy, rage, desire, suffering, and happiness. At the same time we can also try to gain a clearer picture of the Virgin, that prodigious structure of maternality that the West has erected; the foregoing remarks merely record a few episodes in a history that refuses to come to an end.

What is it then, which, in this maternal figure who alone of all her sex departed from the customary ways of both sexes, allowed her to become both an object with whom women wished to identify and an object that those responsible for maintaining the social and symbolic order felt it necessary to manipulate?

3. For example, Jung noted the "hierogamic" relations between Mary and Christ, as well as the peculiar overprotection of the Virgin with respect to original sin, which places her on the fringes of humanity. He also lays a good deal of stress on the acceptance of the Assumption as dogma by the Vatican, which Jung regarded as a significant advantage of Catholicism over Protestantism (Jung, 1964).

gesture, the color, the smell: we live in such things, escapees from our identity cards and our names, loose in an ocean of detail, a data-bank of the unnameable. Between individuals there is no communication but a matching of atoms, molecules, scraps of words, fragments of phrases. The community of women is a community of heirs apparent. Conversely, when the other woman appears as such, that is, in her singularity and necessary opposition, "I" am seized to the point where "I" no longer exist. There are then two possible ways of carrying out the rejection that affirms the other woman as such. Either, unwilling to know her, I ignore her and, "alone of my sex," I amically turn my back on her: hatred that has no recipient worthy of its virulence turns into indifferent complacency. Or else, offended by the other woman's obstinate persistence in believing herself to be singular, I refuse to accept her claim to be the recipient of my hatred and find respite only in the eternal return of physical blows, of hatred striking out—blind, heedless, but obstinate. . . . In this weird feminine seesaw

I want to suggest the following hypothesis: that the "virginal maternal" is a way—and, I might add, not a bad way—of coping with female paranoia.

—The Virgin assumes her female denial of the other sex (of man), but subjugates it by setting a third person against the other: I am a Virgin, *I* conceived not by *you* but by *Him*. This results in an immaculate conception, untainted by man or sex, but still a conception, out of which comes a God in whose existence a woman does therefore play an important part, provided that she acknowledges her subservience.

—The Virgin assumes the paranoid desire for power by turning a woman into the Queen of Heaven and the Mother of earthly institutions—the Church. But she then suppresses her megalomania by kneeling before the child-god.

—The Virgin obliterates the desire to murder or devour through a strong oral investment—the breast; she attaches a positive value to suffering—the sob; and she encourages replacement of the sexual body by the ear of understanding.

—The Virgin assumes the paranoid fantasy of being excluded from time and death, through the very flattering image associated with the Dormition or Assumption.

that swings "me" out of the unnameable community of women into single combat with another woman, it is perturbing to say "I." The languages of great civilizations that used to be matrilinear must avoid, do avoid the use of personal pronouns: they leave it up to the context to distinguish the protagonists, and take refuge in tones of voice to recover a submerged, transverbal correspondence of bodies. A piece of music whose so-called oriental civility is suddenly interrupted by acts of violence, murders, bloodbaths: isn't that what "women's discourse" would be? Wasn't stopping the motion of that seesaw one of the things Christianity wanted to accomplish? Stop it, free women from its rhythm, and install them definitively in the bosom of the spirit? All too definitively. . . .

—Above all, the Virgin subscribes to the foreclosure of the other woman—which fundamentally is probably a foreclosure of the woman's mother—by projecting an image of the One, the Unique Woman: unique among women, unique among mothers, and, since she is without sin, unique also among humans of both sexes. But this recognition of the desire of uniqueness is immediately checked by the postulate that uniqueness is achieved only by way of exacerbated masochism: an actual woman worthy of the feminine ideal embodied in inaccessible perfection by the Virgin could not be anything other than a nun or a martyr; if married, she would have to lead a life that would free her from her "earthly" condition by confining her to the uttermost sphere of sublimation, alienated from her own body. But there a bonus awaits her: the assurance of ecstasy.

Striking a shrewd balance between concessions to and constraints upon female paranoia, the representation of virgin motherhood seems to have crowned society's efforts to reconcile survivals of matrilinearity and the unconscious needs of primary narcissism on the one hand with, on the other hand, the imperatives of the nascent exchange economy and, before long, of accelerated production, which required the addition of the superego and relied on the father's symbolic authority.

Now that this once carefully balanced structure seems in danger of tottering, the following question arises: to what aspects of the feminine psyche does this representation of the maternal offer no answer, or at any rate no answer that is not too coercive for women in this century to accept?

The weight of the "non-said" *(non-dit)* no doubt affects the mother's body first of all: no signifier can cover it completely, for the signifier is always meaning *(sens),* communication or structure, whereas a mother-woman is rather a strange "fold" *(pli)* which turns nature into culture, and the "speaking subject" *(le parlant)* into biology. Although it affects each woman's body, this heterogeneity, which cannot be subsumed by the signifier, literally explodes with pregnancy—the dividing line between nature and culture—and with the arrival of the child—which frees a woman from uniqueness and gives her a chance, albeit not a certainty, of access to the other, to the ethical. These peculiarities of the maternal body make a woman a creature of folds, a catastrophe of being that cannot be subsumed by the dialectic of the trinity or its supplements.

Nor is there any less silence concerning the mental and physical suffering associated with childbirth and, even more, with the self-denial implicit in making oneself anonymous in order to transmit social norms which one may disavow for oneself but which *one must* pass on to the child, whose education is a link to generations past. But, with the ambivalence characteristic of masochism, this suffering goes hand in hand with jubilation, whereby a woman ordinarily averse to perversion allows herself to engage in "coded" perversity, a perversity that is absolutely fundamental, the ultimate basis of all social life, without which society would be unable to reproduce itself or maintain its notion of a normative household. This perversion does not involve a Don Juan-like fragmentation or multiplication of objects of desire. Rather, it is immediately legalized, not to say "paranoized" *(paranoisée)* by the effects of masochism: any sexual "profligacy" is acceptable and therefore insignificant provided a child is born to suture the wounds. The feminine "father-version" *(père-version)* lies coiled in the desire of the law as desire of reproduction and continuity; it raises female masochism to the status of a structural stabilizer—countering structural deviations—and, by assuring the mother of a place in an order that surpasses human will, provides her a reward of pleasure. This coded perversion, this close combat between maternal masochism and the law, has always been used by totalitarian regimes to enlist the support of woman, indeed, quite successfully. Still, it is not enough to "denounce" the reactionary role that mothers have played in the service of "dominant male power." It is necessary to ask how this role relates to the biosymbolic latencies implicit in maternity; and having done that, to ask further how, now that the myth of the Virgin is no longer capable of subsuming those latencies, their surfacing may leave women vulnerable to the most frightful forms of manipulation, to say nothing of the blindness, the pure and simple contempt, of progressive activists who refuse to take a closer look at the question.

Also neglected by the virginal myth is the question of hostility between mother and daughter, a question resolved in magisterial but superficial fashion by making Mary universal and particular but never singular: "unique of all her sex." For more than a century now, our culture has faced the urgent need to reformulate its representations of love and hate, inherited from Plato's *Symposium,* the troubadours, and Our Lady, in order to deal with the relationship of one woman to another. Here again, maternity points the way to a possible solution: a woman rarely, I do not say never, experiences passion—love or hate—for another woman, without at some point taking the place of her own mother—without becoming a mother herself and, even more importantly, without undergoing the lengthy process of learning to differentiate herself from her own daughter, her simulacrum, whose presence she is forced to confront.

Finally, the foreclosure of the other sex (of the masculine) can apparently no longer be done under the auspices of the hypostasized third person through the intermediary of the child: "Neither I nor you but he, the child, the third, the non-person, God, who in any case I am in the final analysis." Since foreclosure does occur, what it now requires, in order for the feminine being who struggles with it to hold her own, is not deification of the third party but counterinvestment in "blue-chip shares," i.e., in redeemable *tokens of power.* Feminine psychosis today sustains itself through passion for politics, science, art, in which it becomes engrossed. The variant of that psychosis that accompanies maternity may be analyzed, more easily perhaps than other variants, in terms of its rejection of the other sex.

The love of God and for God inhabits a hiatus: the space delineated on one side by sin and on the other by the hereafter. Discontinuity, lack, and arbitrariness: the topography of the sign, of the symbolic relation that

What purpose does this rejection serve? Surely it does not allow any sort of pact between "sexual partners" based on a supposed preestablished harmony deriving from primordial androgyny. What it does allow is recognition of irreducible differences between the sexes and of the posits all otherness as impossible. Love, here, is nothing but the impossible.

For a mother, on the other hand, curiously, the arbitrariness that is the other (the child) goes without saying. For her the impossible is like this: it becomes one with the implacable. The other is inevitable, she seems to say, make a God of him if you like; he won't be any less natural if you do, for this other still comes from me, which is in any case not me but an endless flux of germinations, an eternal cosmos. The other proceeds from itself and myself to such a degree that ultimately it doesn't exist for itself. This maternal quietude, more stubborn even than philosophical doubt, with its fundamental incredulity, eats away at the omnipotence of the symbolic. It sidesteps the perverse denial ("I know it, but *still*") and constitutes the basis of social bonding in general (in the sense of "resembling others and, ultimately, the species"). Such an attitude can be frightening if one stops to think that it may destroy everything that is specific and irreducible in the other, the child: this form of maternal love can become a straitjacket, stifling any deviant individuali-

irreconcilable interests of both —and hence of women—in asserting those differences and seeking appropriate forms of fulfillment.

These, then, are among the questions that remain unaddressed even today, after the Virgin. Taken together they point to the need for an ethics appropriate to the "second" sex that some say has recently been experiencing a renaissance.

Nothing guarantees that a feminine ethics is even possible, however; Spinoza explicitly excluded women (along with children and lunatics) from ethics. If it is true that an ethics for the modern age is no longer to be confused with morality, and if confronting the problem of ethics means not avoiding the embarrassing and inevitable issue of the law but instead bringing to the law flesh, language, and *jouissance,* then the reformulation of the ethical tradition requires the participation of women. Women imbued with the desire to reproduce (and to maintain stability); women ready to help our verbal species, afflicted as we are by the knowledge that we are mortal, to bear up under the menace of death; mothers. For what is ethics divorced from morals? Heretical ethics—*herethics*—may just be that which makes life's bonds bearable, that which enables us to tolerate thought, and hence ty. But it can also serve the speaking subject as a refuge when his symbolic carapace shatters to reveal that jagged crest where biology trans-pierces speech: I am thinking of moments of illness, of sexual-intellectual-physical passion, death. . . .

the thought of death. "Hereth-ics" is *a-mort, amour. Eia mater, fons amoris.* Let us listen again, therefore, to the *Stabat Mater,* and to music, all music. It swal-lows goddesses and strips them of necessity.

REFERENCES

Barande, Ilse, 1977. *Le Maternel singulier* (Paris: Aubier-Montaigne).
Jung, Carl Gustav, 1964. *Réponse à Job,* trans. Roland Cahen (Paris: Buchet-Chastel).
Warner, Marina, 1976. *Alone of All Her Sex. The Myth and Cult of the Virgin Mary* (London: Weidenfeld and Nicolson).

CATHARINE A. MACKINNON

If research physicians like Robert Stoller had not recently agreed that the erotic is hopelessly entangled with anger, hostility, and the desire to harm, one would have to return to the days of the early Church Fathers to find a view of sexuality as somber (or a talent for dramatic antithesis as accomplished) as Catharine MacKinnon's.* What MacKinnon says is that attempts to identify rape with violence and not with sex are self-deluding "liberal" efforts to rescue heterosexual sex. At the snaky heart of male sexuality is, precisely, coercion. What Stoller says is that ". . . those qualities in another that produce a feeling of love oppose one's being able to lust" (900), that "humans are not a very loving species and that is especially so when they make love" (909). Stoller does not claim that female sexuality transcends these revenge "scripts" into some realm of purer nobility, nor, in fact, does MacKinnon, who devotes some space to admitting that women can eroticize domination. Indeed, such perversity is inevitable in an erotic context, which is devised overwhelmingly in the interests of men. This context is not just the *only* context; it is backed up by the power of law. According to the law, whether a woman has been raped or not is determined, absurdly, by the state of mind of the man involved, though the injury lies in the meaning of the act to the victim. Women are trapped in a tenacious male hermeneutic according to which female protestation will be interpreted as affirmation. Even when they say "no," they are perceived as meaning "yes." Men tend to pay little attention to what a woman wants, anyway. It is not unusual for a rapist to believe that his victim found the assault in question . . . ravishing. Pornography is both a result of male fantasies about sex and an encouragement, a reinforcement for the perpetuation of these fantasies. Just as ordinary heterosexuality shares with criminal rape the process of penetration, so too is the fantasy of male domination, the right of unrestricted access to a woman, the common theme of pornography and marriage. Sexuality, says MacKinnon, is always already pornography *(Feminism Unmodified:*223). She records the appalling rise in incidents of throat-rape after the release of Linda Marchiano's pornographic film *Deep Throat.* The effect of the film on the general public included not only pressure on prostitutes from clients, on wives from husbands, but also cases of women dead of suffocation from rape of the throat (286). Pornography is not empty imagery or harmless fantasy. "It is sexual reality" (149). Any liberal woman who defends this system on the basis of

* Robert J. Stoller, "Sexual Excitement," *Archives of General Psychiatry,* Vol. 33 (August 1976) No. 8: 899–909. See also MacKinnon, "Sex and Violence" in *Feminism Unmodified* (Cambridge and London: Harvard, 1987) 87–88.

freedom of speech or because she feels fastidious about implicit alliances with the right wing, also in opposition to pornography, is a procuress of women for men (14). MacKinnon, along with her ally Andrea Dworkin, have written and urged passage of antipornography laws that allow people like Linda Marchiano to sue pornographers for the abduction and torture outlined in Marchiano's book *Ordeal*. The laws have been adopted by two Midwest communities, Minneapolis and Indianapolis; but in two cases the laws were struck down. Marchiano has been sued for libel, and *Deep Throat* is protected by the first amendment to the Constitution (11).

Feminism, Marxism, Method, and the State: Toward Feminist Jurisprudence

1983

I

Feminism has no theory of the state. It has a theory of power: sexuality is gendered as gender is sexualized. Male and female are created through the erotization of dominance and submission. The

For A. D. and D. K. H. In addition to all those whose help is acknowledged in the first part of this article, "Feminism, Marxism, Method, and the State: An Agenda for Theory." *Signs: Journal of Women in Culture and Society* 7, no. 3 (Spring 1982): 515–44 (hereafter cited as part 1), my students and colleagues at Yale, Harvard, and Stanford contributed profoundly to the larger project of which both articles are parts. Among them, Sonia E. Alvarez, Jeanne M. Barkey, Paul Brest, Ruth Colker, Karen E. Davis, Sharon Dyer, Tom Emerson, Daniel Gunther, Patricia Kliendienst Joplin, Mark Kelman, Duncan Kennedy, John Kaplan, Lyn Lemaire, Mira Marshall, Rebecca Mark, Martha Minow, Helen M. A. Neally, Lisa Rofel, Sharon Silverstein, Dean Spencer, Laurence Tribe, and Mary Whisner stand out vividly in retrospect. None of it would have happened without Lu Ann Carter and David Rayson. And thank you, Meg Baldwin. Annie McCombs. and Janet Spector.
Marxism appears in lower case, Black in upper case, for reasons explained in part 1.

man/woman difference and the dominance/submission dynamic define each other. This is the social meaning of sex and the distinctively feminist account of gender inequality.[1] Sexual objectification, the central process within this dynamic, is at once epistemological and political.[2] The feminist theory of knowledge is inextricable from the feminist critique of power because the male point of view forces itself upon the world as its way of apprehending it.

The perspective from the male standpoint[3] enforces woman's definition, encircles her body, circumlocutes her speech, and describes her life. The male perspective is systemic and hegemonic. The content of the signification "woman" is the content of women's lives. Each sex has its role, but their stakes and power are not equal. If the sexes are unequal, and perspective participates in situation, there is no ungendered reality or ungendered perspective. And they are connected. In this context, objectivity—the nonsituated, universal standpoint, whether claimed or aspired to—is a denial of the existence or potency of sex inequality that tacitly participates in constructing reality from the dominant point of view. Objectivity, as the epistemological stance of which objectification is the social

1. Much has been made of the distinction between sex and gender. Sex is thought the more biological, gender the more social. The relation of each to sexuality varies. Since I believe sexuality is fundamental to gender and fundamentally social, and that biology is its social meaning in the system of sex inequality, which is a social and political system that does not rest independently on biological differences in any respect, the sex/gender distinction looks like a nature/culture distinction. I use sex and gender relatively interchangeably.
2. This analysis is developed in part 1. I assume here your acquaintance with the arguments there.
3. Male is a social and political concept, not a biological attribute. As I use it, it has *nothing whatever* to do with inherency, preexistence, nature, inevitability, or body as such. It is more epistemological than ontological, undercutting the distinction itself, given male power to conform being with perspective. (See part 1, pp. 538–39, n. 56.) The perspective from the male standpoint is not always each man's opinion, although most men adhere to it, nonconsciously and without considering it a point of view, as much because it makes sense of their experience (the male experience) as because it is in their interest. It is rational for them. A few men reject it; they pay. Because it is the dominant point of view and defines rationality, women are pushed to see reality in its terms, although this denies their vantage point as women in that it contradicts (at least some of) their lived experience. Women who adopt the male standpoint are passing, epistemologically speaking. This is not uncommon and is rewarded. The intractability of maleness as a form of dominance suggests that social constructs, although they flow from human agency, can be less plastic than nature has proven to be. If experience trying to do so is any guide, it may be easier to change biology than society.

process, creates the reality it apprehends by defining as knowledge the reality it creates through its way of apprehending it. Sexual metaphors for knowing are no coincidence.[4] The solipsism of this approach does not undercut its sincerity, but it is interest that precedes method.

Feminism criticizes this male totality without an account of our capacity to do so or to imagine or realize a more whole truth. Feminism affirms women's point of view by revealing, criticizing, and explaining its impossibility. This is not a dialectical paradox. It is a methodological expression of women's situation, in which the struggle for consciousness is a struggle for world: for a sexuality, a history, a culture, a community, a form of power, an experience of the sacred. If women had consciousness or world, sex inequality would be harmless, or all women would be feminist. Yet we have something of both, or there would be no such thing as feminism. Why can women know that this—life as we have known it—is not all, not enough, not ours, not just? Now, why don't all women?[5]

4. In the Bible, to know a woman is to have sex with her. You acquire carnal knowledge. Many scholarly metaphors elaborate the theme of violating boundaries to appropriate from inside to carry off in usable form: "a penetrating observation," "an incisive analysis," "piercing the veil." Mary Ellman writes, "The male mind . . . is assumed to function primarily like a penis. Its fundamental character is seen to be aggression, and this quality is held essential to the highest or best working of the intellect" (Thinking about Women [New York: Harcourt Brace Jovanovich, 1968], p. 23). Feminists are beginning to understand that to know has meant to fuck. See Evelyn Fox Keller, "Gender and Science." Psychoanalysis and Contemporary Thought 1, no. 3 (1978): 409–33, esp. 413; and Helen Roberts, ed., Doing Feminist Research (London: Routledge & Kegan Paul, 1981). The term "to fuck" uniquely captures my meaning because it refers to sexual activity without distinguishing rape from intercourse. At least since Plato's cave, visual metaphors for knowing have been central to Western theories of knowledge, the visual sense prioritized as a mode of verification. The relationship between visual appropriation and objectification is now only beginning to be explored. "The knowledge gained through still photographs will always be . . . a semblance of knowledge, a semblance of wisdom, as the act of taking pictures is a semblance of wisdom, a semblance of rape. The very muteness of what is, hypothetically, comprehensible in photographs is what constitutes their attraction and provocativeness" (Susan Sontag, On Photography [New York: Farrar, Straus & Giroux, 1980], p. 24). See part 1, pp. 539–40, n. 59.
5. Feminism aspires to represent the experience of all women as women see it, yet criticizes antifeminism and misogyny, including when it appears in female form. This tension is compressed in the epistemic term of art "the standpoint of all women." We are barely beginning to unpack it. Not all women agree with the feminist account of women's situation, nor do all feminists agree with any single rendition of feminism. Authority of interpretation—the claim to speak as a

The practice of a politics of all women in the face of its theoretical impossibility is creating a new process of theorizing and a new form of theory. Although feminism emerges from women's particular

woman—thus becomes methodologically complex and politically crucial for the same reasons. Consider the accounts of their own experience given by right-wing women and lesbian sadomasochists. How can patriarchy be diminishing to women when women embrace and defend their place in it? How can dominance and submission be violating to women when women eroticize it? Now what is the point of view of the experience of all women? Most responses in the name of feminism, stated in terms of method, either (1) simply regard some women's views as "false consciousness," or (2) embrace any version of women's experience that a biological female claims as her own. The first approach treats some women's views as unconscious conditioned reflections of their oppression, complicitous in it. Just as science devalues experience in the process of uncovering its roots, this approach criticizes the substance of a view because it can be accounted for by its determinants. But if both feminism and antifeminism are responses to the condition of women, how is feminism exempt from devalidation by the same account? That feminism is critical, and antifeminism is not, is not enough, because the question is the basis on which we know something is one or the other when women, all of whom share the condition of women, disagree. The false consciousness approach begs this question by taking women's self-reflections as evidence of their stake in their own oppression, when the women whose self-reflections are at issue question whether their condition is oppressed at all. The second response proceeds as if women are free. Or, at least, as if we have considerable latitude to make, or to choose, the meanings if not the determinants of our situation. Or, that the least feminism can do, since it claims to see the world through women's eyes, is to validate the interpretations women choose. Both responses arise because of the unwillingness, central to feminism, to dismiss some women as simply deluded while granting other women the ability to see the truth. These two resolutions echo the object/subject split: objectivity (my consciousness is true, yours false, never mind why) or subjectivity (I know I am right because it feels right to me, never mind why). Thus is determinism answered with transcendence, traditional marxism with traditional liberalism, dogmatism with tolerance. The first approach claims authority on the basis of its lack of involvement, asserting its view independent of whether the described concurs—sometimes because it does not. It also has no account, other than its alleged lack of involvement, of its own ability to provide such an account. How can some women see the truth and other women not? The second approach claims authority on the basis of its involvement. It has no account for different interpretations of the same experience or any way of choosing among conflicting ones, including those between women and men. It tends to assume that women, as we are, have power and are free in exactly the ways feminism, substantively, has found we are not. Thus, the first approach is one-sidedly outside when there is no outside, the second one-sidedly inside when someone (probably a woman) is inside everything, including every facet of sexism, racism, and so on. So our problem is this: the false consciousness approach cannot explain experience as it is experienced by those who experience it. The alternative can only reiterate the terms of that experience. This is only one way in which the object/subject split is fatal to the feminist enterprise.

experience, it is not subjective or partial, for no interior ground and few if any aspects of life are free of male power. Nor is feminism objective, abstract, or universal.[6] It claims no external ground or unsexed sphere of generalization or abstraction beyond male power, nor transcendence of the specificity of each of its manifestations. How is it possible to have an engaged truth that does not simply reiterate its determinations? *Disengaged* truth only reiterates *its* determinations. Choice of method is choice of determinants—a choice which, for women as such, has been unavailable because of the subordination of women. Feminism does not begin with the premise that it is unpremised. It does not aspire to persuade an unpremised audience because there is no such audience. Its project is to uncover and claim as valid the experience of women, the major content of which is the devalidation of women's experience.

This defines our task not only because male dominance is perhaps the most pervasive and tenacious system of power in history, but because it is metaphysically nearly perfect.[7] Its point of view is the standard for point-of-viewlessness, its particularity the meaning of universality. Its force is exercised as consent, its authority as participation, its supremacy as the paradigm of order, its control as the definition of legitimacy. Feminism claims the voice of women's silence, the sexuality of our eroticized desexualization, the fullness of "lack," the centrality of our marginality and exclusion, the public nature of privacy, the presence of our absence. This approach is more complex than transgression, more transformative than transvaluation, deeper than mirror-imaged resistance, more affirmative than the negation of our negativity. It is neither materialist nor idealist; it is

6. To stress: the feminist criticism is not that the objective stance fails to be truly objective because it has social content, all the better to exorcise that content in the pursuit of the more truly point-of-viewless viewpoint. The criticism is that objectivity is largely accurate to its/the/a world, which world is criticized; and that it becomes more accurate as the power it represents and extends becomes more total. Analogous criticisms have arisen in the natural sciences, without being seen as threatening to the "science of society" project, or calling into question that project's tacit equation between natural and social objects of knowledge. What if we extend Heisenberg's uncertainty principle to social theory? (Werner Heisenberg, *The Physical Principles of the Quantum Theory* [Chicago: University of Chicago Press, 1930], pp. 4, 20, 62–65). What of the axiomatic method after Gödel's proof? (See Ernest Nagel and James R. Newman, *Gödel's Proof* [New York: New York University Press, 1958].)

7. Andrea Dworkin helped me express this.

feminist. Neither the transcendence of liberalism nor the determination of materialism works for us. Idealism is too unreal; women's inequality is enforced, so it cannot simply be thought out of existence, certainly not by us. Materialism is too real; women's inequality has never not existed, so women's equality never has. That is, the equality of women to men will not be scientifically provable until it is no longer necessary to do so. Women's situation offers no outside to stand on or gaze at, no inside to escape to, too much urgency to wait, no place else to go, and nothing to use but the twisted tools that have been shoved down our throats. If feminism is revolutionary, this is why.

Feminism has been widely thought to contain tendencies of liberal feminism, radical feminism, and socialist feminism. But just as socialist feminism has often amounted to marxism applied to women, liberal feminism has often amounted to liberalism applied to women. Radical feminism is feminism. Radical feminism—after this, feminism unmodified—is methodologically post-marxist.[8] It moves to

8. I mean to imply that contemporary feminism that is not methodologically post-marxist is not radical, hence not feminist on this level. For example, to the extent Mary Daly's *Gyn/Ecology: The Metaethics of Radical Feminism* (Boston: Beacon Press, 1978) is idealist in method—meaning that the subordination of women is an idea such that to think it differently is to change it—it is formally liberal no matter how extreme or insightful. To the extent Shulamith Firestone's analysis *(The Dialectic of Sex: The Case for Feminist Revolution* [New York: William Morrow & Co., 1972]) rests on a naturalist definition of gender, holding that women are oppressed by our bodies rather than their social meaning, her radicalism, hence her feminism, is qualified. Susan Griffin's *Pornography and Silence: Culture's Revolt against Nature* (San Francisco: Harper & Row Publishers, 1982) is classically liberal in all formal respects including, for instance, the treatment of pornography and eros as a distinction that is fundamentally psychological rather than interested, more deeply a matter of good and bad (morality) than of power and powerlessness (politics). Andrea Dworkin's work, esp. *Pornography: Men Possessing Women* (New York: Perigee Books, 1981), and Adrienne Rich's poetry and essays, exemplify feminism as a methodological departure. This feminism seeks to define and pursue women's interest as the fate of all women bound together. It seeks to extract the truth of women's commonalities out of the lie that all women are the same. If whatever a given society defines as sexual defines gender, and if gender means the subordination of women to men, "woman" means—is not qualified or undercut by—the uniqueness of each woman and the specificity of race, class, time, and place. In this sense, lesbian feminism, the feminism of women of color, and socialist feminism are converging in a feminist politics of sexuality, race, and class, with a left to right spectrum of its own. This politics is struggling for a practice of unity that does not depend upon sameness without dissolving into empty tolerance, including tolerance of all it

resolve the marxist-feminist problematic on the level of method. Because its method emerges from the concrete conditions of all women as a sex, it dissolves the individualist, naturalist, idealist, moralist structure of liberalism, the politics of which science is the epistemology. Where liberal feminism sees sexism primarily as an illusion or myth to be dispelled, an inaccuracy to be corrected, true feminism sees the male point of view as fundamental to the male power to create the world in its own image, the image of its desires, not just as its delusory end product. Feminism distinctively as such comprehends that what counts as truth is produced in the interest of those with power to shape reality, and that this process is as pervasive as it is necessary as it is changeable. Unlike the scientific strain in marxism or the Kantian imperative in liberalism, which in this context share most salient features, feminism neither claims universality nor, failing that, reduces to relativity. It does not seek a generality that subsumes its particulars or an abstract theory or a science of sexism. It rejects the approach of control over nature (including us) analogized to control over society (also including us) which has grounded the "science of society" project as the paradigm for political knowledge since (at least) Descartes. Both liberalism and marxism have been subversive on women's behalf. Neither is enough. To grasp the inadequacies for women of liberalism on one side and marxism on the other is to begin to comprehend the role of the liberal state and liberal legalism[9] within a post-marxist feminism of social transformation.

As feminism has a theory of power but lacks a theory of the state, so

---

exits to change whenever that appears embodied in one of us. A new community begins here. As critique, women's communality describes a fact of male supremacy, of sex "in itself": no woman escapes the meaning of being a woman within a gendered social system, and sex inequality is not only pervasive but may be universal (in the sense of never having not been in some form) although "intelligible only in . . . locally specific forms" (M. Z. Rosaldo, "The Use and Abuse of Anthropology: Reflections on Feminism and Cross-cultural Understanding," *Signs: Journal of Women in Culture and Society 5*, no. 3 [Spring, 1980]: 389–417, 417). For women to become a sex "for ourselves" moves community to the level of vision.

9. See Karl Klare, "Law-Making as Praxis," *Telos* 12, no. 2 (Summer 1979): 123–35; Judith Shklar, *Legalism* (Cambridge, Mass.: Harvard University Press, 1964). To examine law as state is not to decide that all relevant state behavior occurs in legal texts. I do think that legal decisions expose power on the level of legitimizing rationale, and that law, as words in power, is central in the social erection of the liberal state.

marxism has a theory of value which (through the organization of work in production) becomes class analysis, but a problematic theory of the state. Marx did not address the state much more explicitly than he did women. Women were substratum, the state epiphenomenon.[10] Engels, who frontally analyzed both, and together, presumed the subordination of women in every attempt to reveal its roots, just as he presupposed something like the state, or state-like social conditions, in every attempt to expose its origins.[11] Marx tended to use the term "political" narrowly to refer to the state or its laws, criticizing as exclusively political interpretations of the state's organization or behavior which took them as sui generis. Accordingly, until recently, most marxism has tended to consider political that which occurs between classes, that is, to interpret as "the political" instances of the marxist concept of inequality. In this broad sense, the marxist theory of social inequality has been its theory of politics. This has not so much collapsed the state into society (although it goes far in that direction) as conceived the state as determined by the totality of social relations of which the state is one determined and determining part—without specifying which, or how much, is which.

In this context, recent marxist work has tried to grasp the specificity of the institutional state: how it wields class power, or transforms class society, or responds to approach by a left aspiring to rulership or other changes. While liberal theory has seen the state as emanating power, and traditional marxism has seen the state as expressing power constituted elsewhere, recent marxism, much of it structuralist, has tried to analyze state power as specific to the state as a form, yet integral to a determinate social whole understood in class terms. This state is found "relatively autonomous." This means that the state, expressed through its functionaries, has a definite class character, is definitely capitalist or socialist, but also has its own interests which are to some degree independent of those of the ruling class and even

10. Karl Marx, *Capital, Selected Works,* 3 vols. (Moscow: Progress Publishers, 1969), 2:120, 139–40: *The German Ideology* (New York: International Publishers, 1972), pp. 48–52; *Introduction to Critique of Hegel's Philosophy of Right,* ed. Joseph O'Malley, trans. Annette Jolin (Cambridge: Cambridge University Press, 1970), p. 139; Marx to P. V. Annenkov, 1846, in *The Poverty of Philosophy* (New York: International Publishers, 1963), pp. 179–93, 181.

11. I am criticizing Engels's assumptions about sexuality and women's place, and his empiricist method, and suggesting that the two are linked. Friedrich Engels, *Origin of the Family, Private Property and the State* (New York: International Publishers, 1942).

of the class structure.[12] The state as such, in this view, has a specific power and interest, termed "the political," such that class power, class interest expressed by and in the state, and state behavior, although inconceivable in isolation from one another, are nevertheless not linearly or causally linked or strictly coextensive. Such work locates "the specificity of the political" in a mediate "region"[13] between the state as its own ground of power (which alone, as in the liberal conception, would set the state above or apart from class) and the state as possessing no special supremacy or priority in terms of power, as in the more orthodox marxist view.

The idea that the state is relatively autonomous, a kind of first among equals of social institutions, has the genius of appearing to take a stand on the issue of reciprocal constitution of state and society while straddling it. Is the state essentially autonomous of class but partly determined by it, or is it essentially determined by class but not exclusively so? Is it relatively constrained within a context of freedom or relatively free within a context of constraint?[14] As to who or what fundamentally moves and shapes the realities and instrumentalities of domination, and where to go to do something about it, what qualifies what is as ambiguous as it is crucial. Whatever it has not accomplished, however, this literature has at least relieved the compulsion

12. Representative works include Fred Block, "The Ruling Class Does Not Rule: Notes on the Marxist Theory of the State," *Socialist Revolution* 33 (May–June 1977): 6–28; Ralph Miliband, *The State in Capitalist Society* (New York: Basic Books, 1969); Nicos Poulantzas, *Classes in Contemporary Capitalism* (London: New Left Books, 1975), and *Political Power and Social Classes* (London: New Left Books, 1975); Goran Therborn, *What Does the Ruling Class Do When It Rules?* (London: New Left Books, 1978); Norberto Bobbio, "Is There a Marxist Theory of the State?" *Telos* 35 (Spring 1978): 5–16. Theda Skocpol, *States and Social Revolution: A Comparative Analysis of France, Russia and China* (Cambridge: Cambridge University Press, 1979), pp. 24–33, ably reviews much of this literature. Applications to law include Isaac Balbus, "Commodity Form and Legal Form: An Essay on the 'Relative Autonomy' of the Law," *Law and Society Review* 11, no. 3 (Winter 1977): 571–88; Mark Tushnet, "A Marxist Analysis of American Law," *Marxist Perspectives* 1, no. 1 (Spring 1978): 96–116; and Klare (n. 9 above).
13. Poulantzas's formulation follows Althusser. Louis Althusser and Etienne Balibar, *Reading Capital,* trans. Ben Brewster (London: New Left Books, 1968). For Poulantzas, the "specific autonomy which is characteristic of the function of the state . . . is the basis of the specificity of the political" *(Political Power and Social Classes* [n. 12 above], pp. 14, 46). Whatever that means. On structural causality between class and state, see p. 14.
14. See Ernesto Laclau's similar criticism of Miliband in *Politics and Ideology in Marxist Theory* (London: New Left Books, 1977), p. 65.

to find all law—directly or convolutedly, nakedly or clothed in unconscious or devious rationalia—to be simply bourgeois, without undercutting the notion that it is determinately driven by interest.

A methodologically post-marxist feminism must confront, on our own terms, the issue of the relation between the state and society, within a theory of social determination adequate to the specificity of sex. Lacking even a tacit theory of the state of its own, feminist practice has instead oscillated between a liberal theory of the state on the one hand and a left theory of the state on the other. Both treat law as the mind of society: disembodied reason in liberal theory, reflection of material interest in left theory. In liberal moments the state is accepted on its own terms as a neutral arbiter among conflicting interests. The law is actually or potentially principled, meaning predisposed to no substantive outcome, thus available as a tool that is not fatally twisted. Women implicitly become an interest group within pluralism, with specific problems of mobilization and representation, exit and voice, sustaining incremental gains and losses. In left moments, the state becomes a tool of dominance and repression, the law legitimizing ideology, use of the legal system a form of utopian idealism or gradualist reform, each apparent gain deceptive or cooptive, and each loss inevitable.

Applied to women, liberalism has supported state intervention on behalf of women as abstract persons with abstract rights, without scrutinizing the content of these notions in gendered terms. Marxism applied to women is always on the edge of counseling abdication of the state as an arena altogether—and with it those women whom the state does not ignore or who are, as yet, in no position to ignore it. Feminism has so far accepted these constraints upon its alternatives: either the state, as primary tool of women's betterment and status transformation, without analysis (hence strategy) for it as male; or civil society, which for women has more closely resembled a state of nature. The state, with it the law, has been either omnipotent or impotent: everything or nothing.

The feminist posture toward the state has therefore been schizoid on issues central to women's survival: rape, battery, pornography, prostitution, sexual harassment, sex discrimination, abortion, the Equal Rights Amendment, to name a few. Attempts to reform and enforce rape laws, for example, have tended to build on the model of the deviant perpetrator and the violent act, as if the fact that rape is a crime means that the society is against it, so law enforcement would reduce or delegitimize it. Initiatives are accordingly directed toward making the police more sensitive, prosecutors more responsive, judges more receptive, and the law, in words, less sexist. This may be progressive in the liberal or the left senses, but how is it empowering in the feminist sense? Even if it were effective in jailing men who do little different from what nondeviant men do regularly, how would such an approach alter women's rapability? Unconfronted are *why* women are raped and the role of the state in that. Similarly, applying laws against battery to husbands, although it can mean life itself, has largely failed to address, as part of the strategy for state intervention, the conditions that produce men who systematically express themselves violently toward women, women whose resistance is disabled, and the role of the state in this dynamic. Criminal enforcement in these areas, while suggesting that rape and battery are deviant, punishes men for expressing the images of masculinity that mean their identity, for which they are otherwise trained, elevated, venerated, and paid. These men must be stopped. But how does that change them or reduce the chances that there will be more like them? Liberal strategies entrust women to the state. Left theory abandons us to the rapists and batterers. The question for feminism is not only whether there is a meaningful difference between the two, but whether either is adequate to the feminist critique of rape and battery as systemic and to the role of the state and the law within that system.

Feminism has descriptions of the state's treatment of the gender difference, but no analysis of the state as gender hierarchy. We need to know. What, in gender terms, are the state's norms of accountability, sources of power, real constituency? Is the state to some degree autonomous of the interests of men or an integral expression of them? Does the state embody and serve male interests in its form, dynamics, relation to society, and specific policies? Is the state constructed upon the subordination of women? If so, how does male power become state power? Can such a state be made to serve the interests of those upon whose powerlessness its power is erected? Would a different relation between state and society, such as may pertain under socialism, make a difference? If not, is masculinity inherent in the state form as such, or is some other form of state, or some other way of governing, distinguishable or imaginable? In the absence of answers to such questions, feminism has been caught between giving more power to the state in each attempt to claim it for women and leaving unchecked power in the society to men. Undisturbed, meanwhile, like the assumption that women generally consent to sex, is the assumption that we consent to this government.

The question for feminism, for the first time on its own terms, is: what is this state, from women's point of view?

As a beginning, I propose that the state is male in the feminist sense.[15] The law sees and treats women the way men see and treat women. The liberal state coercively and authoritatively constitutes the social order in the interest of men as a gender, through its legitimizing norms, relation to society, and substantive policies. It achieves this through embodying and ensuring male control over women's sexuality at every level, occasionally cushioning, qualifying, or de jure prohibiting its excesses when necessary to its normalization. Substantively, the way the male point of view frames an experience is the way it is framed by state policy. To the extent possession is the point of sex, rape is sex with a woman who is not yours, unless the act is so as to make her yours. If part of the kick of pornography involves eroticizing the putatively prohibited, obscenity law will putatively prohibit pornography enough to maintain its desirability without ever making it unavailable or truly illegitimate. The same with prostitution. As male is the implicit reference for human, maleness will be the measure of equality in sex discrimination law. To the extent that the point of abortion is to control the reproductive sequelae of intercourse, so as to facilitate male sexual access to women, access to abortion will be controlled by "a man or The Man."[16] Gender, elaborated and sustained by behavioral patterns of application and administration, is maintained as a division of power.

Formally, the state is male in that objectivity is its norm. Objectivity is liberal legalism's conception of itself. It legitimizes itself by reflecting its view of existing society, a society it made and makes by so seeing it, and calling that view, and that relation, practical rationality. If rationality is measured by point-of-viewlessness, what counts as reason will be that which corresponds to the way things are. Practical will mean that which can be done without changing

---

15. See Susan Rae Peterson, "Coercion and Rape: The State as a Male Protection Racket," in *Feminism and Philosophy*, ed. Mary Vetterling-Braggin, Frederick A. Elliston, and Jane English (Totowa, N.J.: Littlefield, Adams & Co., 1977), pp. 360–71; Janet Rifkin, "Toward a Theory of Law Patriarchy," *Harvard Women's Law Journal* 3 (Spring 1980): 83–92.

16. Johnnie Tillmon, "Welfare Is a Women's Issue," *Liberation News Service* (February 26, 1972), in *America's Working Women: A Documentary History, 1600 to the Present*, ed. Rosalyn Baxandall, Linda Gordon, and Susan Reverby (New York: Vintage Books, 1976), pp. 357–58.

anything. In this framework, the task of legal interpretation becomes "to perfect the state as mirror of the society."[17] Objectivist epistemology is the law of law. It ensures that the law will most reinforce existing distributions of power when it most closely adheres to its own highest ideal of fairness. Like the science it emulates, this epistemological stance can not see the social specificity of reflection as method or its choice to embrace that which it reflects. Such law not only reflects a society in which men rule women; it rules in a male way: "The phallus means everything that sets itself up as a mirror."[18] The rule form, which unites scientific knowledge with state control in its conception of what law is, institutionalizes the objective stance as jurisprudence. A closer look at the substantive law of rape[19] in light of such an argument suggests that the relation between objectification (understood as the primary process of the subordination of women) and the power of the state is the relation between the personal and

17. Laurence Tribe, "Constitution as Point of View" (Harvard Law School, Cambridge, Mass., 1982, mimeographed), p. 13.
18. Madeleine Gagnon, "Body I," in *New French Feminisms,* ed. Elaine Marks and Isabelle de Courtivron (Amherst, Mass.: University of Massachusetts Press, 1980), p. 180. Turns on the mirroring trope, which I see as metaphoric analyses of the epistemological/political dimension of objectification, are ubiquitous in feminist writing: "Into the room of the dressing where the walls are covered with mirrors. Where mirrors are like eyes of men, and the women reflect the judgments of mirrors" (Susan Griffin, *Woman and Nature: The Roaring Inside Her* [New York: Harper & Row Publishers, 1979], p. 155). See also Mary Daly, *Beyond God the Father: Toward a Philosophy of Women's Liberation* (Boston: Beacon Press, 1975), pp. 195, 197; Sheila Rowbotham, *Women's Consciousness, Man's World* (Harmondsworth: Pelican Books, 1973), pp. 26–29. "She did suffer, the witch/ trying to peer round the looking/ glass, she forgot/ someone was in the way" (Michelene, "Reflexion," quoted in Rowbotham, p. 2). Virginia Woolf wrote the figure around ("So I reflected . . ."), noticing "the necessity that women so often are to men" of serving as a looking glass in which a man can "see himself at breakfast and at dinner at least twice the size he really is." Notice the doubled sexual/gender meaning: "Whatever may be their use in civilized societies, mirrors are essential to all violent and heroic action. That is why Napoleon and Mussolini both insist so emphatically upon the inferiority of women, for if they were not inferior, they would cease to enlarge" (*A Room of One's Own* [New York: Harcourt, Brace & World, 1969], p. 36).
19. Space limitations made it necessary to eliminate sections on pornography, sex discrimination, and abortion. For the same reason, most supporting references, including those to case law, have been cut. The final section accordingly states the systemic implications of the analysis more tentatively than I think them, but as strongly as I felt I could, on the basis of the single substantive examination that appears here.

the political at the level of government. This is not because the state is presumptively the sphere of politics. It is because the state, in part through law, institutionalizes male power. If male power is systemic, it *is* the regime.

II

Feminists have reconceived rape as central to women's condition in two ways. Some see rape as an act of violence, not sexuality, the threat of which intimidates all women.[20] Others see rape, including its violence, as an expression of male sexuality, the social imperatives of which define all women.[21] The first, formally in the liberal tradition, comprehends rape as a displacement of power based on physical force onto sexuality, a preexisting natural sphere to which domination is alien. Thus, Susan Brownmiller examines rape in riots, wars, pogroms, and revolutions; rape by police, parents, prison guards; and rape motivated by racism—seldom rape in normal circumstances, in everyday life, in ordinary relationships, by men as men.[22] Women are raped by guns, age, white supremacy, the state—only derivatively by the penis. The more feminist view to me, one which derives from victims' experiences, sees sexuality as a social sphere of male power of which forced sex is paradigmatic. Rape is not less sexual for being violent; to the extent that coercion has become integral to male sexuality, rape may be sexual to the degree that, and because, it is violent.

20. Susan Brownmiller, *Against Our Will: Men, Women and Rape* (New York: Simon & Schuster, 1976), p. 15.
21. Diana E. H. Russell, *The Politics of Rape: The Victim's Perspective* (New York: Stein & Day, 1977); Andrea Medea and Kathleen Thompson, *Against Rape* (New York: Farrar, Straus & Giroux, 1974); Lorenne M. G. Clark and Debra Lewis, *Rape: The Price of Coercive Sexuality* (Toronto: The Women's Press, 1977); Susan Griffin, "Rape: The All-American Crime," *Ramparts* (September 1971), pp. 26–35; Ti-Grace Atkinson connects rape with "the institution of sexual intercourse" (*Amazon Odyssey: The First Collection of Writings by the Political Pioneer of the Women's Movement* [New York: Links Books, 1974], pp. 13–23). Kalamu ya Salaam, "Rape: A Radical Analysis from the African-American Perspective," in *Our Women Keep Our Skies from Falling* (New Orleans: Nkombo, 1980), pp. 25–40.
22. Racism, clearly, is everyday life. Racism in the United States, by singling out Black men for allegations of rape of white women, has helped obscure the fact that it is men who rape women, disproportionately women of color.

The point of defining rape as "violence not sex" or "violence against women" has been to separate sexuality from gender in order to affirm sex (heterosexuality) while rejecting violence (rape). The problem remains what it has always been: telling the difference. The convergence of sexuality with violence, long used at law to deny the reality of women's violation, is recognized by rape survivors, with a difference: where the legal system has seen the intercourse in rape, victims see the rape in intercourse. The uncoerced context for sexual expression becomes as elusive as the physical acts come to feel indistinguishable.[23] Instead of asking, what is the violation of rape, what if we ask, what is the nonviolation of intercourse? To tell what is wrong with rape, explain what is right about sex. If this, in turn, is difficult, the difficulty is as instructive as the difficulty men have in telling the difference when women see one. Perhaps the wrong of rape has proven so difficult to articulate[24] because the unquestionable starting point has been that rape is definable as distinct from intercourse, when for women it is difficult to distinguish them under conditions of male dominance.[25]

Like heterosexuality, the crime of rape centers on penetration.[26] The law to protect women's sexuality from forcible violation/

23. "Like other victims, I had problems with sex, after the rape. There was no way that Arthur could touch me that it didn't remind me of having been raped by this guy I never saw" (Carolyn Craven, "No More Victims: Carolyn Craven Talks about Rape, and about What Women and Men Can Do to Stop It," ed. Alison Wells [Berkeley, Calif., 1978, mimeographed]), p. 2.
24. Pamela Foa, "What's Wrong with Rape?" in Vetterling-Braggin, Elliston, and English, eds. (n. 15 above), pp. 347–59; Michael Davis, "What's So Bad about Rape?" (paper presented at Annual Meeting of the Academy of Criminal Justice Sciences, Louisville, Ky., March 1982).
25. "Since we would not want to say that there is anything morally wrong with sexual intercourse per se, we conclude that the wrongness of rape rests with the matter of the woman's consent" (Carolyn M. Shafer and Marilyn Frye, "Rape and Respect," in Vetterling-Braggin, Elliston, and English, eds. [n. 15 above], p. 334). "Sexual contact is not inherently harmful, insulting or provoking. Indeed, ordinarily it is something of which we are quite fond. The difference between ordinary sexual intercourse and rape is that ordinary sexual intercourse is more or less consented to while rape is not" (Davis [n. 24 above], p. 12).
26. Sec. 213.0 of the *Model Penal Code* (Official Draft and Revised Comments 1980), like most states, defines rape as sexual intercourse with a female who is not the wife of the perpetrator "with some penetration however slight." Impotency is sometimes a defense. Michigan's gender-neutral sexual assault statute includes penetration by objects (sec. 520a[h]; 520[b]). See *Model Penal Code,* annotation to sec. 213.1(d) (Official Draft and Revised Comments 1980).

expropriation defines the protected in male genital terms. Women do resent forced penetration. But penile invasion of the vagina may be less pivotal to women's sexuality, pleasure or violation, than it is to male sexuality. This definitive element of rape centers upon a male-defined loss, not coincidentally also upon the way men define loss of exclusive access. In this light, rape, as legally defined, appears more a crime against female monogamy than against female sexuality. Property concepts fail fully to comprehend this,[27] however, not because women's sexuality is not, finally, a thing, but because it is never ours. The moment we "have" it—"have sex" in the dual sexuality/gender sense—it is lost as ours. This may explain the male incomprehension that, once a woman has had sex, she loses anything when raped. To them we *have nothing* to lose. Dignitary harms, because nonmaterial, are remote to the legal mind. But women's loss through rape is not only less tangible, it is less existent. It is difficult to avoid the conclusion that penetration itself is known to be a violation and that women's sexuality, our gender definition, is itself stigmatic. If this is so, the pressing question for explanation is not why some of us accept rape but why any of us resent it.

The law of rape divides the world of women into spheres of consent according to how much say we are legally presumed to have over sexual access to us by various categories of men. Little girls may not consent; wives must. If rape laws existed to enforce women's control over our own sexuality, as the consent defense implies, marital rape would not be a widespread exception,[28] nor would statutory rape proscribe all sexual intercourse with underage girls regardless of their wishes. The rest of us fall into parallel provinces: good girls, like children, are unconsenting, virginal, rapable; bad girls, like wives, are consenting, whores, unrapable. The age line under which girls are presumed disabled from withholding consent

27. Although it is true that men possess women and that women's bodies are, socially, men's things, I have not analyzed rape as men treating women like property. In the manner of many socialist-feminist adaptations of marxian categories to women's situation, that analysis short-circuits analysis of rape as male sexuality and presumes rather than develops links between sex and class. We need to rethink sexual dimensions of property as well as property dimensions of sexuality.

28. For an excellent summary of the current state of the marital exemption, see Joanne Schulman, "State-by-State Information on Marital Rape Exemption Laws," in *Rape in Marriage,* Diana E. H. Russell (New York: Macmillan Publishing Co., 1982), pp. 375–81.

to sex rationalizes a condition of sexual coercion women never outgrow. As with protective labor laws for women only, dividing and protecting the most vulnerable becomes a device for not protecting everyone. Risking loss of even so little cannot be afforded. Yet the protection is denigrating and limiting (girls may not choose to be sexual) as well as perverse (girls are eroticized as untouchable; now reconsider the data on incest).

If the accused knows us, consent is inferred. The exemption for rape in marriage is consistent with the assumption underlying most adjudications of forcible rape: to the extent the parties relate, it was not really rape, it was personal.[29] As the marital exemptions erode, preclusions for cohabitants and voluntary social companions may expand. In this light, the partial erosion of the marital rape exemption looks less like a change in the equation between women's experience of sexual violation and men's experience of intimacy, and more like a legal adjustment to the social fact that acceptable heterosexual sex is increasingly not limited to the legal family. So although the rape law may not now always assume that the woman consented simply because the parties are legally one, indices of closeness, of relationship ranging from nodding acquaintance to living together, still contraindicate rape. Perhaps this reflects men's experience that women they know meaningfully consent to sex with them. That cannot be rape; rape must be by someone else, someone unknown. But *women* experience rape most often by men we know.[30] Men believe that it is less awful to be raped by someone one is close

29. On "social interaction as an element of consent," in a voluntary social companion context, see *Model Penal Code,* sec. 213.1. "The prior *social* interaction is an indicator of consent in addition to actor's and victim's *behavioral* interaction during the commission of the offense" (Wallace Loh, "Q: What Has Reform of Rape Legislation Wrought? A: Truth in Criminal Labeling," *Journal of Social Issues* 37, no. 4 [1981]: 28–52, 47). Perhaps consent should be an affirmative defense, pleaded and proven by the defendant.

30. Pauline Bart found that women were more likely to be raped—that is, less able to stop a rape in progress—when they knew their assailant, particularly when they had a prior or current sexual relationship ("A Study of Women Who Both Were Raped and Avoided Rape," *Journal of Social Issues* 37, no. 4 [1981]: 123–37, 132). See also Linda Belden, "Why Women Do Not Report Sexual Assault" (City of Portland Public Service Employment Program, Portland Women's Crisis Line, Portland, Ore., March 1979, mimeographed); Diana E. H. Russell and Nancy Howell, "The Prevalence of Rape in the United States Revisited," in this issue; and Menachem Amir, *Patterns in Forcible Rape* (Chicago: University of Chicago Press, 1971), pp. 229–52.

to: "The emotional trauma suffered by a person victimized by an individual with whom sexual intimacy is shared as a normal part of an ongoing marital relationship is not nearly as severe as that suffered by a person who is victimized by one with whom that intimacy is not shared."[31] But women feel as much, if not more, traumatized by being raped by someone we have known or trusted, someone we have shared at least an illusion of mutuality with, than by some stranger. In whose interest is it to believe that it is not so bad to be raped by someone who has fucked you before as by someone who has not? Disallowing charges of rape in marriage may also "remove a substantial obstacle to the resumption of normal marital relations."[32] Depending upon your view of normal. Note that the obstacle to normalcy here is not the rape but the law against it. Apparently someone besides feminists find sexual victimization and sexual intimacy not all that contradictory. Sometimes I think women and men live in different cultures.

Having defined rape in male sexual terms, the law's problem, which becomes the victim's problem, is distinguishing rape from sex in specific cases. The law does this by adjudicating the level of acceptable force starting just above the level set by what is seen as normal male sexual behavior, rather than at the victim's, or women's, point of violation. Rape cases finding insufficient force reveal that acceptable sex, in the legal perspective, can entail a lot of force. This is not only because of the way specific facts are perceived and interpreted, but because of the way the injury itself is defined as illegal. Rape is a sex crime that is not a crime when it looks like sex. To seek to define rape as violent, not sexual, is understandable in this context, and often seems strategic. But assault that is consented to is still assault; rape consented to is intercourse. The substantive reference point implicit in existing legal standards is the sexually normative level of force. Until this norm is confronted as such, no distinction between violence and sexuality will prohibit more instances of women's experienced violation than does the existing definition. The question is what is *seen as* force, hence as violence, in the sexual arena. Most rapes, as women live them, will not be seen to violate women until sex and violence are confronted as mutually

---

31. Answer Brief for Plaintiff-Appellee at 10, People v. Brown, 632 P.2d 1025 (Colo. 1981).

32. Brown, 632 P.2d at 1027 (citing Comment, "Rape and Battery between Husband and Wife," *Stanford Law Review* 6 [1954]: 719–28, 719, 725).

definitive. It is not only men convicted of rape who believe that the only thing they did different from what men do all the time is get caught.

The line between rape and intercourse commonly centers on some measure of the woman's "will." But from what should the law know woman's will? Like much existing law, Brownmiller tends to treat will as a question of consent and consent as a factual issue of the presence of force.[33] Proof problems aside, force and desire are not mutually exclusive. So long as dominance is eroticized, they never will be. Women are socialized to passive receptivity; may have or perceive no alternative to acquiescence; may prefer it to the escalated risk of injury and the humiliation of a lost fight; submit to survive. Some eroticize dominance and submission; it beats feeling forced. Sexual intercourse may be deeply unwanted—the woman would never have initiated it—yet no force may be present. Too, force may be used, yet the woman may want the sex—to avoid more force or because she, too, eroticizes dominance. Women and men know this. Calling rape violence, not sex, thus evades, at the moment it most seems to confront, the issue of who controls women's sexuality and the dominance/submission dynamic that has defined it. When sex is violent, women may have lost control over what is done to us, but absence of force does not ensure the presence of that control. Nor, under conditions of male dominance, does the presence of force make an interaction nonsexual. If sex is normally something men do to women, the issue is less whether there was force and more whether consent is a meaningful concept.[34]

To explain women's gender status as a function of rape, Brownmiller argues that the threat of rape benefits all men.[35] She does not specify in what way. Perhaps it benefits them sexually, hence as a gender male initiatives toward women carry the fear of rape as support for persuading compliance, the resulting appearance of which has been called consent. Here the victims' perspective grasps what liberalism applied to women denies: that forced sex as sexuality is not exceptional in relations between the sexes but constitutes the social meaning of gender: "Rape is a man's act, whether it is male or a female man and whether it is a man relatively permanently or

33. Brownmiller (n. 20 above), pp. 8, 196, 400–407, 427–36.
34. See Carol Pateman, "Women and Consent," *Political Theory* 8, no. 2 (May 1980) 149–68.
35. Brownmiller (n. 20 above), p. 5.

relatively temporarily; and being raped is a woman's experience, whether it is a female or a male woman and whether it is a woman relatively permanently or relatively temporarily."[36] To be rap*able,* a position which is social, not biological, defines what a woman *is.*

Most women get the message that the law against rape is virtually unenforceable as applied to them. Our own experience is more often delegitimized by this than the law is. Women radically distinguish between rape and experiences of sexual violation, concluding that we have not "really" been raped if we have ever seen or dated or slept with or been married to the man, if we were fashionably dressed or are not provably virgin, if we are prostitutes, if we put up with it or tried to get it over with, if we were force-fucked over a period of years. If we probably couldn't prove it in court, it wasn't rape. The distance between most sexual violations of women and the legally perfect rape measures the imposition of someone else's definition upon women's experiences. Rape, from women's point of view, is not prohibited; it

---

36. Shafer and Frye (n. 25 above), p. 334. Battery of wives has been legally separated from marital rape not because assault by a man's fist is so different from assault by a penis. Both seem clearly violent. I am suggesting that both are also sexual. Assaults are often precipitated by women's noncompliance with gender requirements. See R. Emerson Dobash and Russell Dobash, *Violence against Wives: A Case against the Patriarchy* (New York: Free Press, 1979), pp. 14–20. Nearly all incidents occur in the home, most in the kitchen or bedroom. Most murdered women are killed by their husbands, most in the bedroom. The battery cycle accords with the rhythm of heterosexual sex (see Leonore Walker, *The Battered Woman* [New York: Harper & Row Publishers, 1979], pp. 19–20). The rhythm of lesbian S/M appears similar (Samois, eds., *Coming to Power* [Palo Alto, Calif.: Up Press, 1981]). Perhaps most interchange between genders, but especially violent ones, make sense on sexual terms. However, the larger issue for the relation between sexuality and gender, hence sexuality and violence generally, including both war and violence against women, is: What *is* heterosexuality? If it is the erotization of dominance and submission, altering the participants' gender is comparatively incidental. If it is males over females, gender matters independently. Since I see heterosexuality as the fusion of the two, but with gender a social outcome (such that the acted upon is feminized, is the "girl" regardless of sex, the actor correspondingly masculinized), battery appears sexual on a deeper level. In baldest terms, sexuality is violent, so violence is sexual, violence against women doubly so. If this is so, wives are beaten, as well as raped, *as women*—as the acted upon, as gender, meaning sexual, objects. It further follows that all acts *by anyone* which treat a woman according to her object label "woman" are *sexual* acts. The extent to which sexual acts are acts of objectification remains a question of our account of our freedom to make our own meanings. It is clear, at least, that it is centering sexuality upon genitality that distinguishes battery from rape at exactly the juncture that both the law, and seeing rape as violence not sex, does.

is regulated. Even women who know we have been raped do not believe that the legal system will see it the way we do. We are often not wrong. Rather than deterring or avenging rape, the state, in many victims' experiences, perpetuates it. Women who charge rape say they were raped twice, the second time in court. If the state is male, this is more than a figure of speech.

The law distinguishes rape from intercourse by the woman's lack of consent coupled with a man's (usually) knowing disregard of it. A feminist distinction between rape and intercourse, to hazard a beginning approach, lies instead in the *meaning* of the act from women's point of view. What is wrong with rape is that it is an act of the subordination of women to men. Seen this way, the issue is not so much what rape "is" as the way its social conception is shaped to interpret particular encounters. Under conditions of sex inequality, with perspective bound up with situation, whether a contested interaction is rape comes down to whose meaning wins. If sexuality is relational, specifically if it is a power relation of gender, consent is a communication under conditions of inequality. It transpires somewhere between what the woman actually wanted and what the man comprehended she wanted. Instead of capturing this dynamic, the law gives us linear statics face to face. Nonconsent in law becomes a question of the man's force or the woman's resistance or both.[37] Rape, like many crimes and torts, requires that the accused possess a criminal mind (mens rea) for his acts to be criminal. The man's mental state refers to what he actually understood at the time or to what a reasonable man should have understood under the circumstances. The problem is this: the injury of rape lies in the meaning of the act to its victims, but the standard for its criminality lies in the meaning of the same act to the assailants. Rape is only an injury from women's point of view. It is only a crime from the male point of view, explicitly including that of the accused.

Thus is the crime of rape defined and adjudicated from the male standpoint, that is, presuming that (what feminists see as) forced sex is sex. Under male supremacy, of course, it is. What this means doctrinally is that the man's perceptions of the woman's desires often determine whether she is deemed violated. This might be like other crimes of subjective intent if rape were like other crimes. But with rape, because sexuality defines gender, the only difference between

37. Even when nonconsent is not a legal element of the offense (as in Michigan), juries tend to infer rape from evidence of force or resistance.

assault and (what is socially considered) noninjury is the meaning of the encounter to the woman. Interpreted this way, the legal problem has been to determine whose view of that meaning constitutes what really happened, as if what happened objectively exists to be objectively determined, thus as if this task of determination is separable from the gender of the participants and the gendered nature of their exchange. Thus, even though the rape law oscillates between subjective tests and more objective standards invoking social reasonableness, it uniformly presumes a single underlying reality, not a reality split by divergent meanings, such as those inequality produces. Many women are raped by men who know the meaning of their acts to women and proceed anyway.[38] But women are also violated every day by men who have no idea of the meaning of their acts to women. To them, it is sex. Therefore, to the law, it is sex. That is the single reality of what happened. When a rape prosecution is lost on a consent defense, the woman has not only failed to prove lack of consent, she is not considered to have been injured at all. Hermeneutically unpacked, read: because he did not perceive she did not want him, she was not violated. She had sex. Sex itself cannot be an injury. Women consent to sex every day. Sex makes a woman a woman. Sex is what women are *for.*

To a feminist analysis, men set sexual mores ideologically and behaviorally, define rape as they imagine the sexual violation of women through distinguishing it from their image of what they normally do, and sit in judgment in most accusations of sex crimes. So rape comes to mean a strange (read Black) man knowing a woman does not want sex and going ahead anyway. But men are systematically conditioned not even to notice what women want. They may have not a glimmer of women's indifference or revulsion. Rapists typically believe the woman loved it.[39] Women, as a survival strategy, must

---

38. This is apparently true of undetected as well as convicted rapists. Samuel David Smithyman's sample, composed largely of the former, contained self-selected respondents to his ad, which read: "Are you a rapist? Researchers Interviewing Anonymously by Phone to Protect Your Identity. Call. . . ." Presumably those who chose to call defined their acts as rapes, at least at the time of responding ("The Undetected Rapist" [Ph.D. diss., Claremont Graduate School, 1978], pp. 54–60, 63–76, 80–90, 97–107).

39. "Probably the single most used cry of rapist to victim is 'You bitch . . . slut . . . you know you want it. You *all* want it' and afterward, 'there now, you really enjoyed it, didn't you?'" (Nancy Gager and Cathleen Schurr, *Sexual Assault: Confronting Rape in America* [New York: Grosset & Dunlap, 1976], p. 244).

ignore or devalue or mute our desires (particularly lack of them) to convey the impression that the man will get what he wants regardless of what we want. In this context, consider measuring the genuineness of consent from the individual assailant's (or even the socially reasonable, i.e., objective, man's) point of view.

Men's pervasive belief that women fabricate rape charges after consenting to sex makes sense in this light. To them, the accusations *are* false because, to them, the facts describe sex. To interpret such events as rapes distorts their experience. Since they seldom consider that their experience of the real is anything other than reality, they can only explain the woman's version as maliciously invented. Similarly, the male anxiety that rape is easy to charge and difficult to disprove (also widely believed in the face of overwhelming evidence to the contrary) arises because rape accusations express one thing men cannot seem to control: the meaning to women of sexual encounters.

Thus do legal doctrines, incoherent or puzzling as syllogistic logic, become coherent as ideology. For example, when an accused wrongly but sincerely believes that a woman he sexually forced consented, he may have a defense of mistaken belief or fail to satisfy the mental requirement of knowingly proceeding against her will.[40] One commentator notes, discussing the conceptually similar issue of revocation of prior consent (i.e., on the issue of the conditions under which women are allowed to control access to their sexuality from one time to the next): "Even where a woman revokes prior consent, such is the male ego that, seized of an exaggerated assessment of his sexual prowess, a man might genuinely believe her still to be consenting; resistance may be misinterpreted as enthusiastic cooperation; protestations of pain or disinclination, a spur to more sophisticated or more ardent love-making; a clear statement to stop, taken as referring to a particular intimacy rather than the entire performance."[41] This equally vividly captures common male readings of women's indications of

40. See Director of Public Prosecutions v. Morgan, 2411 E.R.H.L. 347 (1975); Pappajohn v. The Queen, 11 D.L.R. 3d 1 (1980); People v. Mayberry, 15 Cal. 3d 143, 542 P.2d 1337 (1975).

41. Richard H. S. Tur, "Rape: Reasonableness and Time," *Oxford Journal of Legal Studies* 3 (Winter 1981): 432–41, 441. Tur, in the context of the Morgan and Pappajohn cases, says the "law ought not to be astute to equate wickedness and wishful, albeit mistaken, thinking" (p. 437). In feminist analysis, a rape is not an isolated or individual or moral transgression but a terrorist act within a systematic context of group subjection, like lynching.

disinclination under all kinds of circumstances.[42] Now reconsider to what extent the man's perceptions should determine whether a rape occurred. From whose standpoint, and in whose interest, is a law that allows one person's conditioned unconsciousness to contraindicate another's experienced violation? This aspect of the rape law reflects the sex inequality of the society not only in conceiving a cognizable injury from the viewpoint of the reasonable rapist, but in affirmatively rewarding men with acquittals for not comprehending women's point of view on sexual encounters.

Whether the law calls this coerced consent or mistake of fact, the more the sexual violation of women is routine, the more beliefs equating sexuality with violation become reasonable, and the more honestly women can be defined in terms of our fuckability. It would be comparatively simple if the legal problem were limited to avoiding retroactive falsification of the accused's state of mind. Surely there are incentives to lie. But the deeper problem is the rape law's assumption that a single, objective state of affairs existed, one which merely needs to be determined by evidence, when many (maybe even most) rapes involve honest men and violated women. When the reality is split—a woman is raped but not by a rapist?—the law tends to conclude that a rape *did not happen.* To attempt to solve this by adopting the standard of reasonable belief without asking, on a substantive social basis, to whom the belief is reasonable and why—meaning, what conditions make it reasonable—is one-sided: male-sided. What is it reasonable for a man to believe concerning a woman's desire for sex when heterosexuality is compulsory. Whose subjectivity becomes the objectivity of "what happened" is a matter of social meaning, that is, it has been a matter of sexual politics. One-sidedly erasing women's violation or dissolving the presumptions into the subjectivity of either side are alternatives dictated by the terms of the object/subject split, respectively. These are alternatives that will only retrace that split until its terms are confronted as gendered to the ground.

Desirability to men is commonly supposed to be a woman's form of power. This echoes the view that consent is women's form of control over intercourse, different but equal to the custom of male initiative. Look at it: man initiates, woman chooses. Even the ideal is not mutual. Apart from the disparate consequences of refusal, or open-

---

42. See Silke Vogelmann-Sine et al., "Sex Differences in Feelings Attributed to a Woman in Situations Involving Coercion and Sexual Advances," *Journal of Personality* 47, no. 3 (September 1979): 420–31, esp. 429–30.

ness of original options, this model does not envision a situation the woman controls being placed in, or choices she frames, yet the consequences are attributed to her as if the sexes began at arm's length, on equal terrain, as in the contract fiction. Ambiguous cases of consent are often archetypically referred to as "half won arguments in parked cars."[43] Why not half lost? Why isn't half enough? Why is it an argument? Why do men still want "it," feel entitled to "it," when women don't want them? That sexual expression is even framed as a matter of woman's consent, without exposing these presuppositions, is integral to gender inequality. Woman's so-called power presupposes her more fundamental powerlessness.[44]

III

The state's formal norms recapitulate the male point of view on the level of design. In Anglo-American jurisprudence, morals (value judgments) are deemed separable and separated from politics (power contests), and both from adjudication (interpretation). Neutrality, including judicial decision making that is dispassionate, impersonal, disinterested, and precedential, is considered desirable and descriptive. Courts, forums without predisposition among parties and with no interest of their own, reflect society back to itself resolved. Government of laws not men limits partiality with written constraints and tempers force with reasonable rule following. This law aspires to science: to the immanent generalization subsuming the emergent particularity, to prediction and control of social regularities and regulations, preferably codified. The formulaic "tests" of "doctrine" aspire to mechanism, classification to taxonomy. Courts intervene only in properly "factualized" disputes,[45] cognizing social conflicts as if collecting empirical data. But the demarcations between morals and politics, the personality of the judge and the

---

43. Note, "Forcible and Statutory Rape: An Exploration of the Operation and Objectives of the Consent Standard," *Yale Law Journal* 62 (1952): 55–56.

44. A similar analysis of sexual harassment suggests that women have such "power" only so long as we behave according to male definitions of female desirability, that is, only so long as we accede the definition of our sexuality (hence, ourselves, as gender female) to male terms. We have this power only so long as we remain powerless.

45. Peter Gabel, "Reification in Legal Reasoning" (New College Law School, San Francisco, 1980, mimeographed), p. 3.

judicial role, bare coercion and the rule of law,[46] tend to merge in women's experience. Relatively seamlessly they promote the dominance of men as a social group through privileging the form of power—the perspective on social life—feminist consciousness reveals as socially male. The separation of form from substance, process from policy, role from theory and practice, echoes and reechoes at each level of the regime its basic norm: objectivity.

Consider a central example. The separation of public from private is as crucial to the liberal state's claim to objectivity as its inseparability is to women's claim to subordination. Legally, it has both formal and substantive dimensions. The state considers formal, not substantive, the allocation of public matters to itself to be treated objectively, of private matters to civil society to be treated subjectively. Substantively, the private is defined as a right to "an inviolable personality,"[47] which is guaranteed by ensuring "autonomy or control over the intimacies of personal identity."[48] It is hermetic. It means that which is inaccessible to, unaccountable to, and unconstructed by anything beyond itself. Intimacy occurs in private; this is supposed to guarantee original symmetry of power. Injuries arise in violating the private sphere, not within and by and because of it. Private means consent can be presumed unless disproven. To contain a systematic inequality contradicts the notion itself. But feminist consciousness has exploded the private. For women, the measure of the intimacy has been the measure of the oppression. To see the personal as political means to

46. Rawls's "original position," for instance, is a version of my objective standpoint (John Rawls, *A Theory of Justice* [Cambridge, Mass.: Harvard University Press, 1971]). Not only apologists for the liberal state, but also some of its most trenchant critics, see a real distinction between the rule of law and absolute arbitrary force. E. P. Thompson, *Whigs and Hunters: The Origin of the Black Act* (New York: Pantheon Books, 1975), pp. 258–69. Douglas Hay argues that making and enforcing certain acts as illegal reinforces a structure of subordination ("Property, Authority, and the Criminal Law," in *Albion's Fatal Tree: Crime and Society in Eighteenth Century England,* D. Hay et al., eds. [New York: Pantheon Books, 1975], pp. 17–31). Michael D. A. Freeman ("Violence against Women: Does the Legal System Provide Solutions or Itself Constitute the Problem?" [Madison, Wis., 1980, mimeographed], p. 12, n. 161) applies this argument to domestic battery of women. Here I extend it to women's situation as a whole, without suggesting that the analysis can *end* there.

47. S. D. Warren and L. D. Brandeis, "The Right to Privacy," *Harvard Law Review* 4 (1890): 193–205.

48. Tom Gerety, "Redefining Privacy," *Harvard Civil Right–Civil Liberties Law Review* 12, no. 2 (Spring 1977): 236.

see the private as public. On this level, women have no privacy to lose or to guarantee. We are not inviolable. Our sexuality, meaning gender identity, is not only violable, it *is* (hence we are) our violation. Privacy is everything women as women have never been allowed to be or to have; at the same time the private is everything women have been equated with and defined in terms of *men's* ability to have. To confront the fact that we have no privacy is to confront our private degradation as the public order. To fail to recognize this place of the private in women's subordination by seeking protection behind a right to that privacy is thus to be cut off from collective verification and state support in the same act.[49] The very place (home, body), relations (sexual), activities (intercourse and reproduction), and feelings (intimacy, selfhood) that feminism finds central to women's subjection form the core of privacy doctrine. But when women are segregated in private, one at a time, a law of privacy will tend to protect the right of men "to be let alone,"[50] to oppress us one at a time. A law of the private, in a state that mirrors such a society, will translate the traditional values of the private sphere into individual women's right to privacy, subordinating women's collective needs to the imperatives of male supremacy.[51] It will keep some men out of the bedrooms of other men.

Liberalism converges with the left at this edge of the feminist critique of male power. Herbert Marcuse speaks of "philosophies which are 'political' in the widest sense—affecting society as a whole, demonstrably transcending the sphere of privacy."[52] This does and does not describe the feminist political: "Women both have and have not had a common world."[53] Isolation in the home and intimate

49. Harris v. McRae, 448 U.S. 287 (1980), which holds that withholding public funds for abortions does not violate the federal constitutional right to privacy, illustrates. See Zillah Eisenstein, *The Radical Future of Liberal Feminism* (New York: Longman, Inc., 1981), p. 240.

50. Robeson v. Rochester Folding Box Co., 171 NY 538 (1902); Cooley, *Torts,* sec. 135, 4th ed. (Chicago: Callaghan & Co., 1932).

51. This argument learned a lot from Tom Grey's article, "Eros, Civilization and the Burger Court," *Law and Contemporary Problems* 43. (Summer 1980): 83–99.

52. Herbert Marcuse, "Repressive Tolerance," in *A Critique of Pure Tolerance,* ed. Robert Paul Wolff, Barrington Moore, Jr., and Herbert Marcuse (Boston: Beacon Press, 1965), pp. 81–117, esp. p. 91.

53. Adrienne Rich, "Conditions for Work: The Common World of Women," in *Working It Out: Twenty-three Women Writers, Artists, Scientists, and Scholars Talk about Their Lives and Work,* ed. Sara Ruddick and Pamela Daniels (New York: Pantheon Books, 1977), pp. xiv–xxiv, esp. p. xiv.

degradation, women share. The private sphere, which confines and separates us, is therefore a political sphere, a common ground of our inequality. In feminist translation, the private is a sphere of battery, marital rape, and women's exploited labor; of the central social institutions whereby women are deprived of (as men are granted) identity, autonomy, control, and self-determination; and of the primary activity through which male supremacy is expressed and . enforced. Rather than transcending the private as a predicate to politics, feminism politicizes it. For women, the private necessarily transcends the private. If the most private also most "affects society as a whole," the separation between public and private collapses as anything other than potent ideology. The failure of marxism adequately to address intimacy on the one hand, government on the other, is the same failure as the indistinguishability between marxism and liberalism on questions of sexual politics.

Interpreting further areas of law, a feminist theory of the state will reveal that the idealism of liberalism and the materialism of the left have come to much the same for women. Liberal jurisprudence that the law should reflect society and left jurisprudence that all law does or can do is reflect existing social relations will emerge as two guises of objectivist epistemology. If objectivity is the epistemological stance of which women's sexual objectification is the social process, its imposition the paradigm of power in the male form, then the state will appear most relentless in imposing the male point of view when it comes closest to achieving its highest formal criterion of distanced aperspectivity. When it is most ruthlessly neutral, it will be most male; when it is most sex blind, it will be most blind to the sex of the standard being applied. When it most closely conforms to precedent, to "facts," to legislative intent, it will most closely enforce socially male norms and most thoroughly preclude questioning their content as having a point of view at all. Abstract rights will authoritize the male experience of the world. The liberal view that law is society's text, its rational mind, expresses this in a normative mode; the traditional left view that the state, and with it the law, is superstructural or epiphenomenal expresses it in an empirical mode. Both rationalize male power by presuming that it does not exist, that equality between the sexes (room for marginal corrections conceded) is society's basic norm and fundamental description. Only feminism grasps the extent to which the opposite is true: that anti-feminism is as normative as it is empirical. Once masculinity appears as a specific position, not just as the way things are, its judgments will be revealed in process and procedure, as well as adjudication and legislation. Perhaps the objectivity of the liberal state has made it appear "autonomous of class." Including, but beyond, the bourgeois in liberal legalism, lies what is male about it. However autonomous of class the liberal state may appear, it is not autonomous of sex. Justice will require change, not reflection—a new jurisprudence, a new relation between life and law.

GAYATRI CHAKRAVORTY SPIVAK

Gayatri Spivak has spoken of the "epistemic violence" necessary for those who want to occupy a place in all three major theoretical projects of our time—Deconstruction, Feminism, and Marxism. These projects, she says, are all "discontinuous" with each other.* Each does valuable work, however, and should be allowed an amicable divorce and asked to procede in their separate directions, on their separate levels, with perhaps an occasional calm exchange on results most recently obtained. Given its explosive possibilities, "Feminism and Critical Theory" is a very gentle and temperate examination of some of these discontinuities. There is no question, however, that while Spivak remains supportive of Feminism, she does see a Feminism at variance with the central preoccupations of the "high feminism" of American university women, whose invocations of male oppression are heard largely in their own tenure struggles, in fact, the only sort of struggle in which most bother to engage.† The implicit comparison made in the essay between the feminist preoccupations of Margaret Drabble in her novel *The Waterfall* and the fate of the 237 female workers who went on strike at a Control Data factory in Seoul, South Korea, in March 1982, makes the same point but with more elegance. "Waterfall" refers to the cherished orgasms of Drabble's central character, who is willing to follow the lead of her body and devise, if need be, an intrepid private morality that condones her untiring pursuit of genital fulfillment. The Korean women meanwhile, hoping for a more modest thrill—a reasonable adjustment in wages —were assaulted by the male Korean workers at the factory where they worked. There were injuries and miscarriages. One woman's miscarriage was dismissed out of hand, however, because she had already had two others without help from anyone. Later in *Ms.* magazine, an executive for the National Organization of Women (NOW) celebrated Control Data as having a superb record in the hiring and promotion of women. Spivak's point is clear: Feminism ". . . is not the determinant of the last instance." Without an economic theory sensitive to the "multinational theatre," bourgeois feminism, gazing in the mirror at its face and genitals (an image from the *"Intervention* Interview") and in *those* terms "adjudicating about woman as such," becomes itself complicit in all sorts of ugly oppression.

*"*Hermes* Interview," by Adam Levy, for the Students and Faculty of Wesleyan University, *Hermes,* Vol. 16, (December 6, 1983), no. 4.
†*"Intervention* Interview," by Terry Threadgold, Cultural Construction of Race Conference, Sydney, Australia (in ms.). The questions were raised at the Sidney convention, then later posed by Frances Bartkowski, Wesleyan University, on 20 August, 1985, and the answers recorded on tape.

But if first-world feminism has been known to fail women, it is not alone. For its part, says Spivak, Marxism has failed women not only by dismissing Feminism's importance but in failing to see the womb as a place of production, failing to see that Marxist categories for assessing value are inadequate for the products of the womb. Psychoanalysis as well has failed Feminism by refusing to consider the acceptance of pain in childbirth within the categories of the normal, as women must. Meanwhile, it is fair to ask Feminism, specifically women's suffrage, to account for its historical antipathy for the cause of workers' unions. The discreet criticism here again seems to be that Feminism has a tendency toward class-bound exclusivity, that for women to acquire power and influence in the system as it is, is not, alas, to procede very far in the direction of justice. One important distinction between Spivak and Fredric Jameson, in fact, is precisely that Spivak is much less blithe about ethical questions, questions of justice, which Jameson seems at times to treat in the beyond-good-and-evil way typical of Hegel, Engels, or at times Marx himself. Yet the ethical Marx exists, too, in the texts, though he is cherished more by the English New Left than the American.**

If Spivak's thought is difficult, it is so not just because her reading is so wide and eclectic; many stages in her arguments are elliptical and would, if developed separately, require very extended treatment indeed. Simply working out some of the topics so generously sown in the essay reprinted here will guarantee a rich harvest of later communications, which in turn will ensure the gratitude of an increasingly large and devoted following.

Feminism and Critical Theory

1985

What has been the itinerary of my thinking during the past few

FEMINISM AND CRITICAL THEORY by Gayatri Spivak from *For Alma Mater: Theory and Practice in Feminist Scholarship,* ed. Paula A. Treichler, Cheris Kramarae, and Beth Staffard. Copyright © 1985 by University of Illinois Press. Reprinted with permission of the publisher, University of Illinois Press.

**For criticisms of middle-class morality by Marx, see *Capital* Vol. I, trans. Ben Fowkes (New York: Vintage, 1977) 516, 481, 375. See Norman Geras, "The Controversy About Marx and Justice," in *Literature of Revolution* (London: Verso Books, 1986) 3–57.

years about the relationships among feminism, Marxism, psychoanalysis, and deconstruction? The issues have been of interest to many
people, and the configurations of these fields continue to change. I
will not engage here with the various lines of thought that have
constituted this change, but will try instead to mark and reflect upon
the way these developments have been inscribed in my own work.
The first section of the essay is a version of a talk I gave several years
ago. The second section represents a reflection on that earlier work.
The third section is an intermediate moment. The fourth section
inhabits something like the present.

I

I cannot speak of feminism in general. I speak of what I do as a
woman within literary criticism. My own definition as a woman is very
simple: it rests on the word "man" as used in the texts that provide
the foundation for the corner of the literary criticism establishment
that I inhabit. You might say at this point, defining the word "woman"
as resting on the word "man" is a reactionary position. Should I not
carve out an independent definition for myself as a woman? Here I
must repeat some deconstructive lessons learned over the past
decade that I often repeat. One, no rigorous definition of anything is
ultimately possible, so that if one wants to, one could go on
deconstructing the opposition between man and woman, and finally
show that it is a binary opposition that displaces itself.[1] Therefore, "as
a deconstructivist," I cannot recommend that kind of dichotomy at
all, yet, I feel that definitions are necessary in order to keep us going,
to allow us to take a stand. The only way that I can see myself making
definitions is in a provisional and polemical one: I construct my
definition as a woman not in terms of a woman's putative essence but
in terms of words currently in use. "Man" is such a word in common
usage. Not *a* word, but *the* word. I therefore fix my glance upon this
word even as I question the enterprise of redefining the premises of
any theory.

---

1. For an explanation of this aspect of deconstruction, see Gayatri Chakravorty
   Spivak, "Translator's Preface" to Jacques Derrida, *Of Grammatology* (Baltimore:
   Johns Hopkins University Press, 1976).

In the broadest possible sense, most critical theory in my part of the academic establishment (Lacan, Derrida, Foucault, the last Barthes) sees the text as that area of the discourse of the human sciences—in the United States called the humanities—in which the *problem* of the discourse of the human sciences is made available. Whereas in other kinds of discourses there is a move toward the final truth of a situation, literature, even within this argument, displays that the truth of a human situation *is* the itinerary of not being able to find it. In the general discourse of the humanities, there is a sort of search for solutions, whereas in literary discourse there is a playing out of the problem as the solution, if you like.

The problem of human discourse is generally seen as articulating itself in the play of, in terms of, three shifting "concepts": language, world, and consciousness. We know no world that is not organized as a language, we operate with no other consciousness but one structured as a language—languages that we cannot possess, for we are operated by those languages as well. The category of language, then, embraces the categories of world and consciousness even as it is determined by them. Strictly speaking, since we are questioning the human being's control over the production of language, the figure that will serve us better is writing, for there the absence of the producer and receiver is taken for granted. A safe figure, seemingly outside of the language-(speech)-writing opposition, is the text—a weave of knowing and not-knowing which is what knowing is. (This organizing principle—language, writing, or text—might itself be a way of holding at bay a randomness incongruent with consciousness.)

The theoreticians of textuality read Marx as a theorist of the world (history and society), as a text of the forces of labor and production-circulation-distribution, and Freud as a theorist of the self, as a text of consciousness and the unconscious. This human textuality can be seen not only *as* world and self, *as* the representation of a world in terms of a self at play with other selves and generating this representation, but also *in* the world and self, all implicated in an "intertextuality." It should be clear from this that such a concept of textuality does not mean a reduction of the world to linguistic texts, books, or a tradition composed of books, criticism in the narrow sense, and teaching.

I am not, then, speaking about Marxist or psychoanalytic criticism as a reductive enterprise which diagnoses the scenario in every book in terms of where it would fit into a Marxist or a psychoanalytical canon. To my way of thinking, the discourse of the literary text is part of a general configuration of textuality, a placing forth of the solution as the unavailability of a unified solution to a unified or homogeneous, generating or receiving, consciousness. This unavailability is often not confronted. It is dodged and the problem apparently solved, in terms perhaps of unifying concepts like "man," the universal contours of a sex-, race-, class-transcendent consciousness as the generating, generated, and receiving consciousness of the text.

I could have broached Marx and Freud more easily. I wanted to say all of the above because, in general, in the literary critical establishment here, those two are seen as reductive models. Now, although nonreductive methods are implicit in both of them, Marx and Freud do also seem to argue in terms of a mode of evidence and demonstration. They seem to bring forth evidence from the world of man or man's self, and thus prove certain kinds of truths about world and self. I would risk saying that their descriptions of world and self are based on inadequate evidence. In terms of this conviction, I would like to fix upon the idea of alienation in Marx, and the idea of normality and health in Freud.

One way of moving into Marx is in terms of use-value, exchange-value, and surplus-value. Marx's notion of use-value is that which pertains to a thing as it is directly consumed by an agent. Its exchange-value (after the emergence of the money form) does not relate to its direct fulfillment of a specific need, but is rather assessed in terms of what it can be exchanged for in either labor-power or money. In this process of abstracting through exchange, by making the worker work longer than necessary for subsistence wages or by means of labor-saving machinery, the buyer of the laborer's work gets more (in exchange) than the worker needs for his subsistence while he makes the thing.[2] This "more-worth" (in German, literally, *Mehrwert)* is surplus-value.

One could indefinitely allegorize the relationship of woman within this particular triad—use, exchange, and surplus—by suggesting that woman in the traditional social situation produces more than she is getting in terms of her subsistence, and therefore is a continual source of the production of surpluses, *for* the man who owns her, or

2. It seems appropriate to note, by using a masculine pronoun, that Marx's standard worker is male.

by the man for the capitalist who owns *his* labor-power. Apart from the fact that the mode of production of housework is not, strictly speaking, capitalist, such an analysis is paradoxical. The contemporary woman, when she seeks financial compensation for housework, seeks the abstraction of use-value into exchange-value. The situation of the domestic workplace is not one of "pure exchange." The Marxian exigency would make us ask at least two questions: What is the use-value of unremunerated woman's work for husband or family? Is the willing insertion into the wage structure a curse or a blessing? How should we fight the idea, universally accepted by men, that wages are the only mark of value-producing work? (Not, I think, through the slogan "Housework is beautiful.") What would be the implications of denying women entry into the capitalist economy? Radical feminism can here learn a cautionary lesson from Lenin's capitulation to capitalism.

These are important questions, but they do not necessarily broaden Marxist theory from a feminist point of view. For our purpose, the idea of externalization *(Entäußerung/Veräußerung)* or alienation *(Entfremdung)* is of greater interest. Within the capitalist system, the labor process externalizes itself and the worker as commodities. Upon this idea of the fracturing of the human being's relationship to himself and his work as commodities rests the ethical charge of Marx's argument.[3]

I would argue that, in terms of the physical, emotional, legal, custodial, and sentimental situation of the woman's product, the child, this picture of the human relationship to production, labor, and property is incomplete. The possession of a tangible place of production in the womb situates the woman as an agent in any theory of production. Marx's dialectics of externalization-alienation followed

---

3. I am not suggesting this by way of what Harry Braverman describes as "that favorite hobby horse of recent years which has been taken from Marx without the least understanding of its significance" in *Labor and Monopoly Capital: the Degradation of Work in the Twentieth Century* (New York and London: Monthly Review Press, 1974, pp. 27, 28). Simply put, alienation in Hegel is that structural emergence of negation which allows a thing to sublate itself. The worker's alienation from the product of his labor under capitalism is a particular case of alienation. Marx does not question its specifically *philosophical* justice. The revolutionary upheaval of this philosophical or morphological justice is, strictly speaking, also a harnessing of the principle of alienation, the negation of a negation. It is a mark of the individualistic ideology of liberalism that it understands alienation as *only* the pathetic predicament of the oppressed worker.

by fetish formation is inadequate because one fundamental human relationship to a product and labor is not taken into account.[4]

This does not mean that, if the Marxian account of externalization-alienation were rewritten from a feminist perspective, the special interest of childbirth, childbearing, and childrearing would be inserted. It seems that the entire problematic of sexuality, rather than remaining caught within arguments about overt sociosexual politics, would be fully broached.

Having said this, I would reemphasize the need to interpret reproduction within a Marxian problematic.[5]

In both so-called matrilineal and patrilineal societies the legal possession of the child is an inalienable fact of the property right of the man who "produces" the child.[6] In terms of this legal possession, the common custodial definition, that women are much more nurturing of children, might be seen as a dissimulated reactionary gesture. The man retains legal property rights over the product of a woman's body. On each separate occasion, the custodial decision is a sentimental questioning of man's right. The current struggle over abortion rights has foregrounded this unacknowledged agenda.

In order not simply to make an exception to man's legal right, or to add a footnote from a feminist perspective to the Marxist text, we must engage and correct the theory of production and alienation upon which the Marxist text is based and with which it functions. As I suggested above, such Marxist feminism works on an analogy with use-value, exchange-value, and surplus-value relationships. Marx's own writings on women and children seek to alleviate their condition in terms of a desexualized labor force.[7] If there were the kind of

4. In this connection, we should note the metaphors of sexuality in *Capital.*
5. I remember with pleasure my encounter, at the initial presentation of this paper, with Mary O'Brien, who said she was working on precisely this issue, and who later produced the excellent book *The Politics of Reproduction* (London: Routledge and Kegan Paul, 1981). I should mention here that the suggestion that mother and daughter have "the same body" and therefore the female child experiences what amounts to an unalienated pre-Oedipality argues from an individualist-pathetic view of alienation and locates as *discovery* the essentialist *presuppositions* about the sexed body's identity. This reversal of Freud remains also a legitimation.
6. See Jack Goody, *Production and Reproduction: A Comparative Study of the Domestic Domain* (Cambridge: Cambridge University Press, 1976), and Maurice Godelier, "The Origins of Male Domination," *New Left Review* 127 (May/June 1981): 3–17.
7. Collected in *Karl Marx on Education, Women, and Children* (New York: Viking

rewriting that I am proposing, it would be harder to sketch out the rules of economy and social ethics; in fact, to an extent, deconstruction as the questioning of essential definitions would operate if one were to see that in Marx there is a moment of major transgression where rules for humanity and criticism of societies are based on inadequate evidence. Marx's texts, including *Capital,* presuppose an ethical theory: alienation of labor must be undone because it undermines the agency of the subject in his work and his property. I would like to suggest that if the nature and history of alienation, labor, and the production of property are reexamined in terms of women's work and childbirth, it can lead us to a reading of Marx beyond Marx.

One way of moving into Freud is in terms of his notion of the nature of pain as the deferment of pleasure, especially the later Freud who wrote *Beyond the Pleasure Principle.*[8] Freud's spectacular mechanics of imagined, anticipated, and avoided pain write the subject's history and theory, and constantly broach the never-quite-defined concept of normality: anxiety, inhibition, paranoia, schizophrenia, melancholy, mourning. I would like to suggest that in the womb, a tangible place of production, there is the possibility that pain exists *within* the concepts of normality and productivity. (This is not to sentimentalize the pain of childbirth.) The problematizing of the phenomenal identity of pleasure and unpleasure should not be operated only through the logic of repression. The opposition pleasure-pain is questioned in the physiological "normality" of woman.

If one were to look at the never-quite-defined concepts of normality and health that run through and are submerged in Freud's texts, one would have to redefine the nature of pain. Pain does not operate in the same way in men and in women. Once again, this deconstructive move will make it much harder to devise the rules.

Freud's best-known determinant of femininity is penis-envy. The most crucial text of this argument is the essay on femininity in the *New Introductory Lectures.*[9] There, Freud begins to argue that the

Press, 1977).

8. No feminist reading of this text is now complete without Jacques Derrida's "Spéculer—sur Freud," *La Carte postale: de Socrate à Freud et au-delà* (Paris: Aubier-Flammarion, 1980).

9. *The Standard Edition of the Complete Psychological Works of Sigmund Freud,* trans. James Strachey, et al. (London: Hogarth Press, 1964), vol. 22.

little girl is a little boy before she discovers sex. As Luce Irigaray and others have shown, Freud does not take the womb into account.[10] Our mood, since we carry the womb as well as being carried by it, should be corrective.[11] We might chart the itinerary of womb-envy in the production of a theory of consciousness: the idea of the womb as a place of production is avoided both in Marx and in Freud. (There are exceptions to such a generalization, especially among American neo-Freudians such as Erich Fromm. I am speaking here about invariable presuppositions, even among such exceptions.) In Freud, the genital stage is preeminently phallic, not clitoral or vaginal. This particular gap in Freud is significant. The hysteron remains the place which constitutes only the text of hysteria. Everywhere there is a nonconfrontation of the idea of the womb as a workshop, except to produce a surrogate penis. Our task in rewriting the text of Freud is not so much to declare the idea of penis-envy rejectable, but to make available the idea of a womb-envy as something that interacts with the idea of penis-envy to determine human sexuality and the production of society.[12]

These are some questions that may be asked of the Freudian and Marxist "grounds" or theoretical "bases" that operate our ideas of world and self. We might want to ignore them altogether and say that the business of literary criticism is neither your gender (such a suggestion seems hopelessly dated) nor the theories of revolution or

10. Luce Irigaray, "La tâche aveugle d'un vieux rêve de symmétrie," in *Speculum de l'autre femme* (Paris: Minuit, 1974).
11. I have moved, as I explain later, from womb-envy, still bound to the closed circle of coupling, to the suppression of the clitoris. The mediating moment would be the appropriation of the vagina, as in Derrida (see Gayatri Chakravorty Spivak, "Displacement and the Discourse of Women," in Mark Krupnick, ed., *Displacement: Derrida and After* (Bloomington: Indiana University Press, 1983).
12. One way to develop notions of womb-envy would be in speculation about a female fetish. If, by way of rather obvious historico-sexual determinations, the typical male fetish can be said to be the phallus, given to and taken away from the mother (Freud, "Fetishism," *Standard Edition*, trans. James Strachey, et al., vol. 21), then, the female imagination in search of a name from a revered sector of masculist culture might well fabricate a fetish that would operate the giving and taking away of a womb to a father. I have read Mary Shelley's *Frankenstein* in this way. The play between such a gesture and the Kantian socio-ethical framework of the novel makes it exemplary of the ideology of moral and practical imagination in the Western European literature of the nineteenth century. See Gayatri Chakravorty Spivak, "Feminism and a Critique of Imperialism," forthcoming in *Critical Inquiry*.

psychoanalysis. Criticism must remain resolutely neuter and practical. One should not mistake the grounds out of which the ideas of world and self are produced with the business of the appreciation of the literary text. If one looks closely, one will see that, whether one diagnoses the names or not, certain kinds of thoughts are presupposed by the notions of world and consciousness of the most "practical" critic. Part of the feminist enterprise might well be to provide "evidence" so that these great male texts do not become great adversaries, or models from whom we take our ideas and then revise or reassess them. These texts must be rewritten so that there is new material for the grasping of the production and determination of literature within the general production and determination of consciousness and society. After all, the people who produce literature, male and female, are also moved by general ideas of world and consciousness to which they cannot give a name.

If we continue to work in this way, the common currency of the understanding of society will change. I think that kind of change, the coining of new money, is necessary. I certainly believe that such work is supplemented by research into women's writing and research into the conditions of women in the past. The kind of work I have outlined would infiltrate the male academy and redo the terms of our understanding of the context and substance of literature as part of the human enterprise.

II

What seems missing in these earlier remarks is the dimension of race. Today I would see my work as the developing of a reading method that is sensitive to gender, race, and class. The earlier remarks would apply indirectly to the development of class-sensitive and directly to the development of gender-sensitive readings.

In the matter of race-sensitive analyses, the chief problem of American feminist criticism is its identification of racism as such with the constitution of racism in America. Thus, today I see the object of investigation to be not only the history of "Third World Women" or their testimony but also the production, through the great European theories, often by way of literature, of the colonial object. As long as American feminists understand "history" as a positivistic empiricism that scorns "theory" and therefore remains ignorant of its own, the

"Third World" as its object of study will remain constituted by those hegemonic First World intellectual practices.[13]

My attitude toward Freud today involves a broader critique of his entire project. It is a critique not only of Freud's masculism but of nuclear-familial psychoanalytical theories of the constitution of the sexed subject. Such a critique extends to alternative scenarios to Freud that keep to the nuclear parent-child model, as it does to the offer of Greek mythical alternatives to Oedipus as the regulative type-case of the model itself, as it does to the romantic notion that an extended family, especially a community of women, would necessarily cure the ills of the nuclear family. My concern with the production of colonial discourse thus touches my critique of Freud as well as most Western feminist challenges to Freud. The extended or corporate family is a socioeconomic (indeed, on occasion political) organization which makes sexual constitution irreducibly complicit with historical and political economy.[14] To learn to read that way is to understand that the literature of the world, itself accessible only to a few, is not tied by the concrete universals of a network of archetypes —a theory that was entailed by the consolidation of a political excuse—but by a textuality of material-ideological-psycho-sexual production. This articulation sharpens a general presupposition of my earlier remarks.

Pursuing these considerations, I proposed recently an analysis of "the discourse of the clitoris."[15] The reactions to that proposal have been interesting in the context I discuss above. A certain response from American lesbian feminists can be represented by the following quotation: "In this open-ended definition of phallus/semination as organically *omnipotent* the only recourse is to name the clitoris as orgasmically phallic and to call the uterus the reproductive extension of the phallus. . . . You must stop thinking of yourself privileged as a

13. As I have repeatedly insisted, the limits of hegemonic ideology are larger than so-called individual consciousness and personal goodwill. Gayatri Chakravorty Spivak, "The Politics of Interpretations: A Response," *Critical Inquiry* 9, no. 1 (September 1982); "A Response to Annette Kolodny," forthcoming in *Signs.*
14. This critique should be distinguished from that of Gilles Deleuze and Felix Guattari, *Anti-Oedipus: Capitalism and Schizophrenia,* trans. Robert Hurley, et al. (New York: Viking Press, 1977), with which I am in general agreement. Those authors insist that the family-romance should be seen as inscribed within politico-economic domination and exploitation. My argument is that the family romance-effect should be situated within a larger familial formation.
15. "French Feminism in an International Frame," *Yale French Studies* 62 (1981).

heterosexual woman."[16] Because of its physiologistic orientation, the first part of this objection sees my naming of the clitoris as a repetition of Freud's situating of it as a "little penis." To the second part of the objection I customarily respond: "You're right, and one cannot know how far one succeeds. Yet, the effort to put First World lesbianism in its place is not necessarily reducible to pride in female heterosexuality." Other uses of my suggestion, both supportive and adverse, have also reduced the discourse of the clitoris to a physiological fantasy. In the interest of the broadening scope of my critique, I should like to reemphasize that the clitoris, even as I acknowledge and honor its irreducible physiological effect, is, in this reading, also a short-hand for women's excess in all areas of production and practice, an excess which must be brought under control to keep business going as usual.[17]

My attitude toward Marxism now recognizes the historical antagonism between Marxism and feminism, *on both sides.* Hardcore Marxism at best dismisses and at worst patronizes the importance of women's struggle. On the other hand, not only the history of European feminism in its opposition to Bolshevik and Social Democrat women, but the conflict between the suffrage movement and the union movement in this country must be taken into account. This historical problem will not be solved by saying that we need more than an analysis of capitalism to understand male dominance, or that the sexual division of labor as the primary determinant is already given in the texts of Marx. I prefer the work that sees that the "essential truth" of Marxism or feminism cannot be separated from its history. My present work relates this to the ideological development of the theory of the imagination in the eighteenth, nineteenth, and twentieth centuries. I am interested in class analysis of families as it is being practiced by, among others, Elizabeth Fox-Genovese, Heidi Hartman, Nancy Hartsock, and Annette Kuhn. I am myself bent upon reading the text of international feminism as operated by the production and realization of surplus-value. My own earlier concern with the specific theme of reproductive (non) alienation seems to me today to be heavily enough touched by a nuclear-familial hysterocentrism to be open to the critique of psychoanalytic feminism that I suggest above.

16. Pat Rezabek, unpublished letter.
17. What in man exceeds the closed circle of coupling in sexual reproduction is the entire "public domain."

On the other hand, if sexual reproduction is seen as the production of a product by an irreducibly determinate means (conjunction of semination-ovulation), in an irreducibly determinate mode (heterogeneous combination of domestic and politico-civil economy), entailing a minimal variation of social relations, then two original Marxist categories would be put into question: use-value as the measure of communist production and absolute surplus-value as the motor of primitive (capitalist) accumulation. For the first: the child, although not a commodity, is also not produced for immediate and adequate consumption or direct exchange. For the second: the premise that the difference between subsistence-wage and labor-power's potential of production is the origin of original accumulation can only be advanced if reproduction is seen as identical with subsistence; in fact, the reproduction and maintenance of children would make heterogeneous the original calculation in terms of something like the slow displacement of value from fixed capital to commodity.[18] These insights take the critique of wage-labor in unexpected directions.

When I earlier touched upon the relationship between wage-theory and "women's work," I had not yet read the autonomist arguments about wage and work as best developed in the work of Antonio Negri.[19] Exigencies of work and limitations of scholarship and experience permitting, I would like next to study the relationship between domestic and political economies in order to establish the subversive power of "women's work" in models in the construction of a "revolutionary subject." Negri sees this possibility in the inevitable consumerism that socialized capitalism must nurture. Commodity consumption, even as it realizes surplus-value as profit, does not itself produce value and therefore persistently exacerbates crisis.[20] It is through reversing and displacing this tendency within consumerism, Negri suggests, that the "revolutionary subject" can be released.

18. I understand Lise Vogel is currently developing this analysis. One could analogize directly, for example, with a passage such as Karl Marx, *Grundrisse: Foundations of the Critique of Political Economy,* trans. Martin Nicolaus (New York: Vintage Books, 1973), p. 710.
19. Antonio Negri, *Marx Beyond Marx,* trans. Harry Cleaver, et al. (New York: J. F. Bergen, 1984). For another perspective on a similar argument, see Jacques Donzelot, "Pleasure in Work," *I & C,* (Winter 1981–82).
20. An excellent elucidation of this mechanism is to be found in James O'Connor, "The Meaning of Crisis," *International Journal of Urban and Regional Research* 5, no. 3 (1981): 317–29.

Mainstream English Marxists sometimes think that such an upheaval can be brought about by political interventionist teaching of literature. Some French intellectuals think this tendency is inherent in the "pagan tradition," which pluralizes the now-defunct narratives of social justice still endorsed by traditional Marxists in a post-industrial world. In contrast, I now argue as follows:

> It is women's work that has continuously survived within not only the varieties of capitalism but other historical and geographical modes of production. The economic, political, ideological, and legal heterogeneity of the relationship between the definitive mode of production and race- and class-differentiated women's and wives' work is abundantly recorded. . . . Rather than the refusal to work of the freed Jamaican slaves in 1834, which is cited by Marx as the only example of zero-work, quickly recuperated by imperialist maneuvers, it is the long history of women's work which is a sustained example of zero-work: work not only outside of wage-work, but, *in one way or another*, "outside" of the definitive modes of production. The displacement required here is a transvaluation, an uncatastrophic *im*-plosion of the search for validation via the circuit of productivity. Rather than a miniaturized and thus controlled metaphor for civil society and the state, the power of the *oikos*, domestic economy, can be used as the model of the foreign body unwittingly nurtured by the *polis*.[21]

With psychoanalytic feminism, then, an invocation of history and politics leads us back to the place of psychoanalysis in colonialism. With Marxist feminism, an invocation of the economic text foregrounds the operations of the New Imperialism. The discourse of race has come to claim its importance in this way in my work.

I am still moved by the reversal-displacement morphology of deconstruction, crediting the asymmetry of the "interest" of the historical moment. Investigating the hidden ethico-political agenda of differentiations constitutive of knowledge and judgment interests me even more. It is also the deconstructive view that keeps me resisting an essentialist freezing of the concepts of gender, race, and class. I look rather at the repeated agenda of the situational produc-

---

21. Jean-François Lyotard, *Instructions païens* (Paris: Union générale d'éditions, 1978). Tony Bennet, *Formalism and Marxism* (London: Methuen, 1979), p. 145 and passim. Marx, *Grundrisse*, p. 326. The self-citation is from "Woman in Derrida," unpublished lecture, School of Criticism and Theory, Northwestern University, July 6, 1982.

tion of those concepts and our complicity in such a production. This aspect of deconstruction will not allow the establishment of a hegemonic "global theory" of feminism.

Over the last few years, however, I have also begun to see that, rather than deconstruction simply opening a way for feminists, the figure and discourse of women opened the way for Derrida as well. His incipient discourse of woman surfaced in *Spurs* (first published as "La Question du Style" in 1975), which also articulates the thematics of "interest" crucial to political deconstruction.[22] This study marks his move from the critical deconstruction of phallocentrism to "affirmative" deconstruction (Derrida's phrase). It is at this point that Derrida's work seems to become less interesting for Marxism.[23] The early Derrida can certainly be shown to be useful for feminist practice, but why is it that, when he writes under the sign of woman, as it were, that his work becomes solipsistic and marginal? What is it in the history of that sign that allows this to happen? I will hold this question until the end of this essay.

III

In 1979–80, concerns of race and class were beginning to invade my mind. What follows is in some sense a check list of quotations from Margaret Drabble's *The Waterfall* that shows the uneasy presence of those concerns.[24] Reading literature "well" is in itself a questionable good and can indeed be sometimes productive of harm and "aesthetic" apathy within its ideological framing. My suggestion is to use literature, with a feminist perspective, as a "nonexpository" theory of practice.

Drabble has a version of "the best education" in the Western world: a First Class in English from Oxford. The tradition of academic radicalism in England is strong. Drabble was at Oxford when the

---

22. See Gayatri Chakravorty Spivak, "Love Me, Love My Ombre, Elle," *Diacritics* (Winter 1984), pp. 19–36.
23. Michael Ryan, *Marxism and Deconstruction: A Critical Articulation* (Baltimore: Johns Hopkins University Press, 1982), p. xiv.
24. Margaret Drabble, *The Waterfall* (Harmondsworth: Penguin, 1971). Subsequent references are included in the text. Part of this reading has appeared in a slightly different form in *Union Seminary Quarterly Review* 35 (Fall–Winter 1979–80): 15–34.

prestigious journal *New Left Review* was being organized. I am not adverse to a bit of simple biographical detail: I began to re-read *The Waterfall* with these things in mind as well as the worrying thoughts about sex, race, and class.

Like many woman writers, Drabble creates an extreme situation, to answer, presumably, the question "Why does love happen?" In place of the mainstream objectification and idolization of the loved person, she situates her protagonist, Jane, in the most inaccessible privacy —at the moment of birthing, alone by choice. Lucy, her cousin, and James, Lucy's husband, take turns watching over her in the empty house as she regains her strength. *The Waterfall* is the story of Jane's love affair with James. In place of a legalized or merely possessive ardor toward the product of his own body, Drabble gives to James the problem of relating to the birthing woman through the birth of "another man's child." Jane looks and smells dreadful. There is blood and sweat on the crumpled sheets. And yet "love" happens. Drabble slows language down excruciatingly as Jane records how, wonders why. It is possible that Drabble is taking up the challenge of feminine "passivity" and making it the tool of analytic strength. Many answers emerge. I will quote two, to show how provisional and self-suspending Jane can be:

> I loved him inevitably, of necessity. Anyone could have foreseen it, given those facts: a lonely woman, in an empty world. Surely I would have loved anyone who might have shown me kindness. . . . But of course it's not true, it could not have been anyone else. . . . I know that it was not inevitable: it was a miracle. . . . What I deserved was what I had made: solitude, or a repetition of pain. What I received was grace. Grace and miracles. I don't much care for my terminology. Though at least it lacks that most disastrous concept, the concept of free will. Perhaps I could make a religion that denied free will, that placed God in his true place, arbitrary, carelessly kind, idly malicious, intermittently attentive, and himself subject, as Zeus was, to · necessity. Necessity is my God. Necessity lay with me when James did [pp. 49–50].

And, in another place, the "opposite" answer—random contingencies:

> I loved James because he was what I had never had: because he belonged to my cousin: because he was kind to his own child: because he looked unkind: because I saw his naked wrists

against a striped tea towel once, seven years ago. Because he addressed me an intimate question upon a beach on Christmas Day. Because he helped himself to a drink when I did not dare to accept the offer of one. Because he was not serious, because his parents lived in South Kensington and were mysteriously depraved. Ah, perfect love. For these reasons, was it, that I lay there, drowned was it, drowned or stranded, waiting for him, waiting to die and drown there, in the oceans of our flowing bodies, in the white sea of that strange familiar bed [p. 67].

If the argument for necessity is arrived at by slippery happenstance from thought to thought, each item on this list of contingencies has a plausibility far from random.

She considers the problem of making women rivals in terms of the man who possesses them. There is a peculiar agreement between Lucy and herself before the affair begins:

I wonder why people marry? Lucy continued, in a tone of such academic flatness that the topic seemed robbed of any danger. I don't know, said Jane, with equal calm. . . . So arbitrary, really, said Lucy, spreading butter on the toast. It would be nice, said Jane, to think there were reasons. . . . Do you think so? said Lucy. Sometimes I prefer to think we are victims. . . . If there were a reason, said Jane, one would be all the more a victim. She paused, thought, ate a mouthful of the toast. I am wounded, therefore I bleed. I am human, therefore I suffer. Those aren't reasons you're describing, said Lucy. . . . And from upstairs the baby's cry reached them—thin, wailing, desperate. Hearing it, the two women looked at each other, and for some reason smiled [pp. 26–27].

This, of course, is no overt agreement, but simply a hint that the "reason" for female bonding has something to do with a baby's cry. For example, Jane records her own deliberate part in deceiving Lucy this way: "I forgot Lucy. I did not think of her—or only occasionally, lying awake at night *as the baby cried,* I would think of her, with pangs of irrelevant inquiry, pangs endured not by me and in me, but at a distance, pangs as sorrowful and irrelevant as another person's pain" [p. 48; italics mine].

Jane records inconclusively her gut reaction to the supposed natural connection between parent and child: "Blood is blood, and it is not good enough to say that children are for the motherly, as Brecht said, for there are many ways of unmothering a woman, or unfathering a man. . . . And yet, how can I deny that it gave me pleasure to see

James hold her in his arms for me? The man I loved and the child to whom I had given birth" [p. 48].

The loose ending of the book also makes Jane's story an extreme case. Is this love going to last, prove itself to be "true," and bring Jane security and Jane and James happiness? Or is it resolutely "liberated," overprotesting its own impermanence, and thus falling in with the times? Neither. The melodramatic and satisfactory ending, the accident which might have killed James, does not in fact do so. It merely reveals all to Lucy, does not end the book, and reduces all to a humdrum kind of double life.

These are not bad answers: necessity if all fails, or perhaps random contingency; an attempt not to rivalize women; blood bonds between mothers and daughters; love free of social security. The problem for a reader like me is that the entire questioning is carried on in what I can only see as a privileged atmosphere. I am not saying, of course, that Jane is Drabble (although that, too, is true in a complicated way). I am saying that Drabble considers the story of so privileged a woman the most worth telling. Not the well-bred lady of pulp fiction, but an impossible princess who mentions in one passing sentence toward the beginning of the book that her poems are read on the BBC.

It is not that Drabble does not want to rest her probing and sensitive fingers on the problem of class, if not race. The account of Jane's family's class prejudice is incisively told. Her father is headmaster of a public school.

> There was one child I shall always remember, a small thin child . . . whose father, he proudly told us, was standing as Labour Candidate for a hopeless seat in an imminent General Election. My father teased him unmercifully, asking questions that the poor child could not begin to answer, making elaborate and hideous semantic jokes about the fruits of labour, throwing in familiar references to prominent Tories that were quite wasted on such . . . tender ears; and the poor child sat there, staring at his roast beef . . . turning redder and redder, and trying, pathetically, sycophantically, to smile. I hated my father at that instant [pp. 56–57].

Yet Drabble's Jane is made to share the lightest touch of her parents' prejudice. The part I have elided is a mocking reference to the child's large red ears. For her the most important issue remains sexual deprivation, sexual choice. *The Waterfall,* the name of a card trick, is also the name of Jane's orgasms, James's gift to her.

But perhaps Drabble is ironic when she creates so class-bound and yet so analytic a Jane? It is a possibility, of course, but Jane's identification with the author of the narrative makes this doubtful. If there is irony to be generated here, it must come, as they say, from "outside the book."

Rather than imposing my irony, I attempt to find the figure of Jane as narrator helpful. Drabble manipulates her to examine the conditions of production and determination of microstructural heterosexual attitudes within her chosen enclosure. This enclosure is important because it is from here that rules come. Jane is made to realize that there are no fixed new rules in the book, not as yet. First World feminists are up against that fact, every day. This should not become an excuse but should remain a delicate responsibility: "If I need a morality, I will create one: a new ladder, a new virtue. If I need to understand what I am doing, if I cannot act without my own approbation—and I must act, I have changed, I am no longer capable of inaction—then I will invent a morality that condones me. Though by doing so, I risk condemning all that I have been" [pp. 52–53].

If the cautions of deconstruction are heeded—the contingency that the desire to "understand" and "change" are as much symptomatic as they are revolutionary—merely to fill in the void with rules will spoil the case again, for women as for human beings. We must strive moment by moment to practice a taxonomy of different forms of understanding, different forms of change, dependent perhaps upon resemblance and seeming substitutability—figuration—rather than on the self-identical category of truth:

> Because it's obvious that I haven't told the truth, about myself and James. How could I? Why, more significantly, should I? . . . Of the truth, I haven't told enough. I flinched at the conclusion and can even see in my hesitance a virtue: it is dishonest, it is inartistic, but it is a virtue, such discretion, in the moral world of love. . . . The names of qualities are interchangeable: vice, virtue: redemption, corruption: courage, weakness: and hence the confusion of abstraction, the proliferation of aphorism and paradox. In the human world, perhaps there are merely likenesses. . . . The qualities, they depended on the supposed true end of life. . . . Salvation, damnation. . . . I do not know which of these two James represented. Hysterical terms, maybe: religious terms, yet again. But then life is a serious matter, and it is not merely hysteria that acknowledges this fact: for men as well as women have been known to acknowledge it. I

must make an effort to comprehend it. I will take it all to pieces. I will resolve it to parts, and then I will put it together again, I will reconstitute it in a form that I can accept, a fictitious form [pp. 46, 51, 52].

The categories by which one understands, the qualities of plus and minus, are revealing themselves as arbitrary, situational. Drabble's Jane's way out—to resolve and reconstitute life into an acceptable fictional *form* that need not, perhaps, worry too much about the categorical problems—seems, by itself, a classical privileging of the aesthetic, for Drabble hints at the limits of self-interpretation through a gesture that is accessible to the humanist academic. Within a fictional form, she confides that the exigencies of a narrative's unity had not allowed her to report the whole truth. She then changes from the third person to first.

What can a literary critic do with this? Notice that the move is absurdity twice compounded, since the discourse reflecting the constraints of fiction-making goes on then to fabricate another fictive text. Notice further that the narrator who tells us about the impossibility of truth-in-fiction—the classic privilege of metaphor—is a metaphor as well.[25]

I should choose a simpler course. I should acknowledge this global dismissal of any narrative speculation about the nature of truth and then dismiss it in turn, since it might unwittingly suggest that there is somewhere a way of speaking about truth in "truthful" language, that a speaker can somewhere get rid of the structural unconscious and speak without role playing. Having taken note of the frame, I will thus explain the point Jane is making here and relate it to what, I suppose, the critical view above would call "the anthropomorphic world": when one takes a rational or aesthetic distance from oneself one gives oneself up to the conveniently classifying macrostructures, a move dramatized by Drabble's third-person narrator. By contrast, when one involves oneself in the microstructural moments of practice that make possible and undermine every macrostructural theory, one falls, as it were, into the deep waters of a first person who recognizes the limits of understanding and change, indeed the precarious necessity of the micro–macro opposition, yet is bound not to give up.

25. As in Paul de Man's analysis of Proust in *Allegories of Reading: Figural Language in Rousseau, Nietzsche, Rilke, and Proust* (New Haven: Yale University Press, 1979), p. 18.

The risks of first-person narrative prove too much for Drabble's fictive Jane. She wants to plot her narrative in terms of the paradoxical category—"pure corrupted love"—that allows her to *make* a fiction rather than try, *in* fiction, to report on the unreliability of categories: "I want to get back to that schizoid third-person dialogue. I've one or two more sordid conditions to describe, and then I can get back there to that isolated world of pure corrupted love" [p. 130]. To return us to the detached and macrostructural third person narrative after exposing its limits could be an aesthetic allegory of deconstructive practice.

Thus Drabble fills the void of the female consciousness with meticulous and helpful articulation, though she seems thwarted in any serious presentation of the problems of race and class, and of the marginality of sex. She engages in that microstructural dystopia, the sexual situation in extremis, that begins to seem more and more a part of women's fiction. Even within those limitations, our motto cannot be Jane's "I prefer to suffer, I think"—the privatist cry of heroic liberal women; it might rather be the lesson of the scene of writing of *The Waterfall:* to return to the third person with its grounds mined under.

IV

It is no doubt useful to decipher women's fiction in this way for feminist students and colleagues in American academia. I am less patient with literary texts today, even those produced by women. We must of course remind ourselves, our positivist feminist colleagues in charge of creating the discipline of women's studies, and our anxious students, that essentialism is a trap. It seems more important to learn to understand that the world's women do not all relate to the privileging of essence, especially through "fiction," or "literature," in quite the same way.

In Seoul, South Korea, in March 1982, 237 woman workers in a factory owned by Control Data, a Minnesota-based multinational corporation, struck over a demand for a wage raise. Six union leaders were dismissed and imprisoned. In July, the women took hostage two visiting U.S. vice-presidents, demanding reinstatement of the union leaders. Control Data's main office was willing to release the women; the Korean government was reluctant. On July 16, the Korean male workers at the factory beat up the female workers and ended the dispute. Many of the women were injured and two suffered miscarriages.

To grasp this narrative's overdeterminations (the many telescoped lines—sometimes noncoherent, often contradictory, perhaps discontinuous—that allow us to determine the reference point of a single "event" or cluster of "events") would require a complicated analysis.[26] Here, too, I will give no more than a checklist of the overdeterminants. In the earlier stages of industrial capitalism, the colonies provided the raw materials so that the colonizing countries could develop their manufacturing industrial base. Indigenous production was thus crippled or destroyed. To minimize circulation time, industrial capitalism needed to establish due process, and such civilizing instruments as railways, postal services, and a uniformly graded system of education. This, together with the labor movements in the First World and the mechanisms of the welfare state, slowly made it imperative that manufacturing itself be carried out on the soil of the Third World, where labor can make many fewer demands, and the governments are mortgaged. In the case of the telecommunications industry, making old machinery obsolete at a more rapid pace than it takes to absorb its value in the commodity, this is particularly practical.

The incident that I recounted above, not at all uncommon in the multinational arena, complicates our assumptions about women's entry into the age of computers and the modernization of "women in development," especially in terms of our daily theorizing and practice. It should make us confront the discontinuities and contradictions in our assumptions about women's freedom to work outside the house, and the sustaining virtues of the working-class family. The fact that these workers were women was not merely because, like those Belgian lacemakers, oriental women have small and supple fingers. It is also because they are the true army of surplus labor. No one, including their men, will agitate for an adequate wage. In a two-job family, the man saves face if the woman makes less, even for a comparable job.

Does this make Third World men more sexist than David Rockefeller? The nativist argument that says "do not question Third World

26. For definitions of "overdetermination," see Freud, *Standard Edition,* trans. James Strachey, et al., vol. 4, pp. 279–304; Louis Althusser, *For Marx,* trans. Ben Brewster (New York: Vintage Books, 1970), pp. 89–128.

mores" is of course unexamined imperialism. There *is* something like an answer, which makes problematic the grounds upon which we base our own intellectual and political activities. No one can deny the dynamism and civilizing power of socialized capital. The irreducible search for greater production of surplus-value (dissimulated as, simply, "productivity") through technological advancement; the corresponding necessity to train a consumer who will need what is produced and thus help realize surplus-value as profit; the tax breaks associated with supporting humanist ideology through "corporate philanthropy"; all conspire to "civilize." These motives do not exist on a large scale in a comprador economy like that of South Korea, which is neither the necessary recipient nor the agent of socialized capital. The surplus-value is realized elsewhere. The nuclear family does not have a transcendent ennobling power. The fact that ideology and the ideology of marriage have developed in the West since the English revolution of the seventeenth century has something like a relationship to the rise of meritocratic individualism.[27]

These possibilities overdetermine any generalization about universal parenting based on American, Western European, or laundered anthropological speculation.

Socialized capital kills by remote control. In this case, too, the American managers watched while the South Korean men decimated their women. The managers denied charges. One remark made by a member of Control Data management, as reported in *Multinational Monitor,* seemed symptomatic in its self-protective cruelty: "Although 'it's true' Chae lost her baby, 'this is not the first miscarriage she's had. She's had two before this.'"[28] However active in the production of civilization as a by-product, socialized capital has not moved far from the presuppositions of a slave mode of production. "In Roman theory, the agricultural slave was designated an *instrumentum vocale,* the speaking tool, one grade away from the livestock that constituted an *instrumentum semi-vocale,* and two from the implement which was an *instrumentum mutum.*"[29]

One of Control Data's radio commercials speaks of how its

27. See Gayatri Chakravorty Spivak, response, "Independent India: Women's India," forthcoming in a collection edited by Dilip Basu.
28. "Was Headquarters Responsible? Women Beat Up at Control Data, Korea," *Multinational Monitor* 3, no. 10 (September 1982): 16.
29. Perry Anderson, *Passages from Antiquity to Feudalism* (London: Verso Editions, 1978), pp. 24–25.

computers open the door to knowledge, at home or in the workplace, for men and women alike. The acronym of this computer system is PLATO. One might speculate that this noble name helps to dissimulate a quantitative and formula-permutational vision of knowledge as an instrument of efficiency and exploitation with an aura of the unique and subject-expressive wisdom at the very root of "democracy." The undoubted historical-symbolic value of the acronym PLATO shares in the effacement of class-history that is the project of "civilization" as such: "The slave mode of production which underlay Athenian civilization necessarily found its most pristine ideological expression in the privileged social stratum of the city, whose intellectual heights its surplus labour in the silent depths below the *polis* made possible."[30]

"Why is it," I asked above, "that when Derrida writes under the sign of woman his work becomes solipsistic and marginal?"

His discovery of the figure of woman is in terms of a critique of propriation—proper-ing, as in the proper name (patronymic) or property.[31] Suffice it to say here that, by thus differentiating himself from the phallocentric tradition under the aegis of a(n idealized) woman who is the "sign" of the indeterminate, of that which has im-propriety as its property, Derrida cannot think that the sign "woman" is indeterminate by virtue of its access to the tyranny of the text of the proper. It is this tyranny of the "proper"—in the sense of that which produces both property and the proper name of the patronymic—that I have called the suppression of the clitoris, and that the news item about Control Data illustrates.[32]

Derrida has written a magically orchestrated book—*La carte postale*—on philosophy as telecommunication (Control Data's business) using an absent, unnamed, and sexually indeterminate woman (Control Data's victim) as a vehicle, to reinterpret the relationship between Socrates and Plato (Control Data's acronym) taking it

---

30. Ibid., pp. 39–40.
31. Spivak, "Love Me, Love My Ombre, Elle."
32. I have already made the point that "clitoris" here is not meant in a physiological sense alone. I had initially proposed it as the reinscription of a certain physiological emphasis on the clitoris in some varieties of French feminism. I use it as a name (close to a metonym) for women in excess of coupling-mothering. When this excess is in competition in the public domain, it is suppressed in one way or another. I can do no better than refer to the very end of my earlier essay, where I devise a list that makes the scope of the metonym explicit. "French Feminism," p. 184.

through Freud and beyond. The determination of that book is a parable of my argument. Here deconstruction becomes complicit with an essentialist bourgeois feminism. The following paragraph appeared recently in *Ms.:* "Control Data is among those enlightened corporations that offer social-service leaves. . . . Kit Ketchum, former treasurer of Minnesota NOW, applied for and got a full year with pay to work at NOW's national office in Washington, D.C. She writes: 'I commend Control Data for their commitment to employing and promoting women. . . . ' Why not suggest this to your employer?"[33] Bourgeois feminism, because of a blindness to the *multi*national theater, dissimulated by "clean" national practice and fostered by the dominant ideology, can participate in the tyranny of the proper and see in Control Data an extender of the Platonic mandate to women in general.

The dissimulation of political economy is in and by ideology. What is at work and can be used in that operation is at least the ideology of nation-states, nationalism, national liberation, ethnicity, and religion. Feminism lives in the master-text as well as in the pores. It is not the determinant of the last instance. I think less easily of "changing the world" than in the past. I teach a small number of the holders of the can(n)on, male or female, feminist or masculist, how to read their own texts, as best I can.

33. *Ms.* 10, no. 11 (May 1982): 30. In this connection, it is interesting to note how so gifted an educator as Jane Addams misjudged nascent socialized capital. She was wrong, of course, about the impartiality of commerce: "In a certain sense commercialism itself, at least in its larger aspect, tends to educate the working man better than organized education does. Its interests are certainly world-wide and democratic, while it is absolutely undiscriminating as to country and creed, coming into contact with all climes and races. If this aspect of commercialism were utilized, it would in a measure counterbalance the tendency which results from the subdivision of labor" *(Democracy and Social Ethics,* Cambridge, Mass.: Harvard University Press, 1964), p. 216.

AN INTRODUCTORY BIBLIOGRAPHY

FERDINAND DE SAUSSURE (1857–1913)

Works available by
Course in General Linguistics, trans. Wade Baskin. New York, Philosophical Library, 1959.

Works available on
Jonathan Culler, *Saussure.* Hassocks, Sussex: Harvester Press, 1976.

ROMAN JAKOBSON (1896–1982)

Works available by
Language and Literature, ed. K. Pomorska and S. Rudy. Cambridge: Harvard University Press, 1987.
Selected Writings, 7 Vols. The Hague: Mouton, 1962 ff.

Works available on
Victor Erlich, *Russian Formalism, History-Doctrine,* 3rd edition. New Haven and London: Yale University Press 1981.

CLAUDE LÉVI-STRAUSS (b. 1908)

Works available by
The Raw and the Cooked, trans. John and Doreen Weightman. London: Cape, 1970.
The Savage Mind. Chicago: University of Chicago Press, 1966.

Works available on
Edmund Leach, *Claude Lévi-Strauss.* New York: Viking Press, 1970.
David Pace, *Claude Lévi-Strauss, The Bearer of Ashes.* Boston: Routledge and Kegan Paul, 1983.

ROLAND BARTHES (1915–1980)

Works available by
A Barthes Reader, ed. Susan Sontag. New York: Hill and Wang, 1982.

The Eiffel Tower, and Other Mythologies, trans. Richard Howard. New York: Hill and Wang, 1979.

Works available on

Jonathan Culler, *Roland Barthes.* New York: Oxford University Press, 1983.

Steven Ungar, *Roland Barthes, The Professor of Desire.* Lincoln: University of Nebraska Press, 1983.

George Wasserman, *Roland Barthes.* Boston: Twayne, 1981.

LOUIS ALTHUSSER (b. 1918)

Works available by

For Marx, trans. Ben Brewster. London: Allen Lane, 1983.

Lenin and Philosophy, trans. Ben Brewster. New York: Monthly Review Press, 1971.

Works available on

Ted Benton, *The Rise and Fall of Structural Marxism.* New York: St. Martin's Press, 1984.

Alex Callinicos, *Althusser's Marxism.* London: Pluto Press, 1976.

Steven Smith, *Reading Althusser.* Ithaca: Cornell University Press, 1984.

MICHEL FOUCAULT (1926–1984)

Works available by

The Foucault Reader, ed. Paul Rabinow. New York: Pantheon Books, 1984.

The History of Sexuality, 3 vols., trans. Robert Hurley. New York: Pantheon Books, 1978 ff.

Madness and Civilization, trans. Richard Howard. New York: Pantheon Books, 1965.

Works available on

Barry Cooper, *Michel Foucault, An Introduction to the Study of his Thought.* New York: E. Mellen Press, 1981.

Karlis Racevskis, *Michel Foucault and the Subversion of Intellect.* Ithaca: Cornell University Press, 1983.

John Rajchman, *Michel Foucault, The Freedom of Philosophy.* New York: Columbia University Press, 1985.

Alan Sheridan, *Michel Foucault, The Will to Truth.* London and New York: Tavistock, 1980.

MARTIN HEIDEGGER (1889–1976)

Works available by
Basic Writings, ed. David Krell. New York: Harper and Row, 1977.
On the Way to Language, trans. Peter Hertz. New York: Harper and Row, 1971.
Poetry, Language, and Thought, trans. Albert Hofstadter. New York: Harper and Row, 1971.

Works available on
Michael Murray, ed. *Heidegger and Modern Philosophy.* New Haven and London: Yale University Press, 1978.
George Steiner, *Martin Heidegger.* New York: Viking, 1979.
Laszlo Versényi, *Heidegger, Being, and Truth.* New Haven and London: Yale University Press, 1965.

GEORGES BATAILLE (1897–1962)

Works available by
Literature and Evil, trans. Alastair Hamilton. New York: Urizen Books, 1973.
Visions of Excess, Selected Writings 1927–1939, Ed. and with an Introduction by Allan Stoekl with Carl Lovitt and Donald Leslie, Jr. Minneapolis: University of Minnesota Press, 1985.

Works available on
Michel Beaujour, "Eros and Nonsense: Georges Bataille," in *Modern French Criticism,* ed. John K. Simon. Chicago and London: University of Chicago Press, 1972.
Michele H. Richman, *Reading Georges Bataille, Beyond the Gift.* Baltimore and London: Johns Hopkins University Press, 1982.

MAURICE BLANCHOT (b. 1907)

Works available by
The Sirens' Song, ed. Gabriel Josipovici. Bloomington: Indiana University Press, 1982.
The Space of Literature, trans. Ann Smock. Lincoln: University of Nebraska Press, 1982.
The Writing of the Disaster, trans. Ann Smock. Lincoln: University of Nebraska Press, 1986.

Works available on
Paul de Man, "Impersonality in the Criticism of Maurice Blanchot,"

in *Blindness and Insight*, 2nd edition, revised. Introduction by Wlad Godzich. Minneapolis: University of Minnesota Press, 1983.

JACQUES DERRIDA (b. 1930)

Works available by
   Margins of Philosophy, trans. Alan Bass. Chicago: University of Chicago Press, 1982.
   Positions, trans. Alan Bass. Chicago: University of Chicago Press, 1981.
   Speech and Phenomena, trans. David Allison. Evanston: Northwestern University Press, 1973.
   Writing and Difference, trans. Alan Bass. Chicago: University of Chicago Press, 1978.

Works available on
   John Llewelyn, *Derrida on the Threshold of Sense*. New York: St. Martin's Press, 1986.
   Rodolphe Gasché, *The Tain of the Mirror*. Cambridge: Harvard University Press, 1986.
   Christopher Norris, *Derrida*. Cambridge: Harvard University Press, 1987.

PAUL DE MAN (1919–1983)

Works available by
   Allegories of Reading. New Haven: Yale University Press, 1979.
   The Rhetoric of Romanticism, New York: Columbia University Press, 1984.

Works available on
   Jacques Derrida, *Memoires: For Paul de Man*, trans. Cecile Lindsay, Jonathan Culler, and Eduardo Cadava. New York: Columbia University Press, 1986.
   Christopher Norris, *Paul de Man: Deconstruction and the Critique of Aesthetic Ideology*. London: Methuen, 1988.

HAYDEN WHITE (b. 1928)

Works available by
   The Content of the Form: Narrative Discourse and Historical Representation. Baltimore: Johns Hopkins University Press, 1987.

Metahistory, The Historical Imagination in Nineteenth Century Europe. Baltimore: John Hopkins University Press, 1973.

GEOFFREY HARTMAN (b. 1929)

Works available by
    Criticism in the Wilderness. New Haven: Yale University Press, 1980.
    Easy Pieces. New York: Columbia University Press, 1985.

EDWARD SAID (b. 1935)

Works available by
    Covering Islam: How the Media and the Experts Determine How We See the Rest of the World. New York: Pantheon Books, 1981.
    The Question of Palestine. New York: Times Books, 1979.
    The World, the Text, and the Critic. Cambridge: Harvard University Press, 1983.

V. N. VOLOSHINOV (1895–?)

Works available by
    Freudianism: A Marxist Critique, trans. I. R. Titunik. New York: Academic Press, 1976.

MIKHAIL BAKHTIN (1895–1975)

Works available by
    The Dialogic Imagination: Four Essays, trans. Caryl Emerson and Michael Holquist. Austin: University of Texas Press, 1981.
    Problems of Dostoevsky's Poetics, trans. Caryl Emerson. Minneapolis: University of Minnesota Press, 1984.
    Speech Genres and Other Late Essays, trans. Vern W. McGee. Ed. Caryl Emerson and Michael Holquist. Austin: University of Texas Press, 1986.

Works available on
    Katerina Clark and Michael Holquist, *Mikhail Bakhtin.* Cambridge: Harvard University Press, 1984.
    Tzvetan Todorov, *Mikhail Bakhtin: The Dialogical Principle.* Minneapolis: University of Minnesota Press, 1984.

GEORG LUKÁCS (1885-1971)

Works available by
    History and Class Consciousness, trans. Rodney Livingstone. Cambridge: MIT Press, 1971.
    Soul and Form, trans. Anna Bostock. Cambridge: MIT Press, 1974.
    The Theory of the Novel, trans. Anna Bostock. Cambridge: MIT Press, 1971.

Works available on
    Agnes Heller, *Lukács Reappraised.* New York: Columbia University Press, 1983.
    George Lichtheim, *Lukács.* London: Fontana, 1970.
    G. H. R. Parkinson, *George Lukács.* London and Boston: Routledge and Kegan Paul, 1977.

WALTER BENJAMIN (1892-1940)

Works available by
    Charles Baudelaire: A Lyric Poet in the Era of High Capitalism, trans. Harry Zohn. London: New Left Books, 1973.
    One-Way Street, and Other Writings, trans. Edmund Jephcott and Kingsley Shorter. London: New Left Books, 1979.
    Reflections, trans. Edmund Jephcott. New York: Harcourt Brace Jovanovich, 1978.

Works available on
    Susan Buck-Morss, *The Origin of Negative Dialectics.* New York: Free Press, 1977.
    Terry Eagleton, *Walter Benjamin, Or, Toward a Revolutionary Criticism.* London: New Left Books, 1981.
    Julian Roberts, *Walter Benjamin.* Atlantic Highlands: Humanities Press, 1983.

THEODOR ADORNO (1903-1969)

Works available by
    Dialectic of Enlightenment, with Max Horkheimer, trans. John Cumming. New York: Herder and Herder, 1972.
    Introduction to the Sociology of Music, trans. E. B. Ashton. New York: Seabury Press, 1976.
    Minima Moralia, trans. E. F. N. Jephcott. London: Verso, 1978.

Works available on
> Martin Jay, *Adorno*. Cambridge: Harvard University Press, 1984.
> ———, *The Dialectical Imagination*. Boston: Little, Brown, 1973.
> Rose Gillian, *The Melancholy Science*. New York: Columbia University Press, 1978.
> Zoltan Tarr, *The Frankfurt School*. New York: Wiley, 1977.

ERNST BLOCH (1885–1977)

Works available by
> *Man on His Own,* trans. E. B. Ashton. New York: Herder and Herder, 1970.
> *On Karl Marx,* trans. John Maxwell. New York: Herder and Herder, 1971.
> *A Philosophy of the Future,* trans. John Cumming. New York: Herder and Herder, 1970.
> *The Principle of Hope,* in three volumes, trans. Neville Plaice, Stephen Plaice, and Paul Knight. Oxford: Blackwell, 1986.

Works available on
> Fredric Jameson, *Marxism and Form*. Princeton, N.J.: Princeton University Press, 1971.
> Wayne Hudson, *The Marxist Philosophy of Ernst Bloch*. New York: St. Martin's Press, 1982.

RAYMOND WILLIAMS (b. 1921–1988)

Works available by
> *Culture and Society, 1780–1950.* London: Chatto and Windus, 1958.
> *Politics and Letters: Interviews with New Left Review*. London: New Left Books, 1979.

FREDRIC JAMESON (b. 1934)

Works available by
> *The Political Unconscious*. Ithaca: Cornell University Press, 1981.
> *The Prison-House of Language*. Princeton: Princeton University Press, 1972.

Works available on
> William C. Dowling, *Jameson, Althusser, Marx: An Introduction to the Political Unconscious*. Ithaca: Cornell University Press, 1984.

HANS-GEORG GADAMER (b. 1900)

Works available by
Philosophical Apprenticeships, trans. Robert Sullivan. Cambridge: MIT Press, 1985.
Philosophical Hermeneutics, trans. and ed. David Linge. Berkeley: University of California Press, 1976.
The Relevance of the Beautiful and Other Essays, trans. Nicholas Walker. Cambridge and New York: Cambridge University Press, 1986.

Works available on
Brice R. Wachterhauser, ed. *Hermeneutics and Modern Philosophy*. Albany: State University of New York Press, 1986.
Robert Holub, *Reception Theory, A Critical Introduction*. London and New York: Methuen, 1984.

HANS ROBERT JAUSS (b. 1921)

Works available by
Aesthetic Experience and Literary Hermeneutics, trans. Michael Shaw, Introduction by Wlad Godzich. Minneapolis: University of Minnesota Press, 1982.
Toward an Aesthetic of Reception, trans. Timothy Bahti, Introduction by Paul de Man. Minneapolis: University of Minnesota Press, 1982.

WOLFGANG ISER (b. 1926)

Works available by
The Act of Reading: A Theory of Aesthetic Response. Baltimore: Johns Hopkins University Press, 1978.
The Implied Reader. Baltimore: Johns Hopkins University Press, 1974.

STANLEY FISH (b. 1938)

Works available by
Is There a Text in This Class? Cambridge: Harvard University Press, 1980.
Surprised By Sin: The Reader in Paradise Lost. London and New York: St. Martin's Press, 1967.

SIGMUND FREUD (1856-1939)

Works available by
Beyond the Pleasure Principle, trans. James Strachey. New York: Bantam Books, 1959.
Civilization and its Discontents, trans. James Strachey. New York: Norton, 1961.
Interpretation of Dreams, trans. A. A. Brill. New York: Modern Library, 1950.
Totem and Taboo, Some Points of Agreement Between the Mental Lives of Savages and Neurotics, trans. James Strachey. New York: Norton, 1950.

Works available on
Bruno Bettelheim, Freud and Man's Soul. New York: Knopf, 1982.
Paul Ricoeur, Freud and Philosophy, trans. Denis Savage. New Haven: Yale University Press, 1970.
Sebastiano Timpanaro, The Freudian Slip: Psychoanalysis and Textual Criticism, trans. Kate Soper. London: New Left Books, 1976.
Richard Wollheim, Sigmund Freud. Cambridge: Cambridge University Press, 1971.

JACQUES LACAN (1901-1981)

Works available by
Écrits, A Selection, trans. Alan Sheridan. New York: Norton, 1977.
Feminine Sexuality, ed. Juliet Mitchell and Jacqueline Rose, trans. Jacqueline Rose. New York: Norton, 1983.
The Four Fundamental Concepts of Psychoanalysis, ed. Jacques-Alain Miller, trans. Alan Sheridan. New York: Norton, 1978.
The Language of the Self, trans. with notes and commentary by Anthony Wilden. Baltimore: Johns Hopkins University Press, 1968.

Works available on
Jane Gallop, The Daughter's Seduction: Feminism and Psychoanalysis. Ithaca: Cornell University Press, 1982.
Anika Rifflet-Lemaire, Jacques Lacan, trans. David Macey. London and Boston: Routledge and Kegan Paul, 1977.
Juliet Flower MacCannell, Figuring Lacan. Lincoln: University of Nebraska Press, 1986.
Sherry Turkle. Psychoanalytical Politics: Freud's French Revolution. New York: Basic Books, 1978.

RENÉ GIRARD (b. 1923)

Works available by
  Deceit, Desire, and the Novel, trans. Yvonne Freccero. Baltimore:
Johns Hopkins University Press, 1965.
  Violence and the Sacred, trans. Patrick Gregory. Baltimore: Johns
Hopkins University Press, 1977.

HAROLD BLOOM (b. 1930)

Works available by
  The Anxiety of Influence, A Theory of Poetry. New York: Oxford
University Press, 1973.
  A Map of Misreading. New York: Oxford University Press, 1975.
  Poetry and Repression: Revisionism from Blake to Stevens. New
Haven: Yale University Press, 1976.

Works available on
  David Fite, *Harold Bloom: The Rhetoric of Romantic Vision.* Am-
herst: University of Massachusetts Press, 1985.
  Frank Lentricchia, *After the New Criticism.* Chicago: University of
Chicago Press, 1980.
  Jean-Pierre Mileur, *Literary Revisionism and the Burden of Moder-
nity.* Berkeley: University of California Press, 1985.

HÉLÈNE CIXOUS (b. 1937)

Works available by
  . *Angst,* trans. Jo Levy. London: Calder, 1985.
  The Newly Born Woman, with Catherine Clément, trans. Betsy
Wing. Minneapolis: University of Minnesota Press, 1986.

Works available on
  Verena Andermatt Conley, *Hélène Cixous: Writing the Feminine.*
Lincoln: University of Nebraska Press, 1984.

JULIA KRISTEVA (b. 1941)

Works available by
  About Chinese Women, trans. Anita Barrows. New York: Urizen
Books, 1977.

Desire in Language, trans. Thomas Gora, Alice Jardine, and Leon Roudiez. New York: Columbia University Press, 1980.
Powers of Horror: An Essay in Abjection, trans. Leon Roudiez. New York: Columbia University Press, 1982.
Revolution in Poetic Language, trans. Margaret Waller. New York: Columbia University Press, 1984.

CATHARINE MACKINNON (b. 1946)

Works available by
Feminism Unmodified: Discourses on Life and Law. Cambridge: Harvard University Press, 1987.

GAYATRI CHAKRAVORTY SPIVAK (b. 1942)

Works available by
In Other Worlds, Essays in Cultural Politics. New York and London: Methuen, 1987.